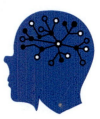

- **Dynamic Study Modules**—help students learn the language of MIS by continuously assessing their activity and performance in real time by adapting to the student's **knowledge** and confidence on each concept. These are available as graded assignments prior to class, and accessible on smartphones, tablets, and computers.

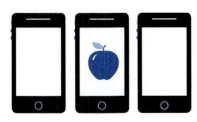

- **Learning Catalytics™**—is an interactive, student response tool that uses students' smartphones, tablets, or laptops to engage them in more sophisticated tasks and **critical thinking** as well as **collaboration** with other class members. Included with MyLab with eText, Learning Catalytics enables you to generate classroom discussion, guide your lecture, and promote peer-to-peer learning with real-time analytics.

- **Reporting Dashboard**—View, analyze, and report learning outcomes clearly and easily, and get the information needed to keep students on track throughout the course with the new Reporting Dashboard. Available via the MyLab Gradebook and fully mobile-ready, the Reporting Dashboard presents student performance data at the class, section, and program levels in an accessible, visual manner.

- **Enhanced eText**—keeps students engaged in learning on their own time, while helping them achieve greater conceptual understanding of course material. The embedded videos, simulations, and activities bring learning to life. to apply the very concepts they are reading about. Combining resources that illuminate content with accessible self-assessment, MyLab with Enhanced eText provides students with a complete digital learning experience—all in one place.

- **Accessibility (ADA)**—Pearson is working toward WCAG 2.0 Level AA and Section 508 standards, as expressed in the **Pearson Guidelines for Accessible Educational Web Media.** Moreover, our products support customers in meeting their obligation to comply with the Americans with Disabilities Act (ADA) by providing access to learning technology programs for users with disabilities.

  Please email our Accessibility Team at **disability.support@pearson.com** for the most up-to-date information.

- **LMS Integration**—You can now link from Blackboard Learn, Brightspace by D2L, Canvas, or Moodle to MyISLab. Professors can acess assignments, rosters, and resources, and synchronize grades with your LMS gradebook.
  Single sign-on provides students access to all the personalized learning resources that make studying more efficient and effective.

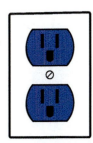

ALWAYS LEARNING

Introduction to Information Systems

Third Edition

Introduction to Information Systems

Patricia Wallace

Johns Hopkins University

330 Hudson Street, NY NY 10013

VP Editorial Director: *Andrew Gilfillan*
Senior Portfolio Manager: *Samantha Lewis*
Content Development Team Lead: *Laura Burgess*
Program Monitor: *Ann Pulido/SPi Global*
Editorial Assistant: *Michael Campbell*
Product Marketing Manager: *Kaylee Carlson*
Project Manager: *Katrina Ostler/Cenveo® Publisher Services*
Text Designer: *Cenveo® Publisher Services*
Cover Designer: *Brian Malloy/Cenveo® Publisher Services*

Cover Art: *Macrovector/Shutterstock; Everything possible/Shutterstock; Rawpixel.com/Shutterstock; Chombosan/Shutterstock; Ktsdesign/Science Photo Library/Getty Images*
Full-Service Project Management: *Cenveo® Publisher Services*
Composition: *Cenveo® Publisher Services*
Printer/Binder: *LSC Communications/Harrisonburg*
Cover Printer: *LSC Communications/Harrisonburg*
Text Font: 10/12 Times LT Pro Roman

Credits and acknowledgments borrowed from other sources and reproduced, with permission, in this textbook appear on the appropriate page within text.

Microsoft and/or its respective suppliers make no representations about the suitability of the information contained in the documents and related graphics published as part of the services for any purpose. All such documents and related graphics are provided "as is" without warranty of any kind. Microsoft and/or its respective suppliers hereby disclaim all warranties and conditions with regard to this information, including all warranties and conditions of merchantability, whether express, implied or statutory, fitness for a particular purpose, title and non-infringement. In no event shall Microsoft and/or its respective suppliers be liable for any special, indirect or consequential damages or any damages whatsoever resulting from loss of use, data or profits, whether in an action of contract, negligence or other tortious action, arising out of or in connection with the use or performance of information available from the services.

The documents and related graphics contained herein could include technical inaccuracies or typographical errors. Changes are periodically added to the information herein. Microsoft and/or its respective suppliers may make improvements and/or changes in the product(s) and/or the program(s) described herein at any time. Partial screen shots may be viewed in full within the software version specified.

Microsoft® and Windows®, and Microsoft Office® are registered trademarks of the Microsoft Corporation in the U.S.A. and other countries. This book is not sponsored or endorsed by or affiliated with the Microsoft Corporation.

Many of the designations by manufacturers and sellers to distinguish their products are claimed as trademarks. Where those designations appear in this book, and the publisher was aware of a trademark claim, the designations have been printed in initial caps or all caps.

Library of Congress Cataloging-in-Publication Data
On file with the Library of Congress.

4 17

ISBN 10: 0-13-463519-1
ISBN 13: 978-0-13-463519-4

To Callie, Julian, and a bright future
of human–centered computing.

About the Author

Patricia Wallace's career spans the fields of information technology, business and management, and psychology, and she has held varied positions, including head of information technology, faculty member, academic administrator, and consultant. She recently retired from Johns Hopkins University, where she was Senior Director, IT and Online Programs, at the Center for Talented Youth for 14 years. Before joining Hopkins, Dr. Wallace served as Chief Information Strategies, at the Robert H. Smith School of Business, University of Maryland, College Park. She currently teaches in the Graduate School of the University of Maryland University College, where she also served as the Associate Vice President and Chief Information Officer for ten years. She earned her Ph.D. in psychology at the University of Texas at Austin and holds an M.S. in Computer Systems Management. Dr. Wallace has published 14 books, including *The Internet in the Workplace: How New Technologies Transform Work* (2004) and *The Psychology of the Internet* (2016), several educational software programs, and numerous scholarly articles.

Brief Contents

Contents

CHAPTER 2

Information Systems and *Strategy*   *32*

CHAPTER **3**

Information and Communications Technologies: *The Enterprise Architecture* 62

CHAPTER **4**

Databases and *Data Warehouses* 94

CHAPTER 5

Information Systems for the *Enterprise* 130

CHAPTER 6

The Web, Social Media, *E-Commerce, and M-Commerce*   *164*

CHAPTER 7

Business Intelligence and *Decision Making*   *198*

CHAPTER 8

Collaborating with *Technology*   *228*

CHAPTER 9

Knowledge Management and *E-Learning*   260

CHAPTER **10**

Ethics, Privacy, and *Security* 294

CHAPTER 11

Systems Development and *Procurement*   328

CHAPTER **12**

Project Management and *Strategic Planning*   *358*

Preface

What's New in the 3rd Edition

The information systems field is fast-moving, and this 3rd edition features a number of new trends that affect organizations around the world. All chapters and case studies have been fully updated with current information and sources.

Major new features include the following:

- Extended coverage of the **Internet of Things** throughout, discussing the explosive increase in connected devices and the data they manage
- Updated Chapter 3 to introduce recent technologies and trends in enterprise architectures
- Revised Chapters 6 and 7 to expand coverage of social media, social and mobile marketing, and digital analytics
- Added several new case studies:
  - *How eBay Scales Its Database Architecture with SQL and NoSQL* (Chapter 4)
  - Salesforce.com: *Taking CRM to the Cloud* (Chapter 5)
  - *LinkedIn: The Social Network and E-Marketplace for Profess*ionals (Chapter 6)
  - *Enabling the Sharing Economy: The Case of Uber Technologies* (End-of-book comprehensive case)

Chapter-Specific Changes

CHAPTER 1: INFORMATION SYSTEMS AND *PEOPLE*

- New key term introduces the **Internet of Things**, a subject that receives expanded attention in this edition
- Updated tables showing social network usage
- Updated table showing important MIS research topics
- New information on Google's Project Loon, to bring Internet access to developing countries
- Updated information on recent data breaches
- Updated case studies on Nasdaq and Twitter with current information and recent sources

CHAPTER 2: INFORMATION SYSTEMS AND *STRATEGY*

- Updated figure showing net profit margins of selected industries
- New examples of recent disruptive innovations and strategic enablers, such as ride-hailing services, 3-D printing, and self-driving vehicles
- Improved figure illustrating cloud computing
- Updated graphs showing average IT spending by industry and per employee
- Updated cases on GameStop and net neutrality using current information and recent sources

CHAPTER 3: INFORMATION AND COMMUNICATIONS TECHNOLOGIES: *THE ENTERPRISE ARCHITECTURE*

- Added **infrastructure as a service (IaaS)** and **platform as a service (PaaS)** as new key terms with discussion
- Updated figures showing market share data for operating systems
- Added recently released 802.11 standards to table

- Added new productivity tips on using speech recognition technology to handle routine tasks, and taking advantage of personal cloud computing
- Reorganized Section 3 on networks and telecommunications to improve flow
- Added discussion of "cord-cutting" to highlight strategic challenges in the telecom industry
- Described software-defined networks in discussion of trends in virtualization
- Updated cases about wearable technologies and Sprint drawing on current information and recent sources
- Deleted older technologies as key terms (WiMax and circuit-switched networks)

CHAPTER 4: DATABASES AND *DATA WAREHOUSES*

- Added **NoSQL DBMS** as new key term, with expanded discussion
- Added new case study "How Ebay Scales Its Database Architecture with SQL and NoSQL," replacing the case study on Colgate-Palmolive
- Add new table to illustrate a "pets" entity for a veterinarian's database
- Updated table showing jobs related to databases with average salaries

CHAPTER 5: INFORMATION SYSTEMS FOR THE *ENTERPRISE*

- Updated discussion of requirements for financial systems
- New "Did You Know" box about Netflix's supply chain for streaming video
- Added discussion of drones in supply chains
- Added new case study, "Salesforce.com: Taking CM to the Cloud," which replaces the case study about CRM in government agencies

CHAPTER 6: THE WEB, SOCIAL MEDIA, *E-COMMERCE,* AND *M-COMMERCE*

- Revised title and chapter contents to add more emphasis to social media
- Added new "Did You Know?" box about cybersquatting on valuable domain names
- Added two new bullets to the features of mobile computing: location awareness and their role in the Internet of Things
- Expanded the digital marketing section to include discussion of social and mobile marketing
- Added new "Did You Know?" box about MOOCs and crowdsourcing
- Added **Bluetooth low-energy (BLE) beacon** as new key term, with discussion of the technology's role in marketing
- Added new case study about LinkedIn, replacing the case study on Pandora Internet Radio

CHAPTER 7: BUSINESS INTELLIGENCE AND *DECISION MAKING*

- Added sections describing different types of metrics used to evaluate websites, social media, and e-commerce applications
- Expanded discussion of artificial intelligence to include emerging technologies
- Added new "Did You Know?" about Microsoft's misguided AI experiment with a chat bot
- Added new table showing sample metrics for mobile apps
- Updated case studies with new information and current sources

CHAPTER 8: COLLABORATING WITH *TECHNOLOGY*

- Added new section on group conversation software, such as Slack
- Added new productivity tip about software to support team projects
- Added new productivity tip about using open source media to enliven student presentations
- Revised and updated data on social networking usage patterns
- Added new "Did You Know?" describing how companies monitor social media for warning signs

- Updated section on virtual reality technology, such as the Oculus Rift headset
- Revised and updated case studies with new information and recent sources

CHAPTER 9: KNOWLEDGE MANAGEMENT AND *E-LEARNING*

- Added new "Did You Know?" box on using knowledge management techniques to combat the Zika virus
- Updated section on organizing knowledge, emphasizing **enterprise content management**, a new key term that describes how organizations manage all types of content through the life cycle
- Deleted expert location system as key term, as these capabilities are embedded in other software
- Added new section on **serious games**, including new key term
- Added brief discussion of the specification called Learning Tools Interoperability (LTI) and the use of badges in learning management systems

CHAPTER 10: ETHICS, PRIVACY, AND *SECURITY*

- New figure summarizing data about organizational policies about software piracy
- New figure and productivity tip advising students to check their own digital footprints occasionally
- Added section on **ransomware,** including new key terms (**ransomware** and **bitcoins**)
- Added new data on the prevalence of insider attacks
- Added new productivity tip suggesting that students adopt multifactor authentication whenever services they use offer this capability
- Updated table on recent events involving information leakage
- Updated case studies on Zynga and Spamhaus using new data and recent sources

CHAPTER 11: SYSTEMS DEVELOPMENT AND *PROCUREMENT*

- Added new section on **application programming interfaces (API)**, including new key term and a discussion of the ways in which APIs improve software development
- Reorganized and revised section on the role of senior managers in procurement, discussing the need to develop policies about software implemented outside of IT departments
- Added new "Did You Know?" about software bugs in computer chips
- Deleted unified modeling language as key term, since its use is declining

CHAPTER 12: PROJECT MANAGEMENT AND *STRATEGIC PLANNING*

- Added new table that compares different IT funding models
- Added brief discussion of disaster recovery as a service
- Updated discussion of technology and industry trends, with revised table showing emerging trends
- Updated case study on Gartner's predictions, using new figure showing recent hype cycle entries with current sources
- Updated case study on JetBlue and WestJet with recent financial figures and current sources

End-of-Book Comprehensive Case Studies

- New case study #2, "Enabling the Sharing Economy: The Case of Uber Technologies" (replaces case on the Red Cross supply chain)
- Facebook case updated and revised to include recent usage and financial data and discussion of "interest-based ads"
- Apple case updated with recent statistics and strategic moves, including self-driving cars
- Federal Government IT case updated with recent examples and data and discussion of changing strategies to manage the immense portfolio

To the Student

Any college student thinking about the job market can't help but notice how valuable it is to have skills related to information systems. In this course you will learn what information systems are all about and why they are so fundamental to business and society. It will be an exciting journey, filled with revelations about business strategies, technology trends and innovations, and also tips that will help you work smarter as a student. Here are the main features of this text and its supplements:

Learn by Doing: The Interactive, Online Role-Playing Simulations

A course on information systems should tap their power for active, experiential learning. This text includes interactive role-playing simulations in MyMISLab™ (mymislab.com) in which students can apply their knowledge and actually experience what each chapter is about, not just memorize key terms and concepts. You will enter realistic and often tense situations, interacting with the characters via a simulated smartphone or laptop, and using email, text messaging, web conferencing, video chat, voicemail, dashboards, ordering screens, and other applications. Each simulation is scored and students receive extensive feedback on the choices they make. Each one also includes key terms from the chapter (with rollover definitions) so you see how they are used in context, which will help you more easily remember their meanings.

The simulations bring the chapter alive, as you enter authentic settings in which people struggle to solve a problem involving information systems. Some examples:

- In World of Mammals (Chapter 1), you help the harried director of a wild animal preserve interview candidates for the CIO position, after the former CIO leaves abruptly. What skills does a CIO need? What kind of experience would fit best?
- Chocolate Lovers Unite (Chapter 7) challenges you to resolve a heated debate over which online marketing pitch works best by conducting tests, analyzing the results, and drawing on data-driven decision making.
- In Green Wheeling, the simulation on software development and procurement (Chapter 11), you join a task force charged with replacing a college's obsolete fund-raising system. You and your team members weigh the pros and cons of "build" or "buy," and you will see how the outcome can change based on your decisions.
- Vampire Legends drops you into a fast-paced, tense situation in which the material in Chapter 10 (Ethics, Privacy, and Security) comes to life in an online game company that is racing to launch a sequel. When troubling things begin happening that involve the company's data center and information security, you will have difficult choices to make.

I've done research on games and simulations in education, and have led several projects to create software that draws on the compelling features of these environments for learning. While online flash cards, Q&A games, and other interactive applications can help students memorize terms or review the chapter contents, simulations that immerse students in a relevant and authentic case can do more. Research shows they create engagement, improve learning outcomes, and build critical thinking skills through active, student-centered involvement. You will find it much easier to learn and remember the material in the textbook when you can engage in simulations like this.

The Human Element in Information Systems

In addition to the simulations, this text brings a fresh perspective to the introductory course in information systems that combines comprehensive and up-to-date coverage with a stronger focus on the human element in businesses, nonprofits, and other organizations. It covers all the major topics for the course in a rigorous way, without skimping on any of the fundamentals. But it enriches those topics with probing discussions about the roles people play in building, shaping, implementing, and sometimes obstructing information systems.

In Chapter 8 on collaborative technologies, for example, students learn how different channels affect the tone of human communications, and how to choose the best technologies for each task to support virtual teamwork, management, negotiation, and leadership. Chapter 12 on project management and strategic planning for information systems shows how human biases can creep into the process.

The text also stresses the processes and policies that people devise to manage information systems. Why do some high-tech companies ban telecommuting, even though employees have well-equipped home offices? Why do organizations implement surveillance?

Exploring Technology Battlegrounds

Grand battles over technology directions help students understand the close links between competitive business strategies and information systems. The stakes are very high in debates about topics such as net neutrality, 4G standards, wireless spectrum auctions, cloud computing, programming languages, mobile operating systems, mobile payment systems, and social network privacy. Billions of dollars are on the line for winners and losers. Yet most people know little about these battlegrounds because the underlying technology issues are out of reach. After reading this text, students will look at online ads, privacy policies, social networks, and their own smartphones with a new appreciation for the fierce business competitions unfolding before their eyes.

Reaching a Changing Student Body

The text recognizes the growth in the number of women, minorities, international students, online students, and nontraditional students who enroll in this course, drawing on examples and settings that will resonate with them. Devon, for instance, is starting her own web design business, and students learn about relational databases by helping her build one for her small business (Chapter 4). International student Prakash is the cofounder of *Leveling UP!*, a smartphone app that is the centerpiece for the interactive role-playing simulation on business strategy (Chapter 2). In the chapter on knowledge management and e-learning (Chapter 9), Sally takes an online course in nonprofit management as she nears retirement and helps her own company build an e-learning course for the coworkers she's leaving behind.

Balancing Coverage of Business, Government, and Nonprofits

This text broadens the coverage about information systems to include all the varied settings in which students work (or will work). It draws on timely examples from multinational corporations, nonprofits, government agencies, midsized businesses, start-ups, charities, volunteer organizations, student clubs, and other settings. The text highlights how these different organizations launch information systems to fulfill their missions, whether that means generating profits, attracting donations, or serving citizens.

The strategies that underlie cell-phone marketing, for instance, work as effectively for nonprofits that want to mobilize citizens as they do for businesses that tempt new customers with discount coupons. And competitive advantage is not just for business. Charities compete for volunteers and donations, and they benefit from customer relationship management systems.

Changing Student Roles

Just as students are gaining employment in a wide variety of organizations, they are taking on more varied roles within them. Though some will become information systems managers, many more will become consultants, business analysts, accountants, marketing professionals, talent development specialists, volunteers, virtual team leaders, forensic experts, legal advisors, and project managers. The text introduces emerging professions, as well, such as data scientist.

Examples in the text, case studies, and simulations feature all these different roles, showing how successful information systems emerge from a broad base of stakeholders with different perspectives and specialties. Carlos, for instance, is the instructional designer on a corporate e-learning development team, adding his knowledge of usability and accessibility for people with disabilities (Chapter 9). In Chapter 11, Lily is a senior manager for an online grocery who comes up with a clever website to capture a valuable market—busy singles who forgot to buy groceries.

Emphasizing Ethics

Ethical concerns weave throughout the text, touching on very human ethical dilemmas such as the one Wikipedia founder Jimmy Wales faced when asked to delete any posts that mentioned the name of a journalist kidnapped by the Taliban. That action was directly opposed to his site's fervent commitment to free speech, and Wales raised a firestorm within the Wikipedia community when he had to make a choice.

A special feature in each chapter titled "The Ethical Factor" explores timely ethical issues such as corporate responsibility in extended supply chains (Chapter 5), or the ethics of massive surveillance and collection of big data by governments and corporations (Chapter 3). In Chapter 10 on ethics, privacy, and security, students take a survey to learn more about how they judge situations that touch on information ethics. The online simulation for that chapter immerses students in a tense situation in which security is compromised and they face some difficult ethical dilemmas.

Here is a list of all the "Ethical Factor" boxes:

1. Ethical Issues Surrounding Information Systems, p. 22
2. Ethical Responsibility in an Extended Value Chain, p. 44
3. Ethical Implications of Big Data, p. 70
4. Ethical Issues in Database Design: The Case of Ethnic Identification, p. 110
5. Ethics and Talent Management, p. 138
6. Website Accessibility: Why Is Progress So Slow? p. 175
7. The Ethics of Tagging Faces in Photos, p. 204
8. Flash Mobs and Free Speech: Should Police Block Mobile Messaging Services? p. 246
9. Knowledge Sharing in Fast-Paced Industries: The Case of Formula One Racing, p. 273
10. Ethical Dilemmas in a Distributed Denial of Service Attack, p. 309
11. Developing Systems That Promote Ethical Decision Making and Social Responsibility, p. 340
12. Code of Ethics for Project Managers, p. 366

Working Smarter, Not Harder: Productivity Tips for Students

Every chapter includes several "Productivity Tips" that suggest ways students can improve their own productivity by applying what they've learned.

In Chapter 2 on information systems and strategy, for instance, a tip invites students to check out the software trial versions that came preinstalled on their computers to see how companies leverage this valuable product positioning, and then remove them to save space and improve the computer's performance. A tip in the section on neural networks in Chapter 7 advises students to alert their credit card companies before traveling abroad because a neural net may trigger a very ill-timed block on the card. Another tip points to solid productivity gains for people who use two monitors, which is especially helpful for students with laptops.

These tips are not only immediately useful. They help you learn chapter material by applying it so you can work smarter, not harder.

Highlighting Globalization and International Contexts

Information systems play a key role in globalization, especially through the Internet and all the creative destruction it unleashed. Examples abound throughout the text, highlighting how Baidu captured the search engine market in China (Chapter 2) or how Ikea manages a global supply chain (Chapter 5). The global financial crises underscore the important work of the International Accounting Standards Board—to promote transparent and enforceable financial reporting for companies around the world using XBRL tags—from the XML family of standards (Chapter 5). The international emphasis also unfolds in working relationships across national borders. For example, the chapter on collaboration (Chapter 8) discusses virtual teams with members from different countries, and offers tips on strategies to use collaborative technologies effectively.

Inspiring Students to Pursue Promising Careers

Finally, an important goal of this text and its supplements is to convey the sheer excitement and limitless potential of this field, with an eye toward inspiring students to go further. Inside are countless examples of how savvy men and women leverage information systems to transform organizations of all stripes, and even build new empires. The text includes many job descriptions, job growth rates, and projected salaries, as well.

Some of the excitement comes from groundbreaking technological advances. The disruptive innovations that topple some industries and open star-studded paths for others are also part of the excitement. GPS dealt a crushing blow to map makers, and the Internet did the same to print newspapers. The ride-hailing services and their mobile apps have shaken up the transportation industry. But all these events opened up vast new territory for innovative start-ups.

To further stimulate interest, each chapter includes short "Did You Know?" snippets to highlight an engaging or amusing application of the chapter's topic. For example, the chapter on hardware, software, and networks (Chapter 3) features a coffee shop whose zany owner constantly renames the free wireless network to different messages, such as "BuyAnotherCupYouCheapskate."

If students catch some of this energy and enthusiasm, they may decide to pursue this field. Those who do will have outstanding career prospects in the private and public sectors, and they'll never be bored.

Supplements

The following supplements are available at the Online Instructor Resource Center, -accessible through www.pearsonhighered.com/wallace:

Instructor's Manual

The Instructor's Manual, assembled by John Hupp, includes a list of learning objectives and answers to all end-of-chapter questions.

Test Item File

The Test Item File, prepared by ANSR Source, Inc., contains more than 1,300 questions, including multiple choice, true/false, and essay. Each question is followed by the correct answer, the learning objective it ties to, a course learning objective, and difficulty rating. In addition, certain questions are tagged to the appropriate AACSB category.

Powerpoint Presentations

The Instructor PowerPoints, prepared by John Hupp, highlight text learning objectives and key topics and serve as an excellent aid for classroom presentations and lectures.

Image Library

This collection of the figures and tables from the text offers another aid for classroom presentations and PowerPoint slides.

TestGen

Pearson Education's test-generating software is available from www.pearsonhighered.com/irc. The software is PC/MAC compatible and preloaded with all of the Test Item File questions.

You can manually or randomly view test questions and drag-and-drop to create a test. You can add or modify test-bank questions as needed. Our TestGens are converted for use in BlackBoard, WebCT, Moodle, D2L, and Angel. These conversions can be found on the Instructor's Resource Center. The TestGen is also available in Respondus and can be found on www.respondus.com.

Alternate Electronic Versions

Pearson is proud to offer alternate versions for students seeking an electronic version of the Wallace text. VitalSource (www.vitalsource.com) provides one option, where students simply select their eText by title or author and purchase immediate access to the content for the duration of the course using a major credit card. Students can also find eBooks through Barnes & Noble, Kindle versions on Amazon, and more through various other eBook retailers.

Available in MyMISLab

- MIS Video Exercises – Videos illustrating MIS concepts, paired with brief quizzes
- Interactive Online Role-Playing Simulations – Require students to apply their knowledge and actually experience what each chapter is about, not just memorize key terms and concepts
- Auto-Graded writing exercises – taken from the end of chapter
- Assisted-Graded writing exercises – taken from the end of chapter, with a rubric provided
- Chapter Warm Ups, Chapter Quizzes – objective-based quizzing to test knowledge
- Discussion Questions – taken from the end of chapter
- Dynamic Study Modules – on the go adaptive quizzing, also available on a mobile phone
- Learning Catalytics – bring-your-own-device classroom response tools
- Enhanced eText – an accessible, mobile-friendly eText
- Excel & Access Grader Projects – live in the application auto-graded Grader projects provided inside MyMISLab to support classes covering Office tools

Acknowledgments

Many thanks go to all the reviewers who took time to comment on manuscripts, simulation storyboards, case studies, and other features of the text. Their feedback and suggestions were extremely valuable, and they help ensure the text and its ancillaries will meet the needs of faculty and students.

Dennis Adams, *University of Houston*

Joni Adkins, *Northwest Missouri State University*

Sven Aelterman, *Troy University*

Solomon Antony, *Murray State University*

John Appleman, *State University of New York College at Brockport*

Bay Arinze, *Drexel University*

Janine Aronson, *University of Georgia*

John Kirk Atkinson, *Western Kentucky University*

Robert Balicki, *Cleary University*

Cynthia Barnes, *Lamar University*

Stephen Barnes, *Regis University*

Peggy Batchelor, *Furman University*

Jon Beard, *George Mason University*

Hossein Bidgoli, *California State University—Bakersfield*

Robert Bonometti, *MGB Enterprises LLC*

Ted Boone, *University of Kansas*

Uptal Bose, *University of Houston; Rainer*

David Bradbard, *Winthrop University*

Jason Chen, *Gonzaga University*

Joselina Cheng, *University of Central Oklahoma*

Steve Clements, *Eastern Oregon University*

Phillip Coleman, *Western Kentucky University*

Emilio Collar, Jr., *Western Connecticut State University*

Steve Corder, *Williams Baptist College*

Dave Croasdell, *University of Nevada, Reno*

Albert Cruz, *National University*

Mohammad Dadashzadeh, *Oakland University*

Don Danner, *San Francisco State University*

Dessa David, *Morgan State University*

Carolyn Dileo, *Westchester Community College*

Michael Douglas, *Millersville University*

Doris Duncan, *California State University—East Bay*

Barbara Edington, *St. Francis College*

Kurt Engemann, *Iona College*

John Erickson, *University of Nebraska at Omaha*

William Figg, *Dakota State University*

David Firth, *The University of Montana*

Anne Formalarie, *Plymouth State University*

Saiid Ganjalizadeh, *The Catholic University of America*

Richard Glass, *Bryant University*

Tanya Goette, *Georgia College & State University*

Sandeep Goyal, *University of Southern Indiana*

Martin Grossman, *Bridgewater State University*

Bin Gu, *University of Texas at Austin*

Laura Hall, *University of Texas—El Paso*

Rosie Hauck, *Illinois State University*

Jun He, *University of Michigan—Dearborn*

Devanandham Henry, *Stevens Institute of Technology*

Michelle Hepner, *University of Central Oklahoma*

John Hupp, *Columbus State University*

Jerry Isaacs, *Carroll University*

Brian Janz, *University of Memphis*

Jon (Sean) Jasperson, *Texas A&M University*

Brian Jones, *Tennessee Technological University*

Junghwan Kim, *Texas Tech University*

Philip Kim, *Walsh University*

Sung-kwan Kim, *University of Arkansas at Little Rock*

Charles S. Knode, *University of Maryland University College*

Brian Kovar, *Kansas State University*

Bill Kuechler, *University of Nevada at Reno*

Louis LeBlanc, *Berry College*

Albert Lederer, *University of Kentucky*

Ingyu Lee, *Troy University*

Mary Locke, *Greenville Technical College*

Sanchita Mal-Sarkar, *Cleveland State University*

Nancy Martin, *Southern Illinois University Carbondale*

Prosenjit Mazumdar, *George Mason University*

Roger McHaney, *Kansas State University*

William McMillan, *Madonna University*

Tonya Melvin-Bryant, *North Carolina Central University*

Kimberly Merritt, *Oklahoma Christian University*

Allison Morgan, *Howard University*

Fui Hoon (Fiona) Nah, *University of Nebraska—Lincoln*

Sandra Newton, *Sonoma State University*

Ravi Paul, *East Carolina University*

Adriane Randolph, *Kennesaw State University*

Betsy Ratchford, *University of Northern Iowa*

Mandy Reininger, *Chemeketa Community College*

Nicolas Rouse, *Phoenix College*

Paula Ruby, *Arkansas State University*

Werner Schenk, *University of Rochester*

Daniel Schmidt, *Washburn University*

Aaron Schorr, *Fashion Institute of Technology*

Paul Seibert, *North Greenville University*

Narcissus Shambare, *College of St. Mary*

Larry Smith, *Charleston Southern University*

Toni Somers, *Wayne State University*

Todd Stabenow, *Hawkeye Community College*

James Stewart, *University of Maryland University College*

Joe Teng, *Troy University Troy Campus*

Evelyn Thrasher, *Western Kentucky University*

Jan Tucker, *Argosy University*

Jonathan Whitaker, *University of Richmond*

Bruce White, *Quinnipiac University*

Anita Whitehill, *Mission College*

G. W. Willis, *Baylor University*

Charles Willow, *Monmouth University*

Marie Wright, *Western Connecticut State University*

Jigish Zaveri, *Morgan State University*

Chen Zhang, *Bryant University*

Many thanks to John Hupp of Columbia State University for his outstanding work on the end of chapter materials and the instructor's manual, and to Jollean Sinclaire of Arkansas State University who contributed to those as well. I am grateful to Robert Mills of Utah State University, who applied his expertise to the questions in the Learning Catalytics system.

Thanks also to the excellent work and innovative ideas of my editor, Samantha Lewis, and also the editors who worked with me in the past, Bob Horan and Nicole Sam. The production team, led by Katrina Ostler at Cenveo Publishing Services, and Ann Pulido with SPi did an outstanding job as well. It is a pleasure to work with all of these people to create a comprehensive set of learning materials that offer faculty unique teaching tools and time-saving strategies, and at the same time, engage students with lively and innovative learning experiences.

And finally, thanks to Julian and Callie, and also Keiko, Lili, and Marlene, a list that includes my very supportive human family and our four-footed companions.

Your Feedback Is Welcome

To all of you who are using this book, as professors, teaching assistants, and students, I welcome your thoughts and feedback. Please email your comments, questions, and suggestions, and I'll be eager to hear how your course goes.

Patricia Wallace, Ph.D.
pwallace@jhu.edu

Introduction to Information Systems

MyMISLab™

- Online Simulation: The World of Mammals: A Role-Playing Simulation on Choosing a New CIO for an Animal Preserve
- Discussion Questions: #1-1, #1-2, #1-3
- Writing Assignments: #1-9, #1-14

LEARNING OBJECTIVES

1 Describe the main roles that information systems play in organizations.

2 Compare the terms *data, information,* and *knowledge,* and describe three characteristics that make information valuable.

3 Describe the four main components of an information system and the role that each plays.

4 Identify several research areas in the discipline of management information systems (MIS).

5 Provide examples of how business, nonprofit, and government managers, as well as information technology departments, depend on information systems knowledge.

6 Explain how information systems present both promises and perils, and pose ethical questions.

An online, interactive decision-making simulation that reinforces chapter contents and uses key terms in context can be found in MyMISLab™.

INTRODUCTION

AT THE HEART OF EVERY ORGANIZATION IS ITS INFORMATION SYSTEMS, and that is what this course is all about. Google, Twitter, Microsoft, and Facebook are all popular companies on the cutting edge of technology, and their innovations and competitive battles make front page news. But even organizations that don't seem very high tech—from a family-owned restaurant to a fitness gym—can hardly do without information systems or without people who know how to build and manage them.

Consider The World of Mammals, for example, the animal preserve featured in the interactive simulation for this chapter. Director Yolanda Whalen is a veterinarian, but she knows very well that this preserve won't succeed without top-notch

information systems and a qualified person to provide leadership. She is asking you, as an enthusiastic volunteer and a student learning about information systems, to help interview potential candidates and join the team that will decide who is best suited for this role. What skills, knowledge, and abilities should this person have—beyond managing payroll and ticket sales—to take advantage of innovative technologies that will make The World of Mammals the most successful preserve in the country?

This opening chapter highlights information systems in action, the nature of information itself, and the four main components of every information system. You will see how the information systems (IS) discipline is changing

THE WORLD OF MAMMALS

A Role-Playing Simulation on Choosing a New CIO for an Animal Preserve

© Meoita/Shutterstock.

and growing and why a solid understanding of this subject will give you a critical edge, regardless of your major or career path. Finally, the chapter examines the promises and perils of information systems and the many ethical issues that arise with the phenomenal power within everyone's reach.

Information is an organization's most important asset. Creating, capturing, organizing, storing, retrieving, analyzing, and acting on information are fundamental activities in every organization. The skill with which you carry out those tasks will be the deciding factor not just for your company's success but for your own as well. This book is about information and the systems that people develop and manage to perform all those tasks and more.

You will see how these systems work, why they are created, how they have become the organization's central nervous system, and why they sometimes fail. You will also learn to tap the power of information systems to help your company compete or your organization become more effective. Finally, you will become more productive yourself—working smarter, not harder—in college, in your career, at home, and throughout your life.

Like the information they manage, information systems cover a very broad scope and contribute to many different activities in an organization. What roles do they play, and how do they transform work? The next section shows the enormous variety of settings in which innovative information systems play a role, well beyond the very useful Google searches.

Describe the main roles that information systems play in organizations.

1 Information Systems in Action

- *Dancing with the Stars* became a smash reality TV hit by engaging millions of viewers in judging the contestants. Hopeful celebrity couples compete each week with a novel dance routine, and audience members cast a vote for their favorite by phoning, sending text messages, or logging into the show's website. An information system on the back end tallies the results, which count for half the couple's score. The system must be able to handle enormous incoming volume in a very short time period to get accurate tallies.

- Hurricane Sandy arrived just before the November 2012 elections in the United States, and many voters could not make it to the polls. Officials in New Jersey decided to let people vote by email, but county clerks were overwhelmed by the volume in their inboxes. Although glitches and security concerns are not uncommon with electronic voting, information systems are playing a more important role every year. Disabled voters, for instance, can now use tablets to vote, eliminating the need for expensive custom-made voting machines.

- Walmart, with more than $485 billion in net sales in 2015, pioneered the globe's most efficient information system to track shipments as they move from supplier factories to warehouses to retail stores. Tags attached to pallets transmit information wirelessly, so Walmart execs know exactly where merchandise is in the supply chain and can spot trouble immediately.

When those bulky computers first entered company basements in the 1970s, the term *information system* brought up images of payroll programs, general ledgers, invoice tracking, and inventory management. Those back-office functions are still critically important, but today's information systems have migrated into every facet of an organization, touching every employee from the mail clerk to the CEO. They also extend well beyond the company's boundaries, reaching out to customers, clients, suppliers, partners, citizens, and all kinds of stakeholders. Their hardware might be as vast as Google's data centers or far smaller than Walmart's pallet tags. And their connections could be the thick fiber-optic cables on the ocean floor or electromagnetic waves in the air around you.

Multinational firms, small businesses, nonprofits, governments, volunteer organizations, self-employed entrepreneurs, universities, and other organizations rely on information systems for a host of reasons, and they continue to adapt, expand, and interconnect them to achieve their strategic objectives. These systems play critical roles in six major areas (Figure 1-1).

Managing Operations

Every successful organization must excel at **operations management**, which involves the design, operation, and improvement of the systems and processes the organization uses to deliver its goods and services. Some of these deal with several very basic functions that are part of every business. Information systems are crucial for tracking employee payroll, taxes, benefits, and timesheets. Accounting information systems are essential to track accounts receivable, to process transactions, to procure goods and services, and to pay the suppliers. Organizations also must manage their assets and inventories, from the computers and the desks they sit on to the massive factories and equipment located in far corners of the globe. Eric Schmidt, former CEO of Google, once remarked that he had no idea how many data centers Google actually managed. He might not have known, but his back-office information systems certainly did.

Information systems designed to handle the processes involved in these functions must also meet compliance standards set by governments and other regulatory agencies, which may change from time to time and also vary by country or state. Reports must be filed, audits passed, and changing regulations followed. Extensive regulations put into place after the global financial crisis of 2009, for example, set tighter standards for accounting practices—particularly in banking—and demanded more transparent reporting.

FIGURE 1-1

The major roles of information systems in organizations.

Many organizations choose commercially produced information systems to handle their back-office information needs, relying on software packages such as SAP, Oracle, NetSuite, or QuickBooks. Some organizations are moving these functions to service providers or even outsourcing them entirely. India became known as the world's "back office" because so many companies moved these applications there,[1] and now the Philippines is becoming the world's biggest operator of call centers.[2]

Depending on their missions, organizations also need information systems to manage industry-specific operations, such as these:

- Manufacturers need systems to manage assembly lines, product quality, production schedules, and just-in-time supply deliveries (Figure 1-2).
- Colleges and universities need systems to manage student academic records, class scheduling, faculty assignments, and student financial aid (Figure 1-3).

FIGURE 1-2

Manufacturing information system displaying production volumes and other metrics.

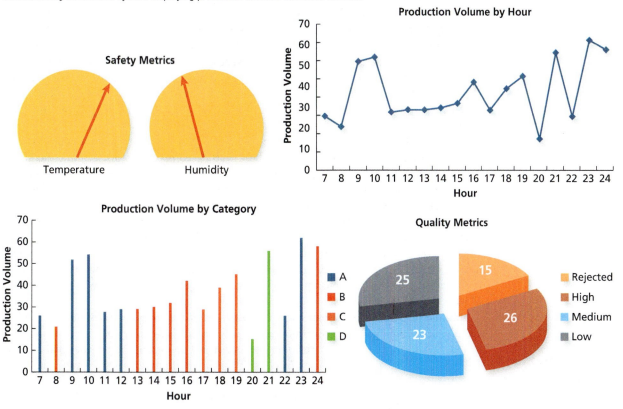

FIGURE 1-3

Student information system with online services for students and faculty.

| MyCollege | MyTools | MyClasses | MyProfile |

Course	Days	Time	Location
Bus 111	MW	14:00–15:00	Macintyre
Bus 111	MW	15:00–16:00	Doyle
Bus 112	T-TH	9:00–10:45	Student Services
Bus 112	-	-	Online
Bus 112	M	9:00–11:45	Garcia
Bus 113	W	1:00–2:45	Doyle

Update contact info / View schedules / Submit request / View requirements / Register for courses

operations management

The area of management concerned with the design, operation, and improvement of the systems and processes the organization uses to deliver its goods and services.

■ Transportation companies rely on information systems equipped with GPS to track their fleets, optimize routes, and conserve gas.

■ Companies that buy products from suppliers around the globe need real-time updates on their global supply chains to manage inventories and reduce costs.

Achieving excellence in operations can provide enormous cost savings and competitive advantage, as companies squeeze every ounce of fat out of their processes without sacrificing quality. UPS drivers, for instance, know to avoid left turns on their delivery routes when possible because they take a few seconds longer, wasting time and gas. Systems that support operations are discussed in Chapter 5.

Supporting Customer Interactions

Interactions with customers, clients, students, patients, taxpayers, citizens, and others who come to your organization desiring a product or service are fundamental to success. Your customers pay the bills. **Customer relationship management (CRM) systems**, discussed in Chapter 5, build and maintain relationships and support all the processes that underlie them.

A brick-and-mortar retail store, for example, needs a sales system that identifies each product in the shopper's basket, tallies the total, feeds the data to the inventory system, and accepts various kinds of payment. Shoppers want fast checkouts, and they get annoyed by clumsy, inefficient processes. When an item lacks its barcode, impatient customers may just abandon it rather than wait for a salesclerk to track it down. Strategies to prevent theft, such as the check on weights added to the bag, also anger shoppers when they do not function properly.

Web-based shopping and self-service transform relationships with customers, freeing them from time-consuming phone calls. These web-based processes often mimic the brick-and-mortar versions, with "shopping carts" and "checkouts" clearly labeled. A web application offers many opportunities to build stronger relationships and also better understand the motives and desires of each person who visits.

Scattered throughout *Amazon.com*'s site, for example, are recommendations based on previous purchases, encouragements to "review this book" or "rate this item," special discounts and coupons, storage space for your wish lists and gift ideas, and many other innovative features to map out your preferences and build a stronger relationship. All of this data contributes to Amazon's customer relationship management excellence and the company's understanding of what each customer wants.

Infinite variations in customer interaction exist, from Southwest Airlines's text reminders about your upcoming flight to the Internal Revenue Service's e-file system. Developing these relationships is not just about improving sales and collecting receipts. It is about building long-term loyalty and satisfaction by listening to customers and learning what is most important to them. That also includes sensitivity to their privacy concerns, as we discuss in Chapter 10.

FIGURE 1-4

How do managers answer questions like these?

Should we offer free wifi to customers?

Should we add more fish to the menu?

Where should we open another branch of our restaurant?

Can we save money by closing an hour earlier?

Source: liza54500/Shutterstock

Making Decisions

How should a restaurant manager make decisions like the ones in Figure 1-4?

Managers make decisions every day, and many rely mainly on their own judgment. In fact, researchers surveyed 250 executives and learned that 40% of major corporate decisions were based on gut instincts.[3] Smart managers, however, know that information systems support **data-driven decision making**, which draws on the billions of pieces of data to reveal important trends and patterns. For example, the sales system will show how much the restaurant makes in the last hour of business, and that data will help the manager make a good decision about closing early.

Business intelligence refers to all the information managers use to make decisions, and it can come from many sources beyond the organization's own information systems. The restaurant manager, for example, might combine customer records with publicly available information about income levels by zip code to help make a smart decision about where to open another branch.

Decision support systems and business intelligence, discussed in Chapter 7, encompass a growing and varied category that blends rapid analysis of information sources with artificial intelligence and human knowledge. For knowledge workers, in particular, the value of knowing how to draw upon those vast mountains of information to make wise decisions is extremely high.

Your online behavior is one of the most important sources of business intelligence. The sites you visit and "like," the apps you download, and the links you click reveal your interests and intentions, and marketers track that data closely. Spending for mobile ads, for instance, could reach $250 per user by 2018.[4]

Collaborating on Teams

Collaboration and teamwork have considerable support from innovative information systems that allow people to work together at any time and from any place. Regardless of where they live and work, participants can hold online meetings, share documents and applications, and interact using microphones, video cameras, and whiteboards. **Social networking sites** support online communities of people who create profiles for themselves, form ties with others with whom they share interests, and make new connections based on those ties. These social groups exploded in popularity as people jumped at the chance to share news, photos, videos, and tidbits. Figure 1-5 shows usage rates for the larger social networking sites. Services that target business users, such as Microsoft's SharePoint, offer additional useful services such as shared calendars and group document editing.

Developing information systems for collaboration takes ingenuity and attention to the ways in which people really do work together. The possibilities are endless, and different groups have different preferences. In online university courses, for example, debates about whether students should turn on their webcams during virtual class sessions are common. Many prefer to keep them turned off, valuing the privacy that invisibility creates. (One can doze off in a virtual class with little concern for detection.)

The information systems that support virtual teamwork, discussed in Chapter 8, are in some respects still in their infancy—especially compared with the more mature systems used to manage operations. Expect many improvements as we learn more about what features work best for different people and different situations.

FIGURE 1-5

Estimated usage for major social networking sites.

Social Networking Site	Estimated Unique Monthly Visitors
Facebook	1,100,000,000
Twitter	310,000,000
LinkedIn	255,000,000
Pinterest	250,000,000
Google+	120,000,000
Tumblr	110,000,000
Instagram	100,000,000
VK	80,000,000

Source: Data from http://www.ebizmba.com/articles/social-networking-websites, eBizMBA, © 2016.

customer relationship management (CRM) system
An information system used to build customer relationships, enhance loyalty, and manage interactions with customers.

data-driven decision making
Decision making that draws on the billions of pieces of data that can be aggregated to reveal important trends and patterns.

business intelligence
The information managers use to make decisions, drawn from the company's own information systems or external sources.

social networking sites
Online communities of people who create profiles for themselves, form ties with others with whom they share interests, and make new connections based on those ties.

Gaining Competitive Advantage

Information systems play what could be their most valuable role when they are tied closely to strategy and to the major initiatives that will help achieve competitive advantage—a topic we take up in Chapter 2. **Competitive advantage**, which is anything that gives a firm a lead over its rivals, can be gained through the development and application of innovative information systems. Information systems are a fundamental part of a company's strategic vision. Indeed, the vision itself is often shaped by what these systems can achieve today and what is possible for the future.

Consider how Apple's iPhone got the jump on smartphone competitors with Siri, the intelligent personal assistant. Siri responds to spoken commands such as "Tell my brother I'll be late" and also answers questions like "Any Italian restaurants near here?" Initially, the iPhone's market share rose to more than 50%, in part because no other smartphone had anything like Siri. But competitive advantage can be fleeting. Microsoft entered the market with Cortana, Google launched Google Now, and Amazon followed up with Echo. Time will tell which personal assistant wins the most hearts.[5]

Strategy is equally important to nonprofit organizations and government agencies, and their information systems break new ground by offering handy services to the public, streamlining operations, and improving decision making. For instance, U.S. citizens can apply for Social Security benefits online rather than wait in line. Government strategies to combat terrorism also involve information systems—and analysis of immense volumes of data. Those strategies raise important ethical dilemmas, discussed in Chapters 3 and 10.

Improving Individual Productivity

Tools to help people improve their own productivity abound, from the smartphones that combine voice calls with web browsing, contact databases, email, music, and games to the many software applications that eliminate tedious work. Even word processing has transformed work in every organization, and many students aren't aware of all the ways that software can make them more productive. You can, for example, automatically create and properly format your term paper references by integrating a bibliographic manager such as Zotero, which captures the citation from a web page.

> **PRODUCTIVITY TIP**
> Time management experts advise that you process your email inbox to zero, flagging important messages, moving others to appropriate categories, and rerouting some using automated filtering tools. Your email system can do quite a bit of work for you if you take time to configure it.

To improve productivity at work, people can choose from a bewildering variety of computer software and electronic devices, but more is not necessarily better. You should select carefully, with an eye to the functions you need most, ease of use, and short learning curves. No one likes reading thick instruction manuals. Throughout this book, you will see productivity tips in boxes—like the one on this page—that will help you improve your own productivity.

Compare the terms *data*, *information*, and *knowledge*, and describe three characteristics that make information valuable.

2 The Nature of Information

Except for words like *the, a, and, if,* and *it,* the word *information* was once one of the most common words on the Internet. No wonder people called the net an "information" storehouse. The term *information* is critical to understanding how information systems work, but it can be very slippery.

Facts, data, intelligence, knowledge, and even tips are synonyms for information, and they all touch on characteristics of the "stuff" that information systems can manage. For our purposes, the term **data** refers to individual facts or pieces of information, and **information** refers to data or facts that are assembled and analyzed to add meaning and usefulness. A patient's single high-temperature reading at a 24-hour walk-in clinic in Maryland is one piece of data.

FIGURE 1-6

Examples of the continuum from data to information to knowledge, as meaning and usefulness grow.

Data	Information	Knowledge
Patient's temperature at walk-in clinic on Dec. 15 = 103.9° F.	Table showing flu diagnoses in region during month of December	Worldwide map of flu outbreaks suggesting pandemic
01010011 01001111 01010011	Binary code for SOS	HELP!!!
Microsoft (MSFT) closing stock price	Graph of Microsoft highs and lows for one year	Combined with analysis of other information, leads to broker's recommendation to buy, hold, or sell stock
CWOT	Complete Waste of Time (text messaging abbreviation)	May be interpreted as an insult
GPS coordinates	Map showing location with push pin	Location of Taj Mahal in India
Invoice #259 Total Amount = $139.23	Total Sales for Southern Region in First Quarter = $2,156,232	Fastest growing sales region; consider broader marketing campaign

But entered into the clinic's information system and combined with the patient's other symptoms and previous medical records, it becomes far more valuable as a diagnostic tool.

We gain even more from this one temperature reading by combining it with data from other patients entering all clinics that week. The patterns may warn of a flu outbreak or even a major epidemic. The health staff at the Centers for Disease Control and Prevention in Atlanta, Georgia, draw on data like this to map the spread of diseases and take swift action to protect the public.

Refining, analyzing, and combining information make it more and more useful and meaningful, and the effort adds to our ability to use it to make decisions and take action. The path from data to information, and then to knowledge, is a continuum, and Figure 1-6 shows some examples. No clear dividing lines separate these categories; they blend together and form a continuum as more meaning and usefulness are created through skillful analysis and human insight.

What Makes Information Valuable?

Separating useful information from the trivial is no easy task given the sheer volume of information on the planet. Three characteristics stand out, however, that contribute to making some information very valuable: (1) timeliness, (2) accuracy, and (3) completeness (Figure 1-7).

Timeliness matters a great deal in some settings, and near real-time information often costs more. For example, people pay monthly fees to financial services to get up-to-the-minute stock prices rather than the delayed price reports shown on free stock tickers you can add to your own browser. Riswan Khalfan of TD Securities says his system can handle a breathtaking 5 million pieces of data per second, far more than most other banks. He points out that "if you fall behind, you're dealing with stale data and that puts you at a disadvantage." With timely, up-to-date trading data, Khalfan's systems can make quicker decisions, which he argues are better (Figure 1-8).[6]

Accuracy may seem like an obvious feature of valuable information, but there actually are degrees of accuracy. The more accurate you want the information to be, the longer it may take to obtain, making extreme accuracy a trade-off to timeliness. A CEO who wants to know how much competitors charge for a rival product, for example, might wait too long for staff to scour all the distribution channels and assemble the data. An approximate but timely answer is more valuable.

FIGURE 1-7

What makes information valuable?

Timeliness

Accuracy

Completeness

---

competitive advantage
Anything that gives a firm a lead over its rivals; it can be gained through the development and application of innovative information systems.

data
Individual facts or pieces of information.

information
Data or facts that are assembled and analyzed to add meaning and usefulness.

FIGURE 1-8
Timeliness is a critical attribute for certain kinds of information, such as stock prices.

Source: Agencja Fotograficzna Caro/Alamy Stock Photo

Completeness adds value, particularly as a means to avoid bias or spin. A marketing survey that polls customers as they enter a store will completely miss those who shop online, for example. The survey results would be incomplete without taking greater care to assess the interests of all the customers. Striving for complete information, however, may also introduce delays that affect timeliness.

PRODUCTIVITY TIP
Many colleges and universities have agreements with software companies to offer discounts to their students. Before you buy software, check with your IT department. Once you leave student status behind, you'll be hard-pressed to find deals like the ones you can get now.

Describe the four main components of an information system and the role that each plays.

3 The Components of an Information System

An **information system**, whether it is a speed camera network, a company's payroll system, or a social networking service, brings together four critical components to collect, process, manage, analyze, and distribute information: (1) people, (2) technology, (3) processes, and (4) data (Figure 1-9).

People

The design, development, launch, and maintenance of any information system involve teams of people. They play a number of different roles—as visionaries, developers, and managers of information systems and also as analysts, liaisons, users, customers, contributors, and sometimes roadblocks. Often underestimated, the human element plays a crucial role in the success or failure of most information systems, and you will see many examples of that throughout this book.

Leaders may be first to propose a system that will accomplish an important strategic objective for the company. However, innovative ideas for such systems come from every level, provided the organization's culture openly encourages people to think about how information

FIGURE 1-9
The four components of an information system.

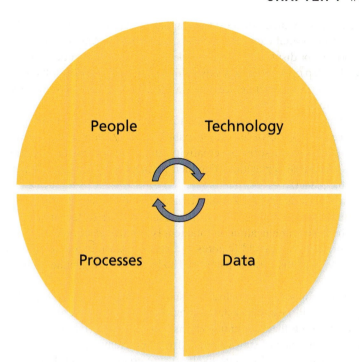

systems can help. Managers and staff from many departments participate on teams with technologists to design a new system or evaluate commercial systems that might be purchased. The information technology team usually works closely with staff in marketing, finance, human resources, and other functional areas to launch user-friendly, people-oriented systems.

Many systems draw from a much wider pool of people, involving users as contributors and developers, not just customers or clients. **User-generated content (UGC)**, for example, makes up most of the information in systems such as Wikipedia, eBay, Craigslist, YouTube, Facebook, and Twitter. These systems would not exist without generous contributions from the community. UGC is an important ingredient in **Web 2.0**, the second generation of web development that facilitates far more interactivity, end-user contributions, collaboration, and information sharing compared with earlier models. Social networking and virtual meetings are all features of Web 2.0.

The people who manage systems that tap UGC work hard to promote the positive contributions and even harder to keep the criminals and pranksters from taking over. For instance, scammers in Texas copied photos from legitimate "Home for Sale" ads, then posted them as "For Rent" on Craigslist. People who wanted to rent one of the houses sent in their deposits to the fake landlord who was "out of town," only to learn later that the home was never for rent at all. Craigslist founder Craig Newmark tirelessly helps the organization deal with issues like that one.

Technology

Information technology (IT) includes hardware, software, and telecommunications. IT is one of the four components of an information system, though people often use the terms interchangeably. Rack after rack of servers in Google's windowless data centers are examples of

---

information system
A system that brings together four critical components to collect, process, manage, analyze, and distribute information; the four components are people, technology, processes, and data.

user-generated content (UGC)
The content contributed to a system by its users.

Web 2.0
The second generation of web development that facilitates far more interactivity, end-user contributions, collaboration, and information sharing compared with earlier models.

information technology (IT)
The hardware, software, and telecommunications that comprise the technology component of information systems; the term is often used more broadly to refer to information systems.

this component, along with all the desktop computers, laptops, netbooks, tablets, cell phones, navigation devices, digital cameras, scanners, and sensors. Anything capable of collecting, processing, storing, or displaying electronic data is potentially part of an information system. The transponder chip on your car's windshield that allows electronic toll collection is another example. The battery-powered device sends a signal to the tollbooth; in some areas, drivers don't even need to slow down.

Software ranges from the code needed to boot up a computer to programs with artificial intelligence and their own learning capabilities. The Internet and the World Wide Web unleashed an explosion of software creativity, transforming businesses around the globe. Organizations can create applications that their partners, suppliers, and customers can access anywhere on the planet.

Telecommunications and networks are also part of IT, and the term **information and communications technology (ICT)** is often used to refer to the broader collection. The main role of the telecommunications component is to move electronic signals from one place to another, route traffic, and add features to improve transmission speeds, eliminate noise, increase security, or analyze traffic patterns. The infrastructure includes both wired and wireless transmission.

Increasingly, people favor wireless transmission because of its flexibility and reduced cost, though speed still lags. Many developing countries that can't afford to build wired networks are transforming their communications and expanding Internet access through wireless transmission. In much of sub-Saharan Africa, for example, copper wiring may never be deployed at all. Wireless is also more likely to stay up and running during storms that bring down utility poles and wires.

While the "people" component and UGC play key roles in Web 2.0 developments, technology is a major driver of what some call *Web 3.0*. As hundreds of millions of sensors are embedded in vehicles, doorways, livestock, warehouse shelves, ocean buoys, wristwatches, and anything else, and all are connected to the net, we begin to glimpse the power of the **Internet of Things (IoT)**. The sensors can pick up geographic location, temperature, motion, wind speed, pollution indicators, heart rate, and much more. When combined with traditional data sources and UGC, these immense, rapidly growing collections are known as "big data," and they offer stunning opportunities for innovation.[7] As the web continues to evolve, new skills and tools will be needed to analyze big data intelligently.[8]

Processes

A **business process** is a set of activities designed to achieve a task. Organizations implement information systems to support, streamline, and sometimes eliminate business processes. Countless decisions are made about how each process should operate, what rules it should follow, how information should be handled from input to output, and especially how the information system will support the process. For example, should the system log every change an employee makes to the data? Will the system require supervisors to electronically approve all purchases or just those above a certain value? What decisions can the information system make on its own based on incoming data and rules, and which ones require human judgment?

Managers develop policies that affect information system processes, and the systems can enforce those policies. A major policy category involves security. How will the system authenticate the user, and what access will he or she be granted? If the system requires a password, how long should it be, and when will it expire?

The steps in any process are affected by thousands of decisions people make, and these are influenced by the way people look at process improvements. For example, some organizations try to design systems that just reproduce what employees were doing, thereby reducing labor. In a college registrations office, employees might send letters to students who could not enroll in a class that they selected to explain why they were denied. One improvement might be to design a feature that automatically generates form letters to those students with their name and address, the class they selected, and a list of the most common reasons they could not register. Instead of typing the letter, the employees can check the reason and stuff the letter into an envelope (Figure 1-10). The staff would be pleased with this handy new efficiency, though students might think the new letters are a bit mechanical.

NARA SELLERS
143 LA GUARDIA STREET
JACKSON, AZ

Dear Student:

We are sorry to inform you that we are unable to confirm your registration for the class listed below for the reason checked:

FALL   BMGT 322   SECTION 5

☐   The class is full.

☐   Your records show you have not fulfilled the prerequisites.

☐   The class is only open to juniors or seniors.

☐   Your tuition payment has not yet been received.

☐   Other_____

Please contact the Registrations Office if you have any questions.

Sincerely,
Registrations

FIGURE **1-10**
Although automatically generating letters like this one provides some process improvement, information systems can do much more. This process could be eliminated entirely.

A closer look at the process, however, might lead to far more radical changes. Moving to online registrations, for instance, could eliminate the process entirely. If a class is full or if the student isn't eligible to take it, the registration system should not allow the student to choose it, thus eliminating the need to send letters at all. This new design, shown in Figure 1-11, would please students because they would get instant confirmation that their class choices

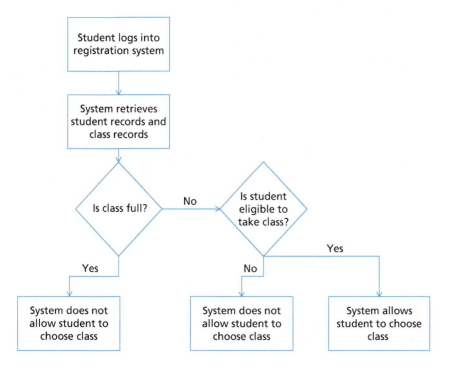

FIGURE **1-11**
Process diagram for a smarter registration system.

information and communications technology (ICT)
The term encompasses the broad collection of information processing and communications technologies, emphasizing that telecommunication technology is a significant feature of information systems.

Internet of Things (IoT)
The network of physical objects that contain sensors and technology that enable them to collect and exchange data.

business process
A set of activities designed to achieve a task; organizations implement information systems to support, streamline, and sometimes eliminate business processes.

were available. Also, they would no longer receive frustrating form letters that foil their academic plans. Registrations staff, however, may worry about layoffs.

Business process management (BPM) is the field that focuses on designing, optimizing, and streamlining processes, taking into account the human element. Analysts look at processes from many different angles to suggest innovative approaches that leverage the power of information systems and propose tweaks at every step. Software is available to simulate business processes and conduct "what if" experiments to assist with the analysis.

Efforts to manage business processes also take into account the overall organizational culture. Does the organization need very tight controls over every piece of information? Banks, hospitals, military units, and many other institutions bear heavy responsibilities to safeguard sensitive information, and their missions affect the way processes are designed. Free use of the Internet may not be permitted, and employees may not be able to take files home on portable USB flash drives to catch up over the weekend. Some organizations even push epoxy glue into the desktop computers' USB ports to prevent anyone from copying data. In contrast, people involved in a freewheeling start-up or a volunteer organization may not be too concerned with where or when people work, how secure their information is, or whether staff post party photos on the company servers.

Business processes and policies must also be reviewed frequently because circumstances change quickly. Numerous corporate scandals, for example, have led to stiff laws about retaining electronic documents. If there is a pending legal case, businesses have a duty to preserve electronic files that might be relevant, including email. **E-discovery** refers to the processes by which electronic data that might be used as legal evidence are requested, secured, and searched. Electronic documents that might be relevant to a case cover a very wide scope, and they can be quite slippery to manage as people edit, cut and paste, and make copies—not just on the company's computers but on their own smartphones and tablets.[9]

Data

Data are the grist for every information system, and these raw facts can present themselves in an enormous variety of shapes and forms. Figure 1-12 shows many examples of data that become part of information systems. Using a mercury thermometer, for example, a patient's temperature reading would appear as the height of the mercury bar in a glass tube. Data reflecting time intervals might appear as seconds on a stopwatch.

Data from the exploding Internet of Things will quickly outpace virtually every other source. In 2014, almost 4 billion devices were connected, but by 2020, that figure is expected to grow to 25 billion.[10] Figure 1-13 shows examples of the many devices that are already part of the Internet of Things.

Regardless of its initial form, incoming data is converted into digital format, which allows it to be integrated in information systems, read by computer programs, and shared across systems. Letters, numbers, money, colors, the tiny dots on an X-ray, air pollution levels, musical notes, vocal frequencies, time intervals, and much more can all be represented in digital format.

Identify several research areas in the discipline of management information systems (MIS).

4 Information Systems, the Discipline

The study of information systems—how people, technology, processes, and data work together—is a lively discipline involving university faculty, private-sector analysts, government researchers, and more. Many refer to the field as **management information systems (MIS)**, and academic departments in colleges and universities often bear that name. (That term also is used to describe a type of information system that supports decision making at the managerial level, discussed in Chapter 7.)

The field draws researchers and practitioners from business, computer science, psychology, sociology, public administration, and many other fields, all of whom have an interest in learning more about how we can create systems to help organizations do more with less, make

FIGURE 1-12
Examples of data.

Photos: Maxim Pavlov/Alamy, D. Hurst/Alamy, Sandra Baker/Alamy, PaulPaladin/Alamy, John Wilhelmsson/
StockShot/Alamy Stock Photo, Rangizzz/Shutterstock

FIGURE 1-13
The Internet of Things.

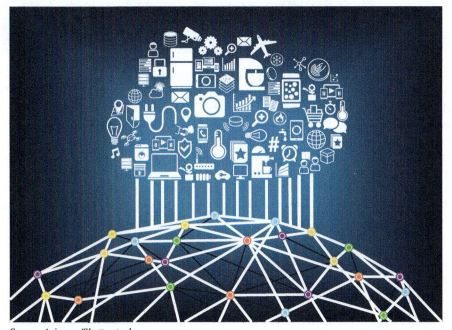

Source: A-image/Shutterstock

business process management (BPM)
Focuses on designing, optimizing, and streamlining business processes throughout the organization.

e-discovery
The processes by which electronic data that might be used as legal evidence is requested, secured, and searched.

management information systems (MIS)
The study of information systems—how people, technology, processes, and data work together. Also used to describe a special type of information system that supports tactical decision making at the managerial level.

FIGURE 1-14
Major research topics in MIS.

Topic	Sample Research Questions
Internet of Things	What kinds of devices can be used to collect data? How should the data be used?
Big data and data analytics	How can organizations collect and analyze big data to achieve competitive advantage?
Development of information systems	What are the best ways to develop new software? How should end users be involved in the development process?
IT in organizations	How should managers introduce change when new systems are implemented? What kinds of IT policies about "acceptable use" work best in different organizations?
IT and individuals	How should IT develop systems for the disabled? What kinds of interfaces are easiest for people to use?
IT and collaboration in groups	Why do virtual teams succeed or fail? How can managers use social networking to promote innovation?
IT and markets	How does the Internet affect the real estate business? How should businesses promote online sales?

companies more competitive, increase productivity, and improve the lot of people around the world. Areas that attract much of the interest are shown in Figure 1-14.[11]

MIS is a young discipline, and researchers strive to keep up with the rapid changes.[12] The Internet of Things, for example, offers tremendous opportunities, as do the analytical tools that enable organizations to capitalize on the big data that those things generate. Another important trend involves the study of e-marketplaces, the kind that are transforming entire industries and threatening traditional players. For instance, Airbnb is a global e-marketplace in which travelers can book a room offered by private individuals, competing fiercely with hotels and motels. The Internet offers remarkable opportunities to invent e-marketplaces for stocks, real estate, music, vacation rentals, used books, rare antiques, and even future spouses. How organizations build trust and make a profit in these worldwide e-markets are very hot topics.

As of 2016, more than 3.3 billion people are Internet users—less than half of the world's population. To improve access for the rest, Google is launching balloons that will float in the stratosphere and provide wireless access. Called *Project Loon*, the balloon experiments are underway in Indonesia.[13]

Research on IT and group collaboration, especially when team members are dispersed around the world, is far more important now because of virtual teams and globalization. The psychology of group dynamics subtly changes when team members use online tools, and the shifts are not always positive. Investigations of successful and unsuccessful teams shed light on strategies people can use to make virtual teams more effective. Most students engage in some virtual teamwork, especially those who take some or all of their courses online. Virtual teamwork and collaboration skills are critical.

The "people" component of information systems is clearly growing in importance, and this book stresses that element. Just making technology work is not enough to create a successful information system.

Provide examples of how business, nonprofit, and government managers, as well as information technology departments, depend on information systems knowledge.

 Information Systems throughout the Organization

Why should you learn about information systems? Consider these comments:

"My career is marketing, developing creative ad campaigns. Those IT folks speak their own language, and I speak mine."

"I'm in human resources—the only system we use is the one the company set up. It's really a disaster, too. We really need a way to train new people faster, before the ones who have all the knowledge here leave."

"We're a nonprofit volunteer organization. We can't spend money on expensive overhead like IT, so what's the point? We don't need anything fancy—just email and word processing."

These people don't realize that the demand for individuals who are savvy about information systems, and how those systems can contribute to the whole organization's success, is skyrocketing.

Information Systems in Business

Information systems underlie most of the business activities and processes that thread their way through every functional business unit, from the CEO's suite to the marketing department. Just about everyone uses email, cell phones, and the Internet, and most also rely on the many information systems that support the company's business processes. Strategic initiatives involving these systems can and should come from any corner of the organization to streamline processes, reduce costs, increase revenue, or launch that "killer app."

Whether your chosen career is marketing, finance, management, human resources, research, sales, law, medicine, manufacturing, or as an entrepreneur, information systems will be fundamental to your success. Consider these examples:

- A marketing manager who knows how to analyze big data from multiple sources will make much smarter decisions about how to spend the marketing budget. This person can finally counter that old joke about marketing: "I know that half the money we spend on marketing is wasted.... I just don't know which half!"
- A talent development professional who has experience launching effective e-learning modules will reach more employees for far less money compared with the trainer who hands out three-ring binders in face-to-face classes. The online learning programs can also be easily updated, while information in the binders grows stale quickly.
- Self-employed consultants with some basic IT skills can launch websites, build social networks, and purchase online ads—all for very little money.

Information Systems in Nonprofits and Government

If your career leads you to service in government, teaching, law enforcement, charities, or other nonprofit areas, information systems will also be critical. In some of these organizations, however, funding for IT may not be high on the priority list. But consider these examples:

- The most successful fund-raisers know how to draw on information systems to reach potential donors and pitch persuasive messages that match their interests. Linking data from Facebook or other sources helps fund-raisers reach the right people compared with those who just blanket a community with postcards or telemarketing.
- UNICEF relief workers who know how to create inexpensive podcasts and "vodcasts" (podcasts with video) can relay the plight of children from war or disasters in troubled parts of the world. Rather than spending money on radio or TV broadcasts, workers freely distribute the short, timely, and compelling video messages worldwide through the net.
- Many people say they want to volunteer to help a worthy cause, but they often don't unless the process is quick and efficient. Do-it, a website that matches volunteers in the United Kingdom to places that need help, does just that. Every 45 seconds someone finds what he or she is looking for, and Do-it's research suggests that 30% of these people wouldn't have started volunteering without the user-friendly online matching system.

Inside the IT Department

The business unit responsible for planning, managing, and supporting information systems is often called *Information Technology, Department of Information Systems, Enterprise Information Systems,* or something similar. Within the department are more specialized groups or individuals who oversee different areas. Figure 1-15 shows a hypothetical department with

FIGURE 1-15
Sample organizational chart for the information systems department.

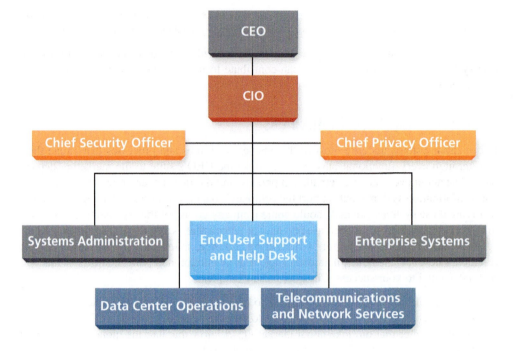

some common subunits, but many variations exist. For instance, organizations might outsource some responsibilities, working with vendors to provide services. Figure 1-16 describes the functions of common subunits.

Heading the department is the **chief information officer (CIO)**, vice president of information systems, or similar title. The CIO might report directly to the CEO or to another vice president—often the one responsible for finance and administration.

What characteristics does a CIO need? Strong leadership abilities, excellent communication skills, and knowledge of information and communications technologies are all important, though the CIO does not need to be an expert in all technology areas. Relevant experience and an educational background in business, information systems, or a related field are also very helpful. As a senior executive, the CIO's job is not just to oversee the department but also to help shape the organization's strategic goals and ensure that the information systems support them.

Working with the CIO, especially in larger organizations and major companies, are more positions with "chief" in their titles, such as those in Figure 1-17. Their roles span the activities of all the IT subunits and, indeed, the whole organization. "Chief" seems to have caught on in IT, as it did in some other business areas. Even "chief wisdom officer" is turning up.

FIGURE 1-16

Common functional areas in an information systems department.

IS Department Areas	Function
Help Desk	Provides services to internal and external customers on technology issues; answers the phone or e-mail "help desk" and troubleshoots problems; installs and maintains desktop equipment.
Systems Administration	Installs, manages, and updates servers.
Data Center Operations	Maintains the environmentally controlled areas in which servers and communications equipment are located; handles backups and archiving.
Enterprise Systems and Applications	Develops, installs, maintains, and oversees the organization's mission-critical software applications.
Telecommunications and Network Services	Installs and manages communications technologies and networks, including voice, cell phones, and wireless networks.

Title	Description
Chief Information Security Officer	Oversees security, ensuring that confidential information is protected from hackers, disasters, accidents, and rogue employees.
Chief Privacy Officer	Manages privacy issues and helps shape policy about how sensitive and confidential data about customers, citizens, employees, patients, and others are handled and protected.
Chief Technology Officer	Position is usually more technical compared to the CIO, overseeing technology solutions and innovative uses.
Chief Knowledge Officer	Manages efforts to improve the organization's ability to capture, nurture, and disseminate knowledge and expertise.

FIGURE 1-17
Besides the CIO, other "chiefs" play leadership roles in an organization.

Collaborating on Information Systems

Nikia Sabri, marketing director at a Los Angeles consulting firm, thought she had a brilliant idea to reduce costs and improve her department's results. Her eight-person staff was frequently shorthanded because of traffic jams, sick kids, or closed schools; however, all of them had computers and Internet access at home. Her boss had rejected work-at-home proposals in the past, but she thought she could make a solid case for it—with the help of the IT department. All staff had phones and email, of course, and most had accounts on a social networking site, but she wanted heightened awareness of one another's presence. Creative marketing people like to bounce ideas off each other, and she was looking for a way to simulate the easy communication that nearby office cubicles create, in which you might roll back your chair and ask your neighbor to take a quick look at your latest drawing. Surely there were web-based applications and tools that would support this.

Where should she start? Her IS department published only a help desk number to submit a trouble ticket, so she tried that first. That unit's software logged the ticket and sent out its automated message. "Thank you for your message. The help desk will respond within 24 hours." Although puzzled by her request, a technician stopped by and installed a headset with microphone, wanting to be helpful and thinking that was what she needed.

Disconnects in communication between IT staff and others in the organization are not uncommon, partly because of the jargon barrier. Frustrations rise when IT doesn't respond immediately to someone like Nikia. Like all functional business units, IT has a full plate of ongoing projects, prioritized by the CIO working with the CEO and other top executives to ensure that resources are wisely spent with a solid return on investment. The technician had to move onto the next trouble ticket and wasn't in a position to decide whether Nikia's project was worthwhile. Does that mean Nikia should forget her project? Absolutely not. Successful organizations rely on innovations like this from people who know their work best. Figure 1-18 lists some tips on how to improve communications between people like Nikia and the IT department, which may sometimes seem impenetrable.

If you have good ideas like Nikia, taking this course will prepare you to interact with the IT staff on projects. In fact, information technology and strategy are so closely integrated with every aspect of business that everyone in the organization is really an "information officer" who can contribute.

If you are in IT or want to be, taking this course will give you a much broader vision of how information systems support strategic objectives and business goals and how you can collaborate with people in finance, human resources, and other units on high-profile projects.

Improving Your Own Productivity

How productive are you? Take the short quiz in Figure 1-19.

To find your score, add up the numbers for all questions except 4 and 6. For those two questions, first reverse the score by giving yourself 1 point if you chose 7, 2 points if you chose 6, and so on. Then add the reversed score to your total. If your total is higher than 50, you have some good habits that are associated with high productivity, including the use of information systems that can help you streamline.

chief information officer (CIO)
The person who heads the department responsible for managing and maintaining information systems and ensuring they support the organization's strategic goals.

FIGURE 1-18

Tips for collaborating on information systems.

For the CIO and IT Staff:

▶ *Focus on business goals.* The objective of a project is not to "upgrade all the servers," but to improve productivity, attract more customers, reduce costs, earn revenue, increase customer loyalty, reduce carbon emissions, etc.

▶ *Avoid jargon.* Learn to speak the language your colleagues in other departments understand, and reserve the technical jargon for internal IT communications.

▶ *Communicate the value of IT.* Although many focus on how much IT costs, the savings or revenue IT generates through improved productivity or added sales are captured in other departments.

▶ *Emphasize return on investment.* Evaluate projects in terms of their ultimate payoff, the same way business managers judge other kinds of initiatives.

▶ *Be proactive.* Propose and support innovative projects with clear business goals, rather than just react to problems and proposals as they arise. Ensure that people like Nikia know how to contact IT to discuss their innovative ideas.

▶ *Embrace customer service.* Strive for the highest level of customer satisfaction for your internal customers, not just the ones who buy your company's products and services.

▶ *Become a hybrid.* The most successful IT professionals have solid technology skills, but are also very well grounded in the business so they can easily communicate.

For People in Other Areas:

▶ *Describe your end goal, not the means to get there.* The more your IT colleagues understand what you want to accomplish, the better equipped they will be to help.

▶ *Learn how to contact IT for different purposes.* If you are not sure, ask.

▶ *Be familiar with how information systems are already supporting your organization.* Explore the company's intranet and review announcements about new initiatives.

▶ *Network.* Keeping in touch with your colleagues in and out of IT builds trust and creates networks of people who can share knowledge.

▶ *Do your homework.* Especially after taking this course, you will be prepared to research your ideas and the information system solutions others have attempted, so you are more familiar with what is possible.

▶ *Be an active partner.* As your project develops, keep in close touch with IT to provide timely assistance and feedback at every step. If you do not, the result may be quite different from what you expected.

FIGURE 1-19

How do you use technology to improve your productivity? Take this short quiz.

	Not at All True for Me					Very True for Me	
1. I empty my email inbox every day.	1	2	3	4	5	6	7
2. I keep a to-do list, and always keep it up to date.	1	2	3	4	5	6	7
3. I use email filters to sort messages by how important they are.	1	2	3	4	5	6	7
4. I stay logged into my social network most of the day so I am alerted when updates occur or messages appear.	1	2	3	4	5	6	7
5. I rarely print anything out.	1	2	3	4	5	6	7
6. I send and receive text messages very frequently, though most are unimportant.	1	2	3	4	5	6	7
7. I focus on the most important projects and can ignore distractions	1	2	3	4	5	6	7
8. I have a clear vision of what I want to achieve and make priorities.	1	2	3	4	5	6	7
9. I keep my calendar online rather than on paper, and I keep it up to date.	1	2	3	4	5	6	7
10. My electronic files are very well organized.	1	2	3	4	5	6	7

High scores on this quiz also suggest you understand that some technologies are distracting and can reduce your productivity. If your total was much lower than 50, you can make many improvements, and you are also not alone.

Learning how information systems support organizations and their missions will be critical to your success. Gaining the technical know-how to increase your *own* productivity is just as important. This book will help you do that. Do you spend too much time hunting for documents? Can you quickly find a phone number when you need it? Are you managing your email and text messages effectively? Do you miss deadlines? Do you rely on easily lost handwritten notes? The tips in each chapter highlight ways to maximize your own personal productivity so you can work smarter, not harder.

Promises, Perils, and Ethical Issues

6 Explain how information systems present both promises and perils, and pose ethical questions.

Google, which became part of Alphabet, Inc. in 2015, boasts that its corporate mission is to "organize the world's information"—a daunting task that stretches the imagination and promises to be an uphill climb. Yet information systems set off game-changing innovations every year, surprising even savvy technology leaders. In 1943, former IBM Chairman Thomas Watson said, "I think there is a world market for maybe five computers." But it was his own company that introduced the IBM-PC, transforming not just the workplace itself but the kind of work each of us is capable of performing.

In the next chapter, examples of the promise of information systems for strategic initiatives are plentiful. Their perils, however, are not inconsiderable, particularly because of the sheer scope of their impact. Information systems are so powerful, and the data they contain so vast and personal, that everyone must appreciate the ethical issues involved in their development and use.

Privacy Breaches and Amplification Effects

Privacy breaches present major risks, and breaches occur very frequently. One especially large one in 2015 involved the U.S. Office of Management and Budget, in which the personnel records for millions of federal employees were hacked. Another incident at health insurer Anthem involved the breach of almost 80 million patient records.[14] Events like these, in which information systems play a central role, seriously threaten privacy and security. As information systems and the underlying computing technologies become ever more powerful and interconnected, the risks rise dramatically.[15] Minor mistakes are amplified; even a misplaced USB drive can erupt into a major crisis.

Reputations are also more vulnerable, given the power individuals have to spread damaging information at lightning speed. Few corporations are equipped to respond to such blitzes—accurate or not—that spread virally through channels such as YouTube. When two disgruntled Domino's Pizza employees uploaded a stomach-turning video shot in the restaurant kitchen showing how they defiled the sandwiches, Domino's corporate office failed to respond for 2 days. The employees claimed it was just a prank, but before it was taken down, the video had been viewed almost 1 million times.[16] Domino's eventually tackled the crisis head-on and earned high marks for limiting the damage, but its response during the first 24 hours was sluggish. Every organization's **crisis management team**, which is responsible for identifying, assessing, and addressing threats from unforeseen circumstances, must be on high alert for signs of any online firestorms. The teams have very little time to take action.

The way modern information systems amplify any communication may put your own reputation and livelihood at risk as well. Any email you send or photo you upload can be forwarded or posted online for millions to view—and for attorneys to collect as evidence. Text, photos, and videos uploaded to your social networking site can

> **PRODUCTIVITY TIP**
> Digital footprints are extremely hard to erase, but services are emerging that try to address people's concerns.[17] With mobile phone app Snapchat, for instance, people can send a photo to a friend's phone, and the image disappears in 10 seconds. Even so, privacy is not guaranteed and users should never assume the photo won't spread far and wide.[18]

easily be distributed to a far wider audience beyond your own network. It is also absurdly easy to make your own blunders by clicking "reply to all" by mistake and sending email to many more people than you intended.[19]

crisis management team
The team in an organization that is responsible for identifying, assessing, and addressing threats from unforeseen circumstances that can lead to crisis situations.

These promises and perils make the study of information systems critically important for us all, regardless of where we work or what kind of work we do. We all share the responsibility for both harnessing the power of these systems and minimizing their risks.

THE ETHICAL FACTOR   Ethical Issues Surrounding Information Systems

Situations like those described in this chapter raise troubling ethical issues:

- Who is responsible for damage caused by accidental leaks of private information? The employee who misplaced a laptop? The information systems professionals who designed a flawed system? The person who found the laptop and didn't return it? The victims who didn't notice problems on their credit card statements?

- In the Domino's case, did the employees who created and then uploaded the video violate ethical principles? Is YouTube partly responsible for allowing uploads of false, damaging, or illegal videos?

- Do people who send harsh emails deserve what they get if the information leaks out? Is it ethical to broadcast a message you receive that was accidentally misdirected?

Many of these questions have no easy answers. People tend to judge the severity of ethical violations partly on the basis of the number of people affected. When the power of information systems and the Internet are involved, the potential for harm is exponentially amplified.

MyMISLab
Online Simulation

THE WORLD OF MAMMALS
A Role-Playing Simulation on Choosing a New CIO for an Animal Preserve

You volunteer at The World of Mammals, the region's largest enclosed animal preserve. Far more than a zoo, the nonprofit preserve provides a reasonably natural habitat for many endangered mammal species and puts the visitors in the "cages" rather than the animals. Miles of chain-link-covered paths crisscross the preserve so people can safely view the animals behaving normally, not pacing back and forth in cramped exhibits. Visitors can also drive around in specially protected jeeps, equipped with night vision goggles, after dark. The preserve's revenue comes from ticket and concession sales, special events, and donations, but veterinary bills keep rising, and personnel costs for the 200-plus employees continue to outpace what the organization takes in.

The chief information officer (CIO) left abruptly, and the preserve's director Yolanda Whalen asked you—a longtime supporter—to help select a new CIO. When you're ready, log in to meet Yolanda, learn about the organization's needs, and start interviewing the finalists....

LEARNING OBJECTIVES

1 Organizations rely on information systems for a host of reasons, and they play critical roles in several contexts: operations management, customer interactions, decision making, collaboration and teamwork, strategic initiatives, and individual productivity.

2 *Data*, *information*, and *knowledge* are terms along a continuum that reflect how raw facts can be combined, assembled, and analyzed to add meaning and value. Characteristics of information that add to its value include timeliness, accuracy, and completeness.

3 The four components of any information system are (1) people, (2) technology, (3) processes, and (4) data. The "people" component covers far more than just the IT staff. It encompasses the human element and involves people from many different parts of the organization. Customers and suppliers also participate in improving processes and eliminating waste. Customers may become contributors through user-generated content (UGC) and Web 2.0 applications.

4 The young discipline of information systems attracts faculty and students from many fields, private-sector analysts, government workers, and more. Research trends show the changing nature of the field. Interest in subjects such as the Internet of Things, big data analytics, e-marketplaces, and collaborative group work has increased considerably.

5 Information systems contribute to success in every functional department and in all different types of organizations. Learning how they make these contributions and how you can lead efforts to leverage their power is important regardless of which career you pursue. This knowledge will also improve your own productivity so you can work smarter, not harder.

6 Although information systems hold extraordinary promise, they also present risks and ethical concerns, especially because of amplification effects. Privacy breaches occur frequently, and the damage can affect millions. Reputations are also more vulnerable because messages, whether accurate or not, can spread so quickly.

KEY TERMS AND CONCEPTS

operations management

customer relationship management (CRM) system

data-driven decision making

business intelligence

social networking sites

competitive advantage

data

information

information system

user-generated content (UGC)

Web 2.0

information technology (IT)

information and communications technology (ICT)

Internet of Things (IoT)

business process

business process management (BPM)

e-discovery

management information systems (MIS)

chief information officer (CIO)

crisis management team

CHAPTER REVIEW QUESTIONS

1-1. What are the six primary roles that information systems play in organizations? How are information systems used in each context?

1-2. How is data different from information? How is information different from knowledge? What are examples of each?

1-3. What are the three characteristics that make information valuable? Why is each a critical attribute of information?

1-4. What are the four components of an information system? Describe each component. What are the five functions that these components provide?

1-5. How are information systems important to managers in a variety of functional business units? What are examples of ways that information systems are important to the success of a marketing department, a human resources department, and a small business owner?

1-6. What are the functional areas that are common to most information technology departments?

1-7. What is the role of the chief information officer?

1-8. How do information systems offer promises to organizations? What are some of the perils of information systems? What are some of the ethical questions associated with the use of information systems?

PROJECTS AND DISCUSSION QUESTIONS

1-9. As customers, students, patients, taxpayers, and citizens, we are surrounded by information systems that support customer interactions. Identify and describe two such systems that you have used. Briefly describe the types of customer interactions you have experienced with these systems and compare what you found to be important features of each one. Are there features or functions that you would change or add to either system?

1-10. Web conferencing has been available for many years. In this market space, products from Adobe, Cisco, Citrix, IBM, and Microsoft compete with lower-cost or free web-conferencing applications from AnyMeeting, Google Hangouts, and others. What are some of the advantages of using a virtual meeting space? Are there disadvantages? Search the web to learn more about online meeting rooms and prepare a 5-minute presentation of your findings.

1-11. Information systems play a very large role in decision making, and many would argue that you can always use more information to make better decisions. But sometimes digging deeply for more information leads to troubling ethical dilemmas. Visit 23andme.com, the website of a company that offers to read your DNA from saliva for a flat fee and provide reports about disease risk factors, ancestral lineage, and more. If you learn of a significant health risk, should you tell siblings who chose not to investigate their own DNA? Should you tell your significant other? List factors you should take into account when making decisions about whether to obtain information like this and how to use it.

1-12. One way to be more productive and manage time is to use the calendar feature of your email system. If you use Microsoft Outlook, visit Microsoft.com and search for "Outlook tutorial" or search the Internet for an Outlook "how to" web page to learn how to set up a calendar. Then create a calendar for the semester that shows class times as well as test dates and project due dates. Which reminder option did you select for class times? Which reminder option did

you select for project due dates? Briefly describe several benefits of using the Outlook calendar feature.

1-13. Although Internet users bemoan the annoying pop-up ads, Netflix has grown to more than 80 million customers who can stream movies and TV episodes to any Internet-connected device or request DVDs by mail. Describe Netflix in terms of (1) the types of information technology it uses and (2) its customer-facing business processes.

1-14. Consider the information that is maintained by a bank. In addition to customer records, the bank maintains records on accounts and loans. Figure 1-20 and Figure 1-21 are

FIGURE 1-20

Customer table.

CustomerID	Name	Address	City	State	Zip
100001	Don Baker	1215 E. New York	Aurora	IL	60504
100002	Yuxiang Jiang	1230 Douglas Road	Oswego	IL	60543
100003	Emily Brown	632 Fox Valley Road	Aurora	IL	60504
100004	Mario Sanchez	24 E. Ogden	Naperville	IL	60563

FIGURE 1-21

Accounts table.

CustomerID	Account Number	Account Type	Date Opened	Balance
100001	4875940	Checking	10/19/1971	2500.00
100001	1660375	Savings	08/10/1973	1200.00
100002	1783032	Savings	05/15/1987	500.00
100002	4793289	Checking	05/15/1987	3200.00
100003	6213690	Checking	02/14/1996	6700.00
100004	1890571	Savings	10/16/2007	5300.00
100004	8390126	Checking	12/02/2008	2700.00

two examples of database tables for a regional bank. How might this data be aggregated and analyzed to create information and knowledge?

1-15. Parking is a problem at many universities across the United States. Is it a problem on your campus? Describe the business process to acquire a parking pass at your school. Can you get a parking pass online? Can you get one in person? How does your process compare with that of an organization that uses a paper form to apply for a parking permit? How can that organization use an information system to improve this business process? Can you think of a business process at your college or university that can be improved with an information system?

1-16. A typical information technology department is composed of common functional areas, and each requires skills and competencies unique to that area. Search the web or visit an online job search site such as careerbuilder.com or monster.com to learn more about the IT functional areas described in Figure 1-15. Select two functional areas and compare job postings for each. In a brief report, contrast the differences in education, experience, and technical certification that are required for each job.

1-17. In June 2010, a security breach in the AT&T network exposed the email addresses of 114,000 Apple iPad 3G owners, many of whom were well-known business executives. The list of subscribers whose data was released included Diane Sawyer of ABC News, New York City Mayor Michael Bloomberg, and former White House Chief of Staff and Chicago Mayor Rahm Emanuel. Work in a small group with classmates to consider the severity of this leak of private information. In this case, is the severity of the breach measured by the number of affected individuals or by the high-profile status of some of the subscribers? What criteria are best for judging the severity of a data leak? Prepare a brief summary of your group discussion.

1-18. Information systems are fundamental to the success of every functional business unit within an organization, from marketing to manufacturing to finance. Work in a small group with classmates to share your career choice and discuss how information systems support processes within your field. Can you name types of software applications that are used in your chosen career?

APPLICATION EXERCISES

1-19. EXCEL APPLICATION: Staff Planning Spreadsheet

Precision Products specializes in custom-manufactured metal parts. The production manager has asked you to create an Excel spreadsheet to help manage operations. The company needs a way to calculate staffing requirements (number of employees) based on different levels of production. The five manufacturing operations are fabrication, welding, machining, assembly, and packaging. One unit of production requires 1.5 hours for fabrication, 2.25 hours for welding, 0.7 hours for machining, 3.2 hours for assembly, and 0.5 hours for packaging. Create the Excel spreadsheet shown in Figure 1-22 to calculate the weekly staffing required, at 40 hours per week, for production levels of 200, 300, 400, and 500 units. How does the total required for each level of production change if Precision Products operates a 45-hour production schedule?

FIGURE 1-22

Managing operations of Precision Products using Excel.

	A	B	C	D	E	F	G	H	I
1				HOURS REQUIRED					
2			Units	Fabrication	Welding	Machining	Assembly	Packaging	Total Hours
3		Weekly Production	1	1.5	2.25	0.7	3.2	0.5	
4			200						
5			300						
6			400						
7			500						
8									
9		Weekly Requirement							Total Requirement
10	Hours	40	200						
11			300						
12			400						
13			500						

Source: Microsoft® Excel, Microsoft Corporation. Reprinted with permission.

1-20. ACCESS APPLICATION:
Information Systems in Business

Seconds Later, a clothing consignment shop, is fast becoming a favorite place to shop. The owner has asked you to create an Access database to help manage inventory. Download and import the information provided in the spreadsheet Ch01Ex02 to create a database with two tables (Consignors and Items). The owner wants you to add a calculated field to the Items table that shows the net selling price after he has paid the commission to the consignors. Start with two reports: an Inventory Report and a Consignor Report. The Inventory Report summarizes the inventory by item type. This report will include the number of items and the total selling price for each item type plus the total sales value of each inventory type. It will also include the potential commission that the consignors will earn if the owner sells all items. The Consignor Report will list the total number of items and the total selling price and commission for each consignor. What other reports could you make with this data that would be useful to the owner?

CASE STUDY #1

Nasdaq's Information Challenges: Facebook's Botched Public Opening and High-Frequency Trading

The world's largest "floorless" exchange handles hundreds of millions of trades every day. Buys and sells happen so fast that each trade has to be time-stamped to the nanosecond. First launched in 2000, Nasdaq OMX is, above all, a technology company, and it successfully competes against the venerable New York Stock Exchange (NYSE) on its breathtaking trading speed.

When most people think of an exchange, they think of NYSE's enormous building on Wall Street, with loud-mouthed traders on the floor shouting orders, racing stock tickers, and giant LCD screens laden with charts, numbers, and ticker symbols. In fact, most exchanges are in data centers, not in neoclassical buildings. And they are also for-profit businesses that compete for companies to list their shares and for investors and brokers to conduct their trades.

Speed matters, and Nasdaq OMX technology can handle 1 million messages per second. It matters so much that some heavy traders—Goldman Sachs, for example—pay Nasdaq OMX for the privilege of locating their own server in Nasdaq's data center, just to avoid the tiny communication delay from Goldman offices. A trader's servers can instantly detect any delay and can then automatically check other exchanges to see if the trade can be rerouted.

As in other businesses, improved information systems and technology drive prices down. In the early 2000s, NYSE and Nasdaq OMX shared 90% of the market, but competition pushed that figure down to 45%. Traders can use other exchanges with cheaper prices, or they can buy and sell stocks in "dark pools"—private groups whose members trade with one another.

Facebook's Public Offering

Nasdaq's focus on technology and lightning-fast trading speed were reasons Mark Zuckerberg chose to use that exchange to take Facebook public in 2012 so people could invest in the company directly. The choice was a major competitive win for Nasdaq, which also carries high-tech companies such as Apple, Google, Groupon, and Zynga. However, Nasdaq lost out to other exchanges for Yelp, LinkedIn, and Pandora. Facebook's initial public opening (IPO) was expected to be one of the largest in history.

During the first few hours of the first trading day, however, technical glitches at Nasdaq caused many delays and chaos, and the exchange had to switch to a secondary system. At some points, orders even had to be completed manually. The botched opening caused many clients to lose millions, and the technical issues added to uncertainty about pricing.

Critics blamed poor decision making at Nasdaq for the costly mess, insisting that the company put profits ahead of risk management. For example, Citigroup claimed that the decision to switch to an untested backup system rather than interrupt trading to fix the problems was a major mistake, one that was mainly driven by a desire to avoid embarrassment during such a high-profile event.

After the first days of trading, Facebook's share price dropped about 18%, and those who purchased the new stock suffered huge losses. While other factors may have contributed to the bungled opening, Nasdaq took responsibility for the technical problems and is attempting to make amends. In 2015, the company agreed to pay investors $26.5 million to settle a class action lawsuit.

High-Frequency Trading

Another looming problem for Nasdaq OMX is computer trading based on algorithms, or "algo-trading." With machines talking to machines, racing with one another to close the deal at the best price, trading volume can skyrocket quickly. Humans use their judgment to craft the mathematical rules; once in place, however, the systems can trigger frenzied rounds of trading.

Some argue that these high-frequency trades make the markets more efficient and equitable, so the big players on the trading floor don't have an advantage. While Nasdaq OMX and other exchanges compete for the growing number of algo-traders, analysts worry that the sheer technological speed introduces serious risks. When markets dropped a gut-wrenching 9% on one afternoon in 2010, some suspected a clumsy algo-trader who accidentally triggered the event (Figure 1-23). Though the real cause of that roller-coaster "flash crash" was never clear, such programmed trades were the clear cause of a similar event back in 1987.

FIGURE 1-23

Flash crash on May 6, 2010.

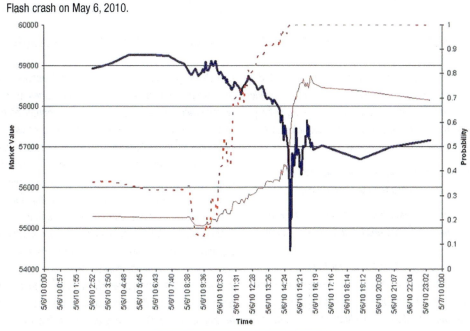

Source: Staffs of the CFTC and SEC to the Joint Advisory Committee on Emerging Regulatory Issues, "Preliminary Findings Regarding the Market Events of May 6, 2010," May 18, 2010. http://www.sec.gov/sec-cftc-prelimreport.pdf (U.S. Securities and Exchange Commission.)

But algo-traders defend their strategy by pointing out that they could not easily trade large numbers of shares at fair prices without the "speed of light" because the trades would signal their intent to other traders. Once that happened, the prices would change dramatically.

The Securities and Exchange Commission and Department of Justice are taking tough stands against suspected misconduct, but unlike the Nasdaq OMX trades, their work is not at the speed of light.

Discussion Questions

1-21. How has Nasdaq's business benefited from the use of information systems?

1-22. What risks do information systems pose for Nasdaq OMX's business?

1-23. This chapter discusses the value of information. What types of information are handled through Nasdaq systems, what are the key characteristics of this information, and how do Nasdaq customers use this information to create value?

1-24. What does the example of Goldman Sachs paying to locate its server in the Nasdaq data center say about the relationship between information systems and physical operations?

Sources: CNBC. (April 24, 2015). Nasdaq to settle Facebook IPO lawsuit for $26.5M. CNBC, http://www.cnbc.com/2015/04/24/nasdaq-to-settle-facebook-ipo-lawsuit-for-265m.html, accessed February 3, 2016.

Cooper, R., Davis, M., & Van Vliet, B. (2016). The mysterious ethics of high-frequency trading. *Business Ethics Quarterly, 26*(1), 1–22. http://doi.org/10.1017/beq.2015.41

Heires, K. (2013). Nasdaq and AX trading look at block trade alternative to HFT. Institutional Investor, http://search.proquest.com/docview/1319779107?accountid=11752, accessed May 30, 2016.

Lynch, S. N. (March 5, 2013). SEC shares expertise with FBII on algorithmic trading. Reuters, http://www.reuters.com/article/2013/03/05/sec-algo-fbi-idUSL1N0BXHRV20130305, accessed May 30, 2016.

Kirchner, S. (2016). High-frequency trading: Fact and fiction. *Policy, 31*(4), 8–20.

McCrank, J. (April 8, 2013). Citi files claim with Nasdaq for compensation from Facebook IPO. Reuters, http://www.reuters.com/article/2013/04/08/us-citigroup-nasdaq-facebook-idUSBRE93713720130408, accessed May 30, 3016.

Rossi, M., Deis, G., Roche, J., & Przywara, K. (2015). Recent civil and criminal enforcement action involving high frequency trading. *Journal of Investment Compliance (Emerald Group), 16*(1), 5–12. http://doi.org/10.1108/JOIC-01-2015-0017

Schaefer, S. (June 8, 2012). Report: UBS lost $350 million on Facebook IPO, prepping suit against Nasdaq. *Forbes*, http://www.forbes.com/sites/steveschaefer/2012/06/08/report-ubs-lost-350-million-on-facebook-ipo-prepping-suit-against-nasdaq/, accessed August 7, 2016.

SEC denies Nasdaq algo plan. (2013). *Compliance Reporter, 12.*

CASE STUDY #2

Breaking News: Twitter's Growing Role in Emergencies and Disaster Communications

When a city councilman in Atlanta, Georgia, spotted a woman on the street suffering a seizure, he quickly pulled out his cell phone. It showed low on battery, so instead of dialing 911 and getting stuck on hold, Councilman Hall tapped out a short tweet:

> "Need a paramedic on corner of John Wesley Dobbs and Jackson st. Woman on the ground unconscious. Pls ReTweet"

Several of the councilman's followers immediately saw his text message and dialed 911. Paramedics arrived quickly to take the woman to the hospital.

Twitter, the microblogging service best known for trivial updates on everyday events that might amuse or bore one's followers, has a growing role in emergency response. The service empowers people with the ability to gather and disseminate information about emergencies and disasters, and this information can be far timelier than anything government authorities or organizations such as the Red Cross can provide.

During the Red River Valley flood in 2009, for example, millions of tweets tracked the location and timing of flooding events, rising in volume with the water. The short messages offered on-the-ground observations of conditions, along with the worry, fear, and finally joy that residents felt when the floodwaters receded. They also passed along—or "retweeted"—official news from regular sources, such as TV or state government. When a rare earthquake hit the East Coast in 2011, Twitter users sent messages to reassure one another, and some of them outpaced the quake itself, so recipients knew it was coming minutes before the news reported it.

Twitter was widely used to communicate during and after Hurricane Sandy in 2012, and more than a third of the 20 million tweets shared news and eyewitness accounts. Tweeters appreciated the real-time updates from fellow victims. For example, they heard first-hand accounts of how high the water was rising on different streets. No news channel carried such detail, and when mistaken information was posted, other Twitter users quickly corrected it.

In the aftermath of a major earthquake in Haiti, a graduate student at the University of Colorado launched a project to improve Twitter's usefulness, called Tweak the Tweet. Kate Starbird's goal was to develop syntax for tweets originating from the disaster sites so they could be better organized and read by computer programs (Figure 1-24). The freewheeling unstructured tweets about victims who needed help were repurposed into more structured messages with "hash tags"—keywords preceded by a pound sign (#). Computer programs can read these to categorize who is involved, what is needed, where the problem is, and what else might be happening. Researchers are also working on strategies to automatically process tweets to detect real-time traffic incidents. People often tweet about accidents they observe, and analyzing those messages can alert authorities about accidents in real time.

The Red Cross and other disaster response organizations recognize that people are relying more heavily on social media such as Twitter for support and information during emergencies. In fact, social media are so prevalent that, in one survey, more than a quarter of the respondents said they would send a direct Twitter message to emergency responders, not realizing that aid organizations are not well prepared to monitor Twitter and other services. They also have few means to assess the value of information received in this way. It may be timely, but is it accurate? It might be a child's exaggerated report or a hoax from some scammer.

Despite the drawbacks, Twitter's value for emergency response and disaster communications may be phenomenal. In a study of Twitter use during a variety of emergencies, researchers found that about 42% of the tweets were posted by traditional and Internet news outlets, and those critical eyewitness accounts made up 9%. Craig Fugate, an administrator at the Federal Emergency Management Center, said, "Social media can empower the public to be part of the response, not as victims to be taken care of."

Discussion Questions

1-25. What are the potential benefits of Twitter and other social media for emergency and disaster communications?

1-26. What are the potential risks of using Twitter and other social media for emergency and disaster communications?

1-27. What types of education would be necessary at the user level to make Twitter and other social media more effective for emergency and disaster communications?

1-28. What would need to happen on the part of aid organizations and traditional media for Twitter and other social media to be effective in emergency and disaster communications?

FIGURE 1-24

Reformatting tweets to improve disaster response.

Original Tweet:
Sherline Birotte aka Memen. Last seen at 19 Ruelle Riviere College University of Porter a3 story school building

Restructured Tweet:
#haiti #ruok Sherline Birotte aka Memen. Last seen #loc 19 Ruelle Riviere College University of Porter #info a 3 story school building

Sources: Atlanta councilman chooses Twitter over 911 to report emergency. (May 19, 2009). EMS World, http://www.emsworld.com/news/10339592/atlanta-councilman-chooses-twitter-over-911-to-report-emergency, accessed May 30, 2016.

Gu, Y., Qian, Z. (Sean), & Chen, F. (2016). From Twitter to detector: Real-time traffic incident detection using social media data. *Transportation Research: Part C, 67,* 321–342. http://doi.org/10.1016/j.trc.2016.02.011

Hotz, R. L. (March 12, 2016). Twitter storms can help gauge damage of real storms and disasters, study says. *Wall Street Journal—Online Edition,* p. 1.

Olteanu, A., Vieweg, S., & Castillo, C. (2015). What to expect when the unexpected happens: Social media communications across crises. *Proceedings of CSCW 2015,* http://works.bepress.com/vieweg/19/, accessed August 7, 2016.

Palen, L., Starbird, K., et al. (2010). Twitter-based information distribution during the 2009 Red River Valley flood threat. *Bulletin of the American Society for Information Science & Technology, 36*(5), 13–17.

Twitter a key source of news for many during Hurricane Sandy. (November 14, 2012). Pew Research Center, http://www.pewresearch.org/daily-number/twitter-a-key-source-of-news-for-many-during-hurricane-sandy/, accessed March 17, 2013.

E-PROJECT 1   Analyzing the May 6 "Flash Crash" with Excel Charts

On May 6, 2010, the stock market showed mind-boggling turbulence for a few minutes, and investigators hypothesize that it was due to a flood of computer-generated trades. This e-project shows how to create charts using Excel, using downloaded stock data from that period so you can see what happened.

1-29. Download the Ch01_AAPL Excel file, which contains the high, low, and closing prices for Apple Computers between May 3 and May 14. (AAPL is the ticker symbol for Apple.) Open the file to see how the data is arranged in columns, with the first row showing the column headers.
   a. What was the closing price for Apple on May 6?
   b. What was the volume of trading for this stock on May 6?

1-30. Create a line graph from the AAPL data, in which the dates are on the *x*-axis (horizontal), and the stock prices are on the vertical (*y*) axis. Include the opening price, high, low, and closing price on the graph. Add a title to the top of your chart.

1-31. Download Expedia stock prices (ticker symbol EXPE) for the same time period (May 3–May 14, 2010) from http://finance.yahoo.com. (Click on "Historical Data" under the current chart and prices.)
   a. Create a line graph to compare the *low* and *closing prices* for Apple stock and Expedia stock. You do not need to include open and high prices on this graph.
   b. How do you compare the activity on those two stocks?

E-PROJECT 2   Gathering, Visualizing, and Evaluating Reports from Twitter and Other Sources During a Disaster

The Ushahidi platform is open source software that organizations use to aggregate, map, and visualize information about disasters or other emergencies. Originally developed to map reports of violence in Kenya after an election, Ushahidi, which means "testimony" in Swahili, continues to be improved by software developers around the world. It can be adapted to the needs of different communities experiencing a variety of emergencies, from social unrest and violence to the major floods that paralyzed parts of the United States in 2016. Combined with another open source product called *Swift River*, the platform can help filter and manage real-time data coming in through Twitter, text messages, email, the web, or other sources.

During the oil spill and recovery in the Gulf of Mexico, Tulane University students worked with the Louisiana Bucket Brigade and a private company to launch a site with Ushahidi to aggregate, map, and verify reports sent in by people using Twitter, text message, smartphone apps, email, and web forms (Figure 1-25). Download the Excel file called *Ch01_OilSpill*, which contains sample reports, and answer the following questions:

1-32. First, select columns B through F and reformat them with word wrap so you can easily see the actual comments people sent in.

1-33. Suppose you have a friend who lives in Bay Champagne. First sort the table by LOCATION, and scroll down to Bay Champagne. How many reports do you find using this strategy? Why would this approach be limited in terms of its ability to find all the events that may have affected your friend?

1-34. For crisis management, timeliness is important, but so is accuracy. How many reports in this sample were not verified (NO in the Verified column)? You can use Excel's countif function to determine the number of NOs and YESes. What is the percentage of total reports that have not been verified?

1-35. Sort the file by CATEGORY then by LOCATION. Take a look at the reports that are categorized as Health Effects in Grand Isle. Why do you think many of these reports are not verified?

FIGURE 1-25

Mapping reports from Twitter, text messages, and other sources during the Gulf Oil Spill.

Source: Copyright © Louisiana Bucket Brigade. Used by permission of Louisiana Bucket Brigade.

CHAPTER NOTES

1. Prater, E., Swafford, P. M., & Yellepeddi, S. (2009). Emerging economies: Operational issues in China and India. *Journal of Marketing Channels, 16*(2), 169–187.

2. At the front of the back office: Business-process outsourcing. (June 23, 2012). *The Economist, 403*, 8790.

3. Wailgum, T. (January 12, 2009). To hell with business intelligence: 40 percent of execs trust gut. *CIO.com.*

4. Digital ad spend worldwide | Statistic. (2016). http://www.statista.com/statistics/237974/online-advertising-spending-worldwide/, accessed February 2, 2016.

5. Martin, J. A. (July 29, 2015). 10 questions for Cortana, Siri, Amazon Echo and Google Now. http://www.cio.com/article/2953989/software-productivity/10-questions-for-cortana-siri-amazon-echo-and-google-now.html, accessed February 2, 2016.

6. Hamm, S. (2009). Big Blue goes into analysis. *BusinessWeek, 4128*, 16–19.

7. Daley, J. (2016). Driven by data. *Entrepreneur, 44*(1), 133–139.

8. Gobble, M. M. (2013). Big data: The next big thing in innovation. *Research Technology Management, 56*(1), 64–66. Retrieved from Business Source Complete, Ipswich, MA, accessed April 14, 2013.

9. Logan, D., & Dulaney, K. (October 24, 2011). Handling e-discovery compliance issues on tablets, smartphones, and other mobile devices. *Gartner Research*, ID:G00217510, accessed July 1, 2013.

10. Tully, J. (2015). *Mass adoption of the Internet of things will create new opportunities and challenges for enterprises.* Gartner Group. http://www.gartner.com/document/2994817

11. Beath, C., Berente, N., Gallivan, M. J., & Lyytinen, K. (2013). Expanding the frontiers of information systems research: Introduction to the special issue. *Journal of the Association for Information Systems, 14*(4), i–xvi.

12. Goes, P. B. (2015, September). Inflection point: Looking back or looking forward? *MIS Quarterly*, pp. iii–viii.

13. Simonite, T. (2015). Project Loon. *MIT Technology Review, 118*(2), 40–45.

14. Frenkel, K. A. (2016). The worst data breaches of 2015. *CIO Insight*, 1–1.

15. Rosenoer, J., & Scherlis, W. (2009). Risk gone wild. *Harvard Business Review, 87*(5), 26.

16. York, E. B., & Wheaton, K. (2009). What Domino's did right—and wrong—in squelching hubbub over YouTube video. *Advertising Age, 80*(14), 1–24.

17. Metz, R. (2013). Now you see it, now you don't: Disappearing messages are everywhere. *MIT Technology Review*, http://www.technologyreview.com/news/513006/now-you-see-it-now-you-dont-disappearing-messages-are-everywhere/, accessed April 10, 2013.

18. FTC settles consumer deception charges with Snapchat. (2015). *Computer & Internet Lawyer, 32*(3), 23–23.

19. Bernstein, E. (March 8, 2011). Reply all: The button everyone loves to hate. *Wall Street Journal*, http://online.wsj.com/article/SB10001424052748703386704576186520353326558.html, accessed July 1, 2013.

2

Information Systems and *Strategy*

- Online Simulation: Leveling UP! A Role-Playing Simulation on Business Strategy for a New Smartphone App
- Discussion Questions: #2-1, #2-2, #2-3
- Writing Assignments: #2-10, #2-12

LEARNING OBJECTIVES

1 Describe Porter's five competitive forces that shape industry competition.

2 Explain how disruptive innovations, government policies, complementary products and services, and other factors affect how the competitive forces operate.

3 Identify the components of the value chain, and explain its extended version.

4 Describe how information systems apply to competitive strategies for business.

5 Explain how information systems apply to strategy for nonprofit organizations and governments.

6 Explain why the role of information systems in organizations shifts depending on whether the systems are deployed to run, grow, or transform the business.

An online, interactive decision-making simulation that reinforces chapter contents and uses key terms in context can be found in MyMISLab™.

INTRODUCTION

COMPANIES COMPETE FOR YOUR DOLLARS, YOUR LOYALTY, AND YOUR ATTENTION, and start-ups face huge challenges as they try to develop a strategy that will lead to success. Dana and Prakash, for example, are the two entrepreneurs in the online role-playing simulation that accompanies this chapter, and they ask you to help them make some important decisions. They're creating a smartphone app that will help high school students prepare for the SAT, but it's not just another boring set of online flash cards or multiple-choice questions. Instead, it's a game called Leveling UP! in which players gain points and advance levels as they get better and better. They are going up against some big names in

this industry, like Kaplan and The Princeton Review, and they need a very sound strategy.

This chapter explores strategy, starting with the forces that shape industry competition and why some industries are more profitable than others. You will see how entire industries are occasionally transformed by events that sweep away dying business models and unleash a flood of new opportunities for clever players like Dana and Prakash. Whether times are calm or stormy, the reasons companies choose one strategy over another—and how they use information systems to implement them—help explain why some companies succeed and others fail.

MyMISLab
Online Simulation

LEVELING UP!

A Role-Playing Simulation on Business Strategy for a New Smartphone App

lipik/Shutterstock

Smart strategy helps explain why the search engine called *Baidu* dominates the Chinese market despite Google's aggressive attempts to take hold in that market. Baidu focuses like a laser on Chinese-speaking Internet users and claims to know them better than Google. On Baidu, they find easier ways to enter keywords and identify relevant websites, all in Chinese. The written Chinese language, with its thousands of complex characters, is not easy to enter for human beings typing on keyboards with a standard QWERTY layout. And a syllable typed in English letters, such as *ma*, could represent different characters with quite different meanings (Figure 2-1). Baidu claims its shortcuts and intelligent interfaces make life a bit easier for Chinese speakers struggling with a keyboard whose grandparent was the typewriter, designed in the United States by English speakers. Baidu earns revenue from online marketers, much as Google does, by showing paid links relevant to the user's search terms.

The strategies companies devise to win customers, earn market share, make profits, and grow their business are tied closely to information systems, like Baidu's search engine or the *Leveling UP!* game. In today's high-tech, globalized business environment, those strategies often rely heavily on innovative information technology (IT) and its application to any area, from marketing and human resources to manufacturing and supply chains. As you will see, some of the IT-related strategies have the potential to completely transform an industry, catapulting the company and its founders into stardom and pushing rivals into bankruptcy.

FIGURE 2-1

The syllable *ma* typed on a QWERTY keyboard can refer to many different Chinese characters with different meanings. The spoken language distinguishes among them through tones, or slight changes in vocal pitch, as the syllable is pronounced.
Source: Kellerkind/Fotolia, Ksysha/Fotolia.

Industries differ, and in some it is more difficult to make a profit—or even survive—than others. Why this is so, and how IT can be such a powerful force for strategists, will become clear, drawing especially on Michael Porter's classic analysis of the forces that affect industry competition and shape strategy.[1,2] We will also see how nonprofit organizations develop strategies involving information systems to dramatically improve their ability to achieve their missions.

Describe Porter's five competitive forces that shape industry competition.

1 Porter's Five Competitive Forces

Glancing at the industries with their average net profit margins as of 2016 in Figure 2-2, you might breathe a sigh of relief if you were not in the oil and gas industry, where plummeting oil prices contributed to severe downturns.[3] Some industries enjoyed healthy margins during this time, with many successful companies. In other industries, the firms struggled just to stay afloat, and many lost money. These conditions are not due to smart managers in the high-profit industries and boneheaded CEOs elsewhere, though the strategies these people implement certainly play a role. Instead, based on Porter's model, the reasons lie with five interrelated forces that influence industry competition (Figure 2-3):

1. Threat of new entrants
2. Power of buyers
3. Power of suppliers
4. Threat of substitutes
5. Rivalry among existing competitors

To see how these forces play out, let's look more closely at graduate students Prakash and Dana, who want to launch that smartphone app for high school students. Needing extra

FIGURE 2-2

Profitability of selected U.S. industries.[18]

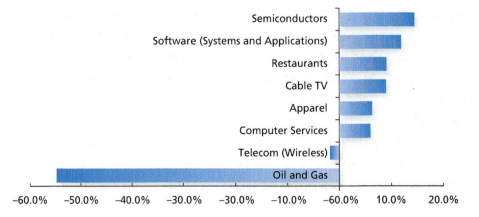

Net Profit Margin for Selected Industries

FIGURE 2-3
The five forces that shape competition in industries.

money, the two plan to develop an appealing way for students to prepare for the SAT. Prakash and Dana know that students are notorious procrastinators, but they also have many small slots of time—usually wasted on daydreaming, game playing, or texting—throughout the day.

To make preparation less painful and also less costly compared to hiring personal tutors for long, tiring sessions, these cofounders want to draw on some of the compelling features of cell-phone games. Rewards, fast-paced action, competition, and special ringtones to indicate a student's advancing level should help motivate students to practice SAT problems whenever they have a spare moment. As students improve, they can make up their own questions to add to the pool. Prakash and Dana like the name *Leveling UP!* for their company, reflecting the game world's jargon for advancing your skills or your character's capabilities. Think about how the strategic concepts in this chapter apply to their innovative idea, and then log into the online simulation to help them plan.

Threat of New Entrants

The **threat of new entrants** in an industry is very high when start-ups like *Leveling UP!* can open shop with little capital, few employees, and next to no experience. Industry incumbents must find ways to ward off newcomers, and profitability often suffers.

Thinking too narrowly about who those new entrants might be can be dangerous. The big players in the SAT preparation business—Kaplan and The Princeton Review—know well that small start-ups can enter relatively easily. But new entrants might also come from established companies in other industries, whose leaders decide to diversify and encroach on one another. At one time, Apple just invented and manufactured computers and consumer electronics, and companies that distributed music and videos on CDs and DVDs didn't think of Apple as a rival. That is, they didn't until Apple launched iTunes and cut deeply into their market.

For their part, the existing incumbents in an industry try to keep newcomers out in many different ways, often drawing on innovative use of information systems. They already have certain advantages, such as higher volumes, which can mean lower costs per unit of production. A large customer base can be significant because of **network effects**, which refer to the increased value of a product or service that results simply because there are more people

threat of new entrants
The threat new entrants into an industry pose to existing businesses; the threat is high when start-up costs are very low and newcomers can enter easily. This is one of Porter's five competitive forces.

network effects
The increased value of a product or service that results simply because there are more people using it.

using it. The value of Facebook, for example, is low if you can only connect a few people. But the more people who use that social network, the more valuable it becomes to everyone.

Groupon offers daily deals by email and was once praised as "the fastest growing company ever." The founder's decision to turn down Google's offer of $6 billion to buy Groupon out was a big mistake. After going public, Groupon's stock price plummeted more than 80%, and the company continues to struggle.[4] The threat of new entrants is high, and the "daily deal" may be a temporary fad.

Incumbents devise strategies to raise **switching costs**, which are the costs customers incur when they change suppliers. Carriers do this by offering a "free" cell phone with a 2-year contract, but the phone is not really free. They increase the monthly fees to cover the phone's initial cost and then charge customers a hefty penalty if they terminate the contract early.

Loyalty programs also raise switching costs and discourage new entrants. Frequent fliers earn valuable rewards for racking up all their flying miles with a single airline, including automatic upgrades and free companion tickets. Travelers go out of their way to stick with their favorite airline and continue to grow their point balance.

For information systems that organizations buy to manage their own records, switching costs can be extremely high. To switch, organizations would pay new licensing fees and would also have to change their business processes, migrate their data, and train their employees on the new system. Companies that use software such as SAP or Oracle to manage their business functions are reluctant to switch, even if their licensing costs go up and competitors offer cheaper pricing. This is one reason the application software industry enjoys very high profitability (Figure 2-2).

Power of Buyers

The **power of buyers** rises when they have leverage over suppliers and can demand deep discounts and special services. If a supplier has a small number of buyers, the supplier is at a disadvantage because losing even one could be devastating. Companies whose main customer is the government, for instance, deal with a very powerful buyer. Buyer power also rises when many suppliers offer similar products and the buyer can switch easily. For airline tickets on the most popular and competitive routes, buyers have high power. Unless passengers are tied to one airline with a loyalty program, they can search for the best price, a factor that holds down the airline industry's profitability.

FIGURE 2-4
Price comparison website.

Arbus Camera 590
$249.99, free shipping   Reviews

★★★★

Arbus Camera 590
$259.95 free shipping

★★★★

Arbus Camera 590
$329.99, free shipping

★★★

The balance of power between buyers and suppliers for many industries shifted dramatically when markets went online and customers could switch from one seller to another with a single click. To make price comparisons for similar products even easier, dozens of websites gather up-to-the-minute prices from sellers so that visitors can easily compare them in a single list (Figure 2-4). On PriceGrabber.com, visitors can enter the product they want and pull up a list of all the merchants who sell it along with their prices. To empower buyers further, the site asks visitors to rate the transaction when they purchase something from a seller on the list. These reviews tip off prospective buyers in case the seller fails to deliver.

Power of Suppliers

The **power of suppliers** is high when they are just about the only game in town and thus can charge more for their products and services. Microsoft is an example. Given the dominance of its Windows operating system on desktop computers, PC assemblers around the world risk losing customers if they don't install it. Not only can Microsoft demand higher prices, but it can also insist on additional perks, such as adding desktop icons for trial versions of its own software products. Windows' lead on desktops is shrinking, though, as Apple gains share and free products attract more customers.

Walmart's thousands of suppliers have far less power than Microsoft. There are few products made by a single supplier for which Walmart couldn't find an alternative close enough to please consumers. Also, Walmart's suppliers have invested in information systems that link their inventories to the company's legendary supply chain system.

> **PRODUCTIVITY TIP**
> Take a close look at the software trial versions that came preinstalled on your computer to see which products the PC manufacturer is promoting with this valuable positioning. As long as you have a recovery disk in case of problems, you can uninstall the ones you don't need to reduce clutter and improve your computer's performance.

High switching costs also add to supplier power. The loyalty programs described earlier do this. An even more powerful way to raise switching costs is through technology. You might spend weeks entering all the addresses and account numbers for your bills into your online banking system, and a competing bank would need to be very persuasive to get you to switch. Companies also promote their own technology formats to raise switching costs. For example, if you wanted to switch from Microsoft Excel to the free Google Sheets, you would need to import all of your spreadsheets and then check to see what features were mangled or lost.

Threat of Substitutes

The **threat of substitutes** is high when alternative products are available, especially if they offer attractive savings. For example, high-quality videoconferencing offers an alternative to face-to-face meetings that can slash a company's travel expenses (Figure 2-5). The technological advances eliminate the distracting choppiness and poorly synched voice transmissions that turned off businesspeople in the past. With tight travel budgets, videoconferencing is a viable substitute for business travel.

Substitutes, which provide the same product or service through different means, can be quite difficult to predict and even harder to combat. What airline executives would have imagined that California-based Cisco, a leader in computer networking products, would grab

FIGURE 2-5
Videoconferencing heightens the threat of substitutes to the business travel industry.

Source: Andersen Ross/Exactostock/SuperStock.

switching costs
Costs that customers incur when they change suppliers.

power of buyers
The advantage buyers have when they have leverage over suppliers and can demand deep discounts and special services. This is one of Porter's five competitive forces.

power of suppliers
The advantage sellers have when there is a lack of competition and they can charge more for their products and services. This is one of Porter's five competitive forces.

threat of substitutes
The threat posed to a company when buyers can choose alternatives that provide the same item or service, often at attractive savings. This is one of Porter's five competitive forces.

their market with its videoconferencing products? Information technology plays a key role in many examples of substitution threats, from online learning modules that replace face-to-face training classes to Internet video that threatens cable TV companies. The number of cable subscribers has been shrinking since 2000, and analysts expect the "cord cutting" trend to continue.

The threat of substitutes may come from any direction, making it critical for strategists to pay attention to developments on a much wider scale. Although drug makers with patented products know that generic substitutes will rapidly take market share once the patent expires, other industries are taken by surprise when potent substitutes arise. The newspaper industry, for instance, failed to grasp how quickly subscribers would switch to the free news available online to save both money and trees. Cutting prices for print subscriptions or classified ads only worsened their financial situations. Today, few print newspapers enjoy healthy balance sheets.

Rivalry Among Existing Competitors

An industry's profitability and its competitive structure are affected by the intensity of **rivalry among existing competitors**, particularly with respect to *how* they are competing and *what* they compete on. If firms compete mainly on price, rivalry is high and the industry as a whole becomes less profitable because price cutting triggers rounds of damaging price wars. Online, price cuts can occur with breathtaking speed, with no need to attach new price tags to physical merchandise. Price wars can also affect the behavior of buyers, who pay more attention to price long after the war ends, and reduce profitability industry-wide.[5] The one who strikes first in a price war may benefit somewhat, but overall, all competitors and their suppliers may suffer. Consumers enjoy terrific deals, though.

Slow growth can also lead to intense rivalry among existing competitors. If sales are flat, any competitive strategy from one company will steal market share from the others, so incumbents will counter every competitive move.

2

Explain how disruptive innovations, government policies, complementary products and services, and other factors affect how the competitive forces operate.

Factors that Affect How the Five Forces Operate

The five forces together determine industry structure and potential for profit. In addition to the strategies companies themselves implement, several external factors affect how those forces operate. Certain innovations, for example, can flood through an industry like a tidal wave, changing everything in their path and forcing every company to either make changes or sink.

Disruptive Technology and Innovations

A **disruptive innovation** is a new product or service, often springing from technological advances, that has the potential to reshape an industry. For example, Kodak, Casio, Olympus, and other companies began offering digital cameras that needed no film in the 1990s, transforming the industry within a few short years. Sales of film rolls and the cameras that used them plunged, along with the businesses that processed the film. Although the early digital cameras had lower resolutions, technological advances quickly made them a very respectable substitute product that almost wiped out film cameras, along with all the services and products surrounding them.

Unlike **sustaining technologies**, which offer important improvements to streamline existing processes and give companies marginal advantages, disruptive innovation is different (Figure 2-6). Often developed by start-ups or industry outsiders, it brings a radical and unexpected breakthrough that first replaces lower-end products but then rapidly overtakes even the high end of the market (Figure 2-7). Companies that cling to the older models may eventually be out of business, although many find ways to adapt. Figure 2-8 shows more examples.

The Internet itself is the kingpin of disruptive innovations in recent decades, and all the innovations it supports are transforming one industry after another. It fundamentally changes aspects of the five forces by, for example, reducing entry barriers for newcomers, empowering

Source: nyul/Fotolia.

FIGURE 2-6
"Innovation is the central issue in economic prosperity."—Michael Porter.

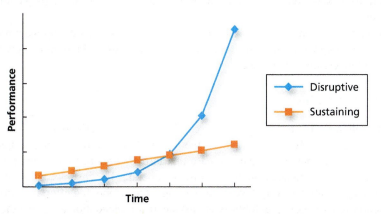

FIGURE 2-7
Comparing disruptive and sustaining innovations on performance over time.

Disruptive Innovation	Disrupted Products and Services
Steamships	Sailing ships
Truck	Horse
Digital cameras	Instant cameras, such as Polaroid, and eventually most film cameras
Desktop publishing software	Dedicated professional publishing
Email	Postal mail
Computer printer	Offset printing press
Word processing software	Typewriter
Music CD	Vinyl record, cassette tape, 8-track tape
Music and video downloads	Music CD/Video DVD
GPS navigation	Printed maps
Internet video	Cable TV
Cloud computing	Local data centers
3D printing	Traditional manufacturing
Smartphones	Cell phones, landlines, digital cameras, laptops
Ride-hailing services	Taxis

FIGURE 2-8
Examples of disruptive innovations.

rivalry among existing competitors
The intensity of competition within an industry. Intense rivalry can reduce profitability in the industry due to price cutting or other competitive pressures. This is one of Porter's five competitive forces.

disruptive innovation
A new product or service, often springing from technological advances, that has the potential to reshape an industry.

sustaining technologies
Technologies that offer improvements to streamline existing processes and give companies marginal advantages.

buyers with far more information about prices and competitors, and virtually eliminating switching costs for many products. It also facilitates a vast, global e-marketplace in which competitors can spring from anywhere. Supported by mobile apps, even individuals can join in the sharing economy to compete against traditional players. For instance, private Uber drivers compete with taxi companies, and Airbnb hosts share their dwellings as alternatives to hotel rooms. Mobile technologies are especially disruptive. In retail industries, for example, buyer power soars when shoppers can scan a product with their smartphones and look for cheaper prices online. Another industry—bus travel between cities—became instantly profitable when young people discovered that they could hop on a bus for much less than traveling by car, train, or plane and surf the web the whole way. With its free wifi, Megabus attracts well-educated 18- to 34-year-olds who want to save money, avoid the hassle of air travel, and also stay online.

Economist Joseph Schumpeter used the term **creative destruction** to describe what happens in an industry when disruptive innovations threaten the established players. Newcomers find ways to capitalize on the new technologies, while many incumbents resist the change and seek ways to protect their old business models.

The music industry may be the poster child of creative destruction. The record labels once dominated this industry, controlling pricing, distribution, and marketing. But Napster found a way for music lovers to share their electronic music files online—for free. The labels fought Napster in court and eventually shut it down for copyright violations, but then Apple entered the picture with its iTunes store and low pricing per song. The labels fought again because it is far more lucrative to sell albums, but consumers flocked to purchase single songs, transforming the industry.

Industry leaders need not be passive observers in the face of such disruptive innovations. Instead, they can assign special teams to work outside their usual hierarchies, giving them freedom to explore creative approaches.[6]

Government Policies and Actions

Government policies and funding priorities can have dramatic effects on how industries operate and how they evolve. Patents reduce the threat of new entrants, for example, while low-cost loans to small businesses can increase that threat. Organizations lobby heavily for government action to influence how the five forces operate. For instance, the government updates its dietary guidelines every 5 years, triggering intense lobbying efforts by food industries. Beef producers, for example, lobbied against any recommendation to reduce the amount of red meat.[7]

Lobbyists for state governments have pressed Congress for years to level the playing field and allow them to collect sales taxes when state residents buy products from online retailers. One Vermont lawmaker complained, "Our retailers have such a hard job, all they are asking for is fairness.... People go in to use [the local business] as a showroom and go home and order on the internet, and do not pay sales tax."[8] Amazon, which has a physical presence in most states, began collecting sales taxes, but regulations remain somewhat murky.[9]

Many lobbying groups fight for government regulation to block new entrants enabled by the Internet. Optometrists once earned profits through contact lens sales, as patients used their new prescription to buy their lenses at the optometrist's store. When 1800contacts.com and other retailers began offering lenses at discounted prices, they lobbied to make it easier for customers to compare prices and buy elsewhere. However, the American Optometry Association also lobbied, and the 2004 "Fairness to Contact Lens Consumers Act" contained regulations to appease both groups. For instance, doctors must provide patients with an original, signed prescription, but online sellers may not accept faxed prescriptions from the consumer without the doctor's confirmation.

Complementary Services and Products in the Ecosystem

Many industries are interrelated, and events in one can influence the others. Desktop publishing software, for example, made the computer and a color printer much more useful to small businesses that save money by developing menus, signs, and brochures in-house. Companies offering specialty paper also benefited.

Companies are embedded in a complex **ecosystem**—an economic community that includes the related industries making complementary products and services, the competitors themselves, the suppliers, and also the consumers. Events in one arena—particularly a disruptive innovation—ripple through the whole community, affecting all the players and the five forces for the industries involved.

In the United States, the ecosystem for gambling consists of casinos, Indian reservations, government regulators, lobbyists, consumer groups, racetracks, financial institutions, hotels, live entertainment, and others. Most forms of online gambling, however, are not legal in the United States, but change may be coming. American gamblers spend more than $100 billion a year at betting websites hosted in places like Antigua, and U.S. casinos would like to see the law changed so they can share in the profit. That would spread throughout the gambling ecosystem, damaging some members, rewarding others, and attracting new entrants with complementary services. Hotels may suffer, but the casinos will have another source of revenue. Cell-phone developers will quickly see a new, user-friendly application—live poker with real bets paid by credit card.

Some of the most powerful strategic moves come from visionaries who propose fundamental changes for all the industries in the ecosystem and persuade the others to come along. Bill Gates did just that early in his career, when he imagined moving computing away from mainframes and onto the desktop. To succeed, they would need a standard operating system so that software developers, peripheral manufacturers, and everyone else could build upon it and quickly enrich the ecosystem with a compelling set of complementary products and services. Microsoft's Windows operating system began its ascent, eventually dominating the industry with almost 90% market share. Other companies that created applications to run on that operating system succeeded as well.

Another example of a strategy that leads a whole ecosystem into new directions involves Salesforce.com. The company promotes cloud computing(discussed in detail in the next chapter), in which an organization's information systems are not installed on servers in its own data center. Instead, employees use the Internet to connect to their systems, hosted by a vendor in a data center shared by many other businesses (Figure 2-9). (The "cloud" is a metaphor for the Internet; a cloud-like shape is often used to depict its complex infrastructure.)

FIGURE 2-9

Sample cloud computing services supported by the Internet.

Source: Nui7711/Shutterstock, Rvlsoft/Shutterstock, Cobalt88/Shutterstock, Maxim Kazmin/123RF

creative destruction
What happens in an industry when disruptive innovations threaten the established players.

ecosystem
An economic community that includes the related industries making complementary products and services, the competitors themselves, the suppliers, and also the consumers.

Companies can purchase subscriptions to use the Salesforce software to manage customer records instead of installing software locally. Cloud computing is gaining a lot of momentum as the next disruptive innovation that overtakes local data centers, including the desktop PC with software installed on the hard drive.

Environmental Events and "Wildcards"

Hurricanes, snowstorms, pandemics, earthquakes, strikes, and civil unrest can all have major effects on entire industries, sometimes without much warning. The East Coast blizzard of 2016, for instance, caused major losses for restaurants, retailers, and other businesses that had to shut down.

Energy costs, conservation initiatives, and concerns over carbon emissions may also trigger waves of change. For example, supply chains that stress just-in-time deliveries may struggle to pay for the extra gas that kind of service requires. E-commerce companies that rely on many small shipments trucked to people's homes may have to raise their shipping fees and experiment with drone deliveries.

For an organization to develop a viable competitive strategy, its leaders take into account the nature of the industry and how the five competitive forces play out. They also consider the factors affecting those forces and how they are changing. But what are their strategic options, and where do information systems fit in? Michael Porter also developed a model that helps strategists think about how the organization actually creates value and where improvements can be made to advance the firm's competitive position.

Identify the components of the value chain, and explain its extended version.

3 The Value Chain and Strategic Thinking

Porter's **value chain model** describes the activities a company performs to create value, as it brings in raw resources from suppliers, transforms them in some way, and then markets the product or service to buyers (Figure 2-10). In the model, the company performs **primary activities** directly related to the process by which products and services are created, marketed, sold, and delivered. **Support activities** encompass all the other processes and offices the company needs, including administration and management, human resources, procurement, and technology support.

FIGURE 2-10
Components of the value chain.

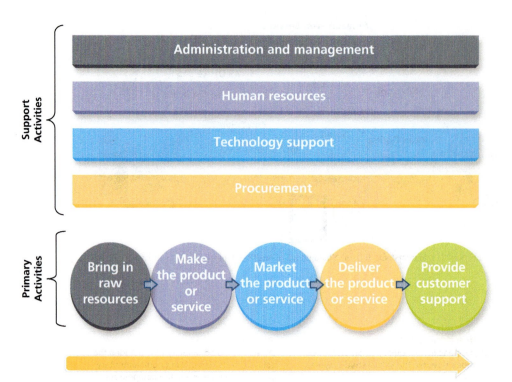

The model may seem to suggest the activities typical in manufacturing companies, but in fact, it applies to many settings. The "raw resources," for example, might be copper ore trucked to a processing plant. They could also be digital journal articles downloaded from online libraries and summarized for a briefing paper needed by a government agency. "Making the product or service" can span many different tasks, from chemical processing of the copper to the consultants' research and analysis.

Extending the Value Chain: From Suppliers to the Firm to Customers

Expanding the model beyond the company's own primary and support activities leads to a better understanding of how all the processes fit together (Figure 2-11). The chain does not actually begin when a truckload of copper is dumped on a processor's doorstep or when the analyst clicks "download" to retrieve a report. The chain also does not end when the buyer pays for the product or service. Events in these external parts of the chain can also offer strategic opportunities and different risks.[10]

A company with shoddy suppliers might benefit from a switch or from strategic alliances with a few of them to help make them more efficient. Toyota, for example, encourages its tiny auto part suppliers to set up shop near its factories so Toyota can provide extensive training and support. Or a company that spots weaknesses in the suppliers' industry might decide to supply its own needs and even compete against its former suppliers.

Downstream, the value chain offers even more intriguing possibilities for strategic advantages. From the buyer's viewpoint, your company is a supplier, and understanding the customers' own value chain is critical. What are the customers' needs, and why are they buying the product? If the customer is another company, what is *its* strategy for creating value from what you provide?

Online, the extended value chain can include contributions from buyers who add value to the company's products or services. For example, Amazon's own customers enrich the retailer's site by contributing their frank and often blunt product reviews. Intuit, the company that offers TurboTax software, launched a user's forum that links directly to the software so that people can ask tax questions for other users to answer. TurboTax doesn't vouch for the answers, but users can rate their quality. The answers are often much easier to understand compared to what they would find in IRS manuals. CNN's *iReport* program solicits videos from people who might just happen to have their cell-phone camcorder turned on to catch breaking news. Web 2.0 offers countless opportunities to incorporate user-generated content.

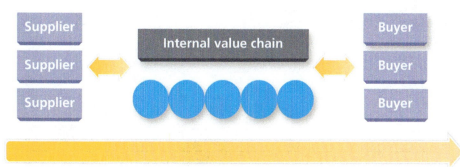

FIGURE 2-11
The extended value chain involving suppliers, the company, and its customers.

value chain model
A model developed by Michael Porter that describes the activities a company performs to create value as it brings in raw resources from suppliers, transforms them in some way, and then markets the product or service to buyers.

primary activities
Activities directly related to the value chain process by which products and services are created, marketed, sold, and delivered.

support activities
Activities performed as part of the value chain model that are not primary; support activities include administration and management, human resources, procurement, and technology support.

Benchmarking Components of the Value Chain

The value chain model offers a way for organizations to compare their performance against industry benchmarks to see how they stack up and also spot areas that should be targeted for improvement. A **benchmark** is a reference point used as a baseline measurement. Often it indicates a measurement that would be considered optimal or best practices within the industry, though it is sometimes simply an industry average.

For the value chain, one benchmark might be the percent of total budget that is spent on each of the primary and support activities. How does the organization's spending compare to industry benchmarks or average expenditures? Does your company spend more than its rivals on human resources, for example? Is your marketing budget a bit slim compared with your competitors'? Analyzing these benchmarks can point to areas that need attention—not necessarily more spending but some thought about why spending is higher or lower than the benchmark. Higher spending on human resources, for instance, might be part of a strategic effort to recruit top talent.

 ## THE ETHICAL FACTOR Ethical Responsibility in an Extended Value Chain

As the extended value chain lengthens, responsibility for harmful consequences becomes more diffuse. Considering the length and complexity of the value chain that leads to a smartphone in a customer's hands, who is ethically responsible when it overheats and injures someone? Suppose a manager allocates smartphones to the salespeople and one person is badly burned while driving. How much responsibility would you assign to each of the links in this chain listed in Figure 2-12?

If you learned that the factory's working conditions were dreadful and the smartphone company made a deal with it anyway because its costs were so low, would your judgments change? Suppose the retailer got a tip that a recall was coming but kept selling the phones to get rid of the inventory. Increasingly, people are rejecting the "plausible deniability" excuse that companies have used in the past to avoid corporate responsibility for mishaps in their extended supply chains. Nevertheless, the drive to reduce costs, particularly for firms that compete for low cost leadership, can lead to ethically questionable decisions. The blurred boundaries along the extended value chain can make it even more difficult to allocate responsibility and easier to point fingers.

FIGURE 2-12

How much responsibility would you assign to each of these links in the extended value chain?

	Not Responsible	Somewhat Responsible	Very Responsible
The retailer who sold it to the consumer			
The smartphone company that designs and markets it under the company name			
The factory that assembles it			
The factory worker who assembled the particular phone			
The small business that supplied battery parts to the factory			
The global shipping company that transported the phones			
The procurement manager who researched the options and selected the phones for the sales staff			
The manager who supplied the smartphones			
The user who didn't read the instruction manual			

IT Benchmarks

Figure 2-13 shows the average percent of total revenue that industries spend on IT.[11] Not surprisingly, software publishing and Internet services spend quite a bit, as do companies in the energy industry. Banks and finance also spend heavily, partly due to the need for extremely high security and fraud control.

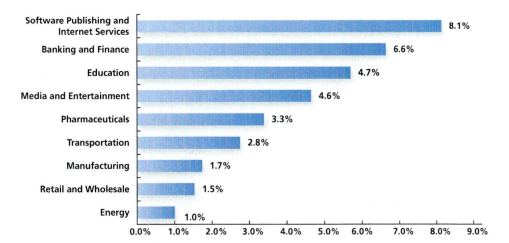

FIGURE 2-13
Average IT spending by industry as a percentage of revenue.

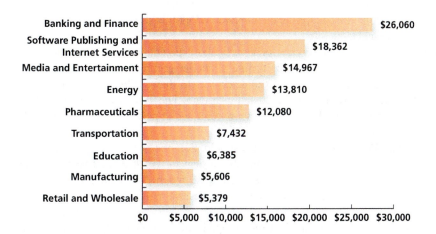

FIGURE 2-14
Average IT spending per employee in a sample of industries.

Another benchmark useful for information systems is the amount spent per employee, and Figure 2-14 shows these averages by the same industries. The amounts range widely, but even the retail and wholesale industry spends more than $4,700 per person. The figure doesn't just include the obvious computer on the desk. It includes all hardware, software, salaries for IT personnel, software licensing, data center costs, telecommunications costs, outsourced IT projects, and others. For education, the $6,000-plus figure might include computer labs, classroom projection systems, online libraries, and antivirus software for students and faculty.

Energy costs affect almost every link in the value chain, and organizations are testing out cheaper sources—including humans. Some fitness gyms connect their exercise bikes, rowing machines, and treadmills to generators so customers can supply some of the building's electricity.

Managers can use benchmarks like these to see how they compare to competitors and also to examine how much every dollar they spend is helping to create value. Each component offers opportunities for either cost savings or improved products and services that offer more value to buyers, both of which can improve the company's bottom line.

benchmark
A reference point used as a baseline measurement.

Describe how information systems apply to competitive strategies for business.

4 Competitive Strategies in Business

Becoming a leader in an industry takes uncanny skill and strategic thinking. Although there are many variables and infinite combinations, Porter identified three basic strategies companies can adopt that are most likely to lead to success.

The **low cost leadership strategy**, which means offering a similar product at a lower price compared with competitors, is one that Walmart, Kia Motors, Southwest Airlines, Lenovo, and many others pursue. To be successful, the company has to cut every gram of fat in the value chain, using information systems to automate and streamline processes and eliminate costly human labor. Southwest Airlines, for instance, reduced inflight service and implemented ticketless reservation systems (Figure 2-15). Walmart's enormous success as a low cost leader in retailing comes especially from its IT-supported supply chain, the envy of its competitors.

Many companies adopt the **product differentiation strategy**—adding special features or unique add-ons for which customers are willing to pay more. The strategy tends to reduce threats from substitute products, and it also erects barriers to new entrants. Apple computer is a clear example that cleverly takes this path over and over again, with its Macintosh computers, iPod, iPad, and iPhone. Pharmaceutical companies adopt this strategy in their search for specialized drugs that can be patented.

Differentiating the product or service for a particular segment of the market is called a **focused niche strategy**. Here, the goal is to find a smaller group of customers who have special preferences and then tailor products and services to them. Ello, for example, is an ad-free social network that promises never to sell user data. The Twitter-like service targets people who are concerned about loss of privacy on other social networks that earn revenue from advertising and data sharing.

Although Michael Porter thought companies should pick one of the strategies and stick with it, not everyone agrees, particularly in the digital age in which those five forces that shape competition in an industry have been shaken up so much. Companies find successful paths with hybrid models, such as shooting for the best value for the lowest price. This contrasts with the low cost approach because it also encourages customers to compare the value of a product and its features against the competition. That can help counter deadly price wars.

Companies also achieve a different kind of success by quickly building a large audience in a brand new market. YouTube took that route by attracting millions of people who wanted to share their homemade videos with friends. The company charged nothing for its services;

FIGURE 2-15

Southwest Airlines stresses low cost leadership strategy.

Source: © EuroStyle Graphics/Alamy.

rather, venture capitalists who know the value of such a faithful following provided the capital. These "angel" investors hope a major company with deep pockets will acquire the new company for far more. As it turned out, Google bought YouTube for more than 40 times the sum those early investors contributed.

The Role of Information Systems in Strategy

All of these strategies leverage information systems to succeed, and those systems are often at the very heart of the company's competitive advantage. Low cost leaders, for example, must automate as much as possible, from their suppliers to their customer support services.

Regardless of which strategic path a company follows, it will reduce costs by using information systems to support all the back-office functions—payroll, benefits, accounting, procurement, inventory tracking, and asset management, for example. Indeed, major savings come from rethinking how these processes are done in the first place, by eliminating steps or avoiding duplication of effort. Converting to self-service in human resources, for instance, is a good example. Rather than asking employees to fill in paper forms that staff in the human resources office have to review and enter into the systems that manage payroll and benefits, companies implement online services so employees enter their own data. They can enter benefit selections and timesheets and also keep track of their information, such as how many vacation and sick days they have left. Mercifully, phone calls to the human resources office drop, along with data entry errors.

Information systems support strategy and reduce cost in every industry, even those that don't spend much on IT. Companies in the transportation industry only spend about 2.8% of revenue on IT (Figure 2-13), but they apply those funds very wisely. For example, shippers are using railroads more and more because of rising fuel costs (Figure 2-16). Freight trains,

FIGURE   2-16
The transportation industry takes advantage of information systems to coordinate cargo transfers.

Source: © soleg/Fotolia.

low cost leadership strategy
A company strategy that involves offering a similar product at a lower price compared to competitors.

product differentiation strategy
A company strategy that involves adding special features to a product or unique add-ons for which customers are willing to pay more.

focused niche strategy
A company strategy that involves differentiating a product or service for a particular market niche.

after all, can move a ton of freight 400 miles on a single gallon of fuel, and en route, the only busy freight train employee is the engineer. But things get very hectic when the train stops at a terminal hub, as trucks converge to drop off or pick up the train's cargo. Information systems avoid chaos by coordinating the trucks' movements—scanning each one and directing it to the right place as the train arrives. Thanks to these systems, truckers are in and out in 3 minutes instead of 20, and the number of accidents is dramatically reduced.

Launching a strikingly differentiated product or service often relies on innovations in IT as well, and not just for high-tech companies. Some grocery stores, for instance, offer shoppers smarter shopping carts with devices that scan a loyalty card and then guide the customer through the aisles. The devices can announce special sales, scan purchases, and total the bill so customers breeze through checkout. The information is transmitted to the store's inventory system, just as it would be if the shopper went through the checkout line. But unlike the data collected at checkout, smart carts can track shoppers' movements and deliver real-time ads that match the customer's interests. For example, if you put hotdogs in the cart, it might offer discounts on buns and relish.

Information Systems: Run, Grow, and Transform the Business

What is that money spent on IT actually used for? How does it contribute to the company's strategy? The computers, laptops, cell phones, and other devices support productivity throughout the organization, in every component of the value chain, whether the employee is in sales, finance, marketing, management, or human resources. The software applications touch every component of the value chain as well, streamlining processes, creating customer friendly portals, or compiling reports about the effectiveness of marketing campaigns.

On average, organizations spend about two-thirds of their IT dollars to just keep things running (Figure 2-17). These costs include IT staff salaries, the data center, the help desk, software licenses, and maintenance of the company's core application software and infrastructure. They are not discretionary, in the sense that the organization can't operate without these capabilities. However, there are many ways to reduce these costs. Some companies are outsourcing their help desks, for example, or moving to cloud computing to reduce data center expenses. Indeed, managers should seek out ways to reduce expenses in this kind of IT spending, just as they would for any other component of the value chain.

Strategic uses of IT that consume the rest of the budget focus on growing the business or transforming the business model. IT is a **strategic enabler**, a role that can potentially make a far greater contribution to success compared to its role in keeping the business running. Information systems can, for example, facilitate a whole new business model, as they did for eBay in the form of specialized software to support online auctions.

Other examples of potentially game-changing uses of IT include 3D printing, robotics, electronic medical records, self-driving vehicles, unmanned drones, smart machines, nanotechnology, and virtual personal assistants (Figure 2-18). Breakthroughs in these and other technologies have enormous potential to transform business models and industries.

FIGURE 2-17

How do organizations spend their IT dollars?

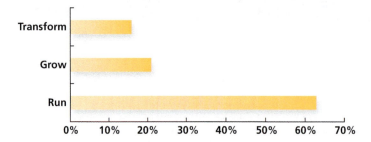

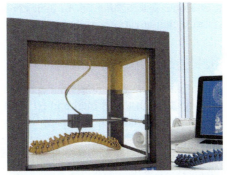

FIGURE 2-18
Breakthroughs in 3D printing, unmanned drones, self-driving vehicles, electronic medical records, and other technologies can lead to major advances and industry disruptions.
Source: Africa Studio/Shutterstock; Belekekin/Shutterstock; Ociacia/ Shutterstock

Information Strategies and Nonprofit Organizations

 Explain how information systems apply to strategy for nonprofit organizations and governments.

Dane R. Grams, the online strategy director at the nonprofit Human Rights Campaign (HRC), recognizes the need for immediacy when a legislative proposal is up for a vote and phone calls from voters can make a difference. "We wanted to call on our most active supporters to act on a moment's notice. … Most people have a single cell phone and it's always with them." HRC arranged to send messages to its members at the right moment, asking them to call their representatives about a pending bill and giving them key points to use in the conversation. Once the message ended, the member was connected to the right office to make the pitch.[12]

Although nonprofit organizations have no shareholders, they can benefit a great deal from strategic use of information systems. Running, growing, and transforming the organization are all very relevant to nonprofits, just as they are to the for-profit world, and information systems play a key role. The operational requirements to run nonprofits are quite similar to businesses, with information systems used for payroll, accounting, and related tasks.

Some of the most innovative strategic uses of information systems come from the nonprofit world, among charities, schools, grassroots projects, religious organizations, government

strategic enabler
The role information systems play as tools to grow or transform the business or facilitate a whole new business model.

agencies, and others. Reaching out to their constituencies is vital, and two areas that reap benefits from such innovations are fund-raising and volunteer management.

Fund-Raising

Many nonprofits rely on donations, and specialized information systems help manage this critical activity. Though direct mail and telemarketing once dominated, much fund-raising is now done online. In 4 years, for example, annual online donations for Chicago's YMCA leaped from a paltry $450 to $24,000, a jump of more than 5,000%. Even a small nonprofit can reach out to a worldwide audience through the Internet, making a case for its mission and motivating people to help.

Nonprofits leverage information systems to learn more about potential donors, their preferences, and their motivations, in the same way that a company like Amazon does. For example, a survey of more than 6,500 people ages 20 to 35 found that this age group has high expectations about a nonprofit's use of technology to encourage donations and attract volunteers. The majority said they preferred to learn about nonprofits through websites, social media, or e-newsletters. They also made it clear they did *not* want to receive texts or voice calls from nonprofits.[13]

Volunteering

Attracting volunteers and sustaining their attachment to the mission are essential tasks for many nonprofits. The efforts are similar to those companies use to build customer relationships and develop employee loyalty. In fact, recognizing the similarity, Salesforce.com created a foundation to help nonprofits use their CRM software, originally designed for businesses to manage customer relationships for the salespeople.

Among the early adopters was Wildlife Victoria, an Australian nonprofit that rescues injured wildlife. Wildlife Victoria implemented Salesforce.com to help manage and extend its network of volunteer wildlife rescuers, coordinate rescue events, and keep track of potential donors. Aiding wildlife at risk can be a complex operation, and the system helps coordinate the many components—from wildlife shelters and transporters to emergency services and rehabilitation.

Helping volunteers find a project that needs their skills is something information systems are very good at. VolunteerMatch.org is a kind of matchmaking service that offers search tools so people can find projects under way near their homes that connect with their interests (Figure 2-19). More than 100,000 nonprofits post their needs on the site, hoping to attract volunteers to teach swimming, mentor children, care for animals, guide museum visitors, and, of course, help build information systems needed by nonprofits. The site adds a Google map with pushpins showing the locations of the opportunities in your area.[14]

FIGURE 2-19

VolunteerMatch.org helps volunteers find opportunities in their areas.

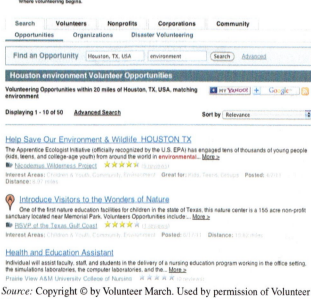

Source: Copyright © by Volunteer March. Used by permission of Volunteer March.

Information Strategies and Government

Like nonprofits, government agencies have similar needs for information systems to "run" the business, handling the operational requirements that all organizations share. They must manage their payrolls, budgets, procurements, assets, and inventories. Agencies also have some very specialized requirements that depend on their responsibilities and the varied services they provide. For example:

- The military needs real-time systems to manage logistics and rapidly deploy personnel to trouble spots.
- The Department of Natural Resources needs easy ways for people to report poachers who damage forests or hunt illegally and offers online tools for that.

■ The U.S. Internal Revenue Service must have information systems to process millions of tax returns.

Two areas that highlight how government strategies involve information systems are in the development of services for citizens and through research.

INCREASING ACCESS AND ENHANCING SERVICES TO THE PUBLIC

E-government involves efforts to make unclassified information available to citizens via the Internet, and offers many interactive online services to save people time-consuming visits to government offices. It has been slow getting off the ground in some areas, but many agency websites are beginning to overflow with resources for the public, such as online car registration and pet licensing. Search engines help visitors track down what they need, and USA.gov serves as a gateway for federal services.

The U.S. Census Bureau (www.census.gov), for example, offers many summaries and tables online and also provides tools to help researchers download data. Business analysts can retrieve detailed records on income, education, marital status, native language, ethnicity, and more.

> **PRODUCTIVITY TIP**
> At the National Do Not Call Registry website (www.donotcall.gov), you can register your phone number to block unwanted telemarketing calls. E-government services continue to improve, so check your state and local government websites for other time-saving services.

FUNDING RESEARCH FOR TECHNOLOGICAL INNOVATION

Government funding is vital to certain research projects that private investors might avoid because of risk or perhaps because the payoff is too far in the future. The project that eventually led to the Internet itself is a key example. A U.S. government agency—Defense Advanced Research Projects Agency (DARPA)—created a computer research program in the 1960s, and it also funded a community of scientists working from other institutions in the United States and the United Kingdom. The working network built with this funding eventually grew into the Internet.

Projects involving green energy and the smart electricity grid also receive funding from governments. Modernizing the grids will require advanced information systems to change the way they operate, which now is mostly one way—from power suppliers to their business and residential customers. However, as more green energy sources come online, many customers can produce their own power. Not only can they reduce their own electricity bills, but they may even earn a profit as the utility company pays them for adding more to the grid than they consumed during the month (Figure 2-20).

New information systems will be a strategic enabler for the grid, with advanced capabilities to monitor power in both directions. The systems will essentially enable the electric meter to run "backward" when the customer is adding electricity to the grid, and they will help consumers see their patterns of daily energy use. Government support can speed this kind of development, as it did for the Internet.

FIGURE 2-20
Smart meters can monitor power transmissions in both directions so consumers can contribute power from their own sources to the grid.
Source: Pi-Lens/Shutterstock

Does I.T. Matter?

6 Explain why the role of information systems in organizations shifts depending on whether the systems are deployed to run, grow, or transform the business.

Nicholas Carr, former editor of *Harvard Business Review*, posed a thought-provoking question: "Does IT matter?"[15] His point is that IT resources have become so commonplace that their strategic importance has diminished. They have become a commodity—a widely available staple, much like electricity or rail transport. Initially, those two disruptive innovations gave early visionaries considerable advantage over competitors. For example, companies that understood how trains could ship large finished products across great distances invested capital in large-scale factories with efficient mass production. With economies of scale and

e-government
The application of ICT to government activities, especially by posting information online and offering interactive services to citizens.

the rail system for transport, these factories soon put the many small, local manufacturers out of business. Over time, though, competitors adopt the innovation as well, so it no longer confers any advantage. Carr argues that IT is reaching that point, and a larger danger now is overspending.

Blindly assuming that IT investments will always increase workforce productivity is also questionable. In fact, economists have struggled to explain the so-called "productivity paradox" for decades.[16] Since the 1970s, the overall amount of IT spending in the United States has not been closely tied to increases in labor productivity. The paradox remains somewhat mysterious, and the way productivity is measured may be partly responsible. In addition, wise IT investments can lead to soaring productivity, but poorly chosen or mismanaged IT projects have the opposite effect.[17]

Spending on Running, Growing, and Transforming

The benchmarks discussed earlier show that companies are looking closely at *how* they spend their IT dollars, not just at total amounts. The funds used to "run" the business are mainly for the kinds of IT resources that now fall into the commodity category. Strategies to reduce those costs are critical, and because price competition for commodities is fierce, opportunities for savings abound. This book examines many ways organizations can avoid wasteful spending in these areas and improve productivity to get the best value for the lowest cost.

In contrast, the funds and human effort applied to growing and transforming an organization are much more closely tied to strategy, innovation, and competitive advantage. It is here where the "people" component of information systems—that human element—is most critical to success. Although many technologies are indeed commodities, the ability to extract their value requires human imagination. Innovative business practices, new products and services, and dramatically changed processes do not spring by themselves from technologies but from talented people who know how to apply them.

Leveling UP!: A Strategic Analysis

How should we evaluate the industry Prakash and Dana are trying to enter, and how does IT fit into their strategy? Their industry is already dominated by powerful and established incumbents such as The Princeton Review, Kaplan, and Cambridge. The products of those companies include costly face-to-face classes, private tutoring, SAT prep books, and other materials. With the growth of e-learning, however, many less expensive alternatives are opening up, making the industry far more competitive. Some incumbents began offering low cost online programs, even competing with the nonprofit College Board that both administers the test and sells online practice programs to students. Newer entrants offer inexpensive video lectures to explain math problems, and some sites offer practice questions for free. Students have many choices, and rivalry is intense.

Fortunately, *Leveling UP!* is a substitute product, quite distinct from face-to-face prep classes. Its unique mixture of fast-paced gaming features with study aids should distinguish it from the incumbents' offerings. Competition never stands still, however, and Prakash and Dana hope the *Leveling UP!* will have more excitement compared with the competitive products so it can be easily differentiated. That should help the entrepreneurs avoid the trap of competing only on price. They know they will have to move quickly and find innovative ways to market their clever approach. Viral marketing through Twitter and YouTube might work, given the customer demographic, using the focused niche strategy to target avid gamers.

How can we describe the value chain Prakash and Dana are creating? It is not a simple one in which the founders buy resources from suppliers, add value to them, and then sell the product to student customers. Because user-generated content (UGC) will play an important role, their value chain is more complex. They will start by writing their own practice SAT questions, drawing ideas from old SATs. The items will reach students by text message, with the software tracking correct answers and advancing levels. But students will become suppliers as they contribute good practice questions and explanations, rated for quality by other students and the cofounders. The best contributors will become high-level wizards, with special rewards and ringtones.

For Prakash and Dana, IT is a strategic enabler to launch *Leveling UP!* They will need specialized software that works flawlessly on smartphone platforms to deliver the SAT questions, dispense rewards, and level up the "players" as they achieve mastery and offer their own questions. The software does not exist, but their time is a major part of the capital they intend to contribute.

Leveling UP! will make an important strategic investment in the mobile application, and the founders will want to get it right. They should spend as little money as possible on the commodities, using free software and their own computing equipment when they can. However, the time and money spent understanding student needs and creating a compelling and effective application to meet them are the key ingredients to their business model. For them, IT definitely matters.

MyMISLab
Online Simulation

LEVELING UP!
A Role-Playing Simulation on Business Strategy for a New Smartphone App

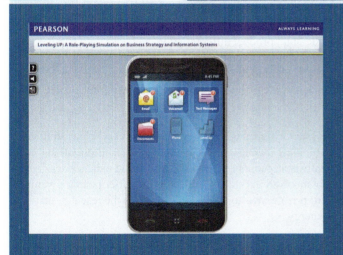

Prakash and Dana asked you to help them brainstorm the strategic direction for their new company, Leveling UP! Your SAT. As this chapter described, their idea is to create a smartphone application that will help high school students practice SAT questions and master the techniques they need to do well on such high-stakes tests. The app will draw on the compelling features of games, though, with rewards, fast-paced action, competition, and special ringtones to indicate advancing levels of mastery, similar to what happens in some of the most popular action and playing games.

Sound like fun? It's a business, though, so you'll need to think about how a company like this with a novel idea can survive, surrounded by very powerful competitors that dominate the industry.

They'll be contacting you with more information, so log in when you're ready.

LEARNING OBJECTIVES

1 The nature of competition in the industry forms the context for every company's strategy, and Michael Porter's model describes the five forces that shape an industry's competitive structure. They help determine how profitable companies operating in the industry will be, and they include (1) the threat of new entrants, (2) the power of buyers, (3) the power of suppliers, (4) the threat of substitute products, and (5) rivalry among competitors.

2 In addition to the strategies of the companies themselves, many external factors affect how the five forces operate. Disruptive innovations, for example, can transform entire industries through the process of creative destruction. Government policies can also affect industry competition through legislation, regulation, and court decisions. Industries that operate in a larger ecosystem are affected by the development of complementary products and services that accelerate trends. In addition, environmental events such as pandemics or earthquakes can reshape industries and call for changes in strategy.

3 Organizations can use the value chain model to understand their options as they strive to compete in an industry. Primary activities (bringing in raw resources, making the product, marketing, delivery, and customer support) and support activities form the major components of the value chain. The extended value chain, which includes suppliers and customers, offers more strategic opportunities. Benchmarks are used to compare a company's performance to industry standards on components of the value chain.

4 Competitive strategies include low cost leadership, product differentiation, and a focused niche strategy for a particular market segment. Information systems support all these approaches by reducing costs, streamlining processes, and adding unique value with new products or features. Their role includes running the organization and, as a strategic enabler, growing and transforming the organization.

5 Nonprofits take advantage of information systems to manage basic operations and also as a strategic enabler in areas such as fund-raising and volunteer management. Governments use information systems extensively for e-government initiatives, especially to increase access and enhance services for the public. Governments are also deeply involved in funding initiatives that offer potential value for the country, but that may be too risky for private investors. Examples include the research that led to the Internet and funding for alternative energy.

6 As technologies become commodities and become widely used by almost all organizations, their strategic value diminishes. The information systems used to "run" organizations, in particular, are readily available and managers should focus on reducing their cost. However, innovative information systems in which creative people leverage technology to grow and transform the organization are critical for effective strategy.

KEY TERMS AND CONCEPTS

threat of new entrants	rivalry among existing competitors	value chain model	product differentiation strategy
network effects	disruptive innovation	primary activities	focused niche strategy
switching costs	sustaining technologies	support activities	strategic enabler
power of buyers	creative destruction	benchmark	e-government
power of suppliers	ecosystem	low cost leadership strategy	
threat of substitutes			

CHAPTER REVIEW QUESTIONS

2-1. What are the five competitive forces that shape industry competition? How are these forces interrelated?

2-2. How do disruptive innovations, government policies, complementary products and services, and environmental events affect how the competitive forces operate?

2-3. What are the components of the value chain? Which components comprise the primary activities? Which components comprise the support activities? What is the extended value chain?

2-4. How do managers use benchmarks to analyze the value chain and IT spending?

2-5. How do information systems apply to competitive strategies for business?

2-6. How are information systems used to run, grow, and transform a business?

2-7. How do information systems apply to competitive strategies for nonprofit organizations?

2-8. How do governments use information systems to improve services and fund research?

PROJECTS AND DISCUSSION QUESTIONS

2-9. Although many people think electronic book readers are too expensive, there is a massive global demand for the devices, and the trend is likely to continue for some time. Search the web to learn more about how digital technology has disrupted the book publishing industry, and prepare a 5-minute presentation of your findings.

2-10. Is a value meal related to a value chain? The value that attracts more than 60 million customers to McDonald's every day comes from capabilities that are based in its value chain. Briefly describe McDonald's value chain and discuss how information systems facilitate each component in the chain. Can you think of a way that information technology could improve your next trip to McDonald's?

2-11. Information technology enables nonprofit organizations to reach out to constituents 24 hours a day, 7 days a week. Visit www.redcross.org and note the various ways this charity is using its website to communicate with volunteers, donors, and people who need assistance. Compare the Red Cross site with your university's alumni association website. Prepare a brief summary of your findings that includes a list of specific services provided on each site. How does each website support the organization's strategic goals?

2-12. Government agencies and corporations have similar information needs. Identify and briefly discuss specific examples of information systems typically used by a law enforcement agency such as a state or local police department. Which of these systems are used to "run" the business? Which are used to fulfill the agency's mission?

2-13. What are the three basic strategies that companies adopt to compete? Describe how information systems support each strategy. What is a "hybrid" strategy? Describe a company, product, or service that adopts each of these four competitive strategies.

2-14. What are network effects? Search the web or visit websites such as Eversave.com and AmazonLocal.com and discuss how network effects can affect the threat of new entrants. Is there an Eversave offering or an AmazonLocal deal in your hometown? How would you describe the long-term value proposition of this online shopping phenomenon? In your opinion, are there any disadvantages for an organization that offers a daily deal?

2-15. The U.S. federal government collects trillions in taxes each year, including individual income taxes, social security/social insurance taxes, and corporate taxes. Visit www.irs.gov and describe how this website enhances services to the public. What types of services are available to individuals? To businesses? To charities and nonprofit organizations? What kind of "tax information for students" does this site provide? Prepare a 5-minute presentation of your findings.

2-16. Why are IT resources described as a commodity? How do IT resources "matter" in terms of the different roles they play in an organization? Which component of an information system is most critical to success in growing and transforming the business? Why?

2-17. According to the Computer History Museum (www. computerhistory.org), the Kenbak Corporation sold the first personal computer in 1971. Since then, several billion PCs have been sold under various brand names. Currently, HP, Dell, Acer, Lenovo, and Asus are the leading brands in the highly competitive PC market.

Work in a small group with classmates to analyze and describe the personal computer industry using the five competitive forces model.

2-18. Work in a small group with classmates to discuss how information technology plays a role in the competitive environment of your college or university. How do you describe the competition to attract and retain students? How do you describe the threat of substitutes in higher education? How does the threat of substitutes affect supplier power in education?

APPLICATION EXERCISES

2-19. EXCEL APPLICATION:
IT Benchmarks

Jay's Bikes is a family-owned and operated business that stocks a wide range of bikes designed to fit the needs of professional riders, your child's first bike, and everything in between. The business has 12 full-time employees. Jay has asked you to create a spreadsheet from the data in Figure 2-21 to calculate average IT spending so that it can be compared with the retail industry average. What is the average IT spending in the retail industry? What is the average IT spending per employee in the retail industry? How do Jay's IT expenditures compare with the industry averages? How much would Jay need to increase spending in order to match the retail industry average?

2-20. ACCESS APPLICATION:
Telethon Call Reports

The volunteer coordinator of the Downtown Emergency Shelter has asked you to use the information provided in Figure 2-22 to create an Access database. (You can download the Excel file called *Ch02Ex02* and import the data into your database.) The coordinator will use the database to manage donor records and help the shelter prepare for an upcoming Phonathon fund-raising event. During the Phonathon, volunteers will call previous donors to ask for donations to this year's fund. Your instructions are to create two tables (donors and volunteers) and prepare a Phonathon Call Report for each volunteer. The shelter manager wants you to add three fields to the donor table: this year's contribution, a calculated field that shows the average contribution per employee, and a calculated field that shows a target contribution that is 5% higher than last year's contribution. The report should list the volunteer's name and number as well as the following donor information: donor number, donor name, company name, phone number, contribution amount from the prior year, number of employees, average contribution per employee, and target contribution for this year. Although address information will not be included on the report, that information will be used to send receipts to the donors at the conclusion of this year's fund-raising event.

FIGURE 2-21

Jay's Bikes revenue and IT expenditures.

	A	B	C
1	Revenue	Apparel & shoes	$ 1,250,000
2		Bike accessories	$ 550,000
3		New bikes	$ 2,650,000
4		Used bikes	$ 18,500
5		Bike repairs	$ 33,000
6			
7	IT Expenditures	Hardware	$ 15,000
8		Software updates	$ 18,000
9		Software licenses	$ 4,500
10		Software support	$ 4,500
11		Employee training	$ 5,000
12		Web site development	$ 5,000
13		Internet access	$ 1,200

Source: Microsoft® Excel, Microsoft Corporation. Reprinted with permission.

FIGURE 2-22

Phonathon data.

	A	B	C	D	E	F	G	H	I	J	K	L
1	Donor No.	Co. Name	Street Address	City	State	Zip Code	Phone No.	2012 Contribution	Employees	Volunteer Number	Last Name	First Name
2	A226	Al's Music Shop	210 W. High Point	Aurora	IL	60506	630-555-5554	$ 945.50	8	J234	Johnson	Bob
3	A657	Downtown Bikes	34 N. Main Street	East Aurora	IL	60508	630-186-7689	$ 1,248.00	12	M173	Miller	Sara
4	C456	Carol's Beauty Shop	265 Peabody	Batavia	IL	60604	312-044-2956	$ 2,365.00	17	H042	Henry	Robert
5	D256	Do It Rental	456 Alexander	Naperville	IL	60602	630-876-3476	$ 3,465.00	19	J234	Johnson	Bob
6	E456	Edies Ice Cream Shop	2093 State Street	Batavia	IL	60604	312-345-7890	$ 5,237.76	24	M173	Miller	Sara
7	A234	All Right Auto Repair	32 N. Central Loop	Aurora	IL	60506	630-345-3333	$ 3,209.00	21	J234	Johnson	Bob
8	F234	The Barbeque Pit	423 Eastview Rd.	St. Charles	IL	60510	312-555-5445	$ 2,926.74	18	M173	Miller	Sara
9	Q349	Hollywood Pet Care	34 Glendale St.	Aurora	IL	60506	630-234-3484	$ 563.00	9	H042	Henry	Robert
10	D345	The Butcher Shop	764 Walnut Street	Batavia	IL	60604	312-456-0080	$ 928.00	5	J234	Johnson	Bob
11	L345	Mia's Nail Salon	435 Hwy. 131	Aurora	IL	60506	630-345-0080	$ 2,644.25	12	H042	Henry	Robert
12	W098	The Book Nook	415 North Second	Yorkville	IL	60607	630-345-5656	$ 5,234.00	26	J234	Johnson	Bob
13	U602	Day & Night Gym	1356 Stadium	Yorkville	IL	60607	630-434-5555	$ 2,535.00	32	M173	Miller	Sara
14	T706	The Little Card Shop	365 S. Main Street	St. Charles	IL	60510	312-455-8876	$ 1,834.00	8	M173	Miller	Sara
15	S493	Perfect Cleaners	156 Third Avenue	Batavia	IL	60604	312-451-0080	$ 2,651.00	11	H042	Henry	Robert
16	E105	Green City Grocers	394 Flood Street	East Aurora	IL	60508	630-123-4598	$ 6,234.45	32	H042	Henry	Robert
17	M697	Alternate Health Spa	3435 Race St.	Batavia	IL	60604	312-341-9979	$ 878.65	3	H042	Henry	Robert
18	W456	Nelson's Gallery	345 Nettleton St.	Aurora	IL	60604	630-345-8235	$ 2,766.00	3	M173	Miller	Sara
19	HU376	Haney Enterprises	190 Johnson Ave.	Naperville	IL	60602	630-345-3767	$ 9,345.00	36	J234	Johnson	Bob
20	A754	Say It With Flowers	3600 Southwest	St. Charles	IL	60510	312-972-3456	$ 2,500.00	14	M173	Miller	Sara

Source: Microsoft® Excel, Microsoft Corporation. Reprinted with permission.

Can GameStop Survive with Its Brick-and-Mortar Stores?

With more than 6,600 stores throughout the United States and 14 other countries, GameStop's management team wants to be the premier destination for gamers. The Texas-based retail chain's major source of revenue is the sale of games, consoles, and other equipment, both new and used. The used market is important because it brings customers into the store to trade in their old games and consoles for store credits. GameStop resells the used games for more than twice what it pays for them.

The business model has, so far, survived the Internet's creative destruction that swept away other brick-and-mortar outlets selling digital products, including Egghead Software and Tower Records. But competition is intense in this industry.

One major rival is Best Buy, which offers customers a chance to trade in their old games for gift cards that can be used at any Best Buy store. Unlike GameStop's store credit, the Best Buy cards can be used to purchase TVs, computers, music, and any other Best Buy merchandise.

Another threat comes from the game developers, who fume about used-game sales because they earn no royalties. To counter used sales, many developers include a coupon with a new game so that purchasers can download special content or a game upgrade. GameStop has to charge people who buy used games a fee to get that coupon, and the total price approaches the cost of the new game. Developers will continue to find ways to combat used-game sales.

Online retailers like Amazon pose another threat, especially combined with price comparison websites that show up-to-the-minute prices from different outlets. The free social games such as Farmville are also luring some gamers away from the costly titles featured at GameStop, such as Call of Duty and Madden.

In addition, widespread access to high-speed Internet has a downside for GameStop. Companies such as Electronic Arts and Blizzard can deliver major upgrades and sequels to their high-end games digitally instead of packaging them into boxes for GameStop to sell. Customers can buy them online, directly from the publisher, rather than making the trip to the store.

GameStop countered these threats by revamping its business strategy and aggressively promoting its online store as a complement to the physical stores. Customers can buy new and used products online and also check out special trade-in deals before they visit the store. GameStop also added pop-culture collectibles, such as Game of Thrones and Star Wars characters, to its inventory.

The company also strives to increase switching costs through a loyalty program called PowerUP Rewards. Members earn points for every dollar they spend but also for telling GameStop about the games they play and their preferences. They can exchange points for gift cards, merchandise, restaurant and movie rewards, and subscriptions to gaming networks. The information GameStop collects about PowerUP members reveals just which promotions might work best for each customer, so the company can save money on marketing. The program also leads to more valuable customers who are far more likely to trade in games, open marketing emails, and buy products. Members spend on average $400 per year at GameStop.

Clearly, the company appreciates the dangerous strategic waters of other brick-and-mortar media companies, many of which have closed their doors due to competition. Sales and net revenue were declining as of 2016, but time will tell if GameStop's strategies will pay off.

Discussion Questions

2-21. Perform a five forces analysis of the online gaming industry. What are the implications of the five forces analysis for GameStop?

2-22. What role have information systems played in the five forces you identified?

2-23. How has GameStop used information systems to compete more effectively?

2-24. What other strategic actions will GameStop need to take to protect its business?

Sources: Colbert, C. (2013). *GameStop Corp.* Hoover's Online Company Database, accessed April 4, 2013.

Hudspeth, C. (2016). *GameStop Corp.* Hoover's Online, *http://subscriber.hoovers.com. proxy1.library.jhu.edu/H/company360/overview.html?companyId=12716000000000*, accessed August 9, 2016.

MarketLine. (2016). *GameStop Corp. SWOT Analysis* (pp. 1–8). *http://search.ebscohost.com/ login.aspx?direct=true&db=bth&AN=113300732&site=ehost-live&scope=site*, accessed August 9, 2016

Mattera, S. (March 11, 2013). How much longer can GameStop survive? *Motleyfool.com*, *http://beta.fool.com/joekurtz/2013/03/11/how-much-longer-can-gamestop-survive/26269/? source=eogyholnk0000001*, accessed March 20, 2013.

Morris, C. (January 29, 2016). Sales declining, GameStop steps into publishing. CNBC, *http://www.cnbc.com/2016/01/29/with-sales-declining-gamestop-gets-into-game-publishing.html*, accessed February 9, 2016.

Seitz, P. (2016). GameStop turns to mobile devices, collectibles as game sales slip. *Investors Business Daily*, 1.

CASE STUDY #2

The Battle for Net Neutrality

Debates over how government should regulate the Internet's evolution heat up whenever anyone mentions "net neutrality." Here are the two sides of the debate:

The Case for Net Neutrality

This side argues that carriers selling Internet access—Verizon, AT&T, and Comcast, for instance—should not discriminate for or against different content providers or applications. All traffic should be routed neutrally, and the carriers should not make special deals to favor some content by giving it more bandwidth so movies will play more smoothly and web pages load faster. Companies that provide content over the Internet, such as Amazon, eBay, Google, Lending Tree, Skype, PayPal, and Netflix, typically support net neutrality, along with nonprofits that advocate for openness, such as the American Civil Liberties Union, American Library Association, and Educause.

The Case Against Net Neutrality

On the other side of the debate are the carriers—AT&T, Verizon, Comcast, and others. They argue that incentives are needed to encourage their investment in the network infrastructure and that their networks have to be managed to provide the best service at reasonable costs. Video downloads, in particular, hog bandwidth to the detriment of other users who just want to read the news or send email. In fact, this issue gained considerable steam when Comcast began throttling download speeds for subscribers who used BitTorrent, software widely used to download movies. Comcast's move, while helpful to most customers, was a violation of net neutrality.

Even though adherence to the net neutrality principle was voluntary, the Federal Communications Commission (FCC) reprimanded Comcast for what it considered an outrageous violation. Comcast sued, and the courts decided the FCC didn't actually have jurisdiction to reprimand anyone because the commission has no authority over broadband communications.

The FCC went on to establish rules supporting net neutrality anyway. In 2015, the FCC reclassified broadband services from a lightly regulated information service to a more heavily regulated telecom service. To no one's surprise, the carriers objected to the FCC's rules, and lawsuits are under way, arguing that the FCC went way beyond its authority. Verizon also claimed that the rules violated the company's freedom of speech by taking away its control over its own property—its networks. Whether network traffic is "speech" is an interesting question, of course.

Another wrinkle in this debate involves Facebook's "Free Basics" service, which the company launched in India to provide mobile access to Facebook and a few other websites that wouldn't count toward the customer's data plan. Critics argued that the service is a kind of "walled garden" that violates net neutrality by giving unfair advantage to the sites Facebook includes. India's regulators agreed with the critics and blocked the service.

All businesses that have an online presence have a lot at stake in this debate, and so do consumers. If the carriers can make deals with some companies so that their pages load faster, big, cash-rich companies might have another edge over small businesses. Or if your carrier favors traffic coming from Amazon Instant Video over Netflix, you might drop your Netflix subscription. On the other hand, your own web browsing would be slower if neighbors who share your cable connection are downloading movies 24 hours a day and the cable company can't throttle them down.

The outcome of the many lawsuits will affect the Internet's future and the way governments treat the net's development.

Discussion Questions

2-25. What are the strategic interests of carriers? What are the strategic interests of websites?

2-26. How do the interests of carriers differ from the interests of websites? What are the implications for websites from a value chain perspective?

2-27. What is the basis for Verizon's lawsuit against the Federal Communications Commission? Why did it claim a violation of free speech?

2-28. What are relevant considerations on the role government could play to resolve differences between carriers and websites?

Sources: Downes, L. (January 24, 2013). The strange resurrection of net neutrality. C|Net, http://news.cnet.com/8301-13578_3-57565561-38/the-strange-resurrection-of-net-neutrality/, accessed May 30, 2016.

Greenstein, S., Peitz, M., & Valletti, T. (2016). Net neutrality: A fast lane to understanding the trade-offs. *Journal of Economic Perspectives, 30*(2), 127–150. http://doi.org/10.1257/jep.30.2.127

Hempel, J. (February 8, 2016). India bans Facebook's basics app to support net neutrality. Wired, http://www.wired.com/2016/02/facebooks-free-basics-app-is-now-banned-in-india/, accessed February 9, 2016.

LaFrance, A. (2016). Not another net-neutrality story. *The Atlantic*, http://www.theatlantic.com/technology/archive/2016/02/net-neutrality-is-interesting-no-really/461943/, accessed August 9, 2016.

Pil Choi, J., & Byung-Cheol, K. (2010). Net neutrality and investment incentives. *RAND Journal of Economics, 41*(3), 446–471.

E-PROJECT 1   Identifying Company Strategy with Online Financial Chart Tools

One useful way to catch up on a company's strategy is to check out trends in its stock price, and the net offers many free tools. Go to Google's finance website (www.google.com/finance) and type the stock ticker symbol for GameStop (GME) into the search bar to pull up current news about the company, including a graph of its share prices, from Google finance.

2-29.   The letters on the graph tie into the news stories, and some of them have major effects on the company's stock. Change the graph to zoom to different periods of time at the top left of the

graph. Do you see any large changes in share price paired with a news story? Does the news shed light on how investors view its strategy or the execution of it?

2-30.   One way to get an idea of how well the company is doing is to compare the trend in its share prices to the Dow Jones Industrial Average. Check the box next to Dow Jones at the top of the graph and compare the trends. How does GameStop's performance compare?

E-PROJECT 2   Analyzing Media Download Times with Excel

In this e-project, you will obtain and analyze information about download times to assess Internet connectivity.

2-31.   Download the file called *CH02_MediaDownloads*. This file shows the approximate file sizes for different kinds of media along with estimated download times.

2-32.   Add a column called Speed Advantage and enter the formula that shows how many times faster the download will be if one uses fast broadband (+d2/+c2). Copy the formula to the remaining rows, and then add a row at the bottom called "AVERAGE." On average, how much faster is it to download media files using fast broadband compared to regular broadband?

2-33.   Add two more columns called Download Time per MB (Fast Broadband) and Download Time per MB (Regular Broadband). Compute these values by dividing the appropriate download time by the file size in MB, and add the average at the bottom.
   a. What is the average download time per MB for fast broadband?
   b. For regular broadband?

2-34.   Download the video file called CH02_TestVideo and time how long it takes.
   a. What is the file's size in MB? If the file size is represented in gigabytes (GB), multiply that number by 1,000 to convert to megabytes (MB).
   b. Using the average download times you computed, what should be the download time using fast broadband? What would it be for regular broadband?
   c. How does your download time compare to these estimates? Do you have fast broadband, regular broadband, or something else?

CHAPTER NOTES

1 Porter, M. E. (1998). *Competitive strategy: Techniques for analyzing industries and competitors*. San Francisco: The Free Press.

2 Porter, M. E. (2008). The five competitive forces that shape strategy. *Harvard Business Review, 86*(1), 78–93.

3 Damodaran, A. (2016). *Margins by sector (U.S.)*. New York, NY: Stern School of Business, New York University, http://pages.stern.nyu.edu/~adamodar/New_Home_Page/datafile/margin.html, accessed August 9, 2016.

4 Groupon announces first quarter 2016 results. (April 28, 2016). *Business Wire,* http://search.proquest.com.proxy1.library.jhu.edu/docview/1785376644/abstract/565883D1AF7B450FPQ/9, accessed August 9, 2016.

5 Sotgiu, F., & Gielens, K. (2015). Suppliers caught in supermarket price wars: Victims or victors? Insights from a Dutch price war. *Journal of Marketing Research (JMR), 52*(6), 784–800. http://doi.org/10.1509/jmr.13.0180

6 Gans, J. (2016). The other disruption. *Harvard Business Review, 94*(3), 78–84.

7 Heid, M. (2016). Experts say lobbying skewed the U.S. dietary guidelines. *Time.com.*

8 Celock, J. (December 5, 2012). States lobby for Internet sales tax bill to pass Congress. *Huffington Post,* http://www.huffingtonpost.com/2012/12/05/internet-sales-tax-state-legislators_n_2246153.html, accessed August 9, 2016. Quote from States Lobby For Internet Sales Tax Bill To Pass Congres by John Celock. Copyright © 2012 by Times Internet Limited.

9 Brachmann, S. (February 1, 2016). Push for online sales tax continues at state and federal levels. Patents & Patent Law, from http://www.ipwatchdog.com/2016/02/01/push-for-online-sales-tax-continues/id=65226/fmu, accessed August 9, 2016.

10 Punniyamoorthy, M., Thamaraiselvan, N., & Manikandan, L. (2013). Assessment of supply chain risk: Scale development and validation. *Benchmarking: An International Journal, 20*(1), 79–105. doi:10.1108/14635771311299506

11 McGittigan, J., Potter, K., Guevara, J. K., Hall, L., & Stegman, E. (2013). *IT metrics: IT spending and staffing report, 2013* (No. G00248502). Gartner Research, http://www.gartner.com/document/2324316?ref=solrAll&refval=162459982&qid=366c11ed28c62744b794855f5e045090, accessed

12 Wallace, N. (February 26, 2009). Google helps charity test its web design. *The Chronicle of Philanthropy,* http://philanthropy.com/article/Google-Helps-Charity-Test-Its/57281/, accessed May 1, 2011.

13 The Millennial Impact Report. (2012). Johnson, Grossnickle and Associates, http://themillennialimpact.com/wp-content/uploads/2012/06/TheMillennialImpactReport2012.pdf, accessed December 31, 2012.

14 Volunteermatch.org. (2016), accessed February 9, 2016.

15 Carr, N. G. (2004). *Does IT matter? Information technology and the corrosion of competitive advantage.* Boston, MA: Harvard Business School Press Books, p. 1.

16 Hajli, M., Sims, J. M., & Ibragimov, V. (2015). Information technology (IT) productivity paradox in the 21st century. *International Journal of Productivity & Performance Management, 64*(4), 457–478. http://doi.org/10.1108/IJPPM-12-2012-0129

17 Brynjolfsson, E. (1993). The productivity paradox of information technology: Review and assessment. *Communications of the ACM, 36*(12), 66–77.

18 Yahoo! Finance. (December 28, 2012), http://biz.yahoo.com/p/sum_qpmd.html, accessed December 28, 2012.

Information and Communications Technologies: *The Enterprise Architecture*

- Online Simulation: Devil's Canyon: A Role-Playing Simulation on Enterprise Architecture for a Mountain Resort
- Discussion Questions: #3-1, #3-2, #3-3
- Writing Assignments: #3-11, #3-12

LEARNING OBJECTIVES

1 Describe the four hardware components of a computer, giving examples of each component.

2 Identify and provide examples of the two major types of software, and describe how software is created.

3 Describe the major types of networks and the transmission media they use, and give examples of network protocols.

4 Explain the importance of the enterprise architecture, describing trends in ICT architecture over time.

> An online, interactive decision-making simulation that reinforces chapter contents and uses key terms in context can be found in MyMISLab™.

INTRODUCTION

THE TECHNOLOGY COMPONENT OF INFORMATION SYSTEMS INCLUDES HARDWARE, software, and telecommunications. This chapter provides an overview of these three important pieces, showing how the parts fit together and why they sometimes don't fit together as well as one might hope.

In the online decision-making simulation called "Devil's Canyon," you will learn about a new mountain resort and the dreams that the young team of entrepreneurs have for it. You will also hear about their challenges as they try to think through what hardware, software, and telecommunications will be the best choices for them. Then you will take on the responsibility for choosing those components. What hardware will they need? Should the resort go with cloud computing or build its own data center? What software should

they implement? Should they buy smartphones for the staff? Should they invest in webcams along the slopes so customers can purchase videos of their ski runs? Costs matter, of course, and you have a budget to work with. But so does making sure all the parts fit together. The choices should also support the team's business objectives and add competitive advantage so the new resort is a smash hit.

Hardware, software, and telecommunications work together to create the **enterprise architecture (EA).** *For a new company like Devil's Canyon, the EA is a guide on what to purchase and install, how long it will take, how everything will work together, why certain decisions were made, and what it will cost. For existing organizations, the EA also describes the current situation and how the EA should be*

MyMISLab
Online Simulation

DEVIL'S CANYON
A Role-Playing Simulation on Enterprise Architecture
for a Mountain Resort

IM_photo/Shutterstock.

changed or upgraded to support the mission, focusing especially on business strategy and the technology required to achieve it. A roadmap describing how to get from the present to that future state guides decision making about technology directions. The EA helps managers navigate through all the choices as they add new information systems and retire older ones.

The knowledge you gain from this chapter will help you understand what the technology options are and how they apply to organizations. People in all parts of an organization have a role to play in designing the enterprise architecture, and input from all stakeholders is needed to ensure the technology matches the business strategy.

enterprise architecture (EA)
A roadmap created by an organization to describe its current situation and where it should head to achieve its mission, focusing on business strategy and the technology infrastructure required to achieve it.

Describe the four hardware components of a computer, giving examples of each component.

1 The Hardware

The physical basis of information systems covers an immense range of hardware, from mainframes and servers in giant data centers to robots, microprocessors, smartphones, printers, scanners, digital cameras, sensors, smart cards, and much more. These devices generally share two important features. First, they are digital, so they all process information using the same binary language of zeroes and ones. Second, they can all be considered computers or computer components.

The **computer** is any electronic device that can accept, manipulate, store, and output data and whose instructions can be programmed. That definition covers equipment you might not ordinarily think of as a computer, such as the smartphone, a game console, or a robotic rat with cameras for eyes and highly sensitive wire whiskers.

Times have changed since 1947 when the world marveled at ENIAC, the first electronic computer (Figure 3-1). Weighing 27 tons, that giant was 26 meters (80 feet) long and contained more than 17,000 vacuum tubes. With every breakthrough and each succeeding generation, the overarching goal is to make technology work for human beings, making the components smaller, less expensive, less power hungry, and considerably more intelligent. Although the details vary considerably, computers typically have four components: input, output, processing, and storage (Figure 3-2).

Input and Output

Figure 3-3 includes various input devices that accept signals and convert them to a digital format that matches the signal's meaning. Some also display the output, such as digital cameras and touchscreens.

HUMAN INPUT

Most input devices rely on human input, so they are designed with human capabilities in mind. Hands can type on keyboards, and each key press is converted into a different string combination of zeros and ones. The **ASCII code** and its variants determine how characters are encoded into digital strings, so that a backspace might send 00001000 and a SHIFT + s sends 01010011, for capital *S*.

Productivity guru David Allen commented on Twitter.com, "Communicating without knowing how to type is like talking with marbles in your mouth." As an interface for human beings, the keyboard is an underappreciated milestone in computer history. Skilled typists can type more than 100 words per minute—faster than most people speak. Managers once disdained keyboards because they seemed linked to low-level clerk-typist jobs, but typing soon became an essential productivity skill for everyone.

FIGURE 3-1

ENIAC, the first electronic computer.

Source: Pictorial Press Ltd/Alamy Stock Photo.

FIGURE 3-2

Hardware components.

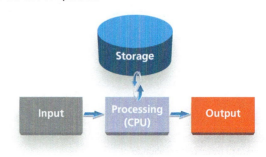

FIGURE 3-3
Input and output devices.

Source: ArchMan/Shutterstock, Pokomeda/Shutterstock, Cliparea/Custom Media/Shutterstock, Igoriale/
Shutterstock, Claudio Bravo/Shutterstock, Algabafoto/Shutterstock, Aperturesound/Fotolia.

Unfortunately, the keyboard layout evolved from the typewriter—originally designed to slow down data entry to prevent collisions of the hammers striking the paper. Because so many people already knew the QWERTY layout, though, attempts to introduce a better design failed. As sometimes happens, a superior technology solution lost out, in this case because human behavior can be so difficult to change.

The ASCII keyboard also helps explain why some countries adopted computing much earlier than others. Although a standard keyboard handily encodes languages that use the Roman alphabet with its 26 letters, 10 numerals, and a few punctuation marks, it is very cumbersome for languages like Chinese and Japanese, which use thousands of characters. Such obstacles are overcome with more intelligent software, but they certainly made faxes more useful in those countries compared to email and delayed widespread computer use.

The mouse, joystick, and graphics tablet are other human input devices, and these can transmit motion and location information. Touch-sensitive screens, for example, respond to finger motions and convert them to digital signals. A screen is organized into *x*- and *y*-axes, and locations can be transmitted as coordinates. Large touchscreens that several people can swipe at the same time are gaining popularity as a way to collaborate. Gloves equipped with sensors can also transmit complex hand movements, such as those used in American Sign Language.

Microphones capture human speech and transmit it in digital format. Although the sounds can be represented digitally just as sounds, speech recognition software can also identify the words.

PRODUCTIVITY TIP

Although the mouse is very useful, it can slow you down as you move your hands from the keyboard. Try the keyboard shortcuts in Figure 3-4 to eliminate some unneeded motion.

FIGURE 3-4
Keyboard shortcuts that improve productivity.

Windows	Macintosh	Function
CTRL+C	Command (⌘)+C	Copy selected text
CTRL+V	Command (⌘)+V	Paste
CTRL+S	Command (⌘)+S	Save current document
CTRL+Z	Command (⌘)+Z	Undo
CTRL+F	Command (⌘)+F	Open a Find window

computer
Any electronic device that can accept, manipulate, store, and output data and whose instructions can be programmed.

ASCII code
A code that defines how keyboard characters are encoded into digital strings of ones and zeros.

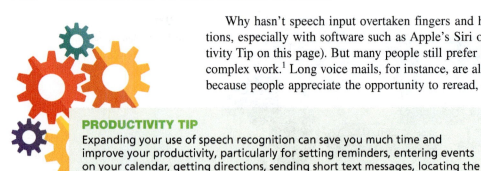

Why hasn't speech input overtaken fingers and hands? It almost has for many applications, especially with software such as Apple's Siri or Microsoft's Cortana (see the Productivity Tip on this page). But many people still prefer typing to speaking for longer and more complex work.[1] Long voice mails, for instance, are all but dead in some organizations, partly because people appreciate the opportunity to reread, edit, and avoid embarrassing mistakes. Human preferences like these play an important role when designing the enterprise architecture.

PRODUCTIVITY TIP

Expanding your use of speech recognition can save you much time and improve your productivity, particularly for setting reminders, entering events on your calendar, sending short text messages, locating the nearest gas station, or conducting simple web searches.

SCANNERS AND SENSORS

Optical scanners capture text or images and convert them to digital format in thousands of settings. They can scan virtually anything into an image, but combined with software or special symbols, they can decipher much more detail. For example, the barcodes that appear on products, price tags, and postal mail represent specific numbers and other symbols, and scanners transmit those details—not just the image (Figure 3-5).

The quick response code (QR code) that appears on magazines, newspapers, and even restaurant menus is another type of barcode. Originally invented by Toyota to track vehicles in the factory, QR codes are now widely used in consumer advertising. Smartphone users can install QR code readers so they can scan the square image and hop directly to the website or other image (Figure 3-6). Such apps often collect user data for marketing purposes.[2]

Scanners, combined with **optical character recognition (OCR)** software, can interpret the actual letters and numbers on a page, creating a digital document that can be edited rather than a flat picture. Banks were early adopters of this technology, which they use to process checks. The unique font is standard throughout the industry, and magnetic ink allows scanners to read the characters even if someone writes over them. Google uses OCR to scan old books so that some contents become searchable, but legal wrangling over copyrights has slowed the project.[3]

Digital cameras are another important input device widely used for surveillance, security, and just entertainment. They monitor traffic patterns, building entrances, hallways, homes, ATMs, baby cribs, and even bird nests. In addition to the fixed cameras, mobile phones equipped with cameras are widespread, so the chances of passing a whole day without appearing in a photo or video are slim.

Radio frequency identification (RFID) tags, another key technology in the Internet of Things, are small chips equipped with a microprocessor, a tiny antenna to receive and transmit data, and sometimes a battery (Figure 3-7). RFID tags can store information on an object's history and whereabouts and can be embedded in anything, including pets, livestock, and human beings. The Department of Energy relies on RFID tags to track shipments of hazardous nuclear material.

FIGURE 3-5

Sample barcode.

Source: Isonphoto/Fotolia

FIGURE 3-6

QR code. If you have a smartphone, download a QR reader for it and scan the image below. Recognize what is in the picture?

Source: U.S. Fish and Wildlife Service.

FIGURE 3-7

RFID tag.

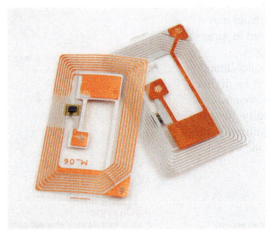

Source: Albert Lozano/Shutterstock.

With the Internet of Things, sensors are spreading extremely rapidly, and the trend is still in its infancy.[5] Environmental sensors on smart buoys capture data such as water temperature and wind speed, and their data is transmitted in real time to the Internet (Figure 3-8).

OUTPUT DEVICES

The familiar flat-panel display is the most common computer output device for desktop computers. Falling prices make a large screen, or even two of them, quite affordable. For human beings, screen real estate is a valuable commodity, making it possible to view several applications at the same time.

On the other end of the spectrum are the small screens used for cell phones and handheld devices and the somewhat larger ones used in tablets and e-book readers. Other common output devices include computer printers and speakers as well as an enormous variety of controllers that operate machinery, from lawn sprinklers and lights to an aircraft's landing gear. Powered USB ports open up opportunities for creative inventors, who came up with several oddball output devices: heated slippers, coffee warmers, and air darts fired off with the mouse.

PRODUCTIVITY TIP
Adding a second monitor can improve your productivity and also reduce the need to print documents. Sales figures show that corporations are buying at least two monitors for more than a third of their employees, and research confirms that most people work more efficiently with more screen real estate. You'll appreciate the second monitor even more if you work with a laptop on a desk.

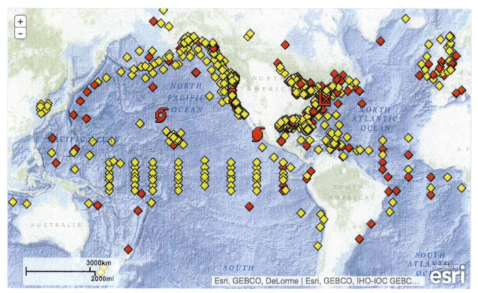

FIGURE 3-8
Buoy sensors collect live data that is made available on the Internet.

Source: National Oceanic and Atmospheric Administration, National Data Buoy Center. http://www.ndbc.noaa.gov/, accessed February 18, 2016.

optical scanners
Electronic devices that capture text or images and convert them to digital format.

optical character recognition (OCR)
The capability of specialized software to interpret the actual letters and numbers on a page to create a digital document that can be edited rather than a flat picture.

radio frequency identification (RFID)
A technology placed on tags with small chips equipped with a microprocessor, a tiny antenna to receive and transmit data, and sometimes a battery that stores information on the tagged object's history.

Processing

The computer's brain is the **central processing unit (CPU)**, which handles information processing, calculations, and control tasks. Early versions used vacuum tubes that frequently blew out, but with the invention of the **transistor**—a small electrical circuit made from a semiconductor material such as silicon—computers switched to using electrical signals to represent zeros and ones. The transistors are packed onto integrated circuits and mass produced at low cost (Figure 3-9).

Decades ago, Intel cofounder Gordon Moore predicted that the number of transistors fitting on a chip would about double every 2 years, a forecast that has proven surprisingly accurate. Now known as **Moore's Law**, his prediction about density also captures advances in processing speed, storage capabilities, cost, and other computer features. Today's low-cost laptop outperforms mainframes from the 1960s—and takes up far less space.

The computing architectures in Figure 3-10 illustrate how the technology has evolved, as each generation took advantage of declining costs, increasing power, and advances that support mobility and ease of use. As we discuss later in this chapter and as you'll see in the Devil's Canyon decision-making simulation, decisions about these computing architectures should fit into the larger picture. Choices depend on the enterprise architecture. For example, a company that still relies on an old software system running on an expensive mainframe would need to keep that running temporarily but plan its replacement in the roadmap.

FIGURE 3-9

Integrated circuits.

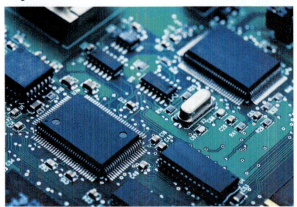

Source: Olga Miltsova/Shutterstock.

FIGURE 3-10

Computing architectures.

Computing Architectures	Description
Mainframe	Developed for large businesses in the 1960s and often called "big iron," mainframes are still used for massive bulk processing tasks and financial transactions requiring high reliability. They are also deployed as servers for large networks. The mainframe market is dominated by IBM.
Supercomputer	Introduced in the 1960s, these high-end computers feature the fastest processors for calculation-intensive tasks in areas such as physics, weather modeling, and molecular analyses.
Minicomputer	Designed to be smaller in size and less expensive than mainframes, minicomputers and the terminals connected to them worked well for small and midsized businesses through the 1990s, after which many were replaced by PC servers. Now they are called "midrange computers," and are used as servers.
Microcomputer	Called PCs for short, these devices proliferated in organizations in the 1990s, replacing the dumb terminals and offering far more capability on the desktop. Powerful PCs are widely used as servers as well.
Laptop	Valued for their integrated display screens and portability, these battery-powered PCs became popular in the late 1980s, facilitating mobility. They could run much of the same software as their desktop cousins, though more slowly. Many newer laptops offer touchscreen sensitivity, similar to tablets.
Netbook	Engineered to be even smaller and less expensive than laptops, netbooks gained attention in the late 2000s as a cost-effective means to wirelessly connect to the Internet. Their low cost also facilitates widespread distribution, especially in developing countries.
Smartphones	Offered initially in the 1990s, these devices combine cell-phone capabilities with data communications for web browsing, email, and text messaging.
Tablet	A mobile device with a large touchscreen and virtual keyboard, a tablet is smaller and thinner than a laptop but larger than a smartphone. They gained popularity with the introduction of Apple's iPad, and many people add a regular keyboard.

Storage

How is all this digital information stored? Fortunately, Moore's Law seems to apply to storage technology, so it is cheaper to satisfy the hungry appetite for more space. Storage capacities are measured using the **byte**, which typically holds eight zeros and ones—the equivalent of one key press for text. Figure 3-11 shows sample storage capacities. The Ethical Factor explores some of the ethical challenges surrounding these huge data repositories, called "big data."

PRIMARY STORAGE

A computer's primary storage, typically on integrated circuits located close to the CPU, includes **random access memory (RAM)**. RAM serves as a temporary storage area as the CPU executes instructions. It is a critical factor in the computer's performance, and you often find extra room so that additional RAM can be inserted. RAM is volatile storage that is erased when power is turned off or lost; however, computers also have other nonvolatile chips that permanently store information.[6]

SECONDARY STORAGE

The massive quantities of digital information are written to secondary storage devices, including computer hard drives. Although easily accessible and searched, hard drives can be a million times slower than primary storage. Their rotating disks and moving heads cannot compare to solid-state integrated circuits, but capacity is higher and costs far lower.

Optical disks (CD-ROMs and DVDs) also offer low cost secondary storage as well as backups for offline storage needed for archiving, disaster recovery, and portability. Magnetic tapes provide cost-effective long-term storage capability.

Solid-state storage with no moving parts is also gaining popularity as prices drop and capacity increases. This category includes flash memory used in USB keys, memory cards for cameras, and hard drive substitutes for rugged laptops.

As prices for primary storage drop and processor speeds increase, developers are beginning to explore **in-memory computing** for certain applications that benefit from very high-speed, real-time access. This term refers to the use of primary storage as the main place information is stored rather than in secondary storage devices. The far slower hard drives are used mainly for backup and recovery. The increase in speed for software applications is phenomenal, particularly for analyzing enormous volumes of big data quickly.[7]

The business drivers that affect storage decisions include access, speed, cost, and safety. Organizations must have their most important data easily accessible to respond to customer queries and process transactions. For safety, all the organization's data must also be backed up, and storage solutions depend partly on how much downtime the organization can risk. Reloading from magnetic tapes stored in secure warehouses will take much longer compared to reinstalling from hard drives. Strategies for storage, backup, and recovery should reflect the organization's needs.

Name	Abbreviation	Capacity	Description
Kilobyte	KB	1,024 bytes	A short, email message
Megabyte	MB	1024^2 bytes	A digital song runs about 3 MB
Gigabyte	GB	1024^3 bytes	About 1 hour of TV recording (not HD)
Terabyte	TB	1024^4 bytes	About 150 hours of HD video recording
Petabyte	PB	1024^5 bytes	Facebook stores more than 300 PB of user data (2016)

FIGURE 3-11

Measures of storage capacity.

central processing unit (CPU)
The brain of a computer, which handles information processing, calculations, and control tasks.

transistor
A small electrical circuit made from a semiconductor material such as silicon.

Moore's Law
A principle named for computer executive Gordon Moore, which states that advances in computer technology, such as processing speed or storage capabilities, doubles about every 2 years.

byte
Measurement unit for computer storage capacity; a byte holds eight zeros and ones and represents a single character.

random access memory (RAM)
A computer's primary temporary storage area accessed by the CPU to execute instructions.

in-memory computing
Refers to the use of primary storage as the main place information is stored, rather than in secondary storage devices such as hard drives, to vastly increase speed.

THE ETHICAL FACTOR Ethical Implications of Big Data

Revelations concerning how much data governments and corporations actually collect about people focus attention on the ethical issues surrounding big data and surveillance.

For business, big data offers valuable opportunities to find patterns and preferences that will help with marketing. A math whiz at Target, for instance, found that pregnant women tend to buy certain products such as unscented lotion, vitamin supplements, and large purses (that might double as diaper bags).[8] His calculations are based on so much data that they can be used to estimate the likelihood that a particular customer is pregnant and also the approximate due date.

Relying on that finding, the company began sending discount coupons for cribs and baby clothes to shoppers most likely to be pregnant. But one outraged father in Minneapolis complained that his teenage daughter was receiving these promotions. "She's still in high school!" he barked at the manager, who had no idea why the company sent those promotions to her. Later, the father admitted that he talked with his daughter and found that she actually was pregnant.

Most consumers don't know how much data companies actually collect on their behavior and how sophisticated the analysis of big data has become. (Chapter 7 explores techniques used to tease valuable information out of the mountains of data now available.) Studies suggest that if consumers did know, they would find it creepy, and many would be downright angry about it. Clearly, consumers are uncomfortable about the use of big data to tailor advertising, especially when the consumers don't really understand how it works.[9] But targeted advertising is extremely important to reduce marketing costs in very competitive industries, so big data will only get bigger and more valuable.

Identify and provide examples of the two major types of software, and describe how software is created.

2 The Software

Processing the zeroes and ones that the hardware stores is the job of **software**—the instructions that direct hardware to carry out tasks. As the "brain" of the information system, software is the most expensive component.

Types of Software

Software has two major functions in an information system (Figure 3-12). **Application software** supports all the work (or play) you want to do, from word processing and spreadsheets to video editing, email, web browsing, and game playing. Databases, discussed in the next chapter, are another major example of application software.

Multiuser application software that is designed for organizations supports transaction processing, human resources management, customer relationship management, collaboration, corporate training, finances, manufacturing processes, supply chain management, customer support, and all the other processes along the value chain. Many programs are industry specific, such as the software real estate agents use to track listings or the routing software used by trucking companies. Businesses spend large sums to develop application software that streamlines operations and helps them deliver excellent services.

System software handles the more basic operations, such as file management, disk storage, hardware interfaces, and integration with the application software. It ensures that the technology tools involved in the information system all work together smoothly, though most of the time you need pay no attention to its activities. System software includes two categories: (1) operating system software and (2) utilities.

The **operating system (OS)** takes care of several basic tasks, without which the computer would not function at all. It handles the interfaces with keyboards, monitors, and other devices; maintains file structures; and allocates memory for its own activities and the needs of application software. It may also support multiple processors, multiple users, and multiple applications running at the same time.

Figure 3-13 shows market shares for the most common operating systems on desktop PCs. Microsoft Windows enjoys

FIGURE 3-12
Types of software.

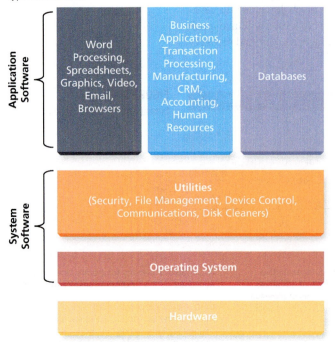

FIGURE **3-13**
Operating system market share: desktops, February 2016.

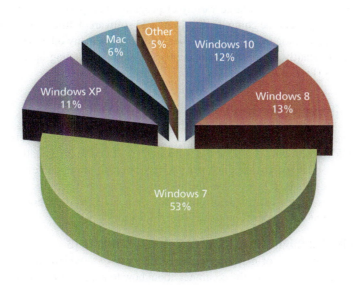

Source: Courtesy of NetMarketShare. www.netmarketshare.com.

almost 90% of this market. (Notice that Windows XP, which Microsoft stopped supporting in 2014, is still in use, partly because people are reluctant to change.) If we just look at data from mobile devices (tablets and smartphones), Android and Apple (iOS) are the major players (Figure 3-14).

Why should businesspeople be concerned about operating systems and their market shares? The OS provides a software platform for application developers, who often write software for just one platform. Companies want to choose an OS that already has a wide selection of business-oriented software available, which is one reason Windows maintains such a lead in the corporate desktop world. They also don't want their IT departments struggling with compatibility issues, so they might reject requests from employees who want an Apple laptop that could require a lot of tweaking to run corporate software.

For mobile devices, though, the market was wide open for new operating systems, and Apple initially took it by storm. Android developers caught up quickly, however.

Although corporations can decide which OS to use for equipment the company purchases for employees, they couldn't easily dictate which mobile device they could buy if they use their own money. This bring your own device (BYOD) trend, in which employees want to use personally owned equipment to access corporate applications, means that IT departments must find ways to support a larger variety of operating systems. Companies are also facing the security challenges of supporting personally owned equipment, where vacation videos and confidential corporate data are mingling.[10]

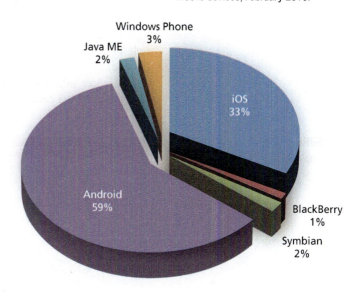

Source: Courtesy of NetMarketShare. www.netmarketshare.com.

software
The computer component that contains the instructions that directs computer hardware to carry out tasks.

application software
The type of software used to support a wide range of individual and business activities, such as transaction processing, payroll, word processing, and video editing.

system software
The type of software that controls basic computer operations such as file management, disk storage, hardware interfaces, and integration with the application software.

operating system (OS)
The category of system software that performs a variety of critical basic tasks, such as handling device input and output, maintaining file structures, and allocating memory.

Utility software includes a large variety of programs that perform specific tasks to help manage, tune, and protect the computer hardware and software. Utilities scan for viruses, perform cleanup routines, log events, back up files, and perform many other tasks. Some of these utilities can significantly improve your own productivity by speeding up your computer and automating tasks (Figure 3-15).

How Is Software Created?

Software is created by teams of programmers working with business analysts, end users, and other stakeholders who envision what the software is intended to do. Creating something like Salesforce.com or TurboTax takes intensive collaboration among people with very different areas of expertise. Chapter 11 explores the systems development process in detail, while this section introduces the technical side of the process, especially to show how software fits into the larger picture of an organization's overall architecture.

PROGRAMMING LANGUAGES AND DEVELOPMENT ENVIRONMENTS

Software is written in one of many **programming languages**, which are artificial languages that provide the instructions for the computer about how to accept information, process it, and provide output. Figure 3-16 lists some common programming languages along with some that are nearly dead. These older languages still survive in **legacy systems**—applications that are still in use because they work reasonably well and are costly to replace.

The **source code** includes all the statements that the programmers write to communicate with the computer and provide instructions. You can see the source code for a web page by right-clicking the page in your browser and selecting "view source." A simple web page might only be a few lines long, but a complex information system might contain millions of lines of code.

Advances in programming languages make it easier for developers to write reliable and easily maintained code. For instance, **object-oriented programming** focuses on "objects"

FIGURE 3-15
Examples of utility software.

Utility Software	Description
Antivirus software	Protects against viruses and other malicious code
Disk defragmenter	Optimizes disk performance by moving parts of the same file to contiguous sectors on the hard drive
Compression software	Reduces file sizes to conserve disk space
Shredder	Makes deleted files completely unrecoverable
Recovery	Assists with the recovery of deleted files
File management	Assists with tasks such as renaming groups of files, changing file attributes, and others

FIGURE 3-16
Examples of programming languages.

Programming Language	Description
COBOL	One of the oldest languages, but more than 200 billion lines of code are still in use for legacy business applications
FORTRAN	Older language used in special projects involving intensive calculations
C++	Widely used object-oriented language with considerable support from vendors
Java	Object-oriented language widely used in web development projects and designed to run on many different platforms
.NET	Microsoft's proprietary language used in its development environment
Python	Dynamic object-oriented language that runs on a variety of platforms, including smartphones; it is growing in popularity
PHP	Open source programming language that can be embedded in HTML that helps create dynamic web pages in software such as WordPress
Swift	Used to create apps for iPhone, Apple Watch, iPad, and other devices

rather than lists of instructions and routines to manipulate data. Programmers define the nature of the data each object contains and also the kinds of operations or behaviors it can do. The modular, reusable objects often simulate real-world objects along with the various states and behaviors they display. A "counter object," for instance, might be used to count visitors to a web page. Its behaviors could include resetting to zero or displaying its current value. An important benefit of object-oriented programming is modularity, so that an object can be independently maintained, reused, or replaced if it breaks down or causes problems. Also, programmers have no need to understand the object's inner workings—only the rules that determine how other objects can interact with it.

Other improvements emerge when software development environments add helpful features that make programmers more productive, much like spell checkers help writers. Swift, for instance, is used to program apps for Apple devices, and it offers programmers a "playground" so they can experiment and see results immediately. Java is popular for web developers and also for projects in which the software should run on any hardware platform, including set-top cable boxes or car navigation systems.

What language should a company use to create new applications? That depends on the nature of the application, the language used to create the company's other applications, the skills of the staff, and also the "age" of the language.[11] Older languages like COBOL are poor choices for new projects because better languages are available and also because the baby boomers who learned COBOL decades ago are retiring.

SOFTWARE DEVELOPMENT AND DEPLOYMENT STRATEGIES

Much software is developed commercially by IT companies and licensed to users. Familiar products such as Microsoft Office, Adobe Premiere, or Quicken are all considered **commercial off-the-shelf (COTS)** software, which means they are ready to buy, install, and use. Although some products, like Excel, are designed for the mass market, others are more specialized for particular business processes. SAS, for example, offers software for statistical analysis, and Practice-Web produces specialty software just for dentists. Source code is not usually included, so buyers can't make changes on their own.

Software as a service (SaaS) is an information system that is owned, hosted, and managed remotely by a vendor. Organizations pay subscription fees to access it via the web, based on their own volumes. This type of cloud computing is part of an emerging trend in enterprise architecture that relieves the need for an organization to maintain its own data center, discussed later in this chapter.

Some organizations develop their own custom software or hire a company to do it for them. This strategy is usually more expensive but works well if commercial products that fit the company's needs are not available. Chapter 11 explores the steps in system development projects.

OPEN SOURCE SOFTWARE

Another approach to software development and distribution is called *open source*. To be considered **open source software**, the licensing terms must comply with several criteria, one of which is free redistribution. The source code must be distributed along with the software so that other people can improve it, build upon it, or use it in new programs. Licensing costs for open source software are zero, though organizations might have higher costs to support the software and train their users.

---

utility software
The category of system software that includes programs to perform specific tasks that help manage, tune, and protect the computer hardware and software.

programming language
An artificial language used to write software that provides the instructions for the computer about how to accept information, process it, and provide output.

legacy systems
Older information systems that remain in use because they still function and are costly to replace.

source code
All the statements that programmers write in a particular programming language to create a functioning software program.

object-oriented programming
A type of software programming that focuses on "objects" rather than lists of instructions and routines to manipulate data.

commercial off-the-shelf (COTS)
Commercially available computer software that is ready to buy, install, and use.

software as a service (SaaS)
A type of commercially available software that is owned, hosted, and managed by a vendor and accessed by customers remotely, usually via the Internet.

open source software
A type of software whose licensing terms comply with criteria such as free distribution, so other people can access the source code to improve it, build upon it, or use it in new programs.

Many open source products are quite successful, earning high market shares against commercial heavyweights. The Linux operating system and the Firefox web browser are examples, and new ones are emerging. Hadoop, for instance, is open source software used to manage and process big data. The licenses are free, but it is more difficult to predict overall costs with open source.[12]

Why would people build software when they don't get paid for their work? Enormous developer communities, often thousands strong, emerge around products such as Linux, and social recognition for valuable contributions is an important motive.[13] The communities may be organized as nonprofits, with a leadership team that determines policies about priorities for enhancement. The nonprofit Apache Software Foundation, for example, supports the collaborative efforts of its members who elect the leaders.

Describe the major types of networks and the transmission media they use, and give examples of network protocols.

3   Networks and Telecommunications

While waiting for her class to begin, part-time student and marketing manager Becca Wells wants to check email on her laptop. She clicks on her wireless icon and then refreshes the list of nearby connections (Figure 3-17). The university's StudentNet signal is usually strong, but today it does not show up at all. Instead, she clicks hopefully on a network called "garage" that she never noticed before. The connection works, but Becca hopes it will be strong enough for the upcoming video chat with her coworker.

Becca's email is on a server thousands of kilometers away, but how those zeros and ones actually travel isn't important to her—as long as the information moves fast and arrives safely. Though networks and telecommunications often stay hidden in the background, they are transforming the workplace in every organization—especially through the Internet and wireless computing.

A **network** is a group of interconnected devices (such as computers, phones, printers, or displays). To understand how networks operate, we begin with the media and protocols they use.

Transmission Media and Protocols

Networks can take advantage of either wired or wireless transmission media, and often include a mix of both. Just as hardware devices use different means to store zeros and ones, transmission media convert digital data to different kinds of signals depending on the nature of the medium. Each has strengths and weaknesses, as well as speed and capacity limitations. Transmission speed is measured in **bits per second (bps)**, and **bandwidth** refers to the maximum amount of information in bits per second that a particular channel can transmit. A bit is a single zero or one, and a string of eight bits makes a byte. For text information, a byte represents a single letter, number, or other character.

WIRED MEDIA

The three major wired media are **twisted pair wire**, **coaxial cable**, and **optical fiber** (Figure 3-18). Twisted pair wires are common in homes because the phone companies already installed them long before they were used to transmit digital data. Transmission speeds have

FIGURE 3-17

Example of wireless networking connection display. The colored bars indicate the strength of the signal, and the lock symbol indicates that the secured network requires password authentication.

Wireless Networks Found

garage   **g**

NorthEnd   **n**

FIGURE   3-18

Types of wired media.

Type	Description		Pros and Cons
Twisted pair wire	Insulated copper wires that are also used for telephones		Somewhat fragile but flexible enough to wind through ceilings and walls
Coaxial cable	Thick cables with a single inner conductor core, usually copper, and a surrounding of mesh		Faster transmission compared with twisted pair and already installed in many homes served by cable TV
Optical fiber	Transmit signals with light pulses along a glass or plastic fiber rather than electrical signals over a conductor		Fastest transmission speed and highest bandwidth; ideal for long distances because signals do not degrade. Requires a different adapter if fiber is connected to a PC

Sources: Courtesy of Patricia Wallace, MyImages – Micha Klootwijk/Shutterstock, Francisco Javier Gil/Shutterstock.

been improved, and these wires remain popular for apartment and office buildings as well. Coaxial cables are also common in homes because the cable TV companies installed them to carry television signals.

Optical fiber cables use light pulses rather than electrical signals, and they carry the most channels at the fastest speeds. Fiber-optic cables the size of a garden hose span all the planet's oceans and form the major arteries for worldwide telecommunications. Although some have occasionally suffered shark bites or other damage, they are proving extremely durable.

WIRELESS MEDIA

Electromagnetic waves, the radiation associated with electric and magnetic fields, can transmit digital information wirelessly (Figure 3-19). These waves include the tiny, atom-sized gamma rays with very rapid frequencies to very long waves with wavelengths stretching

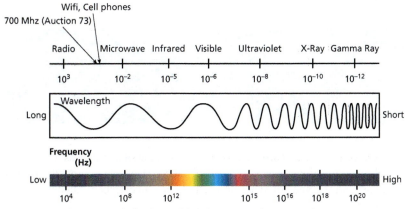

FIGURE   3-19

The electromagnetic spectrum.

Source: Adapted from http://kollewin.com/blog/electromagnetic-spectrum/.

network
A group of interconnected devices, such as computers, phones, printers, or displays, that can share resources and communicate using standard protocols.

bits per second (bps)
The measurement of transmission speed, defined as the number of bits transmitted each second; each bit is a single zero or one, and a string of 8 bits makes up a byte.

bandwidth
The maximum amount of information in bits per second that a particular channel can transmit.

twisted pair wires
The most common form of wired media, these wires consist of thin, flexible copper wires used in ordinary phones.

coaxial cables
Wired medium, initially used for cable TV, consisting of a single inner conductor wire (typically copper) surrounded by insulation, which is then surrounded by a mesh-like conductor.

optical fiber
Cables that transmit bits by means of light pulses along a glass or plastic fiber instead of electrical signals over a conductor; ideally suited for long distances.

FIGURE 3-20

Cellular infrastructure.

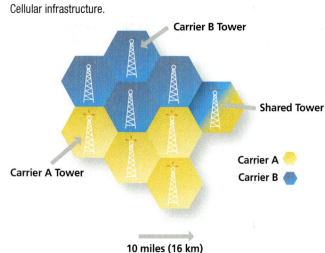

Carrier B Tower

Shared Tower

Carrier A
Carrier B

Carrier A Tower

10 miles (16 km)

to thousands of miles. Electromagnetic waves are also simply called *light*, but what human eyes perceive as light is actually just a small part of this spectrum. **Wavelength** refers to the distance between one peak of the wave to the next, and frequency, measured in **hertz (Hz)**, is the number of cycles per second.

The waves we use for wireless telecommunications are longer than visible light—in the ranges of radio waves and microwaves. **Microwave transmission** sends signals in the gigahertz range to relays in the line of sight. The signals can hop about 70 kilometers when earthbound, but they can also be transmitted to satellites, vastly increasing their flexibility. Networks of microwave relays have been constructed to transmit wireless data, especially in cities where the dishes can be installed on tall buildings.

The cell phone infrastructure (Figure 3-20) relies on radio waves in the 0.8 to 1.9 gigahertz range. Different cell-phone networks use different bands along this range. Companies like Verizon and AT&T also use different technologies to take best advantage of the frequencies available. Carriers negotiate agreements to share the towers and install their own equipment at the tower's base, though not all carriers have equipment at every tower. That explains why carriers publish separate coverage maps for their own networks. Transmission speeds keep increasing with improved technology, and 4G networks support access speeds that compete with home cable connections. Pilots are also underway for even faster 5G service in Japan.

Wifi, short for *wireless fidelity*, refers to a computer network in which connections rely on radio waves at frequencies of 2.4 GHz or 5 GHz. The 2.4 range is also used by cordless phones, which is why they can interfere with one another. The radio signals are sent a few hundred feet out from the antennae of a **wireless router**, which has a wired connection to the network. Signals get fainter as the distance increases, but if your laptop has a wireless adapter to receive the signal, your software will show the ones in range. Most will be password protected. For Becca, though, the "garage" wireless network was unsecured, so she was able to connect without any password. Perhaps whoever installed "garage" in some nearby dwelling simply forgot to set security, or maybe they were offering the free wifi connection as a friendly gesture.

DID YOU KNOW?

CoffeeCompany in Holland chooses names for its free wifi networks to cleverly market its menu items and also make people feel a little guilty if they just freeload. When customers in the cafe open their laptops to connect, they see wifi networks with names like "HaveYouTriedCoffeeCake?" or "BuyAnotherCupYouCheapskate."

Bluetooth, a technology that also uses radio waves in the same range as wifi, is commonly used for wireless connections over very short distances. Devices equipped with Bluetooth adapters, such as a printer and computer or a cell phone and earpiece, can detect one another and communicate.

Networking Basics

How do all these wires and electromagnetic signals connect devices to one another in a network? The industry categorizes network types based on their scale and scope, and how much geographic area they encompass. The **local area network (LAN)** typically connects computers, printers, scanners, and other devices in a single building or home. To describe networks that span smaller or larger geographic areas, the terms in Figure 3-21 are common.

Type of Network	Geographic Area
Personal area network (PAN)	20–30 feet, for devices within reach
Local area network (LAN)	Home, office, school, building
Campus (or Corporate) area network (CAN)	Interconnected LANs encompassing several buildings for a university or a corporate campus
Metropolitan area network (MAN)	Interconnected LANs or CANs for a city
Wide area network (WAN)	Interconnected LANS, CANs, or MANs covering a wide geographic area
Global area network (GAN)	Supports mobile communications across the globe, using a mix of satellite or other strategies

FIGURE 3-21
Types of networks.

PACKET SWITCHING

Most networks now use **packet switching**, in which strings of digital data are broken into segments called *packets* before they are transmitted. The packets contain data about their destination and position in the whole message, and they are reassembled at the receiving end. They may travel different routes, weaving around offline servers or taking longer paths if they hit traffic congestion. Packet switching is quite flexible, and it makes networks far more survivable against natural or manmade disasters.

Packet switching also supports voice calls. **Voice over IP (VoIP)** refers to the technologies that make voice communications across networks using packets feasible, including over the Internet. This disruptive innovation started out as many of them do, attracting people with small budgets and lots of patience for dropped calls or bad audio due to the bursty way packets travel. However, making free phone calls to anyone in the world who has a computer and Internet connection is a compelling draw. Skype, acquired by Microsoft in 2011, has a big lead in the VoIP market, and the service continues to improve—adding videoconferencing capabilities, voice mail, low cost calls to landlines and mobile phones, and better security and voice quality. Businesses can integrate their voice and data communications, making it unnecessary to install separate systems, and some are dropping desk phones entirely. As you will see later, this feature opens up new possibilities for cost savings and innovative business applications.

CLIENT-SERVER AND PEER-TO-PEER NETWORKS

Beyond geographic span and connection styles, we can describe networks in terms of how centralized they are, and how the devices on the network share the workload and provide services to others. A **client-server network** has one or more high-performance hosts running programs and storing data that clients—such as desktop computers, laptops, or smartphones—can access. The workload is shared, and the client runs software that performs some of the

wavelength
The distance between one peak of an electromagnetic wave to the next.

hertz (Hz)
The number of cycles per second of a wave.

microwave transmission
The technology involving signals in the gigahertz range that are transmitted to relays in the line of sight.

wifi
Short for wireless fidelity; it refers to a computer network in which connections rely on radio waves at frequencies of 2.4 GHz or 5 GHz for transmission.

wireless router
A device connected to a computer network that emits signals from its antenna and enables wireless connectivity to the network.

Bluetooth
A technology that uses radio waves for connectivity, commonly used for wireless connections over very short distances.

local area network (LAN)
A network that connects devices such as computers, printers, and scanners in a single building or home.

packet switching
A technology used by networks in which data is broken into segments, called packets, for transmission. The packets contain information about their destination and position in the whole message, and they are reassembled at the receiving end.

Voice over IP (VoIP)
The technologies that make voice communications across networks using packet switching feasible, including those used over the Internet.

client-server network
A type of network in which the workload for running applications is shared between the server and the client devices, such as desktop computers, laptops, or smartphones.

work of interpreting, displaying, and analyzing the data (Figure 3-22). A web browser such as Mozilla's Firefox, for example, is client software. When you open your browser and connect to a host, your client sends the request to the web server, which then sends back the instructions for displaying the page you requested.

The server in a client-server network can be around the corner, deep in your organization's data center, or perhaps across the planet. With any particular request, more than one server may be involved in the response, each specialized for its particular purpose. For instance, the web server may receive your request to display your bank balance, but the data itself is retrieved from a database on a different server. This kind of architecture is called **n-tier**, with a client and one or more servers involved.

The client in a client-server network can do more or less work, depending on how the software is designed, but the trend is to reduce its workload. In fact, much business software now only requires a web browser. This eliminates the need to install special software on all the devices in an organization.

The highly decentralized approach is called the **peer-to-peer network**, in which there is no central server and computers can share files, printers, and an Internet connection with one another. Home networks or small offices are often set up this way, and most operating systems support it. The nodes on a decentralized network are peers in the sense that each one can offer services to the others and none is the centralized server.

On a larger scale, peer-to-peer networks support file sharing and other services on the Internet. BitTorrent is one example that is used to move large files rapidly from one computer to another by breaking them into smaller pieces called *torrents*. People use the software to locate a song, movie, game, or other digital product stored on one of the peer computers in the network, download the pieces, and then make the pieces available for others to download. Implications for copyright violation are acute, however, and lawsuits common.

Skype also uses peer-to-peer networking for VoIP, borrowing a bit of each user's computer power and Internet connection as calls are routed around the globe, hopping from node to node. Unlike the phone companies, which built the vast, wired infrastructure and manage servers that handle call switching, billing, and technical support, Skype enlists the aid of its users and their equipment—though they may not realize it.

Network Protocols

To transmit data from one device to another in a network, both the sender and recipient have to use a protocol of some kind so they understand one another. When you power on your cell phone, for example, the device listens for a special control signal transmitted via radio waves.

FIGURE 3-22
Client-server network.

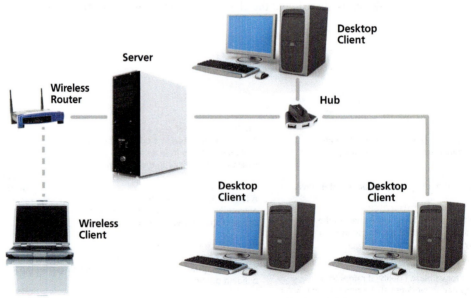

Source: Photos/illustrations: ArchMan/Shutterstock.

If no signal is received, your phone will report "No service." The signal from the cell tower also includes a code that indicates the carrier, and if your phone is using the same carrier, the codes will match. That means your phone is on its home network and not roaming on some other carrier's network.

Networking protocols perform their work in layers, each of which defines how the devices will speak to one another. The lowest layer defines physical connections, such as the shape of the plug. Higher layers define how other connection issues are resolved, such as how the bits will be organized and transmitted, how errors will be corrected, and how the connection will be established. The highest level defines how software applications interface with the user. That "http://" preceding the website is a protocol at this highest level, and it tells your browser how to interpret the incoming data so it shows properly on your screen.

ETHERNET

Ethernet, the protocol widely used for local area networks, has been dominating the market since the 1980s. Technology improvements have increased transmission speed, which is now in the gigabit per second range. The familiar cabling that leads from the back of a desktop computer to a jack in the wall or a home router is very likely an Ethernet cable. It resembles a phone jack, which often appears on the same wall plate, but is a little wider.

TCP/IP AND THE INTERNET'S HOURGLASS ARCHITECTURE

The suite of protocols used for Internet communications that connect Ethernet and other networks together includes the Transmission Control Protocol and Internet Protocol, or **TCP/IP** for short. These two protocols operate in the middle layer and define how data are packaged and transported.

The core design principle of the Internet is an hourglass structure, so the network protocols themselves are really very simple (Figure 3-23). As long as bits are transmitted using the Internet's standardized protocols, new applications for the top end and new communications technologies for the bottom can all be incorporated. For example, long after the Internet was launched using standard phone lines, dozens of new wiring and wireless schemes emerged to increase speed, serve remote areas, or leverage some existing wiring such as coaxial cable. (Some say the Internet is so flexible that two cans and a string will do the trick.)

At the top of the hourglass, the Internet's open architecture has paved the way for astonishing creativity and new applications, such as the World Wide Web, streaming video, e-commerce, VoIP, and multiuser 3D games.

Although the Internet's original design was extremely clever, some features later caused regret. One problem is simply the number of addresses available. The original protocol assigns an IP address to each node or device as a string of four numbers, such as 157.150.190.10, which is currently the United Nations' website (www.un.org). The scheme supports about 4 billion different addresses, which seemed like more than enough at the time. However, with explosive growth and innovations that demand addresses for so many new devices, the pool will soon be exhausted. The latest revision of the IP protocol is **Internet Protocol Version 6 (IPv6)**, and it includes much more breathing room for addresses—quadrillions for

FIGURE 3-23
The Internet's hourglass structure.

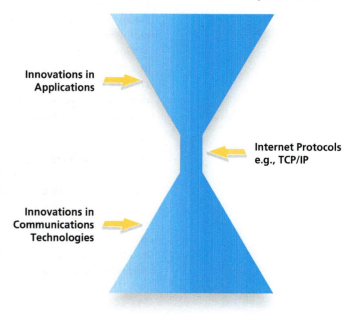

Innovations in Applications

Internet Protocols e.g., TCP/IP

Innovations in Communications Technologies

---

n-tier
Type of network architecture in which several servers, specialized for particular tasks, may be accessed by a client computer to perform some activity, such as retrieving a bank balance.

peer-to-peer network
A type of network in which there is no central server and computers can share files, printers, and an Internet connection with one another.

Ethernet
A communication protocol widely used for local area networks.

TCP/IP
Abbreviation for *Transmission Control Protocol and Internet Protocol;* used for Internet communications.

Internet Protocol Version 6 (IPv6)
The next generation protocol for the Internet, which will support far more IP addresses compared to the current scheme.

every man, woman, and child on the planet. It's just in time, too, given how many nonhuman objects are part of the Internet of Things.

WIRELESS PROTOCOLS

Wireless protocols determine how the electromagnetic spectrum is used to transmit data. A family of standards called *802.11* is widely used for wifi connections, with different versions indicated by a letter appended after the 11. Figure 3-24 compares the standards on several features. The 802.11ac standard, for instance, supports transmission speeds above 1 Gb/s, and even more capable protocols are in development.[14] [15] The faster speeds are especially welcome as video traffic grows. Protocols used for the Internet of Things will need to balance conflicting requirements that touch on range, battery life, security, and bandwidth.

The future for wireless is bright and offers much promise, not just for businesses and consumers but for people in developing countries. Costs for wireless technologies can be far lower than for wired infrastructure, especially for remote areas.

Strategy and Competition in Telecommunications

Few areas of information technology are as fast-moving or competitive as telecommunications, especially because advances happen rapidly and competition among the players is fierce. For instance, companies vie to gain control over portions of the spectrum.

THE WIRELESS SPECTRUM AS OCEANFRONT PROPERTY

The frequencies used for wireless technologies may seem dreadfully dull, but think of them as oceanfront real estate, where supply is short and location is everything—at least in terms of what can be done with the bandwidth. Governments usually regulate the spectrum's use and its allocation because it is a limited public good. Much of the spectrum usable for wireless transmission is already reserved for TV, cell phones, radio, law enforcement, emergency services, defense, and various government agencies. Some of it is left unlicensed and available for any devices to use, such as the bandwidth used for wifi. Since no carrier has control, no fees are charged to use that bandwidth, though some router owners, such as hotels, might want some payment for using their Internet connection and wifi.

Governments also auction these licenses, and the high bidder wins the right to use it for their customers. These auctions can be very high-stakes events, and they raise considerable revenue. The Mexican government, for instance, expects to take in $2.5 billion from carriers who win bids for the rights to use portions of the spectrum for mobile broadband service. Clearly, demand for this "oceanfront property" is booming.[16]

THE LAST MILE

Another tense issue involving telecommunications is that "last mile." For most people, the final leg of wiring to your home is not superfast fiber but twisted pair installed by the phone company carriers or coaxial cable from the cable TV companies. The phone companies initially installed **digital subscriber lines (DSL)** to support Internet traffic, and the cable TV companies also changed their networks to carry signals in two directions. Some companies are also building out fiber networks for select cities with much faster speeds, but even with this kind of service, your devices may still have a short "last mile" in which signals travel via wireless transmission or other media. Your download may travel at light speed most of the

FIGURE 3-24

Comparing 802.11 standards.

Standard	Indoor Range	Frequency	Maximum Data Rate
802.11a	~35 meters	3.7 or 5 GHz	54 Mb/s
802.11b	~38 meters	2.4 GHz	11 Mb/s
802.11g	~38 meters	2.4 GHz	54 Mb/s
802.11n	~70 meters	2.4 or 5 GHz	600 Mb/s
802.11ac	~35 meters	5 GHz	At least 1 Gb/s
802.11ad	~60 meters	60 GHz	Up to 6.75 Gb/s

way, but it hits a bumpy road before it gets to your laptop. The last mile issue is especially important for rural areas and also less developed countries. Fortunately, new technologies are addressing this bottleneck.[17]

CORD CUTTING

Wireless transmission raises further competitive issues, particularly for carriers offering land-line phone service. With improvements in wireless services, "cord cutters" are dropping their landline phone service in favor of cell phones, which also provide reasonably fast wireless Internet connectivity. In addition, cord cutters are dropping their cable TV subscriptions, choosing instead to rely on streamed video services such as Netflix or Hulu.[18] Companies in the telecommunications space will need smart strategies to meet the challenges of these disruptive innovations.

> **PRODUCTIVITY TIP**
> If you live in the United States, visit www.antennasearch.com and enter your own address. The program will map the locations of all the nearby cell towers. Click on the towers nearest your home to obtain some information about them, such as the building they are on or their owner. Knowing their locations will help you avoid unpleasant call interruptions for important conversations.

The Enterprise Architecture

4 Explain the importance of the enterprise architecture, describing trends in ICT architecture over time.

The strange Winchester House in California has about 160 rooms, with countless staircases leading nowhere, and a chimney that stops short of the ceiling. Doors open to blank walls or to steep drops to the garden. It's a tourist attraction, but it wasn't built to be amusing. Owner Sarah Winchester had no master architectural plan for the house, and she just improvised its construction, day after day, year after year. She was wealthy and could afford mistakes; businesses, however, need better planning for their information systems.

The enterprise architecture (EA) is the big picture for the organization, the blueprint that describes the current environment and the target environment the organization hopes to reach to achieve its mission. It also includes a roadmap for moving from the baseline to the target to help managers make better decisions that focus on long-term benefits and not just short-term gains. The architecture is not just about hardware, software, and telecommunications assets, though those are key components. It encompasses the people, technology, processes, and data that make up information systems, and it should be driven by business requirements and the organization's mission.

Figure 3-25 illustrates the enterprise architecture as layers, in which the business mission at the top drives decisions about data and applications architectures. These should then shape the ICT architecture, to include hardware, software, and communications.

FIGURE 3-25
Components of an enterprise architecture.

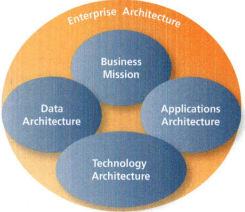

Trends in Enterprise Architectures

The information and communications technology component of the enterprise architecture changes over time as new technologies emerge and businesses build more effective and efficient processes to achieve their missions. Figure 3-26 plots some of the major architectural approaches; mixed environments are not uncommon.

FROM MAINFRAMES TO MICROCOMPUTERS

Beginning in the 1960s, mainframes were the foundation of the architecture. Dumb terminals, with their glowing green-and-black screens, accessed the data center's mainframe, and private leased lines were used to transmit information between corporate sites. When microcomputers entered businesses in the 1980s, they swiftly replaced typewriters, even though the word processing software was very clunky. They replaced the dumb terminals, too, largely because the electronic spreadsheet was such a useful breakthrough. The PC could work like a dumb terminal to access the mainframe's applications, but it could also run its own software locally.

digital subscriber lines (DSL)
Technology that supports high-speed, two-way digital communication over twisted pair phone lines.

CLIENT-SERVER ARCHITECTURES

Local area networks, more powerful PCs, and the development of PC operating systems that could support multiple users opened the path for the client-server architecture described earlier. Software applications that tap the resources of both server and client emerged, with more user-friendly, colorful, and graphical interfaces replacing the dull black screens so familiar to mainframe users.

Businesses enjoyed major savings by retiring expensive mainframes with their costly software and peripherals. They replaced aging systems with new software that ran on PC-based servers and local area networks. Because PC hardware could be obtained from many manufacturers (Dell and HP, for example), prices stayed competitive. Organizations settled on Ethernet as the local area networking standard and adopted strategies for using the Internet for communications rather than leasing private lines from the telecommunications carriers. They also focused on a handful of server operating systems, namely Windows Server, Unix, and Linux. These trends initially brought many cost savings.

THIN CLIENTS

Client-server architecture varies, depending on how the software balances the load. As servers became more powerful, they could take on more of the processing. Servers are also easier for IT staff to manage and update compared with the clients on all those desktops. Increasingly, developers created software that needed nothing more than a web browser, emphasizing the thin client. This trend made it possible for employees to access corporate software from many different devices, including mobile ones.

VIRTUALIZATION

The organization's data center, once home to a mainframe computer and all its components, quickly became jammed with rack after rack of PC servers. "Server sprawl" was rampant, and the numbers kept rising as new applications were implemented. Because many servers in n-tier client-server architectures were originally designed to specialize in one kind of task or one software application, much capacity remained unused. The CPUs might sit idle much of the time, though still drawing electricity and generating heat. To address this, companies began implementing **virtualization** using software that allows multiple operating systems to run on a single physical PC server. To the users, each one appears as a separate, self-contained server that may handle only one software application, but they are actually virtual servers.

Virtualization can cut costs dramatically, not just by lowering electricity bills and hardware expenses but also through reduced maintenance burdens. Virtualization is also an important element in the drive toward environmentally friendly information systems. With fewer servers and improved use of capacity, energy consumption drops.[19]

Virtualization can make managing the network as agile and flexible as it does for servers. The software-defined network (SDN) allows network engineers to respond quickly to changing business needs by managing data traffic, switches, and routers through software rather than having to reconfigure the devices or install new ones. Like server virtualization, SDN helps avoid bottlenecks and make better use of available capacity.

INTEGRATION OF VOICE AND DATA

Since the mainframe era, the infrastructure for voice communications was separated from data. Buildings have been constructed with two sets of cabling to each office or cubicle—one for data communications and the other for voice (Figures 3-26A and 3-26B). The twisted copper pair wiring for voice typically led to **private branch exchange (PBX)** equipment in the data center or off-site, which manages all the office phone lines, voice mail, call transfers and forwarding, conference calling, and other voice services. Many organizations buy such services from phone companies, although larger ones might purchase and maintain their own PBX. Figure 3-26A shows a PBX right next to the mainframe and then later as a smaller, rack-based model (Figure 3-26B).

With VoIP, however, organizations can retire the PBX and design the enterprise architecture quite differently. Voice communications can be integrated with data, traveling over the same networks and managed by software applications on the same servers. Videoconferencing and screen sharing can easily be added as well, as the old PBX is replaced with IP-based

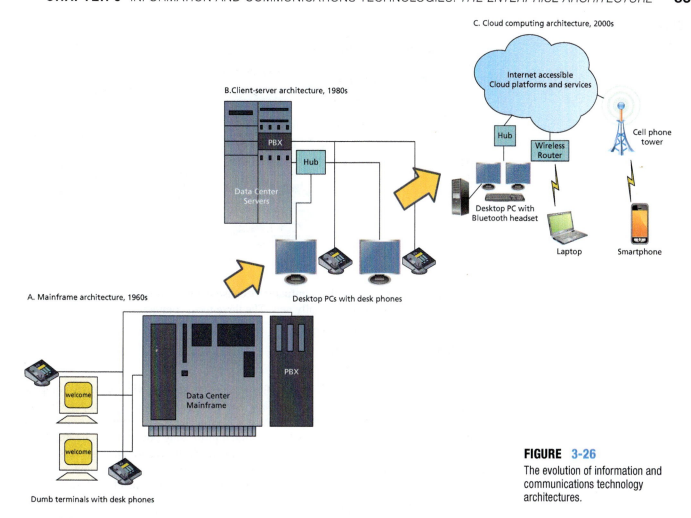

FIGURE 3-26
The evolution of information and communications technology architectures.

solutions.[20] An important advantage for business is that communications can be closely integrated with the other software that a company uses and can tap into the company's databases. For example, the system could bring up a customer's record when that customer calls in without having to ask the customer to key in an account number. The integration would also help avoid duplication of contact information for customers, suppliers, and employees. Voice and data integration is ripe for a great many innovations that will improve productivity, and Chapter 8 describes this trend toward "unified communications" in more detail.

CLOUD COMPUTING

The architecture called cloud computing draws on IT resources outside of the corporation's own data centers and local desktops (Figure 3-27).[21] With an Internet connection, employees can access virtual servers, storage space, video streaming, specialized software, and other cloud-based services from any location, using many different devices. The services are not in a cloud, of course. The physical hardware that supports them is located in very large data centers operated by Amazon, eBay, HP, Google, and other providers. Google cuts hardware costs to the bone by building its own servers from inexpensive parts and distributing the applications over a large number of them. They share the load, and if one goes down, another just takes over.

virtualization
Cost-cutting approach to servers in which multiple operating systems run concurrently on a single physical PC server.

private branch exchange (PBX)
Technology that manages all the office phone lines, voice mail, internal billing, call transfers, forwarding, conferencing, and other voice services.

cloud computing
ICT architecture in which users access software applications and information systems remotely over the Internet, rather than locally on an individual PC or from servers in the organization's data center.

FIGURE 3-27
Cloud-based services.

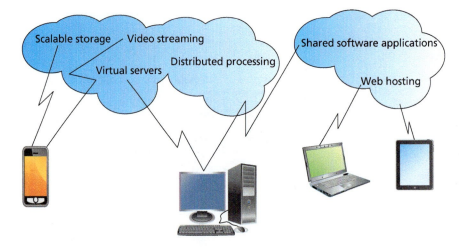

Cloud computing is somewhat confusing because it refers to many different styles and technologies, and some are not actually new. The three most common styles are:

- Infrastructure as a service (IaaS)
- Platform as a service (PaaS)
- Software as a service (SaaS)

With **infrastructure as a service (IaaS)**, the cloud hosting service provides computer resources such as a virtual server, storage space, and processing power. This approach offers major advantages to fast-moving businesses because managers can quickly scale up the resources if demand explodes, perhaps for additional processing power to handle big data.[22] **Platform as a service (PaaS)** refers to situations in which the vendor hosts servers configured with an application development environment along with an operating system and often a database management system (DBMS). Organizations can access the cloud host remotely to create their own software applications.[23] For instance, Microsoft offers its Azure PaaS for developers who work in the .NET application environment. PaaS also typically includes infrastructure services such as storage.

With software as a service (SaaS), the vendor provides access to its full-featured software product, owned and managed by the vendor. Companies like Salesforce.com build software applications in a way that allows many "tenants" to use them for their own organizations.

A drawback of cloud computing is that an extremely reliable Internet connection is a must. Organizations that can't count on that for their operations, perhaps because of their location or harsh weather conditions, would find themselves without access to their mission-critical systems when the net connection failed. Another drawback is that cloud services tend to be "one size fits all" and may not work as well for companies that need special configurations. Game maker Zynga, for instance, started out with its own Dell servers but then switched to the cloud when growth exploded and it couldn't buy servers fast enough. The cloud provider was not able to tune the servers for Zynga's needs, though, so Zynga moved the games back to its own servers and used the cloud to relieve pressure.

To some extent, the drive to rebrand some familiar services as "cloud computing" is more about marketing hype than a brand new architecture, and definitions continue to evolve. However, improvements in virtualization, security, and mobile access are very real, and they offer compelling opportunities to reduce costs and empower the workforce. Eliminating even one corporate data center, for example, can offer substantial savings. As the shift to the cloud gathers momentum, the richness and variety of services will continue to grow, provided vendors can satisfy customer concerns that their data and applications are safe, secure, and utterly reliable. Those concerns are not trivial considering how valuable these resources are.

PRODUCTIVITY TIP
If you want to access your files from different devices, try a personal cloud computing service, such as Microsoft's OneDrive, Dropbox, or Box.com. They offer free versions with some storage space, and you can purchase more if you need it. Cloud services are also useful for backing up your data.

Guiding the Enterprise Architecture

Creating the roadmap to guide the enterprise from its current architecture to its target is a challenge, especially for organizations that have a mix of platforms already in place. Peek behind the counter at your dentist's office, for example, and you may see a PC emulating a dumb terminal, with an old-fashioned text-based display showing your last three appointments. On another desk, you see someone logging into a graphical software application to check on insurance for your dental visit. In the chair, you might watch your dentist pull up vivid X-ray images and medical records on a flat screen. And in a few days, you may be able to check on the insurance claim yourself with your smartphone. Many organizations carry a mix of architectures, implemented over time and with limited integration among them.

The task of creating and guiding the architecture is often led by an enterprise architect (Figure 3-28). This new (and well-paid) position requires a person with deep knowledge of the organization's mission and strategy and a clear understanding of how different architectures can support the company's goals. The architect's role is to lead the effort, promote the value of EA concepts, and coordinate decision making so the organization stays on track. The online simulation called Devil's Canyon that accompanies this chapter gives you a chance to work with a team of entrepreneurs, understand their goals, and make recommendations about the architecture that will work best for them.

The trends in enterprise architecture now under way have a major impact on industries, organizations, their employees, and their customers. Cloud computing offers many valuable business capabilities and the potential for cost savings. But drafting a blueprint that erases the underground data center is far easier than actually dismantling it and reconfiguring it in the cloud. Managers worry about the safety of their data and the reliability of the services. An outage at one of Amazon's data centers brought down major customers, including Netflix, Tinder, and the Internet Movie Database (imdb.com).[24]

Managers also wonder whether their old legacy applications will still run or whether they can get the help they need if the IT department shrinks. IT staff struggle with reduced budgets and also a loss of control over the company's mission-critical systems. The enterprise architect must take into account these human elements when designing a roadmap that will guide the organization into a successful future.

With this overview of information and communications technologies and the different kinds of enterprise architectures we can create with them, we can now move deeper into information systems and the data architecture. The database is a central feature, and the next chapter shows how it works.

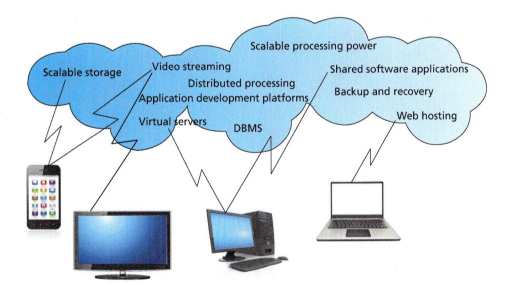

FIGURE 3-28
Cloud-based services.
Source: Nui7711/Shutterstock, Rvlsoft/Shutterstock, Cobalt88/Shutterstock, Maxim Kazmin/123RF

infrastructure as a service (IaaS)
Cloud hosting service provides computer resources such as virtual servers, storage, and processing power, allowing clients to configure the resources as they choose.

platform as a service (PaaS)
Cloud hosting service provides computer resources and also operating systems, application development environments, and often a database management system.

MyMISLab
Online Simulation

DEVIL'S CANYON
A Role-Playing Simulation on Enterprise Architecture for a Mountain Resort

A team of entrepreneurs is building a deluxe mountain resort from the ground up, and they need your help to plan the enterprise architecture. Devil's Canyon is a breathtaking location, and the resort will offer everything from skiing and snowboarding in the winter to rock climbing, white water rafting, hiking, swimming, and fishing in the warmer seasons. These young and enthusiastic entrepreneurs aren't really sure what they'll need, but they want Devil's Canyon to be the premier, 21st-century resort, well equipped with technology to please their demanding target market.

Your job is to get a sense of their vision and how much they can afford and then help them design the enterprise architecture using the interactive design tools. You'll meet the team at the kickoff session, so log in when you're ready to start....

LEARNING OBJECTIVES

1 The four hardware components of every computer are input, output, the central processing unit (CPU), and storage. Input devices convert signals such as a key press on a keyboard or finger motion on a touchscreen into digital information and transmit it to the CPU. Output devices include display screens and printers, and many devices serve both purposes. Scanners and sensors play a large role as input and output, involving technologies such as barcodes, RFID, QR codes, digital cameras, and optical character recognition. Computing architectures vary in terms of size, processing speed and capacities, portability, and other factors. They include mainframes, minicomputers, supercomputers, microcomputers, laptops, netbooks, smartphones, and tablets. Primary storage includes random access memory (RAM), and secondary storage includes hard drives, solid-state drives, optical disks, and magnetic tape. Declining costs for primary storage technologies support in-memory computing, which is much faster compared to secondary storage.

2 Two types of software are (1) application software, which supports all personal activity, business processes, and specific tasks; and (2) system software, which includes the operating system and utilities. Operating systems are important in business because many applications work on only one of them, so business users choose the one that has the most useful software available. Windows dominates the operating system market for desktops and laptops, but operating systems for smartphones and tablets are much more varied. Software is written in various programming languages and software development environments. Managers make choices by taking into consideration staff skills; the availability of training, support, and tools; and other factors. Software created by IT companies such as Microsoft or Oracle and licensed to customers is called commercial off-the-shelf (COTS). Increasingly, web-based applications are licensed as software as a service (SaaS). Unique applications or business processes sometimes call for custom software development. Open source software, with licensing terms that call for free redistribution, is developed by volunteer communities and carries no licensing costs.

3 Networks connect computers and other devices, and their transmission media can be wired or wireless. Wired media include twisted pair, coaxial cable, and optical fiber. Wireless transmission relies on the electromagnetic spectrum, using segments that are either licensed or unlicensed. Wifi, for example, relies on radio waves at frequencies of either 2.4 GHz or 5 GHz. Networks typically use packet switching and can be classified by their geographic areas (such as LAN or WAN) and by their degree of centralization (client-server and peer-to-peer). To connect, devices rely on protocols, such as Ethernet and TCP/IP. The 802.11 family of protocol standards is widely used for wifi. These protocols determine how different layers address connection issues, from the physical layer to the application layer. The Internet's protocols support ongoing innovation because they address mainly the middle layers. Strategies and competition in the telecommunications industry are closely tied to technology development. For example, companies bid on access to portions of the electromagnetic spectrum with which they can develop new wireless services. They also compete on ways to support the "last mile" and deal with the growing number of cord cutters.

4 The enterprise architecture is the organization's master blueprint that describes the current environment, its future state, and the roadmap for achieving that state. It is driven by business needs and helps define and guide the ICT architecture needed to support it. ICT architectures have evolved over time with changes in business needs and technological innovations. Emerging trends include virtualization, the integration of voice and data, and cloud computing. Developing and guiding the enterprise architecture require a keen understanding of the business mission and how ICT architectures can support it.

KEY TERMS AND CONCEPTS

enterprise architecture (EA)

computer

ASCII code

optical scanners

optical character recognition (OCR)

radio frequency identification (RFID)

central processing unit (CPU)

transistor

Moore's Law

byte

random access memory (RAM)

in-memory computing

software

application software

system software

operating system (OS)

utility software

programming language

legacy systems

source code

object-oriented programming

commercial off-the-shelf (COTS)

software as a service (SaaS)

open source software

network

bits per second (bps)

bandwidth

twisted pair wires

coaxial cables

optical fiber

wavelength

hertz (Hz)

microwave transmission

wifi

wireless router

Bluetooth

local area network (LAN)

packet switching

voice over IP (VoIP)

client-server network

n-tier

peer-to-peer network

Ethernet

TCP/IP

Internet Protocol Version 6 (IPv6)

digital subscriber lines (DSL)

virtualization

private branch exchange (PBX)

cloud computing

infrastructure as a service (IaaS)

platform as a service (PaaS)

CHAPTER REVIEW QUESTIONS

3-1. What is the function of each of the four components of a computer? Give an example of each component.

3-2. What is the meaning and significance of Moore's Law?

3-3. What are the two major types of software, and how do they differ? Give an example of each.

3-4. What are the different strategies for creating and deploying software?

3-5. What are the major types of wired and wireless transmission media? What are the strengths, weaknesses, and potential of each?

3-6. What is packet switching, and what are its advantages for networks?

3-7. What is a network protocol? What are the roles of Ethernet, TCP/IP, and wireless protocols?

3-8. What is an enterprise architecture, and what is its role in an organization?

3-9. How have ICT architectures changed over time as new technologies have emerged?

3-10. What is cloud computing? How does it support business objectives?

PROJECTS AND DISCUSSION QUESTIONS

3-11. Smartphones captured the imagination of billions of people, becoming a technology with one of the fastest growth rates in history. Choose a smartphone model and describe its hardware components (input, processing, storage, output), its operating system, and examples of its application software.

3-12. When the "StudentNet" wireless Internet signal did not appear on the list of nearby connections (Figure 3-17), Becca Wells used the "garage" network to check her email. What issues should Becca have considered before connecting to that unknown network? For example, is it ethical to connect through someone's service without permission, even if that person didn't password-protect the access point? What security issues should Becca be concerned about? Search the web to learn more about "wardriving" and prepare a brief summary of your findings.

3-13. Decades ago, analysts predicted the death of mainframe computers. Today, however, many public and private enterprises throughout the world rely on the mainframe as the backbone of large-scale computing. For example,

the U.S. Census Bureau uses mainframe computers to process data about the nation's people and economy. On the other hand, many of today's data centers run on racks of PC servers or large-scale PC server farms. How are mainframe computers different from PCs? How are they similar? Search the web or visit websites such as opensourcemainframes.org and ibm.com to learn more about how mainframes support an IT infrastructure. List and discuss the major uses of mainframe systems.

3-14. When an organization adopts a cloud computing model for its mission-critical data, several new ingredients that may be unfamiliar to the organization's leadership are introduced:

a. Leasing IT resources

b. Depending on a third party to store data

c. Depending on a third party to provide services

List the positive and negative results of these factors as they affect organizations that adopt cloud computing. Outline several reasons why a company might decide to use cloud computing. Are there other issues related to cloud computing?

3-15. Consider the many types of computer input devices available today. Identify two general categories of input devices and provide several examples of each. List and describe several input devices that also serve as output devices. List several input/output devices that you own. Which are your favorites? Why? Which are your least favorites? Why?

3-16. Why are there different programming languages? What is the fundamental difference between Java and .NET? Search the web to learn the origin of the name *COBOL*. How is COBOL used today? How strong is the case that "COBOL is dead"? Why or why not?

3-17. Jackson Real Estate is relocating to new office space, and owner Bella Jackson must decide between a wired or wireless network for 35 on-the-go agents. What are the pros and cons of each type of network for this business environment? Consider the cost, security, and mobility issues of this decision and make a recommendation.

3-18. Work in a small group with classmates to compare three office productivity applications: commercial off-the-shelf software products, such as Microsoft Office; software as a service, such as Google Docs; and open source suites, such as Open Office (openoffice.org) or Libre Office (libreoffice.org). What are the benefits, costs, and risks of each type of application? Discuss why a small business or nonprofit organization might prefer one application instead of another.

3-19. Work in a small group with classmates to explain the effects of Moore's Law on information and communications technology. What is the impact of Moore's Law on your life? Prepare a 5-minute presentation on your findings.

3-20. Work in a small group with classmates to consider the differences between commercial off-the-shelf software and custom software. What are the advantages and disadvantages of each type of software? Why would a company decide to develop its own software rather than use COTS? Investigate the student information system used by your college or university to learn whether the software was custom developed or purchased.

APPLICATION EXERCISES

3-21. EXCEL APPLICATION:
Analyzing Growth in Computer Storage Capacities

Since the computer hard drive was invented in 1956, a constantly increasing data storage capacity has been available at an ever-decreasing cost. Use the historical data of hard drive capacities and prices shown in Figure 3-29 (or download the Excel file named *CH03Ex01*). Modify the spreadsheet so that it includes a new column containing formulas that calculate a common measure of disk size (GB) and a second new column that computes the cost per GB for each year. (Recall 1 gigabyte = 1,024 megabytes; 1 terabyte = 1,024 gigabytes.) Now, create one line graph to show the cost per gigabyte from the period 1995 to 2016. Create a second line graph to show changes in the size of hard disks across the same period. (Tip: Use the "Hide" function to cover the columns you don't need for each graph.) Write a brief summary of the trends you found. What factors have contributed to these trends? What are the implications of these trends?

3-22. ACCESS APPLICATION:
Managing ICT Assets with a Database

Steve Adams Design is an architectural design firm specializing in corporate design projects such as commercial building architecture, interior design, master planning, and sustainable design and consulting. As part of its ICT asset management program, the IT director has asked you to build an Access database to manage the devices used by employees. The database will contain information about each device, such as manufacturer, model, date acquired, condition, purchase price, and current value.

Create an empty database named *Adams*. Download the Excel file Ch03Ex02 and import the two worksheets to tables

FIGURE 3-29

Hard drive capacities and costs by year.

Year	Size	Units	Price
1995	1.7	GB	$1,499
1996	3.2	GB	$ 469
1997	7	GB	$ 670
1998	8.4	GB	$ 382
1999	19.2	GB	$ 512
2000	27.3	GB	$ 375
2001	40	GB	$ 238
2002	100	GB	$ 230
2003	120	GB	$ 168
2004	250	GB	$ 250
2006	390	GB	$ 106
2008	1	TB	$ 200
2010	1.5	TB	$ 220
2011	2	TB	$ 80
2012	3	TB	$ 150
2013	3	TB	$ 119
2014	3	TB	$ 110
2015	4	TB	$ 130
2016	5	TB	$ 130

in your database. Create a totals query to summarize the current value of equipment for each category. Create a report displaying the names and locations of employees who use laptop computers. Create a report displaying the names and locations of employees who use CAD systems.

CASE STUDY #1

Google Glass and Wearable Technologies

Moore's Law is helping companies like Alphabet (Google's parent company) and Apple develop wearable technologies that have considerable computing power, from smartphone watches to heart rate monitors. "Google Glass" broke new ground in this technology category with a headset that resembles a pair of lightweight glasses. The device connects to the Internet wirelessly via wifi, but to be fully mobile, the wearer also needs to carry a smartphone that can work as a hotspot, relying on the carrier's mobile 4G network to stay connected.

Google Glass is a work in progress, but developers envision it as an "always on" device that people can use to take spontaneous pictures and videos, send and receive phone calls and text messages, and post messages on social networks. The small display in the upper corner of the wearer's visual field adds another critical capability, to conduct Google searches, for instance. Air travelers can call up current flight data as they race to the gate. With GPS, the wearer can view navigation maps that match the current position. The device has most of what it needs to function as a standalone computer, including a high-powered processor running the Android operating system.

How does the wearer communicate with Glass? Users can speak a variety of commands, such as "OK Glass, take a picture," or "OK Glass, share this with my network." There is also a tiny touchpad on the headset's frame.

Wearable technologies like this face enormous challenges, however, particularly as head-mounted devices that offer a visual display. Human eyes are not designed to view details on anything so close, so the display has to fool the person's retina with an image that appears to be much further away. Google Glass uses a prism and mirrors positioned over the wearer's right eye to accomplish that.

Another concern is that a visual display could be a safety hazard, especially while driving. Research shows drivers wearing Glass are impaired, though perhaps less so compared to drivers who keep checking smartphones.

The fashion conscious may also reject the austere look of Google Glass, which resembles the headset worn by Levar Burton in Star Trek: The Next Generation.

Some privacy advocates have voiced concerns about Google Glass as well. What does it mean when people are always equipped to record whatever they see and instantly upload it to the Internet without others knowing they are doing it? To some extent, mobile devices already offer that capability, but Google Glass raises the stakes even further. For example, a bar in Seattle banned customers from wearing the device, and other businesses may follow.

Lawmakers worry that Google has the capability to embed its increasingly sophisticated facial recognition software. At some point, the Glass wearer may be able to identify strangers on the street by matching the face to tagged photos on social networks. A group launched the website called StopTheCyborgs.org to draw attention to the many privacy issues surrounding Google Glass, comparing the devices to "human spy drones."

Responding to the criticisms, Google stopped distributing the device in 2015. But company execs say they are still committed to the project. They are also encouraging developers to create new apps for Glass, focusing on work-related applications such as smart glasses for the military or as an aid to football referees. Wearables like Glass will hold key positions in the Internet of Things as the bugs are worked out and concerns addressed.

Discussion Questions

3-23. Identify the major hardware, software, and communications components of Google Glass.

3-24. What are some of the advantages to using Google Glass, and how will they add value to a customer's life?

3-25. What are the major risks associated with Google Glass?

3-26. Why is Google encouraging developers to create apps for Google Glass rather than building those apps itself?

Sources: Cohen, E. (March 13, 2013). The eyes have it: Google Glass and the myth of multitasking. *Scientific American*, http://blogs.scientificamerican.com/guest-blog/2013/03/13/the-eyes-have-it-google-glass-and-the-myth-of-multitasking/, accessed March 23, 2013.
Guarino, M. (March 25, 2013). Google Glass already has some lawmakers on high alert. *Christian Science Monitor*, http://www.csmonitor.com/USA/Society/2013/0325/Google-Glass-already-has-some-lawmakers-on-high-alert.
Metz, R. (2016). Google Glass finds a second act at work. *MIT Technology Review,* https://www.technologyreview.com/s/539606/google-glass-finds-a-second-act-at-work/, accessed February 21, 2016.
Newton, C. (March 8, 2013). Seattle dive bar becomes first to ban Google Glass. c|net, http://news.cnet.com/8301-1023_3-57573387-93/seattle-dive-bar-becomes-first-to-ban-google-glass/, accessed March 24, 2013.
Young, K. L., Stephens, A. N., Stephan, K. L., & Stuart, G. W. (2016). In the eye of the beholder: A simulator study of the impact of Google Glass on driving performance. *Accident Analysis & Prevention, 86,* 68–75. http://doi.org/10.1016/j.aap.2015.10.010

CASE STUDY #2

Rolling Out Its 4G Network, Sprint Corporation Competes with Rivals

Sprint, AT&T, Verizon, and T-Mobile play leapfrog as they upgrade their networks with new technologies that offer faster speeds, more bandwidth, and better coverage for mobile smartphones. However, Sprint has lagged behind both Verizon and AT&T and faces strong headwinds in this market.

Sprint initially invested heavily in a technology called WiMax, pinning its strategy to an early-to-market advantage with the nation's first 4G offering. However, WiMax is slower than 4G services based on a different technology called LTE (long-term evolution), used by Verizon and others. Sprint is phasing out its WiMax networks, but its LTE rollout lags behind its rivals'.

To attract customers, Sprint must provide incentives. The company offers significant discounts and will also pay for any switching fees a new customer might incur. Customers also want faster, reliable service and coverage in more geographic areas. For Sprint, that means installing the towers and transmission equipment that will send and receive the wireless signals in addition to converting to the LTE network.

Before installing 4G antennas, the company has to identify the sites that will provide the best coverage for the area. For cities with tall buildings, large bodies of water, many hills and valleys, and high foliage, those choices are engineering brainteasers. In New York City, for instance, the urban "canyons" create dead spots that cause coverage problems. Sprint Nextel needs thousands of sites to provide adequate service.

Once sites are identified, Sprint must navigate a labyrinth of government agencies, local building codes, citizens' groups, and landowners to obtain approvals. In San Francisco, multiple bureaucracies may be involved, depending on the tower's location. The company may need approval from the California Coastal Commission for sites near the ocean or from the California Department of Transportation. Municipalities may also compete with one another for towers because they are a source of revenue, or they might insist they be constructed on city-owned property.

Some community and homeowner associations may also protest tower construction. Although Californians want 4G, they may value neighborhood aesthetics even more. The Not in My Back Yard (NIMBY) mentality further delays rollouts. Carriers deal with this human element by hiding their towers in church steeples or masking their appearance in other ways. Some are built to resemble trees (Figure 3-30). Sprint is widely known for its "green" environmental initiatives, and the tree-shaped towers support those corporate goals.

Some communities welcome the towers because of the revenue they will earn. For example, a struggling school district in California began negotiating with cell-phone companies to see which one would offer the best deal. Some citizens objected because of possible health risks from radiation, but researchers point out that radiation from the handsets is a much larger risk factor. In fact, handset radiation drops as the number of towers increases because less power is needed to connect.

Despite all these hurdles, Sprint is making progress and continues to expand coverage. The portion of the wireless spectrum that Sprint controls requires more cell sites because the signals don't cover as much territory, but it also offers greater data capacity—something that customers who use a lot of data will appreciate. Step by step, Sprint is jumping through all the hoops to regain lost customers and compete with rivals.

FIGURE 3-30
A cell tower disguised as a pine tree.

Source: Christina Richards/Shutterstock.

Discussion Questions

3-27. What is the relationship between physical infrastructure and services as described in this case study?

3-28. What is the relationship between regulatory considerations and wireless services?

3-29. In the placement of infrastructure, how do the interests of an individual as a customer conflict with the interests of the same individual as a homeowner?

3-30. What other considerations must Sprint consider as it puts its infrastructure in place?

Sources: Carducci, A. (January 25, 2012). Cell-phone towers on California schools to enhance district's bottom line. *Heartland News*, http://news.heartland.org/newspaper-article/2012/01/25/cell-phone-towers-california-schools-enhance-districts-bottom-line, accessed March 29, 2013.

Gruley, B., Moritz, S., & Alpeyev, P. (2016). The eternal sadness of Sprint. Bloomberg *Business Week*, (4461), 50–53.

Segan, S. (2015). Fastest mobile networks 2015. *PCMAG*, http://www.pcmag.com/article2/0,2817,2485838,00.asp, accessed February 22, 2016.

Sprint beats rivals on green initiatives. (March 8, 2013). *Environmental Leader*, http://www.environmentalleader.com/2013/03/08/sprint-beats-competitors-on-green-initiatives/, accessed June 1, 2016.

E-PROJECT 1   Voluntary Distributed Computing

Sharing Some of Your Computer Time for a Worthy Goal

The voluntary distributed computing architecture model relies on the participation of millions of people who offer some spare computer time in exchange for an interesting screen saver and, of course, the good feeling that comes with contributing to a worthy goal. The University of California at Berkeley hosts BOINC, which lists projects that need volunteers (http://boinc.berkeley.edu).

3-31. Visit several BOINC project sites and examine the ways in which the project leaders are engaging volunteers and sustaining commitment. What strategies are they using, and how well do they appear to be working?

3-32. Trust is a significant element for voluntary distributed computing, especially because users are warned about the dangers of downloading executable programs to their computers from unknown sources. Pick two BOINC projects, compare their privacy policies, and look for other ways in which they attempt to convince potential participants that their computer will not be harmed and their privacy will not be violated. How do the two projects compare?

E-PROJECT 2   Using Excel to Analyze Cost Effectiveness for 4G Rollouts

For this e-project, you will analyze data on U.S. municipalities to estimate approximately how many cell-phone towers the city will need and how many people will be able to access each tower. This kind of information helps the carriers decide which markets are most cost effective.

Download the Excel file called *Ch03_Cities* and answer the following questions.

3-33. Sort the cities by land area in square miles, largest to smallest. Which city has the largest land area? Which has the smallest?

3-34. Insert a column after Land Area in Square Miles and label it "Cell Towers Needed." For the first city in that column, enter the formula to divide the Land Area in Square Miles by 10, assuming that one tower will serve about 10 square miles. Copy the formula down to the remaining cities. About how many cell towers will Baltimore require?

3-35. Insert another column to the right of Cell Towers Needed, labeled "Estimated Cost." Enter the formula for the first city as "Cell Towers Needed" * 150000. Format the cell to currency with no decimals, and copy it down the whole column. About how much will it cost to build out the cell tower infrastructure in Chicago?

3-36. Insert one more column to the right of Population, labeled "Cost Per Customer." Insert the formula Estimated Cost/Population for the first city, and then copy the formula down the column. What is the estimated cost per customer for Houston?

3-37. Sort the table on Cost Per Customer from smallest to largest.
   a. Which city would have the lowest cost per customer, and what is the cost?
   b. Which city has the highest cost per customer?
   c. If you live in the United States and your city is listed, which one is it, and what is the estimated cost per customer? If your city is not listed, please select the closest city that is listed.
   d. What is the main factor that accounts for the dramatic differences in cost per customer?

CHAPTER NOTES

1. Begany, G. M., Sa, N., & Yuan, X. (2016). Factors affecting user perception of a spoken language vs. textual search interface: A content analysis. *Interacting with Computers*, 28(2), 170–180. http://doi.org/10.1093/iwc/iwv029

2. Smith, E. J., & Kollars, N. A. (2015). QR panopticism: User behavior triangulation and barcode-scanning applications. *Information Security Journal: A Global Perspective*, 24(4–6), 157–163. http://doi.org/10.1080/19393555.2015.1085113

3. Mullin, J. (October 16, 2015). Appeals court rules that Google book scanning is fair use. *Ars Technica*, from http://arstechnica.com/tech-policy/2015/10/appeals-court-rules-that-google-book-scanning-is-fair-use/, accessed February 18, 2016.

4. Oropesa, I., de Jong, T. L., Sánchez-González, P., Dankelman, J., & Gómez, E. J. (2016). Feasibility of tracking laparoscopic instruments in a box trainer using a Leap Motion Controller. *Measurement*, 80, 115–124. http://doi.org/10.1016/j.measurement.2015.11.018

5. Rao, G. H. (2016). The IoT, data, and great expectations. *CIO Insight*, http://www.cioinsight.com/it-management/expert-voices/the-iot-data-and-the-principle-of-great-expectations.html, accessed February 18. 2016.

6. Greengard, S. (2016). Better memory. *Communications of the ACM*, 59(1), 23–25. http://doi.org/10.1145/2843555

7. Biscotti, F., Pezzini, M., Rayner, N., Unsworth, J., Edjlali, R., Tan, S., Rasit, E., Norwood, A., Butler, A., & Schulte, W. R. (2015). *Predicts 2016: In-memory computing-enabled hybrid transaction/analytical processing supports dramatic digital business innovation* (No. G00293471). Gartner Research, http://www.gartner.com/document/3179439?ref=TypeAheadSearch&qid=62a695e3c7fc3a269865b8402290469d, accessed February 15, 2016.

8. Martin, E. R. (March 27, 2014). EMCVoice: The ethics of big data. *Forbes*, http://www.forbes.com/sites/emc/2014/03/27/the-ethics-of-big-data/, accessed February 18, 2016.

9. Martin, K. (2016). Data aggregators, consumer data, and responsibility online: Who is tracking consumers online and should they stop? *The Information Society*, 32(1), 51–63. http://doi.org/10.1080/01972243.2015.1107166

10. Lannon, P. G., & Schreiber, P. M. (2016). BYOD policies: Striking the right balance. *HR Magazine*, 61(1), 71–72.

11. Driver, M., Duggan, J., Herschmann, J., & West, M. (2015). *IT market clock for programming languages, 2015* (No. G00291012). Gartner Research.

12. Chandrasekaran, A., & Lerner, A. (2015). *Should I use open source in my infrastructure?* (No. G00271630). Gartner Research.

13. Gittlen, S. (February 16, 2016). Open source: Career-maker, or wipeout? *CIO Magazine*, http://www.cio.com/article/3033283/open-source-tools/open-source-career-maker-or-wipeout.html, accessed February 19, 2016.

14. Bellalta, B., Bononi, L., Bruno, R., & Kassler, A. (2016). Next generation IEEE 802.11 Wireless local area networks: Current status, future directions, and open challenges. *Computer Communications*, 75, 1–25. http://doi.org/10.1016/j.comcom.2015.10.007

15. Jones, N. (2016). *Top 10 IoT technologies for 2017 and 2018* (No. G00296351). Gartner Research.

16. Mexico to raise $2.5 billion in spectrum auction—regulator. (February 19, 2016). *Reuters*, http://www.reuters.com/article/mexico-telecoms-auction-idUSL2N15Y06T, accessed August 9, 2016.

17. Ford, N. (2015). Taking bandwidth the last mile. *African Business*, (424), 32–33.

18. Lafayette, J. (2016). Cord-cutting concerns dominate Q4 earnings. *Broadcasting & Cable*, 146(5), 19.

19. Tchana, A., De Palma, N., Safieddine, I., & Hagimont, D. (2016). Software consolidation as an efficient energy and cost saving solution. *Future Generation Computer Systems*, 58, 1–12. http://doi.org/10.1016/j.future.2015.11.027

20. Bhalla, V., & Kowall, J. (March 21, 2013). How to determine readiness for voice, video and unified communications. *Gartner Research* (No. G00247761).

21. Smith, D. M. (2016). *Cloud computing primer for 2016* (No. G00302704). Gartner Research, http://www.gartner.com/document/3287123?ref=solrAll&refval=168595867&qid=bfd65b5b1c398453e54d0771adfcac2a, accessed February 12, 2016.

22. Leong, L. (2016). *How to choose a managed service provider for a hyperscale cloud provider* (No. G00296007). Gartner Research.

23. Vincent, P., Natis, Y. V., & Thomas A. (2015). *Understanding PaaS technologies and architecture to aid cloud strategy* (No. G00292947). Gartner Research.

24. Butler, B. (September 21, 2015). 3 big takeaways from Amazon's latest cloud outage. *Network World*, http://www.networkworld.com/article/2985128/cloud-computing/3-big-takeaways-from-amazon-s-latest-cloud-outage.html, accessed February 21, 2016.

CHAPTER

4

Databases and *Data Warehouses*

LEARNING OBJECTIVES

1 Explain the nature of information resources in terms of structure and quality, and show how metadata can be used to describe these resources.

2 Compare file processing systems to the database, explaining the database's advantages.

3 Describe how a relational database is planned, accessed, and managed and how the normalization process works.

4 Explain why multiple databases emerge and how master data management helps address the challenge of integration.

5 Describe how a data warehouse is created, and explain the challenges and value of big data.

6 Explain how the human element and ownership issues affect information management.

An online, interactive decision-making simulation that reinforces chapter contents and uses key terms in context can be found in MyMISLab™.

INTRODUCTION

EVERY ORGANIZATION IS AWASH WITH INFORMATION RESOURCES OF ALL KINDS, but it takes considerable effort to bring together the people, technology, and processes needed to manage those resources effectively. This chapter explores the structure and quality of information and how people organize, store, manipulate, and retrieve it.

In the online simulation called "Volunteer Now!" you will help a group of college students who have been trying to match people who want to volunteer their time to organizations that need their skills, such as homeless shelters,

hospitals, and animal rescue services. They have been keeping track of all their data using three-ring binders and sticky notes, but mistakes are common. One volunteer who signed up to work in a soup kitchen was given the wrong address and wound up wandering around lost in a deserted warehouse. What Volunteer Now! needs is a database that fits its mission, one that the staff and volunteers can access from their laptops and smartphones at any time of day. You will learn a lot about databases as you help them design it.

MyMISLab
Online Simulation

VOLUNTEER NOW!
A Role-Playing Simulation on Designing the Database
for a Volunteer-Matching Service

mangostock/Shutterstock.

nformation resources are central to any organization's success. And these resources are growing at an astounding rate. Data stored in digital format are multiplying everywhere on a vast array of physical media, ranging from the organization's own computers to hosts that might be located anywhere on the planet. Data also reside on DVDs, CD-ROMs, and tapes and inside people's digital cameras, cell phones, iPods, and flash drives on a keychain. On your own workspace, for instance, objects that *don't* store or display

information of some kind are scarce—perhaps the coffee cup or stapler (Figure 4-1).

People understand that some information is powerful and valuable, but far more is useless junk that should be tossed. We need a strategy to manage information resources so that what is important is secure, organized, and easily accessible to managers, employees, customers, suppliers, and other stakeholders. This enormous challenge is the subject of this chapter.

FIGURE 4-1
The modern workspace:
An information storehouse.

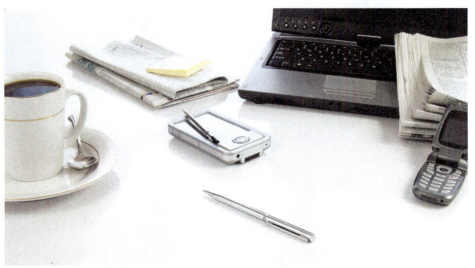

Source: Kathy Burns-Millyard/Shutterstock.

Explain the nature of information resources in terms of structure and quality, and show how metadata can be used to describe these resources.

1 The Nature of Information Resources
Structured, Unstructured, and Semi-Structured Information

Every organization relies on **structured information**, the kind that is usually considered to be facts and data (Figure 4-2). It is reasonably ordered, in that it can be broken down into component parts and organized into hierarchies. Your credit card company, for example, maintains your customer record in a structured format. It contains your last name, first name, street address, phone number, email address, and other data. It would also maintain your purchases, each with a transaction date, description, debit or credit amount, and reference numbers.

Straightforward relationships among the data elements are also relatively easy to identify. A customer's order would be related to the customer record, and the items purchased as part of the order would be related to the order itself. This kind of information is the heart of an organization's operational information systems, with electronically stored customer records, orders, invoices, transactions, employee records, shipping tables, and similar kinds of information. It is the kind that databases are designed to store and retrieve.

In contrast, **unstructured information** has no inherent structure or order, and the parts can't be easily linked together, except perhaps by stuffing them in a manila folder or box. It is more difficult to break down, categorize, organize, and query. Consider a company involved in a touchy lawsuit. Relevant information might include letters, emails, Twitter feeds, sticky notes, text messages, meeting minutes, phone calls, videos, Facebook posts, resumes, or photos.

Drawing information out of unstructured collections also presents challenges. A catering business might have a back room stacked with boxes containing unstructured information on hundreds of contracts. If the owner wants to know which contracts went over budget and then see who handled those, every box would have to be opened. Because unstructured collections

FIGURE 4-2
Types of information resources.

Type of Information Resource	Example
Structured information	A sales transaction with clearly defined fields for date, customer number, item number, and amount
Unstructured information	Manila folder containing assorted items about a lawsuit, such as photos, handwritten notes, newspaper articles, or affidavits
Semi-structured information	A web page with a title, subtitle, content, and a few images

have no means to enforce rules about what types of information must be included, the owner may find little to go on.

A vast gray area exists between the extremes of structured and unstructured information; this is the area within which **semi-structured information** falls. This type includes information that shows at least some structure, such as web pages that have dates, titles, and authors. Spreadsheets can also be semi-structured, especially when they are created by different people to keep track of the same kind of information. One salesperson, for instance, might put a contact's work phone and mobile phone in different columns labeled "Work Phone" and "Mobile," but another might keep them in the same column under the heading "Phones." Resources like these don't have the strong structure, enforced by advance planning, to clearly define entities and their relationships, and they lack controls about completeness and formatting. Nevertheless, such data are easier to query and combine than the unstructured variety.

Metadata

Metadata is data about data, and it clarifies the nature of the information. For structured information, metadata describes the definitions of each of the fields, tables, and their relationships. For semi-structured and unstructured information, metadata is used to describe properties of a document or other resource and is especially useful because it layers some structure on information that is less easily categorized and classified. YouTube's database, for example, contains metadata about each of its videos that can be searched and sorted. A library's card catalog provides metadata about the books, such as where they are physically shelved.

The photo-sharing website Flickr relies on metadata to search its enormous photo collection. A father's beach scene photos, with filenames such as "image011.jpg," become more accessible, meaningful, and sharable for friends and family when metadata are added to their properties, such as location, subject, date taken, and photographer (Figure 4-3).

> **PRODUCTIVITY TIP**
> Adding metadata to the properties of your documents, photos, and videos makes them easier to search and locate later. Right-clicking on the filename usually brings up a menu that includes Properties. You can also remove information from a file's properties so others will not see it.

The Quality of Information

Not all information has high quality, as anyone who surfs the net knows. Here are the most important characteristics that affect quality:

- *Accuracy.* Mistakes in birth dates, spelling, or price reduce the quality of the information.
- *Precision.* Rounding to the nearest mile might not reduce quality much when you estimate the drive to the mall. However, for property surveys, "about 2 miles" is unacceptable.
- *Completeness.* Omitting the zip code on the customer's address record might not be a problem because the zip can be determined by the address. But leaving off the house number would delay the order.
- *Consistency.* Reports that show "total sales by region" may conflict because the people generating the reports are using slightly different definitions. When results are inconsistent, the quality of both reports is in question.
- *Timeliness.* Outdated information has less value than up-to-date information and thus is lower quality unless you are looking for historical trends. The actual definition for what is up-to-date varies. In stock trading, timeliness is measured in fractions of a second.

structured information
Facts and data that are reasonably ordered or that can be broken down into component parts and organized into hierarchies.

unstructured information
Information that has no inherent structure or order and the parts can't be easily linked together.

semi-structured information
Information category that falls between structured and unstructured information. It includes facts and data that show at least some structure, such as web pages and documents, which bear creation dates, titles, and authors.

metadata
Data about data that clarifies the nature of the information.

FIGURE 4-3
Metadata for a beach scene photo.

Photo Metadata	Description
Photo title	Ocean beach scene
Date taken	12/15/2011
License type	Royalty free
Photographer	Felipe DiMarco
Key words	Ocean, waves, outdoors, sunshine, beach, vacation, swimming, swimmers, fishing, surf

Source: Rigucci/Shutterstock.

- *Bias.* Biased information lacks objectivity, and that reduces its value and quality. To make sales seem higher, a manager might choose to include canceled orders, though the CEO might not be pleased.
- *Duplication.* Information can be redundant, resulting in misleading and exaggerated summaries. In customer records, people can easily appear more than once if their address changes.

The data collected by online surveys illustrates many of the problems surrounding information quality.[1] The sample of people who actually respond is biased, and people may race through the questions or turn in more than one survey. Virtual Surveys Ltd., a company that specializes in web-based research, discovered that one person completed an online survey 750 times because a raffle ticket was offered as an incentive.[2] To avoid relying on poor quality data like that, managers must define what constitutes quality for the information they need.

Compare file processing systems to the database, explaining the database's advantages.

2 Managing Information: From Filing Cabinets to the Database

Human ingenuity was applied to the challenges of information management long before the digital age. Before Edwin Siebels invented the lateral filing cabinet in 1898, businesses often organized documents by putting them in envelopes, in rows of small pigeonholes that lined entire walls from top to bottom. The change to vertical manila folders, neatly arranged in cabinet drawers, was quite an improvement for record keeping and much appreciated by file clerks (Figure 4-4). The real revolution, however, occurred in the 1960s when computers entered the picture. These relied on an organizing strategy built around the concept of the record.

FIGURE 4-4

Early information management approaches.

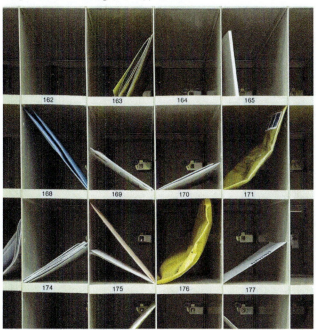 

Source: Edwin Verin/Shutterstock and deepspacedave/Shutterstock.

Tables, Records, and Fields

A **table** is a group of records for the same entity, such as employees, products, books, videos, or some other "thing" that has meaning to people (Figure 4-5). The **record** is a row in the table, and it represents an instance of the entity—a single person, for instance. The record is made up of attributes of that thing, and each of the attributes is called a **field**. The fields are the columns in the table. Fields typically contain numeric data, text, or a combination of the two. Each field should have a **data definition** that specifies the field's properties, such as the type of data it will hold (e.g., alphabetic, alphanumeric, or numeric) and the maximum number of characters it can contain. It also includes rules that might restrict what goes into the field or make the field required.

PetID	Description	Name	Gender	Breed	Birthday
201447	Dog	Champion	M	Mixed	12/1/2014
201448	Dog	Keiko	F	Beagle	5/25/2016
201449	Cat	Sunny	F	Persian	4/15/2015
201450	Cat	Mister	M	Siamese	6/14/2016

FIGURE 4-5

A table for the entity "pets" for a veterinarian's office, showing records (rows) and fields (columns).

table
A group of records for the same entity, such as employees. Each row is one record, and the fields of each record are arranged in the table's columns.

record
A means to represent an entity, which might be a person, a product, a purchase order, an event, a building, a vendor, a book, a video, or some other "thing" that has meaning to people. The record is made up of attributes of that thing.

field
An attribute of an entity. A field can contain numeric data or text, or a combination of the two.

data definition
Specifies the characteristics of a field, such as the type of data it will hold or the maximum number of characters it can contain.

FIGURE 4-6
Data definition for the field "birthdate" in MS Access.

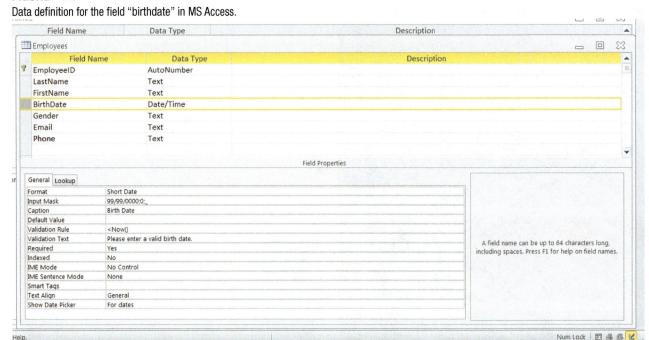

Source: Microsoft® Access, Microsoft Corporation. Reprinted with permission.

Consider, for example, a table that will hold employee records, created using MS Access. The field names might include employee ID, last name, first name, birth date, gender, email, and phone, and the data type appears next to each field name. The properties for BirthDate appear in the bottom half of Figure 4-6. The designer decided to make the field required, make sure users enter it as MM/DD/YYYY, and also only allow dates that are less than today's date.

The Rise and Fall of File Processing Systems

Initially, electronic records were created and stored as computer files, and programmers wrote computer programs to add, delete, or edit the records. Each department maintained its own records with its own computer files, each containing information that was required for operations. For example, the payroll office maintained personnel records and had its own computer programs to maintain and manage its set of files. At the end of the month when it was time to generate payroll checks, the payroll system's computer programs would read each record in the file and print out checks and payroll stubs for each person, using the information contained in the files for that department. That kind of activity is called **batch processing**. The program is sequentially conducting operations on each record in a large batch.

Accounts payable and receivable, personnel, payroll, and inventory were the first beneficiaries of the digital age. Compared to the manual method of generating a payroll, in which deductions and taxes were computed by hand and each check was individually typed, the monthly batch processing of computer-generated checks was revolutionary. However, it didn't take long for problems to surface as other offices began to develop their own file processing systems. Understanding what went wrong is crucial to grasp why the database offers so many benefits.

DATA REDUNDANCY AND INCONSISTENCY

Because each set of computer programs operated on its own records, much information was redundant and inconsistent (Figure 4-7). The payroll office record might list your name as ANNAMARIE, but the personnel office that handles benefits shows you as ANNMARIE. Further, the extra workload involved in resolving redundant records was not trivial and often never got done.

FIGURE 4-7
Data redundancy problems. Separate file processing systems often contain redundant and inconsistent data.

LACK OF DATA INTEGRATION

Integrating data from the separate systems was a struggle (Figure 4-8). For example, the payroll system might maintain information about name, address, and pay history, but gender and ethnicity are in personnel records. If a manager wanted to compare pay rates by ethnicity, new programs were written to match up the records. This clumsy integration affects customers, as well, who fume when they can't resolve inconsistencies in their accounts (Figure 4-9).

INCONSISTENT DATA DEFINITIONS

When programmers write code to handle files, differences in format creep in. Phone numbers may include the dashes and be formatted as a text field in one system but be treated as numbers in another. A more subtle problem involves the way people actually choose to use the system. Data definitions may seem similar across systems, but they are used differently, and summaries become misleading. For example, employees in the personnel department at a retail chain categorize software purchases as "computers." Their coworkers in sales prefer to lump software with pencils, staplers, and clocks as "supplies" because less paperwork is needed to justify the purchase. The CEO lamented that there was no way anyone could possibly know how much this chain was spending on technology because of inconsistent coding (Figure 4-10).

DATA DEPENDENCE

These early systems became maintenance nightmares because the programs and their files were so interconnected and dependent on one another. The programs all defined the fields and their formats, and business rules were all hard-coded or embedded in the programs. Even a minor change to accommodate a new business strategy took a lot of work. IT staff were constantly busy but kept falling behind anyway.

The disadvantages to the file processing approach led to a better way of organizing structured data, one that relies on the database.

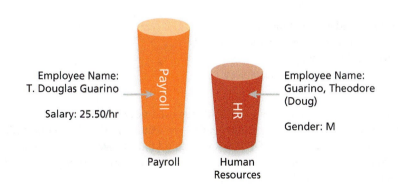

FIGURE 4-8
Information in separate file processing systems is difficult to integrate. For example, a report listing hourly rates by gender would need extra programming effort in this business.

batch processing
The process of sequentially executing operations on each record in a large batch.

FIGURE 4-9
Separate file processing systems lead to a fragmented customer interface, frustrating customers who have to contact several offices to straighten out inconsistencies.

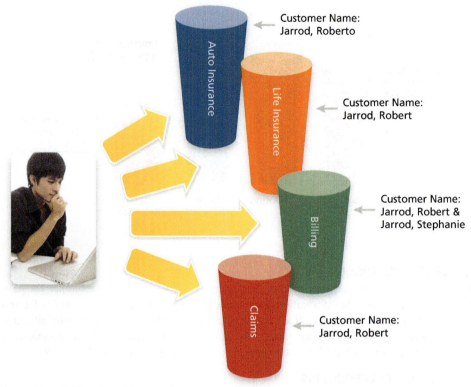

Source: Photo: William Casey/Shutterstock.

FIGURE 4-10
When data definitions are inconsistent, the meaning of different fields will vary across departments and summaries will be misleading. Note how the three departments use categories in different ways.

Department	Object Code	Amount	Category	Description
Sales	4211	1888.25	Computers	Desktop Computers
Sales	4300	249.95	Computer supplies	Image editing software
Sales	4100	29.99	Office supplies	Flash drive
Personnel	4211	59.00	Computers	Stastical software
Personnel	4300	14.95	Computer supplies	Flash drive
Personnel	4211	2500.21	Computers	Laptop Computers
Warehouse	4211	59500.00	Computers	Web server
Warehouse	4211	2500.00	Computers	Printer/copier/scanner/fax

Databases and Database Management Systems

The foundation of today's information management relies on the database and the software that manages it. The **database** is an integrated collection of information that is logically related and stored in such a way as to minimize duplication and facilitate rapid retrieval. Its major advantages over file processing systems include:

- Reduced redundancy and inconsistency
- Improved information integrity and accuracy
- Improved ability to adapt to changes
- Improved performance and scalability
- Increased security

A database management system (DBMS) is used to create and manage the database. This software provides tools for ensuring security, replication, retrieval, and other administrative and housekeeping tasks. The DBMS serves as a kind of gateway to the database itself and as a manager for handling creation, performance tuning, transaction processing, general maintenance, access rights, deletion, and backups.

DATABASE ARCHITECTURE

To be most useful, a database must handle three types of relationships with a minimum of redundancy (Figure 4-11):

- One-to-one
- One-to-many
- Many-to-many

The *one-to-one relationship* is relatively easy to accommodate, and even file processing systems can handle it. For instance, each person has one and only one birth date. The *one-to-many relationship* between records is somewhat more challenging. A person might have one or more dependents, for example, or one or more employees reporting to him or her. The *many-to-many relationship* is also more complicated to support. This might involve a situation in which a person might be working on any number of projects, each of which can have any number of employees assigned to it.

Earlier database architectures offered different strategies to organize and link records (Figure 4-12). For example, one intuitive way to organize information is to follow the organizational chart, and the hierarchical database did just that (Figure 4-13). This approach worked well for one-to-many relationships but stumbled when many-to-many links complicated the chart, such as when a person worked for two bosses. The network database (Figure 4-14) had more flexibility to link entities that didn't fall along a neat hierarchy and could handle many-to-many relationships. But another inventive approach—the relational model—soon won out.

THE RELATIONAL DATABASE

E. F. Codd, a British mathematician working at IBM, invented the relational database, which organizes information into tables of records that are related to one another by linking a field

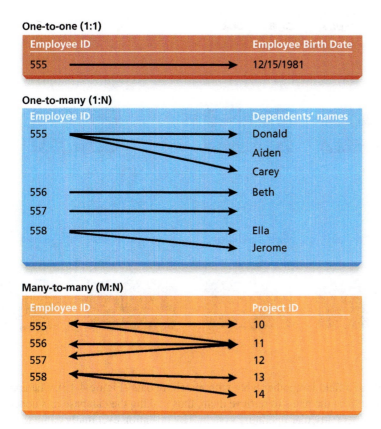

One-to-one (1:1)

Employee ID	Employee Birth Date
555 ⟶	12/15/1981

One-to-many (1:N)

Employee ID	Dependents' names
555	Donald
	Aiden
	Carey
556	Beth
557	
558	Ella
	Jerome

Many-to-many (M:N)

Employee ID	Project ID
555	10
556	11
557	12
558	13
	14

FIGURE 4-11

Relationship types.

---

database
An integrated collection of information that is logically related and stored in such a way as to minimize duplication and facilitate rapid retrieval.

database management system (DBMS)
Software used to create and manage a database; it also provides tools for ensuring security, replication, retrieval, and other administrative and housekeeping tasks.

relational database
The widely used database model that organizes information into tables of records that are related to one another by linking a field in one table to a field in another table with matching data.

FIGURE 4-12

Types of database architectures.

Early Database Architectures	
Hierarchical	Resembles an organizational chart or an upside down tree (Figure 4-13).
Network	Resembles a lattice or web rather than the upside down tree. Records can be linked in multiple ways, supporting many-to-many relationships (Figure 4-14).
Modern Database Architectures	
Relational	Maintains records in rows within tables, and links between the tables are created by linking a field in one table to a field in another table with matching data (Figure 4-15). The relational database is the most widely used.
Object-oriented	Represents information in the form of objects, and uses object-oriented programming languages to access them; used especially for organizing complex data types such as graphics and multimedia.
XML	Organizes data using XML tags; used especially for managing web content and web-based resources.

FIGURE 4-13

Hierarchical database.

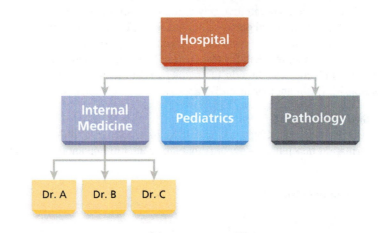

FIGURE 4-14

Network database.

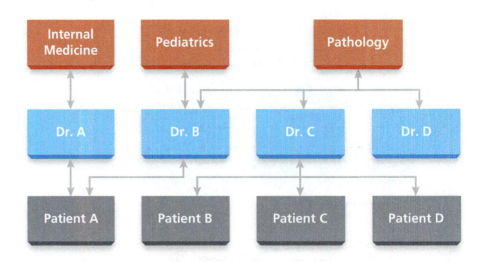

in one table to a field in another table with matching data (Figure 4-15). The approach separates the data from the paths to retrieve them, thus making the database less dependent on the hardware and its particular operating system. His invention eventually came to dominate the field, though it was not well received in the beginning, especially by his bosses at IBM. That company had much invested in selling and supporting its older hierarchical database and the mainframe computers it ran on, and IBM executives were quite critical of Codd's approach. Nevertheless, the relational database survived and flourished and is now a standard in most organizations.[3]

Students

StudentID	LastName	FirstName	BirthDate
54001	Chong	Kevin	12/01/1987
65222	Danelli	Douglas	01/05/1986
54555	Burton	Stephanie	11/12/1978
25553	Washington	Nikia	10/02/1981
96887	Perez	Louis	07/25/1982

Registrations

RegistrationNumber	StudentID	ClassCode	Grade
10011	54001	20083BMGT300A	A
10012	54001	20083HIST450B	C
10013	54001	20083ECON200F	B
10014	54555	20083ECON200F	A
10015	96887	20083HIST410B	I

FIGURE 4-15
Relational database.

To see how the relational database works, consider the tables about students in Figure 4-15. The first table shows the student ID, last name, first name, and birth date. The second table shows student registrations with fields that display registration number, student ID, class code, and grade. Because student ID is in both tables, they can be linked together.

If you have Microsoft Access on your personal computer, you have an offspring of Codd's ingenious approach. Other common relational DBMSs include Microsoft SQL Server, Oracle, and MySQL. These relational databases continue to improve, adding support for large files containing images, video, or audio. Relational systems now also support XML data types as well as spatial information and mapping coordinates.

Developing and Managing a Relational Database

 Describe how a relational database is planned, accessed, and managed and how the normalization process works.

The database is the central information repository, a mission-critical asset of any enterprise. To see how a database is designed and created, we will help Devon Degosta and her colleagues build the database to support DD-Designs, a small business that offers web design services.

Planning the Data Model

The first step is to sit down with Devon and her team to develop the **data model**, identifying what kind of information they want to track and how it is related. The process starts by defining all the entities that will be included, their attributes, and their relationships. A challenging process even for a small business, this model-building step is critical because the database will be the backbone of the company. Also, time spent planning reaps benefits in time saved making changes later.

ENTITIES AND ATTRIBUTES

What entities should be represented for this small business? Employees, clients, projects, invoices, events, and transactions are all candidates, and many more may come to mind as we work with Devon and her team to understand the business and its strategies. Each of the entities in the model will become a table, named with a noun that describes the data contained in the entity. It will have attributes, or fields, that describe the entity. "Employees," for example,

data model
A model used for planning the organization's database that identifies what kind of information is needed, what entities will be created, and how they are related to one another.

is a relatively straightforward entity with attributes such as employee ID number, last name, first name, birth date, email address, and phone number. The "Clients" entity might include attributes such as company name, client ID number, contact person, company phone number, and company address. A single instance of each entity will be a record. Terms such as "rows" and "columns" are also used to describe the components of a table, but records and fields are widely understood.

> **PRODUCTIVITY TIP**
> When you give names to tables and fields, use a consistent naming convention to make it easier for you to remember the names and for others to understand their meaning. One common convention is "CamelCase," which combines capital and lowercase letters to clarify compound words, such as LastName or SalesRegion. The camel's humps are the capital letters in the string. Another convention separates words with an underscore.

PRIMARY KEYS AND UNIQUENESS

Each record in a table must have one **primary key**, which is a field, or a group of fields, that makes the record unique in that table. Devon suggests using each person's last name as the primary key because that is unique. But as the organization grows, there might be two people with the same last name. Devon nods, thinking she might invite her brother to join the company. Some organizations have used Social Security numbers (SSN) to uniquely identify employees, but that has serious drawbacks as well. Non-U.S. citizens might not have one, and that number is confidential and should not be released.

Database developers avoid meaningful information for primary keys, such as an SSN or name. If the key is mistyped or changes, fixing it throughout the database is a complicated affair. Many systems instead simply use **autonumbering** to assign primary keys, in which the DBMS assigns incremental numbers to records as they are created. This approach ensures that each record has a unique primary key and that no one accidentally gives the same ID number to two different people (Figure 4-16). Because the autonumber has no other meaning, there would be no reason to ever change it.

NORMALIZING THE DATA MODEL

Next, we work with Devon to further refine the entities and their relationships. This multistep process is called **normalization**, and it minimizes duplication of information in the tables—a condition that can cause many kinds of problems that diminish the database's integrity.

In the Employees table, for example, one goal of normalization is to make each attribute **functionally dependent** on the employee ID number, which uniquely identifies each employee. Functional dependence means that for each value of employee ID, there is exactly

FIGURE 4-16

Primary and foreign keys in the Employees and Departments tables.

Employees

Primary Key →

EmployeeID	LastName	FirstName	BirthDate	DepartmentID
1011	Jackson	Thomas	12/01/1981	200
1012	Zuniga	Raul	01/05/1983	300
1013	Delany	Nora	11/12/1968	300
1014	Degosta	Dana	10/02/1975	400
1015	Park	John	07/25/1985	200

← Foreign Key

Departments

Primary Key →

DepartmentID	DepartmentName	DepartmentPhone
200	Marketing	251-3621
300	Human Resources	251-1102
400	Finance	209-6656
500	Sales	512-5555
600	Facilities	207-8787

one value for each of the attributes included in the record, and that the employee ID determines that value. For DD-Designs, Devon agrees that there will be just one employee email address, one birth date, one last name, one first name, and one department. In another business, such as theater, that might not work. Actors often work under several stage names.

Devon also wants to add the departmental phone number, and we first consider adding it as a field to the Employees table. On second thought, however, DepartmentPhone is not functionally dependent on employee ID but on the department. If we put it in the Employees table, it might not be too cumbersome with few employees. With hundreds, however, we would create considerable redundancy. Instead, we will normalize by crossing DepartmentPhone out of the Employees table and adding a field to Employees called DepartmentID. Then we create a new table called Departments, with DepartmentID as the primary key. DepartmentPhone is functionally dependent on DepartmentID, along with attributes such as department name, department office number, and department office building (Figure 4-17).

FIGURE 4-17

Normalizing the Employees table by removing Department Phone (A) and placing this field in the newly created Departments table (B).

Employees

EmployeeID	LastName	FirstName	BirthDate	DepartmentPhone
1011	Jackson	Thomas	12/01/1981	251-3621
1012	Zuniga	Raul	01/05/1983	251-1102
1013	Delany	Nora	11/12/1968	251-1102
1014	Degosta	Devon	10/02/1975	209-6656
1015	Park	John	07/25/1985	251-3621

A

Employees

EmployeeID	LastName	FirstName	BirthDate	DepartmentID
1011	Jackson	Thomas	12/01/1981	200
1012	Zuniga	Raul	01/05/1983	300
1013	Delany	Nora	11/12/1968	300
1014	Degosta	Devon	10/02/1975	400
1015	Park	John	07/25/1985	200

B

Departments

DepartmentID	DepartmentName	DepartmentPhone
200	Marketing	251-3621
300	Human Resources	251-1102
400	Finance	209-6656
500	Sales	512-5555
600	Facilities	207-8787

primary key
A field, or a group of fields, that makes each record unique in a table.

autonumbering
Process that assigns incremental numbers to records as they are created to ensure that each record has a unique primary key.

normalization
A process that refines entities and their relationships to help minimize duplication of information in tables.

functionally dependent
For each value of the table's primary key, there should be just one value for each of the attributes in the record, and the primary key should determine that value; the attribute should be functionally dependent on the value of the primary key.

RELATIONSHIPS AND FOREIGN KEYS

The relational model's elegance really shines when the entities are connected to one another in meaningful ways, relying on **foreign keys**. Notice that the field "DepartmentID" is an attribute in the Employees table and a primary key in the Departments table (Figure 4-18). When a primary key appears as an attribute in a different table, as DepartmentID does, it is called a *foreign key*. It can be used to link the records in the two tables together. In DD-Designs so far, we have two tables, Employees and Departments, linked by DepartmentID, which is the primary key in Departments and the foreign key in Employees. This relationship allows us to enter information about employees and information about departments and then link the two together with a minimum of redundancy. It would be easy, for example, to find the list of employees who worked in a particular building, perhaps to make announcements about a broken water pipe.

HANDLING COMPLEX RELATIONSHIPS

Normalization uncovers many-to-many relationships as well. The relational model can't handle these directly but uses a kind of "bridging" table to make the links. For instance, Devon considers project management to be crucial to the company's success, and she wants to track many details about the specific web design project in which each employee is currently involved. We might choose to create a Projects table to manage those attributes and then add ProjectID as a foreign key in the Employees table, similar to what we did for Departments. But we first ask whether Devon's team members might be involved in more than one project at a time, which would make it a one-to-many relationship. She nods enthusiastically, thinking that it is already happening. She plans to bring on a graphic artist who will probably spend time on all the projects. That comment also makes it clear that it is not just a one-to-many relationship of one employee to many projects. It is many-to-many. Each employee can be assigned to more than one project, and each project can have more than one employee assigned. And of course, the sales staff may have no projects, and some projects may not have any assigned employees (yet).

A messy approach would be to create two or more records for the employee, each of which lists a different project. However, this would lead to redundancy because the other

FIGURE 4-18

DepartmentID is the primary key for Departments, but appears as a foreign key in the Employees table so the two tables can be linked together.

Employees

EmployeeID	LastName	FirstName	BirthDate	DepartmentID
1011	Jackson	Thomas	12/01/1981	200
1012	Zuniga	Raul	01/05/1983	300
1013	Delany	Nora	11/12/1968	300
1014	Degosta	Devon	10/02/1975	400
1015	Park	John	07/25/1985	200

DepartmentID is a foreign key in Employees, and the primary key in Departments

Departments

DepartmentID	DepartmentName	DepartmentPhone
200	Marketing	251-3621
300	Human Resources	251-1102
400	Finance	209-6656
500	Sales	512-5555
600	Facilities	207-8787

attributes are all functionally dependent upon EmployeeID and would simply be repeated. When an entity is repeated in the table, updates and deletions are tricky. For example, should Raul's address change, the new address would need to be edited in all the duplicated records for his projects to remain consistent.

Another unfortunate solution, which is sadly rather common in sloppily designed databases, is to include several fields for projects in the record, such as Project1, Project2, Project3, and so on. This introduces other problems, especially in data retrieval. If we are trying to find all the people assigned to the Moon Landing Project, where would we look? It might appear as Project1 for some but in the Project2 or Project3 field for someone else. We would need rather complex queries to go through each of the fields, and we'd waste a lot of storage space with many empty fields.

A more efficient approach is to create a bridging table between Employees and Projects (Figure 4-19). Projects will use ProjectID as its primary key and will include attributes that Devon wants to track—ProjectName, ProjectStartDate, and ClientID. Then, to support the many-to-many relationship between employees and projects, we create a third table, EmployeesProjects, to contain the two attributes that link together employees with their projects: EmployeeID and ProjectID. This new table is very flexible. Thomas Jackson (EmployeeID 1011) is working on three projects, but Devon works on none. Also, a single project such as Recipes (ProjectID 11) can involve more than one employee. Gasoline (ProjectID 14) has no employees assigned. Adding the EmployeeProjectStartDate to EmployeesProject lets Devon track when each employee actually joined a particular project. DD-Designs will be prepared for rapid growth.

Accessing the Database and Retrieving Information

Most people access the database through an application interface with user-friendly web-based forms they can use to securely enter, edit, delete, and retrieve data. The web-based forms make it easy to let customers and suppliers access the database along with staff, with

FIGURE 4-19

Managing many-to-many relationships.

Employees

EmployeeID	LastName	FirstName	BirthDate	DepartmentID
1011	Jackson	Thomas	12/01/1981	200
1012	Zuniga	Raul	01/05/1983	300
1013	Delany	Nora	11/12/1968	300
1014	Degosta	Devon	10/02/1975	400
1015	Park	John	07/25/1985	200

EmployeesProjects

EmployeeID	ProjectID	EmployeeProjectStartDate
1011	10	11/01/2012
1011	11	02/01/2012
1012	12	02/16/2012
1013	11	01/12/2012
1011	13	07/30/2012

Projects

ProjectID	ProjectName	ClientID	ProjectStartDate
10	MoonLanding	251	11/01/2012
11	Recipes	108	01/12/2012
12	Library	212	02/16/2012
13	Dentist	78	07/05/2012
14	Gasoline	85	07/25/2012

foreign keys

Primary keys that appear as an attribute in a different table are a foreign key in that table. They can be used to link the records in two tables together.

appropriate security controls. The customer account records and product catalog on eBay, for instance, are drawn from the relational database, and buyers and sellers have access to certain tables and fields to update their accounts, add purchases, or upload their own product photos.

The application software can be created in many different development environments and programming languages, and DBMS software vendors include their own tools for creating applications. In MS Access, for example, form-generating and report-writing tools help you enter and retrieve the data. Oracle and others provide application development tools as well.

THE ETHICAL FACTOR — Ethical Issues in Database Design: The Case of Ethnic Identification

When a database includes ethnicity, should the designers create a one-to-one relationship with each person? Or should it be one-to-many? For decades, most databases constructed this as a one-to-one relationship with the individual, much like birth date or gender. In the Medicare system, for example, this variable can take one of six different values:

- White
- Black
- Asian or Pacific Islander
- North American Native
- Hispanic
- Other

Only one category can represent each individual in the Medicare files, but ethnicity is clearly not so easily categorized for many people with mixed heritage. Studies of Medicare coding, for example, show that people of Hispanic, Asian, and American Indian ancestry are often miscoded. When Medicare data are used to study ethnic differences in health outcomes, the results can be misleading and biased. The confusion can also affect conclusions about ethnic discrimination in the workplace, scholarship awards, or any other programs that consider ethnic subgroups.

Converting ethnicity to a one-to-many relationship may be feasible in some settings, but how might that affect decisions about program eligibility or conclusions about health care needs? Understanding the human consequences of database design choices takes considerable skill.[4]

As the front end or gateway, the application software performs a number of duties in addition to allowing users to enter, edit, or retrieve information. It may have modules for access control, determining which users can access which parts of the database, and what rights they have with respect to viewing or manipulating data. This interface may also help ensure the integrity of the database by enforcing rules about completeness, validity, or format. For example, it might require users to enter a valid zip code for the address and state.

Although the application software can be developed in any number of programming languages, the main way that they interact with a relational database is through a query language, and SQL is the most popular.

SQL: STRUCTURED QUERY LANGUAGE

Pronounced either as letters or as "sequel," **Structured Query Language (SQL)** is a standard query language, widely used to manipulate information in relational databases. Without much training, end users can create simple queries, such as this one:

```
SELECT LastName, FirstName, EmployeeID
FROM Employees
WHERE LastName = "Park"
```

More complex queries can insert and edit data or delete records. To link tables together, SQL relies on their primary and foreign keys. For example, to retrieve Devon's phone number, which is a field in the Departments table, you would join the Employees and Departments tables on DepartmentID—the primary key in Departments and foreign key in Employees.

OTHER ACCESS AND RETRIEVAL TOOLS

Although the web is a common platform for application software, other platforms are widely used as well. For example, **interactive voice response (IVR)** takes advantage of signals transmitted via the phone to access the database, retrieve account information, and enter data. Callers can make selections from nested menus by entering numbers. Many systems also recognize a limited number of spoken words. Though they can be frustrating for customers, these systems are often the only way to handle massive call volumes.

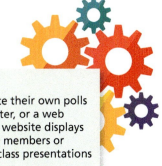

Avis installed an IVR system that "learns"; this helps reduce customer frustration. The system greets the caller by name (based on phone number), and rather than rattling off a long menu, it selects the most relevant options. For example, a customer whose car is expected back tomorrow might be asked, "Would you like to extend your rental time for the Ford SUV?" Avis's CIO insists that IVR is not just a cost-cutting measure. Done well, it can improve the customer's experience.[5]

PRODUCTIVITY TIP
Poll Everywhere (www.polleverywhere.com) helps users create their own polls online, and the audience can vote using a text message, Twitter, or a web browser. The responses are inserted into a database, and the website displays graphed results in real time. If the audience is made up of 40 members or fewer, the poll is free. You can use this service to make your class presentations more interactive.

Mobile phones also offer interfaces to databases, through IVR, text messages, special apps, or the smartphone's web browser. The ability to access a database anywhere, anytime, is a compelling advantage for everything from handling customer orders to voting for your favorite reality TV contestant.

NATURAL LANGUAGE INTERFACES

To many, the holy grail of query languages is the capability to understand and correctly reply to natural language queries, either spoken or typed. Although vendors have attempted to make end-user queries easier to do, the ability to correctly interpret a person's question is still limited, though many promising applications are under way.[6] Apple's Siri, for instance, can interpret a range of spoken questions and search its databases. "What is the best pizza parlor near here?" is something Siri could answer, partly because it knows your location through GPS and it can query Yelp's database of restaurant reviews (www.yelp.com). But it can't easily answer highly unstructured questions or questions that rely on databases Siri cannot access.

For business queries, the natural language query systems work well when the questions use a limited vocabulary. For example, "Which employees make more than $100,000 per year?" could be translated into SQL with reasonable accuracy. However, problems arise when the vocabulary is vague, the attribute names can be confused, or the question itself is not clear. Even the question about the high-earning employees could be interpreted more than one way. For example, did the user intend to include benefits and stock options? Should "employees" include part-time people? Natural language query systems are improving very rapidly, however, as Siri and IBM's Watson demonstrate.

Structured Query Language (SQL)
A standard query language, widely used to manipulate information in relational databases.

interactive voice response (IVR)
A technology that facilitates access to the database from signals transmitted by telephone to retrieve information and enter data.

FIGURE **4-20**
Job opening: Database
administrator (DBA).

> **Applicants Wanted: Database Administrator**
>
> The DBA is responsible for the efficient operation of the company's databases: monitoring and optimizing performance, troubleshooting bottlenecks, setting up new databases, enhancing security, planning capacity requirements, designing backup and disaster recovery plans, and working with department heads and the IT team to resolve problems and build innovative applications.

Managing and Maintaining the Database

The job of database administrator (DBA) is one of the fastest-growing careers in the United States (Figure 4-20). The analysts, architects, and developers who work with the DBA to link business needs and IT solutions also have very attractive job prospects. Figure 4-21 shows some examples.

The DBA must be very familiar with the DBMS software the organization uses. This software will offer many different administrative tools to help keep the databases running smoothly.

PERFORMANCE TUNING AND SCALABILITY

The database needs tuning for optimal performance, and the tuning process takes into account the way the end users access the data. For example, fields that they use to search for records should be indexed for maximum performance. Customers might not recall their customer ID number, so fields such as home phone or email address should be indexed so the representative can find the record quickly.

Although the DBA might be tempted to index everything, that would slow the system down when records are added, so a balance is needed. Designers always strive for balance. DBAs make trade-offs to add speed to certain activities while slowing down others yet always stay attentive to the needs of the employees, customers, and other stakeholders. Optimizing performance for speedy retrieval of information, for example, may require slowing down other tasks, such as data entry or editing. Although managers who query the database frequently would want to optimize for retrieval speed, those who are entering data would have a different preference.

Scalability refers to a system's ability to handle rapidly increasing demand; this is another performance issue. YouTube faced this in its first few months when an initial trickle of visitors became a tsunami. Bigger servers would have helped, but the YouTube team did something that would scale even further. They split the database into "shards," or slices that could be stored separately and accessed on different computers to improve performance. Shards also broke with tradition by storing denormalized data, in which information that users typically retrieve as a whole is stored in the same place, rather than separate, normalized tables. When growth is that fast, the DBA must solve one bottleneck after another. The case study about eBay at the end of this chapter shows how that site addresses rapid scaling.

FIGURE **4-21**

Careers in database administration and related areas.

Job Title	Median annual wage	Suggested Education and Training Requirements
Database administrators	$81,710	BS in MIS, computer sciences; training in DBMS software
Information security analysts	$90,120	BS in MIS, computer sciences, business; proficient in security measures to protect databases, networks, and applications
Web developers	$85,800	BS with experience in web development, including integration with databases
Software developers, applications	$98,260	BS in MIS, computer science, or related field; expertise in one or more programming languages

Source: United States Department of Labor, Bureau of Labor Statistics, Occupational Employment Statistics (2015). http://www.bls.gov/oes/current/oes_stru.htm, accessed September 23, 2016.

INTEGRITY, SECURITY, AND RECOVERY

The DBA manages the rules that help ensure the integrity of the data. For example, a business rule may require that some fields are required or the input must adhere to a particular format. The software can enforce many different rules, such as the **referential integrity** constraint, which ensures that every foreign key entry actually exists as a primary key entry in its main table. For example, when Devon adds a new employee to the employee table and attempts to enter a department ID that doesn't exist in the Departments table yet, the DBMS integrity constraint prevents her from adding the record. She must create a record for the new department before assigning people to it. The constraint would also stop Devon from deleting a department if employees are assigned to it, even if they left the company.

A DBMS will also provide tools to handle access control and security, such as password protection, user authentication, and access control. Although application software often shares the responsibilities for ensuring integrity and security or even handles most of those jobs, the database management system may perform some of them.

When the database locks up or fails, the DBMS offers tools to get it back up and running quickly or to reload all the data from backup media. Some systems use mirroring, so that users are directed to a copy of the database when the main one fails.

DOCUMENTATION

Even a small start-up like DD-Designs will need a database with dozens of tables and many complex relationships. The data model can be documented using a **database schema**, which graphically shows the tables, attributes, keys, and logical relationships (Figure 4-22). The **data dictionary** should contain the details of each field, including descriptions written in language users can easily understand in the context of the business. These details are sometimes omitted when developers rush to implement a project, but the effort pays off later. End users will start to develop their own queries and will become frustrated when the exact meaning of fields is not clear. What does a field named "CustomerTerminationFlag" mean? The DBA may be the only one who recalls the thinking that went into it.

FIGURE 4-22
Sample database schema.
PK = primary key; FK = foreign key.

scalability
A system's ability to handle rapidly increasing demand.

referential integrity
A rule enforced by the database management system that ensures that every foreign key entry actually exists as a primary key entry in its main table.

database schema
A graphic that documents the data model and shows the tables, attributes, keys, and logical relationships for a database.

data dictionary
Documentation that contains the details of each field in every table, including user-friendly descriptions of the field's meaning.

Multiple Databases and the Challenge of Integration

The database was intended to end the frustrations of those early departmental information silos, and it succeeded. However, as organizations grow, some of the same disadvantages creep back into the mix because the number of databases multiplies. This happens when companies merge, and records can't easily be combined. When Delta acquired Northwest Airlines, for example, Delta's CIO said she needed to merge 1,199 computer systems down to about 600. Passengers were annoyed by the frequent snags, and during the transition Delta ranked worst for customer complaints about lost bags, late arrivals, poor flight service, and other frustrations.[8]

Sometimes multiple databases spring up in an organization simply because a fast-moving business needs support for an innovative idea immediately. The managers may choose to buy a separate system for it rather than take the time to build the support into the enterprise database and integrate it fully. Cloud-based services are adding to this trend because they can be implemented so quickly.

Shadow Systems

Although the integrated enterprise database is a critical resource, changes to support new features can be painfully slow. People want to get their jobs done as efficiently as possible, and sometimes the quick solution is to create a **shadow system**. These are smaller databases developed by individuals or departments that focus on their creator's specific information requirements. They are not managed by central IT staff, who may not even know they exist. Shadow systems are easy to create with tools like Access and Excel, but the information they hold may not be consistent with what is in the corporate database. Another hazard is that the department may be left hanging when the creator leaves because no one else knows quite what the shadow system does.

These problems lead to serious headaches for managers who need enterprise-wide summaries to make decisions. They receive many "versions of the truth" from different sources because the information housed in each is not consistent. Companies should try to reduce shadow systems and integrate systems as much as possible so important reports needed for planning or compliance don't mix apples and oranges.

Integration Strategies and Master Data Management

To deal with integration, some organizations build interfaces, or bridges, between different databases; these are used to link common fields. Using this approach, a field that is updated in one database, such as an email address, is then copied over to the same fields in other databases that maintain that information. In the "downstream" databases, the email address would be in read-only format so that end users could not update it there.

A broader strategy to address underlying inconsistencies in the way people use data is **master data management (MDM)**. This effort attempts to achieve uniform definitions for entities and their attributes across all business units, and it is especially important for mergers. The units must agree on how everyone will define terms such as *employee, sale,* or *student.*[9] For example, should *employees* include temporary contractors or student workers?

The most successful efforts at master data management focus mainly on a key area, such as customers, or on a limited number of entities that are most important. Teams from across the company meet to identify the differences and find ways to resolve them. **Data stewards** may then be assigned as watchdogs and bridge builders to remind everyone about how data should be defined.

Master data management has less to do with technology than with people, processes, and governance. Nationwide Insurance launched a master data management initiative to resolve its fragmented environment with 14 different general ledger platforms. The results were slow in coming but eventually were dramatic. It once took the company 30 days to close the books, with much hair pulling to reconcile reports. Within a year, Nationwide cut that time in half.

Another integration strategy, one that is even more effective when master data management efforts reconcile data inconsistencies and improve data quality from multiple sources, is the data warehouse.

Data Warehouses and Big Data

 Describe how a data warehouse is created, and explain the challenges and value of big data.

The **data warehouse** is a central data repository containing information drawn from multiple sources that can be used for analysis, intelligence gathering, and strategic planning. Figure 4-23 shows examples of the many sources that might contribute to the warehouse.

A critical internal source of data for the warehouse is operational data from the company's own systems. That would include customer records, transactions, inventory, assets and liabilities, human resources information, and much more, going back many years. For example, a medical center in New Jersey built a data warehouse based on its surgery patients' electronic health records from 2004 on, including demographic data, lab test results, medications, and survey data from the patients themselves. The goal was to explore longer-term trends that would not be obvious without looking at large numbers of patients over a period of years.[10]

External sources of information can add to the value of the warehouse. For instance, a company that sells high-end jewelry might want to download a table from the U.S. Census Bureau that lists every U.S. zip code along with the median household income for its residents and add that to the warehouse. The customer address table will have zip codes in it for U.S. residents, so that attribute would become a foreign key that can be linked to the primary key in

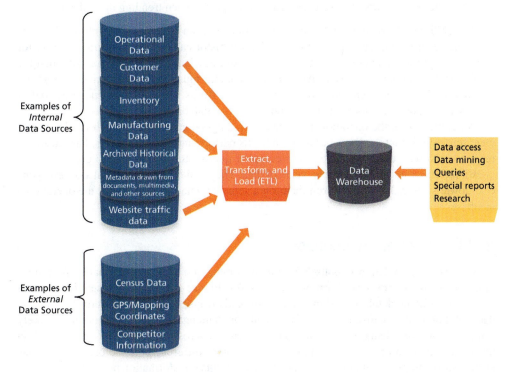

FIGURE **4-23**
The data warehouse.

shadow system
Smaller databases developed by individuals outside of the IT department that focus on their creator's specific information requirements.

master data management
An approach that addresses the underlying inconsistencies in the way employees use data by attempting to achieve consistent and uniform definitions for entities and their attributes across all business units.

data steward
A combination of watchdog and bridge builder, a person who ensures that people adhere to the definitions for the master data in their organizational units.

data warehouse
A central data repository containing information drawn from multiple sources that can be used for analysis, intelligence gathering, and strategic planning.

FIGURE 4-24

External sources of data can be added to the warehouse to increase its value. Here, a table from the U.S. Census Bureau containing the median household incomes for each zip code can be linked to the customers by means of the zip code field.

CustomerAddresses

CustomerID	StreetAddress	City	State	ZipCode
546	321 Smith Avenue	Carson City	NV	89705

← Foreign Key

Primary Key →

USZipCodes (Source: US Census Bureau)

ZipCode	MedianHouseholdIncome
89704	63889
89705	56129
89706	36891

Source: U.S. Census Bureau.

the downloaded table. Figure 4-24 shows how the link between the two tables could be made. By adding this external source of information, managers can learn a great deal about the preferences and behavior of jewelry customers who live in zip codes with different income levels:

- Do customers from high-income neighborhoods tend to shop in the evening?
- Do they respond more to radio promotions or TV ads?
- Over the past 5 years, has the customer income profile been trending up or down?

The ability to draw on high-quality information from an organization's information systems and external sources to spot trends, identify historical patterns, generate reports for compliance purposes, conduct research, and plan strategy is a huge advantage. Although the databases that support the day-to-day business contain much information that goes into a warehouse, the data are typically not in a format that works well for broad analyses. And as we saw earlier, organizations often have more than one database.

A second reason the operational database is not a good candidate for high-level management reporting is that the DBA has to optimize its performance for operations. Fast customer response and data entry come first, not complex queries that answer the bigger, strategic questions. Those queries might span years of data. They will be CPU hogs that slow everyone else down, so it makes sense to run them on a separate data warehouse, not the operational database.

Building the Data Warehouse

How do we create a data warehouse? A common strategy for drawing information from multiple sources is **extract, transform, and load (ETL)** (Figure 4-23). The first step is to extract data from its home database and then transform and cleanse it so that it adheres to common data definitions. As we discussed, this is not a minor challenge, and computer programs rarely can handle it alone. Data drawn from multiple sources across organizations, or even within the same organization, might be defined or formatted differently. If the organization has already made progress with master data management, this transformation process is smoother. Indeed, attempts to build a data warehouse often expose a lot of "dirty data"—inconsistent name spellings, for instance. That leads to more interest in master data management, which is what happened at Rensselaer Polytechnic Institute (RPI).

RPI's president, Shirley Ann Jackson, knew the institute needed better data for strategic planning, and her executive team was frustrated by conflicting reports. The institute's data warehouse effort uncovered many problems that needed cross-functional teams to resolve before data could be loaded into the warehouse. Once they agreed on definitions, data stewards were appointed to watch over how the fields were used.[11]

The transformation process applies to external resources that will enrich the value of the data warehouse for intelligence gathering and marketing. For instance, the U.S. Census Bureau records need to be prepared before they can be loaded into the warehouse, to make sure the zip code fields are the same data type when they are linked. Some reformatting might be necessary whenever the company adds external data to its warehouse.

After transformation, the data is loaded into the data warehouse, typically another database. At frequent intervals, the load process repeats to keep it up-to-date. The DBA optimizes the warehouse for complex reporting and queries without having to worry about slowing down customers and staff. Many data warehouses take advantage of standard relational database architectures, and most DBMS products can be optimized for use as a warehouse. Some include tools to help with the extractions, transformations, and loading as well.

Organizations also use alternative data warehouse architectures, such as those described in Figure 4-25, especially when dealing with truly immense data sets, known as big data.

The Challenge of Big Data

Building a data warehouse from operational databases and adding some external sources are manageable for most organizations and extremely useful. But what about all the other sources of data, especially from the Internet? Think for a moment about the company's website. Even a medium-sized company might have thousands of hits per day, and each visitor might click dozens of times. Consider also how much semi-structured and unstructured information flows through Twitter, YouTube, Facebook, and Instagram, some of which could give the company a competitive advantage if analyzed quickly. A barrage of tweets like the one in Figure 4-26 would certainly get the attention of managers at clothing stores like H&M if their systems could spot the trend fast enough.

Data Warehouse Architectures	
Relational database	Companies often use the same relational DBMS for their data warehouse as they use for their operational database, but loaded onto a separate server and tuned for fast retrieval and reporting.
Data cubes	This architecture creates multidimensional cubes that accommodate complex, grouped data arranged in hierarchies. Retrieval is very fast because data are already grouped in logical dimensions, such as sales by product, city, region, and country.
Virtual federated warehouse	This approach relies on a cooperating collection of existing databases; software extracts and transforms the data in real time rather than taking snapshots at periodic intervals.
Data warehouse appliance	The appliance is a prepackaged data warehouse solution offered by vendors that includes the hardware and software, maintenance, and support.
NoSQL	Database management systems suited for storing and analyzing big data. NoSQL stands for "not only SQL."
In-memory database	Relies on main memory to store the database, rather than secondary storage devices, which vastly increases access speeds.

FIGURE 4-25
Data warehouse architectures.

> **StarlaInBostin**
> **HM is out of hats and gloves..** Idiots you'd think they'd get more in considering the weather
>
> Collapse ← Reply ↻ Retweet ★ Favorite ••• More
>
> 58
> Retweets

FIGURE 4-26
Twitter posts can be part of the big data a company can analyze.
Source: Copyright © by Twitter.

extract, transform, and load (ETL)
A common strategy for drawing information from multiple sources by extracting data from its home database, transforming and cleansing it to adhere to common data definitions, and then loading it into the data warehouse.

The amount of data available is also exploding because so much is gathered automatically—by sensors, cameras, RFID readers, and mobile devices. In consumer electronics, for instance, devices designed to monitor your personal health readings can transmit information to a smartphone app so you can see real-time displays. The rise of the Internet of Things means that data is accumulating at a breathtaking rate—far faster than even Moore's Law would predict.

WHAT IS BIG DATA?

Big data refers to collections of data that are so enormous in size, so varied in content, and so fast to accumulate that they are difficult to store and analyze using traditional approaches. The three "Vs" are the defining features for big data (Figure 4-27):

- *Volume.* Data collections can take up petabytes of storage and are continually growing.
- *Velocity.* Many data sources change and grow at very fast speeds. The nightly ETL process often used for data warehouses is not adequate for many real-time demands.
- *Variety.* Relational databases are very efficient for structured information stored in tables, but businesses can benefit from analyzing semi-structured and unstructured data as well.

BIG DATA TECHNOLOGIES

Relational databases may be part of any effort to analyze big data, but a number of newer technologies are better able to handle the three "Vs." For example, database platforms that don't rely on relational structures are emerging, called **NoSQL DBMSs**, for "Not Only SQL." These don't require fixed schemas with clear data definitions for each attribute. They also don't generally enforce strict rules about data entry or integrity the way a relational database does. Due to volume, data storage is distributed across many servers, often geographically quite far apart.

Another useful technology for big data is Hadoop, which is open source software that supports distributed processing of big data sets across many computers. The software manages file storage and local processing and can be scaled up to thousands of computers in the cloud. Internet radio service Pandora uses Hadoop to analyze billions of thumbs up and down ratings that users click when each song plays. The company can accurately predict customer preferences and create tailored playlists.[12]

FIGURE 4-27

The features of big data.

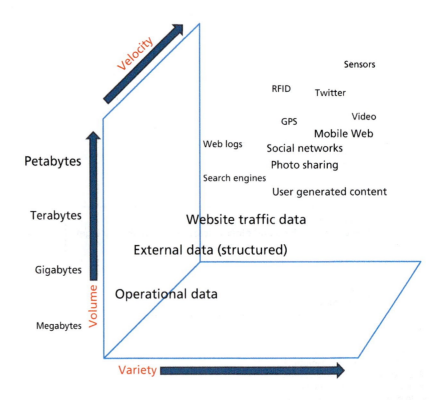

Some software companies also offer in-memory databases where the database itself is stored in main memory rather than on a separate hard drive. This technology vastly increases access speeds, even for extremely large data sets.

While companies still rely mainly on relational database management systems for managing operations, many are deploying NoSQL DBMSs and other alternatives to support emerging needs, especially for storing and analyzing big data. Major database companies, such as Oracle, offer a full range of such products so customers can implement solutions that fit their needs best.

Strategic Planning, Business Intelligence, and Data Mining

Data warehouses and big data efforts should make important contributions to strategic planning. Along with the tools and approaches described in Chapter 7, access to all of this data opens up a wealth of opportunities for managers seeking insights about their markets, customers, industry, and more. They become the main source of business intelligence that managers tap to understand their customers and markets as well as to make strategic plans.

For example, **data mining** is a type of intelligence gathering that uses statistical techniques to explore large data sets, hunting for hidden patterns and relationships that are undetectable in routine reports. For instance, mining the vast amount of data in Facebook turns up some fascinating insights. One study discovered that a person's network size could be increased by more than 60% by optimizing certain activities, especially time between status updates.[13]

The job of "data scientist" is popping up at companies everywhere, and people who can fill that job are in very high demand. Companies need people who have the skills to identify the most promising data sources, build data collections, and then make meaningful discoveries. They need to know the difference between data mining, which leads to important findings, and "data dredging," which sniffs out relationships that might just occur by accident and that have little value. They also must be able to make a compelling case when they do find trends that could add competitive advantage. A successful data scientist is a combination of hacker, analyst, communicator, trusted advisor, and, most of all, a curious person.[14]

The Challenges of Information Management: The Human Element

 6 Explain how the human element and ownership issues affect information management.

As with all technology-related activities, managing information resources is not just about managing technology, databases, and big data. It is also about managing people and processes. Understanding how people view, guard, and share the information resources they need is a critical ingredient for any successful strategy.

Ownership Issues

In the workplace, information resources are found almost everywhere, from file cabinets and desk drawers to the electronic files on portable media and computer hard drives. Although a company may set the policy that all information resources are company-owned, in practice, people often view these resources more protectively, even when compliance and security don't demand tight access controls. Norms about how records are used emerge over time, and though many are unwritten, they can certainly affect employees' behavior.

Salespeople may want to protect access to their own sales leads, or whole departments might want to control who has access to records that they maintain. They may prefer that employees outside the department have the right to *view* one of "their" records but not change it.

---

big data
Collections of data that are so enormous in size, so varied in content, and so fast to accumulate that they are difficult to store and analyze using traditional approaches.

NoSQL DBMS
Flexible database management systems that do not require a fixed data schema with clear data definitions and that do not enforce strict constraints; data storage is typically spread across many servers.

data mining
A type of intelligence gathering that uses statistical techniques to explore records in a data warehouse, hunting for hidden patterns and relationships that are undetectable in routine reports.

Customers themselves raise ownership issues, too. For instance, a customer with no last name (Madonna, for example) might request that the DBA change the last name field to "optional" rather than "required." Ownership issues have to be negotiated among many stakeholders.

Another challenge is simply how long it can take to make changes to an integrated enterprise database when so many people might be affected and will want input. This process takes time, not just for IT staff to analyze the impact but for all the stakeholders to discuss it as well. Changes to the old file processing systems were time-consuming for the IT staff because of the way the code was written. Changes to the integrated database take less time from IT but more from the end users.

Databases Without Boundaries

Another example of how the human element interacts with information management involves databases without boundaries, in which people outside the enterprise enter and manage most of the records. These contributors feel strong ownership over their records. Instagram, for example, heard howls of protest when the company changed its terms of service so that it could sell the photos people upload without their permission and without any compensation. The Facebook-owned photo-sharing site quickly backtracked and changed the policy back, especially after competitors began touting how they would never sell private photos.[15]

Craigslist.com illustrates other ways in which the human element affects information management. Founder Craig Newmark initially sought to help people in San Francisco find apartments and jobs. The site soon became the world's largest database of classified ads, and this major revenue source for print newspapers dried up. Newmark's concerns are less about the database technology than about the health of the community and the relentless threats from spammers and fraudsters who can destroy trust in the site.

Databases without boundaries are also part of emergency disaster relief. Online databases can help victims find missing family members, organize volunteers, or link people who can provide shelter to those who need it. For example, Google launched a "person finder" database after bombs exploded at the Boston Marathon, to help people find one another.[16]

A valuable lesson from the efforts to build databases without boundaries is simply the need to plan for high volume and rapid growth. The growing capabilities of relational databases, along with big data technologies and cloud computing, are essential to support these worldwide repositories.

Balancing Stakeholders' Information Needs

How should managers balance the information needs of so many stakeholders? Top-level management needs strategic information and insights from big data along with accurate, enterprise-wide reports. Operating units must have reports on transactions that match their operations, and they need information systems that are easily changed to support fast-moving business requirements. Customers want simpler user interfaces that work quickly and reliably and don't want to be told that "we just merged and our computer systems don't work together yet." Government agencies want companies to submit compliance reports using government's definitions because they have their own summaries to do.

Meeting all these needs is a balancing act that requires leadership, compromise, negotiation, and well-designed databases. As a shared information resource, the database fulfills its role exceptionally well to provide a solid backbone for the whole organization and all its stakeholders.

MyMISLab
Online Simulation

VOLUNTEER NOW!
A Role-Playing Simulation on Designing the Database for a Volunteer-Matching Service

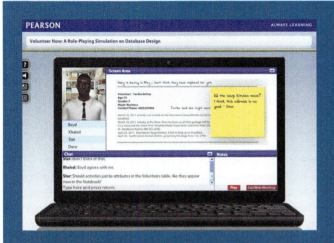

Star and Khaled started their volunteer-matching service a year ago, making lists of local organizations that needed assistance and then posting calls for help on bulletin boards around campus and in local stores. Animal shelters, art museums, soup kitchens, a wildlife rescue station, a children's hospital, and many other worthy organizations benefit from the enthusiastic people who sign up, and students often earn community service points for participating.

The Volunteer Now! loose-leaf notebook is overflowing, and mistakes keep happening. Last week a volunteer called from his cell phone to complain that the address he was given for the soup kitchen was a deserted warehouse, and Star had to pick him up rather than let him wander around on foot. They need a reliable information system with a back-end database to organize the records.

As a frequent volunteer who has some knowledge of databases, you've been asked to offer your input. Log in to meet this well-meaning and energetic team so you can help them get organized.

LEARNING OBJECTIVES

1 An organization's information is a critical resource, and strategies to manage it are essential. Information resources can be described as structured, unstructured, or semi-structured, depending on their characteristics. Structured information is most easily captured by database management systems because it can be broken down into component parts and organized in logical ways. Metadata, or data about data, describes the nature of information and provides details about its structure and properties. The quality of information is affected by several characteristics, such as accuracy, precision, completeness, consistency, timeliness, duplication, and bias.

2 Managing information with the help of computers relies on the use of tables, records, and fields, and each field should have a data definition. Early attempts to manage digital information resources used file processing systems, in which each department maintained its own records. Although they were very valuable, file processing systems had several disadvantages, including data duplication, lack of integration among departmental systems, inconsistent data definitions across departments, and data dependence. The database approach, which uses a database management system, addresses these disadvantages and creates a shared resource with minimal redundancy. Several different database architectures have been developed, and the relational database is now the most widely used. Information is organized into tables in which each row represents a record. Relationships between tables are created by linking a field in one table to a field in another table with matching data.

3 The development of a relational database begins with the planning phase to identify the entities, their attributes, and their relationships. The process involves normalization, in which tables are created in such a way as to eliminate redundancy as much as possible and ensure that tables can be related to one another in a way that reflects their actual relationships. Primary keys ensure that each record in a table is unique, and foreign keys help establish relationships among tables. Most databases are accessed through application software, which serves as a user-friendly gateway to the underlying tables. The database management system (DBMS) provides tools for monitoring and maintaining the database in areas such as documentation, performance tuning, disaster recovery, and security. Information is retrieved from the database using query languages, such as SQL.

4 As organizations grow and expand or when two companies merge, they often wind up with many databases rather than a single integrated one. Employees also launch their own shadow systems to manage just the information they need without the help or oversight of central IT staff. Integration strategies, such as master data management, are needed to coordinate how data are entered and provide enterprise-wide summaries for strategic planning. A data steward helps maintain data consistency across the organization.

5 The data warehouse draws information from multiple sources to create one information storehouse that can be used for reporting, analysis, and research. Sources can be both internal and external. Extract, transform, and load are the three steps used to create the warehouse, which is refreshed with updated information daily or more often. Big data refers to immense data collections that feature the three "Vs" (high volume, velocity, and variety). Relational databases and data warehouses may be used to analyze these collections and conduct data mining along with newer technologies such as NoSQL databases and software that supports distributed processing across thousands of computers.

6 Enterprise information management is not just about technology. It involves a variety of challenges that touch on the human element. Data ownership issues arise, for example, because data have to be shared by all the stakeholders in the organization. Ownership issues also play a major role for databases without boundaries, such as Craigslist, in which most records are entered by people outside the enterprise. Leadership, cooperation, negotiation, and a well-designed database are all needed to balance all the stakeholders' requirements.

KEY TERMS AND CONCEPTS

structured information	batch processing	functionally dependent	shadow system
unstructured information	database	foreign keys	master data management (MDM)
semi-structured information	database management system (DBMS)	Structured Query Language (SQL)	data steward
metadata	relational database	interactive voice response (IVR)	data warehouse
table	data model	scalability	extract, transform, and load (ETL)
record	primary key	referential integrity	big data
field	autonumbering	database schema	NoSQL DBMS
data definition	normalization	data dictionary	data mining

CHAPTER REVIEW QUESTIONS

4-1. What are three categories that describe the nature of information resources? Give an example of each. How do you characterize the relationships within each category of information?

4-2. What is metadata? What does metadata describe for structured information? For unstructured information? Give an example of each type of metadata.

4-3. What are the characteristics of information that affect quality? What are examples of each?

4-4. What were the early design approaches to managing information resources?

4-5. What are the major disadvantages of file processing systems? What are four specific problems associated with file processing systems?

4-6. Following the file processing model of data management, what three architectures emerged for integrated databases? What are the advantages of each? Are there disadvantages?

4-7. What are the steps in planning a relational data model? Are there benefits to the planning stage?

4-8. What are primary keys and foreign keys? How are they used to create links between tables in a relational database?

4-9. What is the typical strategy to access a database? How do users access an Access database? Are there other strategies to access database systems?

4-10. What is the role of the database administrator in managing the database? What is the career outlook for this job?

4-11. What is SQL? How is it used to query a database?

4-12. What is IVR? How is it used to query a database?

4-13. What is a shadow system? Why are shadow systems sometimes used in organizations? How are they managed? What are the advantages of shadow systems? What are the disadvantages?

4-14. What is master data management? What is a data steward? What is the role of master data management in an organization's integration strategy?

4-15. What is a data warehouse? What are the three steps in building a data warehouse?

4-16. What are examples of internal sources of data for a data warehouse? What are examples of external sources of data for a data warehouse?

4-17. What are four examples of data warehouse architectures? Which approach is suitable to meet today's growing demand for real-time information?

4-18. What is big data? What are the defining features of big data?

4-19. What is data mining? What is the difference between data mining and data dredging? What is the goal of data mining?

4-20. What are examples of databases without boundaries?

4-21. How do ownership issues affect information management? How do information management needs differ among stakeholder groups?

PROJECTS AND DISCUSSION QUESTIONS

4-22. Why is metadata becoming increasingly important in this age of digital information? What types of metadata would you expect to see attached to these information resources?
a. Book
b. Digital photograph
c. MP3 file
d. Zappos.com web page for men's athletic shoes

4-23. The concept of relationships is fundamental to relational database design. Briefly describe three relationships that explain how records in a database might be logically related to one another. What are examples of each type of relationship? At your university, what is the relationship between students and courses? What is the relationship between advisors and students?

4-24. Target marketing uses databases and data warehouses to identify potential customers that a business wants to reach based on factors that describe a specific group of people. For example, target markets may be identified by geographic area, by age group, by gender, or by all three factors at one time. One of the leading providers of business and consumer information is infoUSA. com. Visit its website at www.infousa.com to learn how they compile data from multiple sources. (Online at //www.infousa.com/faq/.) How does its process compare to extract, transform, and load (ETL)? Prepare a brief summary of your findings that describes the infoUSA five-step process of building a quality database.

4-25. Visit YouTube.com and search for "R. Edward Freeman Stakeholder Theory" to learn more about stakeholder groups. Are you a stakeholder at any of the following organizations? List several stakeholders at each of these organizations and describe the kind of information each stakeholder needs.
  a. A university
  b. A regional bank
  c. Toyota Motor Corporation

4-26. The idea of data warehousing dates back to the 1980s. Today, data warehousing is a global market worth billions of dollars. What is the relationship between operational databases and data warehouses? Why are data warehouses created, and how do organizations use them? What types of decisions do data warehouses support? Have you ever searched a data warehouse? Visit FedStats.gov and search "MapStats" to see what facts are available for your home state. Prepare a list of five interesting facts about your home state to share with your classmates.

4-27. Lisa Noriega has a problem with unstructured data. As her catering business grows, Lisa wants to analyze contracts to learn if over-budget projects result from using inexperienced project managers. Lisa wants to set up a database, and she wants you to identify the records she will need. Work in a small group with classmates to identify the three entities that have meaning for her catering business. What are the attributes of these entities? What are probable data definitions of the attributes? What is the relationship between records and tables? What is the relationship between fields and attributes? Prepare a 5-minute presentation of your findings.

4-28. The Drexel Theatre is a small, family-owned cinema that screens independent and classic films. The lobby is decorated with vintage movie memorabilia including an original poster of Arnold Schwarzenegger, the Terminator, and his famous quote, "I'll be back." The theatre has a collection of 5,000 movies on DVD. It hires part-time workers for ticket and concession sales as well as janitorial and projection services. It shows one of its movies every evening at 7:00 p.m. The owner of the Drexel plans to implement a relational database to handle operations. He has asked you to develop the data model for managing the film inventory. He wants to track movies, genres (categories), actors, and languages. He wants a description of each entity's attributes, and he wants an explanation of how to use primary keys and foreign keys to link the entities together. Work in a small group with classmates to plan the data model. Prepare a 5-minute presentation that includes an explanation of primary keys and foreign keys.

APPLICATION EXERCISES

4-29. EXCEL APPLICATION:
Managing Catering Supplies

Lisa Noriega developed the spreadsheet shown in Figure 4-28 so that she can better manage her inventory of disposable catering supplies. Download the spreadsheet named *Ch04Ex01* so you can help her with the inventory analysis.

Lisa listed her inventory items in "Case" quantities, but she now wants to analyze items according to "Pack" quantities and create a price list to show to her customers. For example, a case of Heavy Duty Deluxe Disposable Plastic Knives has 12 packs of 24 knives each. She wants to calculate a "Sales Price per Pack" based on her cost plus a 25% markup.

Lisa asks that you complete the following operations and answer the following questions.

- Create columns that list Case Pack, Packs on Hand, and Cost per Case Pack for each item. Use a formula to calculate the Cost per Case Pack.
- Create a column that lists Sales Price per Pack. Use a formula to calculate a 25% markup. Set up an assumption cell to input the percentage markup rather than include the markup value in the formula.
- Format the spreadsheet to make it easy to read and visually appealing.
  1. What is Lisa's total investment in disposable catering supplies?
  2. What is the total sales value of her inventory?
  3. How much profit will she make if she sells all of her inventory at a 25% markup?
  4. How much profit will she make if she uses a 35% markup instead?

FIGURE 4-28

Catering supplies spreadsheet.

	Item No.	Description	Color	Unit	Unit Cost	On Hand
2	630K-C	Deluxe Heavy Duty Disposable Plastic Knives	Clear	Case (12 pk/24 each)	13.61	3
3	630F-C	Deluxe Heavy Duty Disposable Plastic Forks	Clear	Case (12 pk/24 each)	13.61	3
4	630S-C	Deluxe Heavy Duty Disposable Plastic Spoons	Clear	Case (12 pk/24 each)	13.61	3
5	630K-B	Deluxe Heavy Duty Disposable Plastic Knives	Black	Case (12 pk/24 each)	13.61	2
6	630F-B	Deluxe Heavy Duty Disposable Plastic Forks	Black	Case (12 pk/24 each)	13.61	2
7	630S-B	Deluxe Heavy Duty Disposable Plastic Spoons	Black	Case (12 pk/24 each)	13.61	2
8	5454W	54" × 54" Plastic Table Cover	White	Case (24)	19.15	1
9	5454B	54" × 54" Plastic Table Cover	Beige	Case (24)	19.15	2
10	5454BL	54" × 54" Plastic Table Cover	Black	Case (24)	19.15	1
11	549W	54" × 108" Plastic Table Cover	White	Case (24)	30.24	4
12	549B	54" × 108" Plastic Table Cover	Beige	Case (24)	30.24	2
13	549BL	54" × 108" Plastic Table Cover	Black	Case (24)	30.24	1
14	72W	72" Round Plastic Table Cover	White	Case (24)	52.08	3
15	72B	72" Round Plastic Table Cover	Beige	Case (24)	52.08	3
16	72BL	72" Round Plastic Table Cover	Black	Case (24)	52.08	1
17	537	13" × 17" Linen-Like Napkins	White	Case (6 pk/50 each)	45.90	6
18	28500	10" × 10" Linen-Like Napkins	White	Case (8 pk/50 each)	42.00	3
19	1010W	10" × 10" 2-ply Beverage Napkins	White	Case (12 pk/50 each)	18.14	6
20	1010B	10" × 10" 2-ply Beverage Napkins	Black	Case (12 pk/50 each)	18.14	1
21	1010R	10" × 10" 2-ply Beverage Napkins	Red	Case (12 pk/50 each)	18.14	1
22	1313W	13" × 13" 2-ply Luncheon Napkins	White	Case (12 pk/50 each)	25.20	3
23	1313B	13" × 13" 2-ply Luncheon Napkins	Black	Case (12 pk/50 each)	25.20	2
24	1010WED	10" × 10" Wedding Bells Print Napkins	White	Case (12 pk/50 each)	26.46	3
25	1313WED	13" × 13" Wedding Bells Print Napkins	White	Case (12 pk/50 each)	37.80	4
26	CC12	12 oz. Classic Crystal Tall Plastic Glasses	Clear	Case (12 pk/20 each)	78.33	1
27	CC16	16 oz. Classic Crystal Tall Plastic Glasses	Clear	Case (12 pk/20 each)	107.73	1
28	CCR9	9 oz. Classic Crystal Plastic Rocks Glasses	Clear	Case (12 pk/20 each)	53.90	3

Source: Microsoft® Excel, Microsoft Corporation. Reprinted with permission.

4-30. ACCESS APPLICATION:
DD-Designs

Devon Degosta set up an Access database to manage her web design business. She has asked you to create a report that summarizes and identifies projects that are assigned to more than one employee. Recreate the Access database with the table names, attributes, and relationships as illustrated in Figure 4-29. Download and use the information in the spreadsheet Ch04Ex02 to populate the tables. Create a report that lists each project by name and the names of the employees assigned to it. Devon wants the report to include the client name and the project budget. What other reports would Devon find useful?

FIGURE 4-29

DD_Designs database schema.

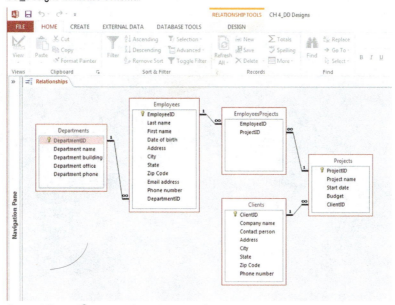

Source: Microsoft® Access, Microsoft Corporation.

CASE STUDY #1

UK Police Track Suspicious Vehicles in Real Time with Cameras and the License Plate Database

Almost every city street in London is under constant video surveillance, partly as a reaction to terrorist attacks. These closed-circuit cameras initially created tapes that could be viewed later, but the technology now is far more capable. The cameras, now also mounted in police vehicles, are equipped with automatic number plate recognition (ANPR) capabilities, which use optical character recognition to decipher the license plate numbers and letters in near real time (Figure 4-30).

The camera's data is sent to the national ANPR Data Centre in north London, which also houses the Police National Computer. Each camera can perform 100 million license plate reads per day. Each vehicle's plate number is combined with the camera's GPS location and a timestamp, so the Oracle database at the data center contains detailed information about the whereabouts of almost every vehicle.

Because the database is linked to the Police National Computer, police on the beat can query it to see whether a nearby vehicle is flagged for some reason. Cross-checking the license plate information against the crime database can turn up vehicles involved in crimes or registered to wanted criminals. In one case, a police constable was killed during a robbery, and police were able to track the getaway car because its license plate was read by the cameras. For cameras mounted on vehicles, the officer does not even need to send a query. An audio alert goes off when the camera's image matches a flagged license plate number, prompting the police to investigate.

Beyond criminal activity, the police database contains extensive information linked to the license plate data. For instance, a car might show that it is registered to someone who owes parking fines or who is uninsured. The data might also show that the license plate is attached to the wrong vehicle, pointing to stolen plates.

The data are maintained for 5 years, creating a rich repository for data mining. One study found that certain cars triggered no flags but seemed to be making impossibly quick journeys from one end of town to the other. Police discovered that car thieves were trying to outwit ANPR by "car cloning," in which the perpetrators duplicate a real license plate and attach it to a stolen car of the same make and model.

Law enforcement agencies see the license plate database, the cameras that feed it, and its integration with police data as a revolutionary advance, even though there are still gaps in coverage and the technology itself is not perfect. For example, rain, fog, and snow can interfere, and the plate itself might be blurred by mud. The plates themselves vary quite a bit, with different colors, fonts, and background images. Despite the drawbacks, police departments in the United States and other countries are rapidly adopting the system, buying camera-equipped cars, and developing smartphone access to databases.

Privacy advocates, however, are concerned about the mounting power of integrated databases and surveillance technologies to scrutinize human behavior. One judge remarked, "A person who knows all of another's travels can deduce whether he is a weekly churchgoer, a heavy drinker, a regular at the gym, an unfaithful husband, an outpatient receiving medical treatment, or an associate of a particular individual or political group." Lawmakers are tightening regulations to provide better protections for citizens in an attempt to balance privacy concerns against the enormous value these databases offer to law enforcement.

FIGURE 4-30

Capturing license plate numbers for law enforcement.

Source: Ann Cantelow/Shutterstock.

Discussion Questions

4-31. Describe the manner in which data elements are linked across databases.

4-32. What technical and physical challenges does this information system face?

4-33. What human capital capabilities for law enforcement are necessary to make the database more effective?

4-34. What are the relevant considerations to balance law enforcement's ability to investigate versus the citizens' need for privacy?

Sources: Chan, T. (February 29, 2016). State lawmakers consider regulations on license plate readers. *WWLP.com*, http://wwlp.com/2016/02/29/state-lawmakers-consider-regulations-on-license-plate-readers/, accessed August 9, 2016.
Du, S., Ibrahim, M., Shehata, M., & Badawy, W. (2013). Automatic license plate recognition (APLR): A state of the art review. *IEEE Transactions on Circuits & Systems for Video Technology* (Feb. 2013), 23(2), 311–325. Retrieved from *Business Source Premier*, April 4, 2013.
Mathieson, S. A., & Evans, R. (August 27, 2012). Roadside cameras suffer from large gaps in coverage, police admin. *The Guardian*, http://www.guardian.co.uk/uk/2012/aug/27/police-number-plate-cameras-network-patchy, accessed March 24, 2013.
National Vehicle Tracking Database, http://wiki.openrightsgroup.org/wiki/National_Vehicle_Tracking_Database, accessed March 24, 2013.
Werner, A. (February 21, 2016). Cost, privacy questions arise about Freeport license plate readers. *CBS New York*, http://newyork.cbslocal.com/2016/02/21/freeport-license-plate-readers-worries/, accessed August 10, 2016.

CASE STUDY #2

How eBay Scales Its Database Architecture with SQL and NoSQL

With more than 150 million users and nearly a billion items listed on its site, eBay IT staff have their hands full. Although the website is known best for its Internet auctions, most of the items listed on the site are actually new. eBay earns revenue from the fees it charges sellers to list and sell their products on the digital commerce site and also from advertising. More than half of eBay's revenue comes from outside the United States, making the platform truly worldwide. Like so many other successful tech companies, eBay continually faced the challenge of extremely fast growth.

eBay's innovative auction platform was initially built in 1995 over a single weekend in a staff member's living room, combining cheap and easily purchased parts from local stores. This architecture maxed out with only 50,000 items listed, so eBay implemented an Oracle database server for the data with additional servers to handle the applications. Initially, eBay was able to scale up the database server to handle bigger loads, but this approach also faced a limit to growth.

The next step was to scale out rather than up by splitting the database into shards so the data could be stored on multiple database servers. This provides a number of advantages, one of which is simply that more servers could be added when needed to further share the database load.

eBay engineers made further adjustments to relieve the load on the database servers by moving some functions that a DBMS ordinarily provides, such as referential integrity, out of the database and into the application instead. For example, the DBMS could be configured to prevent someone from adding a new listing for an item if the item's seller did not yet have a record in the Seller table. The DBMS would check the Seller ID that the seller was trying to enter as a foreign key in the item record to ensure that the same Seller ID is in the Seller table. But that constraint adds workload to the database itself, and the same check could be accomplished in the application that sellers use to create listings. Relieving the DBMS of that kind of work allows it to handle many more transactions and queries without slowing down.

eBay continues to develop strategies to handle growth, ensure security, and add new features, and the company has implemented NoSQL databases along with the relational models. The relational database is "tried and true" for tightly governing how the steps in a transaction are accomplished, ensuring security, and also recovering from glitches, especially those that might happen in the middle of a transaction. The NoSQL approaches, however, excel at handling extremely large data sets with less structure, and processing speeds are extremely fast. For example, eBay uses Hadoop for big data analytics to better understand customer behavior on the site, analyzing petabytes of customer clicks and page views. Companies like eBay must constantly attend to changing business needs, revamping their enterprise architecture as new technologies emerge.

Discussion Questions

4-35. Identify at least three reasons why continuing business growth has been a challenge for eBay database management.

4-36. Identify the risks to data integrity that eBay took when it transferred some of the DBMS functions, such as referential integrity, to the application programs.

4-37. What types of data required eBay to use both relational and NoSQL? Why does eBay use both of these?

4-38. Other than data volume, what other factors have driven eBay to revamp its enterprise architecture?

Sources: Fox-Brewster, T. (2016). eBay fixes "severe" vulnerability but is playing Whack-a-Mole with security. *Forbes.com*, http://www.forbes.com/sites/thomasbrewster/2016/02/03/ebay-severe-security-weakness/#2ee80a0f7736, accessed August 9, 2016.
Hemsoth, N. (November 11, 2013). eBay: NoSQL and RDBMS playing well together. *Datanami*, http://www.datanami.com/2013/11/11/ebay_nosql_and_rdbms_playing_well_together/, accessed August 10, 2016.
Mac, R. (2016). eBay CEO: Company will emerge stronger after tough 2016 for tech. *Forbes.com*, http://www.forbes.com/sites/ryanmac/2016/02/10/ebay-ceo-company-will-emerge-stronger-after-tough-2016-for-tech/#4f8d67581469, accessed August 10, 2016.
Manoharan, A. (October 23, 2015). Apache Eagle: Secure Hadoop in real time. *eBay Tech Blog*, http://www.ebaytechblog.com/2015/10/23/eagle-is-your-hadoop-data-secured/, accessed August 10, 2016.
McLellan, M. (2016). *eBay—Description—Hoover's*. Hoovers, http://subscriber.hoovers.com.proxy1.library.jhu.edu/H/company360/fulldescription.html?companyId=56307000000000, accessed July 12, 2016.
Shoup, R., & Pritchett, D. (2006). *The eBay architecture*. Presented at the SD Forum, http://www.addsimplicity.com/downloads/eBaySDForum2006-11-29.pdf, accessed August 10, 2016.

E-PROJECT 1   Identifying Suspects with a License Plate Database: Constructing Queries with Access

An Access database from a hypothetical small island nation contains simulated license plate information and violation records, and it will illustrate how police are identifying cars involved in crimes or traffic offenses. Download the Access file called *Ch04_Police* to answer the following questions.

4-39.   What are the three tables in the database? For simplicity, the LicensePlates table in this e-project uses LicensePlateNumber for its primary key. Why might that work for a small island nation but not for the United States?

4-40.   Why is PlateImagesID the primary key for the PlateImages table rather than LicensePlateNumber?

4-41.   A police officer spots a car illegally parked on a dark street with license plate LCN5339. Query the database and list any crimes or other violations that are linked to this license plate.

4-42.   A citizen reports a robbery to the police, but she can only remember the first three letters of the car's license plate (JKR). She thinks it was a black or dark blue Toyota. Which car is the best candidate, and who is the owner?

4-43.   Letters such as *G* and *C* are often confused by eyewitnesses. Some witnesses to a hit-and-run accident reported that the license plate started with LGR, but they said they weren't sure. Construct a query to retrieve records that might match either LGR or LCR, and list the candidates.

4-44.   The homicide division learned that a vehicle with a license plate number DYV4437 was observed near a murder scene, and they would like to speak to the owner who might be able to shed light on the case. If the cameras have picked up the license plate at some time, it should be in the PlateImages table. Construct a query to retrieve the latitude and longitude of the car's most recent location.

E-PROJECT 2   Building a Database for Customer Records

In this e-project, you will construct a database of customer purchases for a small concession stand near "Four Corners," the point in the United States at which the Utah, Colorado, Arizona, and New Mexico state lines meet. Much of the data will be imported from Excel files.

4-45.   Open Access and create a new database called FruitStand.

4-46.   Create a table called Products with the following fields:

ProductID (The first field defaults to the name ID, as the table's primary key. Change the name to ProductID. Leave it as autonumber and as the primary key.)
ProductName (Text data type, field size 25 characters)
Price (Currency data type)

4-47.   Enter the records in the following table. Note that you do not enter the ProductID; it is an autonumbering field that generates the next value. Save your work.

ProductID	ProductName	Price
1	apple	$0.45
2	pear	$0.70
3	watermelon	$2.75
4	grapefruit	$1.50
5	avocado	$1.25

4-48.   Download the Excel file Ch04_FruitStand, and import the two worksheets, labeled Customers and Purchases. Identify the CustomerID as the primary key for Customers, and PurchaseNumber fields as the primary key for Purchases, rather than letting Access create its own primary keys.

a.   What fields are contained in the Customers table? Generate a list of all your customers, sorted by CustomerID.

b.   What fields are contained in the Purchases table? What are the foreign key(s) in the Purchases table, and which table(s) do they reference?

4-49.   Use Access to Create Query (Query Design), join Customers to Purchases (on CustomerID) and Purchases to Products (on ProductID), and answer the following questions:

a.   Create a query that returns all the purchases from customers from Nevada (NV). Which fruit do people from that state seem to prefer?

b.   How many pears have been sold? (Click on Totals in the Design Ribbon to bring up options to report grouped totals. Your query should Group By ProductName. Include the Quantity field, and in the Total row, select Sum for Quantity.)

c.   How many watermelons have been sold?

d.   List all the states your customers come from, and the number of customers from each one. (Use COUNT under the CustomerID field from Customers.) From which state do most of your customers come?

4-50.   List the countries your customers come from, sorting the data by CountryName. What problem do you encounter? What would you do to the database to improve your ability to analyze the data by country?

CHAPTER NOTES

1. Greszki, R., Meyer, M., & Schoen, H. (2015). Exploring the effects of removing "too fast" responses and respondents from web surveys. *Public Opinion Quarterly*, *79*(2), 471–503. http://doi.org/10.1093/poq/nfu058

2. Ilieva, J., Baron, S., & Healey, N. M. (2002). Online surveys in marketing research: Pros and cons. *International Journal of Market Research*, *44*(3), 361–376.

3. National Research Council. (1999). *Funding a revolution: Government support for computing research.* Washington, DC: National Academy Press, http://www.nap.edu/readingroom/books/far/notice.html, accessed May 7, 2008.

4. Waldo, D. R. (2005). Accuracy and bias of race/ethnicity codes in the Medicare enrollment database. *Health Care Financing Review*, *26*(2), 61–72. http://www.cms.gov/HealthCareFinancingReview/downloads/04-05winterpg61.pdf, accessed February 19, 2011.

5. Nash, K. S. (2012). Driven to learn. *CIO*, *26*(4), 10–11.

6. Klie, L. (2015). Natural language processing strives to meet STAR TREK STANDARD. *Speech Technology Magazine*, *20*(2), 32–35.

7. Madrigal, A. C. (2013). IBM's Watson memorized the entire 'Urban Dictionary,' then his overlords had to delete it. *The Atlantic*, http://www.theatlantic.com/technology/archive/2013/01/ibms-watson-memorized-the-entire-urban-dictionary-then-his-overlords-had-to-delete-it/267047/, accessed January 19, 2013.

8. Mouawad, J. (May 18, 2011). Delta-Northwest merger's long and complex path. *New York Times*, http://www.nytimes.com/2011/05/19/business/19air.html?pagewanted=all&_r=0, accessed January 20, 2013.

9. O'Kane, B., Judah, S., & Moran, M. P. (2016). *The MDM solution market expands and evolves* (No. G00291294).

Gartner Research, http://www.gartner.com/document/3243517?ref=solrAll&refval=164561303&qid=77fd943360a6ae356ed8d5fee7057245, accessed August 10, 2016.

10. Diet and nutrition disorders; research from St. Francis medical center in the area of obesity described. (2013). *Telemedicine Business Week*, 508. http://search.proquest.com/docview/1266208957?accountid=11752, accessed August 10, 2016.

11. Data stewards and data experts: Roles and responsibilities. (n.d.). Rensselaer Data Warehouse, http://www.rpi.edu/datawarehouse/docs/Data-Stewards-Roles-Responsibilities.pdf, accessed August 10, 2016.

12. Mone, G. (2013). Beyond Hadoop. *Communications of the ACM*, *56*(1), 22–24. doi:10.1145/2398356.2398364

13. Ballings, M., Van den Poel, D., & Bogaert, M. (2016). Social media optimization: Identifying an optimal strategy for increasing network size on Facebook. *Omega*, *59, Part A*, 15–25. http://doi.org/10.1016/j.omega.2015.04.017

14. Noyes, K. (2016). Hoping to land this year's "hottest job"? Here's what you need to be a data scientist. PCWorld.com, http://www.pcworld.com/article/3028002/hoping-to-land-this-years-hottest-job-heres-what-you-need-to-be-a-data-scientist.html, accessed August 10, 2016.

15. McCullagh, D., & Tam, D. (December 18, 2012). Instagram apologizes to users: We won't sell your photos. *cnet News*, http://news.cnet.com/8301-1023_3-57559890-93/instagram-apologizes-to-users-we-wont-sell-your-photos/, accessed August 10, 2016.

16. Ngak, C. (April 15, 2013). Google launches Boston Marathon person finder. *CBSNews*, http://www.cbsnews.com/8301-205_162-57579704/google-launches-boston-marathon-person-finder/, accessed August 10, 2016.

Information Systems for the *Enterprise*

LEARNING OBJECTIVES

1 Explain the role that financial and asset management information systems play in an organization and the importance of financial reporting.

2 Define human capital management, identify its major components, and describe several metrics used to quantify aspects of human capital.

3 Define supply chain management, and describe the metrics, technologies, and information systems that support supply chain processes.

4 Define customer relationship management and its role in an organization, and describe the metrics and information systems that support it.

5 Explain the importance of ERP systems, and describe how they are created, integrated, and implemented.

An online, interactive decision-making simulation that reinforces chapter contents and uses key terms in context can be found in MyMISLab™.

INTRODUCTION

MANAGING ANY ORGANIZATION, LARGE OR SMALL, MEANS KEEPING RECORDS. Those records track transactions, income, employees, customers, suppliers, taxes, assets, and much more, providing a solid backbone for the company's activities. The records also form the data repository needed to generate the endless reports that stakeholders require, both inside and outside the organization. Fortunately, information systems to support most common business processes are widely available, even for start-ups. This chapter examines these systems, showing the business processes they support and the value they provide.

In the online simulation called "Custom Cakes," you will gain first-hand experience with how those systems can be used to manage a business process as you serve as the new

assistant manager at a mall cake store. The store sells cakes with little kits customers can use to add custom decorations and messages, and the cakes are very popular with people who forgot to order in advance for a birthday, graduation, or other occasion. Your job is to decide how many cakes to order from the bakery at closing time, to be delivered to the mall in 3 days. You also need to tell the IT department what data you want displayed on your smartphone ordering screen to help you predict what customer demand will be. Mistakes are costly, as unsold cakes are stored or tossed out. However, if you do run out, you will lose sales and frustrate your customers. The data will come from the company's own information systems, and you can combine them with tips you receive about upcoming events that might boost demand.

MyMISLab
Online Simulation

CUSTOM CAKES
A Role-Playing Simulation on Enterprise Information Systems and the Supply Chain

Otnaydur/Shutterstock

Companies like the mall cake store need robust and flexible information systems to run their businesses. Every organization that handles money and hires people must rely on systems to manage accounting, finances, assets, procurement, supply chains, and human resources. Organizations that serve customers of any kind need information systems to manage operations and build enduring relationships.

This chapter explores the four major categories of information systems that underlie fundamental business processes common to most organizations, each shown with sample functions in Figure 5-1. These are:

- finance and asset management,
- human capital management,
- supply chain management, and
- customer relationship management.

Companies that handle these processes well gain an edge over competitors by reducing costs, adding value, and satisfying employees and customers. Organizations that stumble over these basic functions—dragged down by cumbersome, incompatible, and inconsistent systems—may not stay in business at all, let alone reach the top of their industries. They may struggle just to pay employees, balance the books, and comply with government regulations.

Although these back-office systems are absolutely necessary, experienced managers know they can be difficult to implement and maintain. Their functions weave a path through every organizational unit from the finance office to the sales desk, touching, transforming, and sometimes eliminating business processes. First we will look at individual systems that support major business processes and then at the big picture—how these systems are integrated into full-featured suites of applications.

FIGURE 5-1
Major information systems for managing operations.

Business Process	Sample Functionality for Information System
Finance and Asset Management	Accounts payable, accounts receivable, general ledger, inventory, procurement
Human Capital Management	Human resources management, payroll, benefits, time sheets, talent development, training programs
Supply Chain Management	Supply chain planning software, warehouse management, transportation management
Customer Relationship Management	Contact management, marketing campaign management, email marketing, sales force management, customer service

Explain the role that financial and asset management information systems play in an organization and the importance of financial reporting.

Finance Management

Any organization that handles money—and few do not—needs a robust **financial management system**. These systems lie at the heart of the organization, and companies are held fully accountable for the accuracy of their records. Fuzzy math and accounting tricks that make companies look more profitable than they really are can destroy trust, even if they are legal. Though the endless tables of numbers may seem dry and boring to some, their accuracy, reliability, and trustworthiness could mean enterprise success or failure.

Components of Financial Information Systems

Accounts payable, accounts receivable, procurement, cash management, budget planning, asset management, and the general ledger are examples of the modules typically included in a full-featured financial management system (Figure 5-2). Beyond those, the system may support many related activities and processes, such as collections, debt management, travel and expense management, installment payments, and contracts management.

Nonprofits and government need additional modules for their financial systems. For example, they may need modules to track membership lists, grants from foundations, and gifts from donors.

INTEGRATING THE COMPONENTS
Integration among the modules is especially important to avoid inconsistencies. For example, the details from accounts receivable and accounts payable transactions should automatically

FIGURE 5-2
Sample components for a finance management system.

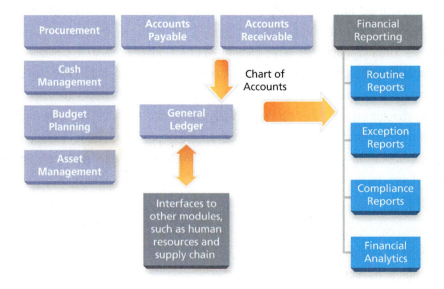

update the general ledger to streamline reconciliation and reporting. Bridges and interfaces to other systems, especially human resources and payroll, also vastly improve accuracy. Time periods and data definitions should match so that, for instance, a monthly report with year-to-date expenditures shows the same payroll totals in both systems.

FINANCIAL WORKFLOWS

The integration of these components supports the development of paperless workflows in an organization. Procurement and accounts payable were some of the first targets for this kind of process improvement. Staff can now use online shopping carts to generate purchase orders from established vendors, routing their requests to supervisors and then to the vendors themselves. The software builds in online, interactive forms so staff can make corrections along the way, using customized workflow tables that determine the routes.

Let's buy some Bluetooth headsets for sales reps at Gulf Travel to see how this works (Figure 5-3):

> Shaun, the office manager in the sales department, browses the web for the best models and then logs in to the financial system. He requests price comparisons for the model he's chosen and finds the lowest prices from TechSmart, Inc., which has a special supplier arrangement with Shaun's company. Shaun enters the order for 10 headsets into the shopping cart, selecting TechSmart as the vendor. Totals and taxes are all computed, and Shaun splits the purchase against two budget numbers—40% for the Northern sales group with four sales reps and 60% for the Southern sales group for its six reps.

> Rania, Shaun's supervisor, logs in and sees a message in her inbox—"Shopping cart approval needed." She is authorized to approve purchases for both budgets, and when she does, the electronic order goes straight to the sales department

FIGURE 5-3
A paperless workflow in procurement to buy 10 Bluetooth headsets.

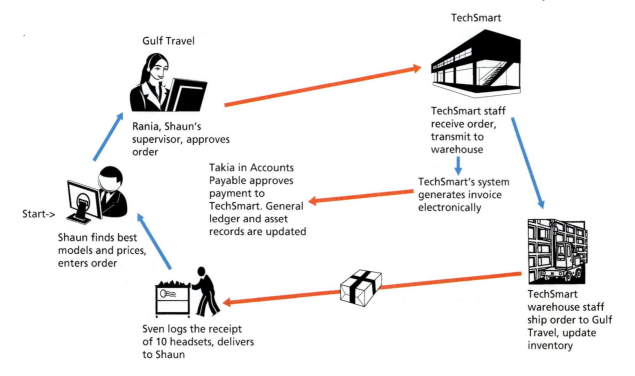

financial management system
Enterprise information system that supports financial accounts and processes, including accounts payable, accounts receivable, procurement, cash management, budget planning, assets, general ledger, and related activities.

at TechSmart because the supplier's contact information is all filled out in Gulf Travel's system.

TechSmart staff receive the order and electronically deliver it to the warehouse for fulfillment. Gulf Travel's system is linked to TechSmart's inventory information, so Shaun already knew that TechSmart had the headsets in stock. TechSmart's warehouse ships the box to Gulf Travel.

Sven, the goods receipt clerk at Gulf Travel, signs for the 10 headsets and logs in to the system to indicate they have been received. He drops the headsets off to Shaun, who hands them out to the sales reps.

TechSmart's system automatically generates the invoice and sends it electronically to Gulf Travel Accounts Payable, where Takia can see immediately that the goods were properly requested, approved, shipped, and received. She approves the electronic transfer of funds to TechSmart's bank account.

The system automatically updates the general ledger and asset records to indicate the company now owns 10 Bluetooth headsets. Other staff may add detail to those records, such as serial numbers or warranty data.

Humans are part of the loop, making decisions, approving actions, and confirming steps in the process. But except for the package's wrapping, paper is not. All the players have real-time access to the same underlying information, so inconsistencies are unlikely. Compare this scenario with one in which orders, approvals, invoices, and payments are all handled manually, moving paper from one person's plastic in-tray to the next, with massive filing cabinets, handwritten signatures, inked stamps, and endless voice mail to clarify stock levels, prices, and shipping dates.

Financial Reporting, Compliance, and Transparency

Reports are the lifeblood of people in finance and accounting, and information systems routinely generate detailed and summary reports on all the organization's transactions and assets.

EXCEPTION REPORTING AND DATA MINING

Financial systems generate considerable data, and they can tag unusual events and anomalies—ones that human beings must review. Such reports and analyses are used to spot mistakes and also patterns that might point to fraud. U.S companies lose hundreds of billions a year to fraud, and the incidence of fraud continues to mount. Exception reports that identify events that fall outside normal ranges and data mining software that picks up unusual trends are powerful tools to help curb this growing problem.[1]

COMPLIANCE REPORTING

Financial systems also carry the major burden of compliance reporting, and in doing so they must conform to local, national, and international regulations that grow increasingly strict. For example, changes in federal banking laws require all banks to report on the assets of American citizens, regardless of whether the bank is in the United States or another country.

The new rules were enacted to ferret out people who try to evade taxes by hiding assets off-shore. Foreign banks objected to the new reporting burden, and some began turning away U.S. customers to avoid having to implement new compliance measures.[2]

XBRL

In the United States, the Securities and Exchange Commission (SEC) mandates many aspects of compliance, and electronic reporting is required, relying on **eXtensible Business Reporting Language (XBRL)**. XBRL is part of the XML family of standardized languages and is specialized for accounting and business reports. The goal is to develop a common language for financial reporting, one that tags every individual item of data to make it understandable, transparent, and also computer-readable for further analysis. "Net profit," for instance, is defined clearly and given a tag, so when it appears on an electronic compliance report, both humans and computer programs know its meaning. This is a huge advance over paper reports and even electronically delivered PDFs.

IMPROVING TRANSPARENCY

Converting to machine-readable financial data can help eliminate manual processes and also greatly improve transparency. Investors and regulators can compare "net profit" from one company to the next, with more assurance that all the figures have been calculated in the same way.[3] BrightScope, for example, is an independent financial information company that obtains machine-readable data on more than 45,000 different retirement plans and then rates each one. HR managers and employees can see for themselves how their retirement plan stacks up against competitors.[4]

The International Accounting Standards Board (IASB) exists to develop and promote a single worldwide set of understandable and enforceable financial reporting standards.[5] Information systems incorporate these as much as possible, though differences among countries still remain. Local political and economic factors can affect a country's decisions about the proper way to report financial figures.

Nevertheless, the growing body of widely accepted accounting standards throughout the world combined with the use of robust financial information systems and languages such as XBRL for business reporting are promising steps. Worldwide trade and investment rely on trust, and the importance of reliable and consistent financial reports can hardly be overstated.

Human Capital Management

2 Define human capital management, identify its major components, and describe several metrics used to quantify aspects of human capital.

Human capital management (HCM) encompasses all the activities and information systems that support effective management of an organization's human capital. The HCM information system includes a growing suite of applications with the employee record as the central element. Together, these applications support recruitment, hiring, payroll, benefits, taxes, career development, training programs, employment histories, employee self-service, and more (Figure 5-4).

Components of Human Capital Management Systems

HUMAN RESOURCES MANAGEMENT

The **human resources management (HRM) system** is typically the heart of the HCM system, tracking each employee's demographic information, salary, tax data, benefits, titles, employment history, dependents, and dates of hire and termination. Some systems also keep

FIGURE 5-4
Components of human capital
management systems.

HCM Module	Description
Core human resources management application	Demographic information, human resources management, payroll, benefits, professional development, education
Workforce management applications	Time and attendance, sick and vacation leave, task and activity tracking, labor scheduling capabilities
Talent management applications	E-recruitment and position applications, employee performance management and tracking, career development, compensation management, e-learning and professional development tracking; visualization and organizational charts
Service delivery applications	Employee and managerial self-service, typically web-based, for entering data and retrieving reports
Social software	Wikis, blogs, social networks

track of performance evaluations, professional development, and training. HRM systems are quite mature, and almost all organizations integrate this information system with the financial system, especially to track payroll expenditures, taxes, and benefits.

WORKFORCE MANAGEMENT

The broader term *human capital management* reflects the fact that traditional human resources management systems have grown into larger software systems that support other employee-related functions. The workforce management module, for example, draws on the data in the core human resource records and adds features to keep track of time and attendance, sick leave, vacation leave, and project assignments. This module is especially useful for labor scheduling and workforce planning. For example, the module can be used to assign the proper number of employees to specific work shifts. The goal is to match staffing with requirements, optimizing the schedules so that employees are assigned when they are most needed but are not standing around with nothing to do during slack periods. This system can also draw on information stored in sales records that shows when peak demand occurs.

TALENT MANAGEMENT

Talent management applications focus on the employee life cycle, beginning with recruitment and extending into onboarding processes, performance evaluations, career development, compensation planning, e-learning, and succession planning after retirement or departure. Visualization and charting tools are adding richness to the way managers view the organization's talent (Figure 5-5). For instance, a constantly updated organizational chart can help with succession planning by highlighting departments in which someone's decision to resign could cause problems because there is no one to fill in. Managers can see the talent throughout their organizations in a more intuitive way, pulling data from several of the organization's information systems.[6]

SOCIAL NETWORKING AND HCM

HCM systems often add social networking software, and organizations are finding innovative ways to use it. Dow Chemical, for instance, wanted to tap the extensive knowledge and skills of its retirees, employees on maternity leave, and others who were loyal to the company but not currently working. It launched a social "alumni" network for this population—well over 40,000 people—and invited them to reconnect with colleagues, search for job opportunities, share news, and mentor less-experienced workers. Part of the company's motivation was the looming skills shortage. Dow encourages scientists to interact with young people who might want to pursue scientific careers.[7]

Dow also invited employees who had been laid off during a business downturn. Some managers feared these members might just vent on the alumni network, but most did not. In fact, some laid-off workers were hired back when business recovered based on their positive attitudes and networking capabilities.[8]

FIGURE 5-5

Talent management applications include visualization and charting tools to display key metrics for human resource professionals.

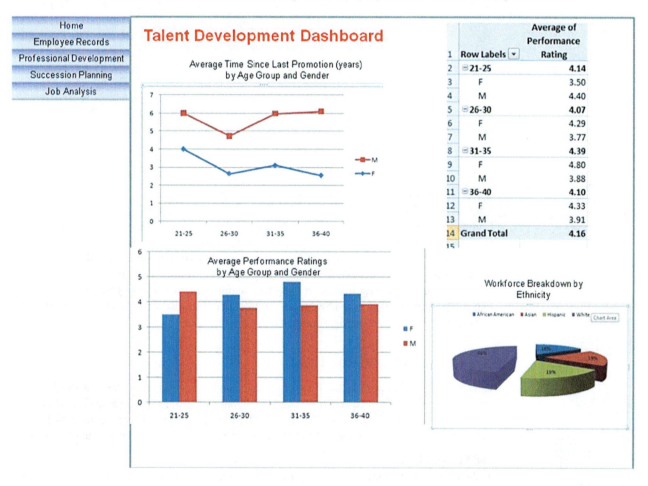

HCM Metrics

Buried in the HCM information system is a wealth of data that can reveal how well the organization is managing and nurturing its human capital.

- Do we have the talent we need to succeed in the future?
- Can we weather the departure of that star over in marketing?
- Are training expenses growing so much because turnover is too high?
- How productive are our full-time employees compared with the part-time people?

Figure 5-6 shows some examples of common HCM metrics. These are less about individual performance than about the overall health of an organization's human capital management. Human resource managers can use these metrics to assess the impact of their strategies on the company's success, often in terms of real dollars. They can also compare their own figures to industry benchmarks.

Human capital management systems have transformed how companies approach human resource issues by introducing a wealth of data that leads to better decisions and strategies. The next section explores systems that support how organizations work with their suppliers.

workforce management module
As part of the HCM system, the workforce management module helps track time and attendance, sick leave, vacation leave, and project assignments.

talent management
As part of the HCM system, the talent management module focuses on the employee life cycle, including recruitment, performance evaluations, career development, compensation planning, e-learning, and succession planning after retirement or departure.

FIGURE 5-6

Metrics drawn from the human capital management system can reveal important information about how well the organization is managing human capital.

Human Capital Metric	Description
Turnover	The percentage of workers who left and were replaced during a time period
Turnover costs	The total of termination costs, hiring costs, training costs, and other costs related to replacing a worker
Cost per hire	Average advertising costs + agency fees + recruiter's salary and benefits + relocation expenses for new employees
Human capital return on investment	The return on investment produced by the organization's expenditures on salaries, benefits, bonuses, and other costs for human talent
Employee satisfaction	Measures of job satisfaction, usually assessed through employee surveys or exit interviews

Define supply chain management, and describe the metrics, technologies, and information systems that support supply chain processes.

3 Managing the Supply Chain

Companies that buy, sell, and ship goods around the world watch inventory levels, weather reports, political news, and customer trends in their quest for excellence in **supply chain management (SCM)**. This term refers to strategies that optimize the flow of products and services from their source to the customer. Depending on your type of business, the chain can be long indeed, stretching from your supplier's suppliers all the way to your customer's customer. The ultimate goal is to align supply with demand so that the right product is delivered to the right place, at just the right time, and at the right price.

Supply Chain Fundamentals

How do companies optimize the flow of products and services as they move along the value chain, especially to meet customer demand? Drawing on the steps in the value chain described in Chapter 2, Figure 5-7 shows the steps that underlie successful management of a next-generation supply chain. These are (1) plan, (2) source, (3) make, (4) deliver, and (5) return.

THE PLANNING STEP

SCM starts with planning, with the goal of building a nimble supply chain that aligns with actual business goals. If the corporate strategy calls for low-cost leadership, for example, the company will strive to reduce costs for transportation and inventory storage. IKEA emphasizes low prices, and the company holds costs down by shipping flat boxes containing furniture parts rather than bulky, fully assembled bookcases or tables. The boxes fit nicely into far

FIGURE 5-7

Steps in supply chain management.

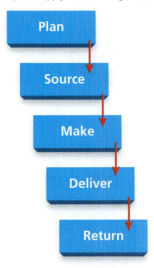

Plan → Source → Make → Deliver → Return

✳ THE ETHICAL FACTOR Ethics and Talent Management

Scenario: The CEO of a large media company with more than 10,000 employees decides to buy out a small business that created a spectacularly successful online role-playing game. The smaller company has about 50 software engineers, and the CEO wants to retain about 20 top performers. The rest will be laid off. The CEO can't obtain performance ratings for the 50 engineers at the online game company, so instead the CEO asks the human resources director to analyze the performance metrics of software engineers at the media company. The CEO's goal is to identify common characteristics of star software engineers to help guide the decision about who should be retained. With the new talent management system, the director can quickly analyze average ratings by job position, years of experience, age, gender, ethnicity, educational background, university attended, marital status, and many more variables.

Suppose the graphs show that, within the media company, average performance ratings are slightly higher for male software engineers under 35 years old compared with women of all ages as well as men over age 35.

Relying on this information to decide who in the game company should get job offers to stay on would not only be unethical, but it could also lead to poor decisions. For instance, the results could stem from past and present discrimination at the media company against people who don't fit a stereotype about software engineers. Human resource professionals need sharp critical thinking skills and thoughtful decision making to use these powerful systems ethically and wisely.

fewer containers traveling by ship or rail. IKEA also grants customers the honor of assembling the products themselves, another huge cost saver.

CHOOSING SOURCES

In step 2, managers make decisions about sources and which suppliers to use. Again, the business strategy should guide many choices, such as whether to commit to long-term contracts or encourage frequent and fierce competition among potential suppliers. For safety, managers may also want to make arrangements with more than one supplier for the same resource in case one fails. Today's global supply chains must be chaos-tolerant; hurricanes, earthquakes, political turmoil, or pandemics can cause major interruptions.

Managers should also check on a supplier's labor practices. After coming under fire because of bad conditions at one of its suppliers in China, Apple started sending auditors to look into some of the factories that make iPhone parts. In one of them, they found more than 70 children working illegally, with forged documents showing false birthdates. Apple reported the violations to Chinese authorities and also helped return the children to their families.[9] Corporate responsibility also extends to the environment, and IKEA audits its suppliers to ensure wood is harvested from sustainable forests.[10] (The Ethical Factor in Chapter 2 discusses ethical responsibility in extended supply chains.)

MAKE, DELIVER, RETURN

The "make" step transforms the resources into something with more value. Supply chain managers track inventory at each stage, fine-tuning the flow so that some parts don't run short while others are overstocked. Managers' keen interest in inventory levels continues through the delivery step, as products are transported to distribution centers and retailers. Finally, SCM includes returns. A very low cost leader might post the "All sales final!" sign, hoping to reduce the cost of that final process to near zero. An online shoe retailer would design a very user-friendly return process, so customers will feel more comfortable about purchasing shoes they haven't tried on.

Measuring Performance in Supply Chains

While company strategy guides decision making throughout the five supply chain steps, accurate and well-chosen metrics tell how well those decisions are working out. How do IKEA's managers know their inventory levels are optimal and that their supply chains are humming along as well as they should?

SUPPLY CHAIN VISIBILITY

Visibility describes how easily managers can track timely and accurate supply chain metrics. Some metrics, such as total sales by product, are easy to get, but a maddening lack of transparency plagues many others. The data might be housed in a supplier's or customer's database with no real-time access, and only slow-moving paper reports transmit critical information. Valuable metrics may also be invisible simply because no one is collecting them. Many are fleeting time durations that are costly and cumbersome to collect.

Netflix, the streaming video and DVD rental company, strives for better visibility on metrics for a critical leg in its supply chain: the U.S. Postal Service. Subscribers choose videos online, and Netflix sends them by mail. When a customer returns a DVD, Netflix processes the return and promptly mails out the next one in the customer's queue. However, the delivery step is highly dependent on USPS timeliness. Customers who wait days to get their new film are annoyed, but Netflix managers may not even know it. Figure 5-8 shows a sample automated email from Netflix, sent in the hope that customers themselves will help make that metric more visible. As you will see, a major goal of SCM information systems is to use technology-supported collaboration to improve visibility for both suppliers and customers.

supply chain management (SCM)
Strategies that optimize the flow of products and services from their source to the customer.

visibility
Describes how easily managers can track timely and accurate supply chain metrics.

FIGURE 5-8

Netflix surveys customers with emails like this one to improve visibility in the supply chain.

> Thank you for your recent DVD return. Please tell us when you mailed back this movie by clicking on the appropriate link below.
>
> I mailed the movie Thursday, Apr 12
> I mailed the movie Wednesday, Apr 11
> I mailed the movie Tuesday, Apr 10
> I mailed the movie Monday, Apr 9

DID YOU KNOW?

As Netflix expands globally with its streamed videos, the company faces many supply chain challenges. Depending on local laws, some movies aren't available in certain countries, but people easily get around that by using a virtual private network service that makes it look like they are logging in from the United States. Netflix is fighting back by cutting off private network providers, trying to stay compliant with each country's laws.[11]

SUPPLY CHAIN METRICS

How do managers decide which metrics to track? Thousands of candidates exist, but no company can excel at all of them; SCM is about optimization, which means trade-offs.

The metric that matters most is **demand forecast accuracy (DFA)**—the difference between forecasted and actual demand. Supply chain managers work with the sales and marketing teams to forecast demand for products, drawing on historical sales patterns, marketing campaign plans, advertising budgets, seasonal promotions, focus groups, demographic shifts, gut instincts, and crystal balls if they have them. As you will learn from the online simulation "Custom Cakes," underestimating demand leads to lost sales and frustrated customers. Overestimates lead to higher inventory and storage costs. Businesses might also have to offer steep discounts to get rid of excess merchandise.

One reason DFA is so critical is the **bullwhip effect**, which describes the distortion in the supply chain caused by changes in customer demand as the orders ripple upstream (Figure 5-9). Small fluctuations in retail sales trigger large swings in inventory levels, as the

FIGURE 5-9

The bullwhip effect in a supply chain.

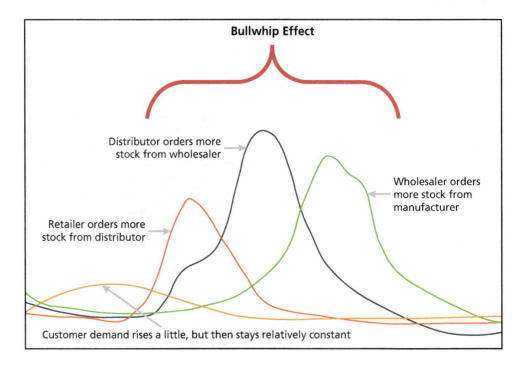

Bullwhip Effect

Distributor orders more stock from wholesaler

Wholesaler orders more stock from manufacturer

Retailer orders more stock from distributor

Customer demand rises a little, but then stays relatively constant retailer sends orders to the distributor to replenish the stock, and the distributor follows up with orders that soon reach the manufacturer. As orders are filled and products shipped, inventory builds up in some places, but shortages occur in others. At times, warehouse shelves are stocked full, but the retailer's display is empty.

REDUCING SUPPLY CHAIN COSTS

Lower costs are also important, so costs must be visible. Total costs are difficult to grasp, though, because they span transportation, inventory storage, warehouse management, distribution centers, customer service for refunds and exchanges, and direct operational costs. Knowing where along the supply chain costs are too high is the first step to finding ways to reduce them. If inventory storage costs are high, a bullwhip effect may be operating and managers will look into better demand forecasting to synchronize the chain's links.

Groundbreaking interventions can sometimes dramatically reduce supply chain costs, especially by omitting whole segments. For example, most computer manufacturers build several models, and ship them first to distributors and then out to retailers such as Best Buy, Staples, or Costco. But Dell bypassed those middlemen altogether. At Dell.com, the customer selects the computer online, customizes it, and then tracks the order until it arrives at the front door, shipped directly from the manufacturer. The monitor, shipped in a separate box, may come from a different manufacturer, but Dell synchronizes the delivery so all the hardware arrives at the same time (Figure 5-10). The trade-off, which sacrifices instant gratification of taking the new PC home the same day in favor of lower cost and customization, was a gamble. But it worked, at least for a while. Dell dominated the PC market with its low cost strategy until rivals mastered their own supply chains.

SUPPLY CHAIN DISRUPTIONS

With companies relying more on suppliers around the world, supply chains are becoming much more complex and varied and more susceptible to disruption.[12] Hurricanes, snowstorms, epidemics, violence, strikes, and many other events can surprise supply chain managers and disrupt the flow of goods. Skyrocketing fuel prices and any restrictions on carbon emissions may also affect supply chains, and managers may need to adjust quickly. Amazon and other online retailers are pushing to deploy drones for delivery, both to increase speed and to bypass potential disruptions (Figure 5-11). Speedy delivery by drones would be especially helpful in the medical supply chain, where expensive products such as antivenom expire in a short time and so must be delivered very quickly, and the location where the serum is needed can't be predicted in advance.

FIGURE 5-10

Dell's supply chain synchronizes delivery of the monitor with the PC so they both arrive at the same time.

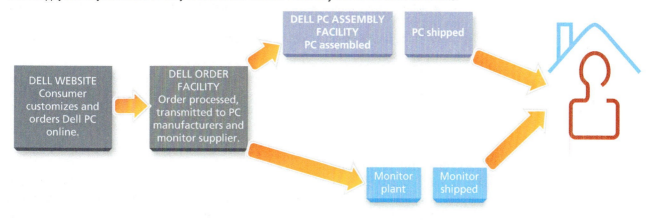

demand forecast accuracy (DFA)
The difference between forecasted and actual demand.

bullwhip effect
Describes the distortions in a supply chain caused by changes in customer demand, resulting in large swings in inventory levels as the orders ripple upstream from the retailer to the distributor and manufacturer.

FIGURE 5-11

Drone deliveries will be a disruptive innovation for many supply chains.

Source: Slavoljub Pantelic/Shutterstock.com.

Information Systems and Technology for Supply Chain Management

Supply chain management software evolved as a patchwork quilt of specialized tools and applications, often developed to address one aspect of the supply chain puzzle in a single industry. A software collection for a manufacturing company, for example, might include:

- Supply chain planning software to predict demand, synchronize with supply, and optimize the whole network
- Warehouse management software (WMS) to manage and optimize inventories, space allocation, shipments, cross-docking, and other warehouse activities
- Transportation management software (TMS) to optimize shipping, logistics, and fleet routing and scheduling
- Manufacturing execution system to manage activities and flow through the manufacturing process
- Global trade management software to ensure compliance for cross-border transactions for importers and exporters

Making all these specialized software applications work together is very challenging, but managers need a clear, end-to-end picture of supply chain performance, not fragmented views of each component. Increasingly, vendors are building software that combines several SCM applications that share data. Also, the major vendors that offer comprehensive financial and human resource management suites are integrating SCM functionality into their suites.

COLLABORATION IN THE SUPPLY CHAIN

The secret to excellence in SCM is collaboration, internally among units and externally with partners, suppliers, and customers. The bullwhip effect, for example, can be better controlled if suppliers have real-time access to up-to-date retail sales data instead of an occasional faxed purchase order from the retailer.

How can organizations share information about real-time inventories and sales? CEOs are understandably reluctant to just hand over a login name and password to suppliers or customers so they can access the company's databases. Instead, firms develop automated bridges to connect their information systems and share data relevant to the supply chain.

Since the 1970s, companies have been using **electronic data interchange (EDI)** to improve visibility about orders, inventories, and data that partners in a chain need to share. This approach to bridge building, which predates the Internet, often relies on private networks and proprietary software and is time-consuming to set up. It improves supply chain performance, but it also tends to lock the partners into their relationship. Having spent so much time and energy building that data bridge, they are less likely to switch partners.[13]

A more flexible way to improve visibility between partners is to use standardized machine-readable formats, especially relying on XML. These collaborative systems are easier to create technically, but they also take time to develop because they require trust between the partners.[14] The biggest players, such as Walmart and Dell, can insist that their suppliers share information electronically to reduce costs and improve the overall supply chain.

SENSING TECHNOLOGIES

Supply chains benefit considerably from sensing technologies that are part of the Internet of Things because they improve visibility during transit and in storage. Commercial shippers, for instance, deploy handheld wireless scanners to read the barcodes on packages and upload the tracking number, date, time, and place to servers. On delivery, the scanners capture the signature and upload that as well to close the loop (Figure 5-12).

RFID chips are especially useful in supply chains. Attached to packages or crates, they can transmit data as they pass by readers at seaports, railway stations, or warehouses. For example, blood products move through a complex supply chain that starts with the donor and usually ends with a transfusion to a hospital patient. But the process can be fraught with errors arising from manual, handwritten forms. In the United States, thousands of units of blood are discarded each year due to record-keeping errors. However, companies are working to add RFID tracking to reduce such errors and ensure patients receive the right blood type.[15]

Source: Tetra Images/Alamy.

FIGURE 5-12

Wireless scanner captures barcode information and uploads to supply chain management system.

electronic data interchange (EDI)

An electronic bridge between partner companies in a supply chain that is used to transmit real-time information about orders, inventories, invoices, and other data.

For high-risk supply chains, organizations use a combination of sensors and tracking software. Chemical companies, for example, must closely monitor the location and status of hazardous materials moving by train. They use satellite communications and sensors in the tank cars, watching for any temperature changes or security breaches. The satellite signals also update the nearest emergency facilities in case of an accident.[16]

Global positioning systems (GPS) are a critical feature of navigation and transportation systems. These devices receive signals from 32 satellites that orbit the earth and transmit time and location data. The GPS receiver computes its own three-dimensional location based on distances from the three or four closest satellites (Figure 5-13). Location is accurate within a few meters. GPS devices help drivers navigate to their destinations keep managers apprised of their fleets. Live GPS tracking software can display the location and movement of an Uber or Lyft car as it heads toward your pickup location. For fleets, GPS devices and displays can show the speed and location of every vehicle overlaid against live traffic maps (Figure 5-14).

The supply chain includes the customer and even the customer's customer. An organization's relationships with its customers are so critical that special information systems have been developed to help manage them, as we see in the next section.

FIGURE 5-13

GPS devices receive signals from nearby orbiting satellites and triangulate location based on the distance each signal travels.

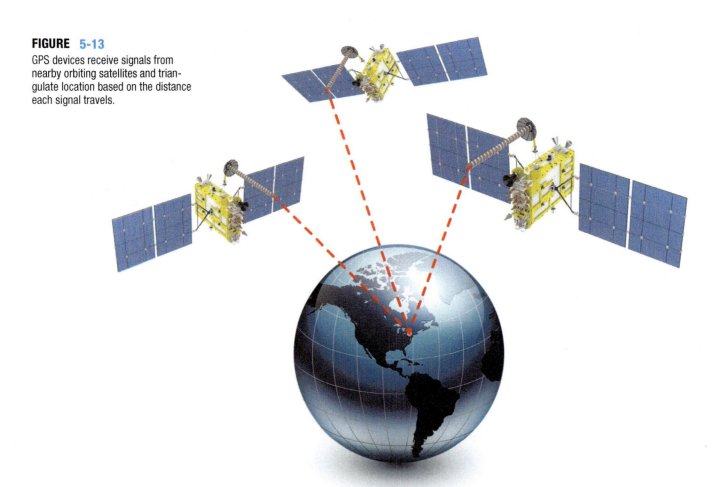

Source: cobalt88/Shutterstock, Mechanik/Shutterstock.

FIGURE 5-14

GPS software tracks the locations of vehicles in a fleet in real time.

Vehicle	Driver	Start Time	Speed
A	5786	4:05 AM Owings Mills	55 MPH
B	5633	7:15 AM Owings Mills	62 MPH
C	6777	9:00 AM Frederick	41 MPH
D	6554	9:21 AM Owings Mills	68 MPH
E	4001	9:45 AM Baltimore	32 MPH

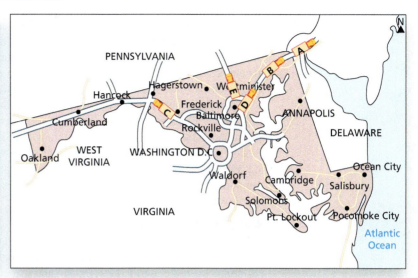

Customer Relationship Management

4 Define customer relationship management and its role in an organization, and describe the metrics and information systems that support it.

How are companies using information systems to manage their relationships with customers? Some customers like to use Twitter to get attention from companies rather than calling an 800 number and getting lost in a phone menu. Andrew Nelson has tweeted complaints to IKEA and Hertz and compliments to Delta Air Lines. When he used Twitter to complain to Sears about a repairman not showing up, the company was quick to apologize and reschedule the visit. Other companies, however, might not even have noticed Nelson's complaint.[17]

Customer relationship management (CRM) covers the strategies, processes, and information systems an organization uses to build and maintain relationships with its current and prospective customers. Those who have direct interactions with the customer, such as sales reps or customer support staff, are on the front lines. But processes in marketing, sales, accounting, product development, and manufacturing can all benefit from a customer-centric focus.[18]

CRM Goals and Metrics

To build stronger customer relationships, managers need clarity about their actual goals. Some common objectives are:

- Improving customer retention
- Improving profitability
- Growing revenue
- Listening to the customers

IMPROVING CUSTOMER RETENTION

Attracting new customers is often more difficult and expensive than retaining existing ones, and the new customer may be less profitable than the old. Strategies for improving retention stress customer satisfaction, loyalty rewards, and perks for returning customers. Farmers

global positioning systems (GPS)
Electronic devices that receive signals from orbiting satellites that transmit time and location data; GPS devices help drivers navigate and keep managers in touch with their transportation fleets.

customer relationship management (CRM)
Encompasses the strategies, processes, and information systems an organization uses to build and maintain relationships with its current and prospective customers.

Insurance Group, for example, uses analytical software from SAS to analyze customers' lifetime loyalty rates and profitability. Its analysis led to a 14% increase in the company's rate of return.[19]

Loyalty and retention can be encouraged in many ways. The UK-based holiday travel site called On The Beach uses CRM to track customer behavior when they visit the site, noting the travel deals each visitor lingers over. Using the data, the company carefully tailors every email to help customers find a perfect beach holiday that matches their tastes. Average retention rate for most travel sites is 18% to 20%, but On The Beach boasts retention approaching 27%.[20]

Analysts project that companies can reduce the loss of profitable customers by at least 10% if they develop a good retention management strategy, which is a very fast return on investment. One metric that organizations gather is simply the number of repeat customers. However, beneath that figure lie other metrics showing *why* customers are returning (or staying away). Close monitoring of the customer satisfaction index is critical, which is why companies bombard customers with requests to complete a survey after any purchase or website visit.

IMPROVING PROFITABILITY

Finding ways to reduce the costs of serving each customer—without also diminishing customer satisfaction—is another important CRM goal. For instance, innovations that encourage customers to stop phoning the company and use other channels instead are worth the investment. A customer who calls FedEx to ask what happened to her package is costly in terms of human resource time, but the same query submitted to the company's website costs FedEx just pennies to answer. Online self-service applications, such as FedEx's package tracker, improve profitability and also please customers who enjoy tracking their package's journey.

Empowering customers with easy access to inventory levels can increase profits and boost customer satisfaction even more. Target, for instance, helps customers avoid pointless car trips by a search tool on its website. Customers can select a special camera, for instance; enter a zip code; and find out which nearby stores have the camera in stock.

GROWING REVENUE

CRM strategies to grow revenue often include finding new customers and markets as well as earning more revenue from existing customers through cross-selling and upselling. The marketing and sales departments champion these efforts, finding new leads, identifying marketing segments, managing campaigns, and building the customer base. They also grow revenue by learning everything they can about each customer and using the data to introduce new products and make additional sales.

PRODUCTIVITY TIP
Many libraries offer online catalogs with "availability" tools to let students and faculty know whether the book they want is on the shelf or already checked out. Some allow you to reserve or recall the book and will send you an automated email when it becomes available.

Capturing new leads, particularly people who show some interest in your service, is crucial to building your customer base. One innovative strategy to capture motivated buyers at just the right time is the "click to chat" button on a website, which opens up a live chat window staffed by a company agent. Although it is widely used by customers who are having trouble completing a transaction, a more proactive use is to intervene when the visitor is just browsing. A pop-up (Figure 5-15) can appear, offering the customer a chance to chat with a live agent who asks, "Can I help you?" Some research indicates that proactive live chat can increase sales as much as 20%. Some companies are adding audio and video options to the text-based chat so that customers can see and hear a live human being.[21]

Live chat in the customer support context offers considerable savings as well. Company representatives can multitask with several customers in different chat windows rather than speaking with just one person at a time on the phone.

LISTENING TO CUSTOMERS

When customers answer one of your surveys, CRM software can easily capture and analyze what they say. Some systems can also do **sentiment analysis**, with software that scans the text comment boxes, blogs, social media, or other user-generated content and employs algorithms to classify the opinions as pro, con, or neutral (Figure 5-16). The sorting isn't perfect,

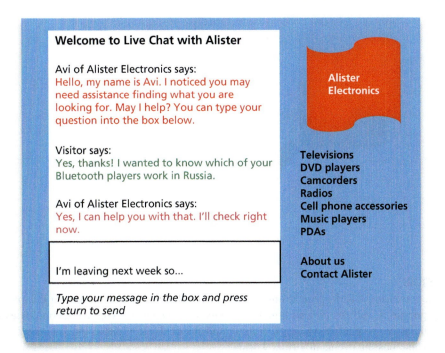

FIGURE 5-15
Click-to-chat functionality to provide just-in-time customer service.

of course, but this kind of social media listening can provide early warnings about customer relationship issues.[22]

For example, an online ticketing company called StubHub used sentiment analysis software to spot a surge in complaints from baseball fans on social media. The stadium mistakenly announced to some ticket holders that a Yankees–Red Sox game was rained out, so the ticket holders requested refunds. The game was only delayed, however, and StubHub initially denied fans' requests. The company quickly reversed that policy when sentiment analysis caught the growing tide of negative posts about StubHub on sports blogs.[23]

CRM Strategies and Technologies

Because CRM touches so many different metrics and areas of the company, the information systems it uses can be quite fragmented, much like those that manage supply chains. These systems cluster into several categories, shown in Figure 5-17, based especially on the business unit that drives the need for them, the kinds of related services they offer, and the metrics they track.

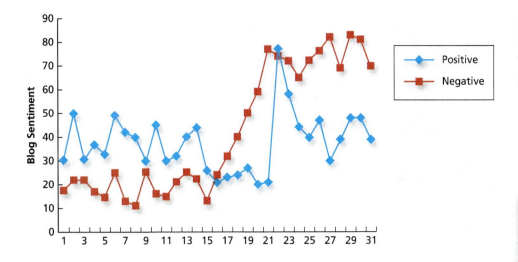

FIGURE 5-16
Sentiment analysis dashboards can show daily trends in positive or negative blog posts, recent Twitter activity, and other relevant information drawn from social media.

sentiment analysis
A capability of specialized software to scan text input surveys, blogs, or other user-generated content and classify the opinions as pro, con, or neutral toward the company or product.

FIGURE 5-17

Customer relationship management systems support activities in several areas of the company, and integrated suites bring these applications together.

MARKETING

Marketers treasure CRM applications, drawing on them to manage marketing campaigns, loyalty programs, and customized email programs. Companies use Web 2.0 technologies for marketing as well—publishing blogs, posting updates on Twitter, launching social networking sites, and hosting events in virtual worlds.

Email marketing is a major focus for CRM applications. JangoMail, for example, offers email marketing software that connects to the company's database to personalize each message and tailor it to the customer's interests. Someone who recently purchased a tennis racket might receive an offer for discounted tennis balls. E-marketing information systems provide extensive tracking capabilities as well, with detailed reports about customer behavior, showing how many opened the message, forwarded it, or clicked on a link.

Technically, the software accomplishes this tracking by embedding in the HTML email a **web beacon** or **web bug**, which is a tiny, invisible image, typically a single pixel with a unique identifier. The image is actually located on the e-marketing server, and when the customer opens the message, a request is sent from the recipient's computer to retrieve the invisible image and download it. The request includes the date, time, and IP address of the computer making the request, and the unique identifier links the request to the customer's email address as well. Beacons are widely used on websites to track visitors.

PRODUCTIVITY TIP

Although web beacons in email provide very useful metrics for marketers, they raise privacy issues. You can prevent much of that tracking by setting your email to open as plain text rather than HTML and disallowing incoming email to load images without your consent.

One promising technology that had a thorny start for CRM is the virtual world, such as Second Life. Early attempts to harness these social 3D immersive worlds for CRM failed, partly because the inhabitants didn't welcome marketers. Virtual gunfights even broke out.[24] However, many companies and nonprofits launch a site on Second Life to engage potential customers and hold live events.

SALES FORCE AUTOMATION

Sales force automation systems boost sales rep performance by helping them track and manage their accounts, contacts, leads, and to-do lists. Some systems also help salespeople develop proposals and quotes for their clients and assist managers in evaluating the success of their sales teams. For mobile sales reps, access to CRM applications via the web and smartphone is essential.

CNN, for example, deployed Salesforce.com to help its sales teams deal with more than 2,000 clients who advertise on the television network. The system is configured with human motivation in mind, especially to encourage sales reps to reach new goals. For example, it provides real-time web-accessible metrics showing number of new accounts for each rep, and it automatically sends emails to the whole organization to recognize and congratulate the top performers.

CUSTOMER SERVICE AND SUPPORT

CRM can help organizations make major improvements in customer service and support and reduce costs as well. The click-to-chat feature described earlier is widely used to interact with customers having login problems or other issues. Online knowledge bases and support sites let customers help themselves to instruction manuals or software drivers. Many companies also try to nurture user communities so that customers can answer each other's questions about the products. IBM, for example, hosts dozens of such communities for developers who use their software tools. The participants discuss issues online and also meet face-to-face in major cities.

Twitter is growing as a way to provide customer support, largely because it can reach customers in near real time. Washington, DC's Metro subway, for instance, tweets about service disruptions. Though tweeting can be very useful and cost-effective, occasional blips occur. Twitter truncates any message down to 140 characters, but Metro workers sometimes forget to stay under the limit:

> "No Line: There is no Blue line train service between Rosslyn & King Street. Shuttle bus service is established. Customers are encouraged to"

Amused followers started tweeting possible endings, such as "...go to the closest bar" or "... ford the Potomac River at their own risk."[25]

Twitter continues to add features that will help businesses use the platform for customer service, partly because so many customers publicly tweet their complaints and electronic word of mouth is so powerful.[26] For example, customer service reps who spot a public complaint can transfer the interaction to Twitter's direct message system. Given the growing volume and public nature of tweets, companies must respond as quickly as possible. On Valentine's Day, complaints poured in about many delayed flower deliveries. Online florist 1800flowers.com responded right away to the tweets, partly because they were public and could be retweeted. But the company took far longer to deal with phone calls.[27]

Call center software can queue calls, let callers know the approximate waiting time, offer menu options for call routing and call backs, and retrieve customer data based on the caller's information so agents can quickly find answers. The software can track performance metrics for the agents as well, such as time spent per call or number of escalated calls. Some even assess the caller's stress level through voice analysis so managers can intervene early. The capabilities of call center systems are expanding to full-featured contact center systems in which agents can interact with customers by phone, through online chat, through email, and inside social networks and community forums.

The Library of Congress stores every tweet to keep a record of how we communicate with 140 character snippets. Will you rethink your tweets? "I could really go for some pancakes" probably isn't a tidbit that merits a place in the history books, but with hundreds of millions of tweets sent each day, the collection will contain a little of everything.

DID YOU KNOW?

MOBILE CRM APPLICATIONS

Mobile access to CRM applications for employees is essential, but what about customers? Incorporating cell phones into marketing campaigns is certainly feasible but fraught with hazards. Most people object to unsolicited cell-phone calls and text messages. Sending an invitation to visit a pizza parlor, known from the cell phone's location to be close by, might provoke irritation—unless it also comes with a hefty discount coupon. Offering customers the choice to opt in helps avoid negative reactions.[28]

PRODUCTIVITY TIP

Many colleges and universities invite students, alumni, and parents to opt in to particular types of targeted messages, such as sports scores, college news, events, or reminders. If available, you should also opt in to your college's emergency email and text messaging service. The service should let you know of any disruptions, such as when bad weather causes classes to be canceled.

web beacon (or web bug)
A tiny, invisible image, typically a single pixel with a unique identifier, used on websites to track visitors.

The cell phone offers endless CRM possibilities, and customers welcome certain approaches. To introduce a brand new car model, Nissan created the car as an avatar that players could drive in *Asphalt 7: Heat*, a popular driving game for mobile phones.[29] This creative use of mobile devices for marketing takes good advantage of their capabilities and engages potential customers.

Offering something the customer really values is essential. To promote its Huggies diapers, Kimberly-Clark created a program to help with toilet training. Parents can text "bigkid" from their cell phones and then request a free toilet training kit. The website has resources and tips for parents, who can also sign up for the second part of the program to schedule cell-phone calls at designated times—for the toddler. On the other end, a Disney character congratulates the child on his or her progress. To encourage sales, the company tempts parents with more Disney voices and phone messages if they submit proof of a Huggies purchase.[30]

The large selection of commercially available information systems for finance, human capital, supply chains, and CRM offers tremendous value as well as some major challenges. Lack of integration is the most severe one, a drawback that enterprise resource planning attempts to solve.

Explain the importance of ERP systems and describe how they are created, integrated, and implemented.

5 Enterprise Resource Planning (ERP): Bringing It All Together

As you saw in Chapter 4, early information systems started out in the past century supporting individual departments: accounting, payroll, human resources, inventory, manufacturing, or sales. Accountants could quickly tally the day's receipts and reconcile their bank deposits. The payroll officer could update salaries in the afternoon and output the payroll checks that evening.

Nevertheless, the departmental information systems operated as separate "silos," and information sharing was difficult. Business processes that crossed departmental boundaries were fragmented, and employees grumbled about delays as paperwork passed from inbox to inbox. Confronted with contradictory reports, managers wondered which ones were correct. Inconsistencies might be due to variations in data formats, definitions, or data-entry procedures. The integrated database for the organization's back-end surmounts these silos and provides much more consistency. However, when departments are implementing separate systems from different vendors, each one has its own back-end database.

Responding to the need to consolidate, major software vendors stepped in to build integrated application "megasuites" with functionality for at least two of the core business processes. Early suites arose from systems that supported "manufacturing resource planning," which was software designed for manufacturing companies that helped manage inventories and materials. When the software vendors added capabilities for sales transactions, accounting, human resources, and other common business functions, the software's name was elevated to **enterprise resource planning (ERP)** to underscore its growing breadth. ERPs have grown well beyond their manufacturing roots and now support back-office business processes for retailers, universities, hospitals, government agencies, and many other organizations.

ERP Components

ERP suites, at a minimum, provide a solid, integrated back-end that supports the company's core functional requirements. Modules typically include financials and asset management, human resources management, and, if applicable, manufacturing. Increasingly, ERPs add CRM, SCM, and many other applications to create a "suite of suites." Figure 5-18 shows examples of the kinds of functionality that an ERP might include.

Major ERP vendors include SAP, Oracle, and Microsoft. SAP's suite, for example, goes well beyond the basics, adding electronic document management, RFID and barcode tracking, event management, product design, business intelligence, data mining, and more. ERP vendors also partner with other companies with attractive products so they can integrate them for customers.

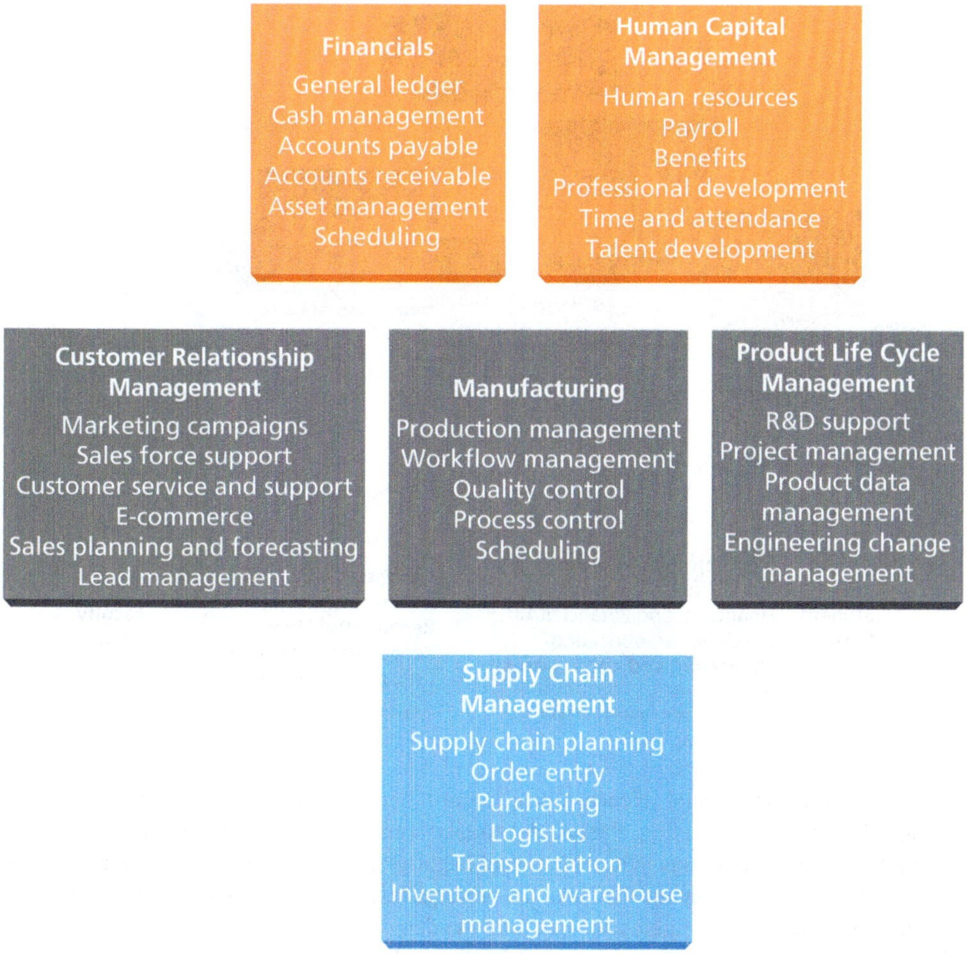

Financials
General ledger
Cash management
Accounts payable
Accounts receivable
Asset management
Scheduling

Human Capital Management
Human resources
Payroll
Benefits
Professional development
Time and attendance
Talent development

Customer Relationship Management
Marketing campaigns
Sales force support
Customer service and support
E-commerce
Sales planning and forecasting
Lead management

Manufacturing
Production management
Workflow management
Quality control
Process control
Scheduling

Product Life Cycle Management
R&D support
Project management
Product data management
Engineering change management

Supply Chain Management
Supply chain planning
Order entry
Purchasing
Logistics
Transportation
Inventory and warehouse management

FIGURE 5-18
Enterprise resource planning (ERP) systems typically include financials and human resources and often also support many other business processes.

ERPs specialized for particular industries are rapidly evolving as well. An ERP for real estate management can manage a portfolio of rental properties, for instance. ERP suites for higher education include modules for financials and human resources and also specialized modules for academic records, financial aid, fund-raising, enrollment management, and others (see Figure 5-19).

STUDENT'S VIEW OF THE ERP

Sophomore Ellen Chang's experience shows how an integrated ERP works at her college (Figure 5-20). Ellen logs in to the student portal to get started. She first checks her account to confirm that her tuition payment is up-to-date and that her partial scholarship is there.

Module	Description
Financials	Tailored for nonprofit, educational institutions, using fund accounting
Human Resources	Human resources and payroll, benefits, time and attendance; system is customized to manage faculty employment conditions, such as tenure and joint appointments
Student Academic Records	Manages classes, courses, student admissions, student registrations, grades, class rosters, faculty assignments
Enrollment Management	CRM tailored to higher education, managing recruitment and retention
Financial Aid	Manages financial aid applications, awards, budgets, and interfaces with aid sources, such as government agencies
Institutional Advancement	Tracks donations, pledges, and gifts, and manages contacts and donor relationships
E-Learning	Provides support for online classes with multimedia presentations, discussion forums, blogs, wikis, assessments, grade books, and other features

FIGURE 5-19
Components of an ERP with modules specialized for higher education.

enterprise resource planning (ERP)
Integrated application suite to support the whole enterprise that includes modules to manage financials, human resources, supply chain, customer relationships, and other business processes.

FIGURE 5-20
Using the portals of an ERP designed
for higher education.

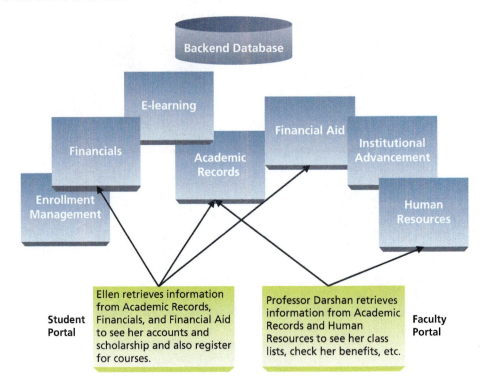

She needs another social science course to fulfill her general education requirements, and because her focus is marketing, she decides to take something in sociology. She searches the schedule of classes and finds SOC 411: Social Demography. But when Ellen tries to register, she receives a message saying she lacks the prereqs. Instead, she looks into SOC 100: Introduction to Sociology and figures she can take the demography course next year. The display shows which sections still have seats, and Professor Darshan has openings. Ellen clicks on the name to bring up a brief bio, office hours, photo, and contact information. She clicks to register and within seconds receives a confirmation email.

THE FACULTY'S VIEW OF THE ERP

Professor Darshan's portal for faculty offers many other self-service tools, such as the ability to update contact information, manage health benefit choices, record expense statements, view student records, and enter grades. The class list for SOC 100 now includes Ellen's name and student ID number, with links to Ellen's contact information. When the class is filled, Professor Darshan will send an email to everyone, welcoming them to the class.

On the back end, Ellen's and Professor Darshan's clicks are generating requests to retrieve information from several ERP modules, such as academic records, human resources, financials, and financial aid. The campus portal controls access for each user, and the integrated database ensures that information is consistent, up-to-date, and unduplicated.

ERP Integration Strategies

How are the ERP modules integrated so the end users have seamless access to whatever organizational data they need? Figure 5-21 shows the major approaches, each of which has pros and cons.

Some products are built from the ground up, so they are engineered with a single architectural foundation and the same programming language. All the components have similar user interfaces, and the back-end database shares common data elements. An employee's email address, for instance, is stored in one place and can be accessed by any module that needs it.

Some vendors enhance their ERPs through mergers or acquisitions, so integration must be added later. SAP and Oracle, the two largest ERP vendors, have both bought numerous smaller companies with attractive software, so then they have to build software bridges to connect the new products and synchronize fields that might be duplicates.

FIGURE 5-21

FIGURE 5-21
Strategies for integrating ERP modules.

Integration Approach	Description	Pros	Cons
The engineered suite	Built from the ground up with consistent user interfaces, integrated backend database, and a single architectural foundation.	Data integrity is high, with consistent, up-to-date, and nonduplicated elements.	Modules are highly interdependent so organizations have to implement and/or upgrade all systems together. Switching costs are high.
Suite with synchronized modules	Vendor provides middleware to connect and synchronize systems that may be running on different platforms.	A common, vendor-provided architecture overlays the systems to improve consistency across the modules.	Modules are integrated at the edges, and the bridges can be fragile.
Best of breed suites	Separate systems, deployed because they each match user requirements closely, but integration is weak and architectural foundations can be very different.	Modules can have very rich functionality and can be implemented individually, reducing risk.	Processes, interfaces, and data may not be consistent across systems. Connections and synchronization, which can be error-prone and costly, may be done in-house or by vendor.

Organizations may also implement a more limited ERP from one vendor but select "best of breed" software for managing customer relationships, supply chain, or some other aspect of their operations. Many universities, for instance, implement an ERP for finances and human resources but build or buy a separate student information system to match their particular requirements. In these cases, the integration effort is often done by in-house IT staff.

MAKING CONNECTIONS WITH MIDDLEWARE

The bridges that attempt to connect different components that might be running on different servers and operating systems are created with software called **middleware**. This software allows one application to access data in another system's database, and it synchronizes data across multiple systems. A customer's email address might be stored in both the finance and CRM modules, and middleware can synchronize the data and propagate an update from the originating system to all the others.

PROS AND CONS OF DIFFERENT INTEGRATION STRATEGIES

The engineered suite offers solid integration on the back-end and consistent user interfaces throughout. Its single architectural foundation can translate to lower IT support costs because staff can focus on just one platform. However, the individual modules may lack all the rich features users want. Also, switching costs are far higher for ERPs in which all the modules are so interdependent.

Another drawback is that tightly integrated ERP systems can be more difficult to modify to meet changing business needs compared with more loosely linked best of breed systems. What seems like a simple change in the structure of a field will ripple throughout the organization with unintended consequences. Making changes in such systems to meet new business needs can often take longer than expected.

Organizations that use either the synchronized or best-of-breed approach must pay close attention to master data management because the same information will appear in more than one system. Avoiding the fate in which the different systems report inconsistent versions of the "truth" is a constant challenge.

Implementation Issues

Implementing an ERP strikes fear into the hearts of CEOs, CFOs, and CIOs alike. Research shows that a very large percentage of such implementations go over budget, take longer than expected, or fail altogether. Finger-pointing about what or who is responsible for such dismal success rates and runaway costs is rampant. Even when an organization successfully launches an ERP, the expected benefits and reduced operating costs may be disappointing.

PREPARING FOR MAJOR CHANGES

The engineered suite, in particular, can be most difficult to implement because it isn't easy to launch the tightly integrated modules one at a time. Instead, organizations use the "big bang"

middleware
Software used as a bridge to integrate separate information systems and synchronize data across multiple systems.

approach, going live with all the core modules at the same time. Simultaneously changing all four tires on a moving car is an apt analogy.

To a large extent, the ERP software requires people throughout the organization to change the way they handle processes, so extensive training before going live is an essential key to success. In principle, the ERP's way of dealing with any particular process embodies best practices, but the organization's old way of doing things might be quite different. The new processes can involve massive changes in terminology, workflow, supervisor approvals, and accounting entries. One school district in Arizona spent several years trying to implement an ERP only to find that employees just didn't want to switch to paperless workflows with streamlined approvals.[31] The need to prepare everyone for new processes is critical.

ERPS AND SOFTWARE AS A SERVICE (SAAS)

The drive to lower implementation costs is pushing vendors toward offering ERPs as software-as-a-service (SaaS) products, in which companies pay subscription fees to access the vendor's software in the cloud via the web. Small and medium-sized businesses with limited IT budgets are especially interested in this model because they can usually get up and running more quickly and don't need their own data center. Larger enterprises are looking closely at the model as well, particularly to become more agile in response to changing business needs. Many cloud-based, best-of-breed products are emerging, and market leaders like SAP, Oracle, and Microsoft offer SaaS versions of their own products.

Although SaaS has many advantages, security and privacy are significant concerns. CEOs are reluctant to house their most valuable assets on servers in the cloud, especially when other companies, even competitors, might be tenants sharing the same servers. Although data on a company's own servers are certainly vulnerable to leaks and attacks, management at least feels some sense of control.

SaaS ERP solutions also may take longer to implement than managers expect. They are not really "instant on" products, and they require just as much training and reengineering of workflows as the on-premise versions. Though IT staff don't install and maintain servers and software, people must configure the software, prepare data for migration, manage the implementation, and train everyone on the new procedures. They may also need to develop interfaces to other systems so that data can be synchronized.[32]

ERP PROS AND CONS

Despite the implementation hurdles, the ERP, at least to integrate finance and human resources, is becoming a near necessity for most organizations. Once in place, it has the potential to enhance operational efficiencies and reduce costs. A key ingredient, of course, is that the organization's employees actually change the way they work to take best advantage of the integrated back end and paperless workflows.

With all its pros and cons, the ERP is, as one business leader put it, something you can't live with and can't live without. Used properly, it can standardize and streamline business processes across the whole enterprise, eliminating the waste and redundancy that creep in when everyone's work is so focused on a single department. An ERP helps people appreciate the full process, spanning departments, not just the part that touches their unit.

Compared to a tangled thicket of poorly integrated systems with rickety electronic bridges running between them, the ERP is an elegant racehorse. It certainly needs a new name, though, given that few remember its roots or what the acronym stands for.

MyMISLab
Online Simulation

CUSTOM CAKES
A Role-Playing Simulation on Enterprise Information Systems and the Supply Chain

The CEO of Custom Cakes is not happy. "Not again! Seems like every day we are either out of stock—which makes our customers mad—or we're loaded with excess inventory that didn't sell. So today it's the line of frustrated customers. I hope you can fix this supply chain and get a handle on that bullwhip effect!"

Custom Cakes is a store in the mall that sells delicious layer cakes with white icing. Inside each box is a special kit with a packet of decorations and several tiny tubes of colored icing that customers use to write their own message on top. Procrastinating customers who forget to order party cakes in advance really appreciate those kits and also buy templates so their cake writing looks more professional.

The company is growing fast, and most of its information systems are supporting business processes well. But its growth is hampered by lost revenue because of supply chain problems. The former assistant manager did his best, but now it is your turn. As the new assistant manager, your job is to get familiar with the company and its information systems and then take on the supply chain problem. Log in when you are ready to get to work....

LEARNING OBJECTIVES

1 The four major categories of information systems that support business processes common to most organizations are finance and asset management, human capital management (HCM), supply chain management (SCM), and customer relationship management (CRM). Finance and asset management systems incorporate modules to support accounts payable, accounts receivable, procurement, cash management, budget planning, asset management, general ledger, and financial reporting. Compliance reporting has become especially important for financial systems, with stringent regulations that require electronic reporting using XBRL, a business report language in the XML family intended to make reports more transparent, consistent, and computer-readable.

2 Human capital management systems include core human resources functionality along with other modules that support a broader range of employee-related applications. Workforce management software offers labor-scheduling tools and also tracks time and attendance, leave, and project assignments. Talent management helps map the employee life cycle, from recruitment through career development and to retirement. Social software is also sometimes included, especially to encourage mentoring. Metrics from these systems, including performance and productivity measures, can help reveal how well an organization is managing and nurturing its human capital.

3 Supply chain management supports processes that optimize the flow of products and services from their source, through the company, and to the customer. The five steps in supply chain management are (1) plan, (2) source, (3) make, (4) deliver, and (5) return. Improving visibility in a supply chain helps managers see metrics that help assess overall effectiveness, in a retailer's real-time sales, for example. The bullwhip effect occurs in a supply chain when visibility is low. Collaboration to improve visibility among suppliers and customers uses electronic data interchange (EDI) or XML. Sensing technologies such as RFID and GPS also help improve visibility.

4 Customer relationship management (CRM) revolves around customer records, especially to improve retention, increase profitability, grow revenue, and listen to customer sentiments. CRM's diverse software applications are especially useful in marketing, sales force automation, and customer service and support. Included in this category are software tools to support email marketing, loyalty programs, marketing campaigns, online customer service, contact management, sentiment analysis, mobile phone advertising, and more.

5 Enterprise resource planning (ERP) systems integrate two or more of the applications that support major business processes common to most organizations, especially finance and human resources. ERPs from major vendors incorporate functionality for CRM, SCM, manufacturing processes, analytics, and other business requirements as well. Some ERPs have tightly integrated modules, whereas others synchronize data across modules that are more loosely integrated, using middleware. Implementing an ERP is a major challenge, partly because so many applications are replaced and so many processes are affected at the same time. SaaS versions are being offered, which can be easier for some organizations. Despite the hurdles, most organizations find the integrated ERP solution very valuable, especially for finance and human resources.

KEY TERMS AND CONCEPTS

financial management system

eXtensible Business Reporting Language (XBRL)

human capital management (HCM)

human resources management (HRM) system

workforce management module

talent management

supply chain management (SCM)

visibility

demand forecast accuracy (DFA)

bullwhip effect

electronic data interchange (EDI)

global positioning systems (GPS)

customer relationship management (CRM)

sentiment analysis

web beacon or web bug

enterprise resource planning (ERP)

middleware

CHAPTER REVIEW QUESTIONS

5-1. What are the four major categories of information systems that support business processes common to most organizations? Which basic business functions does each provide?

5-2. What role does a financial and asset management information system serve in an organization? Why is financial reporting important? What are exception reporting and compliance reporting? Why is each important?

5-3. What is human capital management? What are the major components of a human capital management information system? What are examples of metrics used to quantify human capital? How are these metrics used?

5-4. What is supply chain management? What is the most important metric in supply chain management? What does it measure? What are examples of supply chain management software? How is each used to support supply chain processes?

5-5. What is customer relationship management (CRM)? What are the objectives of CRM? How do organizations measure their customer relationships? How do information systems support each objective of CRM? What are three basic categories of CRM technologies? How do information systems support activities in each area?

5-6. Why are ERP systems important to organizations? What are the typical components of an ERP system? What is meant by the term *a suite of suites*? What are three approaches to ERP integration? What are some of the issues associated with an ERP implementation? What is the primary benefit of a successful ERP implementation?

PROJECTS AND DISCUSSION QUESTIONS

5-7. Sensing technologies are everywhere in the supply chain. Describe some of these sensing technologies and discuss the benefits they provide. Search the Internet to learn more about one of these technologies and how it is used in the supply chain. Prepare a 5-minute presentation of your findings.

5-8. Do you tweet? Twitter claims its users are sending 400 million tweets a day.[33] That's a lot of Twitter chatter! What is sentiment analysis? How do organizations use sentiment analysis to manage customer relationships? Visit www.tweetfeel.com and enter the name of your city to learn what Twitter users are saying about your hometown. Then visit www.tweetfeel.com/biz to learn how organizations can use this online tool to improve customer relations. Describe how TweetFeel works. What are search sets? Does TweetFeel work in real time? How do you think Twitter chatter will change when users learn it is being monitored?

5-9. Does your college or university let you sign up to receive emergency alerts on your cell phone? What are the advantages of this system? How does this differ from using mobile devices for marketing purposes? What are the challenges of implementing mobile CRM targeted to

customers? Describe several approaches to mobile CRM that are welcomed by customers. What are the advantages to employees of providing them mobile access to CRM?

5-10. Many colleges and universities use Banner, a higher education software ERP system. Describe the ERP system at your college or university. Compare the modules described in Figure 5-19 to the system components that you access during the semester. Which modules do you use? How do you use those modules? Which modules are used by university faculty and staff?

5-11. Many CRM systems are integrating social networking technologies to improve customer relationships. Search several social networking sites such as Facebook, Twitter, and YouTube to identify how a specific company such as Dell, Coca-Cola, or McDonald's is using social media to interact with customers. Prepare a 5-minute presentation of your findings.

5-12. Work in a small group with classmates to identify the types of information that you would need for an HCM module to help you identify individuals in an organization who have the potential for promotion. How would you use this information to manage high potential employees?

APPLICATION EXERCISES

5-13. EXCEL APPLICATION:
Performance Bicycle Parts

Ted Stevens owns an Internet-based bicycle accessories website that sells bicycle tires, tubes, chains, sprockets, and seats as well as helmets and water bottles. The bicycle parts aftermarket is very competitive, and Ted realizes that having both a low price and sufficient inventory to offer same-day shipping are critical to his success. He has a global supply chain and relies on many different supplier sources for the quality products his customers demand.

Ted sells more replacement tubes than any other product. For this item, customers expect high quality at a competitive price. Ted spent several months evaluating the quality and performance of six potential suppliers for the most popular replacement tube, the 29" × 1.85"–2.20" presta tube. These suppliers manufacture replacement tubes of comparable quality and performance. With the right price, quality, and availability, Ted expects to sell an average of 12,000 tubes per month, or 400 tubes per day, for $6.50 each. However, he is concerned about the amount of cash or working capital required to support the level of inventory he needs to provide same-day shipping.

Using the information provided in Figure 5-22, create a spreadsheet to analyze the replacement tube cost structure for six potential suppliers. Per unit import duty cost equals the import duty rate multiplied by the sum of per unit base cost and the per unit shipping cost. The per unit warehouse cost is the sum of the per unit base cost and the per unit shipping cost and the per unit import duty cost. The per unit total cost is the sum of the per unit warehouse cost and the average per unit carrying cost.

Required inventory levels are based on projected daily sales times the number of shipping days required for delivery from the supplier to Ted's warehouse. A longer delivery time requires Ted to maintain a higher level of inventory. Thus, he wants to include inventory carrying costs in the analysis. Ted maintains average inventory (units) based on 150% of projected daily sales multiplied by the number of shipping days from the supplier. The average inventory value equals the per unit delivered cost multiplied by the average inventory (units).

Inventory carrying costs include the cost of putting away stock and moving material within the warehouse, rent and utilities for warehouse space, insurance and taxes on inventory, and inventory shrinkage. Ted calculates his total inventory carrying costs at 24% of the average inventory value. The average per unit carrying cost equals the total inventory carrying cost divided by the total number of units sold per year (144,000).

Which supplier source requires the highest investment of working capital or cash for average inventory? Which supplier source provides Ted with the highest percentage of gross profit on the presta replacement tube?

5-14. ACCESS APPLICATION:
VSI Consultants

VSI Consultants Group, Inc., is a professional IT consulting firm that provides business and nonprofit organizations with the highly skilled IT professionals they need to complete IT projects and resolve staffing problems. VSI matches employees with client projects based on employee education, skills, and experience. Emily Loftus, the HR manager, has asked you to use the information provided in the spreadsheet shown in Figures 5-23, 5-24, and 5-25 to create an Access database to manage employees and projects. You can download the Excel file Ch05Ex02 and import the worksheets to tables in your database. Emily wants you to create two queries. The first query identifies the best candidates for three client projects: U.S. Brokerage, Helen's Clothiers, and Solar Systems. The second query matches employees with projects. Specifically, she wants to match projects for two employees: Y326 and T871. What other queries may be useful to Emily?

FIGURE 5-22
Suppliers for Performance Bicycle Parts.

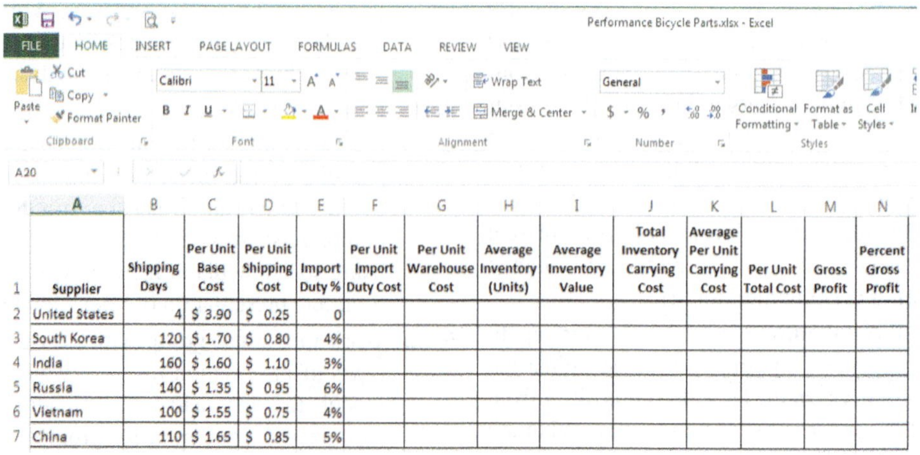

Supplier	Shipping Days	Per Unit Base Cost	Per Unit Shipping Cost	Import Duty %	Per Unit Import Duty Cost	Per Unit Warehouse Cost	Average Inventory (Units)	Average Inventory Value	Total Inventory Carrying Cost	Average Per Unit Carrying Cost	Per Unit Total Cost	Gross Profit	Percent Gross Profit
United States	4	$ 3.90	$ 0.25	0									
South Korea	120	$ 1.70	$ 0.80	4%									
India	160	$ 1.60	$ 1.10	3%									
Russia	140	$ 1.35	$ 0.95	6%									
Vietnam	100	$ 1.55	$ 0.75	4%									
China	110	$ 1.65	$ 0.85	5%									

Source: Microsoft® Excel, Microsoft Corporation. Reprinted with permission.

FIGURE 5-23

Employee data.

	Employee ID	Last Name	First Name	Undergraduate Degree	Advanced Degree	Yrs. Exp.	Skills
1				**Employee Data**			
2	Employee ID	Last Name	First Name	Undergraduate Degree	Advanced Degree	Yrs. Exp.	Skills
3	V321	Victor	Albert	BS Computer Sciences	MS Computer Sciences	3	1,3
4	J045	Johns	Carl	BS Mathematics		2	2,5
5	B195	Barton	Alice	BS Management	MBA	1	1,5
6	C013	Cox	Amanda	BS Accounting		3	2,5
7	Y326	Yee	Han	BS Accounting	MS Accounting	6	5
8	W821	Watson	Helen	BS Computer Sciences		8	2
9	J342	Johnson	Sally	BS Education		7	3,4
10	T078	Thornton	Robert	BS History		4	3
11	R430	Randal	Joyce	BS Economics	MBA	2	5,6
12	N541	Nottingham	Henry	BS Mathematics		3	1,2
13	C427	Cary	Jane	BS Computer Sciences	MS Computer Sciences	5	1,5
14	U039	Underwood	Frank	BS Accounting		2	4,5
15	M432	Morgan	Thomas	BS Mathematics		7	4
16	P549	Palmer	James	BS Electical Engineering		5	2,4
17	B130	Boston	Matt	BS Computer Sciences	MS Computer Sciences	3	4,5
18	S0343	Soloman	Robert	BS Computer Sciences		6	2
19	F430	Francis	Tom	BS Logistics		2	4,5
20	T871	Trenton	Mary	BS Matematics	MS Matematics	3	2,4
21	A321	Alvarez	Hernando	BS Computer Sciences		4	1,2,4

Source: Microsoft® Excel, Microsoft Corporation. Reprinted with permission.

FIGURE 5-24

Skills data.

	A
1	**SKILLS**
2	1 = Database management
3	2 = Business Intelligence
4	3 = Web-design
5	4 = ERP Systems
6	5 = Project management

Source: Microsoft® Excel, Microsoft Corporation. Reprinted with permission.

FIGURE 5-25

Open projects data.

	Client	Project Type	Min. Exper.	Basic Skills	Add'l Skills	Preferred Degree
1			**Open Projects**			
2	Client	Project Type	Min. Exper.	Basic Skills	Add'l Skills	Preferred Degree
3	JM Logistics Inc.	1	4	1	4	BS CS or Math
4	Jefferson Automotive	4	5	4,5	1	MBA
5	World-wide Sourcing	2,4	5	2	4	BS Accounting or MBA
6	Solar Systems	2	2	2		BS Math, BS CS, BS Acctg.
7	Robert's Heating Supply	3	2	3		none
8	Casual Dining, Inc.	2	3	2	1	BS CS
9	US Brokerage	1,2	5	1,2	5	BS CS, BS Math. Or MBA
10	Computer Chips, Inc.	4	3	4,5	1	none
11	Southeast Region Youth Ministries	1,2	4	2	1	BS CS or Math
12	Huston Power Co.	1	5	1		none
13	Helen's Clothiers	4	3	4	1	BS CS, BS Acctg., BS Math.
14	McMasters Printing	3	2	3		none
15	United Grocers	4	5	1,4	5	MBA
16	Shelby County Women's Shelter	1	2	1	5	none
17	National Distributors	1,3	5	1,3	2	BS Accounting

Source: Microsoft® Excel, Microsoft Corporation. Reprinted with permission.

CASE STUDY #1

Salesforce.com: Taking CRM to the Cloud

As the leading CRM software vendor, Salesforce.com is also the pioneering company that launched cloud-based software as a service (SaaS) for enterprise-level applications. Founded in 1999, the company boasts double-digit annual growth, with sales topping $6 billion by 2016. In the early years, however, Salesforce had a difficult time convincing other companies that a cloud-based solution for CRM would work or that their sensitive data would be secure.

Larger enterprises, in particular, were reluctant to move such data off their privately managed servers housed in their own data centers. But Salesforce persisted, offering a "pay-as-you-go" subscription pricing model that allowed companies to identify a small number of users to try out the service. The advanced CRM features that Salesforce offered were often well beyond what the company's own CRM software could do, particularly on mobile devices. Salespeople are on the road quite a bit, and having the ability to manage their leads, tasks, customer communications, and other data important for CRM from anywhere at any time quickly became a "must have." The company's approach essentially propelled the era of enterprise-level cloud computing. Analysts project that 50% of organizations will select SaaS for complex business process support by 2018 as they wind down their private data centers and move applications to the cloud.

Salesforce.com has a growing number of competitors, however, and focuses heavily on continuous innovation for its products. For example, the company added the "Wave Analytics" app to its services so that business users can analyze data in real time and take action from within the app. To encourage innovative thinking, Salesforce.com draws on the ideas of its millions of customers who contribute their thoughts to the IdeaExchange. Other customers can vote on the ideas by clicking thumbs up or down, and those with high vote totals are reviewed by Salesforce staff who decide whether to include the feature in an upcoming release. The IdeaExchange shows the fate of each idea so contributors can see the outcome.

The relentless drive to innovate led company executives to reconsider office space design. Salesforce.com CEO Mark Benioff brought in Buddhist monks to give their thoughts on how to configure the company's skyscraper headquarters in San Francisco. The monks observed that the employees were talking all the time and working constantly and suggested that space should be provided for more contemplation. Benioff added "mindfulness" areas on each floor so that employees would have a quiet place to think and reflect.

Despite very rapid growth, Salesforce.com faces a number of challenges. One involves the need to constantly upgrade its services and technology. For example, it relies on Oracle databases, but the company is considering moving to an open source database solution to reduce costs. It also must ensure that its own platform is constantly available for customers. A major outage in 2016 left customers very frustrated, and 5 hours' worth of data updates were lost.

Perhaps the most important challenge for Salesforce.com is maintaining security, especially because the data's sensitivity is quite high. Concerns about security have always been uppermost in customers' minds, and Salesforce.com continually bolsters the systems used to monitor traffic and access. Its Salesforce Shield, for instance, allows IT administrators to see user activity in real time.

To grow, Salesforce.com spends a large chunk of its revenue on sales and marketing and also technology to improve and expand product offerings. While revenue is growing, the company often posts losses with expenses exceeding income. But with growing adoption of SaaS and cloud computing in general, Salesforce.com should have a promising future.

Discussion Questions

5-15. Identify one way that in the early years Salesforce.com addressed market confidence in its cloud-based systems. Was this way successful? Why or why not?

5-16. How does Salesforce.com use the IdeaExchange for competitive advantage? What benefits does it provide to the company and its customers?

5-17. Explain how office space design in the San Francisco headquarters was changed and why this change is expected to return value to Salesforce.com.

5-18. Identify at least two challenges that Salesforce.com faces and explain why these are important challenges to Salesforce.com.

Sources: Darrow, B. (May 11, 2016). Salesforce negotiates tricky software path. *Fortune.com*, http://fortune.com/2016/05/11/salesforce-two-software-worlds/, accessed August 17, 2016.
Frank, B. H. (2016). Salesforce picks AWS as preferred public cloud provider. CIO, *http://www.cio.com/article/3075532/salesforce-picks-aws-as-preferred-public-cloud-provider.html*, accessed August 17, 2016.
Gallagher, D. (February 25, 2016). How Salesforce.com can keep making it rain. *Wall Street Journal (Online)*, http://www.wsj.com/articles/how-salesforce-com-can-keep-making-it-rain-1456429982, accessed August 17, 2016.
Green, T. (2016). *Salesforce.com, Inc*. Hoover's Online, http://subscriber.hoovers.com.proxy1.library.jhu.edu/H/company360/fulldescription.html?companyId=99297000000000, accessed August 17, 2016.
Konrad, A. (2016). How monks convinced Marc Benioff to install "mindfulness zones" throughout Salesforce's new offices. *Forbes.com*, http://www.forbes.com/sites/alexkonrad/2016/03/07/how-monks-convinced-benioff-to-put-mindfulness-zones-in-salesforce/#6751fd31f79b, accessed August 18, 2016.
Li, M., Kankanhalli, A., & Kim, S. H. (2016). Which ideas are more likely to be implemented in online user innovation communities? An empirical analysis. *Decision Support Systems, 84*, 28–40. http://doi.org/10.1016/j.dss.2016.01.004
Maisto, M. (2016). Salesforce outage results in 5 hours of data loss. *eWeek*, http://www.eweek.com/enterprise-apps/salesforce-outage-results-in-5-hours-of-data-loss.html, accessed August 18, 2016.
Maoz, M., & Manusama, B. (2016). *Magic quadrant for the CRM customer engagement center* (No. G00278086). Gartner Group, http://www.gartner.com/document/3306017?ref=solrAll&refval=168941094&qid=81b8d40ccc92ecfd7fd020f20006a7d0, accessed May 10, 2016.
MarketLine. (2016). *Salesforce.com, Inc*. MarketLine Company Profile, 1–31.
Salesforce.com Website. (2016). http://www.salesforce.com, accessed June 6, 2016.

CASE STUDY #2

Winning the War for Talent: The Mandarin Oriental's Talent Management System

Colleagues is the term that the Mandarin Oriental Hotel Group uses to refer to employees, and a major goal for this luxury chain is to recruit, train, and retain the most productive people in the hospitality industry. Starting in 1963 with a single luxury hotel in Hong Kong called the Mandarin, the company expanded slowly, acquiring a stake in the landmark Oriental Hotel in Bangkok. That hotel first opened in 1865 and enjoyed a grand tradition, having survived several wars and hosted countless authors, celebrities, and government leaders.

Over the years, the Mandarin Oriental Hotel Group grew to more than 40 properties in more than 25 countries. Each hotel is as distinctive as the first two. The company does not want a "monoculture," so each property takes on its own personality to match the local market. But the company's leaders also strongly believe in establishing clear standards and performance indicators for every position and job function. The Hotel Group's HR department in Hong Kong oversees the process so that, for instance, the chef at the Mandarin Oriental in Singapore will meet the same standards as the chefs in Boston, Bangkok, and Bermuda. Locally, each hotel's human resources team can tweak policies and procedures, especially because employment laws and cultural factors differ. But the underlying standards are global.

To manage this empire and ensure that every hotel contributes to its reputation for unsurpassed customer satisfaction, the company relies on a global approach to talent development. With more than 10,000 colleagues speaking many different languages in Asia, Europe, the Americas, Middle East, and North Africa, the company implemented a specialized talent management system. The system relies on SuccessFactors' cutting-edge human capital management (HCM) system, which was purchased by SAP in 2012 to replace SAP's aging HR system.

The HCM system provides the building blocks to assess each colleague's performance, and it also adds a means to determine career development paths and training needs. Both staff and managers can input information about performance, and they can add notes about development plans so that colleagues know what they should do to advance their careers.

The system also supports succession planning because every individual's capabilities and career progression are easily accessed. This helps managers see functional areas that might lack depth and in which a sudden departure of a key employee could be a serious setback. If there is no one with the knowledge and skills to step in easily, either by transferring someone from a different hotel or promoting someone locally, the chain is taking a risk.

Group Director of HR Paul Clark says, "The system is doing the job of tracking careers with the [Mandarin Oriental] group. It helps us to determine who is ready for the next career step and then we actively promote internally." A major advantage is that colleagues are well aware that they have attractive career opportunities, and they know what training they need to pursue them. A side benefit of systems such as this is that the emphasis on career development and interactivity increases the motivation of executives to do performance appraisals with more care.

Companies may never actually win the war for talent, but they must engage in it continually to attract and retain the most productive people. Talent management systems can help them do that.

Discussion Questions

5-19. How does the talent management system help Mandarin Oriental balance the needs of global coordination and local responsiveness?

5-20. Why would it be important for Mandarin Oriental to have an integrated HR database?

5-21. What are the benefits for Mandarin Oriental executives? What are the benefits for Mandarin Oriental employees?

5-22. What further uses could be possible for the data in this system?

Sources: Freyemuth, J. (September 13, 2012). Impact of SuccessFactors acquisition on SAP's HCM strategy. Gartner Research, ID:G00235670.

Mandarin Oriental: Talent everywhere. (March 2010). HRM Asia, http://www.hrmasia.com/case-studies/mandarin-oriental-talent-everywhere/40527/, accessed March 25, 2013.

Ladkin, A., & Buhalis, D. (2016). Online and social media recruitment. *International Journal of Contemporary Hospitality Management, 28*(2), 327–345. http://doi.org/10.1108/IJCHM-05-2014-0218

Otter, T., Freyemuth, J., & Hanscome, R. (March 14, 2013). Magic quadrant for talent management suites. Gartner Research, ID:G00227698.

Schein, A. (2016). Mandarin Oriental International Limited. Hoover's Online, http://subscriber.hoovers.com.proxy1.library.jhu.edu/H/company360/overview.html?companyId=101774000000000&newsCompanyDuns=687029124, accessed March 24, 2016.

SuccessFactors supports Mandarin Oriental Hotel Group global growth strategy. (2009).

S. C. Study, http://www.successfactors.com/docs/Mandarin_CaseStudy_final_art_CRAIG_approved_JM_0121.pdf, accessed March 29, 2013.

E-PROJECT 1   CRM for Human Services Agencies

This e-project explores how human services agencies strive to improve customer relationship management capabilities.

Make a table like the one in Figure 5-26, and then visit the websites of those Departments of Human Services. Attempt to answer the questions for each site, but if you can't find the answer to a question within 3 minutes, enter "Not found."

http://www.oregon.gov/DHS/
http://www.dhr.georgia.gov/portal/site/DHS/
http://dhs.dc.gov/

5-23. How do you compare these departments in terms of how customer-centric their websites are for visitors with different goals?

5-24. What measures are these human services agencies taking to make it easier for people to obtain services that are designed for them?

5-25. In what ways could CRM help agencies improve services and reduce costs?

FIGURE 5-26

How customer-centric are human services agencies' websites?

	Oregon	Georgia	District of Columbia
How do I apply for food stamps?			
Where can I find the nearest homeless shelter?			
What services are available for deaf people?			

E-PROJECT 2   Evaluating Employment and Recruitment Websites

In this e-project, you will compare the major publicly accessible career management websites and test their capabilities.

Founded in 1995, Careerbuilder.com claims to be the largest online job site in the United States. A chief rival is Monster.com, which pioneered digital recruitment in 1994. Its parent company, Monster Worldwide, Inc., also offers similar services in other countries with local listings. Both companies earn revenue from fees charged to employers for posting jobs and searching through résumés for qualified candidates and also from online advertising.

5-26. Visit each site and check out the "About Us" sections to better understand how the two companies differ. Compare and contrast their vision statements.

5-27. Imagine you are a hotel manager looking for a job in a major U.S. city of your choice. Compare the positions you find with Monster to those you find with Careerbuilder.

5-28. Now enter each site as though you are a human resources manager for a luxury hotel, and would like to post a job for hotel manager. Compare the various services and packages that each site offers employers. In which one would you choose to post your ad, and what factors led to your decision?

CHAPTER NOTES

1. Ahmed, M., Mahmood, A. N., & Islam, M. R. (2016). A survey of anomaly detection techniques in financial domain. *Future Generation Computer Systems*, *55*, 278–288. http://doi.org/10.1016/j.future.2015.01.001

2. Rahimi-Laridjani, E., & Hauser, E. (2016). The new global FATCA: An overview of the OECD's common reporting standard in relation to FATCA. *Journal of Taxation of Financial Products*, *13*(3), 9–47.

3. Whitehouse, T. (2016). FASB, SEC offer some new insights on XBRL. *Compliance Week*, *13*(146), 7–8.

4. Thaler, R. H., & Tucker, W. (2013). Smarter information, smarter consumers. *Harvard Business Review*, *91*(1), 44–54.

5. Tysiac, K. (2016). Changes ahead. *Journal of Accountancy*, *221*(3), 81–87.

6. Frigo, M. L., & Ubelhart, M. (2016). Human capital management: The central element of all risk. *People & Strategy*, *39*(1), 42–46.

7. Wilms, T. (May 8, 2012). Dow Chemical: Using social media to educate and train the next generation. *Forbes*, http://www.forbes.com/sites/sap/2012/05/08/dow-chemical-using-social-media-to-educate-and-train-the-next-generation/, accessed April 13, 2013.

8. Baker, S. (April 23, 2009). You're fired—but stay in touch. *BusinessWeek*. p. 54.

9. Osborne, C. (January 25, 2013). Apple discovers underage workers, fires supplier. *ZDNet*, http://www.zdnet.com/apple-discovers-underage-workers-fires-supplier-7000010323/, accessed January 26, 2013.

10. Deligonul, S., Elg, U., Cavusgil, E., & Ghauri, P. N. (2013). Developing strategic supplier networks: An institutional perspective. *Journal of Business Research*, *66*(4), 506–515. doi:10.1016/j.jbusres.2011.12.003

11. Carpenter, S. (2016). PayPal joins Netflix in fight against VPNs. *Forbes.com*, 1–1.

12. Vyas, N. (2016). Disruptive technologies enabling supply chain evolution. *Supply Chain Management Review*, *20*(1), 36–41.

13. Wallace, P. (2004). *The Internet in the workplace: How new technologies transform work*. Cambridge, UK: Cambridge University Press.

14. Giguere, M., & Householder, B. (2012). Supply chain visibility: More trust than technology. *Supply Chain Management Review*, *16*(6), 20–25.

15. Wray, B., 2, & Sanislo, M. (2016). The case for RFID in blood banking. *MLO: Medical Laboratory Observer*, *48*(3), 32–34.

16. Lasisi, A., Bai, L., & Sun, Z. (2012). An empirical study on risk mitigation in transporting hazardous material. *IIE Annual Conference. Proceedings*, 1–10. Retrieved from http://search.proquest.com/docview/1151089925?accountid=11752, accessed June 20, 2013.

17. Smith, A. (January, 2013). Social media for businesses begs for more listening and less marketing. SearchCRM, http://searchcrm.techtarget.com/feature/Social-media-for-businesses-begs-for-more-listening-and-less-marketing, accessed January 28, 2013.

18. Smilansky, O. (2016). How to craft a clear and effective CRM strategy. *CRM Magazine*, *20*(1), 24–27.

19. Farmers Insurance analyzes customer lifetime value with SAS®. (2008). http://www.sas.com/success/farmers.html, accessed May 15, 2011.

20. The frontline. (2010). *Marketing Week* (01419285), *33*(41), 29.

21. Albro, W. (2012). Live chat: Re-engaging remote customers. *ABA Bank Marketing*, *44*(3), 20–24.

22. Saif, H., He, Y., Fernandez, M., & Alani, H. (2016). Contextual semantics for sentiment analysis of Twitter. *Information Processing & Management*, *52*(1), 5–19. http://doi.org/10.1016/j.ipm.2015.01.005

23. Wright, A. (August 24, 2009). Mining the web for feelings, not facts. *New York Times*. p. B.1.

24. Smith, R. (March 9, 2016). Gunfight in the Second Life virtual corral? WRAL.com, http://www.wral.com/business/legacy_local_tech_wire/video/2121937/, accessed September 27, 2016.

25. Hohmann, J. (August 21, 2009). Metro tweets far from short and sweet (or decipherable). *The Washington Post*, http://articles.washingtonpost.com/2009-08-21/news/36872805_1_tweets-twitter-account-140-character-limit, accessed June 20, 2013.

26. Clancy, H. (2016). Twitter Wants to Help Your Customer Service Team. Fortune.com, 32–32.

27. Bigman, D. (2013). Looking for your missing 1800Flowers Valentine's Day delivery? Use Twitter, not the phone, study says. Forbes.com, http://www.forbes.com/sites/danbigman/2013/02/17/looking-for-your-missing-1800flowers-valentines-day-delivery-use-twitter-not-the-phone-study-says/, accessed July 5, 2013.

28. Bacon, J. (2016). Five mobile marketing mistakes and how to fix them. *Marketing Week*, 16–20.

29. Ireson, N. (December 6, 2012). Drive the Nissan Juke Nismo now—in Asphalt 7: Heat. MotorAuthority, http://www.motorauthority.com/news/1080947_drive-the-nissan-juke-nismo-now–in-asphalt-7-heat, accessed January 27, 2013.

30. Chang, R. (August 2009). Getting personal with mobile marketing can boost sales, loyalty. *Advertising Age*, *80*(27), 14.

31. Kanaracus, C. (January 17, 2013). School district options for struggling ERP software project. *CIO Magazine*, http://www.cio.com/article/2389070/cio-role/school-district-weighs-options-for-struggling-erp-software-project.html, accessed August 18, 2016.

32. Hardcastle, C. (2016). *Transforming ERP to Postmodern ERP Primer for 2016* (No. G00292984). Gartner Research.

33. Farber, D. (June 6, 2012). Twitter hits 400 million tweets per day, mostly mobile. *cnet*, http://news.cnet.com/8301-1023_3-57448388-93/twitter-hits-400-million-tweets-per-day-mostly-mobile/, accessed August 18, 2016.

The Web, Social Media, *E-Commerce, and M-Commerce*

LEARNING OBJECTIVES

1 Identify and provide examples of four goals an organization might choose as it develops its web and social media strategies, and explain how websites are named.

2 Provide examples of different website information architectures, explain the importance of usability and accessibility, and describe how websites are created with various software tools.

3 Explain how e-commerce works and why security and trust are critical ingredients.

4 Define m-commerce, and explain how mobile payments work.

5 Explain how organizations manage digital marketing for their website, their social media presence, and their mobile apps.

6 Explain how the evolving web continues to develop by incorporating attributes such as crowdsourcing, expanded data sources, the "Internet of Things," machine learning, and "big data."

> An online, interactive decision-making simulation that reinforces chapter contents and uses key terms in context can be found in MyMISLab™.

INTRODUCTION

EVERY ENTERPRISE NEEDS A WELL-THOUGHT-OUT WEB STRATEGY, one that features its website as the front door. Whether the organization actually sells products, solicits donations, or tries to build mindshare and loyalty, its web presence is a focal point.

In the online simulation for this chapter, you will experience first-hand what it is like to own a start-up that needs a lively web presence. You inherited a gourmet food truck called "Cruisin' Fusion," and business is booming. You and

a couple of partners will get together to plan your website, choose a name, and develop strategies to make the business prosper. You will certainly want customers to find you easily through search engines, and you want to give them easy directions with interactive maps. You'll also need to be wary of scams that prey on websites. The decision-making simulation introduces you to the major concepts in this chapter as a way to learn by doing.

MyMISLab
Online Simulation

CRUISIN' FUSION
A Role-Playing Simulation on Website Development
for a Chain of Concession Stands

Charlotte Lake/Shutterstock.

In "Cruisin' Fusion," the web will be your ally as you build your food truck business. But the web and the Internet itself unleash creative destruction that demolishes other business models. For example, the web bulldozed the newspaper business is short order. Beset by readership losses, layoffs, and plummeting advertising revenue, print newspapers are in deep trouble. Some have already gone bankrupt or drastically cut back their activities. It's not that people aren't interested in news. It is that they can get most of it for free, online, and in much livelier multimedia formats. Even more appealing, they can join the conversation, adding comments, debating opinion pieces, and contributing their own breaking stories.

To thrive, companies must tap the power of the web and social media to engage customers, motivate employees, compete against rivals, and earn revenue. They must also be forward looking about e-commerce as well as mobile commerce (m-commerce). M-commerce is taking off rapidly, and people will be using their smartphones as wallets—in addition to everything else they use them for. This chapter explores these important topics, beginning with an organization's web strategy.

Identify and provide examples of four goals an organization might choose as it develops its web and social media strategies, and explain how websites are named.

 # Developing a Web Strategy

Barely two and a half decades old, the web offers an inexpensive virtual home to any organization, one that is accessible 24/7. An effective web strategy requires a clear vision of the company's goals, whether the goals apply to the company's website, its presence on social media, or both. Who do you want to attract as visitors, and what do you want them to do while there? What do you want to learn about them to find ways to improve the site's effectiveness and lure them back?

Choosing a Goal

Every organization's online presence can accomplish many things, but it can't do everything at the same time. Managers have most success when they stress a few major goals and also design ways to measure how well those goals are being met. Let's look at some examples of major goals.

INFORM OR ENTERTAIN THE AUDIENCE

Organizations that aim to inform an audience or entertain people in some way offer content that drives traffic to the site. To earn revenue, many sell advertising or offer premium access to specialized content for fee-paying members. Online magazines, video sites, and free game sites usually adopt this goal. At AddictingGames.com, for instance, the games are free, but the site's ads target the likely demographic of the players. *Huffington Post*, the online newspaper that features blogs by unpaid celebrities such as Ron Howard, also relies on ad revenue.

An **infomediary** focuses on informing visitors and empowering them with aggregated information about products from different suppliers. *Consumer Reports*, for instance, tests consumer products in its labs and shares its results so consumers can compare brands. Many infomediaries are also **e-marketplaces** that bring together buyers and sellers, often from all over the world. Bizrate.com, with its "Search, compare, conquer" slogan, compares sellers on thousands of items, showing buyers which retailer has the best price. Buyers who check such sites before purchasing can save hundreds every year.

E-marketplaces are often classified based on the buyers and sellers they serve (Figure 6-1). Bizrate and Expedia, for instance, focus mainly on **business-to-consumer (B2C)** transactions, in which many suppliers post their wares and consumers can compare them on pricing and features. E-marketplaces also support **business-to-business (B2B)** relationships. On Alibaba.com, a retailer who needs to restock the inventory for a product can compare wholesale prices, minimum orders, and payment terms from suppliers in dozens of countries.

Consumer-to-consumer (C2C) e-marketplaces include eBay and Craigslist. Individual sellers can post their wares, and shoppers use the search tools to find what they want. **Consumer-to-business (C2B)** relationships, in which consumers sell products or services online to business, are also facilitated by e-marketplaces. Amazon, for instance, pays bloggers a fee when their readers buy something they promote on the blog.

FIGURE 6-1

Types of e-marketplaces.

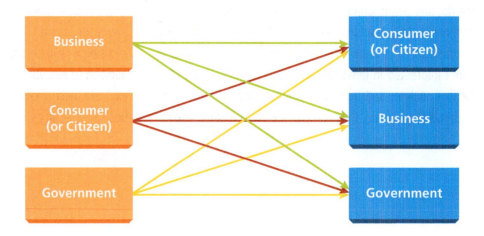

Government websites also support online interactions, so terms such as G2C, G2G, and C2G have appeared. For example, G2C encompasses services such as online payment for car registration renewals, and C2G might include electronic filing of tax forms.

Infomediaries are multiplying because so much information is becoming available in machine-readable forms, typically XML. Innovative start-ups are capturing and analyzing the data and making it available so people can make smart choices. First Fuel, for instance, gathers hourly electric bill data from utility companies and combines that with GPS and hourly local weather data. Customers can see how efficiently their building is using energy and then make changes if needed.[1]

INFLUENCE THE AUDIENCE

Companies that are not actually selling directly to the public online hope to influence their audience in subtle ways through their websites, Facebook pages, or other online presence. They might want to increase brand awareness or persuade visitors to consider new technologies and upgrades. For instance, automobile manufacturers offer numerous tools to construct a virtual car, choose accessories, read reviews, and learn about new options.

Nonprofit organizations, political blogs, campaigns, and public service initiatives might also emphasize influence as the primary goal of their web presence, disseminating information and encouraging visitors to get involved with local activities and events.

SELL PRODUCTS AND SERVICES

Selling is the primary goal of organizations whose websites live and die by e-commerce transactions. Overstock.com, iTunes, and Amazon include many features to help visitors find what they are looking for, read product information or reviews, compile wish lists, and buy online. The checkout process on these sites is critical to customer satisfaction. It must include several payment options, easy shipping solutions, and a simple return policy.

Many nonprofit websites feature e-commerce as well, although the emphasis is on donations to worthwhile causes rather than product sales. They must make a convincing case and then make it very easy for visitors to donate. For instance, a bright red "Donate Now" button is prominently featured on SPCA International's website, a nonprofit dedicated to the safety and well-being of animals.

FACILITATE OFFLINE RELATIONSHIPS

For companies such as hotels, restaurants, ice cream shops, and sports centers, the online presence should facilitate offline relationships. Retail stores might offer online buying with in-store pickup, and restaurants might provide directions and discount coupons. India's Taj Mahal Hotel website features special deals, event planning, virtual tours, reward programs, and food preference surveys along with online reservations.

Websites for colleges and universities typically create engaging tours for prospective students and portals for current students, faculty, alumni, and staff. Along with many online self-service applications, the sites include college news, sports scores, access to digital libraries, and online learning support.

SOCIAL MEDIA GOALS

When companies launch a presence on social media, they should also clearly define their goals, which may overlap with the goals set for the website. But social media offer valuable opportunities to interact with customers in a personal way, responding directly to tweets or engaging in conversations about events. Nike, for instance, uses Twitter extensively to connect with its hundreds of thousands of followers, responding to more than 100 tweets per day. The sporting goods company emphasizes customer service and encouragement as social media goals rather than direct selling or product promotions.

infomediary
Focuses on informing visitors and empowering them with aggregated information about products from different suppliers.

e-marketplace
A website that facilitates transactions by bringing together buyers and sellers from all over the world.

business to consumer (B2C)
E-commerce relationship in which businesses offer products for online sale to consumers.

business to business (B2B)
E-commerce relationship in which businesses can buy and sell products or services online to one another.

consumer to consumer (C2C)
E-commerce relationship in which individual consumers can buy and sell to one another over the Internet.

consumer to business (C2B)
E-commerce relationship in which individual consumers can sell products or services to businesses.

Social media are also very powerful for marketing campaigns, partly because messages can reach much further to people through electronic word of mouth—retweeting, reposting, and sharing. In promoting its adventure camera, GoPro generated considerable online buzz with a GoPro owner's video featuring Didga, a skateboarding cat.[2] The video posted to Instagram earned more than a quarter of a million "likes" and generated thousands of comments.

To be most effective, organizations must coordinate messages across their website and all the different social media platforms and channels, adapting them to the style of each platform. This is another reason companies need clear goals for their online presence. Several online services are available to help companies manage these channels, with capabilities such as organizing content, scheduling posts to different channels, tracking visitors, targeting audiences, launching campaigns, and also following up on responses that might come in the form of retweets, mentions, likes, or new followers.

Naming the Website

Let's follow a group of dog lovers who met while on a study abroad program in Thailand. They learned about dog breeds—like the Thai Ridgeback and Japanese Akita—that originated in their different home countries. The students hope to promote breeds like these and raise money to fund rescue services by creating a website called "Heritage Dogs." Their lighthearted approach will feature a social network in which owners can post messages on their pet's behalf (Figure 6-2).

CLAIMING A URL FOR THE WEBSITE

Selecting a name for the website is a critical first step, and the team hopes to grab the name "HeritageDogs.org" if it hasn't been taken yet. The **uniform resource locator (URL)** is the unique global address for a web page or other resource on the Internet.

Every device connected to the net, whether it is your home videogame console or a major corporation's mainframe, has a unique, numerical IP address, such as 10.181.25.56. These IP addresses are not human-friendly, though, so the Internet's designers added the **Domain Name System (DNS)**—the hierarchical naming system that maps a more memorable URL, such as HeritageDogs.org or cnn.com, to the actual IP address. Mapping responsibilities are distributed to many different servers across the Internet, each of which maintains the mappings within its own domain. A great advantage of DNS is that the URL stays the same even if the organization moves the website to a new server with a different IP address. The new mapping will propagate to all the other name servers on the Internet.

FIGURE 6-2
Heritage Dogs web page.

Source: Keattikorn/Shutterstock.

Component	Examples	Description
Protocol identifier	http://microsoft.com (web page)	Identifies the protocol that will be used to connect to the address following the forward slashes.
Registered domain name	http://www.etrade.com http://www.umd.edu http://www.edu.cn	Maps to the unique IP address of the destination location.
Top-level domain	http://youtube.com http://www.whitehouse.gov http://www.army.mil http://redcross.org http://www.dw-world.de http://canada.gc.ca	The top-level domain typically indicates the type of organization or the country of origin, such as those below. New rules passed in 2011 clear the way for using brand names, cities, or general keywords as well. .com—commercial .edu—education .org—usually nonprofits .gov—U.S. federal government .ca—Canada .de—Germany .cn—China .tn—Tunisia
Filename (optional)	http://www.starhotel.com/ FAQ.htm	Specifies a particular web page within a site, in this case, one with the filename of FAQ.htm.
Port (optional)	http://www.baseball.com:95	Directs the connection to a specific port on the server. If absent, the default http port (80) is used.

COMPONENTS OF A URL

The URL itself is a string of characters, and each component has a specific meaning (Figure 6-3). The first few letters followed by the colon and forward slashes indicate the transmission protocol used to connect to the resource. The most common is **hypertext transfer protocol (http://)**, which shows that the resource is a web page containing code the browser can interpret and display. In fact, the "http://" is so common that most browsers add it automatically if you enter a web address without the protocol. Another is **file transfer protocol (ftp://)**, which indicates that the resource is a file to be transferred.

The actual name of the site follows the protocol, as in www.southwest.com or whitehouse.gov. The last string of letters is the **top-level domain**, such as ".com," ".org," ".gov," or ".mil." The students chose ".org" because this usually signifies a nonprofit organization, which is what they plan for Heritage Dogs.

MANAGING DOMAIN NAMES AND VIRTUAL REAL ESTATE

As the maxim goes, the three most important features of real property are location, location, and location. For online property, the URL is the critical ingredient, not the physical location of the server. Organizations compete to grab the "best" names for their URL, those that visitors will most easily remember or could easily guess.

The students want heritagedogs.org because it nicely reflects their mission and is easy to remember. They can go to one of the domain name registrars, such as www.networksolutions.com or register.com, to see whether that URL is available. If it is, they can pay a small fee to register it.

The Internet started in the United States as a rather obscure technology used mainly by academics and government researchers; as a result, the naming conventions are somewhat U.S.-centric. For instance, the top-level domains ".gov" and ".mil" refer only to U.S. government agencies and military. The net's astounding growth led to the adoption of hundreds of additional top-level domains, including all the two-letter country codes from the Ascension Islands (".ac") to Zimbabwe (".zw").

uniform resource locator (URL)
The unique global address for a web page or other resource on the Internet.

Domain Name System (DNS)
The hierarchical naming system that maps a more memorable URL to the actual IP address.

hypertext transfer protocol (http://)
A URL component that specifies the resource is a web page containing code the browser can interpret and display.

file transfer protocol (ftp://)
A URL component that indicates the resource is a file to be transferred.

top-level domain
The last string of letters in a URL that indicates the type of organization or country code.

The **Internet Corporation for Assigned Names and Numbers (ICANN)** was the nonprofit organization charged with overseeing the net's naming system. ICANN worked out contracts with the organizations that manage URL assignments within each of the top-level domains, accredited the registrars who sell domain names, resolved disputes, and established policies. For instance, the net's naming system originally accepted only domain names written with the Roman alphabet, but ICANN opened the door for other scripts. Egypt was one of the first to apply to use Arabic script for domain names under its ".eg" top-level domain. ICANN also ruled to accept applications from organizations that want to use brand names, city names, or keywords as top-level domains. More than 2,000 applications were submitted, with strings such as ".art," ".paris," and ".nike."[3] Current plans call for ICANN to transition responsibility for several key functions to an international body.[4]

DISPUTES OVER DOMAIN NAMES

Domain name disputes break out, and legal battles are common. Companies take quick action if a name is registered with even a whiff of trademark infringement. A related offense is "cybersquatting," in which someone registers a domain name that is a company's trademark, hoping to resell it to the company at an exorbitant profit. Although laws have been passed to stop the practice, variations on a company's name can still confuse web surfers. "Typosquatting," for instance, is registering a replica site with a misspelling in the trademark name that users might easily mistake for the real thing and enter personal information and passwords for the squatter's fraudulent use.[5] The squatter might also display negative information about the actual company, hoping the CEO will pay a ransom to get the name back. Damage to the brand can be extensive, and many companies want to get control over those rogue sites.

> **PRODUCTIVITY TIP**
> You may need your own website someday, so you might consider reserving a good domain name now for a few dollars a year—before someone else takes it. Most people choose a common pattern such as www.FirstnameLastname. com. Other top-level domains might interest you, such as ".net," ".org," ".biz," or your country code.

Provide examples of different website information architectures, explain the importance of usability and accessibility, and describe how websites are created with various software tools.

2 Building the Website

Once confined to experienced programmers, the task of building the website has been simplified considerably. Nevertheless, creating a professional and well-designed site containing features that support the site's major goals requires skill and careful attention to visitors' interests and motivations.

Website Design

The best-designed website is the one that achieves its goals, and many different approaches work. TripAdvisor.com's strategy has made it one of the most trusted sources of travel advice on the web, with more than 75 million reviews and opinions. Visitors can quickly tap into the collective knowledge of reviewers to read their candid opinions on restaurants, hotels, cruises, and more. Advertisers in the hospitality and travel industries pay top dollar to post ads relevant to the visitor's query. Someone reading reviews for hotels with golf courses in Scottsdale, Arizona, will see ads for just those hotels and perhaps special deals on golf clothing.

The reviews that travelers contribute help build trust in the site; however, malicious or fake reviews may also be posted.[6]

WEBSITE INFORMATION ARCHITECTURE AND NAVIGATION

Just as an architect designs buildings that are easy to use and beautiful to see, web designers strive to reach similar goals with their site's information architecture. Designers must find ways to organize the information, provide navigational tools, and ensure visitors don't struggle to find what they are looking for and complete a transaction.

Figure 6-4 shows some examples of website architectures. Although visitors can enter a website at almost any location, designers consider the home page as the conceptual gateway

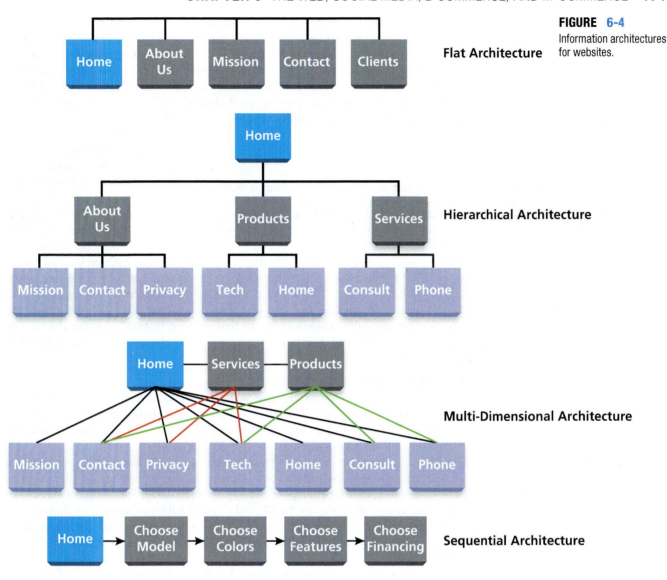

FIGURE **6-4**
Information architectures for websites.

and entrance point, and they build out the information architecture from there. For a very small site, a flat architecture serves well, with a home page linking to four or five additional pages. For larger sites, a common design is the hierarchical website architecture, in which the top-level home page contains links to second-level pages, which then link to further relevant pages. For example, Heritage Dogs will use a hierarchy based on countries, so visitors to the home page can drill down to the images and rescue operations for dogs in each nation. Many organizations start out with a hierarchical design, following their own organizational charts or product lines.

The strict hierarchy has appeal, but frustration mounts if visitors drill down the wrong path, looking for information that doesn't easily fit or that spans categories. For instance, a visitor to a newspaper website who wants to know what time the horse races start would not know whether to drill down into sports, entertainment, or events.

Internet Corporation for Assigned Names and Numbers (ICANN)
The nonprofit organization charged with overseeing the Internet's naming system, establishing policies, and resolving disputes.

hierarchical website architecture
Website structure in which the top-level home page contains links to second-level pages, which then link to further relevant pages.

The **multidimensional website architecture** recognizes that information can be categorized in many ways and that visitors need multiple paths through the site. Panasonic's website, for instance, offers links to different visitor categories in the top navigation bar, including consumers, business, and industrial. Along the right navigation bar, it offers links to product lines, such as printers, audio and video electronics, and others. Amazon.com helps users browse by department, keyword, and sales promotions. Within "Books," visitors can also browse by categories such as best sellers, textbooks, or sales.

> **PRODUCTIVITY TIP**
> Search is a powerful tool, but it works best when you use less common words or strings that are as specific as possible. Search for *graphic design* and you retrieve 164 million web pages. *Graphic design jobs New York City* retrieves far fewer but more relevant web pages. Putting quotation marks around a string will return web pages with an exact match.

A **sequential website architecture** is useful in some settings, particularly when designers want the visitor to proceed step by step through a transaction, survey, or learning module. The example in Figure 6-4 shows how a website might help a shopper design his or her own dream car. Each page would have only one link, often labeled "Next Step."

Search functionality that confines the search to the website rather than the whole web dramatically improves the visitor's ability to find relevant material, particularly on very large websites. One drawback is that a search may retrieve obsolete pages the organization neglected to delete.

USABILITY AND USER INTERFACE DESIGN

Usability refers to the ease with which a person can accomplish a goal using some tool, such as a website, a mobile phone, or a kiosk. Does the user struggle to find directions to the company's address? Do many visitors abandon their shopping carts? Figure 6-5 lists several elements of usability that apply to websites.

Usability relies partly on clear information architecture and also on the user interface design.[7] For example, designers use color to manage the user's attention, drawing on principles of visual perception. Bright red—especially against a darker background—attracts the eye. That color is very often used for the DONATE NOW! button on nonprofit websites. Note how the red button on the left side of Figure 6-6 seems to leap out, even though it is the same size as the dark blue button on the right. Figure 6-7 lists basic tips for designing an effective user interface.

A good way to assess a site's usability is to ask visitors to perform a sequence of tasks and observe the problems they encounter. At the University of Nevada, Las Vegas, for instance, researchers assigned students tasks related to library research, such as these:

1. Find a journal article on the death penalty.
2. Check whether the library is open on July 4.
3. Locate the most current issue of *Popular Mechanics*.

Visitors easily found the library's hours, but they had trouble finding content because they could not easily distinguish between "Journals" and "Articles and Databases" or between "E-Reserves" and "Other Reserves." They tended to ignore the navigation tabs at the top, and

FIGURE 6-5

Elements of website usability.

Element	Sample Metrics
Ease of learning	To what extent can a user accomplish simple tasks on the first visit?
Efficiency	After learning the site's basic design, how quickly and efficiently can a user perform tasks?
Memorability	When a user returns to the site after a period of time, how much effort does it take to regain the same level of proficiency?
Error rates	How many mistakes do users make when they attempt to accomplish a task, and how easy is it to recover from those mistakes?
Satisfaction level	How do users rate their experiences on the site? Do they describe it as pleasant and satisfying, or frustrating?

FIGURE 6-7

Tips for effective user interface design.

▶ Keep it structured. Use a clear and consistent design that is easy for users to recognize throughout the site.

▶ Keep it simple. Make the common tasks very simple to do, so users can accomplish them on the first try without frustration.

▶ Keep users informed. Let users know in clear language when something on the website changes, or the user has completed an action.

▶ Be forgiving of errors. Let users easily undo their actions or return to previous states.

▶ Avoid distractions. Especially when the user is engaged in a sequential task, avoid adding unnecessary links or options.

they also found little use for "Subject Guides."[8] Usability tests are critical to help designers improve the site for the people who actually use it, not the ones who design it.

WEB ACCESSIBILITY FOR PEOPLE WITH DISABILITIES

Web accessibility refers to how easily people with disabilities can access and use web resources. Impaired vision, hearing loss, limited motor skills, and other kinds of disabilities can hinder or even block people from using the web. In the United States, the disabled comprise almost 20% of the population, a figure expected to grow as the population ages. Studies of the websites for large enterprises show that while most large companies have made some improvements, hurdles remain for many users.[9]

Financial institutions are particularly vigorous about fighting cybersquatters because many of those domain names appear in phishing attempts. Customers might receive an email with a familiar link to their bank and never notice that the letter "l" in Capito1Bank.com is really the number one. Never click on such links.

DID YOU KNOW?

The Web Accessibility Initiative (WAI) develops guidelines for web accessibility that are widely regarded as international standards. It also offers tutorials to help organizations improve their sites and understand how design techniques can radically alter a site's accessibility. Its site (www.w3.org/WAI) offers links to a variety of software tools that designers can use to check a site's accessibility against the guidelines. For instance, software is available

multidimensional website architecture
Website structure with multiple links to pages at all levels, allowing visitors multiple paths through the site.

sequential website architecture
Website structure that guides visitors step by step through a transaction, survey, or learning module.

usability
Refers to the ease with which a person can accomplish a goal using some tool, such as a website, a mobile phone, or a kiosk.

web accessibility
Refers to how easily people with disabilities can access and use web resources.

Source: Eveleen/Shutterstock

to assess text and background color combinations that might not work for people with color blindness (Figure 6-8).

Assistive technologies designed to help people with disabilities range from the low-tech magnifying glass for the visually impaired to motorized wheelchairs. When using the web, mouse foot pedals, screen readers, Braille displays, head-mounted pointers, joysticks, and speech-to-text translators for the deaf can all improve access.

Figure 6-9 shows a wireless device that tracks small head motions and converts them to mouse movements, designed for people with limited use of their hands.

Designers should address accessibility issues in the site's information architecture, with design elements that meet the needs of a wider range of users and work well with assistive technologies such as screen readers. Figure 6-10 lists some dos and don'ts for web designers.

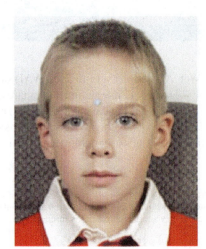

Source: Courtesy of Origin Instruments Corporation.

THE ETHICAL FACTOR Website Accessibility: Why Is Progress So Slow?

Why are organizations so slow to make their websites and mobile apps accessible to people with disabilities? One reason is that the legal obligations are somewhat uncertain, and the technology keeps changing. Companies are reluctant to invest in massive upgrades when they might still be sued for noncompliance.[10]

Some web developers are concerned that there is a conflict between usability and accessibility and that an accessible website will have to bypass many of the rich features and graphical elements that make them pleasing and attention-getting.

Although the challenge of creating accessible websites is not trivial, organizations can make tremendous progress by building in accessibility from the start. A common obstacle for visually impaired people, for instance, is a button that can only be accessed with the mouse. One university's new virtual student union had that flaw on its "Let's get started!" button, so blind students couldn't ever get started.[11] But it is just as easy to program the button to also respond to a key press if the designers keep that feature in mind.

Though many organizations see efforts to improve accessibility for people with disabilities as additional costs, others are learning that accessibility adds strategic benefits in the form of heightened corporate social responsibility and Internet visibility. Making the site more accessible from the beginning also broadens the potential base of customers and thus makes good business sense.

Software Development Strategies for the Web

Creating the website can be as simple as typing into a word processor and uploading some files or as complicated as writing thousands of lines of code from scratch. The goal is to create pages that a visitor can access with a **web browser**—the software application that retrieves, interprets, and displays web resources. Figure 6-11 lists popular web browsers, all of which are free to end users.

> **PRODUCTIVITY TIP**
> Browsers offer many accessibility features that are helpful to everyone. For example, the Windows shortcut to increase text size for most browsers is to hold the Control key down and press the plus sign. On a Macintosh, the shortcut for Safari is Command+.

Do:
- Add alternative text tags for every image, so visually impaired people know what the image is.
- Use self-explanatory links.
- Use "More on cosmetic dentristy" rather than "click here for more."
- Make bold headings, short paragraphs, and orderly paragraph arrangements, so screen readers follow the flow correctly.
- Create text-only alternative versions for devices such as tablets or mobile phones.

Don't:
- Use fixed text sizes, which may make it impossible for visually impaired people to use the site.
- Create very tiny clickable areas, which hinder those with limited mobility or motor function.
- Implement forms that require a mouse click, which prevents keyboard-only users from typing in their information.
- Use overly complicated designs with no simple alternative for browsing on a tablet or mobile phone.

FIGURE 6-10
Design tips for improving website accessibility.

Browser	Market Share on Desktop Computers
Chrome	54.0%
Internet Explorer	27.4%
Firefox	7.7%
Microsoft Edge	5.2%
Safari	4.3%

Source: Data from Netmarketshare, August, 2016. https://netmarketshare.com.

FIGURE 6-11
Major web browsers.

assistive technologies
Devices and software that help people with disabilities, such as screen readers for the visually impaired.

web browser
The software application that retrieves, interprets, and displays web resources.

FIGURE 6-12

Example of how hypertext markup language (HTML) formats text and a link on a web page.

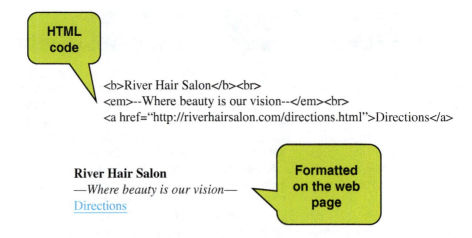

HTML code

```
<b>River Hair Salon</b><br>
<em>--Where beauty is our vision--</em><br>
<a href="http://riverhairsalon.com/directions.html">Directions</a>
```

River Hair Salon
—Where beauty is our vision—
Directions

Formatted on the web page

HTML AND HTML 5

The original language used to create web pages is called **hypertext markup language (HTML)**, which specifies the web page's format and helps put it into reader-friendly output. The language uses tags in angle brackets that browsers can interpret (Figure 6-12), such as <p>, to indicate the start of a new paragraph. Usually, the page will still appear even if the code includes many mistakes in the tags, though it may not be formatted quite the way the designer intended in all the browsers. Competitive battles for market share often lead browser developers to add special features and proprietary tags that work only with their own browser, creating headaches for software developers who must test their code in one browser after another and also in several versions of each browser.

PRODUCTIVITY TIP
Common browsers support many add-ons to boost your productivity and customize your web browsing. Bookmarks, spyware protection, Facebook toolbars, to-do lists, reminders, web page previews, password vaults, bibliographic capture tools, and news feeds are just a few examples. Be selective, though, because some add-ons, or just too many of them, can impede your browser's performance.

The latest version of HTML is HTML 5, which will reduce problems for web developers struggling to support different browsers running on so many different devices, from desktop computers and laptops to smartphones, tablets, and TVs. HTML 5 offers many new features, such as the ability to access location information from a mobile device without having to write special code for each one. Developers can also do fancier graphics and word art rather than having to import such images from software like Photoshop.

HTML 5 reduces the need for web developers to ask customers to download special browser plug-in software, like Adobe Flash, especially for video. Flash was becoming a near universal requirement for browsers because so many videos on the web used the Flash format. But when Apple banned Flash from iPhones and iPads and Google announced that Flash will be banned for display ads, developers quickly began switching to HTML 5.[12]

CREATING INTERACTIVE, MEDIA-RICH WEBSITES

HTML 5 goes a long way toward helping developers build engaging websites. Another popular tool is **JavaScript**, which can be used within HTML to add interactivity to web pages. Pop-up alert boxes, lively images that appear when your mouse rolls over the page, and validation for your input on forms are all examples of what JavaScript can do. A JavaScript library called JQuery contains a growing collection of open source code to help developers create interactive pages that work in many different browsers.

AJAX is a mix of technologies that builds on JavaScript and enlivens the web even more, adding instant intelligence drawn from live data to create interactive displays. Go to www.google.com and try typing the word *computer* into the search box, but type slowly. You will see a rapidly changing list of words as you enter each letter, showing suggestions even before you finish typing. Many interactive maps and charts that show updated data as you move the mouse over different regions also use AJAX, drawing the data from a database (Figure 6-13).

FIGURE **6-13**
Interactive map showing population by congressional district using AJAX.

Source: U.S. Census Bureau.

The **World Wide Web Consortium (W3C)**, of which the Web Accessibility Initiative is one part, is an international body that establishes and publishes standards for programming languages used to create software for the web. Headed by Tim Berners-Lee, the inventor of the World Wide Web, the W3C strives to make sure the web continues to support communication and commerce for all people, regardless of their hardware, software, native languages, or geographic location. So far, its work has helped developers avoid the fate in which the web fragments into islands that can't interact with one another, but there is more to do. Berners-Lee says, "The Web as I envisaged it, we have not seen it yet. The future is still so much bigger than the past."

CONTENT MANAGEMENT SYSTEMS

As websites grow in size and incorporate audio, video, text, graphics, and other kinds of unstructured content, organizations need better ways to manage not just the content but the many tasks and people required to maintain the site. **Content management systems** encompass a large group of software products that help manage digital content in collaborative environments. The web content management system supports website development and maintenance for larger teams.

These systems enable multiple people, often with limited web development and HTML skills, to contribute to the website from any place in the world. The site's overall look and feel, including the navigation bars that should appear on each page, are created as templates with consistent fonts, colors, and layout. The templates include **cascading style sheets (CSS)** that control the fonts and colors to appear when an editor identifies some text as a page heading, a paragraph title, or some other style.

hypertext markup language (HTML)
The original language used to create web pages; HTML specifies the web page's format using tags in angle brackets that browsers can interpret and put into reader-friendly output.

JavaScript
A language used to add interactivity to web pages.

AJAX
A mix of technologies that builds on JavaScript and draws on live data to create interactive online displays.

World Wide Web Consortium (W3C)
An international body that establishes and publishes standards for programming languages used to create software for the web.

content management system
Software used to manage digital content in collaborative environments. The web content management system supports teams that develop and maintain websites.

cascading style sheets (CSS)
The part of a website template that controls the fonts, colors, and styles that appear when an editor identifies some text as a page heading, a paragraph title, or some other style.

Website editors can create new pages using a software environment similar to word processing, and their content is converted to HTML so it will appear nicely formatted on the website, inside the appropriate template. The content management system and its CSS can enforce a consistent look and feel throughout the site, preventing contributors from straying too far from the designer's templates.

Content management systems have many other features to support collaborative website development. For example, they prevent two people from trying to edit the same page at the same time, and they save older versions of each page as the website evolves. The systems also include workflow functionality so that new content can require a supervisor's approval before publication to the actual website.

Explain how e-commerce works and why security and trust are critical ingredients.

3 E-Commerce

E-commerce refers to the buying and selling of goods and services over the Internet or other networks, encompassing financial transactions between businesses, consumers, governments, or nonprofits. Canny marketing promotions, increased consumer confidence in online payments, and even paralyzing snowstorms help steer shoppers to the Internet.

The Online Transaction and E-Commerce Software

Websites whose main goal is selling or soliciting donations need e-commerce capabilities. Many software vendors offer information systems to support online stores with secure web-based financial transactions. These systems help web developers create a catalog of products using a back-end database, conduct online marketing and sales promotions, manage the financial transactions, and handle reporting.

PRODUCTIVITY TIP
The secure connection confirmed by the https:// protocol relies on a certificate issued by a recognized authority such as the VeriSign Trust Network. With most browsers, you can click on the padlock symbol to see encryption details (Figure 6-14).

FIGURE 6-14
Details about the website's security, Note also the "https://" protocol in the URL, indicating transmission is encrypted.

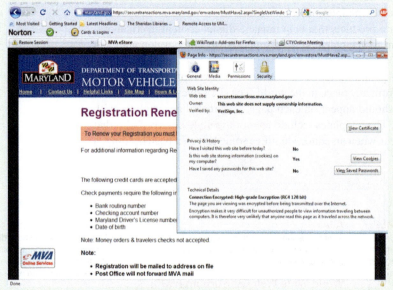

Source: © 2013 Maryland Motor Vehicle Administration (MVA). All rights reserved.

E-commerce systems typically include **shopping cart software** that tracks purchases as customers navigate the site and click "add to cart" as they go. When the customer is ready to check out, the software tallies the purchase, calculates taxes, computes shipping costs, and also posts a discount if the customer enters a valid promotional code. The shopping cart analogy and the software underlying it work well for nonprofits like Heritage Dogs, though it may seem odd to add your donation to a "cart."

E-Commerce Security

The success of e-commerce depends heavily on its security and the perceptions people have about its trustworthiness. Online fraud costs businesses billions every year, but companies are ramping up countermeasures. For example, their information systems rate the risk of any particular transaction by checking data such as order value, past transactions with the card number, and lists of risky accounts.

An e-commerce transaction must be secure from end to end, despite including several steps on different servers that can be geographically quite distant. The web address originating the transaction should show the https:// protocol, indicating the transmission to that server is encrypted and secure.

The credit or debit card information is transmitted to the **payment gateway**, which facilitates online shopping by mediating the interconnections to the merchant's bank, the bank or other entity that issued the card, and then back to the original website. If the transaction is approved, a confirmation is returned to the seller's site. All these connections must also be encrypted and secured. Chapter 10 explores security in more detail.

E-Commerce Trust

Trust is an essential element of e-commerce—buyers need assurance that an organization selling products online is reputable and secure. Well-known brands such as Macy's, Best Buy, and Walmart can rely on their own reputations, built from years of operating physical stores. Some large online retailers that lack actual retail locations, such as Amazon.com and Overstock.com, struggled to build trust over time but now enjoy solid reputations and loyal customers.

Building trust is a daunting task for less well-known organizations and requires close attention to consumers' motivations and buying behavior. Businesses can apply for a "seal of approval" from independent organizations that audit websites to verify their compliance with minimum trust requirements in different countries. TRUSTe gives its approval to U.S. websites that follow strict privacy standards, such as explaining to visitors how personal data is collected.

Another way companies attempt to build trust is by tapping customers' social networks, through social commerce or "s-commerce."[13] Social networks can personalize the shopping experience so that people learn about products from those they know and trust. That feedback is more valuable than the reviews posted by unknown customers, some of which might be fake. Social sites such as Facebook, Pinterest, and Instagram are adding shopping capabilities directly to their own platforms so users don't have to go to the retailer's site to buy a product.

Mobile Devices and M-Commerce

 4 Define m-commerce, and explain how mobile payments work.

Why Mobile Matters

Much of the web's development occurred before mobile devices with high-speed Internet access spread so widely. But these devices are saturating markets around the world very quickly, particularly for younger buyers. Smartphones, for instance, are on track to spread faster than any other technology in history. What makes these devices different—and so appealing? Several features stand out:

- *Small size and light weight.* They fit in a pocket or purse, and no extra bag is needed.
- *Mobile with wireless connectivity.* They stay connected wirelessly, even when their owner is moving at high speed.
- *Versatility.* Although the screen is small, the functionality is remarkable and growing quickly, especially for applications that take advantage of the device's small size and mobility.

---

e-commerce
The buying and selling of goods and services over the Internet or other networks, encompassing financial transactions between businesses, consumers, governments, or nonprofits.

shopping cart software
Computer software that tracks purchases as customers navigate an e-commerce site and click "add to cart" as they go. The software tallies the purchase, calculates taxes based on the customer's location, computes shipping costs, and also posts a discount if the customer enters a valid promotional code.

payment gateway
An e-commerce application that facilitates online shopping by mediating the interconnections to the merchant's bank, the bank or other entity that issued the card, and then back to the original website to approve or decline the purchase.

FIGURE   6-15

Mobile apps versus mobile-friendly websites.

Mobile App	Mobile-Friendly Website
▶ Higher cost	▶ Lower cost
▶ Best for interactive games	▶ Customers don't need to download anything
▶ Customers will use the app regularly and personalize it	▶ Mobile website is accessible across many different devices
▶ The app will perform complex calculations	▶ Customers can find your website with search engines
▶ Customers will want to use the app without an Internet connection.	▶ Easier to update
▶ Easier to delete	▶ Can't be deleted

■ *Location awareness.* With GPS, smartphones can determine their location and can support all kinds of applications that take advantage of this information, from navigation to proximity marketing.

■ *Internet of Things.* Smartphones are important elements in the Internet of Things, sending and receiving signals with and without any user intervention.

The computing industry is affected as well, as PC sales slump and smartphones surge. The major players are companies like Apple and Samsung, not PC makers such as Dell, HP, and Toshiba. Mobile devices upset other industries, too, as people drop their landline telephones.

They also change the way people communicate. Texting, for instance, has created a whole vocabulary of abbreviations to keep messages short and a growing debate about smartphone "manners." The always-available smartphone also creates the expectation that you can be reached at any time. Mobile definitely matters.

Designing Websites and Apps for Mobile Devices

The lively websites designed for desktop computers and larger screens fall short on tiny smartphones. But organizations need to offer a mobile-friendly experience, given the rapid growth of these devices and the new possibilities they offer. For instance, a family looking for a new home might drive by an attractive property. Instead of calling the agent's number on the sign and leaving a voice message, the family could view all the details on a smartphone.

FIGURE   6-16

Mobile-friendly design for Cruisin' Fusion Food Truck.

MOBILE APPS VS. MOBILE WEBSITES

Companies can choose to build separate mobile apps for each of the major mobile operating systems. These are separate applications that customers download from the company website or an online app store and then install on their own devices. Organizations as varied as Zillow, In-N-Out Burger, CVS Pharmacy, E*TRADE, and Major League Baseball all offer innovative apps that tap the special features of mobile devices.

Companies can also choose a lower cost approach in which they develop a companion website optimized for mobile devices that customers can access with their mobile browser. When mobile users visit the full site, they are redirected to the mobile-friendly version. Figure 6-15 compares the pros and cons of apps and mobile-friendly websites.

MOBILE-FRIENDLY DESIGN AND USABILITY

Mobile devices differ from desktop computers in many ways, but two important differences are screen size and the presence (or absence) of the keyboard and mouse. Mobile developers must make the best possible use of screen real estate and ensure that humans can manage choices easily with a single swipe or tap. They must decide what information mobile users might be interested in, display it with fonts large enough to read without zooming, and do so without requiring any scrolling. Any buttons or links should be large enough for clumsy thumbs. The design should be a slimmer, leaner version of the organization's main website so that users recognize the brand. Figure 6-16 shows how Cruisin' Fusion, the food truck company featured in this chapter's interactive decision-making simulation, might slim down a website to make it mobile friendly. Figure 6-17 offers tips on mobile-friendly design.

▶ Display the most important content first.
▶ Avoid popups, Flash animations, and large photos.
▶ Use branding consistent with the main site.
▶ Use a single column design.
▶ Use fonts large enough so that users need not zoom in.
▶ Make links and buttons large enough so that users can click them with
  fingertips.
▶ Ask users to test out your design on different mobile devices.

FIGURE 6-17
Tips for mobile-friendly design.

M-Commerce and Mobile Payments

Mobile commerce (m-commerce) refers to the use of wireless, mobile devices to conduct e-commerce. M-commerce has been going on for quite some time, as customers use their wireless devices to connect to the Internet for banking, shopping, and bill paying. They use credit cards, debit cards, electronic checks, or services like PayPal.

Another type of m-commerce gaining speed is the use of mobile devices as digital "wallets" that actually pay bills on the spot, eliminating the need to carry cash. The trend is further ahead in some countries such as Sweden, where public buses in many cities don't accept cash at all. Riders must use their mobile phones to purchase tickets.[14] The case study at the end of the chapter takes a closer look at the mobile payment industry.

How does a mobile phone pay a bill? The most common approach relies on **near field communication (NFC)**, which is a set of standards for technology that supports communication between mobile devices when the two are very near one another. People with smartphones equipped with NFC chips can tap a special terminal at a café, bus station, sporting arena, or any other participating vendor. The bill is automatically charged to the customer's account.

One advantage NFC systems have over credit and debit cards is that the smartphone can carry many other kinds of information, such as loyalty points, coupons, and customer preferences. And NFC-equipped phones can also communicate with one another, to exchange contact information, for instance.

In some countries, such as China, m-commerce is well established.[15] But adoption lags behind in the United States, and the digital wallet has had a slow start. The competition is fierce, and the systems and companies that eventually win this competition will need to fully protect security and privacy. The cashless society may take some time.

Digital Marketing

5 Explain how organizations manage digital marketing for their website, their social media presence, and their mobile apps.

How do organizations approach digital marketing on such a diversity of platforms? How do they persuade potential customers to visit their website, like or follow them on social media, or download their mobile app? Marketing majors certainly need a deep understanding of how the web works to develop creative and effective approaches. They also need to know how different kinds of people use the web, social media, and mobile apps and why they return again and again to some but ignore others. Let's start with strategies for promoting the website.

Search Engine Optimization

Seeing your website at the top of the first page on the results list from a search engine is a joyful experience for web marketers, especially because most people don't look beyond that first page. **Search engine optimization (SEO)** uses strategies to increase the quantity and quality of traffic from search engines, often by improving the site's position in result lists.

---

mobile commerce (m-commerce)
The use of wireless, mobile devices to conduct e-commerce.

near field communication (NFC)
A set of standards that supports communication between mobile devices when the two are very near one another.

search engine optimization (SEO)
An Internet marketing strategy used to increase the quantity and quality of traffic from search engines, often by improving the site's position in result lists.

FIGURE 6-18

Sample tag cloud for country dog breeds.

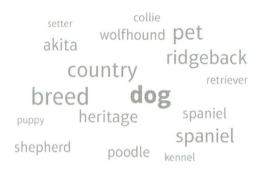

Search engines such as Google and Bing continually send out "spiders"—software programs that crawl the web, visiting sites to analyze the keywords, headers, content, and links to other sites. The spiders update their own databases, and the search engine uses the new information to compute relevance when people enter a search term. Web marketers must understand not only what data search engines collect and how they use it to judge relevance, but also how people use the web to find what they want.

SEARCH TERMS AND KEYWORDS

For users, search terms are key. Developers must guess what people who would be interested in their site might type as a search term and then make sure their site gets a high relevance rating for that term. Choosing the most effective keywords for the descriptors on your pages is critical.

You should always put yourself in the mindset of the website visitor and use more specific phrases rather than generic keywords. For example, the students creating Heritage Dogs should ask what search terms a user who is interested in native dog breeds might enter. Many websites arrange these terms into a tag cloud, which is a visual depiction of keywords related to the search, with font size and position indicating relevance. Figure 6-18 shows an example for Heritage Dogs.

PAGERANK AND RELEVANCE

Search engines rely partly on popularity to determine relevance, and the rules they use to rate popularity take into account the number and quality of external links to the site from other websites. Google's PageRank system, for example, named for cofounder Larry Page, interprets a link from Site A to Site B as a vote, thereby improving B's rank. The ranking system also considers the page that casts the vote, weighing votes more heavily if they come from pages that are themselves highly ranked.

PRODUCTIVITY TIP
Check out the PageRank of your college or university's website by using sites such as www.prchecker.info or www.checkpagerank.net.

Web marketers launch link-building campaigns to improve their search results, contacting sites that might add a link and making deals to do reciprocal linking. Online tools such as www.linkdiagnosis.com help developers keep track of which other sites include links to their web pages and the PageRanks of those sites.

SEARCH ENGINE SCAMS

The drive to improve search results gets so heated that some unscrupulous developers use devious strategies to outwit the engine's ranking system. For example, one technique to build valuable external links is to look for guest books on authoritative sites whose votes would be particularly valuable, such as those in the .gov or .edu domains, and then include a link to the scammer's site in an area that lets any visitor add comments. Scammers also build giant link farms out of servers whose only purpose is to increase the number of external links. Such techniques often result in penalties or outright bans by major search engines.

Some scammers aim to get a competitor's site banned or at least move its site lower in the results. They can inject code onto a competitor's site that repeats the same keyword over and over in a header, which spiders can easily spot and penalize as an unacceptable trick to make the page seem extremely relevant. Scammers might also invite raunchy adult-oriented or gambling sites to add links to the competitor, which can result in penalties and lower ranking.

ONLINE ADVERTISING AND COOKIES

Pop-up ads, floating images, banners, music, and flashy animations appear on many websites, and overall spending for online ad campaigns worldwide is higher than for television. For example, a fitness company that wants its banner ad to appear on top of a sports website pays a fee for a certain number of impressions, perhaps 50 cents per 1,000. Prices vary depending on factors such as the site's popularity or how likely the company thinks people who see the ad will click on it and perhaps buy a product. The **click-through rate (CTR)** is an important metric for such ads, computed as the number of visitors who click on the ad divided by the number of impressions. Typical click-through rates for banner ads are low—about 1/1000 (0.1%).

A **cookie** is a small text file that the website's server leaves on your computer when you visit and then retrieves when you visit again, usually to personalize the site for you. The file typically contains a unique ID and information such as date and time or the page you visited. The cookie can also store information you yourself provide, such as the zip code for a city you intend to visit on a weather site. When you return, the site can immediately display that city's weather.

E-commerce sites rely on cookies to keep track of the products a customer places in a shopping cart. As you collect items, the web server retrieves your unique ID and stores it with the item number in its own database. If you leave the site and return later, the software can retrieve your ID and refill your shopping cart. The site can also deliver targeted ads and recommendations, without asking you to log in, by retrieving your cookie and checking to see what that ID has viewed in the past.

Ad networks such as Brightroll and Casale Media have sprung up that facilitate even better targeting. They deliver banners and other ads to their clients' websites and also deposit their own cookies whenever someone visits one of the client sites. These are called **third-party cookies** because they are not tied just to the site you are visiting. They let the ad network track you as you visit any client site and then serve targeted ads at other sites.

Suppose on your favorite news site you click on an ad for Caribbean cruises designed to appeal to single women in their twenties. The ad network associates that information with the unique ID for you. If you move to a travel site that is also a network client, your cookie will be retrieved and you will see more ads about cruises for young singles. Targeted advertising is growing very sophisticated to improve click-through rates.

> **PRODUCTIVITY TIP**
> You can adjust the settings in your browser to control how it handles cookies as you browse—to prohibit third-party cookies or prompt you for permission to download them, for example. Try overriding automatic cookie handling to see how your favorite sites are using cookies.

SEARCH ENGINE ADVERTISING

Google pioneered a simple advertising approach that relies on your search terms rather than on cookies. Your search terms reveal your current interest, and Google developed the Adwords program to serve small, text-only ads related to your search in a list of sponsored links. Type in "shiba inu," for example, and you will see sponsored links offering puppies for sale. Whether the ad actually appears to someone who submits a keyword the organization has chosen for its ad depends partly on how much the company is willing to spend each day. Unlike buyers of most banner-type ads, these advertisers pay only when someone actually clicks on the ad,

tag cloud
A visual depiction of keywords related to the search, with font size and position indicating relevance.

click-through rate (CTR)
A metric used to assess the impact of an online ad; computed as the number of visitors who click on the ad divided by the number of impressions.

cookie
A small text file left on a website visitor's hard drive that is used to personalize the site for the visitor or track web activities.

third-party cookies
Small text files that a website leaves on a visitor's computer that are not deposited by the site being visited; used by ad networks to track customer behavior across all their client websites.

FIGURE 6-19
Search engine market shares.

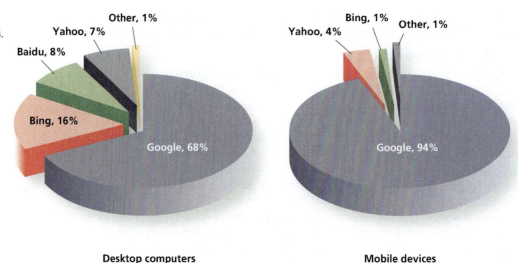

Desktop computers **Mobile devices**

Source: From Search engine market shares, www.netmarketshare.com. Copyright © 2016 by Net Applications.

not each time it appears. Search engine marketing accounts for the vast majority of Google's revenue. Figure 6-19 shows the global market shares for the major search engines. Google dominates on desktops and also on mobile devices.

Social and Mobile Marketing

Marketing leaders recognize that social media marketing and mobile marketing open many promising opportunities to reach out to customers. Social media especially can be amazingly effective because they tap networks of friendships and relationships.[16] Mobile strategies add other advantages, including location awareness and the ability to engage audiences anytime and anyplace.

SOCIAL MARKETING STRATEGIES

Social media platforms provide marketers with unprecedented access to data, not just about customers' search terms or website visits but about their life histories, employment, hobbies, friends, likes and dislikes, and much more. Marketers can target ads quite precisely based on social media profiles, showing an ad for high-tech fitness watches only to people whose profiles suggest they are health-conscious joggers, for instance.

Social media are also valuable because campaigns can involve customers in interactive ways by inviting them to creatively participate in storytelling. Hewlett Packard, for example, launched a campaign called #BendTheRules on Twitter, Vine, and other platforms in which the company invited people to send in videos that showed creative ways to use HP's Pavilion x360 convertible laptop. Customers flocked to the contest, creating many entries that went viral. HP made particular efforts to engage "influencers," people on social media who have large networks and winning strategies.[17] One man, for example, used creative video editing to show how the lid could squeeze an orange and turn it into juice.

Not surprisingly, this kind of engagement builds brand awareness and loyalty. Customers become brand advocates and ambassadors as they use electronic word of mouth to amplify and spread the company's message. Of course, marketers know that negative comments about their brands can also spread virally, so they must be especially diligent about social media marketing.

MOBILE MARKETING STRATEGIES

Marketers seeking to reach customers via their mobile devices must first understand each customer's mobile preferences. The risk of delivering a negative experience, with an ill-timed interruption, for instance, is high.[18] But the potential to reach a customer with the right message at just the right time and place is enormous.

Many retailers initially began mobile marketing by developing a mobile app for their stores. However, consumers are becoming more reluctant to download their mobile apps,

BLE beacon

50% off luggage next to escalator!

Alphaspirit/Shutterstock

FIGURE 6-20
Proximity marketing using BLE beacon signal to nearby smartphone devices

partly because their phones are already saturated. Even when they do download the apps, users ignore them after a short time, focusing on just a few that meet their daily needs. In response, companies are putting more effort into improving the mobile website experience, discussed earlier. This is especially important because Google's relevance rankings favor sites that are optimized for mobile delivery.[19]

Another challenge in mobile marketing is the data caps for cellular plans. People are not thrilled to view bloated mobile ads that are using up their data allotments, and they often install ad blockers to prevent them from appearing.[20] Ad blockers are a controversial subject, and Apple initially refused to add any to its iPhone app store because ads are how many free services and content providers earn revenue.

Despite the challenges, opportunities for effective mobile marketing are huge. For instance, retailers can place **Bluetooth low energy (BLE) beacons** around their stores, which are low-cost, battery-powered devices that broadcast Bluetooth signals to nearby devices (Figure 6-20). A shopper whose smartphone accepts such signals might receive a message about the luggage sale a few feet away. Or, on request, the beacons could offer directions to the restroom. This kind of proximity marketing is getting more popular for large sports stadiums and conferences as well. Apple calls its beacons ibeacons, and Alphabet (Google's parent) uses a technology called Eddystone for Android devices. (These beacons are different from the web beacons mentioned in Chapter 5.)

Online marketing strategies are most effective when the marketers take full advantage of all the tools available to track metrics of success, whether they are sign-ups for newsletters, retweets, or new followers. The next chapter discusses those tools in more detail.

Web 2.0 and Beyond

6 Explain how the evolving web continues to develop by incorporating attributes such as crowdsourcing, expanded data sources, the "Internet of Things," machine learning, and "big data."

In its early days, people compared the web to a vast and rapidly growing library with unlimited shelf space, in which valuable documents could be published alongside trivial junk. As businesses entered and e-commerce matured, the web emerged as a global shopping mall in which tiny start-ups could share space with giant retailers. Marketers and advertisers developed the business approaches, and giant web portals such as Yahoo! and America Online dominated visitors' online experiences.

Innovation exploded and the web also became home to services that offered people opportunities to participate in new ways—gaming, photo sharing, blogging, menu planning, restaurant reviewing, community building, and much more. Web 2.0, as we discussed in Chapter 1, features an emphasis on interaction, conversation, participation, collaboration, and user-generated content. While new technologies continually emerge that support these activities, Web 2.0 is less about the technologies than about the ways in which people and organizations

Bluetooth low-energy (BLE) beacon
Low-cost, battery-powered device that broadcasts Bluetooth signals to nearby smartphones; used in proximity marketing at retail stores, conferences, sports stadiums, and other locations.

are using the web. And the online world continues to grow and develop. Here are examples of some significant trends that help define what some call Web 3.0.

Crowdsourcing and Collective Intelligence

The term **crowdsourcing** describes how tasks can be delegated to large diffuse groups or communities who often volunteer their contributions. Unlike outsourcing, in which an organization contracts with a vendor to do work, crowdsourcing depends on engaging people in tasks they find interesting or rewarding or collecting data about what people are doing anyway as they go about their daily work.[21]

Google, for instance, relies on everyone who clicks on links or embeds links in their websites to continually improve its ranking system. All those clicks and external links are votes that adjust relevance rankings for every website. Amazon's Mechanical Turk site goes one more step, bringing organizations that need human wisdom together with all the people who have a few moments to spare and want to earn a bit of money. Visitors sign up to receive payments and then browse through the thousands of available tasks that are best done by humans rather than computers. For example, one company offers $1.10 to anyone who will transcribe some audio files.

PRODUCTIVITY TIP
Citing Wikipedia entries in your term papers as part of the bibliography is controversial. Many universities and faculty object, due to concerns about bias, reliability, accuracy, and the lack of identified authors. If you do use Wikipedia, include your evaluation of its quality as a source for your topic, just as you would for other web-based sources with unknown authorship.

Wikipedia is another well-known site that amasses collective intelligence and volunteer labor, in this case to create a vast online encyclopedia.[22] Debates over its accuracy and fairness continue, but one early study found that Wikipedia entries compared favorably to Britannica articles.[23]

Expanding Data and Sensory Input: The Internet of Things

Another important trend is the exponential growth of data and innovations in the way organizations collect, use, and value it. The flood of human participation is one contributor to the growing volume, through crowdsourcing and social media, for example. New sensors are adding far more, through RFID technology, smartphones, cameras, camcorders, GPS devices, and other sensory input.[24] The original IP address system is overwhelmed because so many new devices need unique addresses, but the new numbering scheme described in Chapter 3 will make room for quadrillions more to accommodate the Internet of Things.

Companies can achieve distinct competitive advantages when they manage to get control over valuable data collected by all these sensors, organize it into a database, and find ways to understand customers and create new products.

For example, innovative companies leaped at new ways to use GPS data when the U.S. government decided to unscramble some of the data from military satellites. Now a smartphone with GPS can help you navigate to the store, find Italian restaurants near your location, and measure the distance from your golf club to the putting green. Navteq, for instance, creates digital maps for navigation devices—not just for car travel but for walkers and bike riders (Figure 6-21). While GPS innovation toppled the paper map-making business, it added many billions to the economy in new services and applications.

DID YOU KNOW ?

Many of the massive open online courses—MOOCS—rely on crowdsourcing to enrich courses that might enroll thousands of students from around the world. For example, evaluating and providing feedback on each student's work are monumental challenges for a single professor with so many students, but some courses crowdsource the task, using peer assessment strategies.[25]

Source: BartlomiejMagierowski/Shutterstock.

FIGURE 6-21
For China's urban residents, GPS geography analysts add map details relevant to pedestrians or bicyclists who want the quickest routes through crowded streets.

The Learning Web

The massive and ever-growing mounds of data are valuable not just in their own right, as revenue sources for companies or as features to attract more users. They also provide resources for machine learning, making the web and its applications ever smarter. One example shows how Google uses "deep learning" to continually improve its translations from one language to another.[26]

Drawing on an enormous volume of already-translated texts and documents from sources such as the United Nations, Google developed a text translator that acquires its skills directly from the data. The software is not programmed with any rules about semantics or syntax. Instead, it statistically compares phrases from text in one language to its parallel in text that has already been translated by humans into English. Feeding it more paired, translated texts makes the translator ever more powerful. The more data it has to learn from, the smarter it gets. With the mobile app, you can speak a sentence into the microphone and then listen to the translated version.[27]

Google claimed it didn't even use native speakers to double-check any translations, a fact that astonished the CEO of Systran, a rival company that develops translation software relying on language rules and syntax. In one early competition, Systran's software translated an Arabic headline into:

"Alpine white new presence tape registered for coffee confirms Laden."

Google's translation read:

"The White House Confirmed the Existence of a New Bin Laden Tape."

Peter Norvig, who worked on the project at Google, remarked, "We don't have better algorithms. We just have more data."[28]

The web grew from a document-publishing environment to one that supports secure financial transactions and interactivity. Now it is transforming again, even surprising its own creators. As Tim O'Reilly, the person credited with coining the term *Web 2.0*, says, "The Web is growing up and we are all its collective parents."[29]

crowdsourcing
Delegating tasks to large diffuse groups or communities who often volunteer their contributions.

MyMISLab
Online Simulation

CRUISIN' FUSION
A Role-Playing Simulation on Website Development for a Chain of Concession Stands

You inherited a mobile concession truck from your uncle, who sold tacos and bottled drinks at lunchtime. Uncle Al liked talking to people, and his stand had become a local legend. He served only top-of-the-line mahi mahi, chicken, and cheese tacos in freshly baked shells. He also grew his own herbs to make "fusion" sauces that blended flavors from Mexico, Thailand, Korea, and India. His curried chicken taco was a favorite, and long lines formed every day.

You're not sure what to do with the concession truck, but a couple of your friends think Al was onto something with his unusual taco food truck. They want to partner with you to expand, targeting sports events, outdoor concerts, political rallies, holiday marches, and other events where customers might pay a little more for a very distinctive and healthier meal. With the right marketing, this could be a promising business venture. Log in when you're ready to start planning the website. ...

LEARNING OBJECTIVES

1 The Internet is a disruptive technology that causes waves of creative destruction, and an organization's web strategy is increasingly critical to its success. Four major goals that organizations choose to stress for their websites are (1) inform or entertain the audience, (2) influence the audience, (3) sell to the audience, and (4) facilitate or extend offline relationships. An organization may also have a social media presence and should establish clear goals for those platforms and channels. Social media are powerful opportunities for interacting with customers and supporting marketing campaigns. To achieve the greatest value, organizations must coordinate messages across their website and all their social media platforms and channels. The website's name in the form of its URL uniquely identifies the site on the Internet, mapping to its numerical IP address. The URL's components include the top-level domain, such as ".com," ".gov," ".org," ".cn," or ".de," which reflects the organization's mission or country code. Name disputes are common and are resolved by ICANN.

2 Building a website requires paying attention to the site's information architecture, which might adopt a hierarchical, multidimensional, flat, or sequential structure. Usability should be assessed early, and the user interface should follow design principles that will make it easier for visitors to accomplish their goals on the site. The website should also support accessibility for people with disabilities. Software development for websites starts with HTML, the programming language used to format web pages. HTML 5 is the latest version that reduces problems for web developers, reduces the need for browser plug-ins like Flash, and adds new features, especially for mobile devices. Media-rich and interactive websites are created with other programming tools, such as JavaScript, AJAX, Flash, and programming languages that interface with back-end databases. Content management systems enable teams to work together on a website, offering simple ways to format content and providing support for version control and other features.

3 E-commerce is the buying and selling of goods and services on the Internet. E-commerce software, including shopping carts, can support secure and encrypted transmissions, manage product catalogs, and track transactions. Trust is a critical element in e-commerce, and independent organizations audit websites, granting a seal of approval to those that meet minimums standards. Social commerce (s-commerce) also helps tap trust by engaging friendship networks in shared shopping experiences.

4 Use of mobile devices, such as smartphones and tablets, is growing extremely rapidly, and they offer small size and light weight, mobility with wireless connectivity, versatility, and location awareness. They are also important elements in the Internet of Things. Their features require web developers to design mobile-friendly websites and specialized applications. Mobile commerce (m-commerce) takes advantage of these mobile devices to conduct e-commerce on the go. Mobile devices can serve as digital "wallets" to make mobile payments using technologies such as near field communication, eliminating the need to carry cash or credit cards.

5 Digital marketing strategies encompass the website and social media as well as strategies for mobile devices. On the web, strategy should start with search engine optimization (SEO), which seeks to improve a website's position on result lists returned by search engines. Organizations choose appropriate keywords and encourage links from external sites to achieve higher rankings in the search results. Ad networks use third-party cookies to track user behavior across multiple websites, gathering data used to improve targeting. Search engine marketing, in which relevant text ads are served alongside results for the user's query, are most effective. Social media marketing strategies are especially effective because they rely on friendship networks and "influencers." Mobile marketing can take advantage of location with proximity marketing that uses BLE beacons and also the fact that people always carry the device.

6 Web 2.0 and beyond provides examples of how the web continues to evolve. Crowdsourcing draws on collective intelligence and often voluntary labor. Expanded data sources and the Internet of Things open up many new opportunities for innovation. As the web continues to evolve, the massive amount of big data contributed by individuals, companies, governments, and things is greatly enhancing its power and potential. The growing sources of "big data" also support machine learning, so the web can continue to grow smarter.

KEY TERMS AND CONCEPTS

infomediary

e-marketplace

business to consumer (B2C)

business to business (B2B)

consumer to consumer (C2C)

consumer to business (C2B)

uniform resource locator (URL)

Domain Name System (DNS)

hypertext transfer protocol (http://)

file transfer protocol (ftp://)

top-level domain

Internet Corporation for Assigned Names and Numbers (ICANN)

hierarchical website architecture

multidimensional website architecture

sequential website architecture

usability

web accessibility

assistive technologies

web browser

hypertext markup language (HTML)

JavaScript

AJAX

World Wide Web Consortium (W3C)

content management system

cascading style sheets (CSS)

e-commerce

shopping cart software

payment gateway

mobile commerce (m-commerce)

near field communications (NFC)

search engine optimization (SEO)

tag cloud

click-through rate (CTR)

cookie

third-party cookies

Bluetooth low-energy (BLE) beacon

crowdsourcing

CHAPTER REVIEW QUESTIONS

6-1. What are four primary goals an organization might choose to develop its web and social media strategy? What is an example of each? Why are clearly defined goals important of the use of social media?

6-2. How is a URL related to a registered website name? Why does a URL include a protocol identifier? What are the components of a website address? What are typical suffixes that identify top-level domains?

6-3. What is website architecture? What are examples of website architecture?

6-4. What is the difference between usability and accessibility? How do website developers test for usability? How can website design improve accessibility? How do text and background color combinations relate to website accessibility? What are the benefits of designing accessible websites?

6-5. List some software development strategies used for websites. What is an advantage to using basic HTML? How does HTML 5 reduce problems for web developers? What is an advantage to using JavaScript? Why is AJAX used to develop websites? What role does a content management system play in website development? Why do content management systems use templates?

6-6. What is e-commerce? What activities does it include? How do online transaction sites use databases and shopping cart software? Why is security critical for e-commerce success? Which protocol supports secure Internet transactions? Why is trust critical for e-commerce success? Aside from having a well-known brand name, how do online sellers signal their trustworthiness to potential customers?

6-7. What is m-commerce? What is near field communication, and how does it facilitate mobile payments?

6-8. Identify the three primary platforms for digital marketing. Identify which platform uses search engine optimization (SEO) and what SEO is. What are two examples? How do organizations improve their position on search result lists?

6-9. How does web advertising work to target ads for individuals? How does social media marketing influence advertising? How do BLE beacons use mobile advertising?

6-10. What is Web 2.0? What is crowdsourcing? What is an example of crowdsourcing? How do Web 2.0 capabilities change the way in which people and organizations use the web?

PROJECTS AND DISCUSSION QUESTIONS

6-11. VeriSign is a recognized authority on website security, and the VeriSign seal tells online customers they can trust the website to encrypt sensitive data that is transmitted over the Internet. Visit verisign.com to learn more about the VeriSign Trust Seal. In addition to verifying encryption, what else does this seal tell consumers about the websites on which it appears? What is SSL security? How does it work? Prepare a brief report of your findings.

6-12. Pop-ups, such as windows that open to provide a return shipping label, and web browser add-ons, like the Google toolbar, can make browsing more fun or more effective, but sometimes they can slow down your computer or cause the browser to shut down unexpectedly. Most add-ons require user consent before they are downloaded, but some might be downloaded without your knowledge and some may be tracking your browsing habits. How do you know which add-ons are running on your computer? Click on Tools to learn about your browser's settings. How do you allow some pop-ups and disallow others? Review your add-ons. Which ones are allowed on your browser? What specific functionality does each provide? Did you disable any add-ons? Which ones, and why?

6-13. Visit a site that uses AJAX to create interactive maps, such as www.MeasureofAmerica.org. What features does this technology add to make the site more interactive? How might you use this technology to present an interactive map showing the changing incidence of reported cases of flu by geographic area as the flu season progresses?
MyMISLab

6-14. Visit an e-commerce site such as Amazon.com, a nonprofit site such as the Cancer Research Institute (www.cancerresearch.org), and a government website, such as the California Department of Motor Vehicles (www.dmv.ca.gov). For each site, assume you want to accomplish an e-commerce task: purchase a travel guide to Peru, donate $10 to cancer research, and pay a traffic fine online. Compare your overall experiences on each site, and note how easy it is to accomplish the tasks. How do these sites track purchases or donations as users navigate the site? Do all the sites use secure transmissions for e-commerce (https://)? What improvements would you recommend for these sites?
MyMISLab

6-15. Visit joomla.com to learn more about this open source content management system. What types of content does it manage? Who uses Joomla, and what are its advantages? Visit two sites that use Joomla and compare them. How are they similar? How are they different? Prepare a 5-minute presentation of your findings.

6-16. Work in a small group with classmates to evaluate website accessibility issues. Select a website to evaluate, and then choose three pages from the website for your sample. Your sample should be varied but should ideally include pages that contain tables, images, multimedia (e.g., a video or sound file), and a form. Conduct the following tests using at least two different browsers.

a. Turn off images (usually under Tools). Do all the images have alternative text that properly describes the image? Screen readers for visually impaired people will need accurate verbal descriptions to grasp the content of the image.

b. Turn off sound. Is there a text transcription for the narration that hearing impaired people will need?

c. Use the controls on the browser to increase the size of the fonts. Can the fonts be adjusted using the browser? Visually impaired people often need larger fonts to read, but some websites use fixed font sizes.

d. Using just the keyboard, not the mouse, try navigating through the links and the fields on a form. Can you reach all the links, and do they describe what they link to? Can you navigate through the form with the keyboard without using the mouse? This is a good test to see if screen readers will work properly.

e. Print out the three pages using only black, white, and gray. Is there sufficient contrast without color to accommodate color-blind visitors?

f. Compare the results for the different browsers you've tested, and prepare a 5-minute presentation of your group's results.

6-17. What do people look for on the front page of a university website? Work in a small group with classmates to review your university's website. What is the goal or goals of the site? What type of architecture does it have? Describe its usability. Do you struggle to find specific information, or is navigation easy? How many clicks does it take to locate holiday hours of operation for your library? Prepare a list of suggestions for the university web master that describe specific ways to improve your university's website.

APPLICATION EXERCISES

6-18. WEBSITE APPLICATION:
Heritage Dogs

Use Microsoft Word to create a simple website for Heritage Dogs. Launch Word and type "Heritage Dogs" into the document. Click File > Save As and save your file as a Web Page named "index.html" rather than as a Word Document. Save the file as "index.html." (Depending on your version of Word, the default for the file extension may be "htm," which is also recognized as a web page.) Click New to create another page and type "Thai Ridgeback" into the document. Save it as "Thai Ridgeback.html." Create additional web pages for each breed that Heritage Dogs plans to promote. Return to the index page and type "Thai Ridgeback" into the document. Highlight "Thai Ridgeback" and click Insert > Hyperlink and locate "Thai Ridgeback.html." Select the file and click OK. You have just created a hyperlink. After you create additional hyperlinks for each breed, save and close the files. Locate the index file on your computer, and open it with the browser of your choice. Check the hyperlinks. Do they work? What type of website architecture did you create? Explain how this simple website can be expanded to provide additional content for visitors to HeritageDogs.org.

6-19. EXCEL APPLICATION:
Heritage Dogs Website Metrics

The board of directors at Heritage Dogs is meeting to consider how its website is serving the needs of volunteers, donors, and potential adoptive pet owners. The website coordinator has asked you to create an Excel spreadsheet to help her analyze quarterly data for several key indicators including percentage of repeat visitors, page views per visit, and bounce rate. The bounce rate is the percentage of visitors who view only one page. Together, these are a measure of website "stickiness"— the ability to keep visitors interested and coming back for more. Additionally, she wants two line charts that display website usage statistics.

Create the spreadsheet shown in Figure 6-22 and add calculations for Total Visitors, Percentage Repeat Visitors, Page Views per Visit, and Bounce Rate. To calculate Bounce Rate, divide Page Views by Single Page Views.

Create a line chart that shows Visits, Total Visitors, and Page Views. Create a second line chart that shows the Bounce Rate and the Percentage Repeat Customers. For both charts, select a layout that includes a chart title, axis title, and legend.

How would you describe the pattern of website usage in terms of visits, total visitors, and page views? How would you describe the website in terms of "stickiness"?

6-20. ACCESS APPLICATION:
Springfield Animal Shelter

The Springfield Animal Shelter manages a volunteer foster program in which volunteers care for sick and immature animals in their homes and take in injured or abused animals when the shelter facility is full. Animals may be in foster care for a few weeks or a few months, depending on the need. When the animal is healthy and ready to be adopted, the shelter will post its picture and story on the website. Foster parents are given first choice to adopt the animal but are not required to do so. Volunteers enroll in the program on the shelter website, and the information they provide is stored in an Access database. Download the Springfield Animal Shelter database Ch06Ex03 and create three detail reports for the shelter manager. A detail report displays all information for each volunteer.

The first report will list all active volunteers who specified they wish to care for a cat. The second report will list all active volunteers who wish to care for a dog. The third report will list all inactive volunteers regardless of animal preference. Review the information being collected about volunteers and suggest other types of information that may be useful to the shelter manager.

FIGURE 6-22
Heritage Dogs website metrics.

	A	B	C	D	E	F	G	H	I
1					Heritage Dogs				
2					Website Metrics				
3									
4		Q1	Q2	Q3	Q4	Q5	Q6	Q7	Q8
5	Visits	128	143	275	290	365	468	605	681
6	First Time Visitors	82	98	162	172	218	304	436	439
7	Repeat Visitors	12	24	48	28	58	56	98	110
8	Page Views	210	200	480	520	569	780	1004	1265
9	Single Page Views	65	55	125	154	160	250	305	425

Source: Microsoft®Excel, Microsoft Corporation. Reprinted with permission.

Mobile Payments and the Digital Wallet

In a country where cash is king and almost everyone owns a cell phone, Japan's NTT Docomo led a major drive into mobile payments and m-commerce. The mobile phone carrier pioneered the use of near field communication (NFC) chips inside its cell phones, enabling them to exchange data wirelessly over a few centimeters. More than 65 million people subscribe to Docomo's wireless voice network, and they can all pay for their cappuccinos at participating stores by tapping their cell phone against a special terminal or just waving it nearby.

When a customer taps the cell phone to pay, the expense is automatically logged into a digital expense report and charged to the customer's account. Called osaifu keitai in Japanese, the cell-phone wallet frees people from carrying cash. Consumers use their cell-phone wallets to buy subway, train, and airline tickets, and the phone's chip also serves as an electronic key to control access to buildings and homes. Cell-phone wallet holders can check their balances, loyalty points, and purchasing history from the handset and receive promotional discounts.

In the United States, mobile payments have been slow to take off, partly because credit cards are so popular and also trusted. The credit card industry builds in essential safeguards against fraud and also offers incentives such as cash advances, frequent flier miles, or reward points. Switching to mobile payments would be a major change in customer behavior. At most restaurants, you would need to hand over your smartphone to the server instead of offering a credit card because Apple Pay and other major players rely on NFC technology.

While Apple is a major player in the mobile payment industry, the company has had some slip-ups that make customers wary. While waiting for his tech support appointment at a New York Apple store, one customer decided to purchase some headphones. He used the Apple app to scan the barcode and charged the purchase to his iTunes account. Later, when he started to leave with his headphones in a bag, an employee asked to see a receipt. He located the app on his smartphone but then found the transaction had not completed. Instead of letting him click the last button to confirm, the clerk called the police and the customer was arrested for shoplifting.

In Japan, NTT Docomo had to take over a bank to build its osaifu keitai services so it would have the financial backbone to actually handle electronic payments. In the United States, though, the credit card companies or other well-established payment services, such as PayPal, are likely to be major players or partners.

Consumers will need more incentives to try out any of these new services, and they must develop the kind of trust they already have in credit cards, debit cards, checks, and cash. Convenience is one incentive, but creative retailers can tap other features that tie mobile phones to purchasing. Teen clothing chain Aeropostale, for instance, offered an app that let customers choose what music the store would play. The teens hung around the store for 30 minutes or more to hear their selection. The long wait offered plenty of time to shop, and the company learned a great deal about its customers' music preferences.

As mobile payment experiments play out and technologies like NFC become more widespread, those lines at checkout counters may get shorter and shorter. Leather wallets stuffed with credit cards, loyalty cards, photos, and cash may become extinct.

Discussion Questions

6-21. What are the potential benefits of this technology for consumers? What are the potential benefits for retailers?

6-22. What are the risks for consumers and retailers? What are some ways that these risks could be overcome?

6-23. How could this technology affect the telecommunications and consumer banking industries?

6-24. Do you believe this technology would work in the United States? Why or why not?

Sources: Analysis: How has m-commerce evolved? (December 21, 2012). *Retail Week*, http://search.proquest.com/docview/1242202472?accountid=11752, accessed August 17, 2016.

Chaley, C. (March 20, 2013). Partnerships provide the muscle in the mobile payments war. *Fast Company*, http://www.fastcompany.com/3007281/industries-watch/partnerships-provide-muscle-mobile-payments-war, accessed August 17, 2016.

Colbert, C. (2016). NTT Docomo, Inc. *Hoover's Online*, http://subscriber.hoovers.com.proxy1.library.jhu.edu/H/company360/overview.html?companyId=58535000000000, accessed August 17, 2016.

Daştan, İ., & Gürler, C. (2016). Factors affecting the adoption of mobile payment systems: An empirical analysis. *EMAJ: Emerging Markets Journal*, *6*(1), 16–24. http://doi.org/10.5195/emaj.2016.95

NTT Docomo, Inc. (December 7, 2015). LexisNexis Academic, http://www.lexisnexis.com.proxy1.library.jhu.edu/hottopics/lnacademic/, accessed March 30, 2016.

Taylor, E. (2016). Mobile payment technologies in retail: a review of potential benefits and risks. *International Journal of Retail & Distribution Management*, *44*(2), 159–177. http://doi.org/10.1108/IJRDM-05-2015-0065

CASE STUDY #2

LinkedIn: The Social Network and E-Marketplace for Professionals

Founded in 2002, LinkedIn is the premiere social network for professionals, offering a comprehensive platform that stresses career progression and business services rather than updates for family and friends. With more than 400 million users, LinkedIn is far smaller than Facebook, but its user base includes many high-powered professionals, including Fortune 500 business execs, who rely on the service to expand their personal networks, identify career opportunities, recruit talent for their companies, and share information.

LinkedIn invites individuals to create free accounts to post their employment histories, education, and skill sets; connect with colleagues; and identify promising job opportunities. But unlike other networks that rely heavily on targeted advertising as their main source of revenue, LinkedIn enjoys a diverse revenue base with three major product lines.

The company's Talent Solutions line offers a variety of services to recruiters, drawing on the network's user data to help companies identify the best candidates for the positions they have available and encourage them to apply. Sony, for instance, relies on LinkedIn to help find talented professionals not only by searching the database but also by tapping the networks of Sony's own employees, who can offer referrals.

LinkedIn's Marketing Solutions earns revenue from targeted advertising based on user profiles, much like other social media platforms. Companies can also create "sponsored content," in which industry leaders offer their insights and knowledge directly to users who are likely to be interested. CRM software developer Hubspot uses LinkedIn Marketing Solutions to reach marketing professionals and engage them with e-books, webinars, and how-to guides.

The third revenue source is Premium Subscriptions, which offers advanced features that match the user's interests and goals. For example, job seekers can see who has viewed their profile and can compare themselves to other candidates for particular positions. Some plans also offer access to Lynda.com's extensive educational video library, which LinkedIn purchased to make premium membership even more attractive.

College students and recent grads are among LinkedIn's fastest-growing user groups, mainly because the company promotes its services to help grads find their ideal first job. Using data analytics on its big data, LinkedIn recommends positions that are well suited for graduates based on their profiles and majors and also points out openings at companies that have historically hired graduates from the same college. Details on the career paths of those fellow alums will also help the new grad see how to get ahead, perhaps with training through Lynda.com.

In 2016, Microsoft purchased LinkedIn for a whopping $26.2 billion, the company's largest acquisition to date. Microsoft had tried to develop its own social networking platform with little success, but the LinkedIn purchase could be a very promising acquisition. Most people on LinkedIn already use some or all of Microsoft Office products, and integration could uncover opportunities for startling innovations. Imagine, for example, a businessperson heading for the next meeting on the Outlook calendar with the email addresses of the other attendees. Cortina, Microsoft's voice-enabled personal assistant, could offer a briefing on the backgrounds and interests of the other attendees, drawing from LinkedIn profiles. Armed with some personal information, the businessperson could quickly establish a connection that leads to a solid relationship and closed sale.

LinkedIn made some early missteps with overly aggressive tactics to draw in new users. In 2012, the company sent emails to users' contacts with repeated reminders to join LinkedIn, using their names and images. Users sued, complaining that the emails were damaging their reputations, and LinkedIn settled out of court for $13 million. With that mistake in the past, LinkedIn's future looks bright, especially if the company can maintain the trust of its user base and offer useful services and contacts that professionals value as their careers progress.

Discussion Questions

6-25. LinkedIn does not rely heavily on targeted advertising but generates revenue from other sources. Identify other sources of revenue that LinkedIn uses and explain how each contributes revenue.

6-26. What are some of the advantages for college students to use LinkedIn?

6-27. What are some of the advantages and benefits to Microsoft in the acquisition of LinkedIn?

6-28. Describe how Microsoft could integrate its products with LinkedIn to provide greater value to LinkedIn customers.

Sources: Basu, A. (2015). Roles and uses of company websites and social media for Fortune 500. *SIES Journal of Management, 11*(1), 37–42.

Chaykowski, K. (2016). LinkedIn will tell you if you have a shot at that dream job. *Forbes.com*, http://www.forbes.com/sites/kathleenchaykowski/2016/06/07/linkedin-will-tell-you-if-you-have-a-shot-at-that-dream-job/#5728f999387e, accessed August 17, 2016.

Kapko, M. (2016). LinkedIn students app helps graduates get gigs. *CIO*. http://www.cio.com/article/3060049/mobile-apps/linkedin-students-app-helps-graduates-get-gigs.html, accessed August 17, 2016.

Kasson, E. G. (2015). The sourcers' secrets. *HR Magazine, 60*(9), 38–42.

Cother, J. (2016). LinkedIn corporation. *Hoover's Online*, http://subscriber.hoovers.com.proxy1.library.jhu.edu/H/company360/overview.html?companyId=132274000000000, accessed August 17, 2016.

LinkedIn. (2016). http;//www.linkedin.com, accessed June 16, 2016.

MarketLine. (2016). LinkedIn corporation SWOT analysis (pp. 1–10). http://search.ebscohost.com/login.aspx?direct=true&db=bth&AN=113314248&site=ehost-live&scope=site, accessed August 16, 2016.

Mims, C. (2016, June 14). Why Microsoft bought LinkedIn; Microsoft and LinkedIn are a natural fit, and the deal may fare better than Microsoft's past acquisitions. *Wall Street Journal (Online)*, http://www.wsj.com/articles/microsoft-gains-link-to-a-network-1465922927, accessed August 17, 2016.

E-PROJECT 1   Examining Top M-Commerce Sites

The success of m-commerce depends partly on the quality of the user's experience when accessing the site from an Internet-enabled mobile phone. Load time is important, and Figure 6-23 shows the average load time for three retailers in 2016.

6-29. Create the spreadsheet in Figure 6-23 in Excel. Then visit each of the retailers using an Internet-enabled mobile phone. Time how long each one takes to load, using a stopwatch (www.online-stopwatch.com). Enter your data in the "Current load time" column.

6-30. Enter the formula to compute the Percentage Change in the row for Target and copy the formula to the other cells in the column.

6-31. Which retailer's m-commerce site has shown the most change since 2016?

6-32. What factors contribute to a site's load times? Why would your data be different from a classmate's when accessing these sites?

6-33. Conduct an experiment to compare m-commerce at Walmart and Target. Start the stopwatch, load Walmart's site, and search for a Fodor's travel guide to Mexico. Add the product to your cart, check out up to the point at which you would enter a credit card number, and then write down the time from the stopwatch. Do the same experiment at Target's site. How did your time estimates compare for the two m-commerce experiences? Overall, which site do you think offers the best user experience?

FIGURE 6-23
Key metrics for m-commerce sites.

Retailer	Website	Load Time (seconds) 2016	Current Load Time (seconds)	Percent Change
eBay	www.ebay.com	4.14		
Walgreens	www.walgreens.com	3.60		
Best Buy	www.bestbuy.com	6.29		

E-PROJECT 2   Exploring Linkedin's Web Analytics

In this e-project, you will explore the LinkedIn website to learn more about its web model. Then you will examine the site's analytics using Alexa, a web information company that offers a limited amount of free information about traffic to websites.

6-34. Visit www.linkedin.com and scroll down to the footer where the site describes various services. (If you are already a member, stay logged out for this exercise.) Click on Jobs or Search Jobs to find jobs in information technology with no particular location specified. How relevant are the openings listed to your situation? How might that list change if you were logged in and the service had access to your profile?

6-35. Visit www.alexa.com, scroll to where you can enter a website URL, and search for Linkedin.com to retrieve the analytics.

a. What is LinkedIn's Global Traffic Rank, and what does that term mean? Compare LinkedIn's global traffic rank to the site's traffic rank in the United States. How is LinkedIn doing outside the United States?

b. Scroll through the information Alexa provides about the Linkedin.com website. How would you generally describe LinkedIn's main market based on the metrics you are able to see?

c. Which other websites are LinkedIn visitors most likely to come from just before they go to LinkedIn (upstream sites)?

CHAPTER NOTES

1. Thaler, R. H., & Tucker, W. (2013). Smarter information, smarter consumers. *Harvard Business Review, 91*(1), 44–54.

2. Martin, J. A. (October 1, 2015). 11 most memorable social media marketing successes of 2015. *CIO,* http://www.cio.com/article/2988313/social-networking/11-most-memorable-social-media-marketing-successes-of-2015.html, accessed August 17, 2016.

3. Goins, J. D. (2013). Emerging new media issues. *Computer & Internet Lawyer, 30*(1), 13–14.

4. Ribeiro, J. (March 10, 2016). ICANN stewardship transition plan sent to U.S. government. *Computerworld,* http://www.computerworld.com/article/3043201/internet/icann-stewardship-transition-plan-sent-to-us-government.html, accessed August 17, 2016.

5. Isenberg, D. (n.d.). The growing threat of cybersquatting in the banking and finance sector. *Circle ID,* http://www.circleid.com/posts/20160324_growing_threat_of_cybersquatting_in_the_banking_and_finance_sector/, accessed August 16, 2016.

6. Schneider, K. (December 10, 2012). Australian restaurant takes on TripAdvisor over bad review. News.com.au, http://www.news.com.au/travel/news/australian-restaurant-takes-on-tripadvisor-over-bad-review/story-e6frfq80-1226532022053, accessed February 2, 2013.

7. Valdes, R. (2015). *Top 10 mistakes in web and user experience design projects* (No. G00171161). Gartner Research, http://www.gartner.com/document/1184601?ref=solrAll&refval=165312180&qid=78402a8caba685096c74d94abfea1be5, accessed August 16, 2016.

8. Ipri, T., Yunkin, M., & Brown, J. M. (2009). Usability as a method for assessing discovery. *Information Technology & Libraries, 28*(4), 181–183.

9. Gonçalves, R., Martins, J., Pereira, J., Oliveira, M., & Ferreira, J. (2013). Enterprise web accessibility levels amongst the Forbes 250: Where art thou O virtuous leader? *Journal Of Business Ethics, 113*(2), 363–375. doi:10.1007/s10551-012-1309-3

10. Reindl, K., & Linde, S. J. (2016). DOJ postpones website accessibility proceeding: How businesses can prepare in anticipation of a lawsuit and how to maximize insurance once served. *Intellectual Property & Technology Law Journal, 28*(3), 15–18.

11. Parry, M., & Brainard, J. (2010). Colleges lock out blind students online. *Chronicle of Higher Education, 57*(17), A1–A8.

12. Vijayan, J. (2016). Google to stop accepting display ads based on Flash. *eWeek,* http://www.eweek.com/cloud/google-to-stop-accepting-display-ads-based-on-flash.html, accessed August 16, 2016.

13. Chahal, M. (2016). Social commerce: How willing are consumers to buy through social media? *Marketing Week (Online Edition),* https://www.marketingweek.com/2016/03/23/social-commerce-how-willing-are-consumers-to-buy-through-social-media/, accessed August 17, 2016.

14. Landry, M. (2013). Is cash no longer king? *PM Network, 27*(1), 44–49.

15. Li, Y. (February 25, 2016). China Circuit: How mobile payments reshape lifestyles. *The Wall Street Journal Asia,* p. B.1. Hong Kong.

16. Sarner, A., & Wilson, J. (2016). *Social marketing primer for 2016* (No. G00293086). Gartner Research, http://www.gartner.com/document/3187626?ref=solrAll&refval=165383478&qid=187afb8479f181bcbdcc0d7739b5e718, accessed August 16, 2016.

17. Gautam, A. (January 1, 2016). #BendTheRules—HP's genius SMM campaign. *Digital Vidya,* http://www.digitalvidya.com/blog/bendtherules-hps-genius-smm-campaign/, accessed August 16, 2016.

18. Sarner, A., McGuire, M., & Golvin, C. S. (2016). *Mobile marketing primer for 2016* (No. G00293091). Gartner Research, http://www.gartner.com/document/3189317?ref=solrAll&refval=165408229&qid=2710c64a3bae1dc2934a14565bfcce50, accessed August 16, 2016.

19. Bacon, J. (2016). Five mobile marketing mistakes and how to fix them. *Marketing Week,* https://www.marketingweek.com/2016/02/17/five-mobile-marketing-mistakes-and-how-to-fix-them/, accessed August 16, 2016.

20. O'Reilly, L. (2016, March 16). Ads on news sites gobble up as much as 79% of users' mobile data. *Business Insider,* http://www.businessinsider.com/enders-analysis-ad-blocker-study-finds-ads-take-up-79-of-mobile-data-transfer-2016-3, accessed August 16, 2016.

21. Saxton, G. D., Onook, O., & Kishore, R. (2013). Rules of crowdsourcing: Models, issues, and systems of control. *Information Systems Management, 30*(1), 2–20.

22. Ingram, M. (2016). Wikipedia turns 15—will it manage to make it to 30? *Fortune.com,* http://fortune.com/2016/01/15/wikipedia-turns-15-will-it-manage-to-make-it-to-30/, accessed August 16, 2016.

23. Giles, J. (2005). Internet encyclopaedias go head to head. *Nature,* (438), 900–901.

24. Greengard, S. (2016, January 11). How the Internet of Things will connect all things. *CIO Insight,* http://www.cioinsight.com/blogs/how-the-internet-of-things-will-connect-all-things.html, accessed August 16, 2016.

25. Paulin, D., & Haythornthwaite, C. (2016). Crowdsourcing the curriculum: Redefining e-learning practices through peer-generated approaches. *The Information Society, 32*(2), 130–142. http://doi.org/10.1080/01972243.2016.1130501

26. Novet, J. (2016). Google Translate could become more accurate soon thanks to deep learning. *VentureBeat*, https://venturebeat.com/2016/03/10/google-translate-could-become-more-accurate-soon-thanks-to-deep-learning/, accessed August 16, 2016.

27. McDermott, I. E. (2016). Found in translation at the reference desk. *Online Searcher*, *40*(1), 35–37.

28. Stross, R. E. (2009). *Planet Google*. New York: The Free Press.

29. O'Reilly, T., & Battelle, J. (2009). Web squared: Web 2.0 five years on. *Web 2.0 Summit*, http://www.web2summit.com/web2009/public/schedule/detail/10194, accessed August 16, 2016.

Business Intelligence and *Decision Making*

MyMISLab™

- Online Simulation: Chocolate Lovers Unite: A Role-Playing Simulation on Web Analytics
- Discussion Questions: #7-1, #7-2, #7-3
- Writing Assignments: #7-12, #7-13

LEARNING OBJECTIVES

1 Define business intelligence, and describe the three levels of decision making that it supports.

2 Describe the major sources of business intelligence, and provide examples of their usefulness.

3 Explain several approaches to data mining and analytics that help managers analyze patterns, trends, and relationships and make better data-driven decisions.

4 Explain how digital analytics are used as a source of business intelligence and why they are so valuable for understanding customers.

5 Describe how dashboards, portals, and mashups help visualize business intelligence, and explain the role that the human element plays in business intelligence initiatives.

An online, interactive decision-making simulation that reinforces chapter contents and uses key terms in context can be found in MyMISLab™.

INTRODUCTION

MAKING SMART BUSINESS DECISIONS TAKES MORE THAN GOOD JUDGMENT. It takes a clear understanding of the information relevant to solving the problem and knowledge about where that information can be obtained. It also takes insightful analysis, often relying on sophisticated software tools that can do much of the work. This chapter explains what business intelligence is, why you need it, where you can find it, and what decision support tools are available to help you analyze it all. You will also learn how to organize and display the information that is most important to you, which will help you avoid the trap of information overload.

In "Chocolate Lovers Unite," the online simulation for this chapter, you will get first-hand experience with a business intelligence problem. Your job is to help the company decide what works best on the company's website. The managers there have just been guessing (and arguing) about this, but you'll have different photos, taglines, and ad copy to actually try out. Each period, you'll create two versions of the website to compare, and visitors will be randomly directed to one or the other. You'll collect data, and when the experiment is over, you'll analyze the results. Instead of guesswork, you'll have real business intelligence to support the recommendations you make to the CEO.

MyMISLab
Online Simulation

CHOCOLATE LOVERS UNITE
A Role-Playing Simulation on Web Analytics

Adisa/Shutterstock.

Data continues to pile up, turning into the "big data" described in earlier chapters. It comes from databases, the web, social networks, surveys, cameras, smartphones, RFID sensors, digitized books, electric meters, GPS devices, and more. The information systems we use to tap this mother lode intelligently are the subject of this chapter, particularly the ways we can identify trends and patterns to make better decisions. Determining which photos and text work best on a company website is just one decision that can be improved with business intelligence and decision support tools. Here are more:

- How much should we spend for online ads this season? Which ads work best?

- Should we create more fish dishes for our menu? How much can we charge?

- When should we start our phonathon to raise money for disaster relief? Should we invite celebrities to promote it?

- How should we address the bad publicity about our product recalls? Should we ignore it?

Business intelligence (BI), introduced in Chapter 1, is an umbrella term that includes the vast quantities of information an organization might use for data-driven decision making, from within its own data repositories and also from external sources. The term also encompasses the software applications, technologies, and practices that managers apply to the data to gain insights that help them make better decisions.

Define business intelligence, and describe the three levels of decision making that it supports.

1 Levels of Decision Making

Consider the roles that these three people play in a busy city hospital:

- Monica works the evening shift in the call center, scheduling appointments, referring patients, registering callers for hospital seminars, and routing calls.
- Colin just joined the hospital as assistant director of marketing. He will track online campaigns intended to call attention to the hospital's top-ranked specialties, such as sports medicine and cardiology. His business major in college, with its focus on information systems and marketing, was critical to his selection for this position.
- Bora, the hospital administrator, is responsible for the hospital's overall financial and operational health. She plans budgets, sets rates, recruits and hires the medical and administrative staff, and, working with the different teams, develops hospital policies. She earned her MBA and also holds an MS in health care administration.

Each of these people makes dozens of decisions every day, at different levels of the organization and across business units. They draw on written policies, formal training, unwritten norms, business intelligence, and their own insights and gut instincts to make the best decisions they can. At different levels, their decisions all contribute to the success or failure of the whole organization. Figure 7-1 illustrates typical decision-making levels.

Operational Level

Employees working primarily at the operational level make countless decisions as they deal directly with customers and handle routine transactions. Many decisions follow predetermined policies and procedures that spell out how to handle different situations. Monica took training for her call center position, in which rules for dealing with each type of call were specified. She learned how to deal with angry callers, impatient callers, and callers who appear to be in severe distress. Within this structure, however, Monica also makes decisions independently, such as how long to spend with each caller, how to encourage a caller to attend a hospital event, and how sympathetic to sound in each situation.

Business intelligence for use at the operational level is attracting considerable attention as organizations find ways to bring meaningful, performance-related information to all employees. Timely data showing the outcome and effectiveness of their decisions can dramatically affect performance.

At 1-800-CONTACTS, the world's largest contact lens store, operational business intelligence fine-tunes the decision making of every call center agent. Each one has access to a customized screen with color-coded gauges showing daily metrics, such as his or her average calls per hour and average sale size. Bar charts show these metrics, comparing them to the agent's monthly averages. The screens also contain displays updated from a data warehouse every 15 minutes so agents get quick feedback. Bonuses are tied to a formula based on these measures, so motivation to move the needles on their dials is high. After the system was implemented, revenues increased $50,000 per month, with consistently high call quality.[1] Figure 7-2 shows an example of the kinds of screens used in call center settings.

FIGURE 7-1

Different levels of decision making in an organization rely on different mixes of structured and unstructured information.

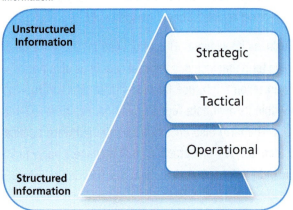

Tactical Level

People at tactical levels draw on business intelligence to make mid-level decisions, the kind that may guide individual business units. Decisions about marketing plans, product development, membership drives, departmental budgets, and other initiatives are generally tactical. A management information system (MIS) supports this kind of decision making, combining data, software, and reporting tools that managers need to carry out their responsibilities. (As we discussed in Chapter 1, the term *MIS* also describes the academic discipline that focuses on the people, technology, processes, and data making up information systems.)

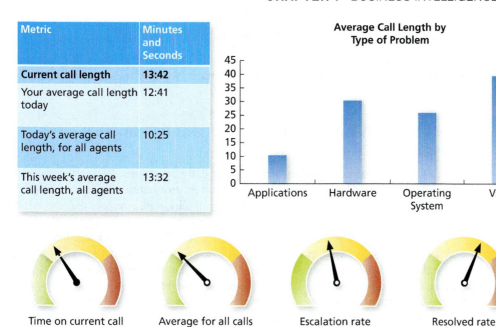

Metric	Minutes and Seconds
Current call length	13:42
Your average call length today	12:41
Today's average call length, for all agents	10:25
This week's average call length, all agents	13:32

Average Call Length by Type of Problem

Time on current call   Average for all calls   Escalation rate   Resolved rate

FIGURE 7-2
Call center agents can see timely data on their own and their coworkers' activities, especially to support operational decision making and improved performance.

Much useful management-level business intelligence comes from the routine weekly or monthly reports that the organization's information systems generate. For instance, Colin needs weekly reports on the number of patients admitted, organized by clinical area. If his department is conducting a marketing campaign featuring the sports medicine clinic, he can use summarized data to check his outcomes.

While operational-level decision making requires detailed, structured information about actual transactions by customers, tactical decision makers need to see trends and summaries, sorted and tallied in different ways, to monitor success and plan next steps.

Strategic Level

The leadership guides longer-term strategy. Decisions at this level can have widespread effects throughout the organization and beyond, to suppliers, customers, and even the whole industry. Each decision could commit huge amounts of capital and people to major initiatives. For instance, hospital administrator Bora may need to decide whether to open a new pediatrics wing or use those resources to enlarge sports medicine.

A high-tech CEO might ask, "Should we make an offer to buy out a rival?" A pharmaceutical company's CFO may wonder how much the company should invest in R&D over the next 5 years. A college president will need extensive data from financial analysts, faculty, and students—both current and prospective—to weigh whether to eliminate an academic department with very few majors rather than lay off people or raise tuition.

The business intelligence that executives need to make better decisions is often less structured than at the operational or even management level. Top-level execs certainly need summary and historical data from the company's own transactional systems and data warehouses. But they also need business intelligence that draws on big data and unstructured data to learn more about their rivals, their industry's landscape, and overall economic trends.

In fact, most people in an organization need decision support at more than one level, depending on the situation. A CEO will want to see the detailed transaction records of a high-value client, and the call center staff can suggest process improvements if they have access to reports showing longer-term patterns. Colin, who usually operates at the tactical level, will be very interested in analyzing the sports blogs to see what people say about the hospital. He'll need tools to tap such external information sources as much as any CEO.

Describe the major sources of business intelligence, and provide examples of their usefulness.

2 Sources of Business Intelligence

A hurdle for business intelligence (BI) projects is not too little information. It's too much. Throughout the organization and well beyond its borders, valuable information sources that can improve decision making at all levels abound.

Transactional Databases, Data Warehouses, and Internal Data Sources

The heart of BI is the transactional system used for daily operations. Within the organization's own databases is a treasure trove of data about its customers, employees, suppliers, and every financial transaction. Data maintained by suppliers or customers are also critical BI sources.

As we discussed in Chapter 4, transactional systems must be tuned for operations. Agents must be able to retrieve a customer's screen in microseconds; however, BI reporting can bog the system down. When a call agent has to say, "I'm sorry, but the system is really slow now," a good guess is that some unwitting manager is running summary reports.

Most organizations build separate data warehouses by extracting part or all of the data from those databases, cleansing it, and then loading it to the warehouse using the extract, transform, and load (ETL) process described in Chapter 4. They might do extractions once a day or even once a week. But with a growing need for real-time intelligence, businesses are finding ways to freshen their data warehouses much more frequently.[2] Satellite TV provider DirecTV, for instance, implemented software to capture the transaction logs and post them to the warehouse in near real time. Within seconds of any transaction, the new data is streamed to the gigantic data warehouse, where agents can draw on it to offer new promotions to customers who are about to switch to a different TV provider.[3]

Valuable intelligence may also be housed in departmental systems, email, electronic documents, filing cabinets, individually maintained spreadsheets, and PC hard drives. These are more difficult to dig into, but as you will see, some progress is being made to unleash these sources.

External Data Sources and Big Data

External databases that are either purchased or publicly accessible are also excellent sources of business intelligence. The U.S. Census Bureau, for instance, maintains many databases with information about demographics, educational levels, income, ethnicity, housing, employment, and more. Figure 7-3 shows an example of output from a query to its extensive international database.

INTELLIGENT AGENTS

Besides retrieving downloadable files from online sources, companies can also use intelligent agents to extract useful business intelligence from publicly accessible websites. These software programs, often called "bots," are sent out to conduct a mission and collect data from web pages on behalf of a user. For example, a tour operator in China might want competitive business intelligence about airline ticket pricing between the United States and Hong Kong, updated daily. Using robot-building software, the operator can design an agent to interact with each airline's website, recording all the steps a human performs to get a listing of first- and coach-class ticket prices (Figure 7-4). The agent can be sent on its mission every day, bringing competitive pricing information home to the company's own data warehouse.

Intelligent agents are useful for many tasks and are growing smarter and more capable each year. Search engines use them to classify and index web pages, and infomediaries deploy them to retrieve current product prices from different vendors.

PRODUCTIVITY TIP
You can create an agent to carry out online searches for recent articles relevant to your upcoming term paper. Yahoo, Google, and many online library databases offer this service, usually called "alerts." Schedule it to run daily and send you an email with its findings.

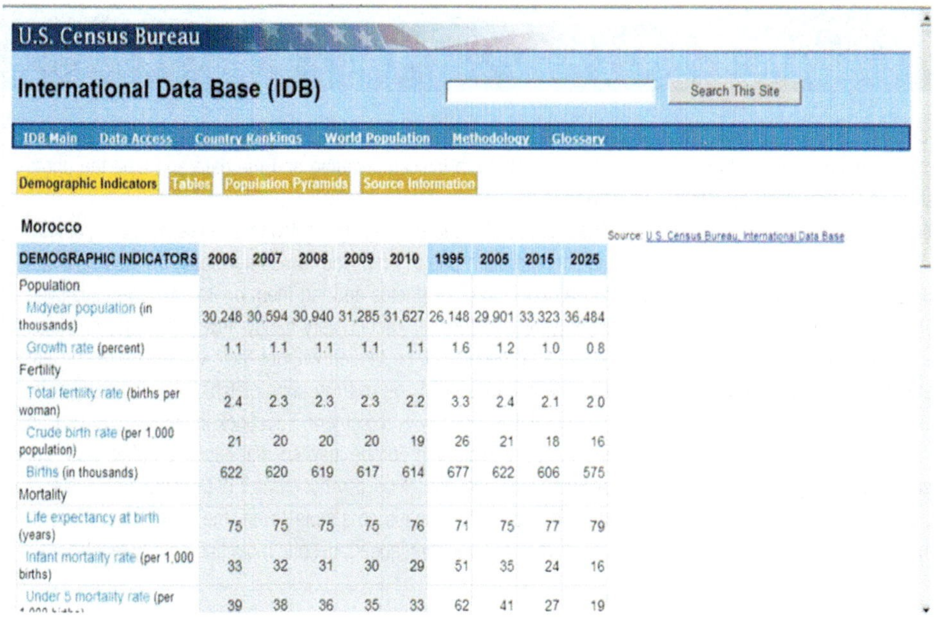

Morocco

DEMOGRAPHIC INDICATORS	2006	2007	2008	2009	2010	1995	2005	2015	2025
Population									
Midyear population (in thousands)	30,248	30,594	30,940	31,285	31,627	26,148	29,901	33,323	36,484
Growth rate (percent)	1.1	1.1	1.1	1.1	1.1	1.6	1.2	1.0	0.8
Fertility									
Total fertility rate (births per woman)	2.4	2.3	2.3	2.3	2.2	3.3	2.4	2.1	2.0
Crude birth rate (per 1,000 population)	21	20	20	20	19	26	21	18	16
Births (in thousands)	622	620	619	617	614	677	622	606	575
Mortality									
Life expectancy at birth (years)	75	75	75	75	76	71	75	77	79
Infant mortality rate (per 1,000 births)	33	32	31	30	29	51	35	24	16
Under 5 mortality rate (per 1,000 births)	39	38	36	35	33	62	41	27	19

Source: U.S. Census Bureau.

FIGURE 7-3
Data useful for business intelligence can be downloaded from the U.S. Census Bureau's website.

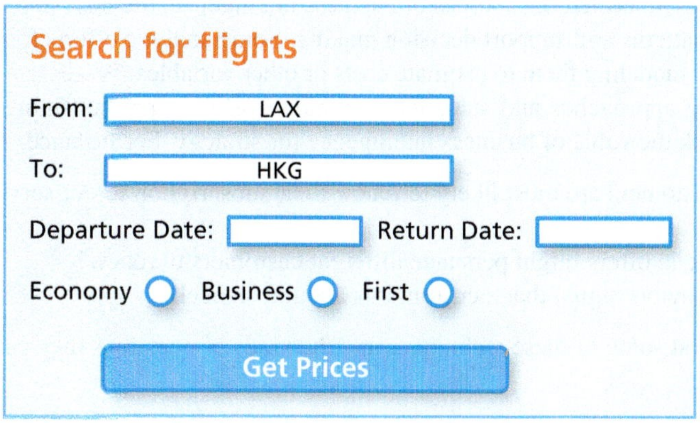

FIGURE 7-4
To build a bot, the designer carries out the steps a human being would perform to capture data on public websites, and the software creates the agent that will carry out the tasks on its own.

BI AND BIG DATA

Big data adds semi-structured and unstructured information in addition to the structured information found in databases or retrieved by agents. As Chapter 4 explained, big data has huge volume, high velocity, and tremendous variety. It might include websites, blogs, wikis, social networks, photo-sharing sites, video repositories, discussion forums, tweets, and text messages, any of which could be useful for business intelligence. A major contributor is the Internet of Things, in which sensors connected to the net collect and send data automatically. That source is rapidly outstripping all others in terms of sheer volume, with input from sensors in smartphones, consumer products, vehicles, animals, lawn sprinklers, medical monitors, and more.[4]

PRODUCTIVITY TIP
How well are you managing your own big data? You might not have petabytes, but you do have great variety and growing volume. Cloud-based services such as OneNote or Evernote offer tools to organize your web links, tweets, online articles, notes to self, and other resources and also make them searchable so you can find them again.

intelligent agents
Software programs or "bots" that are sent out to conduct a mission and collect data from web pages on behalf of a user.

THE ETHICAL FACTOR   The Ethics of Tagging Faces in Photos

Tagging online photos of faces with people's names is wildly popular and very helpful as a means to add structure to information. Those old group photos come alive when you don't have to struggle to recall long-forgotten names. However, these tags are raising serious privacy concerns and ethical dilemmas.

Although you may have no reluctance to tag yourself in your own photos, will your friends and family want you to tag them? They may think the photo is unflattering. Or they may be concerned that their employers will stumble upon tagged images you thought were amusing but that employers think show poor judgment. Parents may also object to tagged images of their children appearing online.

Though photo-sharing sites offer assurances and many choices about privacy, the potential for harm is not trivial, especially because you can't control what others are doing. Uploaded photos might include metadata that you may not even know is attached, such as GPS coordinates that can "geotag" your photo to indicate location and the date and time the photo was taken.

The services offer facial recognition software to ease the tedium of individually tagging each photo. After you tag some faces, the software can find those people in other photos and tag them on its own, even scanning photos on your smartphone. Though very handy, this tool greatly amplifies the chance that people will be tagged without their knowledge or consent and that the information will be used in unpredictable ways by marketers, employers, relatives, or law enforcement. Facebook implemented this kind of service, but regulators in Europe insisted that Facebook offer it as "opt in" for Europeans because of privacy concerns.[5] With cell-phone cameras widespread and photo uploads so simple to do, the "anonymous face in the crowd" may become rare indeed, despite mounting privacy regulations.

Explain several approaches to data mining and analytics that help managers analyze patterns, trends, and relationships and make better data-driven decisions.

3 Data Mining and Analytics

Once a firm has identified the sources of business intelligence, the next step is to start mining them to spot patterns and support decision making. Some analytic efforts focus on describing the patterns or modeling them to estimate costs or other variables. **Predictive analytics** refers to data mining approaches and statistical techniques used to predict future behavior, especially to unlock the value of business intelligence for strategy. For instance:

- Which customers are most likely to renew their subscription to our service at the regular price?
- What special offers might persuade different customers to renew?
- What behaviors signal that a customer is about to cancel?

Let's look at some of these techniques and the kinds of questions they can answer.

Analyzing Patterns, Trends, and Relationships

BI analytical tools are becoming extremely powerful and user-friendly, and many take advantage of in-memory computing so results appear quickly. Some tools are stand-alone BI platforms that the organization can add to its environment to support decision making and link to its data warehouses. Other tools are offered as part of enterprise information systems, and ERP vendors are adding BI capabilities to their product suites. Microsoft adds BI functionality to its SQL Server database, integrating it with its other products, especially Excel.[6]

In addition to the data warehouses that rely on relational databases, many organizations are adding newer platforms that handle less structured big data, such as Hadoop and NoSQL (discussed in Chapter 4).[7] Sears, for instance, saves considerable time by loading terabytes of data into Hadoop without doing the extract, transform, and load process used for a data warehouse.[8]

BI software includes innovative tools to visualize data in new ways that go beyond the usual bar graphs, pie charts, and tables. Color, object shapes, object sizes, 3D views, and interactivity can help display data in human-friendly ways so that meaning is more apparent. For example, Figure 7-5 is an interactive map that shows changes in the population of coastline counties over time. The dynamic display quickly reveals trends in a way that a table of numbers could not.

ONLINE ANALYTICAL PROCESSING (OLAP)

Exploring the data warehouse, with its hundreds of tables, thousands of fields, and dozens of relationships among the tables, is not for the fainthearted. Although programmers and some

Coastline County Population

September 6, 2012

Source: U.S. Census Bureau.

FIGURE 7-5

Data visualization using an interactive map that shows changes in population in coastal counties over time.

power users can write SQL code to frame complex queries, most business users need views into their data that are more intuitive. They want to visualize it in many different ways to find patterns and relationships that don't easily show in routine reports from the transactional system.

Online analytical processing (OLAP) systems allow users to interactively retrieve meaningful information from data, examining it from many different perspectives and drilling down into specific groupings. The software allows users to "slice and dice" massive amounts of data stored in data warehouses to reveal significant patterns and trends. Managers might check sales transactions by customer gender and age group and find relationships that can guide marketing campaigns.

OLAP systems help spot suspicious activity as well. Medicare anti-fraud strike forces, for example, use such systems to detect unusual billing that might point to illegal scams. One analysis found that charges for home health care services in Miami jumped a startling tenfold in just 2 years, though the city showed no noticeable increase in elderly residents. That insight led investigators to bills totaling $155,000 for nurses to help an elderly Miami man inject insulin twice a day. They discovered the man was not diabetic and the nurses did not exist.[9]

OLAP systems achieve their speed and their slice-and-dice capabilities by building multidimensional cubes.[10] These are data structures that contain detailed data and also aggregated values for the dimensions, metrics, and hierarchies the users need. A company might want a cube that managers could use to analyze total sales by store location, by product, or by time

PRODUCTIVITY TIP

Excel is a powerful tool itself, thanks to its pivot tables and charting capabilities. It uses in-memory computing so your charts appear almost instantly, even with very large worksheets.

predictive analytics

Data mining approaches and statistical techniques used to predict future behavior, especially to unlock the value of business intelligence for strategy.

online analytical processing (OLAP)

Software that allows users to "slice and dice" or drill down into massive amounts of data stored in data warehouses to reveal significant patterns and trends.

period (Figure 7-6). These categories could be represented as dimensions of the cube, and time period could also be structured in the cube as a hierarchy. Managers might want to see sales by product, by month, by quarter, or by year. Although the term *cube* suggests that three is the limit for dimensions, these structures can actually incorporate many more than that.

STATISTICS AND MODELING TECHNIQUES

Data mining and predictive analytics often use statistical analysis and models not just to display averages or changes over time but also to identify real patterns—ones that probably did not occur just by chance. Colin's survey of patient families suggests that women rate the pediatrics ward somewhat more favorably than men. But before launching a campaign based on this finding, Colin would use statistics to analyze the data more closely, not just view it on a graph. If the difference is significant, Colin would be confident about a decision to target men in the next campaign.

Statistical relationships can be especially useful to spot. For example, a technique called **market basket analysis** looks for such relationships to reveal customer behavior patterns as they

PRODUCTIVITY TIP
An add-in for Excel that you might want to install is called "Analysis ToolPak." Tools include descriptive statistics with mean, mode, median, standard deviation, correlation, and several modeling and hypothesis-testing tools. Some knowledge of statistics is needed.

FIGURE 7-6
Multidimensional cube created from tables in a data warehouse and used for OLAP.

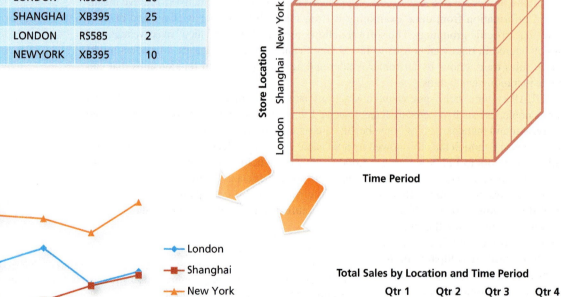

Total Sales by Location and Time Period

	Qtr 1	Qtr 2	Qtr 3	Qtr 4
London	589	685	458	541
Shanghai	325	356	452	521
New York	896	874	785	980

purchase multiple items. Are customers who buy soda more likely to also buy candy? Are people who buy larger TVs more likely to also purchase high-priced speaker systems? Online retailers make very obvious use of the technique to cross-sell. For instance, Amazon's product screens conspicuously show sections titled "Frequently Bought Together" and "Customers Who Bought This Item Also Bought."

FIGURE 7-7
Text mining software can extract useful business intelligence from blogs.

TEXT MINING

Dipping into the vast storehouse of unstructured text-based data contained in emails, blogs, tweets, online product reviews, and comments yields critical business intelligence. **Text mining**, a variation of data mining, is a discovery process in which unstructured text information, rather than structured data, is the source of business intelligence (Figure 7-7). Text min-

> From a blog:
> "The sales rep at Reliance was really rude. He kept insisting that I add more services when all I wanted was a lower price. Made me mad so I canceled completely."
>
> New London Mom

ing software tools rely on keywords, semantic structures, linguistic relationships, parts of speech, common phrases, emotion-laden words, and even misspellings to extract meaningful information.

Choice Hotels uses text mining software to make sense of the comments section of customer surveys. Although it is easy to analyze the quantitative scales on which customers check off responses ranging from "Very satisfied" to "Very dissatisfied," it is far more time consuming to analyze the comments from hundreds of thousands of survey responses. With the software, managers can retrieve graphical displays of problem types expressed in the comments as well as positive and negative comments sorted by location, time of year, and other variables.

Companies are even more motivated to "actively listen" to web and social media chatter with text mining because any anonymous complaint can spread so fast. For instance, travelers reserving a hotel room can check The Bedbug Registry, a website that publishes bedbug reports by state. Even one mention will turn away guests.

Text mining can also help identify fake product reviews. Researchers estimate that a significant percentage of online reviews are likely fakes, created by people paid to write positive comments without actually using the product.[11] Companies like Amazon, Expedia, and Yelp use text mining and other measures to spot suspicious reviews, such as those that just repeat ad copy, and delete them.

> Text mining on historical documents turned up a fascinating tidbit about how views of the United States changed. Authors wrote "the United States are ..." well into the 1800s, when they began using "the United States is ... ." Apparently, Americans didn't think of the United States as a single nation rather than a collection of states until long after the country was born.[12]

DID YOU KNOW?

Simulating, Optimizing, and Forecasting

Decision support systems also include tools that help managers simulate events and make forecasts for the future. Download CH07_Simulations.xlsx to try out the tools described in this section in Excel.

WHAT-IF ANALYSIS

A tool called **what-if analysis** builds a model that simulates relationships between many variables. Excel is popular for building relatively simple models, such as the one in Figure 7-8. Bora is considering launching the hospital seminar series and uses this what-if analysis to play with the variables that contribute to revenue and expenses. She can estimate and change

market basket analysis
A statistical technique that reveals customer behavior patterns as they purchase multiple items.

text mining
A technique used to analyze unstructured text that examines keywords, semantic structures, linguistic relationships, emotion-laden words, and other characteristics to extract meaningful business intelligence.

what-if analysis
A simulation model, often constructed using Excel, that calculates the relationships between many variables; users can change some variables to see how others are affected.

FIGURE 7-8
What-if spreadsheet to estimate revenue and expenses for a hospital seminar series. The user can change the estimates for any variable in yellow, and the spreadsheet recomputes Net Profit/Loss.

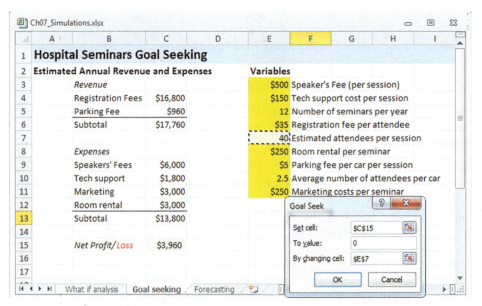

Source: Microsoft® Excel, Microsoft Corporation. Reprinted with permission.

any of the variables in yellow, and the worksheet computes revenue, expenses, and net profit or loss. For example, she calculates the speakers' fees by:

Speaker fee (per session) * Number of seminars per year.

Now Bora can ask, "What if I offer fewer seminars?" or "What if I spend more on marketing?" The model shows how any changes affect the bottom line.

GOAL SEEKING

Goal seeking is similar to what-if analysis but in reverse. Instead of estimating several variables and calculating the result, the user sets a target value for a particular metric, such as profit/loss, and tells the program which variable to change to try to reach the goal. For instance, Bora might wonder what the average attendance at each seminar needs to be for the project to break even. She can use the goal-seeking tool in Excel on her what-if spreadsheet (Figure 7-9). She enters net profit/loss as the cell to set, zero as the goal, and the estimated attendees per session as the changing cell. When she clicks OK, she sees she'll need about 31 guests per seminar to break even.

FIGURE 7-9
Goal seeking. The user sets a target value for one cell, such as Net Profit/Loss, and then enters the cell that Excel can change to reach the target.

Source: Microsoft® Excel, Microsoft Corporation. Reprinted with permission.

OPTIMIZING

In many cases, managers need to use **optimization** tools to find the best solutions that require some juggling of trade-offs. Airlines, for instance, try to optimize profit per flight, taking into account constraints such as fuel costs, ticket discounts, gate availability, airport congestion, and connections. The list grows ever longer and complex as the decision support tools try to balance many competing variables. For example, a Department of Transportation regulation about publicizing each airline's on-time record adds a new constraint. To keep their on-time rating high, most airlines decided to pad their published flight durations so even delayed flights count as "on time." Excel also offers an add-in tool called Solver that helps with optimization problems.

FORECASTING

Forecasting tomorrow's demand, next month's sales, or next year's stock price relies especially on statistical decision support tools. Forecasting tools usually analyze historical and seasonal trends and then take into account existing and predicted business conditions to estimate some variable of interest, such as customer demand or projected revenue. For example, Figure 7-10 is a simple model that shows the historical relationship between weekly snowfall and sales revenue from ski lift tickets. Although not perfect, the correlation between them is reasonably high (+ 0.64): the more snow, the higher the revenue. Using the graph, the weather report for 15 centimeters next week forecasts revenue of about $60,000. More sophisticated models incorporate many other variables that affect the forecast, drawing widely on business intelligence sources.

Artificial Intelligence

Artificial intelligence (AI) describes the capability of some machines that can mimic human intelligence, displaying characteristics such as learning, reasoning, judging, and drawing conclusions from incomplete information. For business, AI makes valuable contributions in

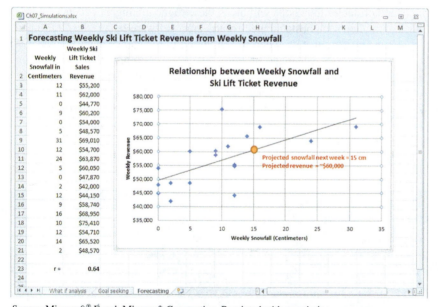

Source: Microsoft® Excel, Microsoft Corporation. Reprinted with permission.

FIGURE 7-10

Forecasting ski lift ticket sales revenue from weekly snowfall based on historical patterns.

goal seeking
A decision support tool, often based on an Excel model, in which the user sets a target value for a particular variable, such as profit/loss, and tells the program which variable to change to try to reach the goal.

optimization
An extension of goal seeking in which the user can change many variables to reach some maximum or minimum target, as long as the changes stay within the constraints the user identifies.

forecasting
A statistical decision support tool used to analyze historical trends and other business intelligence to estimate some variable of interest, such as customer demand.

artificial intelligence (AI)
The capability of some machines to mimic aspects of human intelligence, such as learning, reasoning, judging, and drawing conclusions from incomplete information.

areas such as financial monitoring, scheduling, diagnosing problems, and analyzing customer behavior. Amazon's software, for example, continually learns about each customer to make more relevant recommendations for new purchases.

The AI underpinnings for Watson, IBM's supercomputer that beat human champions in the game show *Jeopardy!*, show extraordinary promise. The stunt demonstrated that AI has a very bright future for interpreting human language and drawing on an immense knowledge base to find answers. Voice-activated personal assistants such as Siri and Cortana tap AI to respond to questions and commands and are rapidly improving. IBM is exploiting Watson-like AI to create even more powerful specialized assistants, especially in medicine. Amazon's Echo home voice appliance and speaker fills a niche for consumers with voice recognition that responds to a variety of commands, such as playing music you request, reporting on traffic and weather, and adjusting lights and thermostats in the home. Amazon, Apple, and other companies are continually adding new features, further pushing the boundaries of consumer-oriented AI.[13]

Artificial intelligence is especially important to handle all the data coming in from sensors. In fast-moving emergency situations, for instance, when the volume of incoming data could overwhelm human decision makers, AI could be enormously helpful. After an earthquake, AI can analyze information from fire alarms, cameras, 911 calls, and other sources to quickly decide how best to allocate ambulances across a city.

Robotic technology also depends on advances in artificial intelligence. The robots that creep around Mars, vacuum airports, assemble cars, defuse bombs, and assist the disabled are specialized to perform certain functions, and they are growing more powerful and useful. The underlying intelligence to vacuum a living room without getting stuck under an armchair is more complicated than it looks.

Unfortunately, AI is also used by scammers who want to pose as human beings, especially as online bots. Companies that offer free email services, for example, do not want bots registering for thousands of accounts. And news sites want to block "blog bots" that post automated comments to articles containing spam or malicious software. Web developers increasingly add obstacles they hope will block these rogue intelligent agents.

FIGURE 7-11

A CAPTCHA designed to ensure visitors are actually human beings and not bots.

Enter the words above

Get another CAPTCHA
Get an audio CAPTCHA

Source: Google and the Google logo are registered trademarks of Google Inc., used with permission.

One such obstacle that thwarts most software bots is the **CAPTCHA**, a test the visitor must pass before continuing to register or enter the site. One variety presents an image of some letters and numbers that the user must correctly read and enter before proceeding (Figure 7-11). The image is fuzzy, and the fonts are irregular. Humans have trouble reading them, but bots have even more difficulty. As technology develops that can discriminate between the mouse movements and keystrokes of bots and humans, CAPTCHAs may no longer be so widespread.[14]

A usability expert calls the CAPTCHA one of the most hated user interactions on the web. Each one can take a user from 10 to 15 seconds to figure out, assuming the user doesn't give up. But the hours aren't totally wasted. Your human eyes help digitize old books with fonts too strange or blurry for optical character readers so the text can be searched. CAPTCHA is an acronym for "Completely Automated Public Turing test to tell Computers and Humans Apart."

Some of the most useful applications of AI for businesses and other organizations are found in expert systems and neural nets, described next.

EXPERT SYSTEMS

An **expert system** mimics the reasoning of a human expert, drawing from a base of knowledge about a particular subject area to come to a decision or recommendation. To build an expert system, developers work with experienced and specialized professionals as they provide answers to questions and explain their reasoning processes. The output is fine-tuned continually as the experts contribute more knowledge to the base, refine the rules, and add additional questions. The process is challenging, often because experts don't quite know exactly how they reach their conclusions. Formally identifying the actual steps is harder than you might think, but the results can be quite dramatic and enormously useful for decision support.

Medical diagnostics reap huge benefits from expert systems, particularly with increases in computer power and available data.[15] These systems can analyze far more than a human physician can, drawing on genetic information, clinical test data, demographics, and more to diagnose the problem, recommend treatments, and also reduce costs.

Mobile AI is also offering much promise. In Kenyan villages, for example, health workers carrying a small test kit visit rural households looking for signs of malaria. They send the results via text message to the expert system, which in just a few seconds returns an automated response about the proper course of treatment based on its analysis. The system also sends additional messages about follow-up treatments and clinic appointments.[16]

DID YOU KNOW?

Microsoft tapped AI to create a lively "chat bot" called Tay, which was designed to learn from interactions with actual people on the Internet. Sadly, Tay learned far too much from Internet trolls and very soon began sending out highly offensive tweets. The company pulled Tay less than a day after its release, expressing regret that the developers focused too much on the technical challenges and not enough on the social challenges.[17]

NEURAL NETWORKS

Neural networks attempt to mimic the way the human brain works, with its vast network of interconnections. Each of the 10 billion-plus neurons connects with thousands of its neighbors, receiving chemical signals from them. The neuron constantly summarizes the input it receives, and the results determine its outgoing transmissions. When repeated input causes signals to travel the same pathway again and again, the connections grow stronger and the pathway becomes more permanent and easier to activate. When you use flash cards to memorize vocabulary words in Japanese, for instance, you are reinforcing the paths connecting the neural underpinnings for the English word with its Japanese equivalent. After many repetitions, when you see *dog,* you easily recall the Japanese word *inu.*

Neural networks are far simpler than the human brain, of course, but they borrow the brain's approach, using digital signals in place of neural ones. The neural net learns from training data selected by humans that contain cases defining the paths from input to output. The net's success depends largely on the number and quality of the cases it can learn from. For example, a neural net being trained to predict housing values could absorb millions of cases in which the input includes location, sales price, square footage, number of bathrooms, and more. For the training data, the output is the actual sales price. Once the net is up and running, the output will be the predicted house value.

Neural nets are widely used on big data, such as in the finance industry where detecting fraud is an important application. Analyzing each card transaction in real time, neural nets compare the specific purchase to the cardholder's regular spending habits and also to

PRODUCTIVITY TIP
Before you travel outside your home country, it's wise to let your credit card company know where you are headed. A neural net may automatically block your card if unexpected foreign charges appear and the card company is unable to reach you.

CAPTCHA
A test created by software developers that the visitor must pass before continuing to register or enter the site; designed to thwart software bots.

expert system
Software that mimics the reasoning and decision making of a human expert, drawing from a base of knowledge about a particular subject area developed with the expert's assistance.

neural network
An information system that attempts to mimic the way the human brain works; often used to spot suspicious activity in financial transactions

FIGURE 7-12

The neural-net called "20Q" plays the game 20 Questions with visitors, very often guessing correctly. The training data includes the millions of games users play at the site (www.20Q.net, from 20Q.net Inc.).

Source: © 1988–2013. 20Q, I can read your mind … and the neural net on the Internet, are registered trademarks of 20Q.net Inc. All related titles, logos, and characters are the trademarks of 20Q.net Inc. All rights reserved.

fraudulent spending patterns. The neural net will certainly pick it up if a retiree who hasn't traveled beyond Costa Rica starts racking up charges for hip blue jeans in Bucharest.

An amusing neural net that encourages web visitors to contribute cases is 20Q (www.20Q.net), based on the game called 20 Questions. The player thinks of an animal, vegetable, or mineral, and the game asks yes or no questions until it makes a correct guess or gives up (Figure 7-12). Relying on the millions of cases visitors have added, the neural net's accuracy is, as one reviewer put it, "scary."

Explain how digital analytics are used as a source of business intelligence and why they are so valuable for understanding customers.

 # 4 Achieving Success with Digital Analytics

The sheer volume of business intelligence available to an organization can be overwhelming, and it is important to focus on the metrics that are most meaningful to the company's goals. Let's see what kinds of digital metrics a company might want to analyze in more detail to uncover trends, patterns, and opportunities.

Capturing Digital Metrics

Each digital measure reveals something a little different that can help describe how people are interacting with the company's website, its social media presence, or its mobile app and also what people might be saying about the company in other channels. As the "front door," the company's website is often the first dataset to analyze.

WEBSITE METRICS

Clickstream data includes every single click by every visitor along with associated data revealing customer behavior patterns, such as time spent on the page, the URL the visitor just left, and the visitor's IP address. With potentially millions of clicks per day, clickstream data adds up quickly. The variety of metrics that can be mined from this BI source is quite large.

Figure 7-13 lists several measures of visitor traffic that are important to all organizations. All the measures refer to a particular time period the analyst selects, such as the previous week, month, or year.

These web metrics come from server logs, and each entry contains detailed information about the date and time, the page, the source, and any clicks on the page itself. The logs also contain information about each user, including his or her IP address and browser. If the site uses cookies, it can collect more information about each user.

Web Visitor-Related Metrics	Description
Visitors	Number of visitors to the website. (Returning visitors will be counted again if they return within the time period.)
Unique visitors	Number of unique visitors. (Returning visitors are not counted again.)
Average time on site	Average amount of time visitors spent on the site.
New visitors	Number of new visitors to the site.
Depth of visit	The number of page views per visit, which shows how extensively visitors interact with and navigate around your site.
Languages	The number (or percentage) of visitors based on the language they configured to use on their computer.
Traffic sources	The sources from which visitors arrive at your site, such as a keyword search in a search engine, an ad, or from a link on related sites. Direct traffic is a visit from someone who used a bookmark or typed the URL in the browser.
Service providers	The number of visits coming from people using different Internet service providers.

Web Content-Related Metrics	Description
Page views	The number of visits per page on the site, showing analysts the most popular content.
Bounce rate	Percentage of visits in which the user left the site from the same page he or she entered it. This can mean that the page the user landed on was not very relevant.
Top landing pages	The number of entrances to your site for each page.
Top exit pages	The number of exits from the site for each page.

FIGURE 7-13
Website metrics.

SOCIAL MEDIA METRICS

Activity on a company's social media site can generate considerable information to analyze.[18] For example, companies that launch a presence on Facebook would certainly want to track the number of fans who clicked "like" in each time period. For any particular post, a marketer would also want to know something about reach—the number of users who have actually seen that post. Reach is important because not all fans will have seen a particular post, and some users may see it who are not fans (yet). Combining these with measures such as the number of comments on a post or the number of times it was shared provides some insight into overall engagement. Figure 7-14 shows examples of a variety of common social media metrics that are useful to assess business impact. Businesses are often tracking changes in these metrics, in response to a particular marketing campaign, for instance.

E-COMMERCE AND ADVERTISING METRICS

If the site includes advertising and e-commerce capabilities, the metrics about actual sales will be very relevant. Which ads attract the most clicks? Which pages do customers view before they purchase something, and which pages do they linger on? Which visitors abandoned their shopping cart, and what pages did they view?

Metric	Platform	Description
Number of fans	Facebook	Number of users who "like" a page
Fan reach	Facebook	Number of users who view a particular post
Number of impressions	Twitter	Number of times users saw the tweet on Twitter
Number of retweets	Twitter	Number of times users retweet a company's post
Engagement	Instagram	Number of likes and comments divided by number of followers
Follower industry demographics	LinkedIn	Profile of followers by the industry in which they work

FIGURE 7-14
Sample metrics for social media activity.

clickstream data
Business intelligence data that includes every click by every visitor on a website along with associated data such as time spent on the page and the visitor's IP address.

FIGURE 7-15
E-commerce metrics.

E-Commerce Metric	Description
Conversion rate	The ratio of visitors who complete some activity (such as buying a product) divided by the total number of visitors.
Clickthrough rate (CTR)	The ratio of clicks on an ad divided by the number of times the ad was delivered.
Cost per clickthrough (CPC)	The amount an advertiser pays each time a visitor clicks on the ad to navigate to the advertiser's site.
Cost per impression (CPM is cost per thousand impressions)	For banner and display ads, the cost the advertiser pays each time the ad loads onto a user's screen from any site on which it appears.
Position on page	The position in which a sponsored link appears on a page in keyword advertising on search engines.

These metrics are also critical to organizations that pay for ads posted to other sites, such as display ads on news sites or ads intended to reach specific audiences on Facebook, on Instagram, or through Google's keyword advertising. All of those services provide extensive metrics about clickthrough rates and other variables. Figure 7-15 shows examples of metrics useful for e-commerce and digital advertising.

MOBILE METRICS

For mobile marketing, organizations focus on what is happening to the mobile app they developed and promoted so users can download it and engage with the company using a smartphone. Certainly, companies will want to track the number of people who download and install the app. Beyond that, information about how often people use the app is critical, partly because so many install the app and then forget about it. They may not bother to uninstall the app, which could be measured, but they may simply not use it. Other metrics can reveal considerable information about users' locations, mobile buying patterns, and the kinds of paths they take through the app. For instance, a game developer could quickly learn that many people abandon the app at a particular level, indicating that the level is too hard. Figure 7-16 shows examples of mobile metrics.

FIGURE 7-16
Sample metrics for mobile apps.

Metric	Description
Number of downloads	Number of users who download the app
Geographic distribution	Describes users by location
Average session length	Average amount of time users have the app open
User paths	Path that users take through the app

FIGURE 7-17
In the online simulation for this chapter called "Chocolate Lovers Unite," you compare the metrics for two versions of the company's website.

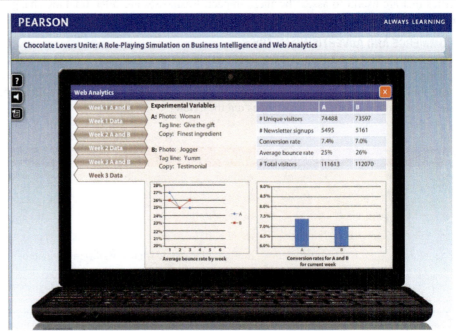

Director, Business Intelligence and Analytics
- ▶ Analyzes web traffic, social media activity, and mobile app performance using business intelligence tools
- ▶ Creates clear and comprehensive reports showing trends and forecasts
- ▶ Provides recommendations on maximizing revenue and improving customer experience
- ▶ Leads efforts to develop effective digital marketing campaigns that increase customer engagement
- ▶ BA required; MBA a plus

FIGURE 7-18
Job posting for a digital analyst.

In the online simulation "Chocolate Lovers Unite," you will focus especially on website metrics, wisely choosing which ones you want to collect and then watching them change each week as you try out different designs for the company's website (see Figure 7-17).

Analyzing Data and Achieving Success

Making sense of these numbers takes considerable skill, and the analyst who has it is in great demand. Figure 7-18 shows part of a job posting for this type of position.

ANALYTICS SOFTWARE

To reap value from all this information, especially given its volume, organizations rely on analytical tools. Products specifically designed to analyze data are growing ever more powerful, with easy-to-use interfaces, graphing capabilities, and advanced statistical techniques. Analysts can quickly see important details about their web traffic, their visitors, and the links that bring customers to their site.

Some products are embedded in content management systems, some are stand-alone products, and others are offered as software as a service. Google's free web analytics, for instance, is a software-as-a-service (SaaS) product. It requires only a short string of code on each page to direct the clickstream data to Google's servers, where the analytical engine does its work. Figure 7-19 shows one example of the kinds of graphs and tables available with web analytics.

REACHING GOALS AND MEASURING SUCCESS

Analytics software spews out thousands of graphs, tables, and charts. To make smart decisions, companies should have a clear notion of the major goals for the campaign so they know

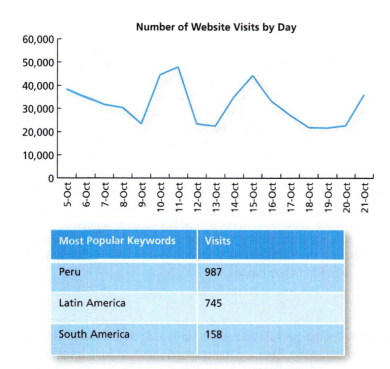

FIGURE 7-19
Sample output from web analytics software, describing the number of website visitors by day and the most keywords used to reach the site.

what to look for and where to find it, particularly because effective campaigns integrate messages across digital channels. These goals will guide them toward the appropriate metrics so they can see whether their decisions bring about improvements.

Depending on the organization's goals, marketers will apply analytic tools to appropriate metrics to help determine return on investment. For example, was that mobile app really worth the money? Are those Facebook ads attracting enough new customers to justify the cost? Was the improvement in brand awareness enough to cover the cost of the video we released on Snapchat? Did we emphasize the most relevant search terms in our ads? (Figure 7-20).

Cost per clickthrough, conversion rates, and the other metrics discussed in this chapter reveal how well campaigns are doing and whether marketing dollars are being spent wisely. Over time, historical patterns can also predict how much the company needs to spend on online campaigns to achieve goals.

Digital marketing is a moving target, though, and analysts should track overall changes in user behavior patterns. For example, the number of people who click display ads has been dropping, and a very small percentage of Internet users actually do most of that ad clicking. Companies are also emphasizing platforms such as LinkedIn, Twitter, and Snapchat in addition to their use of Google keyword advertising. Research demonstrates that short videos are becoming more valuable as a means to engage the audience, so companies are also putting more funding into that kind of content.

FIGURE 7-20

Online ads can include variables to customize the text according to the phrase the user entered as the search term.

Search term: phones for children	Search term: kids' phones
Phones for Children	**Kids' Phone**
The Fun & Easy Way to Find	100s of Kids' Phone
Phones for **Children** at Low Prices	Top **Brands** at **Low** Prices!

 5

Describe how dashboards, portals, and mashups help visualize business intelligence, and explain the role that the human element plays in business intelligence initiatives.

Putting It All Together: Dashboards, Portals, and Mashups

Staying on top of this endless stream of data from so many business intelligence sources can be an immense challenge. Transactional records, competitive business intelligence, clickstream data, news, blogs, tweets, government regulations, and legal cases combine in a barrage of information overload. Access to this universe of information relevant to your job and organization may be a wonderful thing, but you also need strategies for organizing and viewing it in a meaningful way.

Dashboards

Like a plane or car dashboard with its dials, gauges, and other displays of real-time data, the IT **dashboard** is a graphical user interface that helps people visualize information vital to the user's role and the decisions that the user makes (Figure 7-21).

Colin, for instance, wants to track hospital seminar registrations and attendance and also results from the online evaluations each attendee is asked to complete. A dashboard combines those metrics with updated graphs showing clickthroughs for his keyword ads and the number of unique visitors to the web pages he designed as landing pages for the ads.

The dashboard should summarize **key performance indicators (KPIs)**, which are the quantifiable metrics most important to the individual's role and the organization's success. For instance, a chief of police might want to see frequently updated charts showing criminal activity by week or number of crimes solved by type.[19] A regional sales manager launching a major discount promotion might want hourly updates on sales volume by product.

Dashboard capabilities come with most business intelligence software, but users will quickly ignore them if the dashboard isn't relevant, timely, and useful. Figure 7-22 lists some tips on best practices for dashboard design.

Portals

Portals are gateways that provide access to a variety of relevant information from many different sources on one screen. They are content aggregators, making it easier for users to view and drill down into company dashboards, weather announcements, news, traffic reports, stock

FIGURE 7-21

A graphical dashboard example, showing summarized and updated information relevant to a project manager.

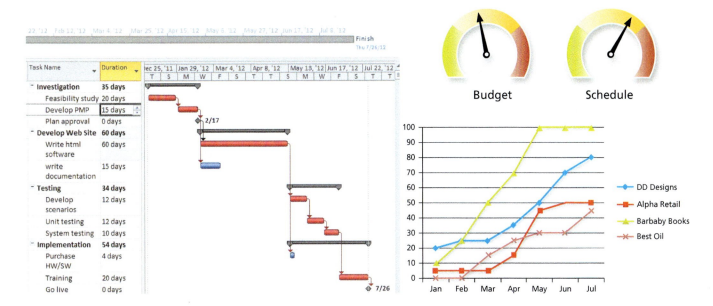

Dashboard Feature	Design Tip
Key performance indicators (KPIs)	Choosing KPIs that are most important to the organization and the person using the dashboard is the most important success factor.
Data quality	Dashboards make data look good, but the charts and graphs are only as useful as the quality of the underlying data. Users should ask for warnings when data is stale or not altogether reliable.
Timeliness	Update the dashboard as often as needed for the user's situation—daily, hourly, or minute by minute, if necessary.
Density	Use seven or fewer graphs, charts, maps, or tables on one dashboard, to avoid information overload.
Chart formats	Keep tables small and charts simple, using familiar types. Avoid 3D and unnecessary animations. Be cautious about pie charts, which can be more difficult to interpret.
Maps and visual displays	When relevant, populate actual maps, seating plans, campus layouts, or other visual displays that combine real images with data.

FIGURE 7-22

Dashboard design tips.

reports, to-do lists, email, and discussion groups. Each bit of content or functionality that a user can customize and add to the display is called a "portlet."

The enterprise portal (Figure 7-23) is a gateway to the organization's resources, usually built and maintained by the IT department using portal software. Working with the business units, IT develops default pages with commonly requested content and builds interfaces to the organization's resources. Communications or human resources offices often play leading roles in the launch, viewing the portal screen as a precious opportunity to disseminate corporate information and reminders quickly. The "Daily Announcements" portlet is often front and center.

Portal users, who might be customers and suppliers as well as employees, access the portal with a company-supplied login ID and password. That login determines which applications users are able to access and what level of access they are granted. From within the

dashboard
A graphical user interface that organizes and summarizes information vital to the user's role and the decisions that user makes.

key performance indicators (KPIs)
The quantifiable metrics most important to the individual's role and the organization's success.

portal
A gateway that provides access to a variety of relevant information from many different sources on one screen; for an enterprise, the portal provides a secure gateway to resources needed by employees, customers, and suppliers.

FIGURE 7-23

An enterprise portal.

Source: © Copyright 2013. SAP AG.

PRODUCTIVITY TIP

If your university or college offers a portal, you can experiment to see what portlets are available, what functionality you can access, and how much you can customize it. Set it as your start-up page in your browser if you find it useful.

portal, users can personalize the display, choosing, for example, email accounts, transactional databases, dashboards, 401(k) retirement accounts, benefits summaries, W-2 tax forms, and other applications. Portlet choices often include some external content as well, such as news, traffic reports, and weather.

Enterprise portals were inspired by the consumer portals offered by web companies that help people combine content to their liking. MyYahoo!, for instance, offers customizable portals with blocks containing snippets of email, news, instant messenger chat, calendars, horoscope, movie show times, stock prices, to-do lists, favorite bookmarks, and more. Depending on the portal service, the portlets might be called *gadgets*, *widgets*, *modules*, or just *stuff*. Many social network sites develop interfaces for these portals, so a block for Twitter, Facebook, or another site can appear on the consumer's portal page as well.

Mashups

Increasing demands for more flexible gateways stretch the limits of portal technology. They also tax IT departments responsible for development and maintenance. Users want to easily aggregate an exploding array of content from countless business intelligence sources, merging maps with customer data; combining dashboards, news sources, and Excel spreadsheet data; adding live camera feeds; and blending information that supports their work roles.

A more flexible approach to aggregating content from multiple internal and external sources on customizable web pages is the **mashup**. This approach relies on Web 2.0 technologies and programming standards such as XML to blend content and updated feeds from various inside and outside sources in flexible ways.

Mashups can incorporate a **web feed**, for example, which is standardized and regularly updated output from a publisher, such as CNN or Weather.com (Figure 7-24). Rather than going to the website itself, users can embed the web feed in their own mashup so they can always see a little content block with the major headlines. The feed includes the text for each update plus XML metadata for some structured data, such as date and author.

FIGURE 7-24

This symbol indicates that the website offers a web feed.

Source: Copyright © 2013 by Yahoo! Inc.

How would end users envision a useful mashup? Sometimes too much flexibility stumps people, so they must understand what information is available, how it might be displayed, and how often it can be updated. Armed with that knowledge, they can focus on the information they need most to do their jobs.

Hospital administrator Bora, for example, might benefit from a mashup that shows KPIs summarized from the hospital's transactional systems, something she can access from a dashboard. She could link seminar attendee data to maps, showing where people who attend the seminars reside. Then, during major storms, she might envision maps drawn from city data sources that could affect emergency room requirements—from traffic accidents or fires, for example. Real-time web feeds showing emergency notifications might improve readiness.

For enterprise mashups, IT departments must ensure security, data quality, and reliability, especially because free services may not provide any assurance of continued existence. Organizations typically use commercial software, which makes it easier for developers to build secure and robust modules that draw on enterprise resources as well as external content. The workload is reduced, though, partly because mashup software already includes pre-built interfaces for common ERPs and other enterprise systems. Also, interfaces are already built for many commonly used external resources, such as Google Maps, YouTube, Facebook, Twitter, and Amazon. Users can mix and match them for their own customized mashups, retrieving timely data as needed.

Business Intelligence: The Human Element

With targeted, timely, and well-summarized business intelligence at our fingertips, we have much of what we need to make smart decisions and try new strategies at every level of decision making. With the information systems described in this chapter, we can use computers to analyze information, drawing on our own organization's structured and unstructured resources. We can also tap the growing mounds of data online, combining public and private information in new ways to sort out options and reveal new trends. Of course, decision making also involves a human element, and humans are not always rational creatures, weighing the evidence the way a computer weighs input.

The most successful BI projects start small, even if the goal is to analyze big data.[20] The people who need the information—from marketing, finance, human resources, operations, or other departments—are at the center; IT plays a supporting role. The focus should always be on obtaining meaningful insights that can reap huge rewards for the organization. Asking the right questions and using the answers wisely are more important than generating page after page of colorful graphs using the latest analytic software.

mashup
An approach to aggregating content from multiple internal and external sources on customizable web pages that relies on Web 2.0 technologies.

web feed
Standardized and regularly updated output from a publisher, such as CNN or Weather.com, that can be embedded in a customized mashup.

MyMISLab
Online Simulation

CHOCOLATE LOVERS UNITE
A Role-Playing Simulation on Web Analytics

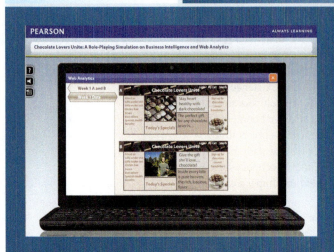

"**C**an you believe this?" whispered the VP to you, as a loud argument broke out among the marketing people, salespeople, web designers, and just about everyone else in the room. They all thought they knew what design would be most effective for Chocolate Lovers Unite (CLU)—an online chocolate retailer with some of the most sumptuous products on the market. The VP asked for quiet in the room and, when everyone settled down, explained that you would be working with them to evaluate different website approaches.

As a web analyst, you were asked to help CLU resolve these arguments using data-driven decision making and business intelligence. Which marketing pitch will work best? Your job is to find out with real data, not guesswork. Time is short with the gift-giving holiday season fast approaching, so you better get started. Check your email and voice messages after you log in....

LEARNING OBJECTIVES

1 Business intelligence encompasses a vast array of information sources that can contribute to better decision making, along with the software applications, technologies, and practices used to analyze it. Levels of decision making that draw on different types of information sources include operational, tactical, and strategic.

2 A primary source of business intelligence is the transactional database, or data warehouse, used by the organization itself for operations or by its suppliers and customers. Data available online can also be sources, including websites, blogs, email, downloadable tables, wikis, and business reports. Along with data from sensors, scanners, and the Internet, these sources form immense big data collections. Both internal and external sources can include structured, semi-structured, or unstructured data.

3 Data mining and decision support tools used to analyze patterns, trends, and relationships rely on data warehouses and newer platforms such as Hadoop that can handle less structured big data. Tools include online analytical processing (OLAP), statistics and modeling techniques, and text mining software. These software systems can analyze immense quantities of data to identify patterns, spot relationships, test hypotheses, and assess sentiments in online comments. Several software approaches are useful for simulating business events, forecasting the future, or determining optimal solutions to business problems given a set of constraints. The what-if analysis, for example, involves building a model based on relationships among variables that the user can change. Other tools in this category include goal seeking, optimization, and statistical forecasting. Artificial intelligence research contributes many important decision support tools, especially in the fields of robotics, expert systems, and neural nets. These all mimic some aspects of human intelligence, such as learning or expert decision making.

4 Organizations can apply digital analytics to many sources of business intelligence, including the main website, their social media pages, their online transactions, and their mobile app. Each platform offers a variety of metrics to gauge success. Total visits, number of unique visitors, traffic sources, page views, mobile app downloads, "likes" on social media, and many other measures will help reveal how well the site is meeting its goals. Choosing the most appropriate metrics depends on developing clear-cut goals so analytical tools are examining meaningful data.

5 Dashboards provide graphic displays that summarize key performance indicators (KPIs), and their content can be customized to meet the needs of individual users. These help reduce information overload and focus attention on the most important metrics. Portals are gateways that aggregate content on the screen and provide access to the individual's resources from a personalized website. Enterprise portals control access to the organization's resources, and the login determines access rights. Mashups also aggregate content and are similar to portals in concept. However, they use Web 2.0 technologies and standards that provide more flexibility to incorporate external resources of all kinds. The human element plays a critical role in decision making, and only people can decide which intelligence to draw on, which tools to use, and how to interpret the results.

KEY TERMS AND CONCEPTS

intelligent agents	what-if analysis	expert system	portals
predictive analytics	goal seeking	neural network	mashup
online analytical processing (OLAP)	optimization	clickstream data	web feed
market basket analysis	forecasting	dashboard	
text mining	artificial intelligence (AI)	key performance indicators (KPIs)	
	CAPTCHA		

CHAPTER REVIEW QUESTIONS

7-1. How do you define business intelligence?

7-2. What are the three levels of decision making that business intelligence supports?

7-3. What are the most important sources of business intelligence inside the organization? What makes them useful?

7-4. What are some examples of external sources of business intelligence?

7-5. How can managers use data mining techniques to analyze patterns, trends, and relationships? How does this lead to better data-driven decision making?

7-6. What is text mining?

7-7. What are examples of statistical techniques that managers can use to simulate business situations, optimize variables, and forecast sales or other figures?

7-8. What are examples of applications that draw on artificial intelligence for decision support?

7-9. How are digital analytics used to assess the effectiveness of websites?

7-10. How do dashboards, portals, and mashups support decision making?

7-11. How does the human element affect decision making?

PROJECTS AND DISCUSSION QUESTIONS

7-12. Why do organizations use external data as a source of business intelligence? What are examples of sources of external data? How might retail giant Walmart use external data to make tactical-level decisions? How might its decision makers use external data to make strategic-level decisions?

7-13. How can an intelligent agent assist with a term paper? Visit your university library's home page to locate the "Search Databases" feature. If your library offers the "ABI/INFORM Complete" database, choose that and enter several keywords (for example, "social media in organizations") into the Basic Search dialog box. (If your library does not offer ABI/INFORM, try doing this exercise on a different database.) Review the results, then select "Refine Search" to select additional databases and/or specify additional search criteria. When you have the results you want, select the "Set Up Alert" option to schedule an alert. Prepare a brief report that describes the alert options that are available for your search. How frequently can you receive updates? How long can you receive updates? Are there options other than frequency and duration? Would you recommend using this intelligent agent to other students working on term papers?

7-14. First Class Salons maintains a company website to promote its chain of 12 health salons. The website includes links to information about its locations, special offers, and FAQs about its services as well as "About Us" and "Contact Us" links. How can First Class Salons use information from its website to gain business intelligence?

Consider the various visitor-related and content-related digital metrics and suggest at least six specific metrics that First Class Salons would want to analyze. Prepare a brief report of your suggestions.

7-15. The Springfield Family Community Center has an outdoor pool that operates May through October. The director is interested to learn whether the center can afford the $57,000 cost of installing a pool-covering dome so patrons can swim year-round. It will also cost about $200 a month for power to keep the dome inflated for 6 months each year. How can the director use forecasting to evaluate the likelihood of selling sufficient tickets to pay for this improvement? Prepare a brief report to the director that explains forecasting. Be sure to include suggestions on both internal and external data that would be useful for this analysis.

7-16. Digital dashboards began to appear in the 1990s as organizations looked for ways to consolidate and display data to make it accessible and useful for busy executives. Visit www.dashboardinsight.com or www.dashboardsbyexample.com or search the Internet to learn more about digital dashboards. What is the relationship between digital dashboards and key performance indicators? Work in a small group with classmates to consider how a digital dashboard can be used by a Radio Shack or other electronics store manager. What specific daily performance indicators would he or she want to see on a digital dashboard? What design tips would you offer to the dashboard developer? As a group, create a hand-drawn sketch of a dashboard design for the Radio Shack manager.

APPLICATION EXERCISES

7-17. EXCEL APPLICATION:
Analyzing Revenue and Expenses for City Hospital Seminars

Figure 7-25 shows the Excel spreadsheet that Bora uses to evaluate the variables relating to the hospital seminar series. She has asked you to use Excel to create a similar spreadsheet to conduct additional what-if and goal seeking analyses. You will need to use the following formulas:

Revenue

Registration Fees = Attendees per seminar × Registration fee × Seminars per year

Parking Fees = (Attendees per seminar/Average number attendees per car) × Seminars per year × Parking fee

Expenses

Speakers' Fees = Speaker's fee per session × Seminars per year

Tech Support = Tech support cost per session × Seminars per year

Marketing = Marketing cost per seminar × Seminars per year

Room Rental = Room rental per seminar × Seminars per year

What-If Questions

After answering each question, be sure to return the variables to their original values shown in Figure 7-25 before testing the impact of changing another one.

1. What is the impact on net profit if the average attendance per seminar increases to 45?

2. What is the impact on net profit if the average attendance drops to 35?

3. What is the impact on net profit if the parking fee is reduced to $3?

4. What is the impact on net profit if the speaker's fee increases to $550 per seminar?

5. What is the impact on net profit of increasing the marketing expense per seminar to $350, which increases average attendance per seminar to 50?

6. What is the impact on net profit of an increase in room rental per seminar to $300?

7. If Bora can negotiate a room rental fee of $160 per seminar, how much will net profit increase?

8. If technical support is included in the room rental per seminar, what is net profit?

Goal Seeking Questions

1. Given the expenses and variables presented in the figure, how many attendees per seminar are required to generate a net profit of $5,500?

2. What parking fee results in a net profit of $4,150?

3. What registration fee per attendee results in a net profit of $5,750?

7-18. ACCESS APPLICATION:
Marketing City Hospital Seminars

Colin is the assistant director of marketing at a hospital that conducts seminars on topics such as sports injuries, arthritis, hip and knee pain, knee replacement, and joint replacement. He is working on a marketing campaign for a new seminar on minimally invasive knee surgery that the hospital is planning to offer. Colin has asked you to help identify potential patients who may be interested in this seminar.

Download the City Hospital database, Ch07Ex02. Write a query that sorts registrants by the type of seminar they have attended. Include the session date as well as attendee information. Modify the query to identify registrants who attended a Knee Replacement seminar. Use the report wizard to create a report that lists the session dates and the names and phone numbers of those who have attended Knee Replacement seminars. This report serves as a "patient contact sheet" that hospital staff will use to call previous attendees to invite them to attend the new seminar. How many patients are listed on the report? Review the attendees table. Is there additional patient information the hospital could collect that may be useful for future marketing campaigns?

FIGURE 7-25

The hospital seminar series data.

	A	B
1	**Hospital Seminars Revenues and Expenses**	
2		
3	**Revenue**	
4	Registration Fees	$16,800
5	Parking Fees	$ 960
6	Subtotal	$17,760
7		
8	**Expenses**	
9	Speakers' Fees	$ 6,000
10	Tech support	$ 1,800
11	Marketing	$ 3,000
12	Room rental	$ 3,000
13	Subtotal	$13,800
14		
15	**Net Profit/Loss**	$ 3,960
16		
17	**Variables**	
18	Speaker's Fee (per session)	$ 500
19	Tech Support cost per session	$ 150
20	Seminars per year	12
21	Registration fee	$ 35
22	Attendees per seminar	40
23	Room rental per seminar	$ 250
24	Parking fee	$ 5
25	Average # attendees per car	3
26	Marketing cost per seminar	$ 250

Source: Microsoft® Excel, Microsoft Corporation. Reprinted with permission.

CASE STUDY #1

Cracking Fraud with Government's Big Data

Driving around Massachusetts, you might notice an RV frequently parked in your neighborhood with Montana license plates. Perhaps it is someone visiting from out west, but it might also be a Massachusetts resident who bought the RV online and registered it in Montana, which has no sales tax. The RV owner saves thousands of dollars, but Massachusetts loses the tax revenue. This kind of fraud is illegal but difficult to catch. A Massachusetts state agency, for example, would not have access to Montana's vehicle registrations and would not be able to match them up against Massachusetts' tax forms or employment records. The data are there, but they are not integrated into big data that can be analyzed.

The health care system is especially plagued by fraud, at both federal and state levels. Analysts estimate that fraud and abuse cost $125 to $175 billion each year, but problems often go unnoticed because they are difficult to identify. Only 3% to 5% of fraudulent cases are discovered, and the detection often happens so late that the funds cannot be recovered.

Predictive analytics are the tools that can spot suspicious activity and unusual patterns. The potential to reduce government waste and fraud in general is enormous; combined with big data, these tools can arm investigators with ways to track fraudulent billing patterns buried in millions of legitimate claims, picking out unusual trends that no human being working alone could ever see.

Health Care Service Corp. (HCSC), for example, implemented a fraud detection system, and it paid off almost immediately. An allergist in Illinois was submitting fraudulent bills, but the individual amounts were never high enough to trigger any suspicion. Something was amiss, however, and the analysts for the insurance company were able to compare what other allergists were charging for the same procedures. The results helped uncover an $800,000 scam.

With access to big data from multiple sources, fraud detection systems can spot a large variety of suspicious activities that need investigation, particularly if data can be drawn from state and federal databases.

In health care, for example, such systems first start with rules that flag unusual behavior in near real time, such as when a provider bills for many services in a short time window or when a person enrolls in Medicaid in more than one state.

Predictive analytics can also learn from the data to build more sophisticated models, especially as the tools have access to more and more data. Fraud rings commit a large number of the scams in health care and government services, and the software can examine relationships. Analyzing the linkages can reap huge benefits and uncover large criminal gangs, even if each individual transaction on its own does not trigger any flags. One ring caught in 2012, for instance, included 107 providers who billed Medicare for more than $400 million in services that were not performed.

Near-real-time analysis is especially important because of the need to spot fraud before any claim is paid. It is much easier to deny payment than to recover funds that have already been paid out. The time window is short, however, given pressure on payers to reimburse quickly. With big data analytical tools, fraud detection systems can operate quickly enough to catch fishy claims before they are paid.

For the 50 states with different information systems and all the counties that maintain their own records, the challenge of reducing fraud is daunting. The goal is to create a big data view of citizens, one that would, for instance, inform a state agency if someone who is receiving benefits purchases a luxury vehicle in a state with no sales tax. With states and counties struggling with budget woes, the drive to catch fraud is strong.

Will "big data" become "Big Brother"? Privacy advocates voice concerns over the growing access to big data across government agencies, particularly as ways are found to integrate the data to paint a meaningful and comprehensive picture of citizens' financial transactions and government benefits. Disclosures about the extent of the government's electronic data gathering for national security have intensified those concerns. Balancing privacy and the need to reduce fraud will be particularly important.

Discussion Questions

7-19. What are some ways that data mining could be used to detect fraud in health insurance claims?

7-20. How could private insurance companies and public government agencies collaborate to combat insurance fraud?

7-21. What types of business skills would be necessary to define the rules for and analyze the results from data mining?

7-22. What business processes are necessary to complement the IS component of data mining?

Sources: Big data and analytics at work. (2015). *Public CIO*, 4–15.

Global big data in healthcare: 2015–2022—key questions answered for the $34.27 billion industry. (February 17, 2016). *PR Newswire*, http://www.prnewswire.com/news-releases/global-big-data-in-healthcare-2015-2022—key-questions-answered-for-the-3427-billion-industry-300221274.html, accessed August 17, 2016.

Hanson, W. (March 19, 2013). Can big data crack fraud? *Government Technology*, http://www.govtech.com/e-government/Can-Big-Data-Crack-Fraud.html, accessed August 16, 2016.

Horowitz, B. T. (December 28, 2012). Big data can fight fraud in health insurance exchanges: Operat. *eWeek*, http://www.eweek.com/enterprise-apps/big-data-can-fight-fraud-in-health-insurance-exchanges-opera/, accessed August 16, 2016.

Ransbotham, S., Kiron, D., & Prentice, P. K. (2016). Beyond the hype: The hard work behind analytics success. *MIT Sloan Management Review, 57*(3).

Schrieber, R. (2013). Examine the broader context to identify healthcare fraud. *Managed Healthcare Executive, 23*(2), 44–45.

Thorpe, N., Deslich, S., Sikula, S., & Coustasse, A. (2012). Combating Medicare fraud: A struggling work in progress. *Franklin Business & Law Journal, 2012*(4), 95–107.

CASE STUDY #2

TV and Twitter: How Nielsen Rates Programs with "Social TV"

To understand the audience for TV shows, TV ratings giant Nielsen relies on electronic "People Meters" placed into a representative sample of homes throughout the United States to track viewing patterns. In half the homes, Nielsen installs "cross-platform" people meters to detect TV viewing on computers or mobile devices and also to track web traffic. The company also asks viewers to fill out paper-and-pencil diaries about their TV viewing habits.

Founded in 1936 when there were very few televisions in the country, Nielsen grew into the ratings giant that can make or break any new program or any TV producer's career. The ratings affect not only the show's survival but the cost of the ads that appear during the show. Super Bowl ads, for instance, are most expensive of all because the Super Bowl has the largest audience of any show on TV.

In the age of Twitter and other social media, however, TV viewing is becoming a social experience that involves many more people than those in a single home. Viewers, especially those in the coveted 18–34 age group, often share their thoughts in real time as they watch a program, trashing the actors, praising the costumes, or mocking the script. Nielsen began measuring the engagement of the TV audience by tracking tweets and posting results on real-time dashboards for the company's clients.

The analytics software picks up tweets related to a particular TV show by using relevant keywords—actors' names, characters, incidents, and other tracking tools. It relies also on the hashtags that identify the topic in many tweets, such as #bigbangtheory, #project-runway, or #gameofthrones. The dashboard shows relevant statistics by time period, such as the number of related tweets with positive or negative spin, and it can scroll the tweets as they flash by. Because the dashboard is showing real-time data, clients can not only see gross statistics such as overall number of viewers. They can also see how viewers are reacting to particular scenes or characters as they appear. The software tracks thousands of programs, so it can generate comprehensive comparison ratings for "social TV" viewers, their demographics, and their preferences.

The use of Twitter feeds to analyze social TV patterns adds a great deal to Nielsen's capabilities. For example, Nielsen's set-top boxes do not easily capture who in the family is actually watching—or even if the set is just turned on and no one at all is watching. Many people leave the TV on so they can record shows they like, though they may not have time to actually view them later. Even if they do, they may fast-forward through the ads. The set-top boxes are also unable to assess viewer attitudes during the show or the ads.

Twitter feeds also have disadvantages as an audience rating tool, however. The tweets are not generated from a representative sample, for instance, so their content is biased toward a certain population of viewers. Those who don't use Twitter are not in the sample, and the feeds may be overwhelmed by a small group of frequent tweeters who are loud and vocal.

Despite the drawbacks, research confirms a relationship between Twitter activity and TV ratings measured by Nielsen's other tools. For example, premiere episodes that generated an 8.5% increase in Twitter volume showed a 1% increase in TV ratings for viewers in the 18–34 age group. The relationship was weaker for other age groups, probably because fewer people outside that group use Twitter.

The relationship between Twitter volume and TV ratings becomes stronger as the season continues and is highest for the season finale. This suggests that Twitter metrics are not just reflecting a show's appeal. The chatter may be creating TV buzz that draws more viewers into the social TV experience.

Social TV may also be drawing people back to viewing shows live rather than recording them. If Twitter volume is high during the show, it means that people have points to make in real time. For instance, they may prefer to weigh in on Dancing with the Stars contestants immediately rather than wait until the next day. This trend may mean more live viewers for the ads as well, a welcome trend for the networks and their advertisers.

Nielsen is expanding its social content ratings by including analytics drawn from Facebook and Instagram in addition to the Twitter feeds, so TV producers will have a rich source of information about how their shows are faring. While Nielsen will not drop its careful sampling techniques and set-top boxes, the company is leading the way toward new ways to learn about social TV.

Discussion Questions

7-23. What potential value does Nielsen intend to add to its ratings by data mining Twitter to analyze social TV patterns?

7-24. What are the drawbacks of using Twitter as a rating tool? Do these disadvantages compromise the value of the Nielsen ratings?

7-25. How might the use of Twitter and other social media be influencing the viewing habits of the American audience?

7-26. As Nielsen extends its data mining of social media to include Facebook and Instagram as well as Twitter, what differences might it expect in the audience being analyzed? Would this analysis have any value to the networks? Why or why not?

Sources: Humphrey, M. (2012). Nielsen acquires social TV metrics company SocialGuide. *Forbes*, http://www.forbes.com/sites/michaelhumphrey/2012/11/12/nielsen-acquires-social-tv-metrics-company-socialguide/, accessed August 16, 2016.

McLellan, M. (2016). Nielsen N.V. *Hoover's Online Database*, http://subscriber.hoovers.com.proxy1.library.jhu.edu/H/company360/fulldescription.html?companyId=42393000000000, accessed April 17, 2016.

New study confirms correlation between Twitter and TV ratings. (March 20, 2013). *PR Newswire*, http://search.proquest.com/docview/1317970375?accountid=11752, accessed June 2, 2016.

Nielsen. (2016). Nielsen to launch "social content ratings" with measurement across Twitter and Facebook. *Nielsen.com*, http://www.nielsen.com/us/en/press-room/2016/nielsen-to-launch-social-content-ratings-with-measurement-across-twitter-and-facebook.html, accessed August 16, 2016.

Nielsen website. (n.d.), http://www.nielsen.com, accessed June 2, 2016.

Pomerantz, D. (2013). Can Twitter save live TV? *Forbes.com*, http://www.forbes.com/sites/dorothypomerantz/2013/03/20/can-twitter-save-live-tv/#3fe69c50711a, accessed August 16, 2016.

SocialGuide website. (n.d.). http://www.socialguide.com, accessed August 16, 2016.

E-PROJECT 1 — Detecting Suspicious Activity in Insurance Claims

Detecting unusual patterns in drug prescriptions is the focus of this e-project. To begin, download the Excel file called *Ch07_MedicalCharges*.

The worksheet contains columns showing a sample of hypothetical prescription drug claims over a period of years.

7-27. Create a pivot table and chart to show the total amounts paid by year for this pharmacy by dragging Year to the Axis Fields box and Amount to the Values box. Be sure you are looking at the sum of Amounts in your chart. Which year had the highest sales for prescription drugs?

7-28. Change the pivot table to show total sales by month by removing Year from the Axis Fields and dragging Month to that box. During which month of the year does this pharmacy tend to sell the most prescription drugs?

7-29. Remove Month and put Prescriber ID in the Axis Fields box. Which prescriber generates the most income for this pharmacy?

7-30. Remove PrescriberID and put PatientID in the Axis Fields box. Which patient generates the most income for the pharmacy?

7-31. Let's take a closer look at this patient by filtering the records. Click on PatientID in the PivotTable Field List and uncheck all boxes except for this patient. Drag Year under PatientID in the Axis Fields box so you can see how this person's spending patterns have changed. Which year shows the most spending?

7-32. Let's see who is prescribing for this patient. Remove Year from the Axis Fields box and drag PrescriberID to the box. Which prescriber has the highest spending total?

7-33. Now, let's see what is being prescribed. Drag DrugName to the Axis Fields box under PrescriberID. What might you conclude from this chart?

E-PROJECT 2 — Analyzing Nielsen TV Ratings with Excel

In this e-project, you will explore TV ratings and analyze them with Excel. Download the Excel file called *Ch07_NielsenRatings*. This file contains ratings for popular network programs for two separate weeks in 2016 (www.nielsen.com/us/en/top10s.html). The rating represents the percent of U.S. households that were watching that channel at the time (of those whose TV was turned on).

7-34. Calculate three new columns:
a. Percent change (up or down) in number of viewers from the July 4 data to the July 11 data.
b. Percent change (up or down) in rating.
c. Absolute change in the number of viewers.

7-35. Answer the following questions:
a. Which show gains the largest number of viewers from July 4 to July 11?
b. Which show is the biggest loser from July 4 to July 11, in terms of change in ratings?
c. Compute the total viewers for these shows for July 4 and for July 11. How many total viewers watched one of the TV shows in this list during the week of March 25.
d. What is the percent change in total viewers for the shows in this list from July 4 to July 11?

CHAPTER NOTES

1 Eckerson, W. W. (Ed.). (2012). Operational dashboards in action. In *Performance Dashboards* (pp. 123–137). John Wiley & Sons, Inc. http://onlinelibrary.wiley.com/doi/10.1002/9781119199984.ch7/summary, accessed August 16, 2016.

2 Dobrev, K., & Hart, M. (2015). Benefits, justification and implementation planning of real-time business intelligence systems. *Electronic Journal of Information Systems Evaluation*, *18*(2), 104–118.

3 Briggs, L. (January 2009). DIRECTV connects with data integration solution. *Business Intelligence Journal*, *14*(1), 14–16. Retrieved May 22, 2011, from ABI/INFORM Global. doi:1673554871

4 Internet of Things market—global industry analysis, size, share, growth, trends and forecast 2015–2021. (December 2, 2015). *PR Newswire*, http://search.proquest.com/abicomplete/docview/1738585703/abstract/74A07776C6B84F7EPQ/18, accessed August 16, 2016.

5 Moscaritolo, A. (2015). EU spurns Facebook Moments app over facial recognition. *PCmag.com*, http://search.proquest.com/abicomplete/docview/1690086250/abstract/1E0D25155CC14FF2PQ/6, accessed August 16, 2016.

6 Parenteau, J., Sallam, R. L., Howson, C., Tapadinhas, J., Schlegel, K., & Oestreich, T. W. (2016). *Magic Quadrant for Business Intelligence and Analytics Platforms* (No. G00275847). Gartner Research, http://www.gartner.com/document/3200317?ref=solrAll&refval=166358693&qid=6460c11df69e31756dea01a16aa0a387, accessed August 16, 2016.

7 Transparency Market Research. (March 28, 2016). Hadoop market is expected to reach USD 37,759.0 million in 2023. *PR Newswire*, http://search.proquest.com/abicomplete/docview/1776117907/abstract/468E63282B784CCAPQ/9, accessed August 16, 2016.

8 Henschen, D. (2013). Big data, big questions. *InformationWeek*, *1349*, 18–22.

9 Sutton, J. (July 1, 2009). Government moves to staunch massive Medicare fraud. *Reuters*, http://www.reuters.com/article/us-usa-medicare-fraud-idUSTRE5604FL20090701, accessed May 22, 2016.

10 Schlegel, K., Sallam, R. L., Yuen, D., & Tapadinhas, J. (2013). Magic quadrant for business intelligence and analytics platforms. Gartner Research, ID:G00239854.

11 Greengard, S. (2015). Shedding light on the dark side of fake reviews. *CIO Insight*, http://www.cioinsight.com/blogs/shedding-light-on-the-dark-side-of-fake-reviews.html, accessed August 15, 2016.

12 McCarthy, M. (February 4, 2013). Text mining revolutionizes academic research. *Digital Discourse*, http://www.siia.net/blog/index.php/2013/02/text-mining-revolutionizes-academic-research/, accessed February 16, 2013.

13 Gold, J. (2016). Report: Apple to chase Echo, Google Home in voice assistant market. NetworkWorld, http://www.networkworld.com/article/3074665/mobile-wireless/report-apple-to-chase-echo-google-home-in-voice-assistant-market.html, accessed August 16, 2016.

14 Chu, Z., Gianvecchio, S., Koehl, A., Wang, H., & Jajodia, S. (2013). Blog or block: Detecting blog bots through behavioral biometrics. *Computer Networks*, *57*(3), 634–646.

15 Bennett, C. C., & Hauser, K. (2013). Artificial intelligence framework for simulating clinical decision-making: A Markov decision process approach. *Artificial Intelligence and Medicine*. doi:10.1016/j.artmed.2012.12.003

16 Sachs, J. D. (2010). Expert systems fight poverty. *Scientific American*, *302*(4), 32.

17 Bass, D. (2016). Microsoft CEO Satya Nadella bets big on artificial intelligence. *Bloomberg Businessweek* (4470), 50–53.

18 Sussin, J., & Rozwell, C. (2014). *Choose social metrics that demonstrate CRM business value* (No. G00252873). Gartner Research, http://www.gartner.com/document/2664015?ref=solrAll&refval=166390963&qid=780dbfed1f8bb35ea5c8c5d58f558920, accessed August 16, 2016.

19 Potter, K. (2016). *Creating and monitoring metrics, dashboards and scorecards primer for 2016* (No. G00293040). Gartner Research, http://www.gartner.com/document/3184119?ref=solrAll&refval=166402096&qid=81af85b1010b71fc362d42584caf7558, accessed August 17, 2016.

20 Marchand, D. A., & Peppard, J. (2013). Why IT fumbles analytics. *Harvard Business Review*, *91*(1), 104–112.

Collaborating with *Technology*

LEARNING OBJECTIVES

1 Describe the major collaborative technologies, and explain the features that each one offers for communications and productivity.

2 Identify and describe Web 2.0 technologies that facilitate collaboration.

3 Explain how unified communications contribute to collaboration.

4 Describe features of online environments that can affect human behavior and group dynamics, and identify strategies to make virtual teams more productive and successful.

An online, interactive decision-making simulation that reinforces chapter contents and uses key terms in context can be found in MyMISLab™.

INTRODUCTION

MANY HUMAN RELATIONSHIPS NOW HAVE SOME VIRTUAL COMPONENT, even for people who see one another every day. Collaborative technologies support these interactions, and they go well beyond email, text messages, and telephone. They transform the way people in organizations work together, whether they are in the next office or across the globe.

In the interactive decision-making simulation for this chapter called "Department of Social Services," you join coworkers at the agency who want to take advantage of collaborative technologies for virtual teamwork. Everyone is tired of long commutes and convinced that they can be more productive if they can be more mobile and flexible. You'll help them put together a proposal for the agency's director that identifies benefits and possible drawbacks. As you work with the team, you'll be using those technologies on a simulated smartphone and laptop equipped with the features you need to make the project work. At one point, the team faces an

MyMISLab
Online Simulation

DEPARTMENT OF SOCIAL SERVICES
A Role-Playing Simulation on Collaborative Technologies
and Virtual Teamwork

Customer : Hello

Advisor: Good afternoon how can I help ...

Customer: I have a problem with ....

Andresr/Shutterstock.

emergency that needs virtual teamwork, and you can help if you're alert and fast enough with the new features of your smartphone.

Collaborative technologies open new possibilities for productive work and social activity, but as you will see in the simulation and read about in this chapter, these online environments affect human behavior and group dynamics in subtle and often unexpected ways. This chapter first covers the major technologies used for collaboration and the facets of human interaction they support. Finally, we explore why they are different from face-to-face interactions and how you can best use them.

Describe the major collaborative technologies, and explain the features that each one offers for communications and productivity.

 # The Evolution of Collaborative Technologies

Samuel Morse inaugurated his telegraph in a grand public demonstration in 1844. Keenly aware of the history-making potential of this technology, Morse chose a dramatic phrase as his first message: "What hath God wrought!"

The late Ray Tomlinson, widely credited with sending the first email message, forgot what it was. He suspected it was something like "QWERTYUIOP." Despite the lack of fanfare, Tomlinson's invention triggered a tidal wave of online collaboration, and billions of messages are now sent daily. Figure 8-1 shows the major generations in the evolution of tools that support online collaboration. Many of them rely heavily on the database and database management systems discussed in Chapter 4. In fact, without a shared database, tools like calendaring, contact management, and social networks could not exist.

Email Technology, Contacts, and Calendars

Technically, email transmission is relatively simple (Figure 8-2), although the steps vary depending on the type of email server that is hosting your mail. You usually start by identifying the servers that will handle your outgoing and incoming mail. For outgoing, you enter the name of the **SMTP server**, which stands for "simple mail transfer protocol." For example, a student in Hong Kong may rely on her university's host. When she types a message to a friend and clicks "send," her message is first transmitted to a special port on the university's SMTP

FIGURE 8-1

Evolution of collaborative technologies.

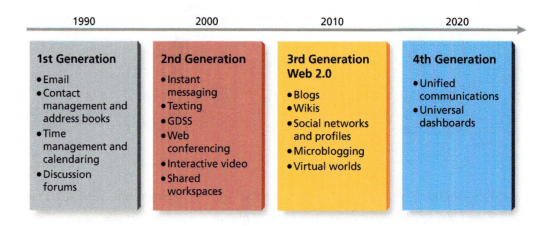

1990	2000	2010	2020
1st Generation • Email • Contact management and address books • Time management and calendaring • Discussion forums	**2nd Generation** • Instant messaging • Texting • GDSS • Web conferencing • Interactive video • Shared workspaces	**3rd Generation Web 2.0** • Blogs • Wikis • Social networks and profiles • Microblogging • Virtual worlds	**4th Generation** • Unified communications • Universal dashboards

FIGURE 8-2

Sending email.

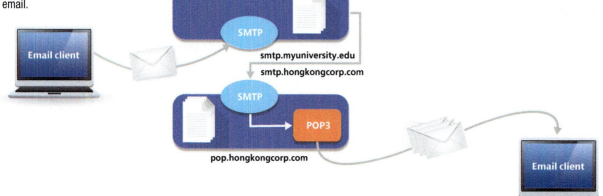

Source: Photos/Illustrations: Lana Rinck/Shutterstock, ezsolee/Shutterstock, Makc/Shutterstock.

server, and then the server software takes over. The SMTP server adds date and time information and then directs the message to the server identified after the @ sign.

Mailbox accounts also specify the name of the server that handles incoming mail. Many begin with "pop," such as pop.myuniversity.edu. Another protocol for incoming mail is **IMAP (Internet mail access protocol)**, in which mail is actually maintained on the server and organized into folders there. IMAP is especially useful when you use more than one device. You can access your mail from your smartphone, tablet, or any other device and also see the symbols that show whether you read or replied to the message. For a mobile workforce, these features are essential.

> **PRODUCTIVITY TIP**
> When you delete email, remember that copies are stored elsewhere, such as on the server's backup media. Legal authorities can retrieve it, and so can employers if it is company email.

Web-based email services, such as Google's Gmail or Yahoo! Mail, are built from the ground up to work within the browser rather than with client software installed on your computer. Many organizations are retiring their locally installed enterprise email servers in favor of outsourcing to such cloud-based services.

THE ADDRESS BOOK, BUSINESS CARDS, AND CONTACT MANAGEMENT

Email's explosive success led to enhancements and new features. Its simple address book expanded to a rich contact management system that supports distribution lists, photos, birthdates, event management, and much more. Keeping all this information about clients and coworkers together, synched to a smartphone, boosts productivity considerably.

The ability to seamlessly share and update contact information electronically is fundamental to contact management. However, the paper business card with all its nonstandard formats and fonts is not going away soon. Sales calls, business meetings, and introductions typically start with an exchange of business cards, and protocol for each exchange may be rigidly prescribed by custom and tradition. Japanese businesspeople, for example, use both hands to offer their cards as a show of respect, and they always make certain the card is oriented so that the recipient can immediately read it.

Scanners with optical character recognition (OCR) software can decipher details on most business cards. Another strategy is to exchange electronic files with your contacts that software can easily read. The "vCard," for instance, is a file format used to exchange business card information electronically. A more versatile approach uses **microformats**, which rely on the XML family of standards to represent metadata. This approach is also used for exchanging contact management data. The "hCard" is an example.

> **PRODUCTIVITY TIP**
> Start building your contacts database in a structured format early. In most email systems, you can add a contact for anyone who sends you an email without having to retype the name or address. Check your email system's help pages and settings to learn how to manage contacts efficiently.

Standardized file formats with business card information can also be exchanged over wireless networks or by means of Bluetooth or infrared connections. In some companies, these electronic exchanges are quite common. However, the business card protocol lives on in most organizations around the world, so it's best to keep some handy.

CALENDARS AND TIME MANAGEMENT

Adding calendars and appointment scheduling capabilities to email clients is a major breakthrough for time management. Although the paper appointment book served well, it could not trigger a "ding" as an alert for an upcoming event. Nor could it send an email, synch with a smartphone, or flag recurring events that stretch out over months or years.

SMTP server
Mail server using the simple mail transfer protocol; handles outgoing email.

IMAP (Internet mail access protocol)
A protocol for handling incoming email.

microformats
A set of formats that rely on the XML family of standards to represent metadata in HTML code and that support electronic exchange of business cards, calendar appointments, and other kinds of data.

Like contacts, calendar events can be transmitted and exchanged using standardized file formats. For instance, the iCalendar format is widely used to transmit calendar data. The .ics extension indicates that the plain text file contains iCalendar code so the programs can recognize it (Figure 8-3).

The calendar's collaborative features eliminate much frustration for event managers. Consider, for example, the struggle to schedule a team meeting, even with the help of email. Asking people for the times and dates they have available can be fruitless and time-consuming with many false starts and delayed responses. But if everyone is sharing calendars, "free" time for all is easier to identify. Personal preferences, cultural factors, and corporate norms all affect the use of calendaring software and how much it adds to overall productivity. Some corporations require its use to streamline meeting arrangements and also to show everyone's whereabouts.

FIGURE 8-3

Example of plain text iCalendar event.

```
BEGIN:VCALENDAR
VERSION:2.0
PRODID://HongKongCorp//NONSGML//EN
BEGIN:VEVENT
DTSTART:20130709T170000Z
DTEND:20130709T190000Z
SUMMARY:Tiger Team Meeting
END:VEVENT
END:VCALENDAR
```

Discussion Forums

The asynchronous discussion forum evolved from the earlier bulletin board as an online site in which people could post text messages, reply to others at any time, and discuss a topic of interest. Employee discussion forums are often used to share company information and coordinate activities or to serve as an online suggestion box.

Forums may be moderated, with someone nurturing the discussion, deleting unacceptable posts, and blocking users who violate the rules. The forum rules may allow people to post under a pseudonym so members feel more anonymous and less identifiable during discussions. That changes how they behave, as we discuss later in this chapter.

Consumer-oriented discussion forums are especially important to electronic word-of-mouth communication. The forums on sites such as OpenTable, Yelp, and TripAdvisor contain valuable tips and reviews that shape customer behavior and attitudes.[1]

Employee discussion forums can be unpredictable. Most are used productively, but occasional posts can tip in a negative direction. At a large European petroleum company, for example, the forum was initially used to post helpful tips about new technology; however, some employees used it to criticize the leadership (Figure 8-4). Discussion forums can be quite valuable when managed properly, with an understanding of how the human element unfolds in online collaboration discussed later in this chapter.

FIGURE 8-4

Sample post from an employee discussion forum.

What happened at Epsilon was almost a Manual of How Not to do Change in Companies. . . People were ill-treated in the face of a restructuring and a merger with another company. They were then left without knowing anything about what to expect [. . .] and ending up learning that there was a "confidential" (!) plan for the restructuring through reading the newspapers.

Source: Based on da Cunha, J. V., & Orlikowski, W. J. (2008). Performing catharsis: The use of online discussion forums in organizational change. Information and Organization, 18(2), 132–156.

Instant Messaging and Texting

Instant messaging (IM), also called "chat," consists of real-time text-based interactions over a network. For quick answers in the workplace, it can be very useful, provided messages don't become too distracting.[2] IM can save you a walk down the hall to a colleague's office or a costly phone call to someone in another country.

IM grew dramatically with the net and the launch of free IM software clients, such as AOL Instant Messenger, Google Talk, Yahoo! Messenger, Skype, and other products targeted to internal business communications or B2B interactions. Some universities provide the service for their students, faculty, and staff so they can chat with one another.

IM AND INTEROPERABILITY

Unlike email, which was designed to be fully open so that anyone can send messages to anyone else regardless of which email software they used, the IM world emerged as proprietary islands. Each product tended to use different protocols that the others could not interpret without special conversion software. For example, WhatsApp is a messaging client for smartphones that relies on Internet connections so users can avoid charges from their cell-phone carriers. However, WhatsApp users can only send and receive messages from other people who have installed that app.

Although some major players develop agreements to allow interaction, the nature of the underlying technology continues to hamper interoperability. In addition, IM providers' competitive strategies do not favor a more open architecture because these firms are not eager to reduce consumers' switching costs.

PRESENCE AWARENESS

IM software introduced a critically important collaborative feature called **presence awareness**, which allows users to display their current status to their contacts, colleagues, or buddy list. The software shows whether the person is logged in and the user can elaborate, adding "working on the team project," "out to lunch," or "pretending to work...." Arguably, this feature was the killer app of IM because it shows whether the person is available to answer a question, pick up the phone, or stop by for a brief meeting. Other kinds of collaborative technologies have since introduced the same feature because of its value.

Presence awareness is one of the subtle advantages that co-located teams have over virtual teams. For example, companies grasp the value of a **war room**, the large area in which team members on the same project work closely together, surrounded by whiteboards, large digital displays, and other tools to facilitate impromptu meetings and smooth collaboration. Working on fast-moving, intense projects, team members in the war room are constantly aware of one another's presence so they can get an immediate response, rather than sending out emails, leaving voice messages, and delaying work. Although not quite as reliable, presence awareness indicators add an important human element to online collaboration, and they are a key reason people adopt the tool within organizations.

> **PRODUCTIVITY TIP**
> Use proper spelling and grammar in your communications at work, at least until you're sure you have a clear understanding of the corporate culture. Also, avoid "textisms," such as "cul8tr" (see you later).

IM is a common collaborative tool even for people in the same building, who may keep the IM client active all day long to receive brief text messages. An IM is much faster than a phone call for short questions, and the social courtesies are not needed (Figure 8-5). People can also multitask during IM exchanges.

TEXT MESSAGING OR TEXTING

Texting blends seamlessly into any collaborative setting, alerting coworkers you'll be a few minutes late, for instance. Interconnections between cellular networks and the Internet now blur the distinction between IM and texting, but the origins of texting were in mobile communications. Texting transforms a cell phone from a single-purpose mobile device into one that can send brief text messages to other mobile devices, transmit photos and videos, and broadcast messages to large groups, as with Twitter. The sender may assume that most people will notice the buzz or vibration on their mobile device that signals an incoming text and, if the situation permits, will take a moment to view it immediately.

Text messaging first gained momentum in Europe and Asia, where it goes by names such as SMS or Short Mail. It now outpaces voice phone calls, with heavy users sending and receiving hundreds of text messages daily. Although texting can be a substitute for a phone call, its characteristics make it a different kind of collaborative tool with its own advantages and limitations. Because people usually carry their cell phones, texting can assist in emergency situations and disaster recovery. In the aftermath of the 2013 Boston Marathon bombing, for instance, phone lines went down and cell phone calls could not get through. However, many could send text messages to let family and friends know they were safe.[3] The Federal Emergency Management Agency also advises people to use texting to communicate at such times to avoid tying up voice lines that are needed for first responders.[4]

---

instant messaging (IM)
Also called "chat." IM consists of real-time text-based interactions over a network.

presence awareness
IM software feature that allows users to display their current status to their contacts, colleagues, or buddy list.

war room
A large area in which team members on the same project work closely together, surrounded by whiteboards, large digital displays, and other tools to facilitate impromptu meetings and smooth collaboration.

FIGURE 8-5

Comparison of time elapsed for a query handled by phone call or IM.

Phone Call	IM
Look up number.	
Dial number.	*Allen clicks on Tamara's icon and types into the chat box:*
Voicemail responds. Allen decides to try again in a few minutes rather than leave a message, not knowing how often Tamara checks her voicemail.	Allen: Tam, can you send me your copy of the August report?
Wait 10 minutes.	*Tamara is on the phone, but can easily multitask.*
Dial number.	Tamara: Sure.
Ring ... ring ...	*Wait 10 seconds.*
Tamara: Hello?	Tamara: AugustReport.xlsx
Allen: Hi, this is Allen, is this Tamara?	Allen: Got it, thanks.
Tamara: Hi, Allen. Yes, this is Tamara. How are you doing?	*Allen clicks on the file and opens the report.*
Allen: Good, and you?	
Tamara: Not too bad, though I'm glad it's Friday!	
Allen: I just had a quick question.	
Tamara: Shoot.	
Allen: I can't find my copy of the August report. Do you have one?	
Tamara: Yes, I'll email it to you.	
Allen: Thanks!	
Tamara: No problem. I'll do that now.	
Allen: That's great. OK, I'll see you later at the meeting.	
Tamara: Talk to you soon.	
Allen: Bye .	
Tamara composes a brief email message to Allen, attaches the report, and clicks send.	
Allen waits for the message to arrive, saves the attachment on his hard drive, and opens the report.	
Time elapsed: ~15 minutes	Time elapsed: ~15 seconds

Text messages also multiply the power of informal networks by allowing users to broadcast information not yet available through traditional means. The first report of the plane that ditched on the Hudson River in New York City in 2009 came from a witness who sent a text message to his Twitter followers: "There's a plane in the Hudson. I'm on the ferry to pick up the people. Crazy."[5] The message spread virally as the followers re-sent it to all their networks, and the emergency water landing was later featured in the film, *Sully*.

Texting is also extremely valuable for real-time micro-coordination, letting people know where and when activities are to be held and coordinating fast-moving crowds. The online simulation for Chapter 9, called "Criminal Investigations Division," shows how texting can be used to coordinate flash mobs.

GROUP CONVERSATION SOFTWARE

Building on the advantages of IM and texting, collaborative technology that supports fluid teamwork has become very popular, with products such as Slack and HipChat.[6] These support persistent group chat, alerts, task reminders, document sharing, search functions, integration with external services such as Twitter, and other features that a fast-paced team needs to coordinate work and facilitate information sharing, whether team members are in an office or on the go with a mobile device. The conversation's persistence is an important element because team members who join late can easily catch up on the team's progress by looking over the conversation's history. Users can create conversation channels for any number of team projects, configuring privacy settings to restrict the conversation to members only or making it public so others can see what is happening.

Team members can also integrate a growing variety of additional tools into their group conversation, ones that are especially relevant to their current work. For example, a team working on an email marketing campaign might add an automated bot that pulls updated campaign statistics into the conversation. Team members don't have to switch apps or log into different programs to see the latest data because the bot presents it to all of them automatically in a timely way.

PRODUCTIVITY TIP

For your next group project, try using group conversation software such as HipChat or Slack. It should help your team coordinate the work and avoid long and confusing email chains. Your university may also offer students free access to similar software.

Group Decision Support Systems (GDSS)

A collaborative technology that helps groups brainstorm and make decisions is called a **group decision support system (GDSS)**. These systems are used for face-to-face group meetings in which each individual is equipped with a computer connected to a shared server, and the group facilitator structures the tasks during the session. The software allows each member to type his or her contributions anonymously as the group moves through the stages of identifying the problem to be solved, brainstorming possible solutions, rating the alternatives, and coming to some consensus about the best course of action. As the contributions, comments, and votes unfold, they appear on the screen—with no names attached.

GDSS was designed to promote novel ideas and high-quality, rational decisions, especially by altering some of the group dynamics that can cause groups to function poorly. High-status members, for instance, have a strong influence even when they are wrong. Group pressure can also squash expression of independent viewpoints that differ from the majority. The anonymity of GDSS helps reduce these effects.

Web Conferencing

Another synchronous collaboration technology is **web conferencing**, which supports online meetings, sometimes called "webinars," via the Internet. Participants join the meeting from their own computers or smartphones and use headsets with microphones or phone conferencing to speak to one another. Browser-based conferencing software, such as WebEx or GoToMeeting, have enriched their offerings to include features such as the following:

- Real-time audio and video support
- Support for PowerPoint or other slide presentations
- Interactive whiteboards, with drawing tools and color coding for each participant
- Text-based chat
- Polling software
- Web-based clients for both desktop computers and mobile phones
- Desktop application sharing, in which the meeting participants or audience can see whatever application the host is running on the desktop
- Archiving recordings so participants who missed the event can play it back
- Registration systems for fee-based enrollments

Web-conferencing applications take advantage of mashups to support shared web browsing, chat windows, video, news feeds, and other modules the meeting participants might need.

group decision support system (GDSS)
Collaborative technology that helps groups brainstorm and make decisions in face-to-face meetings, led by facilitators. Participants can contribute anonymously via their computers.

web conferencing
Technology that supports online meetings or "webinars" via the Internet. Participants join the meeting from their own computers or smartphones.

At Reuters, for example, stock traders in the United States send market data to Asia-based traders as U.S. markets close. The traders can put a webcam image in one corner, a rolling feed of stock prices in another, and an application that calls up news about a particular stock when one of the traders, either in the United States or in Asia, clicks on that ticker symbol.[7]

Web-conferencing tools can make a dramatic dent in travel budgets, and the services see particularly fast growth during economic downturns. They are widely used for corporate training, global project teams, product announcements, virtual sales calls, and other events.

Interactive Video

Interactive video for collaboration is freely available via webcams and software such as Skype and FaceTime and also from web conferencing services that support live video. This capability is described separately because it introduces a significant element for online collaboration by allowing participants to see facial expressions and other nonverbal aspects of communication and not just hear voices or view slides.

The free and lower-end systems often have transmission delays that make it difficult to synchronize the speaker's voice with lip movements, so they may not work well for delicate negotiations. Higher-end interactive video systems can dramatically improve the interaction with crystal-clear images and audio. Some systems rely on leased communications lines to ensure high definition; broadcast-quality images and sound are transmitted to produce the "you are there" feeling of a face-to-face meeting.

The most powerful systems create a sense of **telepresence**, in which the remote participants are almost life-sized and images are vividly clear. Eye contact is more natural, and voices are well synched to lip movements. An executive can turn on the desktop camera and interact with someone across the planet almost as though the person were sitting on the other side of the desk (Figure 8-6). For meeting rooms, larger screens can add remote participants so they seem to be sitting at the same table (Figure 8-7).

Telepresence is also critical for telemedicine. Doctors are in short supply in Switzerland, so a company called Medgate installs high-end interactive video consulting rooms at

FIGURE 8-6

High-end interactive video systems create a sense of telepresence.

Source: Andersen Ross/Exactostock/SuperStock.

Source: FrameAngel/Shutterstock

FIGURE 8-7
Interactive video for meeting rooms.

pharmacies. The patient can consult "face-to-face" with a Medgate physician, who will pre-scribe medication as needed.[8] Multinational corporations find the technology especially useful to bridge barriers between managers in different cultures. These can be difficult to overcome on voice conference calls without the benefit of seeing facial expressions and gestures.

With increasing bandwidth available for cellular networks, the transmission of clear video signals to smartphones with powerful processors is much more feasible. Multisite conference calls with interactive video are possible on these tiny devices. You will experience how they can work in the online simulation for this chapter.

Shared Workspaces

Organizing all the information resources and communications for a team of people takes another kind of collaborative technology. The **shared workspace** is an online area in which team members can post documents, maintain membership lists, feature news and announce-ments, and collaborate on edits and updates.

The core of a shared workspace is the document library, where members can store important information assets and keep track of all the edits. Some software for shared work-spaces, such as Microsoft's SharePoint, offers features for version control to ensure that older copies are maintained and no changes are lost. This centralized document library goes a long way toward eliminating the confusion and dupli-cation that arise when team members are constantly sending revised versions back and forth over email.

Shared workspace software continues to add many new features to help teams collaborate. Some examples are listed in Figure 8-8.

FIGURE 8-8
Shared workspace capabilities for teams.

▶ Discussion forums
▶ Team calendars
▶ Team announcements
▶ Shared task lists with task status, due dates, priorities, and assignments
▶ Email alerts to inform team members of updates to the shared workspace
▶ Member lists with contact information
▶ Search functionality
▶ Content management capabilities with checkout and version control
▶ Collaborative document editing
▶ Workflow management

telepresence
The impression created when remote participants in an interactive video meeting are almost life-sized and vividly clear; useful for sensitive negotiations.

shared workspace
An area on a server in which team members can post documents, maintain membership lists, feature news and announcements, and collaborate on edits and updates.

Identify and describe Web 2.0 technologies that facilitate collaboration.

2 Web 2.0 Collaborative Technologies

Web 2.0 and related advancements introduced powerful tools that encourage widespread participation and end-user contribution to the web. Many of these tools have found their way into corporations to facilitate collaboration and promote information sharing.

Blogs

A **blog**, short for "web log," is one example. The blogger maintains a website composed mainly of ongoing commentary, images, and links to other online resources. The posts are displayed in reverse chronological order so that the most recent appears on top. Blogging software, such as the free versions available through WordPress and Blogger, simplifies the task of creating your own website to express opinions, review products, discuss hobbies, or just rant. Readers can add their own comments to the blogger's posts, joining in the asynchronous discussion.

For organizations, blogs can help create a more intimate connection with customers, employees, or suppliers. For example, the owner of a seafood restaurant might want to blog about favorite fish recipes or add videos of the dock where the owner buys fresh fish. Whole Foods maintains a lively blog that features stories about recipes, healthy eating, and seasonal foods. The company's CEO blogs as well, with entries that focus on business-oriented messages such as discussions of the company's ratings system for responsibly grown fruits and vegetables.[9] Figure 8-9 lists some company blogs that do far more than offer announcements and promotions.

The blogosphere, as pundits call it, also benefits from blogger networks and cross-linking. A post on one blog may intrigue other bloggers and tweeters, creating a viral spread of the item and a rapid increase in page views. When a popular blog links to a post on a relatively unknown site, traffic to that site suddenly skyrockets.

Some blogs are labors of love for friends or hobbyists, with bloggers earning a little revenue when visitors click on ads or contribute to a "tip jar." Other blogs belong to conventional media organizations and employ teams of contributors to update frequently. AOL, for instance, continues to expand its blog empire devoted to finance, politics, music, and other topics, all staffed by freelancers and journalists. These blogs are more like online, interactive magazines, earning revenue from advertising.[10] A key reason people return again and again to favorite blogs is to check for updates, so frequent posting is essential. The sheer volume can lead to quite a lot of junk. One blog reader commented,

> "Give an infinite number of monkeys typewriters and they'll produce the works of Shakespeare. Unfortunately, I feel like I'm reading all the books where they didn't."[11]

Others see it quite differently, noting that user-friendly blogging software gives voice to millions of people outside the mainstream media. For companies, blogging provides a channel for a more personal relationship with customers. Whether you see the blogosphere as a blessing or calamity depends on your point of view, but there is no question that this relatively simple collaborative technology has an immense impact.

FIGURE 8-9

Examples of corporate blogs.

Patagonia	Outdoor clothing	"The Cleanest Line" has the feel of a travel guide, with off-beat stories such as "Skateboarding in Tibet"
Zillow	Real estate infomediary	This site offers useful tips and advice for prospective home buyers.
GE Reports	Electric appliances	General Electric's no frills blog features storytelling to inform the public.
IBM Software Blog	Computer services	Discussions are provided about how software is changing people's lives.
Disney Parks Blog	Amusement parks	The site takes visitors behind the scenes to share what makes the parks successful.

Wikis

Another significant Web 2.0 technology that facilitates end-user contributions and collaborative editing is the **wiki**, a website that allows users to add and edit interlinked web pages. Wiki software usually offers simple text editing tools, so users need not know HTML. It keeps track of versions and lets users view the history of changes to each page, along with discussions about the page's content. Users navigate within a wiki by doing a keyword search or by clicking on the many embedded links to related wiki pages.

Wikis have also emerged as valuable tools within organizations, especially to centralize documents and create knowledge storehouses that employees can edit as needed. The wiki makes it easy for people in any unit or any level of the organization to make contributions from their own personal experience or to update existing articles with current information. Such wikis can become a substantial base of knowledge for an organization, useful for training new employees and organizing all the how-to guides.

PRODUCTIVITY TIP
When you need to enliven your paper or presentations with images, sounds, or videos, visit Wikimedia Commons (http://commons.wikimedia.com). The site is a free media repository, and anyone can contribute to it. For whatever you do use, check the license restrictions, which might ask you to credit the original creator, for instance.

The online encyclopedia called *Wikipedia* is the best-known publicly accessible wiki. With millions of articles contributed by volunteers around the world, the nonprofit Wikipedia is the most popular general-purpose reference work on the net. In general, studies find that the encyclopedia's accuracy rivals more traditional competitors, but critics point to problems with bias, exacerbated by the site's open structure that allows anyone promoting an agenda to edit articles. Corporations and government agencies are known to quietly edit entries about themselves to put out the best spin wherever possible. Occasionally the site blocks people from changing an article, especially when it deals with controversial current events.

More than 85% of Wikipedia's contributors are men, and the lopsided gender ratio appears to lead to some bias in coverage. For instance, articles on baseball cards and videogames are longer and more detailed compared with articles that might have more appeal for women. The site is actively encouraging more women to participate.[12]

Social Networking

Nearly two-thirds of American adults use social networking sites. While younger adults ages 18 to 29 are more likely to maintain one or more sites, usage among older adults age 65 or older has skyrocketed in recent years. Men and women engage in social networking at about the same rates, as do people of different racial and ethnic backgrounds.[13] Social networks have become the de facto platform for collaboration and online asynchronous interaction.

The core element of these sites is the individual or organizational profile, with photos, hobbies, education, and other details. The sites usually include a "wall" on which the user can post updates, adding commentary, links, or images about current happenings.

The value of these social network sites, though, is that the profiles are nodes in a vast, interdependent network of links to other nodes created by other people or organizations

---

blog
Short for "web log," and used to facilitate collaboration and knowledge sharing. Posts are displayed in reverse chronological order so that the most recent appears on top.

wiki
Web software frequently used to build knowledge bases that allows users to add and edit interlinked web pages.

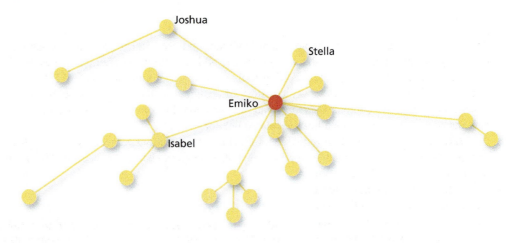

FIGURE 8-10

Interconnected nodes in a social networking site. Emiko's connection to Isabel leads to four more connections, but her link to Stella does not expand Emiko's network yet.

(Figure 8-10). The users build this network themselves as they link to friends or colleagues. Some connections may be suggested by the software itself, perhaps because the other person attended the same college. worked for the same company, or has several connections in common.

For users, the value of social networking sites can be quite high, offering a platform to nurture or renew connections that might otherwise fade away. Network effects, described in Chapter 2, increase the value of these services, simply because more people use them. Social network developers ensure that finding friends is easy because their goal is to increase membership and internal links.

For companies, these sites offer a means to support knowledge sharing in the company and also to reach people who may be interested in their products or services. Network interconnections help messages leap from one network of friends to the next. Ads can be tailored to reach precise target groups based on their members' profiles. Beyond advertising, organizations create their own profiles as a means to connect with their customers, recruit new employees, announce new products, and generally promote their brands.

Traditional brick-and-mortar corporations take good advantage of social media to build awareness in creative ways. Moe's Southwest Grill, for instance, attracted millions of viewers with its wacky YouTube video featuring tomatoes, watermelons, and eggs exploding in a microwave oven. The message was that "Microwaves Ruin Everything" and Moe's restaurant doesn't use them to reheat food.[14]

FIGURE 8-11

Top reasons for taking a break from Facebook.[15]

Was too busy/Didn't have time for it	21%
Just wasn't interested/Just didn't like it	10%
Waste of time/Content was not relevant	10%
Too much drama/gossip/negativity/conflict	9%

Source: From Coming and Going on Facebook by Lee Rainie, Aaron Smith and Maeve Duggan. Copyright © 2013 by Pew Research Center Internet & American Life Project. Used by permission of Pew Research Center Internet & American Life Project.

While Facebook remains the market leader with many more users compared with other social networks, some research suggests that Facebook "fatigue" may be settling in, at least for college students. Concerns about privacy are common, and students expressed annoyance with the level of "drama," the ads, and the constant notifications.[16] Another study found that about 61% of current users said they have taken "Facebook breaks" for several weeks, and 20% stopped using the site altogether. Figure 8-11 lists some of the main reasons users chose to take a break.[17] Advertisers watch such trends closely to focus on obtaining the best return on investment, and time will tell how Facebook fares against the rising popularity of social networking sites such as Pinterest, Tumblr, and Instagram.

Microblogging

Katy Perry, Lady Gaga, and Justin Bieber are among the top Twitter users, with many millions of followers each. They tweet very frequently, with impromptu and intimate 140-character messages that create a constant connection with youthful fans in a way that surpasses the one-way websites that other celebrities build (Figure 8-12).

FIGURE 8-12

Sample tweets from Lady Gaga.

Lady Gaga   REPLY

Going in for surgery now. Thank you so much for sending me love and support. I will be dreaming of you.

Lady Gaga   REPLY

since im living nowhere right now and live on the road with my props+wigs.(which is everything I own) i suppose my fans, in a way, livewithme

---

Microblogging is a form of blogging in which the posts are quite short, containing a brief sentence fragment and perhaps a link to another web resource or video. As in a blog, the entries appear in reverse chronological order. The topics range widely, from simple personal updates to headlines from the *New York Times* or announcements from General Motors. The social media aspect exists because users are able to "follow" other users without having to ask for consent. Then that person's posts constantly appear on followers' computer screens or mobile devices. Followers can reply to posts or repeat them for the benefit of their own followers.

TWITTER

Twitter dominates microblogging, and the terms *tweet* and *retweet* are widely used to describe the basic elements of this collaborative technology. As simple as it sounds, the real-time updates enrich online group dynamics with a level of connectedness that many consider a significant leap for social media, especially because they extend the advantages of text messaging to interconnected social networks. Microblogging offers features that few thought would be valuable when the service was first launched. The news that a distant friend had pancakes for breakfast turned out to be more interesting than expected, at least for some. Even what seems to be pointless babble can serve a role in human interaction.

TWITTER AND MARKETING

Advertisers promote products on Twitter by relying on the social networks. For example, SponsoredTweets.com is a marketplace that brings together people with large followings and advertisers who want them to tweet something nice about their products. Big names can charge thousand of dollars per tweet to reach their followers with a product endorsement.

Companies also use Twitter in creative ways to build stronger ties to customers. For example, Old Spice and Taco Bell engaged and amused their followers by poking fun at one another. @OldSpice tweeted, "Why is it that 'fire sauce' isn't made with any real fire? Seems like false advertising." @TacoBell tweeted back, "Is your deodorant made with really old spices?"

Twitter also offered Vine, in which users could share 6-second videos that loop continuously. Although companies often struggled to find ways to use 6 seconds productively, the format did open up new possibilities.[18] For example, CNN posted Vines that featured "behind the scenes" clips of reporters en route to a breaking news event. Home improvement store Lowe's posted brief "how to" videos, such as one on how to use a magnet to find a stud behind a wall so you can hang a picture. The short format demanded a new kind of storytelling, much like Twitter's text limit required people to communicate in new ways. However, the format didn't catch on as expected, and Twitter pulled the plug on the Vine application.[19]

HASHTAGS

The users themselves added their own conventions to make microblogging more useful. They began using the **hashtag** in which posts on a similar topic all include a keyword prefixed by a #. The practice caught on, especially because it made it easier to search for posts about particular subjects. Twitter encouraged the practice by hyperlinking the hashtags so that a single click would bring up a list of matches. Hashtags have become popular on other social networks as well, such as Facebook and YouTube.

Hashtags are also used to identify trending topics in geographical areas. As users repeat a hashtag and retweet posts containing them, Twitter's information systems tally the results in real time. The ones with the most posts become "Trending Topics" on the front page, and a topic can rise to the top very quickly. Organizations watch this closely in case a public relations storm is brewing that involves them.

Virtual Worlds and Virtual Reality

The **virtual world** is a graphical, often 3D environment in which users can immerse themselves, interacting with virtual objects and with one another using avatars. Sitting at a computer screen with a keyboard, mouse, joysticks, console controls, steering wheels, or foot

---

microblogging
A form of blogging in which the posts are quite short, and especially suitable for mobile devices. As in a blog, the entries appear in reverse chronological order.

hashtag
Microblogging tool invented by web users in which posts on a similar topic all include a keyword prefixed by a #.

virtual world
A graphical, often 3D environment in which users can immerse themselves, interacting with virtual objects and one another using avatars.

pedals, users can explore digitally constructed worlds or pilot vehicles through realistic terrain. They can also change the camera perspective to see their own avatar, a virtual representation of themselves that could be fantastical or quite lifelike.

One hashtag that companies watch closely is #boycott because a consumer protest can mount very quickly. Using sentiment analysis, researchers find that Twitter-generated boycotts often arise to protest human rights abuses, questionable business strategies, corporate failures, or environmental issues. Target, Starbucks, SeaWorld, the Gap, Boston Children's Hospital, and many other organizations have been targets of these campaigns.[20]

These simulated environments create virtual reality, a term that describes what people experience when some of their sensory input is not from the real world but from a computer-generated one. Virtual world inhabitants can often tailor their avatar's appearance and control its movements, facial expressions, and body postures. They type into text chat boxes to communicate or use microphones to speak with other characters in the world, who may be automated bots or avatars controlled by other users.

These engaging online spaces are widely used for multiuser games such as World of Warcraft as well as for training simulations. The U.S. Air Force, for instance, launched its own virtual world called *MyBase* on Second Life. Visitors can take a virtual tour of an Air Force base, fly a P-51 Mustang, and learn more about job possibilities. Virtual worlds are extremely useful for simulating dangerous situations such as combat or urban warfare. They also offer safe ways to train people who work in environments such as offshore drilling platforms and chemical manufacturing plants (Figure 8-13).

Advanced virtual reality systems enhance the illusion of physical immersion in a virtual world even further by adding other technologies, so that immersion is far more complete than it is for the 3D worlds that appear on a computer screen. Stereoscopic goggles, for instance, can present aspects of the virtual world that match the user's actual body posture, movements,

FIGURE 8-13

Virtual worlds can be used to train workers who fight fires or tackle other problems in dangerous environments.

Source: Copyright © by Ambient Performance. Used by permission of Ambient Performance.

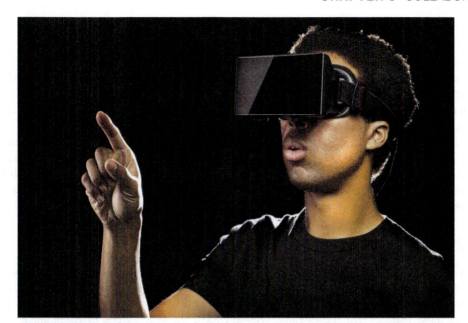

Source: Rommel Canlas/Shutterstock

FIGURE 8-14
Virtual reality headset.

or head turns (Figure 8-14). Specially wired gloves can reproduce the sensations of actually touching and manipulating virtual objects.

The Oculus Rift virtual reality headset is gaining attention from many industries, especially gaming. Combined with specialized software, users can be placed into a variety of game-like environments, such as a rock climbing simulator or a tower defense game.[21] Two or more users in different locations can also enter the same virtual environment at the same time, opening up possibilities for interactions. As the technology improves, many other industries beyond gaming will likely develop software for the devices. Organizations may start using it to hold business meetings in which people who are far apart geographically can shake their virtual hands and sit next to one another in a virtual meeting space.

Beyond business meetings, virtual reality can recreate *any* environment for humans to explore, from a tiny blood cell to the vast emptiness of space. For engineers, the ability to collaborate on the design of component parts, regardless of how small or large, offers exciting possibilities. The opportunities for educators to simulate live classrooms are equally intriguing.

Unified Communications

 Explain how unified communications contribute to collaboration.

A significant advance in collaboration is less about the technologies themselves and more about how they are integrated with one another and how people use them. **Unified communications (UC)** integrates multiple applications and communications channels into a single interface, accessible from many different devices. Although the technologies are not new, a unified approach can bring together real-time communication.[22]

Capabilities for Unified Communications

To succeed at unifying the fragmented communication world most of us now live in, the technology should offer a number of different and seamlessly integrated features:

- Voice calls
- Conferencing (audio, video, web)
- Messaging (email, voicemail)

virtual reality
Describes what people experience when some of their sensory input is not from the real world but from a computer-generated one. Technologies such as stereoscopic goggles and specially wired gloves enhance the illusion of physical immersion.

unified communications (UC)
Technology that integrates multiple communications channels and applications into a single interface, which is accessible from many different devices.

- Instant messaging
- Presence awareness

A unified communications approach should also work well on many different types of clients, from mobile smartphones and tablets to regular desktops and laptops. Ideally, the interfaces should be as similar as possible so people don't struggle with new learning curves. The system should also integrate well with the company's enterprise databases so that contact information for customers, suppliers, and coworkers is not duplicated.

The system should also adjust to communication preferences and adapt to the user's current context. For instance, it might let people who want to reach you know whether you're on a long road trip; if so, you might be available for hands-free cell-phone conversations but not IM or videoconferencing. The driver could direct email to the cell phone's text-to-speech application to have it read aloud.

Universal Dashboards

Universal dashboards are emerging that help people manage their unified communications, providing quick access to context indicators, email, secure instant messaging, voice and video calling, conference calling, corporate tweets, and more. Some software, for instance, integrates those features and allows employees to choose the best method of communicating with coworkers based on their context indicator. When a colleague is talking on the phone, the person's status will automatically switch to show that, so coworkers know that phoning the person at that moment would be a waste of time. The software can also integrate with the company's ERP and customer relationship management system to launch detailed contact information on the screen based on the incoming caller ID. That could help eliminate long pauses when a caller says, "Hi, this is Bill," and you can't quite place the voice. Accessible from desktops or smartphones, the dashboard creates a constant link between the individual and his or her contacts and information resources, one that can be configured based on personal preferences and current status.

The market for unified communications technologies is growing rapidly with fierce competition among vendors such as Cisco, IBM, Microsoft, and others. The integration of communication capabilities also enables new kinds of workplace design in which people can work very productively from different locations. At the same time, the company benefits from reduced travel costs and less need for expensive real estate.[23] Collaborative technologies are constantly improving, not just because bandwidth is increasing but because developers adapt the technologies to human needs and add features that accommodate human behavior, as we see in the next section.

Describe features of online environments that can affect human behavior and group dynamics, and identify strategies to make virtual teams more productive and successful.

 # 4 The Human Element and Collaborative Technologies

Human beings have had thousands of years to refine their strategies for productive interactions in face-to-face settings but only a couple of decades to Figure out how best to collaborate virtually. Much communication is through typed text, and without the nonverbal cues that add richness and meaning to any communication, the unexpected can happen. Missteps lead to miscommunication, hurt feelings, flame wars, dysfunctional teams, lost jobs, and even lawsuits. A key reason for these problems is that online communication is not the same as face-to-face conversation. We also underestimate how much the online environment can affect behavior, just as any environment—from the beach to the office—affects how we behave.

Psychological Characteristics of Online Environments

Online environments vary a great deal, but some common themes that affect behavior appear in many of them (Figure 8-15).

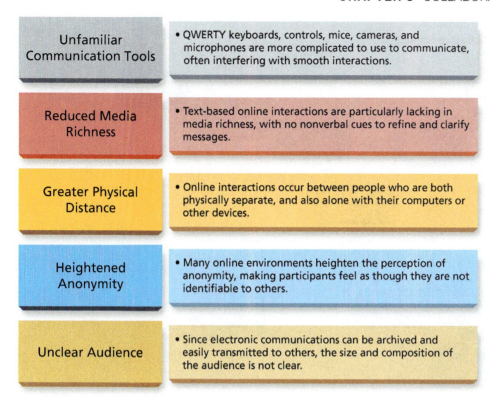

FIGURE 8-15
Characteristics of online environments that distinguish them from face-to-face settings.

UNFAMILIAR TOOLS

We use unfamiliar tools to interact online, often stumbling over them in the effort to make our interactions productive. The QWERTY keyboard is one example, particularly on a smartphone screen. Typing is not the same as speaking, though people often try to use the keyboard to simulate spoken conversations rather than more formal written correspondence. As collaborative technologies add new capabilities, people struggle with complex controls and settings that can cause frustration.

MEDIA RICHNESS

Media richness measures how well a communication medium can reproduce all the nuances and subtleties of the message it transmits. Media richness is usually starkly lower online than face-to-face, even with interactive video. Many communications are text only, leaving out facial expression, eye contact, voice pitch and tempo, gestures, and body posture. Although words carry meaning, most of what people communicate is actually nonverbal. Imagine your boss texting, "you won't be late??" You might interpret that as a simple question or a criticism about tardiness. It's difficult to know if the second question mark was just a keyboard slip.

Figure 8-16 compares various technologies with respect to their support for media richness and interactivity.

PHYSICAL DISTANCE

Another important variable is the combination of physical distance and lack of physical presence. Online interactions typically take place between people who are geographically separate not just from one another but from other people as well. There is no human face looking straight at you as you type, no smile, arched brow, or puzzled expression to signal with immediate nonverbal cues how the other person is reacting. Distance also contributes to a sense of physical safety, so people take more risks with their words.

ANONYMITY

A feature common to online games and public discussion forums is anonymity. When people have a sense that others don't know who they are, their behavior can change considerably. In some settings, this is helpful. GDSS, for instance, relies on moderate anonymity in a small workgroup to encourage people to contribute freely. But in other settings, anonymity can lead to problems because people feel less accountable for their actions.

media richness
A measure of how well a communication medium can reproduce all the nuances and subtleties of the messages it transmits.

FIGURE 8-16

Interactivity and media richness in different collaborative technologies.

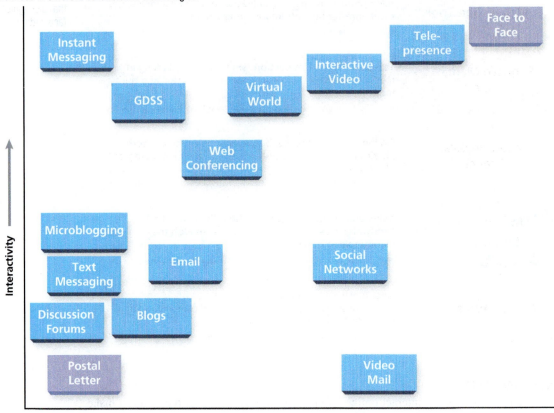

THE ETHICAL FACTOR Flash Mobs and Free Speech: Should Police Block Mobile Messaging Services?

Flash mobs, whether they erupt for a celebration or riot, are difficult to stop. Concerns about the violent variety are mounting, particularly when the rioters smash store windows, loot shops, and attack bystanders. Government officials are struggling to find ways to counter these spontaneous eruptions that are enabled by collaborative technologies.

In certain cases, the participants use mobile group messaging services such as Twitter to organize. The nature of text-based communications promotes a certain amount of disinhibition, and people feel less accountable for their actions.

Some authorities advocate cutting off mobile services in danger zones. Addressing the problem of violent flash mobs in London, former British Prime Minister David Cameron once proposed imposing limits on communications channels that the rioters were thought to be using to organize—in this case, Blackberry Messenger services. In San Francisco, the Bay Area Rapid Transit system shut off cellular signals at some stations, hoping to block riders from using group messaging to organize a protest. Cleveland's City Council voted unanimously to criminalize the use of social media tools to organize unruly flash mobs.

The ethical implications of such measures, and their constitutionality with respect to free speech, are under scrutiny. Cutting off mobile service to certain areas is a drastic move that would also hinder normal communications and 911 emergency calls. Shutting down the Blackberry service in parts of London, for instance, would prevent innocent people from warning their families to stay away. Cleveland mayor Frank Jackson vetoed his council's proposal, saying, "To make a criminal activity of just having a conversation, whether some acts of criminal activity are associated with it or not, it goes beyond reason." When the council voted again, most took a second look and agreed with the mayor.

Police departments are learning how to monitor group messaging and other social media for signs of criminal activity, and these strategies may be more effective than trying to block the services when the flash mob appears. Philadelphia's Police Commissioner stressed, "Social networking is not the issue. It's how people are misusing it to gather and then commit a crime."

AUDIENCE

Online interactions are always somewhat blurry in terms of who is in the audience. When you receive an email with a large distribution list, you might easily click "reply to all" by mistake when you intended to just reply to the sender. This common blunder might be just a minor embarrassment, or it could wreck a career. People often treat online interactions as casual chats, forgetting that email is archived on company servers where it can be resurrected years later. Electronic communications can also be forwarded to others or publicly released—with or without the sender's consent.

PRODUCTIVITY TIP

Choose your communication channel wisely. If the discussion is sensitive or when it must be completely confidential, text-based communication is a poor choice. Also, quickly switch to the phone, interactive video, or face-to-face if text is confusing or tense.

How do these characteristics of electronic communication influence human behavior, social interactions, and virtual teamwork? These technologies are enormously valuable in allowing communication to occur anytime, anywhere, but they also introduce new twists that may cause uncomfortable bumps that hinder smooth working relationships.

Managing Online Impressions

People form impressions quickly using social categories, particularly age, gender, ethnicity, and physical attractiveness. When many of those cues are not obvious, as they are not in the introductory email in Figure 8-17, they use whatever they can to form some kind of impression, and so miscalculations are common online. In the email to Allen Barron, Jun's formal, businesslike approach with its British tilt conveys the impression of someone quite different from the impression he'd make in a face-to-face setting.

FIGURE 8-17

Managing impressions with introductory emails.

1 February 2014

Dear Mr. Allen Barron,

It is with great honour that we join you in this important project to develop a marketing campaign for clients. Please be kindly aware of the large difference in time zones so we hope to agree on acceptable meeting times to create the programme.

Yours faithfully,
Jun Chang

Social media with photos and videos add physical appearance back into the mix, and Jun's profile page shows him as a hip, twentyish motorcyclist. Social networking adds an unusual feature to online impression management that has no parallel in face-to-face settings. Visiting Jun's Orkut site reveals his friendship network, which includes dozens of college-age buddies, one with pink hair and another with tattoos. People will form an impression of Jun based not just on his own profile but also on his friends. The contrast between Jun's professional email and his Orkut profile is stark, and managing online impressions is a challenge for everyone.

PRODUCTIVITY TIP

Employers often visit a candidate's social networking site as a screening tool before making a hiring decision. To manage your online persona, take into account the impression it makes on different audiences and carefully review your privacy settings.

Group Dynamics in Virtual Teams

Organizations are eager to leverage collaborative technologies to create virtual teams, drawing on people's expertise regardless of their physical locations and reducing travel expenses in the bargain. But how do these groups fare compared to the face-to-face variety? How does the online environment affect group dynamics and the success of the group's efforts?

DEVELOPING GROUP NORMS

Within organizations, people usually learn norms from one another as they watch what others do and experience subtle praise or rebuke, often nonverbal. At a face-to-face meeting, for instance, a stony silence from group members

PRODUCTIVITY TIP

Student project teams usually conduct a great deal of their work online, through email, text messages, and shared workspaces, for instance. A team charter that includes elements such as those listed in Figure 8-18 will help establish norms that build productive and trusting relationships and avoid misunderstandings.

when a latecomer arrives will forcefully communicate a "let's always start on time" norm. Online, though, group members can't perceive the nonverbal cues, so group norms can be

FIGURE 8-18

Tips for developing a team charter.

Elements of a Team Charter	Sample Questions to Answer
Leadership	What role does the leader play? How is the leader chosen? What happens when the leader is unavailable?
Meeting Protocols	How often will the group meet using synchronous technologies, and how will meeting times be decided? Will meetings start on time?
Communication	How will the group interact, and what collaborative technologies will it use? How often should each member check email or team workspaces? How quickly are members expected to respond to email? Is it OK for team members to IM each other during meetings? What information is considered confidential, for team members only?
Conflict Resolution	How will the team members resolve disagreements among members? How will members communicate dissatisfaction with the performance of other team members?
Decision Making	How will the team members come to decisions?
Task Definition, Work Allocations, and Deadlines	How will the team define the task, and what constitutes a successful outcome? How will the team allocate work and determine deadlines?
Team Member Evaluation	How will team leaders and members evaluate the performance of each team member? What significance will evaluations have in terms of grade or other outcome?

more difficult to establish. For example, virtual team members often complain that one or two members are free riding and failing to do their share of the work. Norms about how workload should be shared are more difficult to transmit and enforce online.

Successful virtual team leaders compensate for weak norms by making the expectations much more explicit. They may prepare a written team agreement or team charter with very precise language because it helps clarify exactly what is expected from team members without having to rely on nonverbal communication to convey norms.

DISINHIBITION

Online environments often lead to disinhibition, in which people express themselves more bluntly, abruptly, or aggressively than they would in face-to-face settings. Their messages lack the verbal softeners and nonverbal nuances that make consensus easier to reach. Allen might type, "I disagree with Jun," rather than the less assertive, "I am not quite sure I can agree completely with what Jun said." But Allen can't see Jun wince or roll his eyes, so he doesn't know his remark's impact. A smiley face icon may soften the message a little, but that same icon might also be interpreted as sarcasm. And accidentally pressing the CAPS LOCK key so that the communication is sent in all capital letters equates to shouting.

The other aspect of disinhibition is heightened self-disclosure, and this, too, appears more often in online interactions. On blogs, for example, endless streams of highly personal updates are common, partly because the writer can't see his or her followers yawning.

Disinhibition is more extreme in relatively anonymous text-based environments, which is why outrageous flame wars break out in open online forums. Virtual teams are less affected, but distance and lack of media richness contribute to this phenomenon, so misunderstandings can occur even in long-standing teams.

STATUS EQUALIZATION

The online world tends to flatten out hierarchies and equalize status, partly because many of the cues used to establish status are less apparent. A text message, for example, doesn't draw attention to the sender's top-floor corner office or CFO title. Collaborative technologies also empower people to communicate with others and participate on virtual teams regardless of hierarchical boundaries.

Status doesn't go away, of course; even so, virtual team leaders know they do not have the same power as they might in a face-to-face setting. For example, team leaders can bring a face-to-face meeting to closure and end the discussion of a controversial topic more easily than they can terminate a testy email exchange.

Status is partly conveyed through physical appearance, and even variables such as height matter. Other things being equal, taller people tend to have a slight advantage over shorter ones in group discussions because height conveys a sense of power and status. Online, status can sometimes be manipulated in subtle ways by altering how tall the person appears to be. For a video conference, placing the webcam a little too high can make you look shorter, but placing the camera a little lower enhances height, improves your status, and adds to your power to persuade.[24]

PRODUCTIVITY TIP

When you use a webcam or smartphone camcorder for interactive video sessions, consider the position of the lens. A little below eye level will enhance height without creating an eerie, threatening look. To simulate eye contact when you want to make a strong point, look directly into the lens.

The use of avatars adds another fascinating element to perceptions of status in online group dynamics, a feature that becomes more important for interactions involving virtual reality. When people negotiate as avatars, researchers can change their heights far more than a shift in camera angles. People who are given a taller avatar to control tend to negotiate aggressively and win against people assigned to shorter ones, regardless of their actual heights. Interestingly, the effect spills over to subsequent face-to-face interactions, so that the person manipulating the tall avatar continues to negotiate more forcefully after resuming his or her own physical stature, at least for a short period.[25]

TRUST

Trust develops over time, and it is not easy for virtual teams to create it. Working in the same building, coworkers see each other often—at lunch, in the elevator, at nearby shopping centers. They have considerable "face time," even when they are not working on the same project. They learn they can count on one another for a ride home or a small loan.

For virtual teams, especially newly created ones containing members who have never met, trust is fragile. The team can develop a less robust form of swift trust, based on the members' strong task orientation and their frequent communications. But it can break down when people have little knowledge of their teammates' context. Jun's American teammates might not know about a monsoon in Hong Kong that knocked out communications. Instead, they might assume he was slacking off or partying if he misses an important meeting.

Technology glitches are not uncommon, and they also can weaken trust. In one case, a team at an organization's California headquarters planned an interactive videoconference with a remote team in Oregon and began by playing a video for both teams to see. Due to a glitch, the screen in Oregon was blank. The Oregon team assumed they were being intentionally excluded. Miffed, they got up and left. When the video ended, the California participants saw only the empty couch in Oregon on their screen, which made it look as if the Oregon teammates didn't think the meeting was important.[26]

Research shows that an initial face-to-face meeting can enhance trust in virtual teams, often dramatically. Meeting the people you are about to work with, even through interactive video, makes a difference. Instead of having only typed words in an email, your teammates can match a name with a face and a smile.

Making Virtual Teams Work

The challenges of virtual teamwork have led some companies, such as Yahoo, to terminate telecommuting, arguing that people need to interact face-to-face to generate those sparks of innovation.[27] Other companies are creating regional hubs, where remote workers can collaborate without having to commute every day,[28] or experimenting with other telecommuting models.[29]

But even for people who come to a physical workplace every day, virtual teamwork is still critical because so much work is accomplished that way. Knowing how group dynamics unfold online and how collaborative technologies can best support teamwork will help improve the chances for success. Figure 8-19 lists some tips for virtual team members and also for team leaders. Whether the team is composed of students working on a class project, or employees from far-flung corners of a multinational company, these principles can greatly facilitate a team's productivity. They can also make virtual teamwork more satisfying, and more resistant to the pitfalls of online collaboration.

FIGURE 8-19

Tips for making virtual teams work.

Tips for Virtual Team Members

▶ Appoint a leader (if one has not already been appointed) and clarify the leader's role.
▶ Develop a written team charter to ensure team members agree on goals, expectations for work styles, conflict resolution, and team member evaluation strategies.
▶ Agree on a decision-making strategy.
▶ Practice with the technologies before they are needed for intense tasks with upcoming deadlines.
▶ Proactively volunteer for assignments, focusing especially on how your own skill sets can best contribute to the team's success.
▶ Use a high-tech, high-touch approach. Hold an in-person meeting or interactive video session at the start of the project to build trust.
▶ Communicate and share information frequently, even more than required by the team agreement.
▶ Review your communications for any effects of disinhibition that may inadvertently offend.
▶ Let team members know about any change in your context, such as a family emergency, blizzard, or illness.

Tips for Virtual Team Leaders

▶ Get to know each team member, both to build trust and to understand how each person can best contribute.
▶ Arrange a synchronous session and invite members to introduce themselves to kick off the project, using interactive video, in-person meetings, conference call, or chat.
▶ Use the kick-off meeting to raise awareness of any differences in culture or working styles.
▶ Use a relatively structured leadership style, with clearly documented assignments, deadlines, and expectations.
▶ Enhance group cohesiveness and team identity through team-building exercises, team charter, and other means.
▶ Choose collaborative technologies wisely and arrange training to ensure team members know how to use them. Use synchronous collaborative tools, preferably with video, to discuss sensitive topics.
▶ Encourage participation by all members, contacting any who have contributed little to learn why.
▶ Send out frequent reminders about upcoming events and deadlines.
▶ Use encouragement and praise publicly, but convey constructive criticism privately.

MyMISLab
Online Simulation

DEPARTMENT OF SOCIAL SERVICES
A Role-Playing Simulation on Collaborative Technologies and Virtual Teamwork

Everyone at the Department of Social Services in Newton is really tired of wasting time in traffic and paying high gas prices. They want to convince management to allow them to use virtual teamwork part of the time. They have to travel enough as it is, visiting homes, hospitals, shelters, and the county jail. Why do they have to drive to the office every day when they could be meeting virtually to review case files or submitting their paperwork electronically? That would also give them more time to be out in the community. They think the benefits far outweigh the drawbacks, and virtual teamwork would save the department money, too. But it's important to start off right.

As someone who knows something about collaborative technologies, you are asked by your coworkers to join a task force to discuss how to proceed. Log in when you're ready to start brainstorming....

LEARNING OBJECTIVES

1 Collaborative technologies have evolved rapidly, beginning with email and its enhanced features that support contact management with address books and time management with calendaring. Discussion forums, instant messaging, and texting provide support for text-based collaboration, and each technology adds slightly different features to support human interaction. IM, for instance, adds presence awareness, so colleagues can see one another's current status. Texting is widely used for mobile communications and emergency alerts. Group conversation software supports persistent chat among group members and integrates with other external services. Collaborative technologies designed for groups include group decision support systems (GDSS), web conferencing, and shared workspaces. GDSS is usually used for face-to-face group meetings in an attempt to promote brainstorming by allowing members to make contributions anonymously via their computers. Web conferencing supports synchronous online meetings for people at different locations using webcams, audio, interactive whiteboards, desktop application sharing, and other features. Shared workspaces provide teams with server space to support information resource libraries and asynchronous interactions. Interactive video is included in many of these technologies. High-end systems can create a sense of telepresence.

2 Web 2.0 and more advanced technologies provide extensive collaborative support with blogs, wikis, social networking, microblogging, virtual worlds, and virtual reality. Organizations are using these tools to support their own collaborative efforts but also to reach out to customers and suppliers. Social networking sites, for example, offer endless possibilities for targeted marketing based on users' profiles.

3 Unified communications bring together multiple collaborative technologies and applications, simplifying the interfaces and making them accessible through many different devices. With context indicators, users can signal the best way to communicate with them at particular times. Universal dashboards aggregate the collaborative services into a single customizable interface.

4 Key characteristics of online environments that affect human behavior include the unfamiliar tools used to communicate, reduced media richness, greater physical distance, heightened perceptions of anonymity, and unclear audience. Managing impressions can be challenging because of these characteristics. Virtual teams may experience more difficulty developing group norms and building trust, and their members may show more disinhibition. However, online groups tend to show more status equalization. Strategies for making virtual teams work more effectively stress the need to take into account the way online environments affect human behavior.

KEY TERMS AND CONCEPTS

SMTP server	presence awareness	telepresence	hashtag
IMAP (Internet mail access protocol)	war room	shared workspace	virtual world
microformats	group decision support system (GDSS)	blog	virtual reality
instant messaging (IM)	web conferencing	wiki	unified communications (UC)
		microblogging	media richness

CHAPTER REVIEW QUESTIONS

8-1. What are the seven major collaborative technologies? What feature or features does each technology offer for communication and productivity?

8-2. What are the five Web 2.0 technologies that facilitate collaboration? What features does each technology provide?

8-3. What is presence awareness? How does it add value to instant messaging? What are examples of ways that presence awareness facilitates collaboration?

8-4. What are unified communications? What are examples of integrated features of unified communications? How do unified communications contribute to collaboration?

8-5. What are the five distinguishing features of online environments? How does each affect human behavior?

8-6. What are group norms? How does the online environment affect group norms? What is disinhibition? What are other ways in which the online environment influences group dynamics?

8-7. How can virtual team members make their teams more successful? What are some of the things virtual team leaders can do to make their teams more successful?

PROJECTS AND DISCUSSION QUESTIONS

8-8. Email: Do you love it or hate it? How much time do you spend processing your email every day—deciding what it is, deleting it, filing it, answering it, or deferring it for later action? Are there occasions when you would prefer to use instant messaging? Describe the basic functionality of email and instant messaging and discuss the primary uses/purposes of each. What are the advantages of email? Of instant messaging? What are the disadvantages of each?

8-9. The first GDSS was developed in the early 1980s but not by a business; the first GDSS was developed by a university. What is a GDSS? What are the advantages of using a GDSS? Are there disadvantages of using a GDSS? Can you think of specific problems with meetings that cause groups to function poorly that may be overcome by using a GDSS?

8-10. Draw a square and divide it into four equal sections. Label the horizontal axis *Interactivity* and the vertical axis *Media Richness*. Label the first column *Low* and the second column *High*. Label the first row *Low* and the second row *High*. Use this 2-by-2 grid to group the different collaborative technologies into four categories: (1) low interactivity, low media richness; (2) high interactivity, low media richness; (3) low interactivity, high media richness; (4) high interactivity, high media richness. Can you think of a specific organizational communication task that is best suited to the type of technology in each category?

8-11. Social networking sites are fast becoming corporate resources. Consider how Facebook may be used by an organization. Can you think of different ways in which organizations such as Coca-Cola, KFC, or Bank of America can use social networking? What are network effects? Search your favorite social networking site to learn how organizations are using the site.

8-12. Visit YouTube.com and search for "What is SharePoint?" View one or more of the videos you find and prepare a summary that describes how MicrosoftSharePoint is used by organizations. What are the key features of SharePoint? What are "tags," and how are they used? What is version control? What are the advantages of using SharePoint rather than a shared network drive?

8-13. Sorority meetings. Basketball practice. Your part-time job. Your social life. Is it challenging to find time in your schedule for a group project meeting? Work in a small group with classmates to implement shared calendars. Visit calendar.google.com and click on "Sign Up" to get started, or sign in with your Google account. Add your classmates' calendars by entering their contact email addresses. Create a calendar for one full month by adding events for future dates (i.e., classes, work schedule, social events) by using the various options for adding events, and then schedule a group study meeting at a time that is convenient for everyone in your group. Prepare a 5-minute presentation of your group's experience with Google Calendar that includes a list of specific features that are available. What are the advantages of shared calendars? How do they facilitate collaboration?

8-14. Online communication has evolved from newsgroups and listservs to the discussion boards of today where people post and reply to posted messages. Consider the many discussion boards that are available. Search the Internet for "music discussion board" or "movie discussion board" to locate sites such as musicboards.com, a site for musicians and music fans, and chasingthefrog.com, a site with movie games as well as discussion boards. Or visit www.big-boards.com to see a list of the most active discussion boards on the web today. Work in a small group with classmates to consider the use of discussion boards and how they may be used effectively by businesses, nonprofits, and governments. Discuss different ways in which discussion forums may be used internally and externally. Does your university use online discussion boards? If so, how are they used?

APPLICATION EXERCISES

8-15. EXCEL APPLICATION: Going Green!

Everybody talks "green." but some really do it. Marie Chong is a green home designer and builder who is producing a webinar to share her knowledge of green building. She learned that web conferencing requires only a PC and an Internet connection; however, audio conferencing capability is required if she wants to chat with attendees by telephone. Marie is working with a webinar hosting company that charges 10 cents per participant/per minute (ppm) for web conferencing, 15 cents ppm for audio conferencing, and $175 for online registration support. Although Marie will present some content herself, she will hire a professional speaker who is an expert on wind turbines for home use, and she will include audio conferencing so that attendees can interact with the speakers. The registration fee for a 60-minute webinar is $159. Create the Excel spreadsheet shown in Figure 8-20 to determine the number of attendees required for Marie to make a profit. How does that number change if Marie reduces the registration fee to $149? Use formulas for all calculations and Goal Seek to set profit to $1 by changing the number of attendees. If the registration fee is $159, how many attendees are required for Marie to make a profit of $10,000?

8-16. ACCESS APPLICATION: Cloud 9

The ad campaign that Tamara and her team developed for the Cloud 9 chain of nightclubs was a smashing success! Club owners Sally and John Gilbert report membership has doubled and event bookings are sold out months in advance. The Gilberts have implemented an Access database to track membership and events at four nightclubs. Download the Cloud 9 database Ch08Ex02 and use the Report Wizard to create reports that identify which location has the most members and which has the most bookings. Review the structure of the Cloud 9 database. Can you suggest other reports that may be useful to Sally and John?

FIGURE 8-20
Going Green spreadsheet.

	A	B	C
1	Going Green!		
2			
3	**Revenue**		**Total**
4	**Number of Attendees**		
5	Registration Fee	$159.00	
6			
7	**Expenses**		
8	Speaker Fee		$1,500.00
9	Audio Conference Service Fee (ppm)*	$ 0.10	
10	Web Conference Service Fee (ppm)*	$ 0.15	
11	Online Registration Support Costs		$ 175.00
12	Webinar Length (minutes)	60	
13			
14			
15	**Profit**		
16			
17	*per participant/per minute		

Source: Microsoft® Excel, Microsoft Corporation. Reprinted with permission.

CASE STUDY #1

Telepresence Robots Support Remote Collaboration

When a robot resembling a vacuum cleaner topped with a computer monitor rolls by you at work, you might first think it is cleaning carpets. But if it stops to say hello, and you see a coworker's smiling face on the screen, the device is probably a "telepresence robot." Many organizations are experimenting with ways to improve collaboration for remote workers, and these robots are making a very positive contribution.

The remote worker can log in to one of several wifi-connected robots the company might own and control its movements and cameras with a laptop. At meetings, the pilot can swivel the camera around to see everyone present, and the other attendees can see and hear the remote worker's face on-screen.

Several telepresence robots have entered the market, and global demand is expected to reach $7 billion by 2022. They typically have motorized wheels, a microphone, speakers, a camera that faces forward, and another camera that tilts downward so the pilot can avoid obstacles on the floor.

The key ingredient for success is to make the robots easy to drive and manipulate and also ensure they have sufficient battery power so they don't strand the remote worker in a hallway just before an important meeting. The building layout is another consideration. The robot's wheels would get stuck if there are steps, and the robot would need assistance to unlock and open doors.

Reactions to Telepresence Robots

The telepresence robot is a significant improvement over the speakerphone and even over stationary videoconferencing facilities. One remote worker who tried out an experimental version recalled that at first, "The general response was that it was kind of creepy." But very soon colleagues were asking him to roll by their cubicles for a chat. He insists it is far better for collaboration than prearranged video calls. When he is rolling his robot through the halls, people can approach him to start a spontaneous conversation or ask a quick question. He could also move from floor to floor ... if someone pressed the elevator buttons for him.

To be effective, the devices should be simple to operate with a minimum of bells and whistles that might interfere with natural interactions. They should quickly lose their novelty in the workplace so coworkers can get back to work collaborating with one another.

Some workers raise concerns about privacy when they imagine camera-equipped devices creeping up behind them. The robot's design, however, can help mitigate such concerns. A large screen that clearly displays the remote operator's face will probably be perceived as telepresence, but a mobile device with just a tiny camera lens would be interpreted as surveillance. You would wonder who was viewing you and why. Also, efforts to enable the robots to show more nonverbal communication, such as head movements and gestures, may improve the way people interact with them.

Human Resources Issues

Telepresence robots raise numerous questions that don't fit neatly into existing labor policies or laws. For example, if a remote worker lives in Texas but pilots a robot every day in California, where should the person pay taxes? If the remote worker is in another country, does the person need a visa to work? What happens if the robot trips down the stairs or causes an accident?

These issues become even more challenging when the robots do actual physical labor. Employees at a company that manufactures robots were tired of doing the dishes, so they decided to hire someone to pilot a robot to do that task. They advertised online through Amazon Mechanical Turk and found an anonymous Internet worker who learned how to pilot the device. However, employees became uncomfortable with some unknown person rolling about the company's kitchen, listening to their conversations. They decided to wash their own dishes.

Telepresence robots are already making a major contribution in medicine, where specialists can conduct live, virtual consultations with patients. Schoolchildren who can't get to school are also using the devices to "sit" in class, ask questions, and participate in discussions. As the technology improves and prices drop, expect to see these robots in many other places.

Discussion Questions

8-17. What are the benefits of telepresence robots for a company?

8-18. What are the limitations of telepresence robots?

8-19. How does the use of telepresence robots compare with traditional video conferencing?

8-20. In what other settings might telepresence robots be applicable?

Sources: $7 billion telepresence robot market strategies and forecasts, worldwide, 2016–2022—Research and markets. (March 31, 2016, March 31). *Business Wire,* http://search.proquest.com/abicomplete/docview/1776967176/abstract/FF2BBADD39B945B9PQ/4, accessed August 16, 2016.

Bamoallem, B. S., & Bamoallem, Banan S., B. (2016). The impact of head movements on user involvement in mediated interaction. *Computers in Human Behavior, 55,* 424–431.

Leber, J. (April 11, 2013). Does a tele-robot operator need a visa and W-2? *MIT Technology Review* https://www.technologyreview.com/s/513571/does-a-tele-robot-operator-need-a-visa-and-w-2/, accessed August 16, 2016.

Lehrbaum, R. (January 11, 2013). Attack of the telepresence robots. *InformationWeek,* http://www.informationweek.com/byte/personal-tech/mobile-applications/attack-of-the-telepresence-robots/240146106, accessed August 16, 2016.

Markoff, J. (September 4, 2010). The boss is robotic, and rolling up behind you. *New York Times,* http://www.nytimes.com/2010/09/05/science/05robots.html, accessed April 24, 2016.

Raths, D. (2015). 6 ways videoconferencing is expanding the classroom. *T H E Journal, 42*(4), 12–17.

The Pros and Cons of Telecommuting

With gas prices soaring and traffic congestion stealing hours from every commuter's day, organizations around the world have eagerly embraced collaborative technologies and the virtual workplace. Millions of people work at home at least one day a week, and the number continues to climb.

Bucking this trend, Yahoo! decided in 2013 that employees could no longer work from home. Yahoo! CEO Marissa Mayer's decision was accidentally leaked out through a memo signed by Yahoo's human resources director. The memo stated, *"Speed and quality are often sacrificed when we work from home We need to be one Yahoo!, and that starts with physically being together…"*

The policy change at Yahoo! triggered howls of protest from employees, and a firestorm erupted on social media. Twitter lit up with comments such as *"Hey Marissa, 1980 just called, they want their work environment back!"* and *"#Yahoo kills work flexibility and #telework options for employees. CEO is convinced it is still 1994."*

Nevertheless, other companies followed suit by reining in telecommuting options, including Best Buy and Hewlett Packard. Some federal agencies are also redoing telework policies to reduce the number of employees working outside the office.

Telecommuting "Pros"

Employees overwhelmingly support telework for its flexibility, and studies often find that workers are more productive when they are allowed to work from home. The virtual workplace benefits the employee, company, and community as well. For example, employees save as much as $1,700 per year in gasoline and other car expenses, and they add many hours to their days by eliminating commutes. Expenses for clothing, restaurant lunches, parking fees, and tolls also drop. Virtual workers enjoy greater flexibility to balance work and personal lives, which appears to reduce both stress and health problems. Dealing with child and elder care responsibilities is simplified, and disabled workers also benefit.

The company benefits by reducing real estate costs. And with less traffic on the roads, communities benefit by reducing congestion, pollution, accidents, and highway maintenance expenses. Among Fortune magazine's best companies to work for, several in the top 10 feature generous telework policies, including Cisco and Intel. Telework is also a helpful policy to recruit and retain top talent.

Telecommuting "Cons"

Despite the many benefits, research shows that telecommuting can have some serious disadvantages, particularly for high-tech companies that rely on innovation and collaboration. Twitter and Google, for instance, have no specific policy about it, but senior administrators encourage people to work at the office as much as possible to promote face-to-face collaboration. Casual, unscheduled meetings take place more freely, involving people from different departments, and that can break down barriers and spur innovation.

More face-to-face contact can also increase the speed of decision making. For example, an "open office" layout can lead to faster decision making because employees can just meet to work out the details rather than waste time with voice mail or email.

Employees who telecommute most or all of the time may also suffer setbacks in their careers compared with those who work on-site, and they may also experience lower job satisfaction because of the professional isolation. Some studies have found that telecommuters are less likely to be promoted, even if their productivity is high. Just being seen at work makes people think you're a hard worker.

Time will tell how Yahoo! fares in the future, but the decision certainly triggered heated debates about what it means to collaborate in a 21st century workplace.

Discussion Questions

8-21. What are the collaborative technologies that a company like Yahoo! would have to provide to create an effective telecommuting program? How would Yahoo! increase media richness using these technologies?

8-22. In spite of the controversy about CEO Mayer's decision to ban telecommuting, she raises valid points that might affect Yahoo!'s profitability. How could each of her concerns be overcome by providing improved collaborative technologies? Which of Mayer's issues would be insurmountable, if any?

8-23. Describe at least three human behavior challenges with telecommuting, and explain what a company like Yahoo! would have to do to overcome each of them.

8-24. Suppose that you become highly skilled with collaboration technologies and are a seasoned telecommuter. How would this affect your career? How would you represent these competencies and experiences to Yahoo!?

Sources: Allen, T. D., Golden, T. D., & Shockley, K. M. (2015). How effective is telecommuting? Assessing the status of our scientific findings. *Psychological Science in the Public Interest (Sage Publications Inc.)*, *16*(2), 40–68. http://doi.org/10.1177/1529100615593273

Chaey, C. (2013). Marissa Mayer, Yahoo, and the pros and cons of working from home. *Fast Company*, http://www.fastcompany.com/3006538/creative-conversations/marissa-mayer-yahoo-and-pros-and-cons-working-home, accessed August 16, 2016.

Colao, J. J. (2013). Marissa Mayer is wrong: Freedom for workers means productivity for companies. *Forbes.com*, http://www.forbes.com/sites/jjcolao/2013/02/26/marissa-mayer-is-wrong-freedom-for-workers-means-productivity-for-companies/#f039bd6134ee, accessed August 16, 2016.

Elgan, M. (2016). Why it's time to allow employees to work remotely. *CIO Insight*, http://www.cioinsight.com/it-management/workplace/why-its-time-to-allow-employees-to-work-remotely.html, accessed August 16, 2016.

Maucione, S. (February 29, 2016). DISA's backslide on telework heightens employee concerns. *Federal News Radio*, http://federalnewsradio.com/workforce/2016/02/disas-backslide-telework-heightens-employee-concerns/, accessed August 16, 2016.

Suddath, C. (2013). Work-from-home truths, half-truths, and myths. *Bloomberg Businessweek*, (4319), 75.

E-PROJECT 1   Estimating Breakeven Pricing for Telepresence Robots Using a Spreadsheet

In this e-project, you will use a spreadsheet and goal seeking to estimate at what price telepresence robots will become affordable, meaning they generate enough savings to pay for themselves in 1 year. Download the Excel file called *Ch08_Robots*, which includes variables that affect how much in savings will be generated, including the number of employees who will use the systems, how many trips will be saved, and average travel expenses per trip. Let's assume that a high-end robot costs $40,000 to purchase and maintain, as shown in the spreadsheet. The spreadsheet also estimates that the organization will need one robot for every two employees who will be using them.

8-25.   Use goal seeking (under Data/What If Analysis) to determine how much the company can pay for each robot and break even, so that savings minus costs = 0. You will set the cell containing the (Savings – Cost) as the Set Cell, and enter 0 in the To Value input box. The cell that can be changed is the one that represents the unit cost of a telepresence robot. How much can the company pay for each robot, using the assumptions in the spreadsheet?

8-26.   If travel expenses increase to $4,000 per trip, what should the company be willing to pay for each robot and still break even? You can change the average travel expenses, and redo the goal seeking analysis.

8-27.   To be conservative, the CEO insists that any project to implement robots should have a return on investment of at least $100,000. Assuming $4,000 per trip, 100 employees, and 10 trips per year per employee, how much should the company be willing to pay for each robot?

8-28.   It is possible the robots will be so useful that the company needs to assign one for every employee, instead of sharing them. Change the number of robots required so that all 100 employees get their own robot. Then recompute the cost the company can pay per robot, still assuming $100,000 return on investment and $4,000 travel costs. Under these assumptions, how much should the company be willing to pay per robot?

E-PROJECT 2   Estimating Savings for Virtual Work Using an Excel Model

Calculating the effects of a virtual work program requires making many assumptions about gas prices, commuting distances, productivity gains or losses, and other factors. For this e-project, you will create an Excel spreadsheet that models the effects of implementing virtual work for a hypothetical organization.

Download the Excel file called *Ch08_VirtualWorkSavings Model*.

8-29.   How does the model calculate the gasoline savings per virtual worker per year? Click on cell B21 and press F2 to display the variables used in the calculations.

8-30.   Using the assumptions in the model, how much would each virtual worker save in gasoline each year?

8-31.   If the leadership decides to implement a smaller pilot program in which those eligible work at home just 1 day every 2 weeks (0.5 day per week), what would be an employee's average savings on gas per year?

8-32.   Add more variables to the model, to show:
   a. Average cost per square foot per year ($200)
   b. Average square foot per person in an office (80 square feet)

8-33.   Add a conclusion, "Average cost per office per year," and enter the formula to compute this. What is the average cost per office per year?

8-34.   Assume that the company can eliminate an office for every 200 virtual workdays per year (regardless of who is not there). Add another conclusion, "Savings in real estate costs per year," and enter the formula that will compute it.
   a. How much could this organization save in real estate per year if they stick with one virtual workday per eligible employee per week?
   b. How much could this organization save in real estate costs per year if the average number of days per week employees will work from home goes up to 3?

CHAPTER NOTES

1 Shih, H., Lai, K., & Cheng, T. E. (2013). Informational and relational influences on electronic word of mouth: An empirical study of an online consumer discussion forum. *International Journal of Electronic Commerce*, *17*(4), 137–166. doi:10.2753/JEC1086-4415170405

2 Lebbon, A. R., & Sigurjónsson, J. G. (2016). Debunking the instant messaging myth? *International Journal of Information Management*, *36*(3), 433–440. http://doi.org/10.1016/j.ijinfomgt.2016.02.003

3 Ngak, C. (April 15, 2013). Boston Marathon: With no phones, text and social media help get out updates. *CBSNews.com*, http://www.cbsnews.com/8301-205_162-57579692/boston-marathon-with-no-phones-text-and-social-media-help-get-out-updates/, accessed May 11, 2013.

4 Consumer tips: How to communicate during a natural disaster emergency. (2015). https://www.fcc.gov/general/consumer-tips-how-communicate-during-natural-disaster-emergency, accessed April 23, 2016.

5 Deards, H. (January 19, 2009). Twitter first off the mark with Hudson plane crash coverage. *Editorsweblog.org*, http://www.editorsweblog.org/multimedia/2009/01/twitter_first_off_the_mark_with_hudson_p.php, accessed August 16, 2016.

6 Gotta, M., Basso, M., Cain, M.W., Preset, A., Rozwell, C., & Pezzini, M., M. (2016). *Cool vendors in social software and collaboration, 2016* (No. G00299736). Gartner Research, http://www.gartner.com/document/3304917?ref=solrAll&refval=169282054&qid=2760d4ab0eaea74e0beb65c2e865fbf5, accessed August 16, 2016.

7 Fletcher, O. (2010). New markets: Mash it up yourself: Global teams could benefit from evolving web conferencing tools that allow individuals to jointly use browser-based apps. *CIO Insight*, *23*(10). doi:1973263621. Retrieved January 14, 2011, from ABI/INFORM Global.

8 Curtis, S. (February 2, 2013). Cisco telepresence allows doctors to conduct virtual consultations. *CIO*, http://www.cio.com/article/728194/Cisco_Telepresence_Allows_Doctors_to_Conduct_Virtual_Consultations, accessed August 16, 2016.

9 Mackey, J. (January 23, 2016). What's next for responsibly grown. http://www.wholefoodsmarket.com/blog/whats-next-responsibly-grown, accessed August 17, 2016.

10 McLellan. (2016). *AOL Inc.* Hoover's Online, http://subscriber.hoovers.com.proxy1.library.jhu.edu/H/company360/fulldescription.html?companyId=15558000000000, accessed August 16, 2016.

11 Rosenberg, S. (2009). *Say everything: How blogging began, what it's becoming, and why it matters*. New York: Crown Publishers.

12 Dudley, E. (March 14, 2016). Hacking Wikipedia's gender gap. *Southern California Public Radio*, http://www.scpr.org/programs/the-frame/2016/03/14/47186/feminist-edit-a-thons-work-to-close-wikipedia-s-bi/, accessed August 16, 2016.

13 Perrin, A. (2015). *Social media usage: 2005-2015*. Pew Research Center, http://www.pewinternet.org/2015/10/08/social-networking-usage-2005-2015/, accessed August 16, 2016.

14 Daley, J. (2013). The social score. *Entrepreneur*, *41*(1), 132–138.

15 Pew Research Center. (2013). Top reason for taking a break from Facebook: Too busy. http://www.pewresearch.org/daily-number/top-reason-for-taking-a-break-from-facebook-too-busy/, accessed August 16, 2016.

16 Yazdanparast, A., Joseph, M., & Qureshi, A. (2015). An investigation of Facebook boredom phenomenon among college students. *Young Consumers*, *16*(4), 468–480. http://doi.org/10.1108/YC-02-2015-00506

17 Rainie, L., Smith, A., & Duggan, M. (2013). Coming and going on Facebook. Pew Research Center's Internet & American Live Project, http://www.pewinternet.org/~/media//Files/Reports/2013/PIP_Coming_and_going_on_facebook.pdf, accessed August 16, 2016.

18 Johnson, L. (2015). Why brands are ditching Twitter's 6-second Vine app. http://www.adweek.com/news/technology/why-brands-are-ditching-twitter-s-6-second-vine-app-168433, accessed April 24, 2016.

19 Titlow, J.P. (2016). Vine's surprise shutdown leaves video stars out in the cold. FastCompany.com, https://www.fastcompany.com/3065101/vines-surprise-shutdown-leaves-video-stars-out-in-the-cold, accessed October 31, 2016.

20 Makarem, S. C., & Jae, H. (2016). Consumer boycott behavior: An exploratory analysis of Twitter feeds. *Journal of Consumer Affairs*, *50*(1), 193–223. http://doi.org/10.1111/joca.12080

21 Burningham, G. (April 15, 2016). Oculus Rift isn't just coming for hardcore gamers; it's coming for your mom too. *Newsweek (Global Edition)*, *166*(14). http://search.proquest.com/abicomplete/docview/1779510493/abstract/1718CE537D3F4EC4PQ/9, accessed August 16, 2016.

22 Fernandez, M. M., & Elliot, B. (2016). *Magic quadrant for unified communications for midsize enterprises, North America* (No. G00278250). Gartner Research, http://www.gartner.com/document/3329825?ref=TypeAheadSearch&qid=18562cb976a4554d15c5412d6591a210, accessed August 16, 2016.

23 Williams, J., & LaBrie, R. C. (2015). Unified communications as an enabler of workplace redesign. *Measuring Business Excellence*, *19*(1), 81–91. http://doi.org/10.1108/MBE-11-2014-0044

24 Huang, W., Olson, J. S., & Olson, G. M. (2002). Camera angle affects dominated in video-mediated communication. *Proceedings of CHI 2002, Short Papers*. New York: ACM Press. Retrieved January 11, 2011, from ACM Digital Library.

25 Yee, N., Bailenson, J. N., & Ducheneaut, N. (2009). The Proteus effect: Implications of transformed digital self-representation on online and offline behavior. *Communication Research, 36*(2), 285–312.

26 Wallace, P. (2004). *The Internet in the workplace: How new technologies transform work*. Cambridge, UK: Cambridge University Press.

27 Weise, E., & Swartz, J. (February 26, 2013). As Yahoo ends telecommuting, others say it has benefits. *USAToday*, http://www.usatoday.com/story/money/business/2013/02/25/working-at-home-popular/1946575/, accessed August 16, 2016.

28 Johns, T., & Gratton, L. (2013). The third wave of virtual work. *Harvard Business Review, 91*(1), 66–73.

29 Allen, T. D., Golden, T. D., & Shockley, K. M. (2015). How effective is telecommuting? Assessing the status of our scientific findings. *Psychological Science in the Public Interest (Sage Publications Inc.), 16*(2), 40–68. http://doi.org/10.1177/1529100615593273

Knowledge Management and *E-Learning*

MyMISLab™

- Online Simulation: Criminal Investigations Division: A Role-Playing Simulation on Knowledge Management for Crime Scene Police Work
- Discussion Questions: #9-1, #9-2, #9-3
- Writing Assignments: #9-10, #9-11

LEARNING OBJECTIVES

1 Describe the three types of intellectual capital and show how both explicit and tacit knowledge contribute to intellectual capital.

2 Describe the steps in launching a knowledge management program, providing examples of the applicable technologies.

3 Explain how the human element can pose challenges for knowledge management projects and how managers can overcome them.

4 Describe three different approaches to e-learning.

5 Explain how to create an e-learning program and the kinds of technologies that can be applied, including the learning management system.

6 Compare and contrast corporate and educational e-learning as well as e-learning and classroom-based learning.

An online, interactive decision-making simulation that reinforces chapter contents and uses key terms in context can be found in MyMISLab™.

INTRODUCTION

INFORMATION SYSTEMS DO A SUPERB JOB OF TURNING DATA INTO INFORMATION, but the processes of creating, organizing, sharing, and acting on meaningful knowledge are more challenging. How that can be accomplished, using knowledge management and e-learning, is the subject of this chapter.

One obstacle organizations face is that much intellectual capital is semi-structured or unstructured and is also difficult to pin down. A skilled web designer's hard-earned insights about a customer interface might be found in emails, smartphone photos, drawings, videoconferences, blackboard scribbles, presentation slides, or hallway conversations. A salesperson's strategies for using social networks to engage clients might be equally difficult to hand over to others. Yet this kind of knowledge is much too valuable to lose.

In the online role-playing simulation for this chapter, called "Criminal Investigations Division," a police department is facing the loss of vital intellectual capital. Veteran detectives are retiring, and all their knowledge and experience about how to interview witnesses at a crime scene, what information to record, how to secure the chain of evidence, and much more could be lost. The incoming rookies just don't have the experience to manage these investigations on their own, and mistakes keep mounting. The department needs ways to capture this priceless intellectual capital and pass it along, and the detectives want your help to design a knowledge management program that draws on the power of information systems.

Brian A Jackson/Shutterstock

MyMISLab
Online Simulation

CRIMINAL INVESTIGATIONS DIVISION
A Role-Playing Simulation on Knowledge Management for Crime Scene Police Work

In the simulation, you will share the police department's enthusiasm for knowledge management and begin to appreciate how valuable intellectual capital can be. You will also experience first-hand some of the challenges involved, joining the detectives at a "live" crime scene to help them capture some of that knowledge about interviewing a witness.

An organization's assets—land, inventory, cash on hand—are all listed on its balance sheet and are relatively easy to valuate. Its intellectual capital isn't listed, even though it might be the most valuable asset of all. But what exactly is intellectual capital?

Describe the three types of intellectual capital and show how both explicit and tacit knowledge contribute to intellectual capital.

 # The Nature of Intellectual Capital

Intellectual capital (IC) includes all the intangible assets and resources of an enterprise that are not captured by conventional accounting reports but that still contribute to its value and help it achieve competitive advantage. Apple, for instance, might show $110 million in net tangible assets on its balance sheet, even though the firm's estimated market value is more than $500 billion.[1] The term *intellectual capital* highlights the notion that intangible factors, such as the knowledge and expertise of employees, are assets just like other kinds of capital that a firm can apply to the production of goods and services and that help determine its market value. In many cases, it is the one asset that truly distinguishes a successful company from its competitors.

Types of Intellectual Capital

Sally H. is looking forward to her retirement after 22 years with a midsized employment services firm. She gave 60 days' notice, but her swamped coworkers do not have much time to go over all her accounts. They haven't learned her secrets for keeping clients happy or recruiting the best temporary staffer for every position. Sally entered notes about each client into the company's customer relationship management (CRM) system, but the notes are just a pale shadow of her knowledge. She is also concerned that she can't pass on the strong relationships she developed with her contacts, especially in regional business schools where she recruits so much talent.

Sally possesses all three of the main types of intellectual capital, shown in Figure 9-1. They reflect the ways human beings contribute intellectual power to an organization.

HUMAN CAPITAL

Human capital includes the competencies and knowledge possessed by the organization's employees. Education plays a key role in building this capital, as do years of experience working in the field and acquiring successful strategies from experiment or mentors. Sally's vast knowledge of interview techniques, negotiating strategies, mentoring, and coaching is all part of the human capital she adds to the company.

SOCIAL CAPITAL

Social capital describes the number and quality of all the relationships an organization's employees maintain, not just with one another but with clients, customers, suppliers, and prospective employees. Sally has built valuable social capital through her network of university contacts, working closely with the advisors who help students find employment. They have learned to trust her to place students in career-enhancing intern positions that build skills and often turn into full-time jobs after graduation. Sally knew her success depended not just on her relationships with employers with hiring needs but on her long-term ability to find talented students to fill those needs. She invited the students to be "friends" on her social networking site, and her coaching helped them make outstanding impressions from day one.

STRUCTURAL CAPITAL

Structural capital includes the knowledge stored as documentation about business processes, procedures, policies, contracts, transactions, patents, research, trade secrets, and other aspects of the organization's operations and strategies, often stored electronically. Essentially the knowledge left behind when an employee goes home for the day, structural capital is built up over years, although it may not always be well organized. Sally contributed in many ways to the company's structural capital. For example, she developed a handbook that explains legal aspects of temporary employment, and she frequently updated it as laws changed.

Types of Knowledge

In Chapter 1, we discussed the continuum from data to information and finally to knowledge. Knowledge is not just data. At each step along the continuum from data to information and finally to knowledge, the bits and pieces are further refined, analyzed, and combined to create something more valuable and meaningful: actionable knowledge. Much intellectual capital is

FIGURE 9-1

Types of intellectual capital.

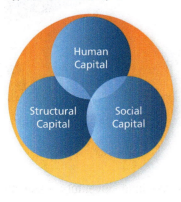

knowledge of one kind or another, and it is helpful to clarify the two major types of knowledge because they require different management approaches.

EXPLICIT KNOWLEDGE

The notes Sally entered into the CRM and the handbook she updated are examples of **explicit knowledge**, or knowledge that can be documented. It is often stored in information systems, on websites, in spreadsheets, or in handbooks and manuals. This kind of structural capital includes all the summarized data that information systems can provide, along with documentation on business processes, procedures, and policies. It can include both structured and unstructured information as well as multimedia content. Sally's notes, for instance, summarized each client's typical hiring needs. The information system already contained each client's pay scales and contract terms, so she didn't need to add those.

TACIT KNOWLEDGE

Employees like Sally and the detectives in "Criminal Investigations Division" possess another kind of knowledge that is more elusive, called **tacit knowledge**. This encompasses the insights, judgment, creative processes, and wisdom that come from learning and long experience in the field, along with many trials and errors. Sally's tacit knowledge, which is so critical to the human capital she contributed to the company, includes her insights about how to interview prospective recruits for different clients, drawing on years of experience in which some of her recruits did well for one client but bombed at another work site.

Some tacit knowledge is so ingrained that the person may not even be consciously aware he or she possesses it or that other people don't share it. A person who is very familiar with the gentle sliding finger motions that control a heat-sensitive smartphone screen might never think to mention that to a new user, who fruitlessly taps the screen harder to no avail.

The distinction between explicit and tacit knowledge can be blurry, partly because strategies to make tacit knowledge more explicit are improving dramatically. Organizations are eager to use technology to prevent so much tacit knowledge from "walking out the door" at retirement or whenever a competitor lures away a talented professional.

Managing Intellectual Capital

The growing understanding that intellectual capital is a critical asset leads to strategies to manage and use it more effectively. Collaborative technologies, in particular, offer exciting possibilities to help coworkers share knowledge.

Knowledge management (KM) refers to a set of strategies and practices organizations use to become more systematic about managing intellectual capital. It is also a field of study in which researchers investigate all the roles these intangible assets play, how they contribute to competitive advantage and productivity, and how human behavior interacts with efforts to capture and share knowledge. It's a spirited field, drawing people from many different disciplines—computer science, information systems, sociology, business administration, management, psychology, and more. Some focus heavily on the role technology plays in capturing and managing intellectual capital. Others stress the human and organizational elements, noting that the success of knowledge management efforts depends as much on people as it does on technology.

---

intellectual capital (IC)
All the intangible assets and resources of an enterprise that are not captured by conventional accounting reports, but still contribute to its value and help it achieve competitive advantage.

human capital
The competencies and knowledge possessed by the organization's employees.

social capital
The number and quality of all the relationships an organization's employees maintain, not just with one another but with clients, customers, suppliers, and prospective employees.

structural capital
The knowledge stored as documentation, often electronically, about business processes, procedures, policies, contracts, transactions, patents, research, trade secrets, and other aspects of the organization's operations.

explicit knowledge
Knowledge that can be documented and codified, which is often stored in information systems, on websites, in spreadsheets, or in handbooks and manuals.

tacit knowledge
Knowledge that encompasses the insights, judgment, creative processes, and wisdom that come from learning and long experience in the field as well as from many trials and errors.

knowledge management (KM)
A set of strategies and practices organizations use to become more systematic about managing intellectual capital. It is also a field of study in which researchers investigate all the roles these intangible assets play, how they contribute to competitive advantage and productivity, and how human behavior interacts with efforts to capture and share knowledge.

Knowledge management is a critical ingredient for combating global health challenges. Fighting the Zika virus, for example, involves many countries, government agencies, hospitals, community organizations, health professionals, and drug companies working on vaccines. Success will depend on all these actors working together across geographical boundaries and quickly sharing information.[2]

Knowledge management is also one of those buzzwords that can be overhyped and over-sold, leading to frustration and abandoned projects. Nevertheless, the failures present key lessons, and the mismanagement of intellectual capital can be so damaging that KM strategies will continue to flourish, although they might appear under different names.[3]

Describe the steps in launching a knowledge management program, providing examples of the applicable technologies.

2 Knowledge Management Strategies and Technologies

Let's take a look at the steps in a knowledge management project, pointing out how different projects can take advantage of various technologies and what pitfalls can spell trouble along the way. Figure 9-2 shows the major steps, beginning with the project's goal.

FIGURE 9-2

Knowledge management steps.

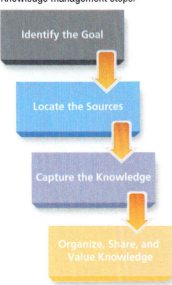

Identify the Goal

The first step is to identify the precise goal of the project, which can best be determined by studying the organization's specific needs. A project with a specific goal and clear aims is more likely to achieve success. The nature of the intellectual capital the organization hopes to capture also guides later steps in the process, such as the methods to capture it and technologies used.

For instance, as car electronics, safety, and emissions systems become more complex, Hyundai's leadership recognized a need for a central call center that could help technicians in all its dealerships diagnose and repair problems. To be effective, the call center agents needed to be fully expert, supported by an extensive knowledge basis with quick and reliable answers. That need drove the goal of the KM project.[4]

Sally's manager identifies a different goal, one that targets the priceless social capital built up by employees who retire or leave the company. With social networking sites so prevalent, employees create complex relationships that can make substantial contributions to the company's success. These sites could help spread news about the company through word of mouth to an employee's social network ties, and they can extend connections to new clients based on recommendations from happy customers.

The aging population is the driver for some KM projects and is especially important to the police department in "Criminal Investigations Division." Demographic trends are creating a workforce crisis for companies in many developed countries, especially Japan and Australia.

Other KM goals, focused more on structural capital, might include documenting and centralizing the organization's policies and procedures, building a collection of presentation templates for salespeople, or creating an online repository for patent ideas.

Locate the Sources

Once the organization identifies its goal, it next locates the sources of relevant knowledge. For projects focused on explicit knowledge and structural capital, much may already be in electronic form, although scattered about in different formats and media types. A common problem is redundancy, worsened by the ease of copying and editing electronic files so that different versions contain inconsistent information. Figure 9-3 shows some possible information sources inside most organizations. These can become excellent starting points for a successful KM project.

The tacit knowledge that employees may not even know they possess is more challenging to locate. Much of it is in the minds of the company's experts, those people everyone else has

Sources of Structural Capital	
Information system	Employee directories
Intranet	Annual reports
Employee manuals	Calendars
Employee handbooks	Presentation slides and videos
Operating manuals	Department bulletin boards
Strategic plan	Marketing materials
Policies and procedures documents	Vendor lists
Lists of frequently asked questions	Human resource forms

FIGURE 9-3
Potential sources of explicit knowledge from structural capital.

learned to turn to when they have a stubborn question in the expert's domain. Locating these sources means finding the experts, wherever they may be working in the organization and at whatever level.

FINDING EXPERTISE

The increasingly digital workplace offers excellent opportunities to find the people in an organization with specific types of expertise based on their education, experience, and activities. Many expert locator tools draw on directories, in which each employee maintains an online profile that includes details about projects, publications, or other hints of expertise. A researcher struggling with a problem on solar panels, for instance, can enter some keywords to retrieve a list of contacts in the company who might have answers. These systems often include workflow tools so that if the first expert doesn't answer, the query is routed to the next. Some include means to control volume so the experts aren't drowned with repetitive questions.

Software can crawl through databases, websites, email, project summaries, and other electronic documents to find relevant expertise. What makes an expert helpful, however, turns out to be more than knowledge about the subject. Trustworthiness, communication skills, and willingness to help are all very important according to user surveys (Figure 9-4). No matter how knowledgeable, a grouch who rejects newcomers' questions will not be a promising candidate to share expertise.

Social media, in particular, can be helpful to flush out desirable traits. Employees who maintain blogs in a specialty area and who respond to comments and questions demonstrate not only their expertise but their communication skills and willingness to help as well.

SOCIAL NETWORK ANALYSIS

Tracking down those key individuals who are tightly integrated into the informal networks through which information flows is a challenge, but **social network analysis (SNA)** can be very useful. This technique maps and measures the strength of relationships between individuals and groups, represented as nodes in the network. The measures provide insights into network clusters and the roles different people play as leaders or connecting bridges to other networks. They also pinpoint the loners who interact with very few others. These connections

FIGURE 9-4
Characteristics people look for when they seek out an expert.

Expert's Characteristic	Average Relative Importance to Users Seeking an Expert
Extent of knowledge	25%
Trustworthiness	19%
Communications skills	14%
Willingness to help	12%
Experience	12%
Currency of knowledge	9%
Awareness of other resources	9%

social network analysis (SNA)
A technique that maps and measures the strength of relationships between individuals and groups, represented as nodes in the network. The measures provide insights into network clusters and the roles different people play as leaders or connecting bridges to other networks.

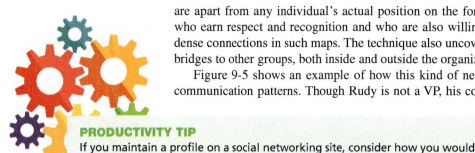

are apart from any individual's actual position on the formal organizational chart. Experts who earn respect and recognition and who are also willing to provide assistance will show dense connections in such maps. The technique also uncovers those who play pivotal roles as bridges to other groups, both inside and outside the organization.

Figure 9-5 shows an example of how this kind of network analysis reveals underlying communication patterns. Though Rudy is not a VP, his connections suggest he is a key hub for his unit and also a bridge to Finance that bypasses the normal reporting lines.

> **PRODUCTIVITY TIP**
> If you maintain a profile on a social networking site, consider how you would modify it if the site were used to identify experts in particular areas. How would you feature your expertise so software could easily find you?

The raw material of a social network analysis is usually data from surveys that ask people who they contact most often for advice. Data drawn from social networking sites is useful as well. The food-packaging giant Mars, for instance, used SNA to trace its scientists' informal networks. It found that some kind souls were overburdened with repetitive questions from advice seekers and also that the scientists were becoming too insulated—perhaps too comfortable with their small cliques. Research shows that having many network connections, even weak ones, contributes to innovation because connections expose people to a wider range of diverse viewpoints.[5] To persuade them to meet new people, Mars launched an unusual convention where attendees wore RFID badges that lit up whenever the wearer approached someone he or she hadn't yet met. Giant screens in the ballroom dynamically graphed new connections on people's growing social networks as they introduced themselves to new people.[6]

> **PRODUCTIVITY TIP**
> Build a social network that includes a wide variety of people, not just those in your own area of interest. Even weak ties contribute to your innovative capacity as you hear different viewpoints.

FIGURE 9-5

Social network mapping shows relationships within a network, which can differ from the organizational chart.

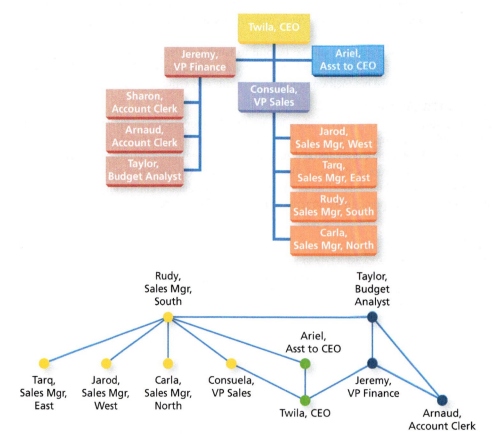

Capture the Knowledge

Before people can take advantage of intellectual capital, it must be captured. The best strategies for doing this depend on the kind of knowledge we seek and how we can store it.

BUILDING A KNOWLEDGE BASE FOR STRUCTURAL CAPITAL

Hyundai's technical knowledge base shows how an organization can gather its structural knowledge assets, organize them electronically, and make them productive for the company. The system started with legacy information from technical bulletins and repair manuals. However, it grew rapidly as technicians found the best ways to resolve problems and then added that knowledge to the system.

The National Oceanographic and Atmospheric Agency (NOAA) created an immense knowledge base of its information about hurricanes and other extreme weather events at answers.noaa.gov. The site is an easily searchable database, built from existing data and frequently asked questions, but it is continually expanded as new information becomes available. Visitors who can't find their answers can also email a question to NOAA scientists from the site and receive a reply within a few days. However, the expanding knowledge base is becoming so extensive that 99% of visitors find what they need through the search engine (Figure 9-6).

STRATEGIES FOR CAPTURING TACIT KNOWLEDGE

Attempts to capture tacit knowledge benefit from less structured approaches that encourage people to describe their knowledge in their own words or through their own actions. The goal is to uncover knowledge the person may not even know he or she has and then find ways to organize, tag, and categorize it so others can access it.

Figure 9-7 describes strategies to capture tacit knowledge. Some strategies in the table, such as after-action reviews, best-practice sessions, narratives, and shadowing, use little technology at this stage, except perhaps to video some of the action. The techniques are powerful, though, because they help shed light on bits of knowledge people may not have considered important and so would not have brought up in a more formal setting.

Collaborative technologies capture and share both explicit and tacit knowledge. For instance, **communities of practice**, which are groups of individuals who come together to learn from one another and share knowledge about their professions, typically rely on online discussion forums, shared workspaces, wikis, blogs, and other social media. Cadbury, a candy

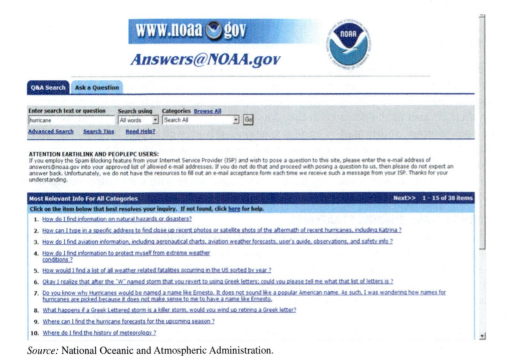

Source: National Oceanic and Atmospheric Administration.

FIGURE 9-6

NOAA's Answer website is a massive, easily searchable knowledge base containing information about oceans and weather.

communities of practice
Groups of individuals who come together to learn from one another and share knowledge about their professions; they typically rely on online discussion forums, shared workspaces, wikis, blogs, and other social media.

FIGURE 9-7

Strategies for capturing tacit knowledge.

Knowledge Capture Strategy	Description
After-action review	A meeting held after a project has been completed to document what worked well and what did not.
Best-practice session	A meeting of people in the same field, or who contribute to the same business process. They share and document their tips for best practices in accomplishing the goal.
Wiki	A website in which users add and edit articles about specific topics and discuss the contents of each article with other editors.
Shadowing	A mentoring strategy in which a new employee works side-by-side for weeks or months with one who is leaving, allowing the veteran to impart knowledge in the context of the actual work.
Community of practice	A group of individuals with common interests who share knowledge because they are in the same profession or job role, often using online tools.
Blog	In the context of knowledge management, a blog can serve to keep coworkers up-to-date about recent developments, new initiatives, and new ideas.
Narrative	An oral history or commentary, often presented as a video interview.
Team workspaces	A collection of online tools that organize and collect a variety of activities for a team, such as team calendars, document and multimedia repositories, blogs, announcements, chat, and discussion boards.

manufacturer in the United Kingdom, creates dozens of such communities for colleagues around the world to share ideas about product development. CHOCNET, for example, engages people in a community of practice working on chocolate products across 36 countries.

Wikis are gaining popularity in corporate settings as a means to capture and share knowledge as well.[7] IBM managers launched wikis for employees as an experiment, just to see how they would be used. The growth rates were extremely high as people flocked to the easy-to-use interface to build document repositories, share information about projects, and manage events. Nokia has also had good success with a homegrown wiki, one that caught on very quickly with employees around the world who used it to collaborate on mobile phone designs. Web 2.0 technologies of various kinds do make it easier for employees to share knowledge, particularly the tacit variety.[8]

Organize, Share, and Value Knowledge

The bits and pieces of knowledge that emerge from all these meeting notes, interviews, documents, and videos will be like a chaotic library with no searchable catalog until they are organized into some kind of repository. The technologies vary, though many companies establish their intranet as the gateway to their knowledge management efforts. Contrasted with the open Internet, an **intranet** is an organization's private web space. It relies on TCP/IP and web browsers, but it is password-protected and accessible only to authorized individuals through the organization portal. Intranets started as a way to organize and distribute employee forms and announcements, but they have grown considerably with knowledge-management initiatives.

ORGANIZING AND SHARING STRATEGIES

An overarching approach to organizing intellectual capital is **enterprise content management (ECM)**, which helps organizations gain control over all kinds of content that might be in the form of documents, videos, web pages, social media posts, or images and then manage changes, updates, or archiving. Software systems to facilitate enterprise content management would include a variety of capabilities to manage different types of content.[9]

For example, ECM would include a **document management system** to manage electronic documents, often converted from paper sources, making them searchable and easily transmitted. In the financial industry, for instance, document management capabilities are essential not just because they save so much in printing and storage costs but because they help institutions more easily comply with regulations.

Using optical character recognition (OCR), which reads typed text, the systems can quickly do much of their own indexing and tagging to process paper forms. The software reads specific zones to decipher document identifiers and shows the scanned form along with the fields the software has read, so human beings can verify the results. Figure 9-8 shows an example in which the software is programmed to capture text in zones where key information appears, such as PO number, date, zip code, and vendor name.

Some systems also incorporate **intelligent character recognition (ICR)**, provided by software that can interpret handprinted text written on paper forms (Figure 9-9). The digital version of the document is displayed on a screen with question marks in the boxes that need human review because the software can't read the letter. OCR and ICR help bridge the gap between paper and electronic record keeping.

Other capabilities for ECM handle different kinds of content. For instance, the web content management systems described in Chapter 6 facilitate control over content on the organization's website. Image processing may also be part of an enterprise content management strategy, using software that extracts features and recognizes patterns in images and video. Image recognition technology is advancing rapidly. For example, facial recognition software is widely used and remarkably accurate. Images of street scenes can also be scanned for visual features that can identify the actual location.[10]

For consumers, Google draws on its unrivaled access to data to offer an image-matching app called "Google Goggles." The user uploads an image taken with a cell-phone camera, and the service searches for possible matches. A photo of a barcode is easy to decipher and will immediately return an image of the product along with web links about it. Popular monuments also hit correct matches, such as the easily recognizable Washington Monument (Figure 9-10).

An important advantage to ECM is that different kinds of content can be managed through their life cycles, from creation and updates to archiving or deletion. Content items can also include tags and metadata to control access, avoid duplication, and make them easier to locate. ECM also helps organizations stay compliant with record management regulations on retention and deletion. Figure 9-11 shows examples of item properties that might be tracked by an ECM system.

While many companies have separate systems that handle some aspects of ECM, they may not be well integrated. However, ECM is an emerging trend, and software vendors are stepping up to develop integrated products that can handle a variety of content in user-friendly ways.

DECIDING WHAT TO KEEP: VALUATION STRATEGIES

Documents and other kinds of content are not always valuable or useful, and much that is captured should be edited or just tossed out. Even as storage costs plummet, the cost, in terms of time wasted, for employees to sift through piles of electronic junk is high. Figure 9-12 breaks down different ways of handling content based on its potential value.

Valuating entries in a knowledge base created by employees is also an important effort. Some organizations engage users to judge the value of entries, by using rating systems. Over time, as the ratings accumulate, the software chooses which entries to promote to the top and which might be deleted.

---

intranet
An organization's private web space. It relies on TCP/IP and web browsers, but it is password-protected and accessible only to authorized individuals through the organization's portal.

enterprise content management (ECM)
An overarching approach to organizing and managing all different kinds of content throughout their life cycles, from creation to updating, archiving or deleting, to include documents, images, videos, web pages, and other types.

document management systems
Systems that manage electronic documents, often converted from paper sources, making them searchable and easily transmitted.

intelligent character recognition (ICR)
Software that can interpret handprinted text written on paper forms.

FIGURE 9-8

Document management systems include forms-processing software that reads the text in specified zones on a scanned form so they can be indexed properly.

PURCHASE ORDER

ATOM OFFICE PRODUCTS
54 S. Girard Street
Boca Raton, FL 33431
Vendor ID Number 58871

The following number must appear on all related
correspondence, shipping papers, and invoices:
P.O. NUMBER: 1672238

TO:	SHIP TO:
Hera Shenar	Hera Shanar
Starfront Real Estate Management	Starfront Real Estate Management
478 West Barkley Street	478 West Barkley Street
Boca Raton, FL 33431	Boca Raton, FL 3331

P.O. DATE	REQUISITIONER	SHIPPED VIA	F.O.B. POINT	TERMS
9-Jul-11				

QTY	ITEM #	DESCRIPTION	UNIT PRICE	TOTAL
5	487-696	Packing material	4.25	21.25
2	878-001	Packing tape	9.95	19.90
1	153-698	Stapler	14.99	14.99
		SUBTOTAL		56.14
		SALES TAX 3%		1.68
		SHIPPING & HANDLING		Free
		OTHER		
		TOTAL		57.82

1. Please send two copies of your invoice.
2. Enter this order in accordance with the prices, terms,
   delivery method, and specifications listed above.
3. Please notify us immediately if you are unable to ship
   as specified.
4. Send all correspondence to:

   ATOM OFFICE PRODUCTS
   54 S. Girard Street
   Boca Raton, FL33431

Authorized by: Date

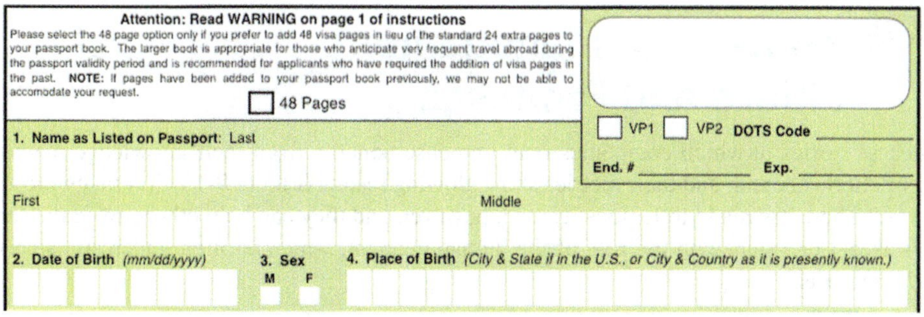
Attention: Read WARNING on page 1 of instructions

Please select the 48 page option only if you prefer to add 48 visa pages in lieu of the standard 24 extra pages to your passport book. The larger book is appropriate for those who anticipate very frequent travel abroad during the passport validity period and is recommended for applicants who have required the addition of visa pages in the past. NOTE: If pages have been added to your passport book previously, we may not be able to accomodate your request.

☐ 48 Pages

☐ VP1 ☐ VP2 DOTS Code ______

End. # ______ Exp. ______

1. Name as Listed on Passport: Last

First

Middle

2. Date of Birth *(mm/dd/yyyy)*

3. Sex M F

4. Place of Birth *(City & State if in the U.S., or City & Country as it is presently known.)*

Source: United States Department of State.

FIGURE 9-9

Intelligent character recognition interprets handprinted text on documents such as this application for additional passport pages.

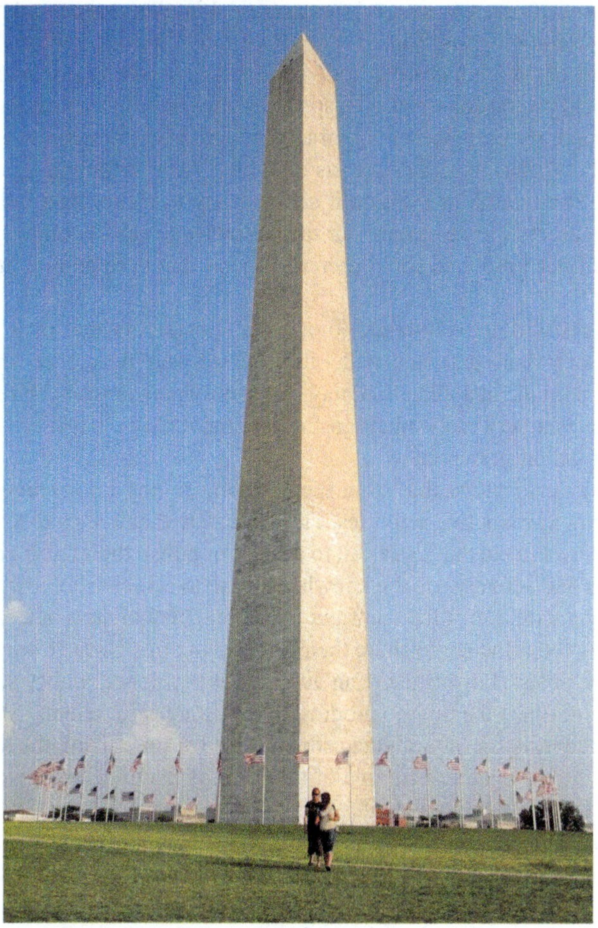

Source: MosamMoments/Shutterstock.

FIGURE 9-10

Google Goggles uses image recognition software to analyze an uploaded snapshot of the Washington Monument and then returns relevant web pages from the National Park Service about the familiar landmark.

FIGURE 9-11

Examples of properties tracked by document management systems.

- Date created
- Date last modified
- Author(s)
- Title
- Document status
- File size
- Keywords
- Latest version
- Date last accessed
- Date last printed
- Security level

Information value ↑

Type of Content	Knowledge Management Strategy
Strategically Valuable Information	Develop strategies to experiment with and invest in this information
Operational Information	Systematically collect and organize, ensuring wide availability throughout organization
Compliance Information	Automate collection and archiving to achieve cost-effectiveness
Low-Value, Nuisance, Redundant Information	Delete

FIGURE 9-12

Strategies for determining the value of captured knowledge.

Explain how the human element can pose challenges for knowledge management projects and how managers can overcome them.

3 Knowledge Management: Pitfalls and Promises

Success stories in which companies reap immense benefits from their knowledge management efforts abound, and their metrics show glowing results (Figure 9-13). Yet many projects do fail. These cases add to lessons learned, however, and they can help others avoid the same mistakes. Let's start with the role of the human element, which is often underestimated for these projects.[11]

The Human Element: Why Share Knowledge?

From a senior manager's perspective, capturing critical intellectual capital and sharing it with other employees seems obvious. But the employee may feel differently. A person's knowledge is a large part of what makes that individual valuable to any organization, and it helps determine salary and promotions. Sally H. spent decades building up her expertise about how to make every temporary employment contract succeed, and she was rewarded for it. Would she think twice about sharing all her secrets on a blog or contributing tips to the company's knowledge base? She would, at least until she is ready to retire. And unlike all the formal documents and contracts she generates, her tacit knowledge is difficult to impart to others. It would take a lot of her time, and she'd prefer to spend that time gaining new clients to earn another bonus.

Some employees will actively hoard knowledge, perceiving that their value to the organization drops as they share expertise with others. A software developer who knows the code inside a specialized financial application may be the only person who can repair bugs and add features. This creates a very risky situation for the organization, but it can certainly translate to job security for the programmer.

Employees may also judge that time spent adding to any knowledge base means time away from their other productive activities. They calculate that it's wiser to contribute as little as possible and instead make that extra call to a client or polish their latest proposal. They may become free riders and actively use the knowledge base to achieve their own goals but not add to it. The free riding would miff the contributors, so they would drop out, too.

People may also be reluctant to share their time-saving tips because employers might then require higher workloads. For instance, an accountant developed a nifty what-if spreadsheet that dramatically cut down the time to produce cost estimates for clients. Sharing this innovation might make requests for last-minute estimates skyrocket, raising the accountant's workload. Figure 9-14 shows another example of this kind of dilemma and gives you a chance to think about what you would do yourself.

Finally, enthusiastic early contributors may get turned off as their content is critiqued by others. A wave of comments that point out faults in a contributor's carefully crafted entry is embarrassing. As we discussed in the chapter on collaboration, online discussions can seem more abrupt and harsh, compounding the problem.

Incentives for Knowledge Sharing

How does an organization encourage people to share their precious knowledge, especially the tacit knowledge that makes them valuable and earns them promotions? Praise and recognition are key ingredients. When employees know that the work they put into knowledge

FIGURE 9-13
Metrics to assess the success of knowledge management projects.

Knowledge Management Project Metrics
Growth in resources attached to the project
Growth in the volume of content
Growth in usage by employees
Survival even after the loss of particular champions who started the project
Evidence of return on investment

FIGURE 9-14
A knowledge sharing
dilemma. What would you do?

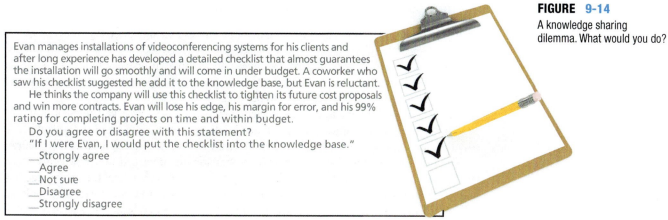

Evan manages installations of videoconferencing systems for his clients and after long experience has developed a detailed checklist that almost guarantees the installation will go smoothly and will come in under budget. A coworker who saw his checklist suggested he add it to the knowledge base, but Evan is reluctant.

He thinks the company will use this checklist to tighten its future cost proposals and win more contracts. Evan will lose his edge, his margin for error, and his 99% rating for completing projects on time and within budget.

Do you agree or disagree with this statement?

"If I were Evan, I would put the checklist into the knowledge base."

__Strongly agree
__Agree
__Not sure
__Disagree
__Strongly disagree

Source: © Alex SlobodkiStock/Getty Images.

sharing is valued, they are more likely to participate. Their contributions also help build their own social capital within the company. If one employee selflessly contributes, others tend to reciprocate.[12]

Moderate monetary rewards can be helpful and can show management support for sharing knowledge. But large cash rewards can have unintended consequences. Big individual bonuses for contributions to a knowledge base can lead to a situation in which employees don't share at all unless they earn what they think is a fair payment. Some will start gaming the system by adding trivial contributions or splitting their content into smaller bites so they get paid more for it. If people earn different amounts based on managers' subjective judgments of knowledge value, protests about fairness erupt.

The annual performance review that rewards people with raises and promotions for sharing also can offer incentives, and it shows management support for a knowledge sharing culture. Emphasizing the team's overall performance can be another effective way to balance competition and cooperation. But annual performance reviews can also hinder knowledge sharing. Microsoft, for instance, once used "forced ranking," in which managers had to rate a fixed percentage of their team as "top performers," "good," "average," "below average," or "poor." This system encouraged competition rather than cooperation, and Microsoft wisely dropped it.[14]

THE ETHICAL FACTOR — Knowledge Sharing in Fast-Paced Industries: The Case of Formula One Racing

In the brutally competitive Formula One racing industry, Ferrari, Mercedes, Honda, and other top automakers vie to build the fastest car on the planet. The engineering teams closely track every tiny change to their rivals' cars, taking photos and videos, chatting with drivers who race for other companies, or picking up tips about technology improvements from suppliers who work with several automakers.

Each company relies heavily on its human capital. The companies value sharing when the results lead to a faster car, even if the "sharing" came from someone they just recruited from a competitor who slipped out carrying the rival's design documents. As one CEO put it, "Every time we take an employee from BMW, or we lose one to Honda, or a Renault man goes to so-and-so, there's always some transfer in information … sometimes it's of tiny value, and sometimes it's worth a tenth or two of a second per lap."[13] The leaks continue despite employment contracts that strictly forbid such knowledge transfers.

Employees are under tremendous pressure to manage their own intellectual capital, hoarding or sharing depending on how they judge the advantages. They may hoard knowledge for job security but freely offer what they know about their former employer's technology. In a fast-moving innovative industry like Formula One, patents and other legal protections are not very useful. By the time a lawsuit is resolved, the intellectual property that was improperly transferred is worth little anyway, so claims of espionage or intellectual property theft are uncommon. Questionable ethical decisions become very tempting in this environment.

Technology Hurdles and Content Issues

Overly complicated technology with long learning curves and high price tags stalls many KM projects. Especially given human concerns about knowledge sharing, systems with novel or awkward user interfaces can turn people away. An intuitive, user-friendly interface encourages people to actually log in. If the technology is smoothly integrated into the systems people use every day anyway, it is more likely to be used.

The quality of the content in the knowledge repository is another key element in its success. If it is stale or inaccurate, people will quickly learn to distrust the entries. Particularly for structural knowledge, a review process should ensure the contents are up-to-date and accurate.

Too little content can also cause people to abandon the project. If they repeatedly search the repository for answers that aren't there, they will look elsewhere and the knowledge base will eventually wither. A critical mass of content is needed from the outset so people see value right away. Hyundai, for instance, populated its knowledge base with stacks of technical documentation that already existed, then rapidly expanded it to incorporate real tips from actual repair jobs.

The Semantic Web

Managing knowledge on the web involves building the **semantic web**, which is a web with meaning, in which online resources and their relationships can be read and understood by computers, relying on machine learning. The web now offers links from one page to the next, and the meaning of that link is clear to human beings who are reading the page. The semantic web, sometimes called "Web 3.0," will make that relationship clear for software agents as well so they can learn as they go and become more effective at complex tasks.

The semantic web relies on the **resource description framework (RDF)** to describe resources and their properties. RDF is written in XML and was developed by the World Wide Web Consortium. It describes a resource and its properties like a sentence, so that the actual relationship between the parts of the sentence can be understood:

- Flipper *is a* dolphin.
- Homo sapiens *is a member of* mammalia.
- Shoes *cost* $25.99.

The semantic web will also make it possible for agents to integrate information from many different databases and collections with different structures, terms, and entity names. Although it is not widely adopted yet, futuristic scenarios about the semantic web show how it might transform the way consumers and businesses interact. If you're hungry, for example, you could send out your agent to check which restaurants are open, which have special deals, and which friends are nearby who might want to join you. It could also check where you ate last night and assume you don't want the same type of food. If you like your agent's choices, it will reserve the table. Your agent will be immune to TV and online advertising, so marketers will have to alter their promotion strategies.

Practical Tips for Launching a Knowledge Management Project

Although the challenges are great, the value organizations can reap by better managing intellectual capital are far greater. The competitive advantages companies strive to maintain are tied up with the knowledge their employees possess and also with the capacity of those employees to leverage collective knowledge for innovation. Every organization is different, and knowledge management efforts will not be the same. In the online simulation "Criminal Investigations Division," for example, the top priority is to capture the knowledge gained by the department's veteran detectives before they retire.

Drawn from years of lessons learned, the practical tips in Figure 9-15 will help you get projects off to a good start and avoid common missteps.

▶ Identify a clear and specific goal, and start small.

▶ Get management buy-in for the project.

▶ Find the assets and human experts in the organization that can help start up the knowledge base, and populate it with valuable, accurate, and up-to-date information.

▶ Choose technology that is simple and user-friendly, and that integrates easily with existing systems.

▶ Introduce the project as a pilot, with a smaller subset of receptive employees.

▶ Develop knowledge-sharing incentive strategies appropriate for the organization.

▶ Actively encourage people to participate, suggest improvements, and add to the organization's collective intellectual capital.

FIGURE 9-15
Practical tips for launching a KM project.

E-Learning

 Describe three different approaches to e-learning.

Carlos, the human resources manager at Sally's employment services firm, is eager to expand the company's training program. Thinking about Sally's skills, he asks her to develop a short course on work visas for noncitizens. Most employees already see her as the resident expert and send her their questions, so Carlos wants to capture this intellectual capital and turn it into a short online course to train new employees. Because Sally had been a trainer earlier in her career, she is happy to give it a try. She taught face-to-face classes, but e-learning will be something new. She also realizes it could help many more people learn the basics compared to her classroom version.

Learning is central to an organization's capacity to build intellectual capital, and e-learning plays an important role. The constraints of time and space that come with a face-to-face classroom session vanish, but new challenges emerge. Technological glitches are not uncommon, with connections breaking down or microphones failing. But organizations can reap huge benefits if they take advantage of the online medium for learning and not just try to replicate a class session.

Comparing E-Learning Approaches

E-learning refers to a varied set of instructional approaches that all depend on information and communications technologies, especially the Internet, to connect trainees with learning materials and also with their instructors and other trainees. E-learning approaches can be quite different, and the jargon used to describe them can be confusing. Let's sort out the major categories.

SELF-PACED E-LEARNING

Instruction might be designed as self-paced e-learning, in which students use online materials independently with little or no instructor involvement. They might read texts, watch narrated presentations, play videos, and then take quizzes. Their successful completion of the course demonstrates mastery of the material and readiness to move on to more advanced topics.

These self-paced learning programs are especially useful for gaining structural knowledge about company policies or information systems. Rather than waiting for HR to schedule a face-to-face class, new employees can log in to take a self-paced course whenever it suits them. SAP, for instance, maintains a vast inventory of online, self-paced courses in several languages that teach how to use the ERP software. Self-paced learning is also widely used for technical training. At nuclear power plants, employees who work long shifts in remote areas can log in to take self-paced courses on nuclear physics or other subjects.

INSTRUCTOR-LED E-LEARNING

Instructor-led e-learning, as its name suggests, involves a teacher who guides students through the course, often using virtual classrooms, email, phone, web conferencing, discussion forums, and other collaborative technologies. The course can include synchronous events

---

semantic web
A web with meaning, in which online resources and their relationships can be read and understood by computers as well as human beings.

resource description framework (RDF)
Part of the XML family of standards, RDF is used to describe online resources and their properties for the semantic web.

e-learning
A varied set of instructional approaches that all depend on ICT, especially the Internet, to connect trainees with learning materials and also with their instructors and other trainees.

in which students and instructors interact using online tools at the same time, although from different geographic locations.

One of the early versions of e-learning was the interactive video network, in which classrooms equipped with video cameras and TV monitors were constructed in different locations and proprietary network lines connected them to one another (Figure 9-16). The instructor taught as usual from one classroom location and could see the students at the remote location in a large TV monitor. At the other location, the students could see the instructor on their own TV monitor.

With increasing Internet bandwidth, synchronous e-learning events were no longer limited to specially constructed interactive video classrooms and networks. Instead, they could bring together instructors and students wherever they resided, using their own computer screens, speakers, microphones, webcams, and Internet connections. Instead of viewing the instructor speaking from a podium on a TV monitor, students might view presentation slides while the instructor narrates, or they might share an online, interactive whiteboard.

Instructor-led e-learning also incorporates asynchronous activities, in which students can log in at any time to work through online course materials, submit assignments, take assessments, or send messages. Some modules developed for self-paced learning might be embedded in an instructor-led course. Also, synchronous activities might be recorded so students can log in to review them later.

FIGURE 9-16

Interactive video network linking physically separated classes.

HYBRID PROGRAMS

Hybrid e-learning blends online activities with in-class sessions to create a rich learning experience. Trainees might attend a daylong class at the corporation's national conference and then continue to advanced topics using e-learning after they go home. Or they might enroll in an instructor-led e-learning course that includes a weekend at the plant for hands-on activities and class sessions.

Face-to-face courses increasingly use online tools to communicate and store materials as well. An instructor might post the course's PowerPoint slides, for instance, so students do not need to take detailed notes during the class session.

Creating an E-Learning Program

 Explain how to create an e-learning program and the kinds of technologies that can be applied, including the learning management system.

Almost any technology used to develop web resources, collaborate online, or organize existing resources into a coherent course can add to e-learning programs. While a vast array of tools are available, Carlos relies on a well-designed strategy that focuses first and foremost on the content and how best to present it. He wants it to be clear, comprehensive, lively, and easy to update as work visa policies change.

Course Development

Unlike a face-to-face class, where the learning experience relies so heavily on the instructor's knowledge of the content and skill as a teacher, a successful e-learning course needs a team.

Sally will fill the role of **subject matter expert**, the person who possesses the content expertise and knows what should be covered. She has all the government checklists and forms as well as extensive knowledge about all kinds of visa scenarios and immigration issues.

Peyton from Carlos's office will join the team as **instructional designer**, the person who brings the knowledge and skills about what strategies work best for e-learning. Peyton will help Sally clarify the goals of the course, develop an effective e-learning strategy based on the needs of the trainees, and design assessments that will confirm the trainees have mastered the material (Figure 9-17). The designer helps bring the content to life and also ensures people with disabilities can access it so it is compliant with government regulations.

The project's sponsor is typically the manager who defines the project's goals and pays the bills. In this case, Carlos fills that role, as head of the HR office where the corporate training budget resides. Depending on the project, skills might also be needed from writers, programmers, technicians, videographers, and graphic artists. Finally, a project manager coordinates all these activities, tracking progress from kickoff to completion. Peyton, the instructional designer, will handle that role.

The team strives to create a course that will effectively accomplish its goals and that students and instructors will find easy to use—and also to update. Figure 9-18 shows some items often used to judge whether an online course is properly designed.

Learning Objects

Sally brings her PowerPoint slides and a collection of documents to the kickoff meeting with Peyton and Carlos, and they can see she has already started to flesh out the substance. As they

---

Job Opening: Instructional Designer

As instructional designer, you will join the Human Capital Development Office to help create engaging e-learning courses for corporate training. You will work with subject matter experts and corporate sponsors to assess learner needs, develop learning content, create assessments, and evaluate e-learning programs. Knowledge of content authoring tools, web-based application development, and learning management systems required. Bachelor's degree in instructional design or related field required.

FIGURE 9-17

Job description for an instructional designer.

---

subject matter expert
The person on an e-learning development team who knows what content should be included in the course and possesses the content expertise.

instructional designer
The person on an e-learning development team who brings the knowledge and skills about what strategies work best for e-learning.

FIGURE 9-18
Sample items from online course assessments.

	Strongly Agree	Agree	Disagree	Strongly Disagree
▶ The introduction to the course provides a clear orientation for the student.	☐	☐	☐	☐
▶ Course layout is easy to navigate and understand.	☐	☐	☐	☐
▶ Course policies, such as grading standards, plagiarism, attendance, and late penalties, are clear.	☐	☐	☐	☐
▶ Guidelines for contributing to group discussions are clearly stated.	☐	☐	☐	☐
▶ Self-introductions are encouraged to help build the learning community.	☐	☐	☐	☐
▶ Instructions for obtaining technical support are readily available.	☐	☐	☐	☐
▶ The learning objectives for the course are clearly stated.	☐	☐	☐	☐
▶ Course resources are easily accessed.	☐	☐	☐	☐
▶ Course resources and activities are relevant and closely tied to learning objectives.	☐	☐	☐	☐
▶ All instructional resources are appropriate for the online environment.	☐	☐	☐	☐
▶ Technologies used support the learning objectives.	☐	☐	☐	☐
▶ Course technologies support and encourage interaction.	☐	☐	☐	☐

go through the material, Sally's outline is falling into place, with six major units and four or five topics under each one. She estimates people will need about 8 hours to go through all the material.

The goal is to take each topic and create a **learning object**, a digital resource that can be embedded in Sally's course in its proper place and that can be edited and reused for other purposes if needed. Unlike a lengthy classroom lecture, the learning object is smaller, more self-contained, and more reusable. Each learning object will have metadata to describe its contents, author, date created, and other features, making it easy to locate later and reuse. Many learning objects are quite short, offering "bite-sized" lessons. An employee who just needs to brush up on the requirements for the H2B visa program, for instance, will not have to trudge through long texts, videos, or slide presentations. The learning object in Sally's course that deals just with that topic will be easily found and updated as rules change.

Content Authoring Tools

A learning object might be as simple as a text document converted to a web page or a PowerPoint presentation or as complicated as a custom-built multiplayer interactive game. A common theme in e-learning is that "content is king," so the substance should always drive the technologies, not the other way around.

NARRATED PRESENTATIONS
Presentations with a live or recorded audio soundtrack are popular for e-learning, especially because many people are familiar with PowerPoint. Narrating the presentation is essentially what instructors would do during a face-to-face class session, so this type of learning object can be easy to develop. The presentation can include text, images, diagrams, videos, animations, and other features.

INTERACTIVE PRESENTATIONS
A number of content-authoring tools support interactivity beyond just moving slides forward or turning the audio on or off. For instance, some software helps developers create interactive diagrams that students can explore with the mouse, pop-up text boxes, or narration that explains each component (Figure 9-19). Other varieties might include online flash cards,

crossword puzzles, drag-and-drop matching exercises, and guided tours through a series of images, with a question to answer at the end of each series.

Computer programmers were once essential to develop interactive learning objects, but with advances in content-authoring tools, people with no programming knowledge can create engaging resources. For instance, presenters can create animated flash cards just by entering the content for both sides.

SCREEN CAPTURES

The computer screen itself can be an important element in any e-learning program, especially if the topic is about software or programming. A trainer might want to walk students through the process of adding a record to a database, for example, or show them how to download files from a website. Screen-capture software, such as Camtasia or Adobe Captivate, is used to make a video of such sessions, complete with audio soundtrack for the narration and special effects that highlight mouse clicks.

For one of her learning objects, Sally creates a 10-minute virtual tour of the resources available online from the Department of State. As she is explaining how to access the site and navigate through the materials, she will capture the tour in a video file to post in her class.

SIMULATIONS

Online activities that simulate a scenario and invite the learner to make choices that lead to different consequences help encourage active, experiential learning. These immersive activities can be especially engaging and also valuable to promote critical thinking skills. Students take an active role in decision making and also deal with the consequences of their decisions.[15] Figure 9-20 shows the start of a simulation that will be part of Sally's course.

In the online role-playing simulations that accompany this text, you enter different situations that call for smart decisions and quick action as you interact with the characters through simulated smartphones, web conferencing, email, texts, and other methods. Your decisions affect the outcome, and all the situations relate to the content of each chapter. The simulations also include key terms so you hear how they are used in context and can more easily remember them.

A great advantage of simulations is that they offer people a chance to practice skills without risk to themselves or their organizations. Business students can practice budgeting without risk of bankruptcy. Medical simulations allow physicians to diagnose and prescribe for simulated patients, and military simulations let officers try out battle tactics in different settings. With improvements in virtual reality, simulations will become even more valuable in such environments.

SERIOUS GAMES

Given how engaging online games can be, it's a natural leap to apply their compelling features to organizational training programs.[16] The term **serious game** refers to a game designed for useful purposes beyond entertainment and is often used in

FIGURE 9-19

Interactive diagram as a learning object. Clicking on each segment of the visa triggers a pop-up and audio, explaining what that segment means.

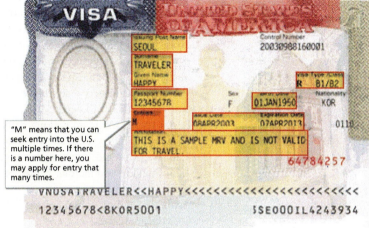

Source: U.S. Customs and Border Protection.

FIGURE 9-20

For each choice the student makes in a simulation, the program proceeds down that path and provides feedback at the end.

Jeanne is a citizen of the Philippines and a highly qualified nurse. City Hospital would like her to join their staff, and is relying on you and your team to help her obtain the visa she needs.

Select an appropriate visa type to proceed.

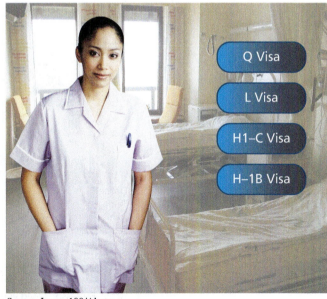

Source: Image 100/Alamy.

---

learning object
A self-contained digital resource embedded in an e-learning course that can be edited and reused for other purposes.

serious game
A game designed for useful purposes beyond pure entertainment.

industries such as defense, education, health care, or emergency response. Many simulations might also be called serious games, as they draw on gaming features such as levels, hints, rewards, role play, and fast-paced, competitive action.

Corporations develop such games for a variety of purposes. Sun Microsystems, for example, created Rise of the Shadow Specters, a 3D serious gaming simulation set in an alternate universe that helps new hires learn the company's structure, values, and innovative culture. Wandering colonists settle one of the worlds, and their goal is to create an information network with a knowledge base to make sure colonists don't get lost again. In the game world, Sun is the groundbreaking company that founds the network. The military also uses games such as Virtual Battlespace 2 in its training programs to simulate ambushes, evacuations, and other fast-paced action so trainees improve the split-second decision-making and visual attentions skills they will need.[17]

Software to create serious games varies, and some applications are relatively straightforward, allowing educators to embed their own content in templates such as Snakes and Ladders. More advanced game engines used to create rich 3D environments similar to the kind found in commercial games have longer learning curves and may require programming skills.[18] While some engines are proprietary, other companies encourage educators and students to use their game engines.[19] Epic Games, for example, freely offers its Unreal Engine for education.

Collaboration Tools

E-learning, especially when it is instructor-led, takes advantage of many of the collaboration tools described in Chapter 8. Discussion forums, shared workspaces, blogs, and wikis offer useful ways for instructors and students to interact asynchronously. Virtual worlds, web conferences, and interactive video systems support synchronous interaction.

Web conferencing systems are widely used for virtual business meetings, but they have features that make them ideal for e-learning as well (Figure 9-21). Participants all see what the meeting host selects to show—presentation slides, a software application, a website, or an interactive whiteboard, for example. They can interact using webcams and microphones or submit comments and questions using text chat. The host might want to walk them through an Excel worksheet, show some websites, or write on the shared whiteboard. Other features

FIGURE 9-21
Virtual classroom session.

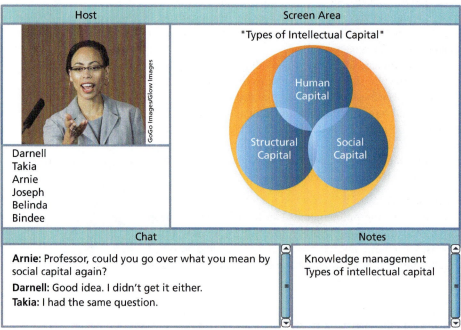

Source: GoGo Images/Glow Images.

include file sharing, polling, and "breakout rooms" so small groups can work together privately and then come together to report back.

Students can express themselves with a few of those nonverbal nuances that help teachers gauge how the class is going. Even if they aren't using their own webcams, students can indicate status by clicking icons to signal they are laughing, clapping, raising their hand, or nodding their heads in agreement. They can also pass private "notes" to one another. Simulated web conferencing is widely used in the interactive decision-making simulations for this text.

Strategies to Prevent Cheating

A thorny problem for online learning is cheating, particularly when higher stakes such as a promotion or academic credit are involved.[20] Was it really the student who took the final exam? If it was, did he or she break the rules by opening the textbook or doing a Google search?

Most e-learning programs require users to log in with a password, and some use fingerprints or other biometric identification. For tests, course authors might require the student to agree to an honor code before starting or take the test in a proctored setting. Some organizations require the student to turn on a webcam, pan the room so the remote proctor can confirm the student is alone, and then leave the camera on while the student takes the test. New technologies are also under development, such as software that tracks eye movements, monitors the browser, or recognizes each student's typing patterns.

"Telepresence robots" help students who can't join a face-to-face class but really want to. A 10-year-old girl with cancer, for example, logs into a motorized robot at school equipped with a video monitor, microphone, speakers, and wheels. Steering her robot from home on her iPad, she can attend classes, chat with classmates, and participate in small groups.[21]

Learning Management Systems

Carlos manages the company's whole e-learning program with a corporate **learning management system (LMS)**. The LMS is an information system used to deliver the e-learning courses, track student progress, and manage educational records. Many offer other features, such as online registration, assessment tools, collaborative technologies, and payment processing. They also offer tools for creating or importing content.

Once considered niche software, the LMS has grown in importance as organizations focus on knowledge management and talent development, striving to nurture their employees and build intellectual capital. It also has become a crucial feature in industries such as hazardous materials or financial services, where compliance with regulations requires many specialized training programs and certifications.

LEARNING OBJECTS, ASSESSMENTS, AND STANDARDS

The LMS hosts the e-learning content and assessments and provides a range of tools to create learning objects, quizzes, and tests. For a lesson, the instructor might insert text, images, or video into a sequence of pages through which the student will progress. To assess learning, the instructor can create tests with instant feedback and many options for grading, timing, and retaking. Many LMSs offer tools to create more advanced content, such as adaptive learning modules, as well. This technology adjusts the way the material is presented to students based on their responses or preferences, especially to avoid boring those who already know the material or confusing those who need more instruction.

Learning objects created with content authoring tools in the LMS work nicely in that environment, but they may not be usable in another LMS. A student's score on a quiz, for example, might not be captured correctly. As LMS vendors strove to raise switching costs by

learning management system (LMS)
An information system used to deliver e-learning courses, track student progress, and manage educational records. Such systems also support features such as online registration, assessments, collaborative technologies, payment processing, and content authoring.

adding proprietary features that made it difficult for clients to move their content to a rival LMS, the need for interoperability and industry standards for e-learning content became clear.

Several standards for learning objects emerged, and the LMS vendors added tools so clients could export and import learning objects. One set of standards is called the **Sharable Content Object Reference Model (SCORM)**. These guidelines govern how e-learning objects communicate with the LMS on a technical level, so a user can import a SCORM-compliant object to any LMS that supports the standard. Another example is Learning Tools Interoperability (LTI), a specification that establishes standard ways of integrating rich, cloud-based content from remote hosts into an organization's LMS.

Another emerging trend involves badges so that learners earn recognition for smaller chunks of learning as they progress through a course or a program. The concept comes from gaming where badges and other signs of accomplishment are common. Assuming the LMS vendors conform to open standards, the badges may become open credentials that employers recognize.[22]

SOCIAL LEARNING PLATFORMS

The long history of knowledge management efforts makes it clear that people learn at least as much from their peers and mentors on the job as they do from formal learning programs and instructors. People are so accustomed to social networking and other Web 2.0 applications that it is an easy step to build these tools into e-learning environments. Many LMS vendors are doing this by adding support for wikis, blogs, news feeds, personal profiles, discussion forums, and virtual classrooms. Organizations that already have social software in place for knowledge sharing can tie the activities that happen in those venues to their e-learning programs. For example, an instructor leading a course on web analytics can start a blog accessible to the whole organization to highlight key points from the course and how they apply to current events in the company. Using social software to blend the e-learning programs with what happens day-to-day is a powerful way to make learning timely, relevant, and just-in-time.

Compare and contrast corporate and educational e-learning as well as e-learning and classroom-based learning.

 ## E-Learning in Education

Sally is no stranger to e-learning. When she and her husband decided to retire, she enrolled in an online course on nonprofit management. She registered online and then received her login name and password to the college's LMS. Her course hadn't started, but she could click on links to view the syllabus, assignments, textbooks, and also an introductory video. Professor Altman encouraged all the students to complete their profiles and upload a photo so classmates could get to know one another.

On the first night of class, Sally logged into the virtual classroom and was immediately welcomed by the professor using a webcam: "Welcome, Sally, I'm glad you could make it tonight. Can you hear me OK? Try using your mike to make sure it works." Several other students were already there, conversing in the scrolling chat window.

As the small class progressed, Sally and her classmates read the e-textbook, visited websites, watched videos, completed assignments, sent endless emails and text messages, and contributed to discussions in the forum. They added comments to the professor's blog, worked on team projects, and shared personal news in the virtual lounge.

For each assignment, the professor sent detailed feedback and talked with Sally by phone as well. They held virtual classes weekly, but the classes were all recorded so Sally could skip a few when she was busy at work and watch them later.

Sally's experience with e-learning featured frequent attention from the professor. Another model gaining momentum in higher education is the **massive open online course (MOOC)**. A MOOC is usually offered by a college or university through a third party, and anyone can enroll for free or very low cost. Coursera, for instance, hosts courses contributed by many universities, such as Introductory Human Physiology (Duke University). Millions have enrolled in MOOCs, although most never actually finish a course.

Most MOOCs rely on computer-based testing and feedback rather than feedback from instructors, and some also ask participants to evaluate one another's work. Most MOOCs do not carry any academic credit, although some universities are considering it by adding proctored tests or other requirements. Corporations are also exploring their value for training and also marketing.[23] How MOOCs will affect traditional education is a hot topic, given their potential to reach anyone with a desire to learn.

Differences Between Corporate and Education E-Learning

Initially, universities and corporations took different approaches to e-learning. Corporations built many self-paced e-learning modules that employees could take on their own time to improve their skills or achieve certifications. Many modules were professionally developed with excellent production values or licensed from providers who developed specialized commercial software. Instructor-led training was conducted mainly in classrooms, not online.

> **PRODUCTIVITY TIP**
> Before you start an online course, navigate around the site to get comfortable with the tools you can use. Check out all the links to make sure you know where to find all the course content and assignments. Sometimes links are deeply buried and easy to miss.

In contrast, colleges and universities leaned toward simulating the learning experience of a face-to-face class led by a faculty member. The faculty pioneers who experimented with e-learning created their own courses.

One consequence was that LMS developers targeted *either* the corporate market *or* the educational market, and the products were different for each. The LMS for business emphasized integration with human resources, compliance training, and professional development tracking. The educational products followed a course model, with syllabus, library access, gradebooks, test banks, and many collaborative tools—wikis, blogs, forums, profiles, and more. While business software developers focused on corporate needs, the educational market became dominated by companies such as Blackboard and Desire2Learn as well as open source products such as Moodle. Over time, however, the requirements are converging, especially as corporations seek to build social software into their e-learning programs and a growing number of LMS vendors respond with competitive products.

Comparing E-Learning and Classroom Learning

E-learning is one of those disruptive innovations with the potential to overturn existing industries in waves of creative destruction, not just in corporations but in colleges and schools as well. Fiery debates about it are not uncommon. Educators and corporate trainers worry that they could suffer the same fate as travel agents, whose numbers diminished as people migrated to online services to plan trips and buy tickets.

Many argued that e-learning is a poor substitute for a live classroom in which students and teacher can interact face-to-face. The lecture method of teaching and learning is more than 700 years old, first used in medieval universities in Paris. Perhaps its resilience speaks to its effectiveness as a gold standard for learning. Indeed, a nagging question for corporations and educational institutions alike is whether e-learning "works." Do students learn and retain as much from an e-learning course as from one offered in a face-to-face classroom?

In general, research that compares student outcomes for e-learning and classroom-based learning shows few differences. In many studies, online students actually do better in certain respects.[24] However, the results are variable, and as we discussed, e-learning comes in many forms, from Sally's intimate online class to the gigantic MOOCs. Conventional classrooms vary as well due to the talent, expertise, and energy of the teacher.

As for technologies, Figure 9-22 shows which ones might be useful in different settings, from the asynchronous e-learning conducted at "different times, different places," to the "same time, same place" classroom experience.

Sharable Content Object Reference Model (SCORM)
A set of standards that govern how e-learning objects communicate with the LMS on a technical level, so a user can import a SCORM-compliant object to any LMS that supports the standard.

massive open online course (MOOC)
An online course usually offered by a college or university through a third party for free or very low cost, with open enrollment and often very large volume.

FIGURE 9-22

Comparing e-learning and classroom-based instructional technologies based on whether students and instructor are in the same or different locations, and whether their interactions occur at the same time (synchronous) or different times (asynchronous).

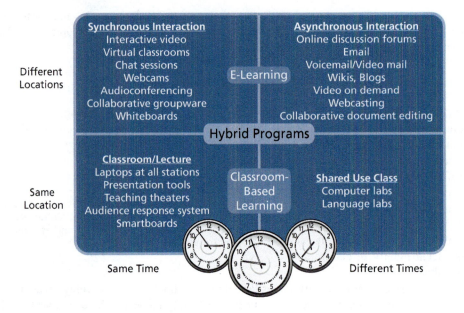

Finally, the nature of the student counts. Success in e-learning courses depends heavily on the students' ability to adapt to this learning format and apply top-notch time-management skills. Figure 9-23 offers some useful tips.

E-learning and classroom learning are complements to one another, and organizations can blend them in creative ways by offering online resources to students enrolled in classroom-based programs, for instance. They can also tie in-person events into e-learning or develop hybrid programs that leverage the best aspects of each.

Learning is an essential building block in any effort to manage intellectual capital in a broader sense, and e-learning is a powerful tool for knowledge management. It supports formal courses, and combined with social media tools, it promotes informal, just-in-time learning among colleagues. To speed learning for a new CRM system, for instance, the company might offer face-to-face classes, e-learning courses, and also an easy-to-use wiki in which employees can ask each other questions about specific screens, post their own solutions and tips, and access the training manuals and videos. When information systems help integrate learning smoothly into day-to-day work, it does not feel like "learning" at all. Instead, it adds to the organization's culture of knowledge sharing and cooperation and constitutes real progress toward effective knowledge management.

FIGURE 9-23

Tips for succeeding in e-learning.

▶ Manage your time effectively. Create a calendar with to-do list and deadlines that match the course requirements and your own schedule. (Time management mishaps are a major cause of failure in e-learning.)

▶ Practice navigating the course and the learning management system before class starts. Be sure you know how to turn in assignments and take online tests. Locate any FAQs or online help files and keep them handy.

▶ Post a personal profile that humanizes your presence in the class, adding hobbies and career interests. Include any special expertise to help with expert location.

▶ Polish your skills with the collaborative technologies offered. Try practicing with one classmate first to avoid making a major blunder that all will see.

▶ Communicate often in the class discussions, wikis, blogs, virtual classroom, or whatever medium is offered. This is your only way to show that you are "present" in the class.

▶ For group projects, build trust and develop agreement by creating a team charter, volunteering, meeting deadlines, offering assistance, and documenting work assignments. (See Chapter 8 for more tips on virtual teamwork.)

▶ Help build the learning community by asking questions and offering comments, not just to the instructor, but to other students.

▶ After the course ends, invite classmates you worked well with to join your social network, continuing to build your social capital.

MyMISLab
Online Simulation

CRIMINAL INVESTIGATIONS DIVISION
A Role-Playing Simulation on Knowledge Management for Crime Scene Police Work

The deputy police commissioner who heads the Criminal Investigations Division looks over the roster and sighs. "So, another rookie just brought in a suspect's computer as evidence but forgot to initial the sealing tape. With so few experienced officers, we just can't afford to put one on every team to avoid mistakes like that. And we're going to lose them in a year or two, anyway, and that means an awful lot of knowledge going out the door. We've got to do something now before that happens."

The commissioner chimed in. "The recruits have some savvy of their own that they could share. They're right on top of the way flash mobs are using Twitter and Facebook. Our older officers don't know much about that."

Much of what those veteran detectives know about solving cases comes from many years of investigating crime scenes, interviewing witnesses, interrogating suspects, gathering and processing forensic evidence, and chasing down leads. The training the new recruits receive helps, but there is so much to remember and little time to look things up when officers are out in the field. For their part, the recruits could really be helpful to show the other officers how the flash mobs organize so quickly and how police could get to the scene more quickly.

The commissioner thinks you should be able to bring in new ideas about how to capture this priceless intellectual capital and make it available to all the officers. The leadership is open to suggestions, so log in when you're ready to learn more about the challenges they face and how you can help ...

Chapter Summary

LEARNING OBJECTIVES

1 Intellectual capital includes all the intangible assets and resources of an enterprise that are not captured by conventional accounting reports but that still contribute to its value and help it achieve competitive advantage. The three types are human, social, and structural capital. Explicit knowledge can be documented and codified, but tacit knowledge is more difficult to capture because it includes insights, judgment, creative processes, and even wisdom from experience. Organizations launch knowledge management initiatives to better manage their intellectual capital.

2 Knowledge management (KM) refers to a set of strategies and practices organizations use to become more systematic about managing intellectual capital. A knowledge management project begins with the identification of the goal; projects with clear and focused objectives are more likely to succeed. The second step is locating the sources of knowledge. Search tools can crawl through corporate data sources to find expertise, and social network analysis can also identify key people in specific fields. The third step is to capture the knowledge using a variety of techniques such as after-action reviews, best-practice sessions, wikis, shadowing, and blogs. Communities of practice are also widely used to capture knowledge. Knowledge must be organized, shared, and valuated to be most useful to an organization, and the organization's intranet often becomes the focal point for these steps. Organizations use enterprise content management (ECM) to organize and track content items of all different types, such as documents, images, videos, or web pages. ECM systems offer a variety of capabilities. For example, document management systems rely on optical character recognition (OCR) and intelligent-character recognition (ICR) to convert paper-based information to searchable electronic format. To determine value and decide what to keep, organizations consider compliance requirements, operational effectiveness, and strategic value.

3 The human element's role in KM efforts is critical, especially because many incentives exist to hoard valuable knowledge rather than share it. The right incentives can encourage employees to share. KM projects are also prone to fail when the technologies underlying them are too complicated or the content is not useful. The semantic web offers considerable potential for large-scale knowledge management across enterprises by describing relationships among entities with the resource description framework (RDF).

4 E-learning is an important ingredient for building intellectual capital and developing talent. Approaches include self-paced e-learning, instructor-led e-learning, and hybrid programs that combine face-to-face classes with e-learning.

5 E-learning programs begin with clear objectives, and courses are created by teams that include subject matter experts, instructional designers, a sponsor, and others. Different approaches to e-learning include self-paced, instructor-led, and hybrid instruction. Learning objects are digital resources that each cover one topic. Technology helps developers to create narrated slide presentations, interactive presentations, screen captures, simulations, and serious games. E-learning courses also may include collaborative technologies to support synchronous and asynchronous interactions between instructors and students. Learning management systems (LMS) support e-learning programs with features such as online registration, powerful content-authoring tools, tools to create tests and assessments, progress tracking, gradebooks, social networking, and other Web 2.0 technologies. Standards such as SCORM and LTI help ensure compatibility with multiple learning management systems and make it easier for instructors to draw from cloud-based learning resources. Strategies to prevent cheating include proctored tests, webcams, and biometric authentication.

6 Corporate e-learning emerged with an emphasis on self-paced modules, while e-learning in higher education tended to replicate a classroom experience. The two are growing more similar as corporations add more collaboration. Although there are many varieties of both e-learning and classroom-based learning, research generally confirms that outcomes for e-learning are equal to or slightly better than face-to-face classes.

KEY TERMS AND CONCEPTS

intellectual capital (IC)

human capital

social capital

structural capital

explicit knowledge

tacit knowledge

knowledge management (KM)

social network analysis (SNA)

communities of practice

intranet

enterprise content management (ECM)

document management systems

intelligent character recognition (ICR)

semantic web

resource description framework (RDF)

e-learning

subject matter expert

instructional designer

learning object

serious game

learning management system (LMS)

Sharable Content Object Reference Model (SCORM)

massive open online course (MOOC)

CHAPTER REVIEW QUESTIONS

9-1. What is intellectual capital? What are the three main types of intellectual capital? How is each type of intellectual capital acquired?
MyMISLab

9-2. What is explicit knowledge? What is tacit knowledge? How does each contribute to intellectual capital? Why do they require different management approaches?
MyMISLab

9-3. What are the steps in launching a knowledge management program? What types of information technology can be used in a KM program?
MyMISLab

9-4. How can human behavior pose challenges for a KM project?

9-5. What is the semantic web?

9-6. What are three approaches to e-learning? How are these approaches similar? How are they different?

9-7. How are e-learning programs created? What types of technology are used to create e-learning programs? What is a learning management system? What role does it serve?

9-8. How are corporate learning and educational learning similar? How are they different?

9-9. How are e-learning and classroom-based learning similar? How are they different?

PROJECTS AND DISCUSSION QUESTIONS

9-10. In 1998, Buckman Labs was recognized for its leadership in building knowledge communities. In 2000, Bob Buckman was named one of the 10 Most Admired Knowledge Leaders for world-class knowledge leadership. Buckman Labs has received the Most Admired Knowledge Enterprise (MAKE) Award eight times, and Buckman's book, *Building a Knowledge Driven Organization* (2004), is regarded as one of the seminal books on knowledge management. Search the Internet (search "Fast Company Buckman knowledge management") to learn how Buckman created a culture of knowledge sharing. Why did he develop a KM system? How did he motivate employees to share their knowledge?
MyMISLab

9-11. Are you one of the more than 1 billion users of Facebook? Consider your Facebook page and what it may look like in the future when you have completed your degree program and become an expert in your field. Log on to Facebook, select "Profile," and then select "Edit Profile." How would you change your basic information, profile picture, featured people, and philosophy to reflect your future professional status? Would you change the information in other categories such as activities and interests or contact information? Describe how your profile could help identify you as an expert in some area.
MyMISLab

9-12. Microsoft maintains a vast searchable knowledge base containing information about its various products and services. Visit support.microsoft.com. Note the different product categories including Windows, Internet Explorer, Office, and Xbox. Select a product such as "Windows Phone" and then search the top solutions to see various support topics. Return to the product categories and select a Microsoft product you use. Search the solutions to find a topic relevant to your use of the product. What are the advantages of using this site? What are the disadvantages? Prepare a brief summary in which you recommend (or don't recommend) this knowledge base to your coworkers.

9-13. How can collaborative technologies facilitate knowledge management? Recall the types of collaborative technology discussed in Chapter 8. Work in a small group with classmates to create a list of suggestions for your university, outlining how it could use different types of collaborative technology to manage knowledge.

9-14. Work in a small group with classmates to explore the kinds of graduate programs in business that are available online. Are e-learning programs offered online or in hybrid formats? Choose three programs and prepare a brief summary to compare and contrast the way each one uses e-learning that you can share with the class.

APPLICATION EXERCISES

9-15. EXCEL APPLICATION:
Top Talent

Top Talent Employment Services provides both temporary and permanent employees to clients in a tri-state area. Top Talent uses an online customer satisfaction survey that makes it easy for clients to provide feedback about the services and the employees provided by Top Talent. Jill Simons, sales and marketing manager at Top Talent, has asked you to analyze the survey data from the past 3 months to identify areas of company performance that may need improvement. Download the Top Talent Survey Excel file Ch09Ex01 and provide descriptive statistics (mean, mode, minimum, maximum, standard deviation) for each survey item. Use formulas to calculate statistics. Create a line chart to display the survey results (the means of all survey items). Which areas have shown the greatest improvement in customer satisfaction? Which have shown a decline in customer satisfaction?

9-16. ACCESS APPLICATION:
Top Talent

Recall the e-learning course that Sally was asked to develop at the beginning of this chapter and assume it was a success. Now her firm has decided to create a simplified version of an expert location system in order to capture the experience of its professional staff. Carlos plans to launch the system using an Access database. His goal is to identify members of the staff who have specialized expertise and to provide access to that knowledge in a searchable format. Download the TopTalent Excel file Ch09Ex02 and import the worksheets to create the database shown in Figure 9-24. Create a report that lists each expert by name within each category of expertise.

FIGURE 9-24
Access database for Top Talent.

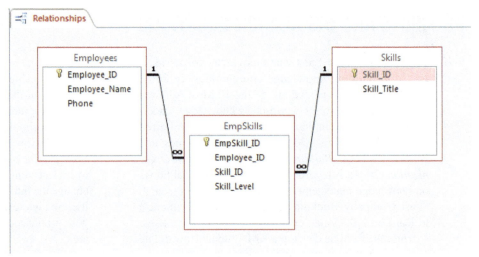

Source: Microsoft® Access, Microsoft Corporation. Reprinted with permission.

Lynda.com: How an E-Learning Entrepreneur Rides Waves of Change

Lynda Weinman, cofounder of the online learning company called Lynda.com, says, "The first time I ever used a computer, I went to the manual to try to teach myself how to do it, and I was mortified by how it was written." Like many others, she struggled to teach herself and decided there had to be a better way.

Weinman first decided to write a book on web design, one that became a widely used textbook at universities and colleges around the world. She and her husband Bruce Heavin moved to California and began offering face-to-face classes on web design, and many of their eager students were trying to start high-tech businesses of their own—the so-called "dot-coms." Business was booming, and the couple began exploring new instructional strategies—recorded videos, in particular.

But in the spring of 2000, the dot-com bubble started bursting. Most of those high-tech online companies took huge hits in their stock prices; Amazon.com, for example, went from $107 per share to $7. Many companies—like Pets.com, which sold pet supplies on the Internet and was becoming a household name with ads airing during the Super Bowl—failed completely, and investors lost more than $300 million. (The URL pets.com now belongs to retailer PetSmart.) As their funding dried up, the dot-coms stopped sending students to Weinman, and business plummeted.

Changing the Business Model

The 9/11 terrorist attacks in 2001 hit the U.S. economy even harder, and CEOs slashed spending on travel and training. Weinman, however, saw an opportunity to fill a need and decided to try a new business model. She and her husband had a growing library of training videos, but rather than sell them individually as DVDs, they decided to offer them as an online library with paid subscriptions. Subscribers could watch any video in the growing library for a flat monthly rate.

The switch was risky, especially because most of their revenue was coming from DVD sales. Weinman and Heavin frankly admit that marketing was never their strength, but they stuck to their decision. Unlike most of the dot-com entrepreneurs who wanted to build a business quickly and then sell it, the pair wanted to stay with this adventure. Because the subscription price includes the whole library, Lynda.com encourages browsing and developing new computer skills. Those who took one course were tempted to try others.

Their strategy worked, and subscriptions began to soar. Companies that could not afford travel bills and instructor-led training purchased volume subscriptions for their whole organization. Government agencies and universities began buying campus-wide subscriptions, and the New York Public Library purchased access to share with library visitors.

The company received $103 million in venture capital to expand worldwide. By 2013, sales topped $22 million and Lynda.com employed 450 people—teachers, designers, content developers, and support personnel.

Riding the Next Wave

Lynda.com began before the explosion of free online videos, and the company will need to find new ways to compete if it maintains the subscription model. YouTube, for instance, features thousands of free instructional videos—from pruning fruit trees to using Excel pivot tables. Many are contributed by experts in the field. YouTube mainly earns revenue through advertising. Khan Academy also offers thousands of free instructional videos, mostly in math and science. That site has no advertising but attracts funding from donors such as the Gates Foundation. The massive open online courses (MOOCs), which are also free, present another challenge to Lynda.com's subscription model. For-profit Coursera, for example, offers hundreds of free online courses contributed by dozens of universities.

Lynda.com focuses on excellence in teaching, high production values, and advanced training in software development; so far, that strategy is succeeding. Recent releases, for example, feature Universal Windows app development, HTML 5 projects, and new features in AutoCad 2017, the 3D design tool. But competing against the growing volume of free videos that help people acquire high tech skills will be one of Lynda.com's next challenges. The professional network LinkedIn purchased Lynda.com in 2015 to offer those educational services to its members, and then Microsoft purchased LinkedIn a year later, so Lynda.com will have plenty of backup and capital to face those challenges.

Discussion Questions

9-17. When Lynda.com began offering subscriptions to a library of e-learning courses, what new value did the company provide to its customers? What advantages did e-learning from Lynda.com have over traditional in-person education?

9-18. What kind of changes to company's information systems would be needed to support this new business model?

9-19. What types of training would Lynda.com have difficulty providing customers? What kinds of education are less appropriate for e-learning than traditional in-person courses?

9-20. What kind of challenges does Lynda.com face today? How might the business be changed to address these?

Sources: Collins, A. (2013). Tech, media & telecom: Lynda.com acquires Video2brain. *Mergers & Acquisitions Report*, *26*(7), 24.

Lynda.com. (2016). *Hoover's Online*, accessed August 16, 2016.

Lynda.com, NYPL explore librarywide access model. (2013). *Library Journal*, *138* (1), 24.

Lynda.com fuels growth and innovation with $103 million funding. (January 16, 2013). *Business Wire*, http://search.proquest.com/docview/1269628604?accountid=11752, accessed August 16, 2016.

Microsoft to acquire LinkedIn. (June 13, 2016). Microsoft.com website, accessed August 16, 2016.

Sorvino, C. (2016). A Q&A with mother of the Internet Lynda Weinman, cofounder of Lynda.com. Forbes.com, http://www.forbes.com/sites/chloesorvino/2016/06/05/a-qa-with-mother-of-the-internet-lynda-weinman-cofounder-of-lynda-com/#6b5461554c63, accessed August 16, 2016.

CASE STUDY #2

Diplopedia: Managing State Department Knowledge with a Wiki

The U.S. State Department's Diplopedia wiki started in 2006 with just a handful of articles. The project was driven partly by the need for improvements in collaboration and knowledge management at the department that the 9/11 Commission recommended.

U.S. diplomats and other State Department employees move frequently from country to country, and they needed a much better way to capture and transmit knowledge. They might take 6 months to a year to get up to speed when they were transferred to a new country. They could email or phone other department employees who had lived there, but the wiki solution is far superior.

The wiki is a rapidly mounting collection of constantly updated articles on subjects critical to diplomats. For instance, it contains the desk officer manual that helps newcomers decipher departmental jargon or tips on getting a newly nominated ambassador confirmed by the Senate. As an internal wiki, Diplopedia is only accessible to authorized employees.

The idea for the State Department's wiki as a knowledge repository came from Jimmy Wales, founder of Wikipedia. Diplopedia uses the same open source software and also follows many of its guidelines, as shown in Figure 9-25. Unlike Wikipedia, however, the State Department's wiki requires strict governance, given that much of the information in it may be sensitive. Wikipedians rely on people behaving like adults, so their guidance to the department about governance was basically to tell employees: "Don't be a jerk."

The Office of eDiplomacy at the State Department oversees Diplopedia and provides clear guidelines for contributors. A founding principle of Diplopedia is to assume people's good intentions. As a check, however, Diplopedia does not permit anonymous contributions, as Wikipedia does, and no "sock puppets" are allowed.

Disputes about content are also handled differently compared with Wikipedia. At the public encyclopedia, editing battles can erupt in which anonymous contributors keep changing one another's posts, often until the controversy just dies down on its own or the contributors tire out. On rare occasions, Wikipedia's administrators might freeze an article to prevent further editing. At Diplopedia, however, the Office of eDiplomacy might form a panel of experts to settle the dispute.

Diplopedia's success surprised many observers because the department was not known for any pioneering IT initiatives. Chris Bronk, a professor at Rice University who studies the agency, remarked that "science and technology have a somewhat tarnished history at State." Even though the department is fully wired, its communication patterns have changed little since the days of the telegraph and cable, although email is used instead.

Diplopedia is not open to the public, though its contents are unclassified. The site's disclaimer reminds users that the articles may be informative, but they are not official government documents. Especially after WikiLeaks obtained and publicly released thousands of classified diplomatic documents in 2010, the security for online government documents receives considerable scrutiny, yet breaches still occur.

Diplopedia's contributors must keep in mind that their contributions are not confidential. Leaks are not uncommon, and leakers are rarely prosecuted. Contributors must be careful what they post; nonetheless, the site still provides a valuable platform for information that helps diplomats adapt as they move from one country to another. The State Department encourages them to make contributions of enduring value, ones that will capture and document the richness of their experiences and expertise about their country. Most important, their knowledge will not be lost when their plane takes off for the next assignment. And it won't go out of date, either, as newly assigned members of the diplomatic corps correct, expand, and enrich the wiki knowledge base.

FIGURE 9-25

Strategies for KM success for Diplopedia.
Diplopedia's Guidelines.

▸ If something is wrong, change it.
▸ If something is missing, add it.
▸ Use plain language.
▸ Use the Discussion tab to discuss an article.
▸ Use a neutral point of view.

Discussion Questions

9-21. In 2010, the website WikiLeaks posted more than 250,000 U.S. diplomatic cables. What are some potential implications of this posting for Diplopedia?

9-22. What key issues will need to be addressed for Diplopedia to be more widely used by diplomatic personnel?

9-23. How can the State Department benefit from Diplopedia?

9-24. What types of knowledge are appropriate for Diplopedia?

Bronk, C. (March 2010). Diplomacy rebooted: Making digital statecraft a reality. *Foreign Service Journal*, 43–47.

Bronk, C. (2010). Diplopedia imagined: Building State's diplomacy wiki. Proceedings of the 2010 International Symposium on Collaborative Technologies and Systems.

Perez, E., & Prokupecz, S. (March 1, 2015). Sources: State Dept. hack the 'worst ever.' CNN.com, http://www.cnn.com/2015/03/10/politics/state-department-hack-worst-ever/, accessed September 30, 2016.

Pozen, D. (2013). The leaky leviathan: Why the government condemns and condones unlawful disclosures of information. Columbia Public Law Research Paper No. 13-341.

Sources: About Diplopedia. (July 15, 2015). U.S. State Department website, http://www.state.gov/m/irm/ediplomacy/115847.htm, accessed August 16, 2016.

E-PROJECT 1 — Exploring the World of Online Courses

Thousands of courses are available for free on the web, and in this e-project you will explore some of them to learn what technologies they use and how they compare to your own courses.

9-25. Visit the MIT Open Courseware project (http://ocw.mit.edu) and review the many courses available. Note the icons at the top of the course listings that explain what resources are included. Find a course that you have already taken at your college or university.

    a. What resources are included in the online course?

    b. What technologies does the course rely on for its learning objects?

    c. How does this course compare to the one you took at your university?

9-26. Visit the Khan Academy (www.khanacademy.org) to learn more about a growing list of online course materials posted on YouTube. Salman Khan started this nonprofit organization with the aim of making education freely available to anyone who wants it at any time. Courses are arranged as "playlists," and students are encouraged to start from the beginning unless they need a quick refresher on a specific topic. Choose a course that you have already taken, look over the list of topics, and watch the first video.

    a. What technologies does the course rely on?

    b. How does this approach to online courses compare with MIT's open courseware?

    c. How does it compare to the course you took?

E-PROJECT 2 — Managing the Human Element on Wikipedia with Technology

In this e-project, you will explore Wikipedia's strategies for managing the largest online knowledge repository in the world, learning more about how technology is used to manage the human element.

First, visit Wikipedia's main page (http://en.wikipedia.org/wiki/Main_Page) for an overview of the site. Next, go to the article titled "Smartphone" (http://en.wikipedia.org/wiki/Smartphone).

9-27. Click on the Talk tab at the top.

    a. What is the purpose of this section?

    b. What issues and debates are underway regarding the content of the article on smartphones?

    c. How does this technical support for discussion about the contents of an article help manage the human element?

9-28. Go back to the article and click on the Edit tab.

    a. What is Wikipedia's policy regarding the disclosure of your IP address if you are not logged into your account and choose to edit the contents of an article?

    b. Why would Wikipedia's leadership allow account holders to hide their IP addresses?

9-29. Wikipedia has special policies for controversial topics.

    a. How does Wikipedia define "edit warring?"

    b. What strategies does Wikipedia use to handle editors who have disputes over content?

    c. Overall, how do you evaluate Wikipedia's strategies for managing the human element?

CHAPTER NOTES

1. YCharts. (2016). *Apple Market Cap (AAPL)*. https://ycharts.com/companies/AAPL/market_cap, accessed August 16, 2016.

2. Kott, A., & Limaye, R. J. (March 31, 2016). To fight Zika, coordinating agencies must prioritize effective knowledge management. *New Security Beat*, https://www.newsecuritybeat.org/2016/03/fight-zika-coordinating-agencies-prioritize-effective-knowledge-management/, accessed August 19, 2016.

3. Hobert, K.A. (2015). *Revive knowledge management with the digital workplace* (No. G00289855). Gartner Research, http://www.gartner.com/document/3146417?ref=solrAll&refval=167022770&qid=b2db813afab6d38c643d29d57b343d27, accessed August 19, 2016.

4. Call center case study. www.knowledgesys.com/solutions/print-call-center-case.pdf, accessed April 28, 2016.

5. Byosiere, P., et al. (2010). Diffusion of organisational innovation: Knowledge transfer through social networks. *International Journal of Technology Management, 49*(4), 401–420.

6. Patton, S. (June 15, 2005). Who knows whom, and who knows what? *CIO, 18*(17), 1.

7. Majchrzak, A., Wagner, C., & Yates, D. (2013). The impact of shaping on knowledge reuse for organizational improvement with wikis. *MIS Quarterly, 37*(2), 455-A12.

8. Nath, A. K. (2015). Web 2.0 for knowledge management in organizations and their effects on tacit knowledge sharing and perceived learning. *Journal of Accounting, Business & Management, 22*(2), 11–22.

9. Shegda, K. M., & Chin, K. (2015). *Critical capabilities for enterprise content management: Compliance and records management* (No. G00274701). Gartner Research. http://www.gartner.com/document/3176520, accessed August 18, 2016.

10. Doersch, C., Singh, S., Gupta, A., Sivic, J., & Efros, A. A. (2015). What makes Paris look like Paris? *Communications of the ACM, 58*(12), 103–110. http://doi.org/10.1145/2830541

11. Jimenez-Jimenez, D., & Sanz-Valle, R. (2013). Studying the effect of HRM practices on the knowledge management process. *Personnel Review, 42*(1), 28–49. doi:10.1108/00483481311285219

12. Yong, S. H., Byoungsoo, K., Heeseok, L., & Young-Gul, K. (2013). The effects of individual motivations and social capital on employees' tacit and explicit knowledge sharing intentions. *International Journal of Information Management, 33*(2), 356–366.

13. Solitander, M., & Solitander, N. (2010). The sharing, protection and thievery of intellectual assets: The case of the Formula 1 industry. *Management Decision, 48*(1), 37–57.

14. Mankins, M., Bird, A., & Root, J. (2013). Making star teams out of star players. *Harvard Business Review, 91*(1), 74–78.

15. Lovelace, K. J., Eggers, F., & Dyck, L. R. (2016). I do and I understand: Assessing the utility of web-based management simulations to develop critical thinking skills. *Academy of Management Learning & Education, 15*(1), 100–121. http://doi.org/10.5465/amle.2013.0203

16. Curry, J., Price, T., & Sabin, P. (2016). Commercial-Off-the-Shelf-Technology in UK Military Training. *Simulation & Gaming, 47*(1), 7–30. http://doi.org/10.1177/1046878115600578

17. Mead, C. (2013). *War play: Video games and the future of armed conflict*. New York, NY: Eamon Dolan/Houghton Mifflin Harcourt.

18. Meloni, W. (2015). Rev up your engines. *Computer Graphics World, 38*(1), 18–23.

19. Allal-Chérif, O., & Makhlouf, M. (2016). Using serious games for human resource management: Lessons from France's top 40 companies. *Global Business & Organizational Excellence, 35*(3), 27–36. http://doi.org/10.1002/joe.21668

20. Kapoor, K. (2014). Preventing high-tech cheating. *Claims, 62*(9), 11–11.

21. St. George, D. (November 28, 2015). Peyton's awesome virtual self, a robot that allows girl with cancer to attend school. *Washington Post*, https://www.washingtonpost.com/local/education/peytons-awesome-virtual-self-a-robot-that-allows-girl-with-cancer-to-attend-school/2015/11/28/ad481a00-9258-11e5-a2d6-f57908580b1f_story.html, accessed August 18, 2016.

22. Lowendahl, J. M., Thayer, T.-L. B., & Morgan, G. (2016). *Top 10 strategic technologies impacting higher education in 2016* (No. G00294732). Gartner Research, http://www.gartner.com/document/3186323?ref=solrAll&refval=167133314&qid=ae8887ac44711793c56069ace51b3f49, accessed August 16, 2016.

23. Dodson, M. N., Kitburi, K., & Berge, Z. L. (2015). Possibilities for MOOCs in corporate training and development. *Performance Improvement, 54*(10), 14–21. http://doi.org/10.1002/pfi.21532

24. Means, B., et al. (2009). Evaluation of evidence-based practices in online learning: A meta-analysis and review of online learning studies. Office of Planning and Policy Development. U.S. Department of Education: Washington, DC.

LEARNING OBJECTIVES

1 Define ethics, describe two ethical frameworks, and explain the relationship between ethics and the law.

2 Explain how intellectual property and plagiarism pose challenges for information ethics, and describe technologies that are used to deal with them.

3 Describe information privacy and strategies to protect it, and explain why organizations may implement surveillance.

4 Explain the steps that organizations use to manage security risks, identify threats, assess vulnerabilities, and develop administrative and technical controls.

5 Explain why human behavior is often the weakest link for ethics, privacy, and security, and provide examples of strategies that can be used to counteract the weaknesses.

> An online, interactive decision-making simulation that reinforces chapter contents and uses key terms in context can be found in MyMISLab™.

INTRODUCTION

IN "VAMPIRE LEGENDS," THE ONLINE DECISION-MAKING SIMULATION FOR THIS CHAPTER, you join a fiercely competitive company in the multiplayer game business. It is about to launch a sequel to its wildly successful first game, and the stakes are very high. The company must roll the game out on time, stay within budget, and do a brilliant marketing campaign. It also must be sure its IT infrastructure can handle whatever happens. With pressure so high, the team must make tough decisions as it confronts choices dealing with ethics, privacy, and security.

This chapter and the simulation explore the responsibilities organizations and individuals share to treat data with care, make ethical decisions about its use, and protect it from countless threats. Game companies face intriguing problems in these areas, with the vast amount of private information they store and the endless hacking attempts. In addition, their customers are often very devoted to their online games and avatars.

VAMPIRE LEGENDS

A Role-Playing Simulation on Ethics, Privacy, and Security in the Multiplayer Online Game Business

Pavel L Photo and Video/Shutterstock

Ethics, privacy, and security issues underscore how the human element is so tightly interwoven with the other three components of information systems: technology, processes, and data. People decide how to build a system, manage it, secure it, and use the potentially price-less information it contains. Let's begin with ethics and the kinds of ethical dilemmas people and organizations face in the digital world.

Define ethics, describe two
ethical frameworks, and explain
the relationship between ethics
and the law.

 # Ethics

How do people decide on the right course of action? What makes an action right or wrong? Most people try to do the right thing, but it is not always easy to decide what that is. **Ethics** refers to a system of moral principles that human beings use to judge right and wrong and to develop rules of conduct.

Ethical Frameworks

Innumerable ethical frameworks have arisen throughout human history, but two are especially widely adopted (Figure 10-1). One framework emphasizes **natural laws and rights**. It judges the morality of an action based on how well it adheres to broadly accepted rules *regardless* of the action's actual consequences. "Thou shalt not steal," for example, is one of Christianity's Ten Commandments, and religious principles form the basis for many underlying rules. Others, such as "Keep your promises," "Protect private property," and "Defend free speech," emerge from beliefs about fundamental and natural rights that belong to human beings. The U.S. Declaration of Independence, for instance, lists life, liberty, and the pursuit of happiness as inalienable human rights.

A second framework, called **utilitarianism**, considers the *consequences* of an action, weighing its good effects against its harmful ones. "First, do no harm" is a precept of medical ethics ensuring physicians will heavily weigh the possible harmful consequences of each remedy. When you try to judge what action would create the greatest good for the greatest number, you are using a utilitarian scheme.

In many situations, both ethical approaches will lead people to the same conclusion about the proper action. But ethical dilemmas arise when they lead to different judgments. For example, Wikipedia founder Jimmy Wales is committed to the principle of free speech on the site. But when *New York Times* reporter David Rohde was kidnapped by the Taliban, the newspaper begged Wales to suppress mention of it. At first Wales asked his team to edit out any updates about the event, playing a deadly game of "whack the mole." When that failed, he blocked Rohde's Wikipedia entry. Wales's ethical framework was sorely challenged when the consequences of sticking to those rules might cause grave harm. Fortunately, Rohde escaped to safety.

Ethics and the Law

Laws are often grounded in ethical principles, such as the prohibition against murder and theft or the protection of private property and free speech. The U.S. Bill of Rights codifies many ethical principles into the Constitution, such as freedom of religion, freedom of the press, and the right to trial by jury. Its Fourth Amendment, about protection from unreasonable search and seizure, helps shape expectations about privacy, as we discuss later in this chapter.

However, some laws have less to do with ethics and instead result from the pushes and pulls of lobbying efforts and political pressures. For example, when cable television was first introduced, the TV networks lobbied hard for laws to slow cable's growth. Their goal is to erect legal barriers against newcomers, and online services are a key target. Taxi companies around the world lobby for laws restricting ride-hailing services such as Lyft and Uber, with some success. Argentina, for instance, banned the services entirely.[1]

FIGURE 10-1
Major ethical frameworks.

Ethical System	Description	Examples
Natural laws and rights	Actions are judged to be ethical or unethical according to how well they adhere to broadly accepted rules derived from natural law.	Thou shalt not kill. Right to privacy. Right to a free press. Liberté, égalité, fraternité.
Utilitarianism	Actions are ethical or unethical based on their consequences and outcomes.	The greatest good for the greatest number. The needs of the many outweigh the needs of the few.

Laws don't cover all ethical principles, so just because an action is legal does not mean it is ethical. Depending on the circumstances, lying might be legal but, at the same time, grossly unethical. A Missouri woman created a fake profile of a fictitious teen boy on the social networking site Myspace and then used the account to torment a neighbor's daughter, who eventually committed suicide. Based on existing laws, the woman's only misbehavior was a violation of the Myspace terms of service.[2]

Ethical Issues and Information and Communications Technologies

Before reading this section, take the short survey in Figure 10-2.

For questions like number 1, both ethical frameworks would lead to the conclusion that stealing a book is not right and warrants punishment. In a few areas, though, questions could lead to a debate that depends on the ethical framework. On number 5, for instance, a natural law approach would lead people to say punishment is warranted, similar to the punishment assigned to the theft in question 1. But a utilitarian approach might argue that helping a sick friend is a greater good compared to the harm done to the copyright owner.

Information and communications technologies (ICT) also add important new elements to ethical decision making. First, they change the scope of effects, especially for the consequences of an action. Their worldwide, viral reach amplifies the extent of both good and harm, turning what might be a minor blunder into something far greater. Twitter's spontaneous nature often leads to trouble—and sometimes unemployment. For example, a congressman's young staffers tweeted about partying in the office at taxpayer expense; they were all fired.[3]

FIGURE 10-2

Take this short survey on ethical decision making. Do you judge these actions as completely right, completely wrong, or somewhere in between?

	Completely right, no punishment 1	2	3	4	5	6	Completely wrong, severe punishment 7
1. In a book store, accounting student K.F. slips an expensive CPA Exam Prep book into a shopping bag, then leaves the store without paying for the book.	O	O	O	O	O	O	O
2. Marketing manager L.D. posts some negative reviews about a competitor on a review website, pretending to be various dissatisfied customers.	O	O	O	O	O	O	O
3. Business student F.W., who asked to take the midterm early due to travel, meets several friends for coffee after the test, to tell them all the questions on it.	O	O	O	O	O	O	O
4. Late for work, Assistant Manager J.T. cuts and pastes large segments from a website to finish a report on time, without citing the source.	O	O	O	O	O	O	O
5. A sick friend asked M.B. for a special book on alternative medicines, so M.B. downloads a pirated copy without paying, and e-mails it to the friend.	O	O	O	O	O	O	O
6. Frustrated by incompetent managers who only promote their relatives, scientist R.P. secretly takes photos of the designs for the company's groundbreaking new medical device, then offers to bring them to the company's rival for a higher paying position there.	O	O	O	O	O	O	O

ethics
A system of moral principles that human beings use to judge right and wrong and to develop rules of conduct.

natural laws and rights
An ethical system that judges the morality of an action based on how well it adheres to broadly accepted rules regardless of the action's actual consequences.

utilitarianism
An ethical system that judges whether an act is right or wrong by considering the consequences of the action, weighing its positive effects against its harmful ones.

Information technology also affects decision making, especially because of the way the online world can affect human behavior. As we discussed in Chapter 8, people often become disinhibited when they interact online and the psychological distance between them is greater. People may underestimate the harm their actions might inflict—out of sight, out of mind. For instance, research shows that college students judge actions differently depending on whether technology is involved. They consider cheating on tests, plagiarizing term papers, and illegal copying of intellectual property to be somehow more acceptable if they use the computer and the Internet to do them.[4]

For the survey in Figure 10-2, add up your points for questions 2, 4, and 5, and compare that total to the sum of your points for 1, 3, and 6. If you tend to judge ethically questionable actions as less serious when they involve technology, your total score for 2, 4, and 5 is lower.

Explain how intellectual property and plagiarism pose challenges for information ethics, and describe technologies that are used to deal with them.

2 | Information Ethics

The ethical issues most important for managing information systems touch especially on the storage, transmission, and use of digitized data. As that mound of data grows, the scope of information ethics grows with it, and so do the controversies.

Figure 10-3 lists many dilemmas involving information ethics. Intellectual property (IP), which is now overwhelmingly digitized, is one example. Some consider IP protection to be a natural right. Others argue that the greater good is served when information is as widely distributed as possible.

Intellectual Property and Digital Rights Management

Intellectual property (IP) includes intangible assets such as music, written works, software, art, designs, movies, creative ideas, discoveries, inventions, and other expressions of the human mind. Most societies have developed a maze of copyright laws, patents, and legal statutes to protect intellectual property rights. These give the creator of the property the right to its commercial value.

ENFORCING IP LAWS

Enforcing IP laws is extremely challenging, however, when the IP is digitized. Media giant Viacom, for example, unsuccessfully tried to sue YouTube for $1 billion for allowing its copyrighted movies to play on the video site. But when many hours of video are uploaded to YouTube *every minute*, spotting one pirated clip is a daunting task.[5]

Laws also vary by country, adding more hurdles. Mexico, for instance, outlaws hyperlinks that link to other servers if they contain unauthorized works.[6] Google, YouTube's owner, decided to block viewers in Germany from seeing videos of a meteorite shower taken by a passing motorist in Russia because the car's radio was playing in the background.

FIGURE 10-3

Information ethics issues and the dilemmas they present.

Information Ethics Issue	Sample Dilemma
Intellectual property rights	Is it more important to protect intellectual property (IP) rights or to make information as widely available as possible? Will IP creators stop creating if there are fewer incentives?
Hacking	Is it ethical to break into the corporate network, not to do harm, but to demonstrate that the company needs better security?
Plagiarism	When a person gets an idea from reading another's work and then paraphrases it in a paper without crediting the source or even remembering where it came from, is that plagiarism? Or is it just forgetfulness?
Parasitic computing	Is it ethical to borrow a few CPU cycles from thousands of private computers without the owners' consent when they are not being used? What if the purpose is to do medical research?
Spam	Is it ethical to harvest millions of email addresses from websites and send them unsolicited commercial messages?

Google was unsure whether the strict German laws would require payment for playing copyrighted songs.[7]

PIRACY

Estimates about the worldwide cost of digital piracy range well into the hundreds of billions, a figure that especially affects the entertainment and software industries.[8] The Business Software Alliance reports alarming financial losses to businesses due to software piracy, estimating that 43% of the software installed on microcomputers around the world is not licensed properly. In its survey of companies, BSA found that only 35% had written policies about software piracy. The survey also found an "awareness gap," with many IT managers saying that their company had written or at least informal policies while many of the workers knew little about them (Figure 10-4).[9]

Yet efforts to fight piracy can lead to unfortunate results. The Recording Industry Association of America (RIAA) initially battled the music piracy problem by suing a few end users for up to $150,000 per downloaded song, targeting music lovers like Brianna, a 12-year-old child in New York. The litigation strategy was so unpopular that RIAA finally gave it up. Instead, it launched anti-piracy teams who send millions of "take down" notices to rogue websites, using software to locate them. RIAA files lawsuits against the larger websites, but their operators can be very elusive.[10]

Most people conform to laws because they agree with the underlying ethical principle or fear punishment. Many think it is not a very serious ethical violation to break IP laws when the material is digitized. They see no victim and no harm to the IP owner—not even a lost sale if the violator had no intention of purchasing a legal copy. Unlike a DVD in a jewel case, a digital copy costs next to nothing, and violators may believe they are unlikely to get caught.

To complicate matters, not everyone agrees that strict legal protection for software is the best ethical decision. The Free Software Foundation, for example, advocates for less restrictive software copyright laws, insisting that users should have the freedom to run, copy, distribute, and improve software products. The foundation argues that access to the source code is essential so independent developers can examine it, fix bugs, and add new features.

Nevertheless, intellectual property is a bedrock of an organization's intellectual capital and competitive advantage. Trade secrets, software, patents, and copyrighted works are all part of what creates that advantage, and many organizations use technology to protect it themselves rather than relying on law enforcement.

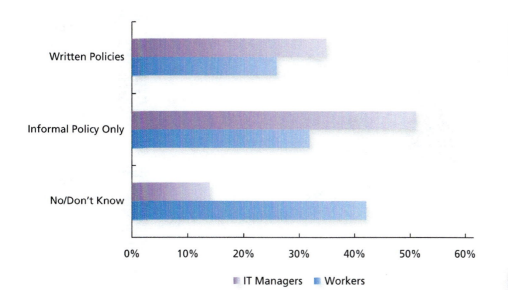

FIGURE 10-4
Does your company/organization have a policy about the use of unlicensed software?

Source: Data from Business Software Alliance. (2014). *The Compliance Gap: BSA Global Software Survey.* Retrieved from http://globalstudy.bsa.org/2013/downloads/studies/2013GlobalSurvey_Study_en.pdf, accessed October 7, 2016.

intellectual property (IP)
Intangible assets such as music, written works, software, art, designs, movies, creative ideas, discoveries, inventions, and other expressions of the human mind that may be legally protected by means of copyrights or patents.

PROTECTING IP WITH TECHNOLOGY AND NEW BUSINESS MODELS

Digital rights management (DRM) refers to technologies that software developers, publishers, media companies, and other intellectual property owners use to control access to their digital content. For example, one scheme requires end users to first connect to a content service to request the material; a request is then sent to another server to obtain the license for actually viewing it (Figure 10-5).

Some cumbersome DRM schemes may be thwarting legitimate users more than pirates, though. For example, e-book distributor Fictionwise angered its customers when one of its publishers decided to stop supplying e-books.[11] People whose computer crashed couldn't get another copy of a book they had already purchased. DRM often interferes with screen readers as well, frustrating the visually impaired who use them to turn on-screen text into speech.

Apple takes a unique approach to music piracy with its iTunes Match service. For an annual fee, the service scans users' hard drive for music files—pirated or not—and stores them in iCloud so users can access their music from their devices. Apple turns over a percentage of the revenue to copyright holders. Users believe they are paying Apple for a useful service, but the business model is actually helping pay for those pirated songs. As new technologies and business models develop, companies will find ways to give IP holders protection for their products without inconveniencing customers.[12]

PRODUCTIVITY TIP

When you purchase digital content, keep copies of online receipts, serial numbers, and confirmation numbers, just in case you have to contact customer support to reinstall it over DRM schemes.

Plagiarism

A type of intellectual property theft that mushroomed with online "cut-and-paste" is plagiarism, which involves reproducing the words of another and passing them off as your own original work without crediting the source.

Plagiarism scandals have tarnished some prominent authors, but technologies are also available to track this kind of activity. Ironically, just as the Internet made plagiarism easy to do, it also made it easy to track. Turnitin.com, for example, offers an "originality checking" service that color-codes documents submitted to it, showing the sources of passages

FIGURE 10-5
Digital rights management scheme.

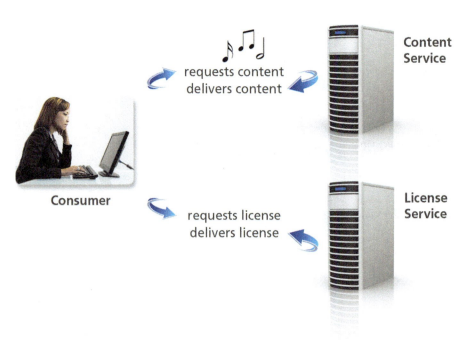

Consumer

♪♫♪ requests content
delivers content

Content Service

requests license
delivers license

License Service

Photos/Illustrations: iofoto/Shutterstock, Blue Vista Design/Shutterstock.

FIGURE 10-6
Checking written work for originality
and possible plagiarism.

Source: Courtesy of iParadigms LLC. Turnitin is a registered trademark of iParadigms LLC
in the United States and other countries.

that match existing written work (Figure 10-6). The company's database includes the billions
of pages on the public Internet and also term papers, journals, and books. Its software even
applies automated translation technology to spot passages in foreign languages that appear
to be translated directly from sam-
ples of English text without crediting the source. Universities are
increasingly adopting the software
and requiring students to check
their own work for unintentional
plagiarism.[13]

> **PRODUCTIVITY TIP**
> Students can use free originality-checking software, such as www.writecheck.
> com, to examine their own work for unintentional plagiarism. The output will
> show which sections are not original and will need citations.

Privacy

3 Describe information privacy and
strategies to protect it, and explain
why organizations may implement
surveillance.

> *"You have zero privacy anyway. Get over it."*
>
> —Scott McNealy, cofounder, Sun Microsystems

> *"If you have something that you don't want anyone to know, maybe you
> shouldn't be doing it in the first place."*
>
> —Eric Schmidt, former CEO, Google

Stern warnings like these—from technology leaders who should know—are stark reminders
of how elusive privacy has become. On a typical day, you might visit hundreds of websites,
enter dozens of search terms, download a free screen saver, collect dozens of cookies, upload
a batch of photos, and click on some ads. Security cameras snap your photo, and stores swipe
your credit card. Your ID badge, your car's EZ pass, your mobile phone, your passport, and
your GPS device track your whereabouts.

Your profiles on social media show your profession, hobbies, friends, and family members. Information about many of your life events is publicly available online—birth, marriage,
home purchase, awards, criminal offenses, and death. And you never know whose cell phone
is silently capturing you in a video, then uploading it to YouTube.

The power to weave all these tidbits into a rich portrait is a marketer's dream because it
might point to products you will buy, investments you might make, or charities you choose

**digital rights management
(DRM)**
Technologies that software
developers, publishers, media
companies, and other intellectual
property owners use to control
access to their digital content.

FIGURE 10-7
Elements of privacy.

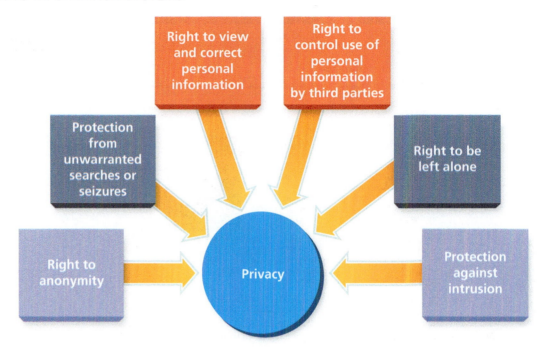

to support. No wonder more than two-thirds of U.S. adults say they are seriously concerned about identity theft. The ease with which information systems can collect and interconnect data makes privacy a top ethical issue. But what exactly is privacy?

The United Nations identified privacy as a fundamental human right in 1999, but its definition remains hazy. Governments, legal bodies, and privacy advocates identify a number of features that might be included (Figure 10-7), though countries certainly vary in the degree to which they respect these elements.[14] Nevertheless, societies from ancient history onward recognize the concept. The Qur'an, the Bible, and Jewish law all refer to elements of privacy, and legal protections against privacy violators—such as peeping toms and eavesdroppers—have existed for hundreds of years.

Information privacy, which refers to the protection of data about individuals, is a special concern. When data was on paper or in separate systems with clumsy interconnections, information privacy was easier to achieve. Now, it mainly rests on the decisions people, organizations, and governments make about what to collect, use, and distribute. Facial recognition software, for example, is a valuable tool for police officers, who can snap a photo and check the image against the department's database of suspects. But the same kind of software can crawl the web to start automatically tagging faces. Some will object to being publicly identified without their consent.

What happens to a person's digital assets when he or she dies? Do the heirs inherit all the iTunes songs and Kindle e-books? What about all the photos and videos on social networking sites or the level 99 warrior in an online game? A few states have passed laws to clarify the issue, but it remains muddled and will be tested in courts. While some valuable digital assets may pass to heirs, most people do not want anyone rummaging through their private email and texts, even after their death.[15]

Trading Privacy for Convenience and Freebies

People are surprisingly willing to disclose personal data to marketers for a little convenience or a discount coupon. Allowing a site to leave cookies, for instance, means we experience a more compelling site on our next visit, one that features promotions tailored to our interests. Grocery chains have no difficulty persuading patrons to carry barcoded loyalty cards, and drivers trade privacy for convenience when they purchase EZ passes so they can zip through tollgates.

To earn trust, organizations should clearly state in their privacy policies what they are collecting and why. They must also take great care to protect the data they do collect and adhere to their own policies. But blunders abound. For instance, Google's camera-equipped cars were identifying wifi hot spots as they maneuvered around taking street view images. But the equipment also picked up data traffic going through unsecured wireless networks from people working in their homes. Google argued that it never meant to harvest such data.[16] Oops.

Anonymity

At one time, the cartoon caption about no one knowing you are a dog when you surf the web was mostly true.[17] Now, however, with advanced technologies that collect, store, and analyze big data, anonymity is far more difficult to achieve than people assume.

Not everyone agrees that online anonymity should be protected as a right. On the positive side, anonymity is important for whistleblowers, police tipsters, news sources, and political activists in oppressive regimes. It also protects people who participate in online support groups where they reveal personal details without fear of disclosure. However, anonymity also protects terrorists, criminals, spammers, and even vengeful posters.[18]

Online identity can be obscured by using fake names, nicknames, free email, and public computers. Erasing digital tracks entirely, however, is far more challenging. Any network connection requires a handshake between the device and the server, so that the device's IP address, along with its location, is exposed. Hiding that information usually requires handing off the transmission to a **proxy**, an intermediary server that receives and analyzes requests from clients and then directs them to their destinations. The transmission then appears to come from the proxy, not the actual sender (Figure 10-8).

FIGURE 10-8

Proxy servers can be used to mask a web surfer's IP address.

| Web surfer IP address 10.210.222.5 | Anonymizing Proxy Server IP Address 14.85.90.20 | Web Destination receives transmission from 14.85.90.20 |

Photos/Illustrations: Luna Van-doome/Shutterstock, Blue Vista Design/Shutterstock, Saskin/Shutterstock, Vector-RGS/Shutterstock.

information privacy
The protection of data about individuals.

proxy
An intermediary server that receives and analyzes requests from clients and then directs them to their destinations; sometimes used to protect privacy.

FIGURE 10-9
A network of distributed servers can relay a transmission and hide its source.

Photos/Illustrations: iofoto/Shutterstock, Maxim Kazmin/123RF, Cliparea\Custom media/Shutterstock, Blue Vista Design/Shutterstock, Alex Kalmbach/Shutterstock.

A drawback to using the proxy server to ensure anonymity is the need to rely on the company that operates the proxy and its promise to protect its customers' identities. Another approach used by the Tor network depends instead on a distributed network of servers. The encrypted transmission is relayed from one server to the next, and no single server has access to all the addresses that relayed any particular message (Figure 10-9).

> **PRODUCTIVITY TIP**
> Tor is a free service operated by volunteers (www.torproject.org) that anonymizes web surfing. An add-on is available for some browsers so that users can enable it only when needed because it can be slow.

Even with these tools, rock-solid anonymity online is very difficult to maintain. Your browser's cookies, for instance, might reveal information about you even if your IP address doesn't. Or some nodes on the Tor network might be compromised. A resolute tracker can usually detect even very faint digital footprints.[19]

Surveillance

Surveillance technologies to monitor email, texting, web surfing, and other online communications are readily available to government agencies for law enforcement. In the business world, many employers also adopt these technologies. Surveys show that employers lean toward surveillance for several reasons:

- Concerns about employer liability for allowing harassment or hostile work environments
- Need to protect security and confidentiality
- Concerns about employee productivity and "cyberslacking"
- Concerns about bogging down corporate servers with personal files

Liability is a powerful driver, given several legal findings that hold employers responsible for employees' offensive online behavior. Continental Airlines was hit with a harassment suit when its first female pilot complained that male employees were posting harassing and insulting comments to an online discussion group called "Crew Members' Forum." The courts eventually held Continental responsible, even though the forum was not hosted by the airline.

Security concerns about trade secrets also prompt employers to keep tabs on communications. A pro football team, for instance, implemented software to track leaks of the team's playbook secrets. Any message that included the phrase "first 15," meaning the first 15 plays of the game, triggered an alarm. Employers sometimes step up surveillance on departing employees who might decide to take confidential data with them.

Preventing leaks is especially challenging when employees are IT professionals. Edward Snowden, who leaked information to the press about the U.S. government's own surveillance programs, was working as an infrastructure analyst for private contractor Booz Allen at the time. Even with tight security and employee surveillance, the company could not prevent the leaks.[20]

Although sound reasons for surveillance exist, the downsides are not trivial. Despite concerns about "cyberslacking," surveillance itself can sometimes cause a drop in productivity, as it suggests a lack of trust between management and staff.[21] Monitored employees may also suffer more stress, resulting in increased absenteeism and lower productivity. Whatever policies the company chooses to implement, managers should make sure everyone understands what those policies are and the reasons for adopting them.

"The Right to Be Forgotten"

Growing concerns about "big data" and how permanent it is are leading to debates about whether a new privacy right is needed: the right to be forgotten.[22] The European Union's strict data protection laws require companies to ensure many safeguards for personal data, and citizens have the right to demand that it be corrected or deleted under some circumstances. The issue emerged when a Spanish citizen insisted that Google delete pointers to embarrassing and obsolete reports about his former debts. Google finally removed the information from results generated by its search engine,[23] but the debate continues, with thousands of similar requests being submitted.[24]

Some legal scholars argue that the "right to be forgotten" conflicts with freedom of speech, and that freedom is strongly protected in the United States.[25] Whether or not some versions of the right to be forgotten do become law in the United States and other countries, technology innovations are helping

PRODUCTIVITY TIP
Google yourself periodically to see what information is publicly available. If you find sensitive personal information or explicit photos that were shared without your consent, you can request that Google remove links to them by using the company's online form, "Remove Information from Google." Also contact the site that hosts the information to request removal.

people erase some of those footprints or at least make them a little less permanent. For example, the Snapchat app allows users to send self-destructing photos that vanish in seconds after receipt. Nothing is foolproof, though, and recipients can take a screenshot or snap a photo of the photo with another camera. Figure 10-10 offers some tips about how people can at least reduce their digital footprints, if not entirely erase them.

Tips for Reducing Digital Footprints

▶ Check your privacy settings on all of your social networking sites.

▶ Remove accounts that you no longer use.

▶ Before you post something online, think about whether you'd mind if it appeared in a national newspaper, with your name attached.

▶ If your posts include information about other people, think about whether they would mind if that information appeared in a national newspaper.

▶ Try using the Tor browser.

▶ Wipe clean all information on digital devices before you recycle them.

FIGURE 10-10
Tips for reducing digital footprints.

Explain the steps that organizations use to manage security risks, identify threats, assess vulnerabilities, and develop administrative and technical controls.

4 Information Security

Information security broadly encompasses the protection of an organization's information assets against misuse, disclosure, unauthorized access, or destruction. Like most aspects of information systems, it draws on the four familiar pillars: technology, processes, people, and data.

Risk Management

Companies spend millions on earthquake-proof vaults, video cameras, secure access cards, and many other security precautions to protect assets. But with countless threats and limited budgets, organizations can't eliminate all risks. Instead, they must make careful assessments to manage them. Risk managers consider many issues, beginning with a clear understanding of what information assets need protection (Figure 10-11). Laws play a large role here, requiring organizations to safely secure medical records, financial information, Social Security numbers, academic records, and other sensitive data. Governments in turn must secure classified documents, and companies must protect their trade secrets.

Identifying Threats

Figure 10-12 shows examples of the many threats to information security that arise both inside and outside the organization. They can be natural events or human-made, accidental or deliberate.

MALWARE AND BOTNETS

Human-made threats pound servers and computers every minute with automated attempts to install all types of **malware**—malicious software designed to attack computer systems (Figure 10-13). To help track down the attackers, security software companies sometimes set up "honeypots," which are computers configured with specific vulnerabilities so they can attract different varieties of malware in the wild, study their properties, and find out who started them.

FIGURE 10-11

Issues for risk managers.

- ▶ What information needs protection?
- ▶ What are the major threats from inside or outside the organization?
- ▶ What are the organization's weaknesses, strengths, and vulnerabilities?
- ▶ What would be the impact of any particular risk?
- ▶ How likely are each of the risks?
- ▶ What controls can be used to mitigate risks?

FIGURE 10-12

Types of information security threats.

Human Threats

Accidental misuse, loss, or destruction by employees, consultants, vendors, or suppliers

Actions by disgruntled employees, insider theft, sabotage, terrorism, hackers, spam

Information Assets

Environmental Threats

Fire
Floods
Earthquakes
Hurricanes
Industrial accidents
Dust
Power failures
Lightning

Malware	Description
Computer virus	A malicious software program that can damage files or other programs. The virus can also reproduce itself and spread to other computers by email, instant messaging, file transfer, or other means.
Spyware	Software that monitors a user's activity on the computer and on the Internet, often installed without the user's knowledge. Spyware may use the Internet connection to send the data it collects to third parties.
Keylogger	Monitoring software that records a user's keystrokes.
Worm	A self-replicating program that sends copies to other nodes on a computer network and may contain malicious code intended to cause damage.
Trojan horse	A seemingly useful, or at least harmless, program that installs malicious code to allow remote access to the computer, as for a botnet.

FIGURE 10-13
Examples of malware.

Many attacks are launched by criminal gangs that build and manage enormous **botnets**. The term combines "robot" and "network" and refers to a collection of computers that have been compromised by malware, often through some vulnerability in their software or operating system. The Barmital botnet, which infected more than 8 million Windows computers, led people to malicious websites when they clicked on what they thought were legitimate links returned by a search engine. This botnet was not just stealing victims' confidential data. It also created fraudulent clicks for online advertisers that they have to pay for, so it was disrupting the whole online advertising business.[26]

The gangs activate their botnets to capture user IDs, passwords, credit card numbers, Social Security numbers, and other sensitive information. They can then transfer funds, steal identities, and purchase products, or they might just sell the information to other criminals. They also rent out their zombie armies to various customers, such as spammers who use them to relay the millions of unsolicited messages that comprise the vast majority of Internet email traffic.

Malware often infects a computer when an innocent user downloads a screen saver or other freebie. Without the user's knowledge, the infected computer becomes a "zombie," added to the gang's growing botnet. Some analysts estimate that up to one-fourth of the world's computers contain botnet code that can be activated whenever the commander chooses. The Gameover ZeuS botnet spanned millions of computers for years and led to the loss of $70 million before government authorities in the United States and other countries finally shut it down.[27] The challenges of coordinating legal investigations across national boundaries can make these gangs especially difficult to prosecute.

DISTRIBUTED DENIAL OF SERVICE

Another grave threat posed by the botnets is the **distributed denial of service (DDoS)** attack, in which zombies are directed to flood a single website with rapid-fire page requests, causing it to slow to a crawl or just crash. Someone with a grudge can rent a botnet for a day to damage corporations, political enemies, or universities. One massive attack targeted Twitter, Facebook, and several other sites in an attempt to silence a single blogger posting about the conflict between Russia and Georgia. DDoS attacks cost organizations many millions of dollars in downtime, lost business, and lost client goodwill (Figure 10-14).

information security
A term that encompasses the protection of an organization's information assets against misuse, disclosure, unauthorized access, or destruction.

malware
Malicious software designed to attack computer systems.

botnet
A combination of the terms *robot* and *network* referring to a collection of computers that have been compromised by malware and used to attack other computers.

distributed denial of service (DDoS)
An attack in which computers in a botnet are directed to flood a single website server with rapid-fire page requests, causing it to slow down or crash.

FIGURE 10-14

Distributed denial of service attack (DDoS). Under the control of the botnet, the zombies send rapid-fire page requests to the targeted site, bringing down the server and blocking out regular customers.

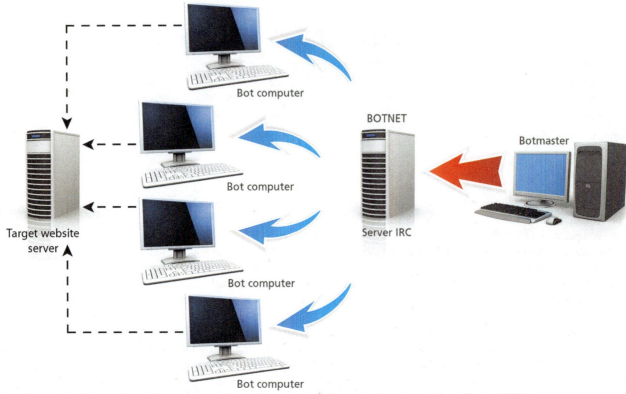

Photos/Illustrations: Blue Vista Design/Shutterstock, ArchMan/Shutterstock, Alex Kalmbach/Shutterstock, Maxim Kazmin/123RF.

PHISHING

Because the botnets mask the actual source of the millions of incoming messages, they are often used for **phishing** attacks. These typically start with an email such as the one in Figure 10-15, which cleverly lures taxpayers to click on a link. Recipients land on what appears to be a genuine website, where they innocently type in their passwords, credit card number, Social Security number, or other sensitive details. The lure can be anything that gets users to enter personal information into a malicious website, from emails offering employment to fake messages that say you need to confirm your account information and reset your password now.

"Spear" phishing is a sophisticated version in which the attackers create messages tailored to a specific individual, often a high-level company executive. These can be very persuasive, and more than a quarter of such attacks are successful.[28] Figure 10-16 shows an example; opening the attachment will download malware.

RANSOMWARE

A type of malware that encrypts files on the victim's computer is called **ransomware** because the attacker demands a ransom payment to provide the codes that will unlock the files. The criminals often want payment in **bitcoins**, which are a form of online virtual currency that is not issued by any governments and instead is valued based on market demand. Bitcoin transactions are quite difficult to trace because they aren't tied to particular individuals.[29]

For example, an attack on a hospital in California made it impossible for the staff to access patient records, X-rays, and other critical

FIGURE 10-15

Sample phishing email.

From: Internal Revenue Service [mailto:admin@irs.gov]
Sent: Wednesday, March 01, 2006 12:45 PM
To: john.doe@jdoe.com
Subject: IRS Notification - Please Read This.

Internal Revenue Service
United States Department of the Treasury

After the last annual calculations of your fiscal activity we have determined that you are eligible to receive a tax refund of **$63.80**. Please submit the tax refund request and allow us 6-9 days in order to process it.

A refund can be delayed for a variety of reasons. For example submitting invalid records or applying after the deadline.

To access the form for your tax refund, please **click here**

Regards,
Internal Revenue Service

Source: Internal Revenue Service.

THE ETHICAL FACTOR   Ethical Dilemmas in a Distributed Denial of Service Attack

Scenario: An elementary school librarian is trying to install some free software to create avatars from students' photos so they won't be tempted to upload their own photos. He fails the first time, but rather than phone the vendor, the librarian tries turning off the firewall and antivirus software. That works, and the librarian turns the security back on.

Two weeks later, the school's whole network goes down. The school's IT technician can see that the server's CPU is overloaded with Internet traffic but can't do anything. By noon, the harried principal is wondering whether to close the school because so much depends on computers, from bus scheduling and reporting to communications and academic records. At 1:30, the principal receives a call from the security officer of a government agency in Canada, who says the school's server was turned into a zombie by a botnet and used in a denial of service attack against the agency. The agency's minister insisted on stopping the attack at once, so the officer triggered a counterattack to target the zombies as quickly as possible. First embarrassed, then angry, the principal says, "But this is an elementary school! You

can't just bring it down like that without telling us. It's not ethical. What if this were a hospital?!" The principal ponders suing someone but isn't sure whom to blame. The officer complains that no one can identify who created the botnet or who paid to use it to launch this DDoS.

The well-intentioned librarian took a shortcut to install software and made the school's network vulnerable. Once the malware was installed and the DDoS against the government agency got under way, the security company in Canada used intrusion-detection techniques to identify the zombies by their IP addresses. That company was tasked with stopping the DDoS, so its staff quickly shut down the zombies with a counterattack, without taking time to learn who they were or what impact that decision might have. Recovering from this event will cost the school considerable time and money.

The scenario involves many players: the librarian, the principal, the school's IT technician, the security officer in Canada, the agency's minister, the botnet creator, and the one who purchased use of the botnet and set off the DDoS. How would you evaluate their ethical decision making?

data and forced them to rely on handwritten notes. The hospital paid 40 bitcoins (about $17,000) to restore the files.[30] Although law enforcement urges people not to pay ransoms, victims often comply to avoid downtime or lost data. Unfortunately, that just drives more ransomware attacks.

INFORMATION LEAKAGE

The threat of information leaks comes not just from cybercriminals. Employees can lose laptops and smartphones, mail containing backup media may go astray, and people may drop unshredded sensitive documents into the dumpster. These accidental leaks are not uncommon, and governments have passed numerous laws imposing huge fines on organizations that lose customer data. Organizations need to inform everyone whose information has been compromised. Although the laws may help stop identity theft, the sheer volume of leaked credit card and Social Security numbers has made this information rather cheap to obtain. In the underground market where it is bought and sold, oversupply drives down prices. The thieves might sell 100,000 Social Security numbers in a bulk transaction for a penny each. A full profile for a single individual might go for $30.[31] Figure 10-17 lists examples of information leaks.[32]

FIGURE 10-16

Sample spear phishing email.

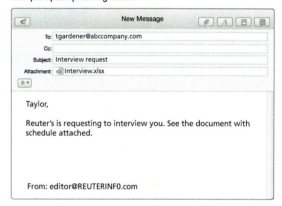

Assessing Vulnerability

An organization's risk assessment must examine its vulnerabilities to determine how effective its existing security measures are. Are employees ignoring warnings not to share passwords? Does the information

PRODUCTIVITY TIP
Check your credit card statements carefully for any unauthorized purchases, and get free credit reports from www.annualcreditreport.com. The three credit services will each provide one free report per year, so you can check for suspicious activity every 4 months.

phishing
An attempt to steal passwords or other sensitive information by persuading the victim, often in an email, to enter the information into a fraudulent website that masquerades as the authentic version.

ransomware
A type of malware that encrypts the victim's files, and the attacker demands a ransom payment to provide the codes to unlock them.

bitcoins
An online virtual currency that is not issued by a government and instead is valued based on market demand; transactions are difficult to trace.

FIGURE 10-17
Sample information leakage events.

Organization and Date	Event
Internal Revenue Service February 10, 2016	Automated cyberattack on the e-filing system, leaking e-file PINs
Snapchat March 4, 2016	Successful phishing scam targeting the company's payroll department
BeautifulPeople.com, April 26, 2016	Hackers gained personal information on 1.1 million users of the online dating site
Office of Personnel Management, June 4, 2015	21.5 million government personnel records hacked, exposing employees' personnel data

Source: Based on Chronology of data breaches—Security breaches 2005–Present. Privacy Rights Clearinghouse.http://www.privacyrights.org/, accessed October 7, 2016.

system maintain a log of every access attempt? Are administrators alerted about water in the data center?

When an Apple employee left a prototype of the newest iPhone in a California bar, the vulnerability posed by the human element—in this case, accidental loss—became glaringly apparent. Apple is known for the impenetrable security surrounding its super-secret product development, but that single iPhone slipped through.

DID YOU KNOW ?

According to an IBM report, 60% of cyberattacks on its clients are carried out by insiders, typically an employee or someone else who has been granted access to a company's information systems. About 75% of such attacks are malicious and deliberate, while the rest are inadvertent.[33] The public often doesn't hear of those insider attacks because companies prefer to avoid the publicity.

Once vulnerabilities have been analyzed, the organization can evaluate controls that fill in security gaps and protect against specific threats. Industry standards are often used for this step. Examples include the federal guidelines for information security in government agencies and the security self-assessment questionnaire developed by the Payment Card Industry Security Standards Council for companies that operate e-commerce sites and accept credit cards. The questionnaire helps organizations identify measures required to achieve compliance.[34]

Vulnerability depends partly on how likely any particular event may be. A major earthquake in Mexico City rates as highly likely, but hurricanes in that region are very rare. Even very unlikely events might pose serious risks, however, when their impact would be immense if they did occur. Risks also differ depending on the threat. A major information leak would compromise confidentiality, for example, while a power outage would affect availability by bringing down the systems.

The **risk matrix** lists the vulnerabilities in a table, and managers rate the level of risk each one presents in areas such as confidentiality, company reputation, lost revenue, or downtime. The matrix also includes an estimate of how likely that event might be, and managers may add other metrics to further refine the analysis for their own organizations. The matrix helps focus attention on the vulnerabilities that pose the greatest potential dangers. Figure 10-18 shows a simplified example using rating scales of 1 (low risk) to 10 (high risk).

FIGURE 10-18
Simplified risk matrix.

Vulnerability	Leak of Confidential Data	Lost Integrity, Reputation	Systems Unavailable	Financial Risk	Likelihood That Event Will Happen	Total Impact Rating
No backup power for a workstation	1	2	8	2	4	4
Loss of unencrypted backup data	10	10	4	7	3	6.8

Administrative Security Controls

Administrative security controls include all the processes, policies, and plans the organization creates to enhance information security and ensure it can recover when danger strikes. Some controls may establish information security policies that restrict the Internet sites that employees can visit or that deny Internet access altogether. Such policies might add protection by prohibiting employees from downloading data to smartphones or USB drives. Industries that routinely handle sensitive information will need to put very strict policies in place and take measures to enforce them. Leaving a workstation without logging out, for example, may be trivial in some settings but disastrous in others.

The processes and policies that control employee access to systems are some of the most sensitive. Knowing how angry some terminated employees might become, some employers cut off their access before they deliver the pink slip. IT employees pose greater threats because of their expertise and higher-level access.

Administrative controls to enhance information security extend beyond the organization to its vendors, suppliers, and customers. For example, what background checks and due diligence should the organization do before signing an agreement with a cloud computing vendor? How should the organization monitor access to its systems by suppliers and customers?

> **PRODUCTIVITY TIP**
> The administrative controls you establish for your own computer will help protect your information assets. Turning off the computer at night, for instance, will reduce your exposure to intrusion attempts, and save energy, too.

To avoid chaos and missteps when something happens, the organization should also have a clear **incident response plan** that staff use to categorize the threat, determine the cause, preserve any evidence, and also get the systems back online so the organization can resume business (Figure 10-19).

Technical Security Controls

The technologies available to protect information assets help with three important tasks:

- deterring attacks,
- preventing attacks, and
- detecting that an attack occurred.

Surveillance cameras, for instance, can deter unauthorized entry. Even the automated message on a system's login screen, issuing dire warnings of criminal penalties for misuse, will deter most people from trying to break in. Figure 10-20 shows how technical and administrative controls work together for several security areas.

AUTHENTICATION STRATEGIES

Technical controls for preventing unauthorized access draw on technologies that can authenticate people and determine what access privileges they should be granted. Most authentication strategies rely on:

- Something the user *knows*, such as a user ID, password, PIN, or answer to a security question;
- Something the user *has* in his or her possession, such as an ID badge, credit card, or RFID chip; or

FIGURE 10-19

Steps in an incident response plan.

Identify the threat
- Communicate with crisis management team.

Contain the damage
- Stay calm.
- Restrict systems access.
- Take systems offline.

Determine the cause
- Investigate logs.
- Preserve evidence.

Recover the systems
- Restore from media known to be undamaged.
- Get organization up and running.

Evaluate lessons learned
- Prosecute offender.
- Improve systems.
- Reevaluate risk matrix.

risk matrix
A matrix that lists an organization's vulnerabilities, with ratings that assess each one in terms of likelihood and impact on business operations, reputation, and other areas.

incident response plan
A plan that an organization uses to categorize a security threat, determine the cause, preserve any evidence, and also get the systems back online so the organization can resume business.

FIGURE 10-20
Examples of administrative and technical controls.

Category	Administrative Control Examples	Technical Control Examples
Account management	The organization requires appropriate approvals for requests to establish accounts.	The information system automatically disables accounts after a time period defined by the organization.
	The organization monitors for atypical usage of information system accounts.	The information system automatically logs any account creations, modifications, or termination actions.
Access controls	The organization defines the information to be encrypted or stored offline in a secure location.	The information system enforces approved authorizations for access to the system.
	The organization defines the privileged commands for which dual authorization is to be enforced.	The information system prevents access to any security-relevant information contained within the system.
Information flow	The organization defi nes the security policy that determines what events require human review.	The information system enforces the organization's policy about human review.
Separation of duties	The organization separates duties of individuals as necessary to prevent malevolent activity without collusion.	The information system enforces separation of duties through access control.

- Something the user *is*—a biometric characteristic that uniquely identifies the user, such as a voice pattern, fingerprint, or face.

Reliance on user knowledge is the simplest strategy, although in many ways the weakest and easiest to crack. Financial institutions especially have expanded password security to require the user to have several pieces of knowledge or to link each login to a particular IP address. They also take the precaution of sending the PIN to account holders by mail in a letter separate from the user ID.

Biometric identifiers are also widely used, especially for physical security, because they are more difficult to crack or forge. Most computer vendors offer laptops equipped with fingerprint scanners, for example, and the technology is used for smartphones as well.

Multifactor authentication combines two or more authentication strategies, creating much stronger security against unauthorized access. For example, a user might need to swipe an ID badge and then also enter a password to gain access.

PRODUCTIVITY TIP
Many online services offer multifactor authentication, often by sending a code to your smartphone if the site detects a login from an unknown IP address. You will be prompted to enter the code before proceeding, thus confirming that the phone number you registered on the service is in your possession. This adds strong protection against hackers.

ENCRYPTION

A powerful technical control that protects sensitive data is **encryption**. This process transforms the data into an unreadable form using mathematical formulas, so that no one can read it unless they know the key to unscrambling it. Encryption is used for both storage and data transmission. For storage, you can encrypt individual files on your computer, or the whole disk drive, by adding a password, but you will not be able to retrieve the information if you forget it. Encryption is so effective that if an organization loses sensitive information that was encrypted, the notification laws described earlier do not apply. If the backup tapes shown in the matrix in Figure 10-18 were encrypted, the risk assessments would be much lower.

Secure data transmission relies on either symmetric or asymmetric encryption. In the symmetric version, both the sender and receiver use the same key to encrypt and decrypt the message. For asymmetric transmission, one key is used to encrypt the message and another to decrypt it.

For Internet transmission, a popular strategy is **public key encryption**, which uses asymmetric transmission. One key is public, widely shared with everyone, but the other is private, known only to the recipient. For example, when you want to communicate with a company's website securely, your browser uses the organization's public key to encrypt the data you send, and the organization uses its private key to read it. Though the keys are mathematically related, the formulas are too complex and the keys too long for anyone to decipher the private key from its paired public key.

Because symmetric transmission is faster and simpler to use, the first exchange using public key encryption—between your computer and a secure website, for instance—is one designed to share the same private key. Once both parties have the same key, they can switch to symmetric transmission.

Organizations typically obtain security certificates for websites that need encryption, purchased

> **PRODUCTIVITY TIP**
> Before entering sensitive data into any form on a website, check for the *https://* in the address bar to be sure transmissions are encrypted. Click on the padlock symbol to see security details.

from a third party such as VeriSign. The certificate confirms that all communications between your computer and the website are encrypted, and it also certifies the site's identity.

INTRUSION PREVENTION AND DETECTION SYSTEMS

Astronomer Clifford Stoll tells an old detective story of how he was asked to look into a 75-cent accounting error on his lab's server. The logs showed that someone took 9 seconds of computer time without paying for it. His curiosity piqued, Stoll began to track down the intruder. Few detection tools existed in those years during the Cold War, but Stoll attached printers to incoming lines to record any intrusions. He added some fake files that sounded super-secret, and the hacker took the bait. The intruder was selling information to the Soviet KGB, but Stoll's sting operation put a stop to it.[35]

Many more tools are available now to prevent unauthorized traffic from entering the network and to detect any intrusions that do make it through. But the attackers' tools improve, too, and criminals constantly test defenses and hunt for vulnerable points.

FIREWALLS

The most important defense is the **firewall**, a technical control that inspects incoming and outgoing traffic and either blocks or permits it according to rules the organization chooses. The firewall can be a hardware device or a software program, and its rules regulate traffic based on different levels of trust. Servers in the same domain would be considered trustworthy, so traffic would pass easily between them. External traffic from the Internet, however, would need different rules. The firewall might prohibit any Internet traffic from reaching its database servers, for instance, but allow incoming requests to its public web server.

Other rules might control which ports on the machine can accept traffic or which IP addresses or domain names should be blocked. Organizations that prohibit use of YouTube, for instance, can customize their firewalls to block access.

Firewall systems also include features to detect suspicious events and alert managers immediately. For example, a failed attempt to log in as the computer administrator may trigger a text message to designated smartphones so IT staff can investigate.

BLOCKING SPAM

Spam continues to be a costly menace, and intrusion prevention systems are also needed to filter traffic. Combating spam has become even more critical as messaging moves to mobile devices, where calling plans might charge users for every kilobyte received. Many organizations install special email content-filtering appliances inside their firewalls so that all messages are examined for telltale signs of spam before they are delivered to any employees (Figure 10-21). Adjusting the filters is an ongoing challenge. The goal is to trap spam but avoid false positives in which important messages are blocked or labeled junk mail. These

---

multifactor authentication
A combination of two or more authentications a user must pass to access an information system, such as a fingerprint scan combined with a password.

encryption
Technique that scrambles data using mathematical formulas so that it cannot be read without applying the key to decrypt it.

public key encryption
A security measure that uses a pair of keys, one to encrypt the data and the other to decrypt it. One key is public, widely shared with everyone, but the other is private, known only to the recipient.

firewall
A defensive technical control that inspects incoming and outgoing traffic and either blocks or permits it according to rules the organization establishes. The firewall can be a hardware device or a software program.

FIGURE 10-21

Blocking spam.

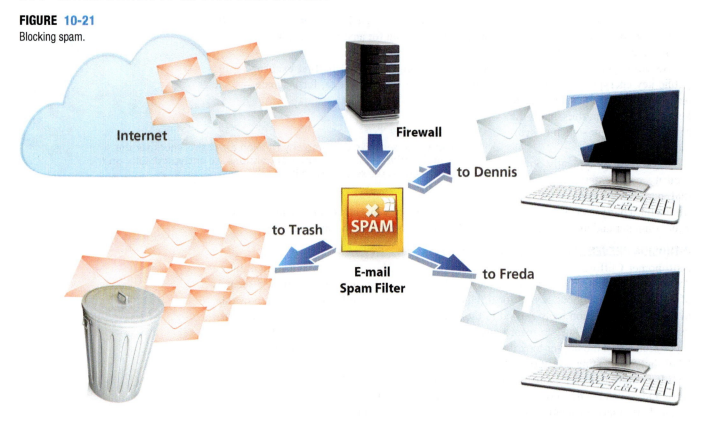

Internet

Firewall

to Dennis

to Trash

SPAM

to Freda

E-mail
Spam Filter

Photos/Illustrations: Broukoid/Shutterstock, ArchMan/Shutterstock, TyBy/Shutterstock, Spectral Design/Shutterstock, Login/Shutterstock, Alex Kalmbach/Shutterstock.

technology advances are helping, although spam still constitutes the majority of global email traffic.

Information Security and Cloud Computing

The trend for businesses to move toward cloud computing, where their mission-critical applications and data are hosted by a service off-site and accessed via the Internet, is largely driven by cost savings and convenience. But IT managers worry about security for cloud computing and whether cloud providers can adequately protect the organization's most valuable assets. With countless information leaks and security breaches, they have cause for concern.

PRODUCTIVITY TIP
Your college or university probably has spam blocks in place, but no filter is perfect. Check your junk mail occasionally in case messages you want to receive were trapped by the filter. Identify any false positives as "not junk" so the sender's messages are not trapped again.

Data protection laws present another issue for cloud computing. They vary by country, and they tend to assume that a citizen's data is actually located somewhere within the country's boundaries. But with cloud computing, the data may be stored anywhere, and it moves a great deal as vendors open new data centers to accommodate growth.

Although cloud computing raises difficult security issues, it offers advantages as well. Most organizations with their own data centers are struggling with security, too, and information leaks are not uncommon. It takes considerable effort and resources for a company to continually upgrade security and comply with laws. Budget pressures, along with the growing challenge of recruiting qualified information security staff, are leading even skeptical organizations to take a closer look at cloud computing.

Another problem cloud computing helps address is the loss of data when employees download it to their portable devices and then lose them. When their data is cloud-based and they can retrieve it from any device, these leaks may shrink.

Given cloud computing's momentum, determined efforts are under way to develop security standards and best practices, along with transparent auditing mechanisms that will help assure potential clients that their information will be safe. The success of this important trend in enterprise architecture will partly hinge on robust security.

The Human Element in Information Ethics, Security, and Privacy

5 Explain why human behavior is often the weakest link for ethics, privacy, and security, and provide examples of strategies that can be used to counteract the weaknesses.

Human behavior and decision making play a central role in almost any situation combining information ethics, privacy, and security. Indeed, human beings are very often the weakest link for a number of reasons.

Cognitive Issues and Productivity

The sheer complexity of computers and information systems challenges even the brightest humans. It is not surprising that people will turn off their security features for a few minutes to install software, as the librarian did in the DDoS scenario described earlier. We prefer to apply our cognitive skills to productive pursuits, and when security policies and procedures seem to get in the way, we may bypass them. In most cases nothing happens, but occasionally calamity results.

WEAK PASSWORDS

The limits of human memory (and patience) make the password a serious vulnerability.[36] On their own, people tend to create weak passwords that are easy to remember and easier to crack. A security breach at RockYou.com released millions of passwords, and almost 300,000 people chose "123456." Pet names ranked high along with the word "password" and "NCC1701" (the ID number of the starship *Enterprise*).

Although technical controls can force users to embed numbers and nonalphabetic characters and change them frequently, the results are still not promising. Users then tend to write passwords down and reuse them on less secure systems, such as online games. Indeed, hackers break into corporate networks by offering employees free access to new services. An alarming number will reuse their corporate login to create the account.

We can't easily remember a long string of random letters and symbols, but we have no difficulty remembering such strings if they represent meaningful chunks of information. For example, mhBs*124MTH is a strong password, but it is easy for an aspiring bowler to memorize: my highest Bowling score * 124 Must Try Harder. Figure 10-22 offers tips on creating secure passwords.

REDUCING COMPLEXITY

To reduce the complexity and cognitive load associated with multiple passwords, many organizations implement the **single sign-on**, which is a gateway service that permits users to log in once with a single user ID and password to gain access to multiple software applications.

Password "vaults" can also help reduce complexity. These services store and enter your login credentials for the sites you visit, so you only need remember the master password for the vault. They also generate secure passwords for your sites to help you avoid the practice of reusing passwords.

Complexity hampers privacy decisions as well. Few people read the terms of service before they click "I agree," although those terms often contain troubling conditions that trade privacy away. Social networking sites balance users' privacy concerns against their own need to generate advertising revenue through targeted marketing that relies on the data you share with the site.

single sign-on
A gateway service that permits users to log in once with a single user ID and password to gain access to multiple software applications.

FIGURE 10-22
Creating secure passwords.

▸ Do not include personal information such as names, addresses, or phone numbers.

▸ Avoid real words.

▸ Mix different character types, including lowercase, uppercase, and special characters.

▸ To reduce the cognitive load of memorizing the password, create "pass phrases" with meaningful chunks and use the first letter of each word, such as "I love whitewater rafting_Done it 15 times" (Ilwwr_Di15t).

▸ Use different passwords for each login you want to secure, so loss of one does not compromise the others.

▸ Change your passwords every few months, or as required by the application.

Social Engineering and Information Security

Human beings are very vulnerable to **social engineering**, which manipulates them into breaking normal security procedures or divulging confidential information.

One weak spot is simply the human desire to help others. People routinely pass virus-laden hoaxes along to friends and neighbors, trying to be helpful. An employee who swipes his or her ID badge to open a secure door and then courteously holds it open for the person behind may be falling for a common social engineering trick to bypass physical security. The pressure to be helpful is even greater if the follower is holding packages or using crutches (Figure 10-23).

Respect for authority is another common human tendency that intruders exploit, relying on uniforms, titles, or verbal hints that the company president wants something done. Intruders gain easy access to office equipment just by wearing a tool belt.

Humans are certainly not immune to greed, and scammers tap this human frailty routinely to persuade people to turn over confidential information or money. The so-called 419 scam, named after a section of Nigeria's criminal code, has conned many people out of thousands of dollars. The scam usually starts with an unsolicited email inviting the recipient to participate in a scheme to gain large sums from a foreign bank, simply by allowing the sender to cleanse the funds through the target's bank account. The target is eventually asked to pay an advance fee of some kind, or a transfer tax, after which "complications" may require the payment of additional fees.

FIGURE 10-23
Social engineering: Would you hold the door for these people so they don't have to search for their ID badges?

© Juice Images/Alamy Stock Photo.

Ironically, another highly effective bit of social engineering relies on the human desire to *avoid* malware. When a pop-up appears that says your computer is infected and provides a link for you to buy software to remove the virus, you may have become a victim of "scareware." The virus didn't exist. The "removal" software might be harmless, or it might actually be malware. As real threats grow, more and more people fall for these scareware attacks (Figure 10-24).

Security Awareness and Ethical Decision Making

Organizations should have robust security awareness programs to help educate and continually remind people about the risks that lax security presents. The program should cover the organization's own policies and procedures as well as laws and regulations about how information should be handled to ensure compliance. Figure 10-25 lists several relevant laws that touch on information security and privacy.

Beyond legal compliance, a security awareness program should also alert people to the many ways in which social engineering can exploit human tendencies toward kindness, helpfulness, greed, or just productivity. It should provide training in tools such as encryption and help people spot areas where breaches are most likely.

Finally, it should reinforce the principle that the organization has an ethical responsibility to maintain information security. Consider, for example, the extent of harm each of these actions might inflict on other people:

- A sales rep copies customer data to her smartphone and quickly drops it into a jacket pocket. Corporate policy forbids taking confidential documents out of the building, but she just wants to work on them at home to catch up. She leaves her jacket on the subway but says nothing to her supervisor about the incident.
- A sixth grader finds a USB drive in a school computer and sees the names and addresses of all the students and teachers. He uploads it to his social networking account so all his friends have contact information.
- A university employee looks up old academic records of political candidates and sends some provocative tidbits to the press.
- A coworker suspects an employee of accessing illicit websites at work but hesitates to mention it because it might get the employee in big trouble or even fired.
- The CFO asks someone in IT to delete his whole email account from the server and backup media because it contains messages that suggest criminal behavior.

How would you judge the actions of these people? These cases show how closely tied ethics, privacy, and security are and how humans make decisions about such issues almost daily. Sometimes they are easy to make, but often they present dilemmas that challenge even people who understand security and who try hard to make ethical decisions. As information systems grow even more powerful and interconnected, the race to protect these valuable information assets will become ever more urgent.

FIGURE 10-24

Scareware persuades people that a computer is infected when it is not. The solution the victim pays for may be harmless or it may install its own malware.

Law/Regulation	Description
Privacy Act of 1974	Establishes requirements that govern how personally identifiable information on individuals is collected, used, and disseminated by federal agencies.
Health Insurance Portability and Accountability Act (HIPAA)	Includes provisions to protect the privacy and security of individually identifiable health information.
Family Educational Rights and Privacy Act (FERPA)	Establishes privacy rights over educational records. For example, federally funded educational institutions must provide students with access to their own educational records and some control over their disclosure.
CAN-SPAM Act	Prohibits businesses from sending misleading or deceptive commercial emails, but denies recipients any legal recourse on their own. The act also requires companies to maintain a do-not-spam list.
Gramm-Leach-Bliley Act	Stipulates how financial institutions are required to protect the privacy of consumers' personal financial information and notify them of their privacy policies annually.
Driver's Privacy Protection Act of 1994	Limits the disclosure of personally identifiable information that is maintained by state departments of motor vehicles.
State Security Breach Notification Laws	Require organizations to notify state residents if sensitive data are released. The wording varies by state.
European Union's Data Protection Directive	Establishes privacy as a fundamental human right for EU citizens. The law is more restrictive than U.S. laws. For example, it requires companies to provide "opt out" choices before transferring personal data to third parties.

FIGURE 10-25

Examples of laws touching on information security and privacy.

social engineering
The art of manipulating people into breaking normal information security procedures or divulging confidential information.

VAMPIRE LEGENDS
A Role-Playing Simulation on Ethics, Privacy, and Security in the Multiplayer Online Game Business

The massively multiplayer online game business is lucrative but very competitive. Your company has poured millions into the game, adding vivid graphics, tense storylines, and many features to support collaboration and team play, and the strategy is paying off. You are very proud of the way you were able to use social media to spread the word and persuade people to try it out. Most noticed right away that the avatars move very smoothly and that they are much easier to configure and control compared with other games. That's thanks to the terrific IT staff, who also made programming breakthroughs so players could do more quests from their smartphones. A number of celebrities even play the game, although under false names and in disguise.

Now that the game's sequel is ready to release, you and the other senior execs must work out the strategy and budget. Everyone thinks Ancient Age of Vampires will be even more successful than the original game, and analysts project a significant revenue increase. Log in when you're ready to get to work....

Chapter Summary

LEARNING OBJECTIVES

1 Ethics is a system of moral principles used to judge right from wrong. One ethical framework focuses on natural laws and rights. A second, called utilitarianism, emphasizes the consequences of actions. Although many laws are grounded in ethical principles, actions can be legal but not ethical or ethical but not legal. Most people tend to judge unethical behavior, such as plagiarism or intellectual property theft, less harshly when the violator uses a computer and the Internet compared with similar acts committed in face-to-face settings.

2 Information ethics focuses on the storage and transmission of digitized data and raises both ethical and legal issues. Although most countries protect intellectual property (IP), digitized IP is extremely difficult to protect, and many companies use digital rights management technologies to safeguard their assets. Plagiarism has also become very difficult to prevent because of ICT, although it can also be much more easily detected with originality-checking tools.

3 Privacy is under considerable pressure because of the growing volume of personal information online, the complexity of privacy settings and privacy policies, and users' willingness to trade privacy for convenience. Services that use proxies can offer anonymity for online activity. Surveillance poses threats to privacy, but employers often choose to implement surveillance because of concerns about liability, security, confidentiality, and productivity. Some governments are debating whether to pass laws that give people the "right to be forgotten" with respect to information that companies collect about them online.

4 Information security ensures the protection of an organization's information assets against misuse, disclosure, unauthorized access, or destruction. Organizations use risk management to identify assets needing protection, identify the threats, assess vulnerabilities, and determine the impact of each risk. Threats arise from both human and environmental sources and include accidental events, intentional attacks from insiders or external criminals, fires, floods, power failures, and many more. Distributed denial of service and phishing attacks are common threats that result in significant downtime and leakage of sensitive information. Administrative controls encompass the policies, procedures, and plans the organization creates and enforces to protect information assets and respond to incidents when they occur. Technical controls are implemented by the information systems and include strategies such as encryption and user authentication. Intrusion prevention and detection systems block traffic and activity based on the rules the organization develops and alert managers if suspicious activity occurs. The firewall is an important element for intrusion prevention. Standards for information security for cloud computing are under development but are critical to the future of this architectural trend.

5 Human beings prize productivity highly and may neglect security when it interferes. Social engineering tactics take advantage of human behavioral tendencies to manipulate people into disclosing sensitive information or bypassing security measures. Training in security awareness and the relationships between security, ethics, and privacy can help counteract these tendencies.

KEY TERMS AND CONCEPTS

ethics	proxy	ransomware	public key encryption
natural laws and rights	information security	bitcoins	firewall
utilitarianism	malware	risk matrix	single sign-on
intellectual property (IP)	botnets	incident response plan	social engineering
digital rights management (DRM)	distributed denial of service (DDoS)	multifactor authentication	
information privacy	phishing	encryption	

CHAPTER REVIEW QUESTIONS

10-1. What are ethics? What are two broad categories of ethics? What approach does each category take? What are examples of each category of ethics? What is the difference between ethics and the law?
MyMISLab

10-2. What is intellectual property (IP)? What are the information ethics associated with IP? What is the impact of digital media on the information ethics of IP? What are examples of technologies used to control access to digitized intellectual property?
MyMISLab

10-3. What is plagiarism? What are the information ethics associated with plagiarism? What is the impact of digital media on the information ethics of plagiarism? What are examples of technologies used to detect plagiarism?
MyMISLab

10-4. What is information privacy? What is anonymity? What are strategies that may be used to achieve anonymity on the Internet?

10-5. Why do organizations implement surveillance? What are the advantages of surveillance? What are the disadvantages of surveillance?

10-6. What are the steps that organizations take in order to manage information security risks and build a risk matrix? What is involved in each step of this process?

10-7. What are the two types of threats to information security? What are examples of each type of threat?

10-8. What are information security vulnerabilities? How do organizations assess vulnerability?

10-9. What are examples of administrative controls that organizations implement to improve security?

10-10. What are examples of technical controls that organizations implement to improve security?

10-11. Why is human behavior often the weakest link for information ethics, information privacy, and information security? What are examples of strategies that organizations can implement to counteract the weaknesses in human behavior and decision making that have a negative impact on information security and privacy?

PROJECTS AND DISCUSSION QUESTIONS

10-12. According to Wikipedia.org, digital rights management is used by organizations such as Sony, Amazon, Apple, Microsoft, AOL, and the BBC. What is digital rights management? Why do organizations use technology to protect intellectual capital? Describe a typical DRM application that can be used to manage access to digital content. Are there disadvantages to using DRM?
MyMISLab

10-13. Two dreaded "P" words for college students are *procrastination* and *plagiarism*. Does the first action necessarily lead to the second? Visit Plagiarism.org to learn more about the various forms of plagiarism. How are the different types of plagiarism similar? How are they different? What are the consequences of plagiarism at your university? Consult your student handbook to learn how plagiarism is defined by your school and how faculty members may respond to cases of plagiarism. What are the options for discipline in cases of plagiarism? Prepare a 5-minute presentation of your findings.

10-14. The Identity Theft Resource Center® is a nonprofit organization dedicated to helping users understand and prevent identity theft. Visit Google.com and search for "ITRC Fact Sheet 101" or visit www.idtheftcenter.org and use the Search box to enter "ITRC Fact Sheet 101" to locate "ITRC Fact Sheet 101: Are You at Risk for Identity Theft." Answer 20 self-test questions relating to document disposal, Social Security number protection, information handling, and scams to determine your ID theft risk score. Are you savvy about identity theft risks, or do you need to take some corrective actions? Prepare a 5-minute presentation to share with your classmates.

10-15. Do you trade privacy for convenience? Visit Google.com and select "About" at the bottom of the page to locate the "Privacy" link located at the bottom of that page. Follow this link to the "Privacy Policy." Does Google place cookies on your computer or other devices? Why do they use cookies? What are location-enabled services? Does Google have information about your actual location? Under what circumstances does Google share personal information with other companies? How do you describe the information security measures that Google takes to safeguard access to personal information? Is there anything in the privacy policy that makes you uncomfortable? Are you likely to change your Google search habits as a result of reviewing its privacy policy?
MyMISLab

10-16. Malware is malicious software that is developed for the purpose of causing harm. What are different types of malware? How does malware infiltrate a computer system? What is a botnet? Why do criminals use botnets? What is a distributed denial of service attack? What are three ways that DDoS attacks affect organizations? Visit Microsoft.com and select Support. Search for "malicious software removal tool." How frequently does Microsoft release a new version of this tool? Search Microsoft.com to learn more about how to boost your malware defense and protect your PC. Prepare a brief summary of your findings.

10-17. Why is it important to verify the identity of computer users? What are three authentication strategies? Which is the strongest form of authentication? Which is the weakest? What credentials does your university use to verify your identity for access to email and other web-based information such as personal financial aid information and online course materials? Is this strong or weak authentication? What is a security token? Visit Wikipedia.org to learn how security tokens are used to authenticate users and prepare a brief report of your findings. Do you think it is a good idea to use security tokens to authenticate students? Why or why not?

10-18. Did you ever wonder why junk email is called "spam"? The Monty Python sketch on spam has been viewed more than 5 million times on YouTube. That's a lot of spam! Work in a small group with classmates to consider why spam is one of the biggest problems facing the Internet today. Approximately how much email traffic is made up of spam? Is spam a problem on mobile devices? Why is spam a problem for consumers? Why is it a problem for organizations and Internet service providers? What types of technical controls do organizations use to combat spam? Prepare a brief report of your group discussion.

10-19. Recall from Chapter 3 how cloud computing generally requires leasing IT resources, depending on a third party to store data or provide services. Work in a small group with classmates to consider the security risks associated with cloud computing. Why are IT managers concerned about protecting cloud-based information assets? What is the IT industry response to concerns about cloud computing? What is the Cloud Security Alliance? Consider the class registration application at your university. Does your group consider this a mission-critical application? Why or why not? Prepare a 5-minute presentation of your discussion that includes a recommendation for or against using cloud computing for critical applications at your university.

APPLICATION EXERCISES

10-20. EXCEL APPLICATION:
Citywide Community College

The IT Department at Citywide Community College developed a computer security incident response plan that requires users to provide information for each security incident. Louis Hermann, the IT manager, inventoried the major components of the college's computer systems and created a spreadsheet to track the equipment by manufacturer, model number, and serial number. He decided to confine the list to major computer components, and he does not try to track keyboards, mice, and so forth. Louis then created a spreadsheet to track systems security incident facts including information about the department reporting the incident, target-specific information (host machine name, etc.), source-specific information (source IP address), and information about the type of security incident or attack. Louis has asked you to use the data provided in the CCC Security spreadsheet, Ch10Ex01, to identify (1) the department reporting the highest number of security incidents and (2) the most prevalent type of intrusion. Use the "countif" function to count the number of security incidents in which the computer system was compromised. Use a memo format to submit a summary of your findings to Louis.

10-21. ACCESS APPLICATION:
Citywide Community College

Louis Hermann, IT manager at Citywide Community College, is working with two spreadsheets to manage computer security incident reporting. One spreadsheet tracks the major components of the college's computer systems, and the other spreadsheet tracks security incident facts. To provide for better reporting capabilities, Louis wants you to set up an Access database that tracks college departments, computer systems, and security incidents. Download the spreadsheet Ch10Ex02 and import the worksheets to create the database shown in Figure 10-26. Create a report that lists the number of security incidents reported by each department. Create a second report that lists the number of attacks in which the system was compromised for the department having the greatest number of security incidents. What other reports would Louis find useful?

FIGURE 10-26
Citywide Community College security database.

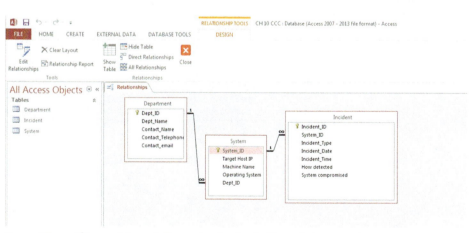

Source: Microsoft®Access, Microsoft Corporation. Reprinted with permission.

CASE STUDY #1

Zynga Kills Petville and Angers Virtual Pet Owners

Social game developer Zynga started as a leading player in the industry, with millions of active users around the world. It features popular titles such as Castleville, Mafia Wars, Farmville 2, Words with Friends, and Zynga Poker. Most people play the games with their friends on Facebook or on Zynga's own site (Zynga. com). Founded by Mark Pincus in 2009, Zynga's popularity peaked in 2012, when revenue topped $1.2 billion.

Unlike most online game companies, Zynga earns most of its revenue from in-game purchases of virtual goods rather than advertising. The games are free to play, but advancement can take a long time. Players who want to advance more quickly can purchase game currency, energy points, or virtual goods.

Social games rise and fall in popularity, and when Zynga's share prices began to plummet in 2012 following some missteps, the company began cost-cutting. Zynga pulled the plug on underperforming games, and one that was killed off with barely 2 weeks' notice was Petville. Devoted players were outraged. Many had invested years in nurturing and caring for their digital pets, sharing the adventure with their friends and family on Facebook. Thousands posted their sadness and anger on social media sites, with comments like those in Figure 10-27.

Clearly, the players had an emotional investment in their virtual pets and also in the social dimension of the game that Zynga's software specifically encourages. For example, players earned points by visiting neighbors, who were actually real-life friends with their own virtual pet in the game. Points mounted up quickly as more neighbors joined and exchanged gifts.

Zynga tracks and analyzes player behavior closely and uses the big data to add features that ensure players log in frequently to develop that strong attachment. Zynga wisely chose not to let someone's virtual pet die from hunger if the player did not feed it daily. However, the pet was taken to the pound, and the owner had to find ways to earn enough cash to retrieve it.

Zynga offered credits for its other games, but Petville players were quite dismayed by the company's lack of sensitivity. Certainly, companies have to shut down badly performing products, but there is a difference between terminating a line of shampoo and killing off a game like Petville. Customers are not likely to mourn the loss of a favorite hair product in the same way they would a virtual puppy they have been nurturing for years.

Even though the terms of service agreement gave the company vast leeway to terminate services or close down games and Zynga's metric-driven business strategy justified the shutdown, its approach generated a lot of ill will. At best, it was a customer relations blunder, but it also raised ethical questions. The company's software is specifically designed to create such emotional ties, so observers thought that the company should have recognized they existed and arranged for a more sensitive closing. Certainly more advance notice was warranted. Rather than assume players would happily switch to another game and forget about their pets, Zynga might have held online ceremonies to bid farewell or planned a clever happy ending in which the pets founded their own world together.

As of 2016, Zynga continues to struggle, posting large losses despite the popularity of some of its games. Founder Mark Pincus stepped down as CEO for the second time, unable to turn the company around. Zynga has a wealth of talent, however, and time will tell whether Zynga can use its big data to better understand its own customers and develop a profitable business.

FIGURE 10-27

Comments from players who objected to Zynga's decision to shut down Petville.

▶ "I loved my bunny now I will never get to see her again—it is not fair at all."

▶ "My autistic son and I had played Petville together for two years…I wish you 'people' could have seen the streams of tears running down both our faces as we played our last session. We even took photographs. I guess money trumps everything!"

▶ "This is the last day my little friend will be alive. So sad."

▶ "My daughter is heartbroken."

▶ "Zynga [stinks]!! And I will NEVER play any of your games again. You can take your lousy credits and shove them! I hope Karma comes around to get you and you think back on how many people you upset and lost due to [the] stupid, greedy decision to remove Petville."

Discussion Questions

10-22. When Zynga dropped Petville abruptly, virtual pet owners protested that they had been harmed. This ethical argument uses a utilitarian framework. How might you argue from a natural laws and rights ethical framework that Zynga was wrong?

10-23. The suddenness of Zynga's action created a firestorm of customer discontent. What are other ways that Zynga might have handled the discontinuance of a failing game without creating such protest?

10-24. How is the ownership of digital information determined? Is it ethically wrong to deny people access to owned information if that denial causes harm?

10-25. When virtual pet owners invested emotionally and financially in "their" pets, should they have been considered at least partial owners of the digital information? Why or why not?

Sources: Farewell to Fido: A lesson in digital customer relationship management. (January 30, 2013). Knowledge @ Wharton, http://knowledge.wharton.upenn.edu/article.cfm?articleid=3178, accessed May 25, 2016.
Green, T. (2016). *Zynga, Inc.* Hoover's Online, http://subscriber.hoovers.com.proxy1.library.jhu.edu/H/company360/fulldescription.html?companyId=161848000000000, accessed August 22, 2016.
Needleman, S. E., & Minaya, E. (My 4, 2016). Zynga results boosted by cost cuts; Maker of "Words with Friends," "FarmVille" reports decline in daily users. *Wall Street Journal (Online),* http://www.wsj.com/articles/zynga-results-boosted-by-cost-cuts-1462392621, accessed August 22, 2016.
Seitz, P. (February 11, 2016). Zynga stock getting dogged by declining user base. *Investors Business Daily,* p. 1.

CASE STUDY #2

Community Policing on the Internet: Spamhaus Targets Worldwide Spammers

Silently protecting the inboxes of billions of people worldwide is an international nonprofit organization called Spamhaus, which describes its mission as:

- Tracking the Internet's spam operations and related threats.
- Providing dependable real-time intelligence about threats to the Internet's major networks.
- Working with law enforcement agencies to identify and pursue spam and malware sources worldwide.

With headquarters in the United Kingdom and Switzerland, Spamhaus maintains a "block list" containing the IP addresses believed to originate spam. Many governments, corporations, universities, and other organizations check the list before delivering mail, blocking any messages whose senders match an entry on it.

Identifying and Fighting Spammers

How do senders wind up labeled as spammers and placed on the block list? Spamhaus defines spam as any mail that is both unsolicited and sent in bulk. Mail that meets this definition may not be illegal in many places, including the United States, so Spamhaus is the target of lawsuits claiming damages for lost business. For example, a Chicago email marketing firm called e360 Insight sued Spamhaus for more than $11 million in damages. A U.S. court eventually awarded e360 $27,000, but Spamhaus refused to pay even that amount, insisting that e360 is a spammer. The U.S. Court of Appeals reduced the amount to $3, overturning the judgments of previous courts. Although e360 is now out of business, its main employee complained bitterly about this kind of community policing that works outside of traditional law enforcement. "Spamhaus.org is a fanatical, vigilante organization that operates in the United States with blatant disregard for U.S. law," he said.

Although the cause is noble, the stakes are extremely high, so the work itself can be both dangerous and secretive. Larry, Spamhaus's chief technical officer, who prefers not to reveal his last name, says,

"We get threats every day. In the U.S., it is people bringing lawsuits against us. And then there are organized criminals in Russia and Ukraine, who use different methods." Police have advised Steve Linford, head of Spamhaus, to be suspicious of any unexpected packages delivered to his home.

In March 2013, a massive distributed denial of service (DDoS) attack, one of the largest in Internet history, hit the Spamhaus website. The attackers used "DNS reflection," in which the Internet's domain name servers, which resolve URLs to their corresponding IP addresses, are spoofed into sending huge traffic streams to one website. Spamhaus crashed, and the enormous attack left many wondering if the whole Internet might be in danger.

Sven Kamphuis quickly took credit for the attack, accusing Spamhaus of trying to "control the Internet through underhanded extortion tactics." Kamphuis heads a company named CyberBunker; this company offers a hosting service that does not keep any traffic logs, so there are no records for police to confiscate. Spammers and copyright violators flock to hosts like this, and Spamhaus had blocked several of CyberBunker's clients, some of whom volunteered to launch the DDoS attack.

Fighting spam becomes more challenging as the Internet grows, and many new top-level domains (TLDs) are approved. While the registrars for .com, .net, and other major TLDs do a good job of monitoring for spam, some TLDs are rife with it. Figure 10-28 shows the worst offenders.

Pros and Cons of Community Policing

Industry analysts know that community policing is not perfect and that block lists can contain false positives that harm legitimate businesses. It is time-consuming and expensive for companies to work through the process to get cleared. But as one analyst put it, "These [spammers] aren't just a nuisance. They're a cancer on society. And Linford has taken it upon himself to do something about them. That these cops are self-appointed is troubling. But marketers would do well to understand that without Spamhaus, people's inboxes would be unusable."

FIGURE 10-28

Some top-level domains with the worst reputations for spam operations, identified by Spamhaus. https://www.spamhaus.org/statistics/tlds/, accessed August 22, 2016.

Top-Level Domain	% Bad Domains
.download	83.6%
.work	74.1%
.uno	71.3%
.click	67.5%

Discussion Questions

10-26. How do the interests of computer users differ from the interests of spammers?

10-27. Do you agree with the Spamhaus methodology to reduce spam?

10-28. What other approaches could be taken to reduce spam?

10-29. What are the relevant legal issues in this case?

Sources: Constantin, L. (2013). DDoS attack against Spamhaus was reportedly the largest in history. *CIO*, (13284045), http://www.cio.com/article/2387217/internet/ddos-attack-against-spamhaus-was-reportedly-the-largest-in-history.html, accessed August 22, 2016.

Constantin, L. (2016). Maintainers of new generic top level domains have a hard time keeping abuse in check. *CIO (13284045)*, http://www.cio.com/article/3041338/maintainers-of-new-generic-top-level-domains-have-a-hard-time-keeping-abuse-in-check.html, accessed August 22, 2016.

Ducklin, P. (July 13, 2015). Lad who attacked Spamhaus in DDoS attack avoids prison, given a second chance. https://nakedsecurity.sophos.com/2015/07/13/lad-who-attacked-spamhaus-in-ddos-attack-avoids-prison-given-a-second-chance/, accessed August 22, 2016.

Kirk, J. (2013). Spamhaus warns marketers to keep email databases tidy. *CIO*, (13284045), 39.

Riley, M., Matlack, C., & Levine, R. (2013). CyberBunk: Hacking as performance art. *Bloomberg Businessweek*, (4324), 33–34.

The Spamhaus Project. (2016). https://www.spamhaus.org/, accessed May 25, 2016.

Vijayan, J. (2013). Spamhaus attacks expose huge open DNS server dangers. *CIO*, (13284045), 35.

E-PROJECT 1 — Tracking the Trackers: Investigating How Third-Party Cookies Steer the Ads You See

This e-project will show how third-party cookies read by a browser can shape the user's online browsing experience across websites.

First, you will need to remove existing cookies so you can conduct the experiment with a clean slate. Once they have been removed, configure your browser to accept new third-party cookies. (Check your browser's "help" if you need assistance.)

Next, visit online retailer Zappos (zappos.com) and look around for a product you would never actually purchase. Examine the product, clicking on features, and then add it to your cart. The goal is to add the third-party cookies about your visit and your shopping interests. Don't buy anything, of course. Zappos participates in quite a few ad networks, and each one will place a cookie on your computer.

10-30. Browse to several sites that carry advertising, such as yahoo.com, latimes.com, time.com, aol.com, and bloomberg.com. Search each page to see if there are any Zappos ads. Which websites show an ad from Zappos? Which ones did not show any Zappos ads? What was the content of the ads?

10-31. Remove all your cookies again, and revisit the same list of sites. What Zappos ads do you see now?

10-32. Explain the results that you found in this e-project. (Don't forget to reconfigure your browser to the privacy settings you prefer.)

E-PROJECT 2 — Analyzing Spammers by Country Using Excel Pivot Tables

In this e-project, you will explore Spamhaus's Registry of Known Spam Operators (ROKSO), a list the organization maintains and posts on its website.

Visit www.spamhaus.org and click on ROKSO. How does Spamhaus determine who or what should be in the registry?

Download the file Ch10_SpamHaus, which contains a list of known spammers from 2016.

10-33. Sort the list by the TopTen column. Which entry is considered the number-one spammer?

10-34. Next, you will generate a pivot table and chart showing the list of countries, with the count of each country's known spammers. Select the data in all columns and then choose Insert, Pivot

Chart. Change the chart type to Column if needed. Drag and drop Country to the Axis Fields, and Name to the Values box, so the chart shows the count of spammers by country.

a. Which country has the most known spammers?

b. Which country is second in terms of the number of known spammers on this list?

10-35. To view a chart containing just the Top Ten offenders by country, click on IsOnTopTen in the Field List, and then click the down arrow to the right. Uncheck "no" so the analysis will only include spammers who are on the top 10 list. Drag the IsOnTopTen field to the Report Filter box. Which countries have the most spammers in the top ten?

CHAPTER NOTES

1. Woody, C. (April 15, 2016). A court in Argentina has ordered a crackdown on Uber's operations. *Business Insider*. http://www.businessinsider.com/argentina-crack-down-on-uber-2016-4, accessed August 22, 2016.

2. Zimmerman, M. (2009). Judge overturns Lori Drew misdemeanor convictions. Electronic Frontier Foundation, http://www.eff.org/deeplinks/2009/07/judge-overturns-lori, accessed June 4, 2016.

3. Spitznagel, E. (2012). Great moments in Twitter blunders. *Bloomberg Businessweek*, (4283), 88–89.

4. Molnar, K., Kletke, M., & Chongwatpol, J. (2008). Ethics vs. IT ethics: Do undergraduate students perceive a difference? *Journal of Business Ethics, 83*(4), 657–671.
   Molnar, K. K. (2015). Students' perceptions of academic dishonesty: A nine-year study from 2005 to 2013. *Journal of Academic Ethics, 13*(2), 135–150. http://doi.org/10.1007/s10805-015-9231-9

5. Google, Viacom settle landmark YouTube lawsuit. (March 18, 2014). *Reuters*, http://www.reuters.com/article/us-google-viacom-lawsuit-idUSBREA2H11220140318, accessed August 22, 2016.

6. Llanes, M. (2016). Mexico: Copyright infringement by hyperlinking. *Managing Intellectual Property*, http://www.managingip.com/Article/3532490/Mexico-Copyright-infringement-by-hyperlinking.html, accessed August 22, 2016.

7. Farivar, C. (February 20, 2013). Germans can't see meteorite YouTube videos due to copyright dispute. *Ars Technica*, http://arstechnica.com/tech-policy/2013/02/germans-cant-see-meteorite-youtube-videos-due-to-copyright-dispute/, accessed August 22, 2016.

8. Kos Koklic, M., Kukar-Kinney, M., & Vida, I. (2016). Three-level mechanism of consumer digital piracy: Development and cross-cultural validation. *Journal of Business Ethics, 134*(1), 15–27. http://doi.org/10.1007/s10551-014-2075-1

9. Business Software Alliance. (2014). *The Compliance Gap: BSA Global Software Survey*. http://globalstudy.bsa.org/2013/downloads/studies/2013GlobalSurvey_Study_en.pdf, accessed August 22, 2016.

10. Legrand, E. (2016). The Takedown Squad. *Music Week*, 18–19.

11. Schiller, K. (2010). A happy medium: Ebooks, licensing, and DRM. *Information Today, 27*(2), 1–44.

12. Hasshi, S. (March–April, 2013). Effectiveness of anti-piracy technology: Finding appropriate solutions for evolving online piracy. *Business Horizons, 56*(2), 149–157.

13. Bruton, S., & Childers, D. (2016). The ethics and politics of policing plagiarism: a qualitative study of faculty views on student plagiarism and Turnitin. *Assessment & Evaluation in Higher Education, 41*(2), 316–330. http://doi.org/10.1080/02602938.2015.1008981

14. Geller, T. (2016). In privacy law, it's the U.S. vs. the world. *Communications of the ACM, 59*(2), 21–23. http://doi.org/10.1145/2852233

15. Antoine, H. (2016). Digital legacies: Who owns your online life after death? *Computer & Internet Lawyer, 33*(4), 15–20.

16. Bradshaw, T., Menn, J., & Schafer, D. (May 18, 2010). Google faces German and US probes over harvested wifi data. *Financial Times* (London), http://search.proquest.com/docview/250289768?accountid=11752, accessed August 22, 2016.

17. Steiner, P. (July 5, 1993). On the Internet, no one knows you're a dog (cartoon). *The New Yorker*, p. 61.

18. Wallace, P. (2016). *The psychology of the Internet* (2nd ed.). New York, NY: Cambridge University Press.

19. Minárik, T., & Osula, A.-M. (2016). Tor does not stink: Use and abuse of the Tor anonymity network from the perspective of law. *Computer Law & Security Review, 32*(1), 111–127. http://doi.org/10.1016/j.clsr.2015.12.002

20. Shane, S., & Sanger, D.E. (June 20, 2013). Job title key to inner access held by Snowden. *New York Times*, http://www.nytimes.com/2013/07/01/us/job-title-key-to-inner-access-held-by-snowden.html?pagewanted=all&_r=0, accessed August 22, 2016.

21. Chory, R. M., Vela, L. E., & Avtgis, T. A. (2015). Organizational surveillance of computer-mediated workplace communication: Employee privacy concerns and responses. *Employee Responsibilities and Rights Journal, 28*(1), 23–43. http://doi.org/10.1007/s10672-015-9267-4

22. Werfel, E. (2016). What organizations must know about the "right to be forgotten." *Information Management Journal, 50*(2), 30–32.

23. Vijayan, J. (2016). Google reportedly to further enforce EU's right to be forgotten mandate. *eWeek*, http://www.eweek.com/cloud/google-reportedly-to-further-enforce-eus-right-to-be-forgotten-mandate.html, accessed August 22, 2016.

24. Pike, G. H. (2016). The right to be forgotten. *Information Today, 33*(3), 13.

25. Shuntich, S. (2016). The life, the death, and the long-awaited resurrection of privacy. *Human Rights, 41*(4), 2–13.

26. Kirk, J. (February 7, 2013). Microsoft, Symantec take down Barmital click-fraud botnet. *Computer World*, http://www.computerworld.com/article/2494639/malware-vulnerabilities/microsoft–symantec-take-down-bamital-click-fraud-botnet.html, accessed August 22, 2016.

27. Gross, G. (2016). Detecting and destroying botnets. *Network Security, 2016*(3), 7–10. http://doi.org/10.1016/S1353-4858(16)30027-7

28. Greengard, S. (January 21, 2016). How spear phishing puts businesses on the hook. *CIO Insight*, http://www.cioinsight.com/security/slideshows/how-spear-phishing-puts-businesses-on-the-hook.html, accessed August 22, 2016.

29. Meiklejohn, S., Pomarole, M., Jordan, G., Levchenko, K., McCoy, D., Voelker, G. M., & Savage, S. (2016). A fistful of bitcoins: Characterizing payments among men with no names. *Communications of the ACM*, *59*(4), 86–93. http://doi.org/10.1145/2896384

30. Ransomware expands, attacks hospitals and local authorities, and moves to new platforms. (2016). *Network Security*, *2016*(3), 1–2. http://doi.org/10.1016/S1353-4858(16)30022-8

31. Skowronski, J. (July 27, 2015). What your information is worth on the black market. *Bankrate.com*, http://www.bankrate.com/finance/credit/what-your-identity-is-worth-on-black-market.aspx, accessed August 22, 2016.

32. *Chronology of data breaches—Security breaches 2005–Present*. Privacy Rights Clearninghouse, www.privacyrights.org/data-breach, accessed May 4, 2016.

33. IBM. (2016). *IBM's 2016 cyber security intelligence index*. http://www-03.ibm.com/security/data-breach/cyber-security-index.html, accessed August 22, 2016.

34. Payment Card Industry Security Standards Council Website. (n.d.). https://www.pcisecuritystandards.org, accessed May 4, 2016.

35. Stoll, C. (1990). *The cuckoo's egg: Tracking a spy through the maze of computer espionage*. New York: Simon and Schuster.

36. Everett, C. (2016). Are passwords finally dying? *Network Security*, *2016*(2), 10–14. http://doi.org/10.1016/S1353-4858(16)30017-4

11 Systems Development and *Procurement*

LEARNING OBJECTIVES

1 Describe the seven phases of the systems development life cycle (SDLC).

2 Describe three major software development strategies.

3 Explain why organizations choose one software development strategy over another for particular projects.

4 Explain how organizations decide whether to build or buy and the steps they use if they choose to buy an information system.

5 Identify several ways in which the human element is important for systems development and procurement.

An online, interactive decision-making simulation that reinforces chapter contents and uses key terms in context can be found in MyMISLab™.

INTRODUCTION

HOW DO INFORMATION SYSTEMS COME INTO BEING? SOME START OFF IN A PROGRAMMER'S BASEMENT, and a few of those burst out to earn billions for their creators. Most, however, are built or bought in response to a business need.

In the online simulation for this chapter called "Green Wheeling," the business need is clear. A university launched a campaign to contact alums, local corporations, wealthy residents, and potential donors to ask for donations to purchase electric vehicles for the campus so students wouldn't need cars. The problem, though, is that the information system they rely on to manage this campaign is in shambles and must be replaced. Duplicate names abound, and the volunteer fund-raisers—including you—are irritating donors with multiple phone calls. You join a task force to identify what the real problems are, what features you need most, and how you will go about getting this new information system. You'll learn what trade-offs people make as they push for the features that matter most to them, and you will also weigh the pros and cons of buying software versus building it.

GREEN WHEELING
A Role-Playing Simulation on Systems Development
for a Fund-Raising Application

This chapter traces the life cycle of an information system, from the birth of the idea and the planning phase to the system's implementation and maintenance. A lot can go wrong in this cycle, and many projects fail along the way. We will see why that can happen and the kinds of choices people make as they navigate all the options. We also examine how information systems—like the university's crumbling fund-raising system—age and why they eventually must be replaced.

Describe the seven phases of the systems development life cycle (SDLC).

 # Systems Development Life Cycle

Bored at the thought of another frozen lasagna dinner, Lily looks closely at her refrigerator's shelves and spots parmesan cheese, garlic, cream, and other odds and ends. Her cabinets also hold chicken stock, tomato paste, and olive oil, so there must be something creative to make. Her few cookbooks have tempting recipes, but none match her supply. If only she could find one that uses what she has on hand. If a system had that information, could it do a matching process to recommend some dishes she hasn't considered?

Innovations often spring from frustrations like this one, and Lily starts mulling over a web application to fill this gap. As a senior manager for an online grocer that delivers to a 20-mile radius, she is also thinking about competitive advantage and how this application, her "What to Make with What You Have" cookbook, might help the company. Lily is no stranger to web development; she was charged with implementing the company's main e-commerce website. She starts making notes, planning to bring the idea up at the next managers' meeting.

The **systems development life cycle (SDLC)** is the process that begins with planning and goes through several phases until the system has been implemented. It then enters its maintenance period. In theory, the process encompasses seven sequential steps (Figure 11-1), although, of course, the real world is often more unruly. The seven steps are planning, analysis, design, development, testing, implementation, and maintenance.

Planning

The goal in this step is to define the business need for the project, assess its importance to the company, and determine whether the project is actually feasible. Most organizations are not short of ideas for information system projects, but they all have limited time and funding. Indeed, many have a long queue of ideas to enhance or replace existing systems or to implement brand new ones, many of which may seem worthwhile. Lily's cookbook project may face some tough competition for the company's resources. A steering committee with business stakeholders and IT staff often leads the planning phase and makes the case for the new system.

ASSESSING BUSINESS NEED

Three major factors that bolster business need and determine where to allocate funding for systems development projects are:

- Return on investment (ROI)
- Competitive advantage
- Risk management

If the project will either save or earn more money than it will cost, the *return on investment (ROI)* is positive. For some projects the ROI is relatively easy to calculate. For example, when two school districts in Canada merged into one, they each had separate phone systems. They decided to replace the systems with unified communications and IP phones that rely on Internet connections at a cost of $500,000. The combined district saved $200K a year, returning the investment in just 2 ½ years. The school also benefits from many added features such as paging, public address system, videoconferencing, and free call forwarding.[1]

ROI can be much harder to estimate in other projects. Lily envisions that her system will promote online grocery sales by including a feature to suggest recipes that will also work well—except for one or two items the customer is missing. The program would offer a discount coupon for those and promise speedy delivery. Since the customer would already be paying the delivery charge, the promotion might also suggest some other items to complement the customer's pantry. Leveraging information systems for *competitive advantage* is a powerful driver for systems development, and Lily thinks this aspect should be stressed in the proposal. Thinking about the site in those terms, she decides to add a loyalty feature for repeat customers who can earn points toward free deliveries. She also describes a commenting and reviewing function so that customers can rate the recipes and

FIGURE 11-1

Systems development life cycle phases.

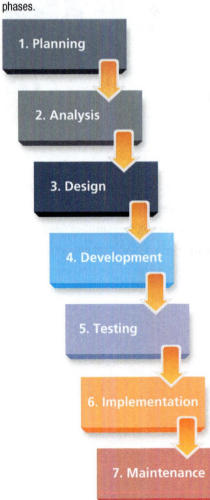

share their tips. That would help build a community of creative people who like to cook something fun on the spur of the moment with little advance planning.

Risk management is a third driver of information systems development, one that usually touches on security, privacy, safety, and regulatory compliance. For example, the company's CIO might insist on new software development to improve information security for customer data. The development effort won't increase sales, but it will protect the company from security threats. Lily's project doesn't reduce risk, so it can't be justified on that basis. In fact, it may raise new privacy concerns. Customers might not be willing to divulge food preferences in connection with personally identifying information because they might hint at medical problems or just awful eating habits. A strong privacy policy will be needed, and Lily will cover this in her proposal.

> Software bugs are inevitable, but some can be very embarrassing. One of Intel's early Pentium computer chips, for instance, made mistakes when calculating certain division problems. Intel tried to downplay the severity of the problem, making the public relations problem even worse. The company finally offered to replace the chip for anyone who asked.[2]

FEASIBILITY STUDY

The **feasibility study** is an important part of the planning process that examines whether the initiative is viable from technical, financial, and legal standpoints. It may not be technically feasible if the technologies either don't exist yet or are not mature enough to support the project's goals. Financially, the return on investment may be promising, but the organization may lack capital to fund it. A legal review may uncover risks that could expose the company to lawsuits. Disputes over technology patents are particularly common.

The feasibility of Lily's project depends partly on whether she can get access to recipes in a format that can be analyzed according to ingredients. Her company already has a huge database of grocery products, so that side of the matching is already in place.

Analysis

Once the project has approval to proceed, the next step is to analyze and document what the system should actually do from the business (as opposed to the technical) perspective. During **requirements analysis**, stakeholders identify the features the system will need and then prioritize them as mandatory, preferred, or nonessential.

Gathering these requirements entails many meetings, interviews, and reviews of the way existing processes unfold. The person who leads this analysis needs a solid background in business management and information systems but also outstanding listening and consensus-building skills. The stakeholders will have different views about how processes actually work and how they should be improved, especially when their own jobs are involved. You will see that happening in the Green Wheeling simulation.

PROCESS DIAGRAMS AND BUSINESS PROCESS IMPROVEMENT

The analysis will develop a clear understanding of the processes the system will support, usually using **process diagrams**. These trace how each process operates from beginning to end in a way that is clear to all the stakeholders. Figure 11-2 shows an example.

---

systems development life cycle (SDLC)
The process that describes the seven steps in the life of an information system: planning, analysis, design, development, testing, implementation, and maintenance.

feasibility study
Part of the information system planning process that examines whether the initiative is viable from technical, financial, and legal standpoints.

requirements analysis
The process by which stakeholders identify the features a new information system will need and then prioritize them as mandatory, preferred, or nonessential.

process diagrams
Graphical representations that trace how each process that a new information system will support operates from beginning to end.

FIGURE 11-2

Sample process diagram.

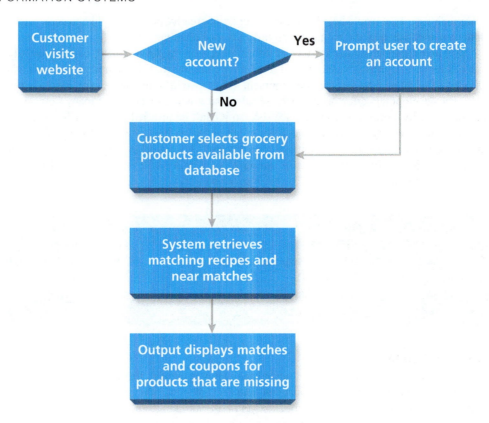

A well-done requirements analysis should also uncover opportunities to optimize business processes and even eliminate some of them. As we described in Chapter 1, attention to how information systems can improve business process management (BPM) can yield rich dividends. For instance, a process that includes routing a supply purchase to a supervisor for approval might not be needed at all if the rules the supervisor uses to make decisions can be built into an expert system. Manual data entry from handwritten forms is a major target for elimination, drawing on intelligent character recognition or customers who will happily input their own data on the web.

When you buy an airline ticket on the carrier's website, you do all the data entry yourself, including your passport number if it is an international trip. Contrast that with a phone call to an airline reservation specialist, who will charge you a fee for making the arrangements and entering your data for you. As an added bonus, customers have a strong motivation to avoid errors in their own data, so accuracy improves.

An early form of BPM introduced in the 1990s was called **business process reengineering (BPR)**. In his article with the provocative subtitle "Don't Automate, Obliterate," Michael Hammer proposed BPR as a means to make sweeping changes that eliminate all processes that did not add value.[3] Following his advice, many companies went through wrenching, expensive, and ultimately unsuccessful projects to redesign processes throughout the organization. It soon became clear that the human element is key to managing and improving business processes, and by 1995, BPR was criticized as a fad that "forgot people." BPR's objectives are sound, though, if the techniques are used in a more focused way on smaller projects in the context of new system development and overall business process management.[4]

REQUIREMENTS DEFINITION DOCUMENT

The output of the analysis phase is the **requirements definition document (RDD)**, which specifies in detail what features the system should have, prioritized by the stakeholders. It also includes assumptions and constraints that affect the system, such as the need to migrate and possibly reformat data from an existing system. In addition to the system's actual features,

Types of Requirements	Examples
Functional requirements	System features, prioritized by stakeholders; description of processes the system will support, and the system's input and output
Usability requirements	Ease of learning the software, task efficiency, screen attractiveness
Accessibility requirements	Accessibility for people with disabilities
Performance requirements	Response time, reliability, availability, scalability
Interface requirements	User navigation, data display
Security requirements	Authentication, privacy, encryption
Compliance requirements	Processes and reports required for compliance
Integration requirements	Interfaces with other systems
Language requirements	Support for English, Spanish, and/or other languages

FIGURE 11-3
Types of requirements included in a requirements definition document.

the document should address the kinds of requirements listed in Figure 11-3. Stakeholders sign off on the document, confirming that this is indeed the system they need, specified as precisely as possible.

> **PRODUCTIVITY TIP**
> You can optimize one of your own processes by leveraging information systems. Before you run errands, make a checklist. Then use a navigation app to find the most efficient order for your destinations and the best routes to take.

BUILD OR BUY?

Once the stakeholders agree on what is needed, a review of commercially available information systems may take place. The RDD becomes a feature guide to help compare the fit of each candidate to the organization's requirements. A general rule of thumb is that if an organization can buy or license software that meets at least 75% to 80% of its requirements, and costs are within reason, the "buy" option is probably a favorable approach. "Buy" is also typically the best choice when the system supports common business functions, such as financial or human resource management. We will come back to the procurement process later in this chapter. For now, we continue with systems development when the choice is to build it from scratch. Design, development, testing, and implementation might proceed with in-house IT staff, or the project might be outsourced to a software development company. In either case, the RDD is the road map.

Design Phase

In the design phase the RDD is translated into a workable technical design. Here, the team makes decisions about the system's architecture and draws up plans that describe the technical details.

ARCHITECTURAL DESIGN

The choice of software development environments and hardware architecture is a critical one. As we discussed in Chapter 3, the organization has to consider the enterprise architecture as a whole. Although a particular software development environment might be marginally more efficient for a specific project, the disadvantages of a fragmented, poorly integrated architecture are too costly to ignore.

The choice will also be affected by the experience and capabilities of the IT staff. A company whose IT staff is very experienced with the Java programming language, Linux servers, and MySQL databases, for example, would lean in that direction for new projects to leverage its existing expertise. If the staff is experienced only in older technologies, however, the

business process reengineering (BPR)
The design and analysis of workflows in an organization with the goal of eliminating processes that do not add value.

requirements definition document (RDD)
A document that specifies the features a new information system should have, prioritized by stakeholders. It also includes assumptions and constraints that affect the system, such as the need to migrate and possibly reformat data from an existing system.

organization's chief architect will want to take this opportunity to train staff in new tools, ones that align with the enterprise's future architecture.

SERVICE-ORIENTED ARCHITECTURE

A growing trend in software design is **service-oriented architecture (SOA)**, in which systems are assembled from relatively independent software components, each of which handles a specific business service. For example, one chunk of code might "get the customer's credit rating," and different applications and business units could interface to this chunk to perform the same common task rather than build it separately. The approach is especially useful in fast-moving, agile companies that need to make many changes to business rules and processes and that also want to streamline common business services across the enterprise.

Verizon developers, for instance, built a service to "get the customer service record." The underlying software code was not pretty—it had to retrieve a complex jumble of data from 25 different systems. But other developers who needed that service for new web-based applications didn't have to worry about the innards—they only had to write a single link to interface with the service's outside wrapper. Without the service, those developers would have had to write interfaces to all those 25 systems independently, and the results that were returned for each customer may not have been consistent. Worse, when a 26th system is added, from a merger perhaps, every one of those systems would need changes, not just the one service.

APPLICATION PROGRAMMING INTERFACES (API)

Software development benefits even more from the enormous and rapidly growing number of **application programming interfaces (API)** offered by third parties. These are sets of routines and protocols that specify how software components should interface with one another. Consider, for instance, how an electrical plug forms the interface between a hair dryer that needs 120V to run and the utility services that deliver the current. An API is like that plug; much innovation can take place in how the utilities generate and distribute electricity and also in the electrical devices as long as the service delivered stays the same and the devices can use it.[5]

Many companies offer APIs to access their services via the Internet, such as mapping, payments, billing, and others. Google, for instance, makes its mapping APIs available, so any organization that wants to show pushpins on maps need not write code from scratch. Instead, the developer can just write a few lines to pass the required parameters to the API, such as latitude and longitude. Clients of Salesforce.com, the cloud-based CRM vendor, rely heavily on Salesforce's APIs to integrate customer data with their other information systems.[6] The API economy is exploding because it contributes so much productivity to software development and supports so much innovation.[7]

Microsoft Graph illustrates that company's vision for an API ecosystem. Graph's tools allow developers access to information users maintain in their cloud-based Office 365 products, so they can design new apps that leverage integration. For example, one software application helps sales people draw from Office calendars, documents, and presentation templates to quickly schedule and prepare a proposal for an upcoming meeting. Microsoft purchased LinkedIn in 2016, planning to expand these capabilities even further by enabling access to the vast storehouse of professional data on more than 400 million LinkedIn users.[8] Cortana, Microsoft's personal digital assistant, may help that salesperson even more by offering a briefing on each attendee, drawn from LinkedIn.[9]

Like many companies, the online grocer where Lily works has a mix of architectures because some systems were purchased from software vendors and integrated with others that were custom-built. However, the grocery product database is in a MySQL database, and the web applications are all developed with the open source programming language called PHP. That architecture makes the most sense for the cookbook project, and it will take advantage of APIs for mapping services.

Whatever architecture is selected, the organization must also consider size and capacity issues because the application will put new pressures on it. For example, more server space might be required, whether in the data center or in the cloud.

DATA MODELS AND DATABASE DESIGN

The design phase captures all aspects of how the system's components will function together to accomplish the goal, using descriptions, models, and diagrams. It is the technical blueprint for the whole system, with all the fine print and details. The analyst and IT staff will look this over very closely because fixing mistakes now helps avoid costly corrections later.

The database schema described in Chapter 4, for instance, will show all the details for the database's tables, the fields for each table, and the relationships between the tables. The **use case diagram** will show how different types of users will interact with the system (Figure 11-4). (Stick figures really are used to represent users.) Other diagrams document specific business processes and rules, screen layouts, and navigation.

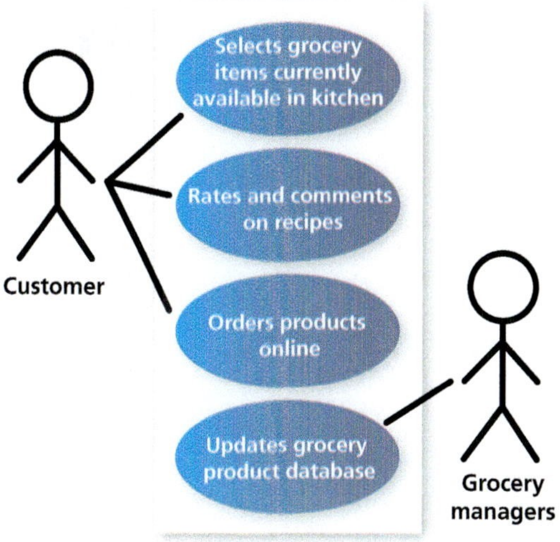

Designers rely on standardized graphics symbols and notations to improve communication and clarity, creating visual models and blueprints that document the system's components, as well as the behaviors it is expected to perform.

The design phase also addresses usability and considers the needs of all the different end users who will interact with the system. For a customer website, a positive user experience adds business value and encourages visitors to come back. Eager buyers return again and again to Amazon because usability is high; customers can easily locate what they need, enter shipping information, and complete the purchase. Usability does not mean flashy graphics and slow-to-load animations, which can often discourage customers rather than attract them.

Designers also consider end users with disabilities in this phase and ensure the design complies with legal requirements. Although those requirements continue to evolve, lawsuits are mounting, often resulting in settlements rather than trials.[10] Accessibility features will not just meet legal requirements; they will also broaden the customer base.

FIGURE 11-4
Simplified use case diagram.

Development Phases

Converting the design into an operational information system is the goal of the development phase. Depending on the system's scope, this phase might require teams of developers to work for months, each constructing one portion of the system.

Software developers use their own information systems to streamline work and keep one another informed about progress or challenges. For example, **version control software** tracks versions of the code, acting like a library with checkout procedures to prevent developers from writing over one another's files. To work on a program, the developer checks it out of the library. Other developers can still view it and see who has it, but they can't make their own changes. When the developer has finished, the code is checked back into the library as the latest version, and another developer can then check it out.

Project- and issue-tracking software offers useful features to help developers stay abreast of all aspects of their projects. Developers can upload diagrams and documentation, comment on activity, describe challenges, report bugs, and request assistance. The software maintains a complete history of project activity, including dates showing when each module was started and completed and who has been assigned each task. It also offers customizable dashboards so developers can see at a glance how the project is coming along and which activities they need to complete today (Figure 11-5). Software tools are available to facilitate **code review**, a peer review process in which programmers familiar with the project and the development environment check over one another's work to ensure it is

---

service-oriented architecture (SOA)
A set of design principles in which systems are assembled from relatively independent software components, each of which handles a specific business service.

application programming interface (API)
Set of routines and protocols that specify how software components should interface with one another in a standardized way.

use case diagram
Diagrams that show how different types of users will interact with the system.

version control software
A type of software that tracks versions of the source code during development, enforcing checkout procedures to prevent developers from writing over one another's files.

code review
A peer review process in which programmers check over one another's work to ensure its quality.

FIGURE 11-5

Project- and issue-tracking software.

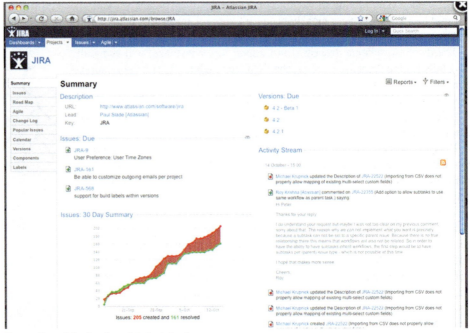

Source: From Atlassian.Copyright by Atlassian.

well documented and properly written. Software can check for security vulnerabilities in the code so they can be fixed early.

PRODUCTIVITY TIP

When creating a new document for one of your courses, you need a way to track versions. Try using a standardized file-naming convention that combines the course code, short paper title, and version number, such as BUS101_SDLC_ v01. Don't fall into the trap of tacking the word *new* onto the filename for the latest version. "*New*" becomes old very quickly.

Testing Phase

Testing goes on during the development phase, as individual modules are completed. When the system has been completed, it undergoes much more rigorous testing to ensure that the whole system works smoothly together, not just its individual modules. Figure 11-6 lists examples of the kinds of tests developers might perform.

Each test mimics events the system will handle when it goes live. The test cases are carefully documented so the developers can make corrections in case of any failures. Software tools help tremendously with this testing as well. For example, once developers have created a library of test cases, software tools can automatically run them against the system as it evolves to test for errors. The software can simulate an army of customers, simultaneously trying to

FIGURE 11-6

Types of testing for information systems.

Types of Testing for Information Systems	Description
Unit testing	Programmers can check the functionality of small modules of code during the development phase.
System testing	Both end users and IT staff test the functionality of the entire system.
Stress testing	Tests are conducted by IT staff to assess how well the system performs under peak loads.
Parallel testing	Using the same input, developers compare the new system's output to the output generated by the system it is replacing.
Integration testing	End users and IT staff test the new system's interfaces with other software components it links to.
Acceptance testing	End users perform final testing to determine whether the project is complete as specified.

FIGURE 11-7

Software testing tool to examine web applications for various types of problems, such as missing text descriptions for images.

Source: http://achecker.ca, developed by the Adaptive Technology Resource Centre—University of Toronto. http://atrc.utoronto.ca.

complete a web-based form with different data, different input errors, different browsers, and different expected outcomes. For Lily's cookbook, the test cases would include a range of people, some whose cupboards are almost bare and others who have rare spices and specialty foods.

Other software tools can check for security holes, compliance with accessibility regulations, performance under loads, broken web links, and more (Figure 11-7). These tools, and also independent testers, are critical because programmers are not the best testers of their own code. They know how the code actually works and unconsciously avoid the odd key presses and clicks that end users try.

Kentico Software found a creative way to motivate end users to report bugs they spot in its web content management software. The company plants a tree in the bug finder's honor and maintains a Tree Gallery with photos of every tree planted, the name of the person who reported the bug, and the tree's location.[11]

Implementation

As the go-live date approaches, tasks shift to the needs of the end users who will be using and managing the system. They will need documentation and training to understand clearly how the new system works and how it differs from the old one, if there was one. Their jobs may change considerably, and they must feel confident they can handle the new roles.

Organizations have several choices about how to implement a new system:

- Parallel implementation
- Phased implementation
- Direct implementation

A **parallel implementation** launches the new system while the old one is still running. Employees either do their jobs twice, once on each system, or two separate teams handle the same processes, one team on each system. An advantage to this approach is that both systems are processing the same cases, so if the new one is operating properly, the output should be the same. However, parallel implementation is very expensive and thus is usually in place for only a short period. Also, if the old system is being retired because it bungled some processes, the comparisons might not be valid.

parallel implementation
A type of implementation in which the new system is launched while the old one it is replacing continues to run so output can be compared.

A **phased implementation** launches modules in phases rather than all at once. For example, an ERP might start with human resources, then phase in components of the financial modules. The implementation team and trainers can focus on one departmental group at a time, helping them become accustomed to the new software while the developers watch for glitches. A disadvantage is that the new system's modules may be tightly integrated, so implementing one without the others may create some confusion and require temporary interfaces to the old systems. For example, the human resources system will include payroll data that must be passed to the old general ledger if the new ledger isn't up and running yet. Consistency is also an issue if information is maintained in more than one place as the modules are phased in.

Direct implementation switches off the old system and launches all the modules of the new one on a single, very hectic go-live date, sometimes called the "big bang" (after the way astronomers describe the universe's explosive origin). Often employees go home at night and come back in the morning to find the new system all in place. A major advantage is that all those temporary bridges between old and new modules are unnecessary, and people whose job roles span modules do not have to switch back and forth. The strategy works well for smaller systems and may be the only logical choice for them. However, the risks can be high for large-scale implementations of complex software such as the ERP, involving thousands of employees.

Often the type of system determines which implementation plan is feasible. Lily's application, for instance, can easily be implemented in phases, with the matching feature that compares pantry contents to the recipe database launched first. Company staff will be trained to enter and maintain the grocery and recipe databases, with the IT staff prepared to respond to tech support questions. Customers can start populating the system with the contents of their larders and retrieve recipes immediately. The online grocer's marketing team will favor this sequence because it offers a quick win in terms of competitive advantage. The customers will be more likely to come back once they devote all that effort to enter their own data. Later phases can add user comments, reviews, and targeted promotions to further boost loyalty.

Maintenance

During the first weeks, dedicated support people are usually on call to resolve technical glitches, train users, correct documentation, and make sure everyone has access to all the functionality they need. As things settle down, the system moves into maintenance mode, in which the regular help-desk team can provide support. Maintenance does not mean changes are not being made to the system, however. Most information systems continue to evolve to fix bugs and respond to changing conditions.

BUG FIXES AND CHANGE REQUESTS

Despite extensive testing, no system with any complexity is bug-free. The test cases used to pound the system into shape touch on only a small subset of all the possible events and combinations. Once the system has gone live, users introduce more cases and bugs surface.

Bugs also arise because the surrounding technologies evolve. For instance, Internet Explorer, Firefox, Safari, and other browsers are constantly being upgraded to new versions. Sometimes those upgrades cause trouble in systems that were tested with earlier browser versions; this is why you often see notices that say, "works best with [browser name, version number]." Databases such as Oracle or SQL Server also upgrade to new releases, and migrating to the latest version can cause some components of the software to break.

Maintenance includes the work needed to support changing business requirements. In a merger, for instance, staff will need to integrate data or build new interfaces between two information systems. Each company might have a comprehensive database of suppliers, but they can't easily be consolidated because the fields don't match or there are too many duplicates.

For example, airline mergers often result in a decline in service

PRODUCTIVITY TIP
When you find a bug in one of your college's systems, immediately take a screen shot, write down what you were doing at the time, and add any details that might help the IT staff replicate it, such as the browser you're using and the version number. Forwarding this information is much more productive for you, IT, and the whole organization compared with a vague report that just says "it isn't working."

quality, partly because it takes time to integrate their information systems.[12] The merger between United and Continental Airlines created a long list of systems maintenance issues. Frequent flier account balances and reward rules had to be harmonized along with records on the two companies' airplane fleets. Creating a single roster of employees with accurate human resource records is another challenge, complicated by different union seniority rules that govern work assignments for pilots and other positions.[13]

Changes in government regulations also drive systems maintenance. For example, when states began passing legislation that required organizations to notify customers affected by a breach of their personal information, companies raced to encrypt the data, whether it resided on servers, laptops, smartphones, backup media, or other places that might leave data exposed. As long as the data files are encrypted, the notification requirements do not apply.

Most systems continue to evolve as new features and enhancements are added after the initial launch. Lily plans to collect feedback from everyone who uses the "What to Make with What You Have" website to help her decide which features to add to make the site more compelling and effective.

To manage all the bug fixes and change requests, organizations put into place a **change control process**. IT staff help clarify the change requests and estimate the resources required to accomplish them. They then work closely with business units and executive management to determine priorities. Backlogs of these fixes can grow very long, especially as the system gets older.

WHEN INFORMATION SYSTEMS GROW OLD

Unlike mechanical gear, software doesn't wear out with use. Information systems do age, however, and eventually need replacement. Over time the maintenance burden may grow very heavy. All the changes pile up inside the code, adding patches and workarounds that clog what was once streamlined code. Maintenance projects needed to keep a system secure and up-to-date with the latest versions of the underlying technology are often deferred, as business units devote resources to new features that offer competitive advantage. Like an old house whose owners add a lovely rose garden rather than replace the faulty copper wiring, information systems accumulate hidden signs of aging. The systems become harder to adapt to changing business needs, and they can also present risk of catastrophic failure.

For example, almost every system needed maintenance work to dodge the inevitable breakdowns associated with Y2K, the computing problem that loomed in the late 1990s. Most systems had been designed to store the year as a two-digit field rather than four digits to save space on hard disk drives. Thus, as December 31, 1999, neared, maintenance teams devised ways to avoid confusion by increasing the field size or adding rules that determined whether "00," for instance, meant 1900 or 2000. But many organizations used the imminent event to replace their **legacy systems**, older systems built on aging or obsolete architectures that continue in use because they still function reasonably well and replacing them is costly.

Software Development Strategies

> **2** Describe three major software development strategies.

The system development life cycle (SDLC) describes an orderly progression from planning to maintenance and eventual replacement, with discrete steps in between. However, actual projects may deviate from a straightforward step-by-step approach, using alternative development methods. The SDLC aligns closely with the waterfall method, which we discuss first.

---

phased implementation
A type of implementation in which the modules of a new information system are launched in phases rather than all at once.

direct implementation
A type of implementation in which all the modules of a new information system are launched at the same time and the old system is turned off; also called the "big bang" approach.

change control process
A process organizations use to manage and prioritize requests to make changes or add new features to an information system.

legacy systems
Older systems built on aging or obsolete architectures that continue in use because they still function reasonably well and replacing them is costly.

THE ETHICAL FACTOR Developing Systems That Promote Ethical Decision Making and Social Responsibility

Just as organizations can develop innovative information systems that streamline operations and build competitive advantage, they can build in requirements for new systems that promote ethical decision making and social responsibility. For instance, software can promote the goal of "going green" by automatically reminding employees of the environmental cost each time they choose to print out a document. Systems that track each user's print usage and provide frequent reports also achieve that goal because they increase individual accountability.

To promote ethical decision making in procurement, the software can automatically compare current prices offered by qualified suppliers. When the buyer can see the comparisons and knows that others can see them, too, he or she is more likely to make an objective choice rather than favor a supplier whose sales rep brought a nice gift on the last call. Ensuring transparency about the details of any decision is a powerful tool to promote ethical behavior.

Employees can also be alerted with special messages or color coding whenever they view confidential information about customers as a reminder to avoid privacy breaches. Systems can prevent employees from downloading such data as well.

When managers develop the requirements for new information systems, they should consider what features might facilitate ethical decision making. While the systems must meet minimum compliance requirements, they can do much more toward promoting high ethical standards and corporate social responsibility.

Waterfall Software Development

In the **waterfall software development method**, the SDLC tasks occur sequentially, with one activity starting only after the previous one has been completed (Figure 11-8). The analysis phase nails down the requirements, and at that point the developers estimate the time and resources needed to complete the project. Programmers don't start writing any code until all the previous phases have been completed, including the detailed design. Different people may be engaged in each task, and they hand off their work to the next team when their part is done.

FIGURE 11-8
Waterfall method of software development.

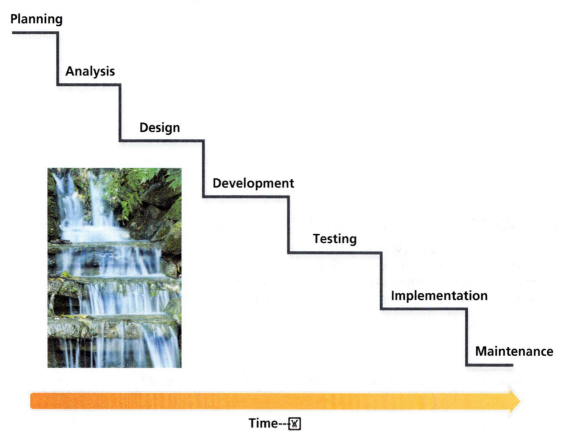

Source: Digoarpi/Shutterstock.

In theory, the progression continues forward from one task to the next. In practice, though, requirements often change after later stages have already begun, forcing the waterfall to run back uphill. The design has to be changed, and then the programming must be changed as well. Although the waterfall method has been used for decades, success rates are often quite disappointing, especially for large projects that take a long time to complete. Over the year or more that design and development are under way, the organization's needs are quite likely to change, so the system the developers are building is already obsolete. The rework is costly and time-consuming, resulting in blown budgets and missed deadlines. These frustrations led to the development of alternative approaches that are better able to adapt to changes in the business landscape.

Iterative Methods

Iterative software development methods compress the time horizon for development, partly to reduce the impact of fast-changing business needs and the resulting rework. They focus on the time available until the next release, or iteration, and the development team determines how many of the requirements it can deliver in that timeframe. While the waterfall method estimates time and resources needed based on the analysis of requirements, the iterative methods do the reverse. Given available time and staffing, what features can we deliver?

Iterative approaches vary, but most incorporate the tasks in the SDLC rapidly, and they overlap. Figure 11-9 shows how the tasks might be undertaken for a project expected to release in 6 months. Notice how the tasks are sequenced, but they don't end before the next task begins.

A common approach used in iterative methods that helps software developers bring an application to life more quickly is called **rapid application development (RAD)**. Developers create a software prototype that they can share with users and get their feedback to make corrections and improvements before more time is spent building a fully functioning version. End users are much more helpful when they can see a prototype even if most of it doesn't actually work. The approach works well with the overlapping phases typical of iterative development, and it is often used in other software development approaches as well.

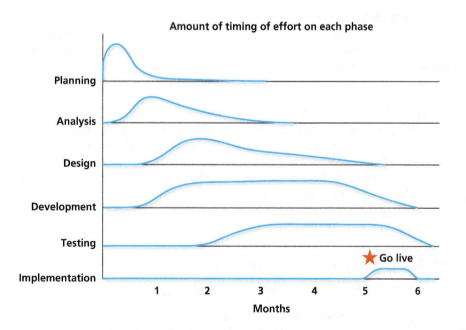

Amount of timing of effort on each phase

Planning

Analysis

Design

Development

Testing

Implementation

⭐ Go live

1   2   3   4   5   6
Months

FIGURE 11-9

Task phases in an iterative software development approach, preparing for a release in 6 months.

waterfall software development method

Method in which the systems development life cycle tasks occur sequentially, with one activity starting only after the previous one has been completed.

Iterative software development methods

Strategies that compress the time horizon for software development, partly to reduce the impact of changing business needs and the resulting rework. They focus on the time available until the next release, or iteration, and the development team determines how many of the requirements it can deliver in that timeframe.

rapid application development (RAD)

A strategy in which developers quickly bring up prototypes to share with end users, get feedback, and make corrections before building the fully functional version.

Agile Methods

Agile software development methods use a less structured approach in which tasks are not sequenced according to the SDLC. Instead, many activities occur simultaneously. The development team is typically very cohesive and usually collocated rather than geographically distributed as teams in a waterfall project might be. An agile team also includes one or more business users dedicated to the project. The duration for development, called the "time box," is quite short, often just 2 to 6 weeks.

In 2001, developers who were using various agile methods came up with a "manifesto" that clarifies the key features (Figure 11-10). The methods stress a team-oriented approach that includes end users and an unconcern for strictly defined processes, written documentation, and contracts. Many different varieties of agile methods exist, but two examples are Scrum and XP.

FIGURE 11-10

The Agile Manifesto.

We value

▶ **Individuals and interactions** over processes and tools

▶ **Working software** over comprehensive documentation

▶ **Customer collaboration** over contract negotiation

▶ **Responding to change** over following a plan

SCRUM

The most widely used agile method is called **Scrum**, which offers a framework for software development that relies on tightly knit, cohesive teams that do "sprints" of 2 to 4 weeks each. The customer's voice on the team is called the "product owner," and this person makes sure the project adds business value. He or she might be a marketing executive if the project involves customer relationships or a manager from finance if the new feature will improve the billing process. Lily would be the product owner for the "What to Make with What You Have" website. The project manager gets the colorful name of Scrum Master. The term *scrum* is actually a move in the sport of rugby, in which the team members pack together, acting in unison to get the ball down the field.

At the start of a sprint, the product owner prioritizes the backlog of requirements for the software, and the team decides which ones are feasible for the next sprint. Once the team has confirmed the requirements, they are fixed for the sprint's duration so the team can get right to work. Short sprints, close collaboration, and daily meetings help ensure that developers don't work for months on a set of requirements only to face the waterfall problem: Business needs have already changed. The goal is to have workable software with the new features at the end of each sprint.

EXTREME PROGRAMMING (XP)

Another team-based agile method, **extreme programming (XP)**, focuses on frequent releases of workable software and time boxes for development. The approach stresses four fundamental principles: coding, testing, listening, and designing. A project starts with user stories, often written on 3 × 5 index cards, and the team arranges these into a plan for the features that will be in the next software release.

A distinguishing feature of XP is that developers work in pairs, reviewing one another's work, providing each other with feedback, and testing the code as it is written. Often the pair will sit side by side, viewing the same monitor and pushing the keyboard and mouse back and forth as they collaborate to come up with good coding solutions. XP's strong emphasis on testing is also an important feature, and one reason for its development was to improve software quality. Poor software quality costs the U.S. economy an estimated $59 billion annually, and more thorough testing can help reduce that waste. While not many companies use "pure" XP as a methodology, many adopt some its practices, especially the emphasis on testing.[14]

Explain why organizations choose one software development strategy over another for particular projects.

3 Comparing Software Development Approaches

How do organizations choose which method to use? While some developers are fanatical about one method, all can work well or poorly, depending on the situation and the people using them.

Type of Project

First, the choice of a development approach depends heavily on the type of project. For example, an iterative approach will work well for projects in which the requirements can be launched in discrete phases as releases. The clarity of requirements can also affect the choice. A waterfall method would work when the requirements are clear, stable, and easy to define well in advance. When business needs are changing rapidly, lengthy projects based on the waterfall method will fail and an agile approach should be used.

Organizational Culture

The organization's culture is also an important element. Moving to an agile development approach means much more than programming in pairs or adopting the colorful Scrum vocabulary. It is a cultural shift that many development teams may find uncomfortable. After years of using the waterfall method, for instance, some developers resist changes to the requirements after the analysis phase has been done. They see it as rework, and they try to lock down the requirements through written documents, contracts, and user sign-offs. Agile methods require developers who welcome changes in requirements because they understand that the ultimate goal is to develop software that users really want, not just to finish a project on time.

Another cultural shift is from the "me" mentality to "we." The waterfall method stresses sequenced tasks, so developers who complete their task on time consider themselves successful even if the project itself is falling behind. But agile teams are collectively responsible for delivery, and team members must help one another achieve the goal to be successful. The team must be cohesive and trusting, since each member's job and career may depend on the whole team's performance.

Is Waterfall Dead?

Excitement surrounding the nimble iterative and agile methods has led to predictions of doom for the waterfall method. But surveys show that the older approach is still widely used, despite its disappointing track record.[15] One reason it persists is that business managers are comfortable with its logical and familiar structure. The cultural challenges associated with agile methods are also larger than some organizations anticipate. They find that agile development needs more discipline, not less, especially for larger projects, and employees need coaching and time to adjust to a team-oriented approach. Some prefer not to make that switch.[16]

Outsourced software development also tends toward waterfall methods. Once the requirements phase is complete, the contractor uses the results to determine the cost of the whole project before signing a contract. If the client wants changes to the requirements in midstream or adds features outside the scope of original requirements, the price would go up.

However, to avoid the risks of the traditional waterfall method, companies are adapting the method to much shorter timeframes and more focused goals, using the "incremental" waterfall method, and often adding agile methods into the mix. Those prolonged projects in which the software is delivered years after requirements were collected are, for the most part, a thing of the past.

Software Procurement: The "Buy" Strategy

Explain how organizations decide whether to build or buy and the steps they use if they choose to buy an information system.

As commercial software companies add more features and reduce licensing costs, organizations are increasingly considering the "buy" strategy rather than custom development. Especially for business functions that don't offer very much competitive advantage, commercially produced software may be the best choice. These options go beyond the software products that an organization can license from the vendor and install on its own servers. They also include free, open source software. The rapidly evolving software-as-a-service (SaaS) products described in previous chapters expand options still further. Organizations can lease just the subscriptions they need, and employees can access the cloud-based application with their web browsers or smartphone apps.

---

agile software development methods
Development strategies involving cohesive teams that include end users and in which many activities occur simultaneously rather than sequentially to accelerate delivery of usable software.

Scrum
An agile process for software development that relies on tightly knit, cohesive teams that do "sprints" of 2 to 4 weeks each.

extreme programming (XP)
A team-based agile method that features frequent releases of workable software, short time boxes, programmers who work in pairs, and a focus on testing.

Pros and Cons of Build and Buy

Figure 11-11 highlights the major pros and cons associated with custom systems development and commercial software. As mentioned earlier, commercial, prepackaged software that handles at least 75% of the organization's requirements could be an excellent choice. But the decision is really more complicated than that, and many factors should be considered. Strategic value, overall cost, time needed to deploy, the need for customization, and the availability of IT resources should all enter the equation.

The Procurement Process

Figure 11-12 shows the SDLC, including the steps organizations take when they decide to pursue a "buy" strategy.

RFI AND RFP

During the early phases of the SDLC, IT staff and business users should be systematically exploring the landscape of commercially offered software that might fit the organization's needs. As the list of user requirements develops, they will send out a **request for information (RFI)** to a

FIGURE 11-11

Pros and cons of custom systems development and prepackaged software.

	Pros	Cons
Custom System Development	Is tailored closely to the organization's needs	Usually has higher overall cost
	May offer strategic value that contributes to company's competitive advantage	Requires more time before going live
	May not require employees to change their processes	Requires ongoing in-house maintenance, upgrades, and compliance
Prepackaged Software	Handles processes using industry best practices	Does not match all the organization's requirements
	Requires shorter implementation time	Might overstate product's capabilities and vendor support
	Usually carries lower cost	Requires organization to change business processes and develop interfaces to other systems
	Can include vendor's new features and maintains compliance requirements	May not include new features needed by the organization
	Works best for applications that offer few competitive advantages	May not fit enterprise architecture

FIGURE 11-12

SDLC including steps for the "buy" option.

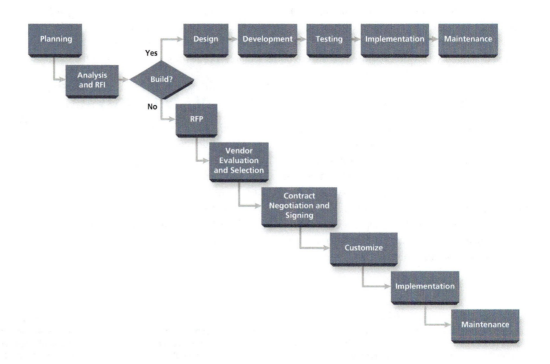

large number of potential vendors to serve as their initial market scan of the options. The RFI describes the new system in broad, high-level terms, and interested vendors send responses describing their products and services.

At this point, the steering committee decides whether to proceed with the design phase or buy. If the responses to the RFI and the committee's own research show some promising candidates, the committee will develop a **request for proposal (RFP)**, which is an invitation to software companies to submit a formal proposal, including a detailed description of their products, services, and costs. The RFP details the requirements that were developed in the analysis phase and also information about the organization's architecture, staffing, and other relevant details. This invitation is sent to the most promising commercial vendors and possibly also to companies that specialize in implementing open source products.

Releasing an RFP does not commit the organization to the "buy" approach, and the steering committee may decide to custom-build the product after all. But the RFP provides the platform for vendors to compete fairly and present their best cases for meeting the organization's needs. The RFP process is also typically used to procure the services of a software development company to custom build the system, if the organization decides to outsource the project rather than build it in-house.

EVALUATING THE OPTIONS

For large projects, especially ones that involve major systems for multinational corporations or large government agencies, the procurement process can be lengthy and complex. The bidders might offer many options with different prices, and as part of their bid they may include consulting companies that will serve as implementation partners.

The steering committee checks references, explores software demos, visits sites where the software products are in use, and narrows down the list. The finalists are invited to do presentations for the stakeholders, and the steering committee develops an evaluation strategy that prioritizes the criteria it will use to rate the solutions. For example, the spreadsheet in Figure 11-13 shows five weighted criteria. The stakeholders rate each vendor's responses on the criteria and start contract negotiations with the winning vendor.

The criterion "vendor architecture" deserves special attention because of the need to consider the overall enterprise architecture and the other systems the company is using. Some organizations choose a **best of breed** approach, in which they procure the best systems for each application regardless of the vendor. The CRM may be a cloud-computing solution, for instance, while the finance and human resources systems are on company premises and from

FIGURE 11-13

Evaluating responses to an RFP on weighted criteria.

Weight	30%	20%	10%	20%	20%	100%
Scale (1=very poor to 5=very good)	Matches Requirements	Vendor Experience	Vendor References	Vendor Architecture	Cost	Totals
Commercial Software Vendor 1	5	3	2	1	1	2.7
Commercial Software Vendor 2	4	2	3	1	2	2.5
Open-Source Solution	2	1	4	2	4	2.4
SaaS	4	1	4	4	3	3.2

request for information (RFI)
A request sent to software vendors containing a high level description of the information system an organization needs, so that vendors can describe their products that may fit.

request for proposal (RFP)
An invitation to software companies to submit a formal proposal, including a detailed description of their products, services, and costs. The RFP details the requirements developed in the analysis phase and also includes information about the organization's architecture, staffing, and other relevant details.

best of breed
An approach used by organizations in which they procure the best systems for each application, regardless of the vendor, and then build interfaces among them.

a different vendor. With these different architectures, the firm must build interfaces that allow its systems to interact with one another and pass data back and forth.

Another approach is **unified procurement**, in which organizations lean toward systems that are offered by a single vendor, especially the one that supplies the ERP. Even if the ERP's customer relationship management system does not fit as well, the company may decide to choose it over competitors to keep integration problems to a minimum and maintain a consistent enterprise architecture.

Adaptation and Customization

When the packaged solution meets 75% or more of the organization's needs, what happens to the other 25%? One possibility is for the company to adapt its own processes to match what the software will support. Many vendors, especially the large ERP companies, strongly recommend this path, arguing that their software products build in the industry's best practices for standard business processes. At Johns Hopkins, for example, hospital employees were paid every 2 weeks (26 per year), but university employees were on a twice-monthly scheme (24 per year). Rather than customize the new ERP to handle two payroll schedules, Hopkins switched everyone to the same calendar.

Another possibility for that 25% is to customize the software, either by paying the software vendor or another company to do it or by making the code changes in-house. For processes that are not so easy for an organization to alter or ones that support features that add strategic value and competitive advantage, customization may be the best approach.

The drawbacks to customization are not trivial, however, and managers should consider them carefully. Although tailoring some features to the organization's processes may make implementation easier, problems arise later. Adding customized code to a major software product can introduce errors that may not be discovered until well after going live, especially in large systems with tightly integrated modules. The vendor may also refuse to support customized code it did not build. When bugs crop up, it is hard to tell whether the errors lie in the vendor's product, in the organization's custom-developed segments, or somewhere in between. Identifying just who is responsible for fixing the problem is important when support contracts are in place.

Another drawback involves upgrades. The vendor will continue to improve the product with new features, but organizations that add custom code have work to do for each new release. They must add their customizations to the new version and test the whole system to make sure everything still works. In some cases, companies decide not to take advantage of a new release because of these headaches. Over time, the company's customized software might drift further and further behind the vendor's current offering. Many of the vendor's upgrades will address rising security threats, so a version that lags behind will not only lack new features. It will also entail greater risk. The vendor may decide to drop support for older versions, leaving the organization entirely responsible. These lessons have been learned painfully over time, and most organizations wisely try to keep customization to a minimum.

Identify several ways in which the human element is important for systems development and procurement.

5 The Human Element in Systems Development and Procurement

The logical approaches to systems development and procurement described here do not always unfold quite so tidily. Communication on cross-functional teams, for instance, can be challenging.

Working in Teams

Especially in the planning, analysis, and implementation phases, people who don't often work together will join cross-functional teams, and communication problems may arise. IT staff might not quite understand what the marketing team members mean when they talk about a system that will "delight" customers. And people in sales will scratch their heads when the IT person mentions RDDs or time boxes. Communication gaps and different priorities may also appear between different business units, such as marketing and accounting. The accounting people must ensure compliance, but marketing people may stress customer relationship management features. Whether the team decides to build or buy, the members will need to bridge the gaps to be successful.

During the planning and analysis phases, the cross-functional team members will try to describe how processes work and what the requirements for a new system should be. But most employees will only have a firm grasp on the part of a process that they deal with. They may find it challenging to design a system that can streamline the process from end to end and still satisfy all the requirements from accounting, finance, marketing, and sales. The exercise is often quite productive, though, as cross-functional teams with members from different parts of the company share knowledge and ideas. The analyst who leads this effort can promote this knowledge-sharing aspect of systems development because it offers added benefits for the whole organization.

Communication problems also can arise in global software development teams, in which people from around the world are working on different tasks. Many kinds of miscommunication can interfere with team efforts, as described in Chapter 8. That chapter also includes tips for making virtual teams successful.

The Role of Senior Management

Senior managers play a key role in systems development and procurement, one that should stress the strategic value of the new information system to the organization. They can inspire employees to work together and ensure the resources the project team needs are available. Through their leadership, they can also prepare the organization for change. Implementing new processes can be both challenging and threatening, especially to employees whose duties will change dramatically or disappear entirely.

The industry trend that promotes cloud computing and software as a service (SaaS) also affects how decisions about systems development and procurement are actually made as well as who makes them. Because IT support is not as much needed to manage servers or maintain software, technology-savvy employees are increasingly developing solutions or procuring applications on their own, sometimes without IT staff's knowledge. These often start as the shadow systems described in Chapter 4, but senior managers need to recognize the value that these "citizen developers" can offer in terms of agility and also employee engagement. At the same time, they also must establish policies to monitor and govern those applications, especially when they border on mission-critical. At some point, the application may need to transition into IT to ensure proper security and support.[17] CIOs and senior managers in the business units must maintain close communication to implement cloud services wisely.

Working with Consultants

Implementing a new system, especially a large one from a commercial vendor, often means engaging consulting services to help configure, customize, and launch the software. The consultants might be employees of the software vendor, or they might work for a separate company with expertise in that software product and a history of successful implementations in other organizations. The consultants can take on many roles to help make the project a success, such as those listed in Figure 11-14.

ADVANTAGES AND DISADVANTAGES

One advantage of engaging consultants is that it gives the organization access to experts who know the software well. Experienced consultants have seen how different companies implement the product, and they know where the trouble spots are. For example, some modules may need extra attention and training because the user interface is confusing, and others

FIGURE 11-14

Common roles for information systems consultants.

▶ Requirements gathering and clarification
▶ Customization services
▶ Data cleansing and migration
▶ Software configuration
▶ Systems integration services
▶ Documentation
▶ User training
▶ Training of IT staff
▶ Project planning
▶ Communications
▶ Implementation support

unified procurement
An approach used by organizations in which they prefer systems from a single vendor, especially to avoid the need to build interfaces.

might have known bugs that require workarounds. The organization's own IT staff would not have this knowledge.

A special kind of consultant called a **systems integrator** has expertise in making the different hardware and software components of an information system work together. The components, such as scanners, servers, smartphones, software, and database, may all come from different vendors, and the systems integrator takes responsibility for making them function smoothly with one another.

Another advantage of consulting services is that the organization does not have to assign so many key people to the project full-time and then backfill their positions. The director of marketing, for example, can participate in a project to implement a CRM but still maintain oversight of the marketing unit.

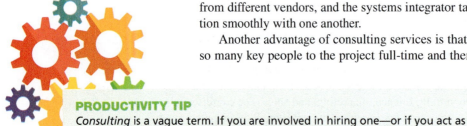

PRODUCTIVITY TIP
Consulting is a vague term. If you are involved in hiring one—or if you act as one yourself—be sure to clarify the scope of work, payment, due dates, and other arrangements in writing.

Consultants are not a cure-all, however, and they come with disadvantages. The organization's own employees will be less involved in many of the development and implementation tasks, so they will miss opportunities to learn the ins and outs of the software. They may also feel less ownership of the project and be less committed to all the changes that new processes will mean to their units.

Clients sometimes file lawsuits when a project involving consultants falters or goes way over budget. For example, California's Marin County sued Deloitte Consulting for $30 million, accusing Deloitte of fraud when its consultants claimed extensive knowledge of the ERP system the county was implementing. That suit was eventually settled, but such disputes are not uncommon. It can be difficult to determine where the fault lies.[18]

CONTRACT MANAGEMENT

The frequent need to engage consultants increases the value of an important skill information systems professionals need: *contract management*. The people who oversee such contracts will be negotiating terms and conditions, documenting any changes to the agreements, tracking progress, and ensuring that both the consulting company and the organization meet their obligations on time. The CIO and IT staff will help write the language for these contracts. They will also monitor the project and flag potential problems because many IT-related tasks will not be familiar to business users. If the consultants are customizing the software and charging by the hour, the change control process will be especially important. Business managers will need a clear understanding of how changes in the requirements can escalate costs or delay the go-live date.

Regardless of whether the organization builds or buys the information system, successful implementation will depend heavily on effectively managing the project from start to finish. Dealing with budgets, timelines, escalating requirements, and the many "people" issues that go along with massive changes in the way the organization functions are all part of project management, and missteps are easy to make. The next chapter takes up this important topic and how projects fit into the much larger picture of strategic planning for information systems.

MyMISLab
Online Simulation

GREEN WHEELING
A Role-Playing Simulation on Systems Development
for a Fund-Raising Application

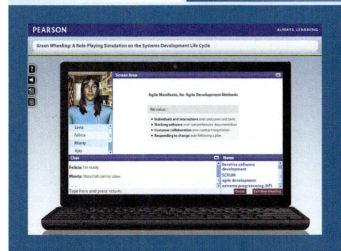

Green Wheeling! That's the campaign you're working on for a university, trying to raise funds from rich alums, donors, and corporate foundations. You get a list every week from the Development Office, and you try to contact each name to persuade these donors to help purchase a fleet of electric vehicles for student rentals so they don't need cars on campus.

The campaign is a mess. Your lists always have wrong numbers or people who have never heard of the university. Yesterday, you visited a foundation that another rep had just contacted last week. The administration knows it needs an information system to manage this calamity, and you've been asked to join a task force to get one. Meetings will use web conferencing, so log in when you're ready....

systems integrator
A consultant who ensures that the hardware and software components of an information system work together when they come from different vendors.

LEARNING OBJECTIVES

1 The systems development life cycle (SDLC) includes seven steps. During the planning phase (1), the business need for the system is established and a feasibility study is conducted to ensure the project is feasible. In the analysis phase (2), the project team identifies the requirements for the system to create the requirements definition document (RDD), drawing process diagrams and listing features the system should support. The design phase (3) translates the RDD into a workable architectural design, addressing issues such as data models, databases, usability, accessibility, and others. In the development phase (4), programmers translate the design into a working system, taking advantage of techniques such as version control and code review. During the testing phase (5), the unit modules are tested independently, and the whole system undergoes tests to ensure the units can work together properly. The system goes live in the implementation phase (6), which can be parallel, phased, or direct. Finally, the system enters the maintenance phase (7) in which bugs may continue to arise that need to be fixed, and the organization may choose to add enhancements.

2 Software development strategies include the waterfall method, iterative methods, and agile methods. In waterfall software development, one phase of software development starts after the previous one has been completed. Iterative strategies compress the development process by focusing on the next release date and working only on features that can be included in that. The SDLC phases often overlap. Agile development methods are more unstructured, with activities occurring at the same time. Two examples are extreme programming (XP) and Scrum.

3 The choice of software development method depends on the type of project and the organizational culture. Agile methods require a team-oriented approach, for example. Waterfall methods are useful when organizations outsource development to external contractors.

4 The decision about whether to build or buy the system should consider whether a purchased system can handle at least 75% of the organization's requirements and whether the system is important for strategic reasons. Other factors include cost, time to deploy, architecture, and skill sets. Procurement usually starts with a request for information (RFI), followed by a request for proposal (RFP) to the leading candidates. The RFP process is also used to select a software development company to custom build the system, if the organization chooses to outsource the project.

5 The human element affects systems development and procurement, partly because people from different parts of the organization work together in cross-functional teams, and communication issues may arise. Senior managers should emphasize the system's strategic value and inspire employees to work together. Organizations are increasingly hiring consultants to assist with systems implementation, so information systems professionals need to develop effective contract management skills.

KEY TERMS AND CONCEPTS

systems development life cycle (SDLC)

feasibility study

requirements analysis

process diagrams

business process reengineering (BPR)

requirements definition document (RDD)

service-oriented architecture (SOA)

application programming interface (API)

use case diagram

version control software

code review

parallel implementation

phased implementation

direct implementation

change control process

legacy systems

waterfall software development method

iterative software development methods

rapid application development (RAD)

agile software development methods

Scrum

extreme programming (XP)

request for information (RFI)

request for proposal (RFP)

best of breed

unified procurement

systems integrator

CHAPTER REVIEW QUESTIONS

11-1. What are the seven phases of the systems development life cycle? What activities occur in each phase?

11-2. What is the waterfall method of software development? How do the SDLC tasks occur in this method of development? What are the success rates for systems developed using the waterfall method? Is the waterfall method dead? Why does the waterfall methodology persist despite its track record?

11-3. What is the iterative method of software development? How do the SDLC tasks occur in this method of development? What role does time play in this development methodology?

11-4. What is the agile method of software development? How do the SDLC tasks occur in this method of development? What role do teams play in agile software development? How does the time frame for agile development differ from that of iterative development?

11-5. Why do organizations choose one software development methodology over another? What are two factors that affect this decision? Why do organizations consider each of these factors when selecting a software development strategy?

11-6. What are the advantages and disadvantages of custom-building software?

11-7. What are the advantages and disadvantages of buying prepackaged software?

11-8. What rule of thumb do business analysts recommend for making the decision to buy or custom-build software? What other factors affect this decision?

11-9. What steps do organizations take when they decide to buy rather than build software? What activities occur in each step? How is an RFI different from an RFP? Does the logical approach to systems procurement always prevail? What are examples of ways in which the human element affects information systems procurement decisions?

11-10. Why are cross-functional teams needed for systems development and procurement? What kinds of problems might they experience?

11-11. What role should senior managers play in systems development and procurement?

11-12. What are the advantages and disadvantages of engaging consultants to assist with implementation? What kinds of skills do IS professionals need to work effectively with consultants?

PROJECTS AND DISCUSSION QUESTIONS

11-13. Lily's cookbook project faces some tough competition for the company's resources. She knows her coworkers, Stan and Rohit, are working on a proposal to incorporate a DVD rental feature on the company's website, and she needs to make a strong case for her "What to Make with What You Have" online cookbook if she wants approval for her project. You are on the steering committee that will help Lily in the planning phase, and your job is to help her identify and summarize the business need for the project. What are the major factors that support a business need and determine where to allocate funding for a systems development project? Which factors has Lily considered? Can you think of other potential benefits of this project? Are there any feasibility issues with this project? Prepare a brief summary of Lily's case that outlines the facts relating to the proposed online cookbook.

11-14. Consider Lily's online cookbook and describe the requirements for that system. Which requirements do you think are most important for Lily's website? Which are least important? Prepare a brief summary that prioritizes the requirements of Lily's online cookbook.

11-15. Recall from Chapter 3 that enterprise architecture describes the blueprint of the information technology and organizational resources that are used to execute business processes. At what stage in the systems development life cycle do stakeholders determine the architecture they will use to build an information system? What is SOA? Visit YouTube.com and search for "infoclipz: service oriented architecture." View this 3-minute video by InfoWorld and prepare a brief summary that includes a discussion of the benefits and challenges of SOA.

11-16. The first software bug was a moth. Really. Visit the Computer History Museum at www.computerhistory.org to learn how Grace Hopper, a rear admiral in the Navy, made history in the computer field with the first software bug. The rigorous testing that takes place during the development phase of the SDLC encompasses much more than looking for bugs. What are the six types of testing that may be performed in the development phase? What occurs in each test? How are scenarios used in the software testing process? How do software tools facilitate software testing? Is it a paradox to use software to test software?

11-17. If software doesn't wear out, which phase is generally the longest phase in the SDLC? Maintenance begins in the first few weeks of implementation and may last for many years until such time as the system is declared obsolete. For example, changes that occur at a university often require maintenance of the system. Describe the software modifications that might be needed if the university changed all the classes offered by a particular academic department to e-learning so that no classrooms were needed. Describe the changes that might be needed to accommodate students who have more than one email address.

11-18. Work with a small group of classmates to develop a process diagram that illustrates the steps necessary to register for a class at your university. Use standard flowchart notation to represent processing steps with rectangles, decisions with diamonds, and the ordering of steps (i.e., flow control) with arrows. Prepare a PowerPoint presentation of your process diagram to share with your class.

APPLICATION EXERCISES

11-19. EXCEL APPLICATION:
Jay's Bikes

Heather and Jay Madera started Jay's Bikes in the family garage. Cycling is their passion! They moved to their bicycle-friendly community because of its three great bike trails that were built by the city to promote tourism and strengthen the downtown area. Jay's Bikes' business is booming and now Heather and Jay are operating three retail stores with 18 full-time employees. The stores stock a wide range of bikes and apparel for both casual and professional riders, and they have become gathering points for local bike enthusiasts and tourists alike.

Jay is currently using an old version of point-of-sale (POS) software and he wants you to create the spreadsheet shown in Figure 11-15 to evaluate the alternatives for a new system. Jay has weighted the selection criteria according to his preferences. Create a formula to calculate the total weighted score for each software alternative. Be sure to include a formula to calculate the total weight of all factors and use absolute cell references where appropriate. Based on the initial evaluation shown here, the best option for Jay's Bikes is SaaS for retail.

Questions

1. Which alternative scores highest if the "matches requirements" criterion is weighted at 50% and the "vendor architecture" is weighted at 0%?

2. Which alternative is best if the "matches requirements" criterion is weighted at 40%, "vendor architecture" is weighted at 0%, and "cost" is weighted at 30%?

3. Which alternative is best if the "matches requirements" criterion is weighted at 50%, "vendor architecture" is weighted at 0%, and "cost" is weighted at 20%?

11-20. ACCESS APPLICATION:
Managing a Recipe Collection

Steve and Gail Horton are cooking enthusiasts who want to use a database to manage their collection of recipes. They have asked you to help them create the Access database shown in Figure 11-16. Use the information provided in the Horton spreadsheet Ch11Ex02 to create and populate the tables. Create a report that lists the vegetarian recipes first, in descending order by the number of servings. Include the recipe ID number and the recipe name. Review the tables in the database and suggest other reports that Steve and Gail would find useful.

FIGURE 11-15

Vendor evaluation for Jay's Bikes POS system.

	A	B	C	D	E	F	G
1	Weight*	30%	20%	10%	20%	20%	100%
2	Alternatives	Matches Requirements	Vendor Experience	Vendor References	Vendor Architecture	Cost	Total
3	POS Vendor #1	5	3	2	1	1	2.7
4	POS Vendor #2	4	2	3	1	2	2.5
5	Open Source POS	2	1	4	2	4	2.4
6	SaaS for retail	4	1	4	4	3	3.2
7							
8	*Scale: 5 = very good, 1 = very poor						

Source: Microsoft® Excel, Microsoft Corporation. Reprinted with permission.

FIGURE 11-16

Managing a recipe collection with Access.

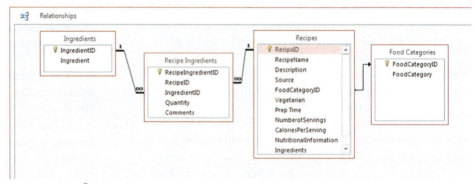

Source: Microsoft® Access, Microsoft Corporation. Reprinted with permission.

Baby Steps toward Scrum: How BabyCenter.com Made the Cultural Transition to Agile Software Development

BabyCenter.com's website pioneers some of the most interactive and engaging tools for parents and parents-to-be, with birth announcements, customized pregnancy calendars, a baby names finder, emails timed to child development stages, and tips to help parents survive an 8-hour plane ride with children. Like many Internet companies, however, it started in a very fragile, understaffed, and chaotic development environment. Its network operations team consisted of just three people, and programming staff spent 85% of their time fighting fires and fixing bugs. Priorities for developing the site's new features kept changing, and attempts to use the waterfall method were frustrated by delays in nailing down requirements and delivering design specs.

Something had to change. While recovering from back surgery, the company's VP for engineering read about agile development, particularly Scrum. Intrigued, he started a pilot project. The Scrum team held daily standup meetings, usually 15 minutes or less. The "product owner," who was the business manager from the department requesting the new features, collaborated closely with the developers to prioritize requirements. The pilot worked well, but the company's developers continued to struggle with competing priorities, complaining that they were splitting their time 50/50/50: "I'm spending 50% of my time on Project X, 50% on Project Y, and 50% on Project Z." Developers were still racing between projects and maintenance activities, and most were engaging in "cowboy coding," bypassing access controls and good programming practices to quickly fix bugs and get at least a few new features installed.

In the next phase, the VP demanded a more disciplined approach, blocking the developers out of the production system and drawing on Scrum principles. The most wrenching cultural change was management's drive to clear the company's backlog of requirements and establish priorities based on their strategic value or return on investment. Previously, business stakeholders would individually bring ideas to the developers, who did their best to decide which to work on first. The shift to using strategic value and ROI to prioritize projects dismayed managers whose requirements were pushed down the list, but it ensured that developers would work on high-value projects rather than managers' personal agendas. Now developers could say, "Sorry, that's not on my sprint. Go see the product owner."

More Scrum features were adopted, such as the full-time assignment of a product owner and at least two developers on every team. Product owners became accustomed to deeper involvement in the features they were requesting, attending the standup meetings and working much more closely with the software than before. Some of the developers had been used to the freedom of choosing which projects they thought were important, but they came to appreciate the value of Scrum's structure.

The Scrum sprints provided another way to add discipline to BabyCenter's software development environment. Managers came to respect the planning meetings because they knew that requirements are fixed once the sprint starts. They also took more pains to review the software early to avoid winding up with something that wasn't what they wanted but couldn't change for at least 2 weeks.

BabyCenter started with baby steps, but gradually it put into place a highly disciplined agile development environment that ensures its software projects align with business goals. The results speak for themselves, as they do in other companies that have adopted agile software methods. The company won its 13th Webby Award in 2016, testifying to the success of its software development strategies. BabyCenter reaches more than 45 million parents a month with websites in many different languages.

Discussion Questions

11-21. Describe the previous software development process at BabyCenter.com.

11-22. Describe the new software development process at BabyCenter.com. How has the software development process changed?

11-23. What cultural changes were required for BabyCenter.com employees to adapt to the new software development process?

11-24. What might BabyCenter.com business stakeholders and developers not like about the new software development process? How could BabyCenter.com executives respond to these concerns?

Sources: BabyCenter wins the esteemed Webby "People's Voice Award." (May 20, 2016). *PR Newswire,* http://www.prnewswire.com/news-releases/babycenter-wins-the-esteemed-webby-peoples-voice-award-300272242.html, accessed August 23, 2016.

Babycenter.com. (2016). http://www.babycenter.com/, accessed May 28, 2016.

Benton, E. (March 25, 2010). Tina Sharkey, CEO of BabyCenter. Fast Company, http://www.fastcompany.com/1597709/tina-sharkey-ceo-babycenter, accessed August 24, 3016.

Melo, C. de O., Cruzes, D. S., Kon, F., & Conradi, R. (2013). Interpretative case studies on agile team productivity and management. *Information and Software Technology, 55*(2), 412–427.

Nottonson, K., & DeLong, K. (2008a). Baby steps: Agile transformation at BabyCenter.com. IT Professional, *10*(5), 59–62.

Nottonson, K., & DeLong, K. (2008b). Crawl, walk, run: 4 years of agile adoption at BabyCenter.com. AGILE '08 Conference.

Schein, A. (2016). *BabyCenter, L.L.C.* Hoover's Online. http://subscriber.hoovers.com.proxy1.library.jhu.edu/H/company360/overview.html?companyId=60450000000000, accessed August 23, 2016.

CASE STUDY #2

Extreme Programming at the U.S. Strategic Command

The agile software development method called extreme programming (XP) has its enthusiasts and detractors, and the jury is still out on whether it is a better choice compared with the more popular agile approaches such as Scrum. Mindful of how important agility is for military software, the U.S. Strategic Command launched a pilot XP project.

XP shares many principles in common with Scrum, including the early and continuous delivery of functionality, close collaboration between developers and end users, and responsiveness to changing requirements. XP developers are less plan-driven and do much less documentation to define requirements. XP also features "pair programming," in which two developers work together, often on the same computer, and frequent testing is a fundamental component.

For the military project's pilot, the XP team's job was to add new search functionality to SKIWeb, the Command's strategic knowledge and information website used to share information about military operations and world events across the whole command and intelligence communities. All team members were contractors, except for the government functional manager who served as user collaborator. The two programmers sat next to one another in a cubicle, and the user collaborator's office was on the same floor. Other team members were either in the same building or nearby, so no one was participating in virtual mode.

The project got off to a rocky start when one of the two developers announced that she'd tried pair programming before and wasn't willing to do it again. The team didn't try to enforce it but did encourage her to work closely with her programming partner to solve thorny logic problems together. Other agile practices were welcomed and adopted easily. For instance, the practice of delivering frequent small releases rather than infrequent major ones was already in place. Having the customer on-site is another critical element, and the user collaborator was right down the hall.

The daily meetings were very successful, but problems in work assignments and communications arose. XP team members are supposed to be fully assigned to the project to avoid distractions, but this project's team members were often pulled off for other assignments or emergencies. Midway through, they found they needed someone with expertise in interface design, but that person was skeptical about joining the XP project, and communication suffered. One team member complained that there was resistance to change from a traditional hierarchy to the more collaborative XP style of communication.

Research with undergraduates suggests that paired programmers do about as well as the best performer of the pair but no better, raising doubt about whether "two heads are better than one" for programming tasks. However, the students enjoyed the programming task more when working in pairs, and the weaker member gained some confidence. Further research on XP suggests that paired programming itself may not be a key ingredient for XP's success. The factors that make XP work are really the collective ownership of the project by the whole team, the involvement of the client, and a strong focus on code standards and testing.

In the U.S. Strategic Command's pilot, the team members' perceptions about the project were positive, despite the snags. They believed that the XP approach led to very good-quality software, even better than the team might have produced using the old approach. As more and more organizations switch to agile methods such as XP, we will better understand just what it is about these methods that makes them successful.

Discussion Questions

11-25. How did the U.S. Strategic Command adjust to unexpected issues as it implemented extreme programming?

11-26. What types of changes accompany the extreme programming methodology?

11-27. Why could a methodology such as extreme programming be good for a military project? What might be its disadvantages?

11-28. Does the research mentioned at the end of the case study influence your view of XP?

Sources: Balijepally, V., Mahapatra, R., et al. (2009). Are two heads better than one for software development? The productivity paradox of pair programming. *MIS Quarterly, 33*(1), 91–118.

Bissi, W., Serra Seca Neto, A. G., & Emer, M. C. F. P. (2016). The effects of test driven development on internal quality, external quality and productivity: A systematic review. *Information & Software Technology, 74*, 45–54. http://doi.org/10.1016/j.infsof.2016.02.004

Choi, K. S. (2015). A comparative analysis of different gender pair combinations in pair programming. *Behaviour & Information Technology, 34*(8), 825–837. http://doi.org/10.1080/0144929X.2014.937460

Fruhling, A., McDonald, P., et al. (2008). A case study: Introducing eXtreme programming in a U.S. government system development project. Proceedings of the 41st Hawaii International Conference on Systems Science. http://www.computer.org/portal/web/csdl/doi/10.1109/HICSS.2008.4, accessed May 27, 2016.

Tilk, D. (2016). 5 steps to agile project success. *Internal Auditor, 73*(2), 57–61.

Wood, S., Michaelides, G., & Thomson, C. (2013). Successful extreme programming: Fidelity to the methodology or good teamworking? *Information & Software Technology, 55*(4), 660–672.

E-PROJECT 1   Watching Babycenter.com Change over Time with the Internet Archive

The Internet archive (www.archive.org) is a nonprofit organization that builds the Internet's library, the "wayback machine." Copies of websites are archived at intervals for researchers, historians, and scholars. In this e-project you will take a look at Babycenter.com's website at different stages. (The archive doesn't maintain all the images and graphics, so often a page will not be displayed correctly; some links won't work.)

Visit www.archive.org and retrieve the historical files for www.babycenter.com.

Right-click on each of the following dates one at a time, and open each page in a new window to make it easier to compare.

February 8, 2004
February 4, 2006
February 7, 2008

(The archive sometimes removes pages, so if any date is not available, choose one that is reasonably close.)

Open another window with the current website for www.babycenter.com.

11-29. How has the website changed over this time period? What new features or services were added or removed?

11-30. What advantages does Scrum offer to the development of this website?

E-PROJECT 2   Analyzing Software Defect Rates Using Excel

Excel is a useful tool to analyze data from software development. In this e-project, you will analyze the pattern of software defects that are identified on each day of a 14-day programming project. Download the Excel file called *Ch11_SoftwareDefects*.

For each type of graph or chart you create, copy the image to the worksheet labeled Output, so you will be able to compare them at the end of the e-project.

11-31. Create a line graph that shows the number of severe defects on each day of the 14-day period. The *x*-axis should show the day number, and the *y*-axis should be labeled "Number of Severe Defects."

11-32. Now create another line graph that shows Minor Defects. One way to do this is to hide the "Severe" column by right-clicking at the top of the B column and click Hide. (To unhide, select Columns A and C, right-click again, and choose Unhide.)

11-33. Next, create a stacked-column chart, and include Severe, Minor, and Total Defects.

11-34. Create another version of your stacked-column chart so that it only includes Severe and Minor Defects.

11-35. Create a clustered bar chart using Severe, Minor, and Total Defects columns.

11-36. Create a 100% stacked area chart using Severe, Minor, and Total Defects columns.

11-37. Compare the pros and cons of the different representations for this data set. Which representations do you think developers will find most useful? Which one do you think could be misleading to developers?

CHAPTER NOTES

1. Duffy, J. (June 18, 2010). Unified communications saves Canadian school district $200K/year. *NetworkWorld,* http://www.networkworld.com/news/2010/061810-pembina-schools-unified-communications.html, accessed July 8, 2013.

2. Pogue, D. (2014). 5 most embarrassing software bugs in history. *Scientific American,* http://www.scientificamerican.com/article/pogue-5-most-embarrassing-software-bugs-in-history/, accessed August 22, 2016.

3. Hammer, M. (July/August, 1990). Reengineering work: Don't automate, obliterate. *Harvard Business Review,* 104–112.

4. Grant, D. (2016). Business analysis techniques in business reengineering. *Business Process Management Journal,* 22(1), 75–88. http://doi.org/10.1108/BPMJ-03-2015-0026

5. Berlind, D. (2015). The API economy delivers limitless possibilities. http://www.programmableweb.com/news/api-economy-delivers-limitless-possibilities/analysis/2015/12/03, accessed May 6, 2016.

6. Vukovic, M., Laredo, J., Muthusamy, V., Slominski, A., Vaculin, R., Wei Tan, … Branch, J. W. (2016). Riding and thriving on the API hype cycle. *Communications of the ACM,* 59(3), 35–37. http://doi.org/10.1145/2816812

7. Malinverno, P. (2016). *The API economy: Turning your business into a platform (or your platform into a business)* (No. G00280448). Gartner Research, http://www.gartner.com/document/3217617?ref=TypeAheadSearch&qid=fe767d8c249eac79e0a038704323666d, accessed August 22, 2016.

8. Davenport, T. H. (June 13, 2016). 7 ways Microsoft can make LinkedIn worth $26 billion. https://hbr.org/2016/06/7-ways-microsoft-can-make-linkedin-worth-26-billion, accessed June 14, 2016.

9. Perez, S. (2016). How Microsoft will put LinkedIn to work in Office. http://social.techcrunch.com/2016/06/13/how-microsoft-will-put-linkedin-to-work-in-office/, accessed August 22, 2016.

10. Reindl, K., & Linde, S. J. (2016). DOJ postpones website accessibility proceeding: How businesses can prepare in anticipation of a lawsuit and how to maximize insurance once served. *Intellectual Property & Technology Law Journal,* 28(3), 15–18.

11. Kentico website (n.d.) http://trees.kentico.com/, accessed May 8, 2016.

12. Steven, A. B., Yazdi, A. A., & Dresner, M. (2016). Mergers and service quality in the airline industry: A silver lining for air travelers? *Transportation Research Part E: Logistics and Transportation Review,* 89, 1–13. http://doi.org/10.1016/j.tre.2016.02.005

13. Schlangenstein, M., et al. (2010). United and Continental reach for the sky. *Bloomberg Businessweek,* (4178), 19–20.

14. West, M., & Sobejana, M. (2016). *Making sense of the agile methodology wars* (No. G00278387). Gartner Research, http://www.gartner.com/document/3217417?ref=solrAll&refval=167471927&qid=e0201583986c73a9035fb5726a6b2fc1, accessed August 22, 2016.

15. Hotle, M., & Wilson, N. (2016). *The end of the waterfall as we know it* (No. G00291841). Gartner Research, http://www.gartner.com/document/3188962?ref=solrAll&refval=167381724&qid=0a1efc78e1db757db1ca316cbe687bcb, accessed August 22, 2016.

16. Wilson, N. (January 25, 2013). Managing the agile project. Gartner Research, ID: G00245859.

17. Driver, M., Howard, C., Wong, J., & West, M. (2015). *Citizen development is fundamental to the digital workplace.* Gartner Research, http://www.gartner.com/document/3113317?ref=TypeAheadSearch&qid=f802e77f0601b7648e0304aed186d483, accessed August 22, 2016.

18. Kanaracus, C. (January 11, 2013). Marin County settles legal claims against Deloitte, SAP over software project. *ComputerWorld,* http://www.computerworld.com/s/article/9235619/Marin_County_settles_legal_claims_against_Deloitte_SAP_over_software_project, accessed August 22, 2016.

LEARNING OBJECTIVES

1   Define a project, and explain how time, cost, and scope affect it.

2   Describe the five processes of project management.

3   Explain how project management software helps managers plan, track, and manage projects.

4   Identify the main factors that cause projects to succeed or fail.

5   Explain the importance of strategic planning for information systems, and provide examples.

6   Explain how the human element affects strategic planning.

An online, interactive decision-making simulation that reinforces chapter contents and uses key terms in context can be found in MyMISLab™.

INTRODUCTION

PROJECTS THAT INVOLVE INFORMATION SYSTEMS NEED SKILLED OVERSIGHT, and poor project management is often the reason new information systems go off track. This chapter explores the phases of a project from the beginning, in which a plan is first developed, through the processes used during each phase. You will also learn about the project manager's role and the software tools that help track progress on tasks, work assignments, and expenses.

In the online simulation for this chapter called "eXtreme Virtual Reality," you will get first-hand experience acting as that project manager, helping this start-up company get

ready for opening day. The company creates high-tech virtual reality experiences such as hot-air balloon rides and underwater adventures. You'll need to coordinate all the software testing so they can open on time, with reliable systems that work smoothly to create these amazing rides. But tasks outside IT are also essential, such as marketing and legal reviews. They all must be carefully planned and monitored. As in any project, however, you should also expect surprises.

The second part of the chapter explores strategic planning for information systems, and projects like the one in the

EXTREME VIRTUAL REALITY
A Role-Playing Simulation on Managing a Project to Open a New Business

pasphotography/Shutterstock.

online decision-making simulation play a key role. Strategic planning charts the course for all the organization's information system resources and all the people who will use them. It lays out the guiding principles and vision, showing how the organization's strategies align with its goals. But the strategic plan is not just a list of projects or a tally of anticipated hardware expenses. It is the roadmap that clarifies how information systems contribute to the company's mission and strategy for the future and what needs to be done to protect the organization's assets and ensure its success.

Define a project, and explain how time, cost, and scope affect it.

What is a Project?

Successful project management starts with knowing what a project is and what it isn't. A **project** is a temporary activity that is launched for a specific purpose to carry out a particular objective. Figure 12-1 lists common characteristics for most projects, from landing a spacecraft on Mars to running for political office. Launching virtually any new information system, whether it is a new web portal for customers or a whole new financial system, is a project.

Projects Versus Processes

Projects are temporary, with their own budgets, timelines, and sponsor. In contrast, a business *process* is a series of events designed to deliver a product or service that is repeated over and over. Projects are unique, but processes are recurring. For instance, publishing the next edition of a monthly magazine is not a project, even though all the stories and puzzles are fresh. It is a process; tasks repeat each month, such as assigning stories, designing graphics, and scheduling print runs. Projects are one of a kind, and they involve uncertainty. People are doing things that are new to them, so their predictions about how long tasks will take may be well off the mark. In contrast, a process should be tweaked so that the underlying activities are streamlined, efficient, predictable, and cost-effective. Figure 12-2 contrasts the tasks

FIGURE 12-1
Common characteristics of a project.

A project

▶ is a temporary endeavor

▶ has a specific, unique purpose

▶ has a primary customer or sponsor, as well as stakeholders

▶ requires resources, staff time, and expertise from different areas

▶ includes an element of uncertainty

▶ has metrics for success

FIGURE 12-2
Projects versus processes.

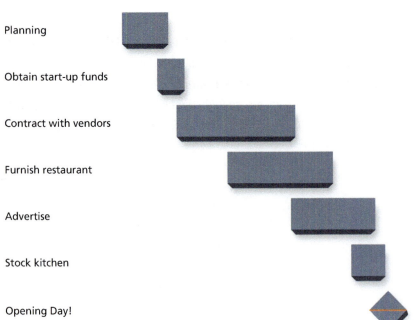

PROJECT: Opening a new restaurant

PROCESS: Procuring office supplies

involved in a unique project to open a new restaurant and a frequently repeated procurement process.

Often, whether a particular event is a process or project depends on your point of view. For example, a wedding is a one-time project for the couple, but it would be a process to a wedding planner who handles all the details routinely.

Project management skills are essential for projects incorporating information systems. However, many activities in IT are business processes that repeat, and they should be made as streamlined, routine, and cost-effective as possible. Help-desk support, information system maintenance, software updates and patch installation, user training, and backups are all processes, not projects.

> **PRODUCTIVITY TIP**
> You can improve your own productivity by distinguishing between projects and processes and managing them wisely. Term papers, for example, have many features that are "process-like." Create term paper templates with standard headers, footers, styles, and naming conventions, and develop streamlined strategies for organizing your references. Don't treat everything as a unique project.

The Triple Constraint: Time, Cost, and Scope

Every project is constrained by three fundamental forces: time, cost, and scope. These three are interrelated; if one changes, the others are affected (Figure 12-3).

Often one of the constraints is fixed for a particular project, so the other two forces must be adjusted if change is needed. For a new website feature, for example, a manager might say $100,000 is the limit, not a penny more—thus fixing the costs. To stay within budget, the project's scope can be reduced.

New financial information systems usually must launch at the beginning of the fiscal year, so the time constraint is critical. Managers face tough decisions when the go-live date nears if tasks remain undone. Training time may be cut to the bone, and any nonessential software features might be abandoned to avoid having to wait another year to go live. To implement its ERP on the cutover date, one state government agency went live with almost no accounting reports yet available. A frustrated budget analyst said, "With no reports, it's like driving wearing a blindfold." The alternative, though, might have been to spend another year using the legacy system.

FIGURE 12-3

Time, cost, and scope: The triple constraint.

Project Management

2 Describe the five processes of project management.

As the theme park's newly hired assistant director for social media, Stan M. is eagerly anticipating his first assignment. The park's mammoth new waterslide, the largest in the region, is scheduled to open at the start of the summer, and the CEO wants a blockbuster social media campaign to promote it. With a background in business and information systems, Stan knows that managing a project like this without a plan is like launching a Broadway musical with no score and no script, so he gets to work.

Project management is a systematic approach to project planning, organizing, and managing resources, resulting in a project that successfully meets its objectives. It requires knowledge and skills in many areas and a clear understanding of the processes that underlie a successful project.[1]

---

project
A temporary activity launched for a specific purpose, to carry out a particular objective.

project management
A systematic approach to project planning, organizing, and managing resources, resulting in a project that successfully meets its objectives.

FIGURE 12-4

The five project management processes.

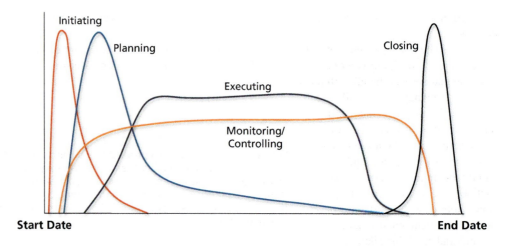

The Five Project Management Processes

Every project has five underlying processes that require management, beginning with the very first stage in which the project is conceived. Each process becomes more intense at certain phases of the project, as shown in Figure 12-4.

- Initiating
- Planning
- Executing
- Monitoring and controlling
- Closing

INITIATING

The **initiating processes** lay the groundwork for the project by clarifying the value it will bring to the organization, setting its objectives, and estimating the project's length, scope, and cost. Projects might be proposed by different people, but in this early phase managers should identify the major players in the project, including the sponsor, the project manager (PM), the team members, and other stakeholders.

A key document that authorizes the project is the **project charter**. The charter shows that the project has the backing of senior management, an essential element for success. It should also include a clear statement of objectives, estimated start and end dates, the names of the relevant people and their roles, a tentative budget, criteria for success, and any other pertinent information to get the project off to a good start.

Some managers might depend on informal emails to authorize a project or assume that some comments made at a meeting should get things rolling. But those approaches put a fledgling project on shaky footing. If the manager leaves or decides to reassign a key team member, the project could be left hanging. The charter helps to avoid unexpected surprises later. Stan drafted the simple charter shown in Figure 12-5. More complex and costly projects will have charters with more detail that go through several versions before formal signoff.

Another initiating process is the kickoff meeting, where the stakeholders meet one another, sometimes for the first and only time. Led by the project manager, the team reviews the charter and discusses next steps.

PLANNING

The **planning processes** should start very early with the overarching **project management plan**. This will be the roadmap and guide for executing the project, and it describes the components needed to ensure success. The plan will include an organizational chart, a description of the work to be performed, schedule information, success metrics, and notations about any information systems that will be used. It should also identify the **deliverables**, which are the products, documents, or services that will be delivered to the sponsor during the course of the project. For Stan's project, those will include the new blog and website, video clips, mass emails, a Facebook page, sample Twitter output, and reports showing the analytics on page views and other metrics. Given the uncertainty that is part of any project, the plan should include steps stakeholders take to make changes and get them approved.

Project: Social Media Campaign for The Wild River Waterslide Ride

Start and End Dates: April 2 – June 30

Key Participants:
- ▶ Project Manager: Stan M.
- ▶ Sponsor: Consuela T., Director of Marketing
- ▶ Estimated budget: $38,000 (includes personnel salaries)
- ▶ Team Members:
  - ▶ Bailey L., Programmer/Analyst
  - ▶ John C., Copywriter
  - ▶ Lucinda V., IT Support

Project Objectives: Develop, launch, and track a social media campaign to promote the waterslide throughout the region. The goal is a 20% increase in number of park visitors from June 15 to July 15, compared to the same period last year. Additional metrics will include (1) web analytics on the blog and other online assets, such as percent change in the number of video views and unique visitors, and (2) survey of Wild River riders to determine how they learned about the ride.

Project Approach: With IT's support, launch a blog containing comments, images, and videos of employees and guests who experience the ride before opening. Post videos to YouTube and distribute links to popular bookmarking sites. Invite loyal customers who maintain their own blogs to a "Wild River Preview" day. Capture leads from the blog by offering discount coupons.

Signatures:

FIGURE 12-5

Sample project charter.

The project management plan should clarify the scope of the project, and sometimes this requires a separate document. Stakeholders with different interests may quarrel over what is inside or outside the project scope, advocating for the features they prefer. A strategy for changing the scope that everyone agrees upon in advance will help resolve such disputes and avoid scope creep, in which features are added in an uncontrolled way, often without considering the impact on the budget or timeline.

The project management plan will also include strategies for managing time, quality, human resources, communications, cost, risk, and overall integration, as shown in Figure 12-6.

FIGURE 12-6

Project management planning areas with sample outputs.

Area	Description	Sample Outputs
Integration	Overall management of the project	Project charter; project management plan
Scope	Clarifying what work is part of the project, and what is not	Scope statement; work breakdown structure; scope management plan
Time	Ensuring the project meets its deadlines	Project schedule; Gantt chart; critical path analysis; time management plan
Cost	Determining the budget, analyzing any need for changes, and ensuring the project's costs are tracked and managed properly	Cost estimate; running expenses; net present value analysis; return on investment analysis; cost management plan
Quality	Ensuring the project deliverables meet quality standards for the project	Quality standards, project metrics; quality management plan
Human resources	Managing the people involved in the project, motivating stakeholders, allocating tasks, monitoring workloads	Project organizational chart; assignment matrix; human resources management plan
Communications	Providing updates and status reports to stakeholders; presenting project to sponsor(s)	Status reports; meetings; project dashboard; website; communications management plan
Risk	Managing risks that may impact the project; implementing mitigation strategies	Risk management plan; risk register

initiating processes
Processes that lay the groundwork for the project by clarifying its business value; setting its objectives; estimating the project's length, scope, and cost; identifying team members; and obtaining approval.

project charter
A document that authorizes a project that includes a clear statement of objectives, estimated start and end dates, the names of the relevant people and their roles, a tentative budget, criteria for success, and other pertinent information.

planning processes
The processes in project management that focus on planning how the project will be executed.

project management plan
The roadmap and guide for executing a project that includes information such as an organizational chart, a detailed description of the work to be performed, information about the schedule, details about meetings and reviews, success metrics, and notations about any information systems or project monitoring tools that will be used.

deliverables
The products, documents, or services that will be delivered to the sponsor during the course of a project.

scope creep
A term that refers to the way in which features are added in an uncontrolled way to a project, often without considering the impact on the budget or timeline.

The project manager might work with the project team to create separate documents for each of these, depending on the project's size and complexity.

The project's scope includes a work breakdown structure (WBS), which is an orderly listing of actual tasks that the project team must complete to produce the project's deliverables. The **Gantt chart** is a handy visual guide that lists the tasks on the WBS along with each task's projected start and finish dates in graphical format (Figure 12-7). The bars graphically show the sequence of tasks and their duration, and the diamonds indicate milestones for the project.

These documents, along with many other planning and tracking aids, are typically generated through project management software, described later in this chapter.

EXECUTING

Executing processes include all the coordinating efforts that ensure the tasks on the WBS are carried out properly. For the project manager, tasks to execute include communicating with stakeholders, assigning tasks, negotiating contracts, coaching team members, holding meetings, writing updates, doing presentations for the board, and much more. The best project managers, however, spend a little more time on the other processes—especially planning—and a little less on executing. Inexperienced project managers often try to do everything themselves rather than learn how to manage the project by good planning, delegating, and team building.

MONITORING AND CONTROLLING

Monitoring and controlling processes track progress from start to finish, pinpointing any deviations from the plan. The project manager pays close attention to reports that might show early warning signs that some tasks have fallen behind. If a team member gets sick, the project manager must find a way to fill in.

Most tasks on the WBS have **predecessors**, which are the other tasks that must be completed before the particular task can begin. For example, Stan wants to have the project charter done before he holds the kickoff meeting, so the charter task is a predecessor of the meeting. In Figure 12-7, the connecting arrows show the predecessors. Other tasks are less

FIGURE 12-7

Gantt chart for the Wild River Water-slide social media campaign.

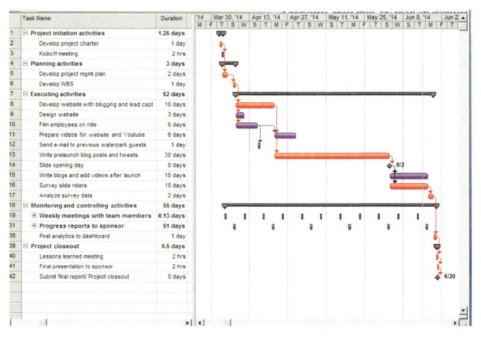

Key:
Bars show the projected start and end dates for tasks.
Red bars indicate tasks along the critical path.
Black diamonds indicate project milestones.
Connecting arrows indicate the sequence for tasks.

dependent on previous activity, so the project manager has some flexibility about when to schedule them.

The **critical path**, shown in red in Figure 12-7, is the longest path through the project, and it identifies those tasks that can't be delayed without affecting the finish date. In Stan's project, the IT department has to build the website before the blog can launch, so the website is a predecessor of the blog. Both of these tasks are red, indicating that they are on the critical path and must finish on schedule. In contrast, the task in which employees film themselves on the ride could slip a bit without affecting the schedule, so that task is in blue, indicating it is not on the critical path. Monitoring tasks that fall along the critical path is especially important, and you'll be making decisions about them in the online simulation.

CLOSING

Closing processes will formally end the project in an orderly way. The sponsor may need to sign off that all deliverables have been received and accepted, and the team members may be reassigned to their regular jobs. Usually the project manager holds a final meeting with the team to celebrate (or mourn).

The closing phase should also include a process to capture lessons learned to add to the organization's knowledge base. Stan and his team will have much to say about how to make social media work better the next time and also how to better manage any project for the theme park.

Unfortunately, many organizations neglect the lessons-learned component of closing processes, partly because of pressure to move on to the next project. People are also reluctant to document lessons learned when the project fails

> **PRODUCTIVITY TIP**
> Take time to document your own lessons learned after each project in which you're involved. You can use these to make recommendations to the next team or improve your own performance as project manager.

because they don't want to admit mistakes or risk blame. Despite the challenges, smart managers in a high-performing organization will develop incentives to encourage team members to share what they learned about project management.

The Role of the Project Manager

The PM needs leadership skills, excellent communication abilities, and strong team-building skills (Figure 12-8). Although technical competence in the task at hand is valuable, "people" skills are equally so. The job is demanding, and project success can depend so heavily on the PM's skills that many organizations require professional certification, especially for those charged with managing large projects. The Project Management Institute (PMI) offers programs to certify project managers who can demonstrate their qualifications and agree to PMI's code of professional conduct and ethics.[2]

Another knowledge area project managers must master is **change management**, which is a structured approach to the transition employees must make as they switch from their existing

FIGURE 12-8

Characteristics of effective project managers.

- ▶ Strong leadership skills
- ▶ Excellent communication abilities
- ▶ Outstanding "people" skills
- ▶ Technical competence in project area
- ▶ Good listening skills
- ▶ Strong team-building skills
- ▶ Excellent presentation skills
- ▶ Good problem-solving and critical-thinking skills
- ▶ Ability to balance priorities, stay organized, and keep the team on track

---

Gantt chart
A graphic showing the tasks on the work breakdown structure along with each task's projected start and finish dates.

executing processes
All the coordinating efforts that ensure the tasks on the work breakdown structure are carried out properly.

monitoring and controlling processes
Processes that track a project's progress from start to finish, pinpointing any deviations from the plan that must be addressed.

predecessors
The tasks that must be completed in a project before a particular task can begin.

critical path
The longest path through the project, which identifies those tasks that can't be delayed without affecting the finish date. Monitoring tasks that fall along the critical path is especially important.

closing processes
Processes that formally end the project in an orderly way; they include a signoff by the sponsor confirming that all deliverables have been received and accepted.

change management
A structured approach to the transition employees must make as they switch from their existing work processes to new ones, especially with the introduction of a new information system.

THE ETHICAL FACTOR   Code of Ethics for Project Managers

Project managers adhere to a code of ethics, and one widely used in the field is from the Project Management Institute.[3] The values that form the foundation for this code emphasize responsibility, respect, fairness, and honesty.

For example, PMs are expected to make decisions and take actions based on the best interest of society, public safety, and the environment. They must also accept assignments only when the position matches their background, experience, skills, and qualifications. They can accept "stretch" assignments provided they keep the key stakeholders informed about areas in which they have gaps.

The PMI code stresses that project managers have an obligation to avoid any conflicts of interest. Such conflicts are not uncommon, and they present a major challenge to the profession. For example, a PM employed by the company sponsoring the project should answer questions like these:

■ Have you done any consulting work for any of the vendors who will be bidding on the project?
■ Have any of your close relatives done such work?
■ Do you own stock or have investments in any of the companies that might be hired for this project?

The prohibition against conflicts of interest extends to even the appearance of it, because that could compromise the PM's effectiveness. The code of ethics establishes a very high standard of ethical behavior for project managers that will serve them and their employers well.

---

work processes to new ones. Much change accompanies the introduction of new information systems, particularly when some processes are drastically revised or eliminated through business process management efforts. Resistance to change can sink an entire project.

Explain how project management software helps managers plan, track, and manage projects.

3   Project Management Software

The market for project management software is very strong, and project managers enjoy a broad range of tools that can help manage and track a project. Although it is possible to use Excel or even a word processor to create a work breakdown structure, fill in timelines and due dates, and assign people to tasks, specialty software offers far more capabilities.

Managing Time

Project management software provides extensive tools to help the PM manage time, one of the three constraints in any project. For instance, the software automatically adjusts start and end dates as the PM creates the work breakdown structure. Stan enters the approximate duration for each task and then identifies each task's predecessors, shown in Figure 12-7. For instance, he estimates that task 17—analyzing the survey data from customers who ride the waterslide—will take 2 days. The predecessor is task 17, to survey slide riders. If the team needs a couple of extra days for the survey, Stan can increase the duration of that task, and the dates for his analysis will automatically adjust.

The PM can also use the project plan as the baseline schedule. Once the project starts, the PM can enter actual completion dates for each task or percent completed, and the software can display two bars for each task, one for the baseline and one for the actual progress. Figure 12-9 shows that Stan took a bit longer to develop the project charter than he projected. The software adjusts the schedule for Stan's project, delaying the kickoff meeting and later tasks to compensate. Stan will have to find ways to tighten the schedule later to finish on time. It takes skill to balance resources and time constraints, especially to avoid burning out the team toward the end.

Managing People and Resources

Another useful feature in project management software is the ability to assign people to tasks and then track their workloads and duties across the project. The PM can enter the people along with their working calendars and planned vacations. Team members can each be assigned to the appropriate tasks in the work breakdown structure, and reports will show the level of effort required of each person each day. If someone is overloaded for a period of time,

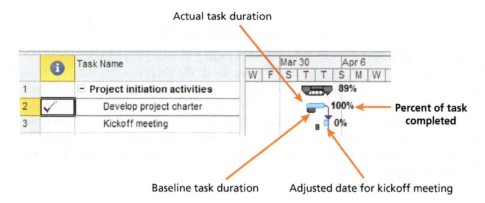

FIGURE 12-9
Comparing the project's baseline to actual progress (2 and 3). The gray bars under each subtask show the original baseline, and the blue bar above that indicates actual progress and schedule adjustments for future tasks.

perhaps because the schedule calls for that person's skills on two overlapping tasks, the PM can use the software to test scenarios that stretch out some tasks or delay others so the project team doesn't have to put in so much overtime. Stan can see he is overloaded in the beginning of the project, but he decides to work on weekends rather than delay the slide's opening.

The reports showing everyone's schedule are especially useful because many projects include team members who work in other departments or projects, and their skills have to be shared. The smart PM will keep team members and their supervisors well informed about the timing for their tasks so they can plan ahead and avoid unpleasant surprises that affect work in their own departments.

Stan assigns Bailey to develop the website with blogging capability, and the duration estimate assumes that Bailey will work full-time on that. Bailey is also needed for the kickoff and various weekly meetings, and the software can generate a report showing Bailey's projected schedule. If the timing on tasks changes, Stan can send out updated schedules. The cooperation of Bailey's supervisor is essential because her department's ongoing work has to adapt to her absence.

Managing Costs

Salaries, consulting fees, equipment, travel, rentals, and other expenses can all be estimated up front with project management software and then tracked against the baseline as the project progresses. The PM might enter team members' hourly rates for regular hours and for overtime if the rates are higher. Equipment costs can be added to the task that uses them as a one-time expense or be spread over the duration of the project. If the project is charged for the use of meeting rooms, those fees can be added, too.

The software calculates the baseline costs for the project and provides reports on variances as the project proceeds. Figure 12-10 shows a sample report that alerts the PM to cost variances by task. For example, the extra time Stan spent on the project charter affects not only the schedule for the project but also its costs because of his salary. If the website takes longer to build, that will add to costs as well. Juggling the three constraints is a constant challenge for project managers, and Stan may need to check with the project sponsor about whether to reduce the scope so that the project comes closer to the original budget and timeline.

Wild River Waterslide Project: Budget Report

Task	Baseline Cost	Actual Cost	Variance
Develop project charter	1,280.00	1,920.00	640.00
Kickoff meeting	670.00	670.00	0
Develop project management plan	1,280.00	1,280.00	0
Develop WBS	640.00	640.00	0
Develop website with blogging capability	8,800.00	11,440.00	2,640.00

FIGURE 12-10
Tracking the Wild River Waterslide social media marketing budget.

Identify the main factors that cause projects to succeed or fail.

4 Why Projects Succeed and Why They Fail

After investing more than $300 million in modernizing its financial information systems, the Veterans Administration (VA) has little to show for it. The first project failed, and the major components of the second were canceled over doubts that the project could ever be successfully executed within the budget.[4] And the VA is certainly not alone. The troubled rollout of the Healthcare.gov website, along with the decisions by several states to abandon their own attempts to build health care exchanges, further highlights the costly risks. Analysts estimate that the cost of failed government projects involving information systems may be as high as $20 billion per year.[5]

Why Do Projects Fail?

Several critical factors contribute to failure:

- Lack of executive support
- Lack of stakeholder involvement
- Unclear requirements
- Technology problems
- Scope creep and excessive customization
- Unclear roles and responsibilities
- Unrealistic time frames
- Poor communications
- Poor change management

Although technical problems do contribute to failures and delays, most fail factors have more to do with the way projects are managed, monitored, communicated, and supported by senior execs. Some spectacular failures happen because of the **escalation of commitment** phenomenon. People hesitate to pull the plug on a project in which huge sums have already been invested. Instead of weighing the value of further investment, they forget that sunk costs are bygones and should not guide future decision making. The VA's $300 million investment was a sunk cost, and the project managers wisely decided not to escalate their commitment any further.

Success Factors for Project Management

The success factors are almost the mirror image of those that contribute to failure. Figure 12-11 lists characteristics that describe projects that have the best chance of succeeding, grouped by category. In the category called "People factors," executive support tops the list, just as lack of that support does for failed projects.

Clarity is essential, especially at the very start of the project when stakeholders, project manager, team members, and sponsor all must agree on the project's objectives, success

FIGURE 12-11
Success factors for projects.

	Does the project have...
People factors	Executive support and sufficient resources allocated? Talented and motivated personnel assigned to the project? Leaders with project management expertise? A strategy to manage conflicts among stakeholders?
Organizational factors	Involvement and buy-in from a broad range of end users? An objective that is perceived to be aligned with business goals?
Project factors	A clear objective and a well-defined scope? A design that will allow any new systems to interact with existing systems?
Project management factors	A well-defined system development methodology that is appropriate for the project? Appropriate project management software and other tools? A clear change control process for managing scope creep? A strategy for assessing quality? A clear process for monitoring and tracking progress?
External factors	Well-understood and binding agreements with vendors and consultants?

criteria, scope, and other details. The project charter is an effective tool to achieve this clarity and ensure everyone is on the same page.

Project managers also need to be willing to make unpopular decisions and communicate unpleasant truths. The PM has to clearly define the time, cost, and scope constraints as the project unfolds. Features that the stakeholders were expecting may have to be dropped if sticking to the budget and launching on time are judged more important.

Another factor that should not be underestimated is the need for end-user training and hand-holding after launch. If help is readily available, employees will master the new processes and software much more quickly and with much less frustration.

On the technical side, the growing complexity of many software projects adds to the uncertainty. As you learned in Chapter 10, systems development often involves many components and services, often from third parties. It also might involve many players who might be geographically quite distant. Successful project managers must manage these challenges and be prepared to adjust as surprises occur.[6]

Most organizations have several projects under way simultaneously that incorporate information systems and technology, so strategic planning is essential for establishing priorities and resources for the project portfolio. For information systems, strategic planning also entails several other essential activities, discussed in the next section.

> **PRODUCTIVITY TIP**
> If you take on the role of project manager for a student team project or a project at work, pay close attention to the factors that contribute to success or failure. The project manager shoulders much of the blame for failures and delays, deserved or not. You should also use a team agreement, as described in Chapter 8.

Strategic Planning for Information Systems

5 Explain the importance of strategic planning for information systems, and provide examples.

Information systems are like the nervous system of an organization, with neurons that extend into and support every organ and muscle fiber. Because information systems are so central to success and strategic competitiveness, organizations create a strategic plan to provide a roadmap that charts the course.

This roadmap should take into account significant trends in the environment, and it should be aligned with the strategy the company establishes, as we described in Chapter 2. Whether that strategy is low cost leadership, product differentiation, or something else, the strategic plan for information systems should be closely aligned and used to guide decision making. While the CIO typically leads the effort, stakeholders from across the organization also participate. Some of the major areas the plan covers are:

- Vision, principles, and policies
- Project portfolio management
- Disaster recovery and business continuity
- Technology and business trends

Let's take a closer look at each.

Vision, Principles, and Policies

Vermont's information technology strategic plan begins with a vision that "Vermonters are *the* one. We will think as one … act as one … and have one mission." That statement shows a clear focus on an enterprise-wide approach that will guide information systems planning. This vision lays the groundwork for strategic decision making and indicates that integration and online customer service will be major themes.

The organization's vision, mission, and culture determine the principles that guide how its information systems are managed and used, and how resources are allocated. A risk-averse

escalation of commitment
The tendency to continue investing in a project, despite mounting evidence that it is not succeeding; often comes about because people mistakenly let sunk costs affect decision making rather than weighing the value of further investment.

FIGURE 12-12
Comparing IT funding models.

Model	Description	% in use
Subsidy model	No chargebacks; costs are allocated to business units	30%
Cost center model	Similar to subsidy, but some chargebacks are in place	30%
Service center model	Chargebacks for IT services	30%
Profit center model	Services billed at market rates to help fund new IT projects	10%

financial company will lean toward strategies that protect assets and ensure compliance with regulations. But a high-energy start-up might stress innovation and ease of collaboration, establishing principles that promote creativity.

FUNDING MODELS

The vision and the principles that drive it are translated into policies and procedures that reach down into business processes and workplace culture. For example, the procurement policy may require all technology purchases to be approved by the IT department to ensure compatibility and to help build a consistent enterprise architecture. If your company only supports Windows laptops, your plea for a MacBook will fall on deaf ears. Your manager may also deny a request for a desktop printer because "going green" is a fundamental principle.

The organization's guiding principles also influence how it allocates IT expenses and recovers costs. Some IT organizations use a cost center or service center model, in which business units are charged back for some or all IT services, such as help-desk calls, hardware purchases, or storage space, so department managers receive a bill each month. Other companies rely on a subsidy model in which costs are allocated to the business units based on employee headcount, or they just treat IT as overhead and don't charge departments directly. More recently, some IT organizations are emerging as a profit center, charging the business units market rates for services and using the profit for new IT investments (Figure 12-12)[7]

Funding models like these have effects on behavior, and they sometimes lead to unintended consequences. For example, a manager in a chargeback setting might scrimp on new computers to save the department's budget, leaving workers struggling with outdated machines. Or an employee may hesitate to call the help desk and instead spend many wasted hours trying to remove a virus. Without chargebacks, though, managers lack information about how their departments are using IT, and they have less incentive to watch costs. Some departments are branded IT "hogs" that elevate everyone's share of costs. Educating employees about the pros and cons of different funding models helps avoid such problems.

ACCEPTABLE-USE AND SECURITY POLICIES

The organization's principles also guide the **acceptable-use policy**, which explains what employees are allowed—and not allowed—to do with company IT resources. These policies touch on the services each employee will be provided, whether and how much they can use company resources for personal use, and what surveillance is in place (Figure 12-13). Policies also stress legal requirements, such as rules against copyright infringement or exporting encryption software. Harassment, fraudulent use, and any attempts to disrupt information systems or circumvent authentication are covered as well.[8]

Acceptable-use policies should contain clear language describing the organization's security and confidentiality requirements. For instance, the policy might require all PCs and laptops to be encrypted and secured with a password. With the dramatic rise in lawsuits related to email, many organizations establish specific email policies. Some require employees to add disclaimers to their email signatures designed to diminish legal threats to the company, such as those in Figure 12-14.

Acceptable-use policies are expanding to cover how employees use technology outside work as well. For example, IBM encourages employees to contribute to blogs, tweet, and join virtual worlds, but the company publishes social computing guidelines. One reminds employees never to post anything about a client without the client's approval.[9]

Personally owned devices are also coming under acceptable-use policies. With so many employees wanting to link their own smartphones to corporate systems, managers are struggling to develop practical policies for the world of "BYOD" (bring your own device), especially to ensure security and maintain privacy.[10] For example, should the company insist that

▶ What IT services are provided to each employee?

▶ Can employees access the Internet?

▶ Is access to certain websites prohibited?

▶ What kind of surveillance and monitoring is in place?

▶ Are employees permitted to use the company's IT resources for personal use? If so, what are the constraints?

▶ How does the organization respond to violations? What are the penalties?

▶ Can employees download and install software without IT approval?

▶ Can employees send mass email to colleagues about personal issues, such as "kittens are ready to adopt" or "donuts available"?

▶ Can employees use IT resources for fund-raising or commercial ventures?

▶ Can employees use the company name when they post on blogs or other social media?

▶ Security requirements

▶ Password construction and change schedules

▶ Encryption requirements

▶ Prohibition against sharing accounts

▶ Confidentiality requirements

FIGURE 12-13
Elements of an acceptable-use policy.

Potential Threat	Purpose of Disclaimer
Breach of confidentiality	The disclaimer can warn recipients against disclosing information contained in the email.
Accidental breach of confidentiality	If the email contains confidential information intended only for the recipient, a third party (such as the postmaster) might receive it accidentally. Wording that the message is intended only for the addressee provides some protection.
Transmission of viruses	The disclaimer can warn recipients that they are responsible for checking the message for viruses.
Implied contractual obligations	An employee's email might contain wording that implies a firm contract. The disclaimer can add that any contract must be confirmed by the employee's manager.
Negligent misstatements	The company may be liable if an employee provides advice that the recipient then relies on. The disclaimer can include wording to protect the company from this.
Employee misuse	Absent a disclaimer, the employer may be held responsible for an employee who misuses email and violates the company's policies, for example by making libelous or defamatory statements in email.

FIGURE 12-14
Why do companies require employees to add disclaimers to their emails?

it can remotely wipe an employee's iPhone clean if it is misplaced to protect any confidential data it might contain? The data would vanish, but so would all your personal photos, videos, and music. Mobile device management can address some of the technical challenges, particularly to improve security. But others remain difficult to resolve, and a survey of U.S. businesses found that more than half had not yet implemented formal policies.[11]

"BYOD" (bring your own device) seemed like a great solution for a law firm whose attorneys liked to dictate memos. Instead of buying dictation equipment for each lawyer, the IT department told them to install a $1.99 app on their personal smartphones. That worked fine until the app developer went out of business, and the attorneys lost all their recordings. IT support in these hybrid environments is quite a challenge.[12]

acceptable-use policy
An organizational policy that describes what employees are allowed to do with IT resources and what activities are disallowed; employees agree to the policy before gaining access to IT resources.

ENTERPRISE ARCHITECTURE

As we discussed in Chapter 3, the enterprise architecture is the organization's overarching ICT environment, and the plan for this architecture should address its current and target state. As new systems are added and old ones retired, the components of the architecture continue to change. With a strategic plan to guide the architectural decisions, changes will lead toward the target. Systems that don't talk to each other now could be replaced by new systems that more easily interface. Redundant and inconsistent data will decline, and consistent hardware choices will help streamline and reduce support costs. Strategic planning for a flexible and forward-looking enterprise architecture will ensure the organization can meet its current needs and be positioned for future success.

Project Portfolio Management

The strategic plan should outline how the organization will guide investments in new information systems projects, especially to show how they will support business goals. **Project portfolio management** is a continuous process that oversees all the projects for an organization, selecting which projects to pursue, and then managing the whole portfolio. The process also includes culling those projects that have a poor prognosis, such as the Veterans Administration's troubled financial system.[13]

DECIDING WHICH PROJECTS TO PURSUE

Most organizations are not short of project ideas that rely on technology. Almost every proposal for developing new products and services, reducing costs, or increasing revenue has some IT-related element. Some projects are rejected early, perhaps after the feasibility study in the planning phase of the systems development life cycle. Managers may learn that the system they imagined is too expensive or that the technology is still too buggy.

To choose among the rest, the organization must decide on selection criteria and a strategy to determine which projects fit best. Costs can be very high, so strategically choosing projects for the portfolio is important. The typical criteria for selecting projects (Figure 12-15) include:

- Contribution to competitive strategy
- Return on investment
- Compliance and risk reduction

Projects that contribute to competitive strategy and distinguish the company from rivals always deserve attention. For example, managers at the unstructured document management service called Evernote stress features that add to the site's usefulness. Users can clip web articles, upload photos, add voice or text notes, and store them all for free in an organized and easily searchable online repository. But Evernote offers premium services for paid subscribers. Any project that tempts users to pay the fee gets highest priority.

Return on investment (ROI) is another important criterion, although it is not always easy to estimate. Savings for a project to replace individual servers with a smaller number of virtualized servers may be straightforward. But sometimes project costs rise unexpectedly, and boosts in revenue are hard to predict. For instance, managers often underestimate the cost of customizing commercial software, especially because of scope creep and the need to maintain

FIGURE 12-15
Criteria for comparing the value of projects.

Criterion	Example
Contribution to competitive strategy	Projects that advance the organization's competitive position should be rated highly. One example is Carfax.com's web-based software to access a used car's history of accidents or defects based on the vehicle identification number.
Return on investment	Projects that offer a substantial return on investment earn high ratings. For example, Oregon Corrections switched to Voice over IP for its call center, staffed by prison inmates, reducing monthly telecom charges by 40%.
Compliance and risk reduction	Reducing risk and ensuring proper compliance are especially important drivers in some industries. Companies in the financial services industry spend more than 8% of their net income on IT projects and services, much of it to ensure compliance and mitigate risk.

the custom code throughout the information system's life cycle. Those costs will continue to grow as long as the system stays in use.

Savings can be elusive, too. A supply chain management system might save considerable time for staff in the procurement office, and the original ROI projection included reduced personnel costs. But those workers might not be let go. Instead, they are assigned to other duties, so personnel costs don't drop. Nevertheless, organizations can reap very substantial returns on many of their information systems investments, even though the actual figures can be a challenge to predict.

Compliance and risk reduction are also important drivers for projects. For instance, businesses must invest heavily in projects to comply with requirements established by the payment card industry for e-commerce. Of course, the cost of noncompliance can be much higher. Fines for a single security breach are hefty, and restitution paid to customers whose data are compromised can reach into the millions of dollars. The credit card issuers can also prevent a noncompliant merchant from accepting credit cards for online transactions, which is devastating for retailers.

MANAGING THE PORTFOLIO

By some estimates, *Fortune* 500 companies sink well over half their strategic initiatives into projects, but many executives do not have a clear picture of how they all are faring. To better manage the portfolio, many organizations establish a **program management office (PMO)** that oversees all the projects under way and also provides project management training, software, and support. These offices help resolve any conflicts that arise between project managers vying for IT staff or other resources. With the organization's goals in mind, the PMO can make the tough decisions about how scarce resources are assigned.[14]

To track progress on all the projects, the PMO collects data from each one to build a larger picture of the overall health of the whole portfolio. On the dashboard, summary charts show how well all the projects are doing in terms of cost, schedule, or other metrics, and managers can drill down into specific projects to see where each one stands. Figure 12-16 shows a dashboard with sample output summarizing all IT projects at federal agencies. Collecting reliable data is a challenge for the PMO. What do green, yellow, and red really mean, for instance? Yellow might indicate that a few tasks are a little behind, but it could also signal serious

Projects	% Completed	Priority	Expense to Date	Risk Rating
Mobile Device Encryption	15%	1	$157,844	1
M-commerce initiative	69%	2	$258,333	5
Mobile App	20%	1	$15,006	5
Mobile Device Management	88%	2	$58,774	2
Social Media Presence	100%	1	$5,688	3
Data Analytics Project	0%	3	$0	5

Portfolio Status, May 25

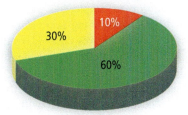

Source: IT Dashboard, USA.Gov.

FIGURE 12-16

Example of output from a project portfolio dashboard.

project portfolio management
A continuous process that oversees all the projects for an organization, selecting which projects to pursue and which ones to terminate.

program management office (PMO)
The part of an organization that oversees all the projects going on throughout the organization and provides project management training, software, and support.

FIGURE 12-17
Types of disasters and possible
consequences to information systems.

Types of Disasters	Possible Consequences
Natural disasters (floods, fires, hurricanes, snowstorms, earthquakes, volcano eruptions)	Electrical outages, destruction of technology infrastructure; disruption of supply chains
Security breaches (unauthorized break-ins, employee theft, denial of service attacks, information leaks)	Release of confidential information, disabled servers, corruption or alteration of data, malware infections
Pandemics	Massive absenteeism
Environmental hazards (hazardous materials spills, radiation, letters containing white powder)	Evacuation; system disruptions; inability of staff to work in the company's facilities

problems. Time estimates also vary. One overconfident programmer might estimate 10 days for a task, but a more cautious person might double that estimate rather than risk a yellow or red flag. Managers should stay alert to such differences in reporting styles.

Disaster Recovery and Business Continuity

The CIO of Entergy, a New Orleans–based energy company, recalls the day Hurricane Katrina hit the city. "That was not a good day," said Ray Johnson. "But it is not a unique event for us. We've got our disaster plan nailed." Thanks to the frequent reviews and drills, Entergy was able to move its primary data center after the storm devastated the Louisiana facility. Employees brought the systems back online from backup tapes at the recovery site in Little Rock, Arkansas, well out of the storm's path.[15]

Disaster recovery refers to all the procedures, documentation, and resources the organization puts into place to prepare for a disaster and recover the technical infrastructure. The list of possible disasters is very long, from the hurricanes and snowstorms that damage facilities and knock out power grids to security breaches, environmental hazards, pandemics, and terrorism (Figure 12-17).

Recovery from disaster is not just about bringing the systems back online, however. It also means ensuring **business continuity**. Faced with many different disaster possibilities, the organization must develop plans for maintaining its business operations to avoid a devastating revenue loss and damaged reputation. How will employees communicate with each other, and where will they work? How will they access the information systems?

The company also needs to prioritize the information systems to help decide which ones should be recovered first. An online retailer, for instance, should make recovering its e-commerce website a top priority. A utility company focuses on power distribution systems. An airline will need its reservation and plane scheduling systems back online.

Other features of the analysis include:

- Data backup schedules
- Off-site storage locations for backup media
- Recovery sites where the data can be restored
- Procedures for restarting the systems

Testing the plan is important, and often the devil is in the details. When the insurance company USAA tested its evacuation plan, employees were efficiently ushered out of the office building. But then they stood in the sweltering Texas sun for more than 2 hours, waiting to get into the alternate site. Most left their car keys behind, so they had no way to get home without re-entering the evacuated building.[16] USAA managers learned from these slip-ups and revised the plan accordingly.

To help manage disaster recovery and business continuity efforts, many organizations turn to companies that offer "disaster recovery as a service," with options for cloud-based solutions, subscription pricing, and access strategies.[17] These can be especially helpful to small and midsized businesses.

Technology and Industry Trends

Strategic planners must be well aware of trends in technology and the industry that might be relevant as well as those that might affect the roadmap. The explosion in the use of mobile

Trend	Description
Digital mesh	Increasing connections and interactivity between a wide range of devices and human beings.
Advanced machine learning	With so much more data and computing power available, artificial intelligence is gaining considerable ground.
3D printing	Printers can use a wider variety of materials, including biologics, to print parts on demand.
Internet of Things	Sensors embedded in objects to connect to the Internet continue to expand.
Security threats	The emerging "hacker industry" poses far greater threats to organizations.

Source: Cearley, D. W., Burke, B., & Walker, M. J. (2016). *Top 10 strategic technology trends for 2016* (No. G00291954). Gartner Research, http://www.gartner.com/document/323 1617?ref=solrAll&refval =167664853&qid=79eac2bb15ddd0fab8e747e43814c2db, accessed August 22, 2016.

FIGURE 12-18
Technology trends.

devices, for instance, is important for any strategic plan involving IT. Launching a major corporate information system without considering mobile access would be a major mistake.

Figure 12-18 lists some examples of technology trends under way that affect strategic planning in some way. For example, the "digital mesh" refers to the growing connections between the physical and virtual worlds, with computing capability embedded in objects all around us, even within us, and virtual reality becoming more accessible.[18] Smart machines, 3D printing, advanced security threats, and the Internet of Things are all important trends that strategic planners take into account.

> When a massive earthquake struck Japan, the Otis Elevator Company was prepared. In regions with high earthquake risk, each elevator carries a seismic detector. If the device senses vibration, the elevator is programmed to return to the ground floor. Doors open so passengers can exit, but further use is blocked pending safety checks. All 80,000 elevators worked flawlessly during the quake, and no one was trapped inside any of them.[19]

Industry trends are equally important for planning. As technology companies change course, merge, drop products, or go bankrupt, their clients' roadmaps must adapt. The outcome of the competition among mobile payment schemes, for example, affects planning for m-commerce, discussed in Chapter 6. The growing maturity of software as a service (SaaS) is changing how IT departments work with the business units, which affects IT staffing, training, and retention.

Planners keep a close eye on trends in government regulations and laws. For example, the outcome of the debate over whether technology companies must provide law enforcement access to encrypted devices, such as Apple's iPhone, will certainly affect how those companies plan their strategies for new products.[20]

Planning for the Future: The Human Element

 Explain how the human element affects strategic planning.

Every strategic planning effort calls for human judgment. Planners must assess the current environment, drawing on what they hope is reliable and up-to-date information about trends and patterns. Ideally, they have access to the rich analyses that business intelligence systems can provide to help them see a clear picture of strengths, weaknesses, opportunities, and threats—not just within the organization but for suppliers, customers, and competitors as well.

disaster recovery
The procedures and documentation the organization puts into place to prepare for a disaster and recover the technical infrastructure.

business continuity
The maintenance of the organization's operations in the event of disaster or disruption.

Planners then must make predictions about the future, stating what their assumptions are and how they arrived at them. How fast will m-commerce grow? Will software developers be in short supply and high demand? How reliable will cloud computing become? Will that new technology explode in popularity or become just another flash in the pan? Will any of our software vendors go out of business?

Cognitive Biases and Strategic Planning

Crystal balls are in short supply, and making predictions about events that affect information systems planning is a considerable challenge. Although hard data and business intelligence can inform the plan and keep it grounded in reality, human beings make mistakes. The quotes in Figure 12-19 show how far off the mark people can be. One reason for such mistakes is that humans show certain biases that can cloud how they interpret data.

A **cognitive bias** is a common human tendency to make systematic mistakes when processing information or making judgments. Figure 12-20 lists some examples. For instance, people show **confirmation bias** by choosing information to examine that supports the view they already hold and ignoring data that might refute their hypothesis. A CIO who favors cloud computing might skip over research on security flaws, pointing instead to case studies highlighting benefits. From the CIO's perspective, the reviewed data support the decision, but the choice the CIO made about which data to review was biased.

Stan's confirmation bias might play out as he analyzes the survey data. He is convinced that social media are a powerful marketing tool, so he might give less weight to survey respondents who said they learned about the ride from the billboard in the park.

Another bias is *overconfidence* in the accuracy of our own estimates. When students are asked to estimate how long it will take to finish a senior thesis, they very frequently underestimate the time. Even when they said they were 99% confident that they would meet a particular deadline, fewer than half actually met it.[21] For project managers, this kind of

---

FIGURE 12-19

Missing the mark: Some of the worst predictions about ICT.

"There is no reason anyone would want a computer in their home."—*Ken Olson, president, chairman, and founder of Digital Equipment, mini and mainframe computer manufacturer, 1977.*

"I have traveled the length and breadth of this country and talked with the best people, and I can assure you that data processing is a fad that won't last out the year."—*The editor in charge of business books for Prentice Hall, 1957.*

"I think there is a world market for maybe five computers."—*Thomas Watson, chairman of IBM, 1943.*

"The wireless music box has no imaginable commercial value. Who would pay for a message sent to no one in particular?"—*Associates of David Sarnoff responding to the latter's call for investment in radio in 1921.*

"The Americans have need of the telephone, but we do not. We have plenty of messenger boys."—*Sir William Preece, chief engineer, British Post Office, 1878.*

"This 'telephone' has too many shortcomings to be seriously considered as a means of communication. The device is inherently of no value to us."—*A memo at Western Union telegraph company, 1878.*

"When the Paris Exhibition closes, electric light will close with it and no more will be heard of it."—*Erasmus Wilson, Oxford professor, 1878.*

FIGURE 12-20

Examples of cognitive biases that can affect strategic planning.

Cognitive Bias	Description
Confirmation bias	The tendency to choose information to review that supports our existing position and ignore conflicting evidence
Overconfidence	The act of having more faith in our own estimates than is realistically justified
Planning fallacy	The tendency to underestimate the time it will take to complete a task
Anchoring	Reliance on one piece of information, however irrelevant
Availability bias	The tendency to judge the probability of an event based on how easily examples come to mind
Hindsight bias	The belief that an actual event was predictable even if it was not

FIGURE 12-21
Which causes the most deaths—
shark attacks or vending machines?

(a)   (b)

Source: TK Kurikawa/Shutterstock, Martin Prochazkacz/Shutterstock.

overconfidence can lead to many adjustments in the schedule, as team members take longer than they estimated.

People often rely too heavily on one piece of information to adjust their estimates, even if it is irrelevant. The phenomenon is called **anchoring**. For instance, suppose someone throws out a wild guess to estimate the costs for a future software project, say $100,000, but the requirements are extremely vague. That one guess becomes the anchor. The CIO might adjust it up or down a little, but the anchor has a powerful influence on the project's actual cost estimate.

For strategic planning, anchoring biases influence time estimates as well as budgets. If managers are asked to draw up a 3-year plan, that duration itself will be an anchor on their estimates about how long it will take to accomplish the plan's objectives. Chances are, you will find quite a few projects on the plan with 3-year timeframes.

Which causes more deaths, shark attacks or vending machines (Figure 12-21)? Most people choose the shark because such attacks get so much publicity in the news. But deaths caused by a falling vending machine, though still quite unusual, are actually many times more common. The example illustrates the **availability bias**, which is the tendency for people to judge the likelihood of events based on how readily they come to mind.

Availability biases can affect how people develop disaster recovery plans, and especially what disasters they judge most likely. Major security break-ins by hackers get considerable media attention, but the costs from more common but less widely publicized threats, such as scareware and careless employees, can be far higher.

The Black Swan

Until the 18th century, people in Europe thought the black swan was either very rare or nonexistent because they had seen only white ones. The bird actually thrives in Australia, but the term **black swan** became a symbol for those extremely rare events that are difficult or nearly impossible to predict (Figure 12-22). Though the odds might be less than 1%, these rare events have an immense impact in areas such as technology, finance, and science, and they pose enormous challenges for strategic planners. Examples of black swans include events such as World War I; the attacks on September 11, 2001; or inventions such as the personal computer or the rise of the Internet.

FIGURE 12-22
The black swan.

Source: NAN728/Shutterstock.

cognitive bias
A common human tendency to make systematic mistakes when processing information or making judgments; cognitive biases can distort strategic planning.

confirmation bias
The human tendency to choose information to examine that supports the person's view but ignore data that might refute that view.

anchoring
The tendency for people to rely too heavily on one piece of information to adjust their estimates, even if it is irrelevant.

availability bias
The tendency for people to judge the likelihood of events based on how readily they come to mind rather than their actual likelihood.

black swan
Used to describe an extremely rare event that is difficult or nearly impossible to predict but that can have an immense impact in areas such as technology, finance, and science; black swans pose enormous challenges for strategic planners.

How might black swan events affect strategic planning? A CIO who systematically rates potential threats according to their likelihood might judge a terrorist attack on the data center so unlikely as to make costly and controversial precautions unnecessary. Building cinderblock protective walls and arming the staff are expensive measures that seem less important compared to intrusion-detection software or off-site backups. Unlike announcing new killer apps or brilliant marketing campaigns, preparing year after year for a highly unlikely disaster that never happens is a thankless task.

Yet improbable events do occur, however rarely, and they can cause enormous damage. Smart managers in every business unit will need to balance all the risks and rewards and at least consider how to handle a highly unlikely black swan.

Hindsight, they say, is 20/20. The **hindsight bias** refers to the human tendency to think an unusual event was (or should have been) predictable once they know it actually happened. This tendency explains why people heap blame on strategic planners who are caught off guard by the black swan.[22] Bill Gates, for instance, was soundly criticized for not predicting the Internet's potential.

The disruptive innovations we discussed in this book are black swans that reshape entire industries, and Bill Gates is not the only savvy technology leader who missed some. Those very smart people quoted in Figure 12-19 failed to predict the technology black swans that soon transformed much of the world. Their predictions may also have been blinded by wishful thinking. Ken Olson, for example, founded Digital Equipment Corporation (DEC), and his company's entire business model rested on large mainframe and minicomputers with proprietary operating systems. While IBM's leaders reinvented the company after the PC disrupted the mainframe industry, DEC foundered and eventually vanished.

What black swans are swimming in the marshes now? We may not be able to predict them, but given how suddenly black swans appear and how fast they spread, organizations will need strategic plans that are agile and responsive, not carved in stone. Like Stan and those waterslide riders in the social media project described in this chapter, we're in for a wild river ride.

MyMISLab
Online Simulation

EXTREME VIRTUAL REALITY
A Role-Playing Simulation on Managing a Project to Open a New Business

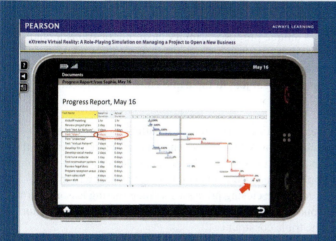

"**J**ust try this on … see what you think," says Theo. You reluctantly put on the headgear and gloves and then enter a dimly lit glass chamber in a room surrounded by computer gear. Theo helps you settle into the swing and clicks the seat belts, saying, "We'll just do a short one." He signals to Trina, sitting at one of the terminals, and you hear the sound of rushing air. An explosion of bright light reaches your eyes, and you're now suspended far above the earth for a VR hot-air balloon ride! You swoop down low over an orchard so you can reach out and grab what feels just like a real orange and then climb high into the stratosphere, where you touch the icy cold metal of an orbiting satellite. Exhilarating! Trina programs the balloon to land gently near the orchard, with a strong orange fragrance.

Theo and Trina are the founders of eXtreme Virtual Reality, a company with plenty of venture capital funding and about 30 employees—mostly programmers and graphic designers. It will open its first locations within a couple of months. Right now, it has several VR adventure scenarios programmed, including the hot-air balloon ride, a breathtaking underwater adventure, and a planetary mission to Mars. They also have one VR training program for health workers in development to practice suturing techniques on virtual patients.

You joined the company as a project manager, and the upcoming opening is your first assignment. Log in when you're ready to get started....

hindsight bias
The human tendency to think an unusual event was (or should have been) predictable, once they know it actually happened.

Chapter Summary

LEARNING OBJECTIVES

1 A project is a temporary endeavor with a unique purpose, primary customer or sponsor, and stakeholders. It also involves an element of uncertainty because the project team takes on tasks that may be unfamiliar. Projects differ from processes, which are repeated activities, and should be managed differently. All projects are subject to the triple constraints of cost, time, and scope.

2 Project management has five major processes: initiating, planning, executing, monitoring and controlling, and closing. The project usually begins with a project charter that authorizes it, and the project manager develops a comprehensive project management plan that includes a work breakdown structure, Gantt chart, and additional subplans as needed to explain how the project will manage scope, human resources, risk, and other areas. The closing processes include sharing lessons learned to document what went right and what could be improved. The project manager is responsible for coordinating the project and managing the triple constraints.

3 Project management software provides tools to help manage all aspects of a project and track its progress. The software can automatically adjust start or end dates for tasks and alert managers when team members are overloaded. It can also compare ongoing progress to a baseline established during the planning phase and provide reports on cost variances.

4 Primary reasons that projects fail include poor project management, lack of executive support, lack of stakeholder involvement, unclear requirements, and technology problems. The opposites of these, such as strong executive support and user involvement, contribute to success. Other success factors include clear objectives, well-defined scope, a team with some project management experience, and a strategy to manage conflicts.

5 Information systems are central to an organization's success, so strategic planning is needed to ensure they continue to align with and support the organization's vision, mission, and goals. The plan should clarify the underlying principles that guide policy development and include topics such as funding models, acceptable-use policies, security requirements, and enterprise architecture planning. The strategic plan should also cover the organization's approach to project portfolio management, explaining how projects are selected and managed. The disaster recovery and business continuity plan should clearly identify the time-sensitive and mission-critical systems that must be recovered first after a disaster and explain how the organization will handle the event. Business continuity issues also include how employees will communicate with one another and where they will work. In addition, planners should take into account major trends in technology and in the industry, including changing laws and government regulations.

6 The human element plays out in strategic planning for information systems because cognitive biases systematically affect the way people process data and make predictions. For example, humans show a confirmation bias in which they tend to ignore or downplay information that doesn't agree with their position or prediction. Strategic planning must also encompass strategies to deal with black swans—events that may be extremely unlikely but can have enormous impact if they do occur. Organizations should be prepared to respond in fleet-footed, agile ways when the unexpected happens.

KEY TERMS AND CONCEPTS

project	Gantt chart	escalation of commitment	cognitive bias
project management	executing processes	acceptable-use policy	confirmation bias
initiating processes	monitoring and controlling	project portfolio	anchoring
project charter	processes	management	availability bias
planning processes	predecessors	program management	black swan
project management plan	critical path	office (PMO)	hindsight bias
deliverables	closing processes	disaster recovery	
scope creep	change management	business continuity	

CHAPTER REVIEW QUESTIONS

12-1. What is a project? How do projects differ from business processes? What three forces constrain every project? How does each constrain a project?

12-2. What are the five processes of project management? What are examples of activities that occur in each process of project management?

12-3. What role does a project manager play in overseeing a project? What skills do project managers need? What are the characteristics of effective project managers?

12-4. How does project management software help plan, track, and manage projects?

12-5. What is the purpose of a Gantt chart? How is it used in project management?

12-6. How is a work breakdown structure used in project management?

12-7. What are the main factors that cause projects to fail? What are the main factors that enable projects to succeed?

12-8. Why is it important for an organization to have a strategic plan for information systems? What major areas are covered in an organization's IT strategic plan?

12-9. What are two IT funding models that organizations use to determine how IT expenses are allocated and

costs recovered? How are IT expenses charged in each model? How does each funding model affect human behavior?

12-10. What is an acceptable-use policy? What are example elements of an acceptable-use policy? Why do organizations implement an acceptable-use policy? How do acceptable-use policies affect human behavior?

12-11. What is project portfolio management? Why do organizations need project portfolio management?

12-12. What is the purpose of a program management office (PMO)? What are typical services provided by a program management office? How does a PMO use dashboards? Why is collecting consistent data a challenge for the PMO?

12-13. What is disaster recovery? What are the major tasks associated with disaster recovery?

12-14. What is business continuity? What are the major tasks associated with planning for business continuity?

12-15. What is a cognitive bias? What are examples of cognitive biases? What is a black swan phenomenon? How do cognitive biases and black swan phenomena affect strategic planning for information systems?

PROJECTS AND DISCUSSION QUESTIONS

12-16. Project management skills are at the top of the list of skills desired by employers, and those with project management credentials are sought by many organizations because they understand the role of the project management discipline in delivering successful projects. The Project Management Institute (PMI) is a leading nonprofit association that sets standards of good practice and certifies project management expertise. Visit www.pmi.org to learn more about the Project Management Professional (PMP) certification and code of ethics. What are the benefits of PMP or similar project management credentials? Click on Business & Government, then click on Case Studies in the left column to locate the Case Study Library, a collection

of brief case studies that highlight the effective use of project management methods. Select and review a case study, and prepare a brief summary of a case that includes a discussion of at least one project management process presented in this chapter.

12-17. The Wild River Water Park is excited to open its new waterslide this summer. Following an established project management methodology, Stan drafted the project charter, illustrated in Figure 12-5, to launch the waterslide social media campaign project. What are the characteristics of Stan's charter that link to factors listed in Figure 12-11 to suggest his project will be successful? What factors do you think need more attention to ensure the success of Stan's project?

12-18. Which project management phase has a component that is neglected in many organizations? Why is this process ignored? Is there one reason or many reasons why this process is ignored? What are the benefits of completing this phase in a thorough manner? Prepare a brief summary that highlights the challenges of this phase of project management.

12-19. In the planning phase, Stan identified the deliverables for his project: a new blog and website, video clips, mass emails, a Facebook page, sample Twitter output, and reports showing the analytics on page views and other metrics. Now he is concerned about scope creep. What is scope creep? How does scope creep affect a project? What steps can Stan take to manage scope creep? Describe three documents he can use to minimize scope creep.

12-20. Recall the characteristics of effective project managers listed in Figure 12-8. How do these characteristics relate to change management? What is change management? Briefly describe the skills that Stan used to resolve the change management issues on his social media campaign project.

12-21. Interview a friend or family member who works for a small to midsized company to learn whether they have a disaster recovery or business continuity plan. Does the plan include data backups or off-site storage of data? Does the plan include a designated recovery site? Prepare a brief summary of your interview to share with classmates.

12-22. Work in a small group with classmates to consider the work breakdown structure for Stan's project. (See Figure 12-7.) What is the purpose of a work breakdown structure? What activities did Stan schedule for the initiation phase? What is the purpose of a kickoff meeting? Describe the activities in the executing phase of the project. Identify which activities are likely to be concurrent and which have predecessor tasks. What is a critical path? Which tasks make up the critical path for Stan's project? Prepare a brief summary of your group discussion.

12-23. Most universities require faculty and students to be aware of and comply with an acceptable-use policy regarding the use of information technology and email. Do you recall agreeing to abide by your school's acceptable-use policy? Work in a small group with classmates to find the policy on your school's website and review it. Does the policy address copyrighted computer software? Computer ethics? Game playing or electronic chatting? What are the consequences of failing to comply with the policy?

APPLICATION EXERCISES

12-24. EXCEL APPLICATION:
Creating a Gantt Chart with Excel

In 1920, Henry Gantt, a U.S. engineer, developed the scheduling and monitoring diagram that bears his name. At the time it was an innovation. Today, the Gantt chart is a standard management tool used by project managers around the world to chart the progress of their projects. Project managers likely use specialized software such as Microsoft Project to create Gantt charts. Another option is to use Excel.

You can create a Gantt chart with Excel by customizing a stacked bar chart. Enter the data from Figure 12-23 into Excel.

- Select the headers and data for Tasks, Start Date, and Duration (Days) and create Stacked Bar Chart.
- Right-click on the chart and click Select Data.
- In Legend Entries (Series), remove Duration (Days).
- Click on Add to add a new series with Series Name "Start Date" and Series values B4:B11.
- Click on Add again to add another new series, with Series Name "Duration (Days)" and Series values C4:C11.

FIGURE 12-23
Data for Gantt chart.

	A	B	C	D
1	Project Management Gantt Chart			
2				
3	**Tasks**	**Start Date**	**Duration (days)**	**End Date**
4	Task 1	6/1/2013	7	6/8/2013
5	Task 2	6/2/2013	5	6/7/2013
6	Task 3	6/3/2013	9	6/12/2013
7	Task 4	6/8/2013	13	6/21/2013
8	Task 5	6/12/2013	22	7/4/2013
9	Task 6	6/13/2013	11	6/24/2013
10	Task 7	6/16/2013	24	7/10/2013
11	Task 8	6/29/2013	14	7/13/2013

Source: Microsoft® Excel, Microsoft Corporation. Reprinted with permission.

- Click on the *y*-axis, select Format Axis, and check the box "Categories in reverse order" to put the rows in order.
- Right-click on the first part of the first stacked bar and choose Format Data Series. Choose Fill, then click No Fill to make those parts of the stacked bar invisible.
- To start the chart at the project's start date, you need to correct that axis. Excel converts June 1, 2013, to 41426, which you can see for yourself if you change the format of the cell to numeric rather than date. Now click on the *x*-axis at the top of the chart, and select Format Axis. Change the Minimum to Fixed, and then enter 41426.
- Finally, delete the legend at the right. Your Gantt chart should look similar to the one in Figure 12-24.

If you need more help, you can find videos that walk you through the process on YouTube by using the search terms "Excel Gantt Chart."

12-25. ACCESS APPLICATION:
Apprentice Project Managers

Your manager asked you to create a database to track the project management skills of a recent group of candidates applying for the project manager position at your company. Create a database that includes two tables: the Applicant table to store applicant data and the Skills table to store the characteristics of effective project managers listed in Figure 12-8. Use the Lookup Wizard to look up values from the Skills table and insert them into the Applicants table to identify each applicant's primary skill (PrimarySkill), secondary skill 1 (SS1), and secondary skill 2 (SS2).

Record the relevant data for the 16 applicants listed in Figure 12-25 that includes rating scores on three skills: leadership, communication, and people. Write a query that identifies the contestant(s) whose primary skill is leadership. Modify the

FIGURE 12-24

Gantt chart created from Excel.

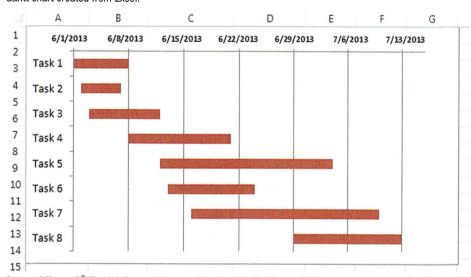

Source: Microsoft® Excel, Microsoft Corporation. Reprinted with permission.

FIGURE 12-25

Rating the applicants on project management skills.

	A	B	C	D	E	F	G	H
1	Applicant_ID	Contestant_Name	PrimarySkill	SS1	SS2	Leadership	Communication	People
2	1	Tyana Alvarado	7	8	5	6	8	6
3	2	Kelly Smith Beaty	1	3	5	10	9	9
4	3	Poppy Carlig	3	5	6	7	8	10
5	4	Stephanie Castagnier	1	2	3	10	9	8
6	5	Nicole Chiu	3	5	2	7	6	10
7	6	Alex Delgado	3	2	6	6	9	10
8	7	Gene Folkes	1	3	5	10	8	9
9	8	Wade Hanson	6	3	2	6	7	9
10	9	David Johnson	1	8	9	10	7	6
11	10	Brandy Kuentzel	1	2	6	10	9	5
12	11	Steuart Martens	8	2	7	7	9	7
13	12	Lisa Mucheru-Wisner	2	1	3	9	10	8
14	13	Clint Robertson	6	5	7	6	8	6
15	14	Mahsa Saeidi-Azcuy	1	3	2	10	6	9
16	15	Anand Vasudev	3	5	8	7	7	10
17	16	James Weir	6	2	3	6	9	8

Source: Microsoft® Access, Microsoft Corporation. Reprinted with permission.

query to identify the applicant(s) whose primary skill is leadership and SS1 is communication. Modify the query to identify the applicants whose critical thinking skills are rated primary, SS1, or SS2.

Create a calculated field in the query to calculate a weighted "Score" for each applicant wherein leadership is weighted highest, communication is weighted second highest, and people is weighted third highest. Use the following formula to calculate score. When you type the expression in the Field row, be sure to put the field names inside brackets.

$$Score = ([Leadership]*3) + ([Communication]*2) + ([People]*1)]$$

Based on this weighted score, which candidate should the company hire to be the project manager?

CASE STUDY #1

Predicting the Future: Gartner's Research Informs Strategic Planning

As the world's leading research and advisory company on all matters relating to information technology, Gartner, Inc., attempts to see far into what is often a hazy future. Founded in 1979, Gartner's thousands of research analysts and consultants rely on in-depth research, surveys, interviews, and countless analytical studies to examine every aspect of information technology. CIOs, business leaders, government agencies, and professional organizations depend on Gartner's research to help them with their own strategic planning.

A major competitive advantage for this company, worth more than $2 billion, is simply size. Gartner analysts are in contact with thousands of organizations worldwide, so they gather information from large and small companies in every industry and also from government agencies and nonprofits. This breadth gives them insights into patterns and trends that others do not have. Daryl Plummer remarked, "Thought leadership is mostly about insight—making connections that others have not yet made…. We have a lot of topics, a lot of customers, and a lot of analysts. Insight flows from those intersections."

Hype Cycles

One of Gartner's most useful planning tools is the legendary "hype cycle," which tracks the evolution of technologies or IT-related business trends. A cycle begins with a technology trigger, often a disruptive innovation or a start-up company that gains attention. The innovation's popularity rises quickly through the "Peak of Inflated Expectations." But then it promptly begins falling into the "Trough of Disillusionment," as organizations learn the pitfalls and real-world challenges. If it survives, the innovation starts coming out on the other side and eventually reaches the "Plateau of Productivity," becoming a standard technology or business practice that makes solid contributions.

The hype cycle analysts also estimate the time period for each prediction because some people adopt certain technologies with breathtaking speed, like smartphones and tablets. Figure 12-26 shows Gartner's hype cycle predictions about several innovations, including when (or whether) they will reach the plateau.

Virtual worlds, discussed in Chapter 8, will be mature technologies that contribute to productivity in 2 to 5 years. But the ecosystems that application programming interfaces (API) will help create, described in Chapter 11, are in an emerging category, in the technology trigger phase. Crowdsourcing (see Chapter 6) is emerging from the trough of disillusionment and is likely to make it the plateau of productivity in just a few years.

"Gamification" is a technology in which game-like features are used to engage people in educational and business scenarios, such as customer interactions and employee training. The online role-playing simulations that accompany each chapter in this text are an example of gamification in education.

Some technologies never make it out of the trough before they reach the plateau of productivity, although they may stay around on the sidelines. Gartner forecasts this future for the open source financial systems that some colleges adopted, particularly because solid commercial systems are available and the open source community may not be able to continue maintaining the software for the few colleges that used it.

How Accurate Are Gartner's Predictions?

Gartner occasionally audits its own predictions, to see when they are off track. In 2005, for instance, Gartner predicted that organizations would routinely be using alternatives to Microsoft's Office suite by 2009. That didn't happen. They also missed the mark when they underestimated the success of Apple's iPhone.

But many other predictions were on target. For example, in 2009, Gartner predicted that major social networks would offer privacy management features by 2013, and that turned out to be correct. But as the case study about Facebook and Instagram at the end of the text explains, more progress is needed.

Although strategic planning is fraught with pitfalls, companies such as Gartner offer a window into the future that can help organizations move in the right directions. Arguably, they also play a role in shaping that future by influencing the choices organizations make.

FIGURE 12-26

The Gartner hype cycle.

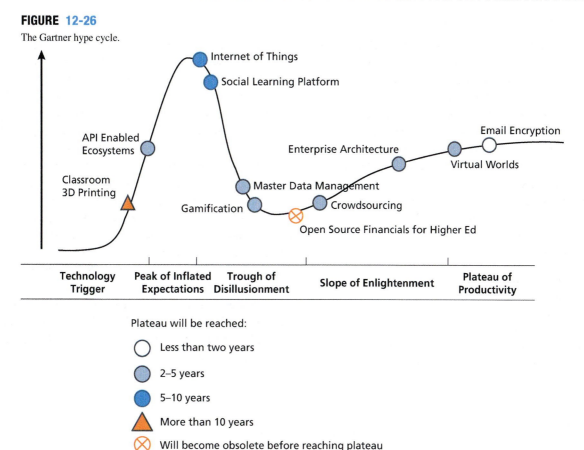

Plateau will be reached:

○ Less than two years

◔ 2–5 years

● 5–10 years

▲ More than 10 years

⊗ Will become obsolete before reaching plateau

Source: Data include innovations drawn from several Gartner hype cycle charts from 2015–2016.

Discussion Questions

12-26. What does this case tell us about the relationship between information systems and strategic planning?

12-27. What other information do company executives need to have beyond the type of information provided by Gartner?

12-28. How could organizations apply the Gartner hype cycle to their strategies?

12-29. What is the value of having Gartner review its past predictions?

Sources: Anderson, A. (2016). *Gartner, Inc.* Hoover's Online, http://subscriber.hoovers.com.proxy1.library.jhu.edu/H/company360/newsList.html?companyId=16598000000000&newsCompanyDuns=097220180, accessed August 22, 2016.

Burton, B., & Allega, P. (3015). *Hype cycle for enterprise architecture, 2015* (No. G00277792). Gartner Research, http://www.gartner.com/document/3103125?ref=solrAll&refval=168515293&qid=486ebd5fbf2ee04869554b098a71768b, accessed August 22, 2016.

Drakos, N., & Sussin, J. (2016). *Hype cycle for social software, 2015* (No. G00277657). Gartner Research, http://www.gartner.com/document/3100230?ref=solrAll&refval=168515286&qid=486ebd5fbf2ee04869554b098a71768b, accessed August 22, 2016.

Fenn, J., & Raskino, M. (July 2, 2013). Understanding Gartner's hype cycles. Gartner Research, ID: G00251964.

Ganly, D, & Montgomery, N. (2015). *Hype cycle for ERP, 2015* (No. G00276492). Gartner Research, http://www.gartner.com/document/3101918?ref=solrAll&refval=168515216&qid=486ebd5fbf2ee04869554b098a71768b, accessed August 16, 2016.

Lowendahl, Jan-Martin. (2015). *Hype cycle for education, 2015* (No. G00277499). Gartner Research, http://www.gartner.com/document/3090218?ref=solrAll&refval=168514847&qid=196b274f84552bb1fb6b2af73adf7f7e, accessed August 22, 2016.

CASE STUDY #2

JetBlue and WestJet: A Tale of Two Software Implementations

The reservation system is more than just automated ticketing for an airline; it is the interface that customers come to know and love (or hate) as they find cheap flights, select seats, upgrade for more leg room, and cash in their frequent flyer points. Two discount airlines, JetBlue and WestJet, both chose to replace their aging systems with software from Sabre, the company that handles reservations for more than 200 other airlines. The similarity in their software implementation projects ends there, however, and the differences between them offer some important lessons.

WestJet's Bumpy Software Implementation

WestJet, Canada's second-largest airline, was in the unfortunate position of going first. Company executives wisely decided to make the cutover during the winter, when passenger count was lower, but they didn't try to lower the volume further by limiting the number of tickets sold. They also decided against warning passengers that a change was coming until the go-live date. WestJet VP Bob Cummings commented, "We didn't want to telegraph dates so a competitor would put on a big fare sale."

For the cutover, WestJet had to transition 840,000 customer accounts to the new system for passengers who had already purchased tickets, migrating the data from WestJet's servers in Calgary to Sabre's servers in Tulsa, Oklahoma. The migration suffered from glitches, and WestJet's website crashed. Customers suffered long waits and angry bloggers posted their complaints.

JetBlue Learns from WestJet

WestJet had kindly invited JetBlue staffers to observe the transition, and the visitors eagerly absorbed the lessons. First, they knew they could avoid the website crash by bringing up a backup site. They also learned to emphasize communications and they alerted customers and other stakeholders weeks ahead. The JetBlue blog was the platform they used to explain how the company was preparing for the software implementation. JetBlue managers wanted to keep the number of passengers low when the cutover occurred, giving employees more time to troubleshoot problems, so it pre-canceled 56 flights and restricted ticket sales on the remainder. To make sure customers didn't have to wait in long phone queues, the company hired 500 temporary reservation agents and kept them on board for two months. Rick Zeni, the JetBlue VP who led the project, said the extra agents were "one of the wisest investments we made."

Although glitches occurred and not all kiosks immediately functioned properly, observers gave JetBlue high marks. The whole company pitched in, and even executives were in the airport in shifts, solving problems and helping out. Changing an airline's reservation system is an enormous project with major risks, one that airlines do very rarely. JetBlue learned from WestJet's missteps, so its "brain transplant" caused minimal disruption.

Once these airlines got past their software implementations, they both fared well. As the numbers in Figure 12-27 illustrate, WestJet and JetBlue both showed higher net profit margins by 2015 compared with the industry medians.

FIGURE 12-27

Comparing JetBlue and WestJet (2015). Data from Hoover's Online.

Metric	WestJet	JetBlue	Industry Median
Annual sales	$2.91B	$6.42B	–
Net profit margin	9.12%	11.35%	1.63%
12-month revenue growth	1.33%	8.63%	3.13%

Discussion Questions

12-30. What are some key differences between the JetBlue and WestJet software implementations?

12-31. What are the advantages and disadvantages of communicating a major project in advance?

12-32. What are the advantages and disadvantages of adjusting business volume during a major business project?

12-33. Beyond not being the first firm to implement a particular piece of software, what other more general lessons apply for software implementation?

Sources: Anderson, A. (2016). *WestJet Airlines Ltd.* Hoover's Online, http://subscriber. hoovers.com.proxy1.library.jhu.edu/H/company360/competitiveLandscape.html?companyId =100814000000000&newsCompanyDuns=252892591, accessed August 22, 2016.
Canada, Y. F. (October 19, 2009). WestJet's "slick new reservation system." The Wings of the Web, Airliners.net, http://www.airliners.net/aviation-forums/general_aviation/read. main/4582650, accessed April 30, 2013.
Carey, S. (2010). Two paths to software upgrade. *Wall Street Journal* (Eastern Edition). *255*(85), B6.
Disgraceful, http://www.flyertalk.com/forum/westjet-frequent-guest/991443-westjet- switching-sabre-2.html, accessed May 25, 2016.
MarketLine. (2016). *JetBlue Airways Corporation SWOT analysis* (pp. 1–8). http:// search.ebscohost.com/login.aspx?direct=true&db=bth&AN=113282582&site=ehost- live&scope=site, accessed August 22, 2016.
MarketLine. (2015). *WestJet Airlines Ltd. SWOT analysis* (pp. 1–8). http://search.ebscohost. com/login.aspx?direct=true&db=bth&AN=110508796&site=ehost-live&scope=site, accessed August 22, 2016.

E-PROJECT 1   Checking on Gartner's Predictions

Gartner makes many very concrete predictions about how different technologies or business practices will fare in the future and even how particular businesses will evolve. For this e-project, conduct an "audit" to determine whether Gartner's predictions panned out.

12-34. In 2009, Gartner analysts were very impressed by Amazon's strategic efforts to become customer-centric and predicted that by 2011 the company would have the highest customer-satisfaction score among Internet retailers on the American Customer Satisfaction Index (ACSI). Visit www.theacsi.org and learn how this organization rates companies on customer satisfaction. Check out

Amazon's performance during the last few years by going to ACSI Results and clicking on Benchmarks by Company. How accurate was Gartner's prediction? How is Amazon doing now?

12-35. Figure 12-28 shows the predictions Gartner made in April 2013 about mobile operating systems and their projected worldwide market shares. How accurate are these so far? You can find market share data at several websites, such as www.netmarketshare.com and gs.statcounter.com.

FIGURE 12-28

Gartner's predictions about market share for mobile operating systems worldwide.

Mobile Operating System	2013	2014	2017
Android	36%	42%	50%
Windows	15%	16%	19%
iOS/MacOS	12%	14%	17%
RIM (Blackberry)	1%	1%	1%
Others	36%	27%	13%

Source: Data from Gartner.com, http://www.gartner.com/newsroom/id/2408515, accessed May 5, 2013.

E-PROJECT 2   Analyzing Airline Performance with Excel Pivot Tables

In this project, you will download departure data for JetBlue and other airlines, using flights that depart from Los Angeles. The project will help you learn to use Excel's Pivot Table function to analyze large data sets.

Download the Excel file Ch12_Airlines. Select all the columns containing data, and then choose Insert/Pivot Chart.

12-36. Drag Carrier Code to the Axis Fields (Categories) box, and drag Departure Delay to the Values box. If the chart is showing the Count of Departure Delay, change that to Sum by clicking on the down arrow, choosing Value Field Settings, and selecting Sum. Which airline had the highest number of delay minutes in this time period?

12-37. Because the airlines have a different number of departures, the average (mean) of delay minutes is a better metric than the sum. Click on the Sum of Departure Delays and select Value Field Settings. Change the setting to average. Which airline has the shortest average departure delay?

12-38. Now let's examine the delays in terms of where planes are headed. Click on the black arrow inside the Carrier Code symbol in the Axis Fields box, and choose Remove Field. (You can also just drag the Carrier Code symbol out of the box to remove it, or just uncheck the box next to Carrier Code in the field list.) Drag Destination airport to that location to break down the average delays by destination. Which destination experienced the largest average departure delay for flights from Los Angeles, and what is the average departure delay for this destination?

12-39. That result could mean that Milwaukee's February weather is partly the cause. But now drag Carrier Code back into the Axis Fields Box, and place it just above Destination Airports. Which airline operates flights from Los Angeles to MKE?

12-40. The file also includes columns that break down the delays based on what caused them. What factor is causing most of the delays for the flights from Los Angeles to Milwaukee?

CHAPTER NOTES

1. *A guide to the project management body of knowledge*, 5th ed. (2013). Newtown Square, PA: Project Management Institute.

2. Project Management Institute website. (2016). http://www.pmi.org, accessed May 9, 2016.

3. Project Management Institute code of ethics and professional conduct. (n.d.) http://www.pmi.org/~/media/PDF/Ethics/PMI-Code-of-Ethics-and-Professional-Conduct.ashx, accessed May 9, 2016.

4. Censer, M. (July 26, 2010). VA cancels financial management system in wake of federal IT squeeze. *Washington Post*, p. X.

5. Hendershot, S. (2015). Reformat and reboot. *PM Network*, 29(5), 8–10.

6. Yadav, V. (2016). A flexible management approach for globally distributed software projects. *Global Journal of Flexible Systems Management*, 17(1), 29–40. http://doi.org/10.1007/s40171-015-0118-9

7. Gomolski, B., & Naegle, R. (2016). *Key concepts in IT financial management: Transparency, budgeting, funding and allocation* (No. G00299489). Gartner Research, http://www.gartner.com/document/3261825?ref=solrAll&refval=167605126&qid=de7f0a3c4819765c4f6665df2be2a4d5, accessed August 22, 2016.

8. Gartner Research. (2016). *Best practices for creating an acceptable use policy to manage risk* (No. G00295872). http://www.gartner.com/document/3188919?ref=TypeAheadSearch&qid=2ac6dcfca20793cd8bc47fc42ba7cae6, accessed August 22, 2016.

9. IBM social computing guidelines: Blogs, wikis, social networks, virtual worlds, and social media. (n.d.). IBM, http://www.ibm.com/blogs/zz/en/guidelines.html, accessed May 9, 2016.

10. Lannon, P. G., & Schreiber, P. M. (2016). BYOD policies: Striking the right balance. *HR Magazine*, 61(1), 71–72.

11. Half of U.S. firms lack formal BYOD policy. (2016). *Information Management Journal*, 50(1), 13.

12. Londis, D. (March 14, 2013). How BYOD can complicate support. InformationWeek.com, http://www.informationweek.com/byte/personal-tech/consumer-services/how-byod-can-complicate-support/240150754, accessed August 22, 2016.

13. Handler, R.A. (2016). *Applying project portfolio management with scarce resources to optimize business value primer for 2016* (No. G00292982). Gartner Research, http://www.gartner.com/document/3187625?ref=solrAll&refval=167621988&qid=cf6d8f7fbef5a940f5db3c04d5c445e3, accessed August 22, 2016.

14. Schoen, M. (2016). *Seven best practices for a highly effective PMO* (No. G00300627). Gartner Research http://www.gartner.com/document/3245617?ref=TypeAheadSearch&qid=f41e1d460046690c8758737418919467, accessed August 22, 2016.

15. Overby, S. (September 16, 2005). Lessons from Hurricane Katrina: It pays to have a disaster recovery plan in place. *CIO.com*, http://www.cio.com/article/11931/Lessons_from_Hurricane_Katrina_It_Pays_to_Have_a_Disaster_Recovery_Plan_in_Place, accessed August 22, 2016.

16. Slater, D. (2015). Business continuity and disaster recovery planning: The basics. *CSO Online*, http://www.csoonline.com/article/2118605/disaster-recovery/pandemic-preparedness-business-continuity-and-disaster-recovery-planning-the-basics.html, accessed August 22, 2016.

17. Blair, R., & Morency, J. P. (2016). *10 strategic questions to ask potential DRaaS providers* (No. G00302860). Gartner Research, http://www.gartner.com/document/3262217?ref=solrAll&refval=167662704&qid=1c93a0a4e74ba51f05bc0bd91b674839, accessed August 22, 2016.

18. Cearley, D. W., Burke, B., & Walker, M. J. (2016). *Top 10 strategic technology trends for 2016* (No. G00291954). Gartner Research, http://www.gartner.com/document/3231617?ref=solrAll&refval=167664853&qid=79eac2bb15ddd0fab8e747e43814c2db, accessed August 22, 2016.

19. Pike, G. H. (2013). Internet sales tax proposals back on the table. *Information Today*, 30(4), 24.

20. Grossman, L. (2016). Inside Apple's code war (cover story). *Time*, 187(11), 42–49.

21. Buehler, R., Griffin, D., & Ross, M. (1994). Exploring the "planning fallacy": Why people underestimate their task completion times. *Journal of Personality and Social Psychology*, 67, 366–381.

22. Yudkowsky, E. (2008). Cognitive biases potentially affecting judgement of global risks. In Bostrom, N., & Cirkovic, M. (Eds.), *Global catastrophic risks*. Oxford University Press: Oxford, UK, 91–119.

Case Studies

CASE STUDY #1
Facebook and Instagram: Privacy Challenges

Facebook—along with Instagram, the photo-sharing site that the company purchased in 2012—struggles with thorny privacy and ownership issues (Figure 1-1). The site's loyal users rely on it to share news, photos, videos, and special moments with their friendship networks, but their personal information and preferences can leak out in ways they often don't understand.

FIGURE 1-1
Facebook Statistics

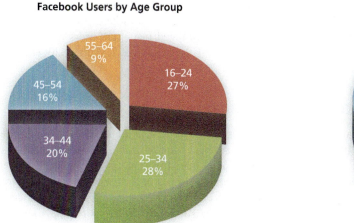

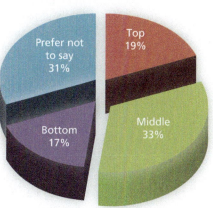

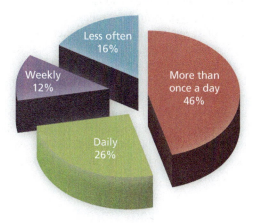

Data drawn from Global Web Index. (2016). *Facebook Profile Report*. London, UK http://www.globalwebindex.net, accessed July 15, 2016.

Facebook's Privacy Policies: A Moving Target

Facebook frequently changes its privacy policies, and every tweak can either reassure users that their data is safe or cause further alarm. In 2005, when the site was called "Thefacebook," the policy was very simple: *No personal information that you submit will be available to any user of the website who does not belong to at least one of the groups specified by you in your privacy settings*. Years later, the privacy policy stretches to thousands of words in legalese. Lawyers write much of this text, using language they hope will satisfy regulators and privacy advocates but that often confounds users.

One change that users called "creepy" happened in 2007, when Facebook launched a service that could track people's actions on third-party websites and broadcast that information to their Facebook friends. Users objected to this lack of control, and Facebook soon dropped the practice. In 2010, the company decided to have the user's privacy account settings default to "everyone," so that anyone could view the information unless the user proactively altered the privacy settings to limit access to friends. After privacy advocates protested, Facebook reversed course and changed the default to more restrictive settings.

The Facebook Places service, launched in 2010, raises additional concerns about privacy. This service allows you to "check in" so others can see your current location on a map. Facebook defaulted the setting to "friends only," having learned from experience that a default to "everyone" would trigger objections. The service also offers you the option to broadcast your location to other users who happen to be nearby but are not in your friends network; however, that was prudently disabled by default.

Just after Facebook purchased Instagram in 2012, the company promptly announced a change in Instagram's privacy and ownership policies to take effect in 2013. According to the new policy, Facebook claimed a perpetual right to license all public Instagram photos, allowing it to sell the photos to companies for advertising purposes. Imagine for a moment how Instagram might sell your vacation photos to the hotel where you stayed to use in its ads without paying you or even notifying you. Outraged Instagram users brought on an online firestorm, and Facebook backed off some of the language. The company still claimed the right to associate sponsored ads with users' photos, though.

Social Marketing and S-Commerce

Facebook is in a unique position for marketing because the site has so much information about what you like, who your friends are, and what *they* like. While search engine marketing relies on the keywords you enter, social marketing can tap into a deeper understanding of your behavior patterns. It can also draw on whatever influence you have on your friends and turn products into overnight sensations through viral marketing. For instance, Facebook introduced "Sponsored Stories" as a way for advertisers to let your friends know whenever you click the "Like" button on their brand or check in at one of their stores.

With more companies establishing a Facebook presence, more Facebook users are going through those pages to make purchases, often based on the "likes" of their network friends. This kind of social commerce (s-commerce) is a powerful marketing strategy, making the privacy issues even more important. Privacy advocates argue that there should be some way for users to opt out of Sponsored Stories. Many people don't want their "likes" to be shared and don't want their faces appearing in ads targeting their friends.

Facebook offered to settle with Facebook users whose name or image appeared in Sponsored Stories without their permission. More than 614,000 people filed a claim, and they each received about $15. Facebook retired Sponsored Stories and launched "interest-based ads," which offers opt-out. This approach takes into account not only the actions you perform on the Facebook site but your visits to other websites outside of the social network with which Facebook partners.

Facebook Apps from Third Parties

The third-party companies that develop applications for Facebook have also come under fire for privacy breaches. These companies make agreements with Facebook so that users can access social games and activities. However, some applications were collecting information about users in a way that violated Facebook's own privacy rules, all without the user's permission. In one case, the information was transmitted to a company that compiles dossiers on individuals to use for targeted advertising. Facebook disabled the applications involved in the scandal, and the company continues to block apps that violate its policies.

Social gaming and online marketing have become so complex, however, that it is possible some of the third-party developers did not even know they were breaching privacy rules. Facebook's policies prohibit the third-party apps from transferring personal information to marketers, but the technical challenges of complying are daunting.

Challenges Ahead

Managing privacy becomes more complicated for Facebook as the site's capabilities expand. The myriad privacy settings confuse users, although Facebook has made headway by revising its interface, trying to make each setting more comprehensible (Figure 1-2). The company's default and recommended settings may permit more sharing than you prefer, but you can further restrict access to each category of information to just friends, specific friends, friends of friends, or just yourself. Facebook also introduced a "hide" setting so you can identify certain friends in your network who should not be allowed to view photos or other categories.

The fact that users don't have much control over what other people upload is another challenge for privacy. Once a friend uploads a photo that tags your image with your name, the friend's privacy settings have control over who sees that photo on his or her page, and those settings might cause trouble. Facebook added a "Report/Remove tag" feature so a user who objects to a photo posted by someone else can at least remove the tag that identifies him or her and also ask the poster to take the photo down.

With a worldwide footprint, complying with privacy laws in all the countries in which users live is another immense challenge. European regulators, for example, insist that Facebook should safeguard user data according to the EU's privacy rules. They also recognize, however, that laws vary from one country to the next in the European Union, so they are trying to harmonize the maze of privacy rules for online data. In the meantime, legal battles continue, as European authorities slam Facebook with lawsuits and fines for violating data privacy laws.

Finally, a nagging challenge is whether fickle fans will get "Facebook fatigue" and begin dropping Facebook in favor of other social networks or possibly choose to use none at all. Growth in active users has slowed, while growth rates for services such as Pinterest and Tumblr are increasing.

Privacy could well become a much bigger threat to Facebook's future, as more people decide to opt out altogether. Despite all the tweaks to improve privacy controls and the reassurances about data protection, people may decide that liberal information sharing is just too risky, whether on Facebook or any other social network.

The risk is certainly real. Facebook users were shocked to learn that the company maintains "shadow" profiles on each of them. These invisible profiles combine data that users willingly upload to the site with other data Facebook obtains about them. For example, a friend might upload an address book that contains your private cell phone number; Facebook links that to your shadow profile.

FIGURE 1-2

Examples of Facebook privacy options.

Examples of Facebook Privacy Options
Setting the audience that can see posts by me.
Determining who can comment on my posts.
Deciding who can see different aspects of my profile.
Adjusting settings for interest-based ads.
Determining who can see my social actions that may be paired with ads on the site.
Reviewing tags that people add to my posts before they appear.

To earn revenue, however, Facebook must monetize its most valuable asset: user data. If advertisers can't benefit from Facebook's "big data" for marketing, they won't pay for ads. This puts Facebook in an awkward position.

Since its launch in 2004, Facebook has continually broken new ground. Perhaps it is not surprising that founder Mark Zuckerberg admitted candidly, "Basically, any mistake you think you can make, I've probably made it, or will make it in the next few years."

Discussion Questions

1. How might privacy and user considerations differ for an application such as Facebook, which is used primarily by individual users, compared with an application such as an ERP system that is used primarily by corporations?
2. How does the default selection of sharing versus not sharing information affect the subsequent choices of individual users?
3. What is the likely perspective of marketers on privacy issues at Facebook?
4. How do app developers fit into the social media industry?

Sources

Beaubien, G. (2013). Instagram modifies privacy policy after sparking Internet outrage. *Public Relations Tactics*, *20*(1), 6.

Global Web Index. (2016). *Facebook Profile Report*. London, UK, http://www.globalwebindex.net, accessed July 16, 2016.

Hill, K. (June 27, 2013). Only 614,994 Facebook users to get paid for appearing in "Sponsored Story" ads, http://www.forbes.com/sites/kashmirhill/2013/06/27/only-614994-facebook-users-to-get-paid-for-appearing-in-sponsored-story-ads/, accessed September 9, 2016.

Lomas, N. (2016, March 2). Facebook faces German antitrust privacy probe. *TechCrunch*, http://social.techcrunch.com/2016/03/02/facebook-faces-german-antitrust-privacy-probe/, accessed September 9, 2016.

Matsa, K. E. (2016). *Facebook, Twitter play different roles in connecting mobile readers to news*, http://www.pewresearch.org/fact-tank/2016/05/09/facebook-twitter-mobile-news/, accessed September 9, 2016.

Pogue, D. (2013). Term of confusion. *Scientific American*, *308*(3), 35.

Rainie, L., Smith, A., & Duggan, M. (2013). Coming and going on Facebook. Pew Research Center, http://pewinternet.org/Reports/2013/Coming-and-going-on-facebook.aspx, accessed May 17, 2016.

Ribeiro, J. (2016). Facebook faces restrictions in France on data transfer to US, tracking of users. *CIO.com*, Facebook faces restrictions in France on data transfer to US, tracking of users, accessed September 9, 2016.

CASE STUDY #2
Enabling the Sharing Economy: The Case of Uber Technologies

Uber Technologies offers an outstanding example of how an information system can become a strategic enabler for what is called the "sharing" economy. Uber is known best as a ride-hailing service, in which passengers can summon a nearby Uber driver using Uber's mobile app. The model enables people to share underutilized assets, matching up someone who needs a lift with a person with a car and time to spare.

Uber started out as a luxury limo service in San Francisco but quickly blossomed into "everyone's private driver" as the concept took off. The key element for this model is the information system that serves as the platform for its e-marketplace.

How Do Uber Apps Work?

Uber developed two apps, one for drivers and the other for riders, and both rely heavily on the mobile phone's GPS capabilities. The rider's app shows a map with a pushpin indicating current location and defaults the pickup point to that spot. Riders can change that to a different address if needed and then pick the type of vehicle that they need, such as four-passenger car or something larger. The map displays the locations of nearby drivers, and the software estimates how many minutes it will take the nearest driver to arrive at the pickup point. Riders can also enter their destination and get a price estimate before requesting a driver. Once the rider requests a car and a driver accepts the request, the software shows details, including the driver's name and photo, as well as the type of car. The rider can text or phone the driver if needed, perhaps to ask if it's OK to bring along a dog.

The app developed for drivers includes a "Go online" button to indicate that the driver is ready to accept riders. When the driver's location is the closest Uber car to a rider making a request, the app will signal the driver, allowing 15 seconds for the driver to accept the request. If the driver doesn't respond, the software signals the next closest driver. The driver who accepts the request can bring up the navigation screen to plot the best route to the pickup point. Drivers tap "Arriving now" in the app to send a text to the rider's phone. Drivers also tap to start and end the trip, so the software collects the details to determine price.

Uber's technology also handles all the payments from riders, charging the credit card they initially signed up with, so riders do not need to carry cash or pay by credit card on the spot. To help ensure quality, Uber's software includes a reputation system in which both drivers and riders can rate one another after each trip, and Uber can block access to the app for poor ratings.

Expanding the Apps

Uber continues to expand and improve its information systems, enabling further capabilities. For example, the company launched UberPOOL, which lets riders split the cost of a ride with other people headed in the same direction, as a kind of carpooling.

It also encourages other companies to take advantage of its application programming interfaces (API). Grocery stores, for instance, can embed UberRUSH into their online checkout app to offer customers on-demand delivery. A luggage company that developed GPS-equipped suitcases lets people track their bag's location, and the company embeds Uber technology in its own app so that lost bags can be returned to their owners promptly. The app also detects when a passenger with the company's carry-on lands at the airport and then scans for available Uber drivers.

Uber and the Sharing Economy

Uber, along with other companies that develop computer-based platforms to enable peer-to-peer connections, supports a sharing economy that raises many new issues. Ride-hailing platforms offer tremendous potential benefits, including reduced traffic, emissions, accidents, and drunk driving. Reliable transportation is another important advantage, particularly for the suburbs, low-income areas, and other locations far from hotels and airports, where taxis gather. Some decide they don't need a car of their own and can instead rely on Uber and mass transit. Uber also offers very flexible employment opportunities, as drivers decide when, where, and how long to work.

Controversies, however, plague Uber, and legal battles erupt frequently. Damage to the taxi industry, for example, is severe in many cities, and taxi companies protest loudly about Uber's unfair advantages. Taxis are highly regulated in most cities, with stiff licensing fees and requirements and caps on the number of cabs. Cities also pass laws to protect certain industries; one requires people who want a limo to request it at least an hour in advance so limos don't compete with taxis. Some city governments refuse to allow Uber to operate or slap strict requirements that the company resists. Uber stopped serving Austin, Texas, when the government demanded that Uber drivers be fingerprinted. In many cases, Uber launches in a city even though the city's laws forbid the model, relying on its popularity to pressure city politicians to make regulatory changes.

Uber categorizes its drivers as "independent contractors," which means they are not subject to minimum wage requirements or workplace safety laws, and they don't receive any benefits. Uber's employment approach also protects the company from liability if drivers have accidents. Some argue that this employment arrangement exploits workers who can't unionize.

Uber Takes on the World

Despite the controversies, Uber forges ahead to new frontiers, launching its platform and attracting riders and drivers in cities around the world. It operates in dozens of locations in Europe, the Middle East, Asia, South America, and Africa and pioneers models that fit the location. In Indonesia, for instance, the Uber platform offers uberMotor so riders can hail a driver on a motorbike, a popular transport option in the traffic-clogged streets of Jakarta.

Uber faces stiff competition and challenges, as other companies develop apps that also support the sharing economy, taxi companies protest, and governments restrict or block the model. In China, for instance, Uber competes with a Chinese ride-hailing company that has an enormous lead along with a $1 billion investment from Apple.

The information systems that enable the sharing economy propel companies in industries beyond transportation, as people test out ways to share underutilized resources with one another. For example, Airbnb offers a platform for sharing overnight accommodations, and Figure 2-1 lists more examples. Time will tell how this model grows and matures and which sharing platforms survive.

Discussion Questions

1. Uber has two different apps: one for the drivers and the other for the riders. How are these different? Briefly describe how each works and identify the benefits to each of these kinds of users.
2. Identify at least three ways Uber is expanding its apps and describe how this expansion might give Uber a competitive advantage.

FIGURE 2-1

Examples of sharing platforms.

Sharing Platform	Description
Airbnb	E-marketplace for people to list, discover, and book accommodations.
Neighborhoods	Platform for people to list tools and other household items to share with neighbors.
Lyft	Ride-hailing platform, competitor to Uber.
TaskRabbit	Platform to connect people with skilled workers in the neighborhood to do chores.

3. Despite the advantages that Uber offers, its shared-economy approach brings disadvantages. Identify at least three disadvantages of Uber's approach and describe how these affect the market and workers.

4. Consider the sharing of underutilized resources and the opportunities for businesses in that model. Would you work for a company using that model? Why or why not? If you owned such a company, what would you do to address the disadvantages of the sharing-economy? Describe how each of your proposed actions might address the disadvantages.

Sources

Chafkin, M. (2015). What makes Uber run? *Fast Company, 199*, 110–142.

Hoover's Online. (2016). *Uber Technologies, Inc.,* http://subscriber.hoovers.com.proxy1.library.jhu.edu/H/company360/overview.html?companyId=13895459&newsCompanyDuns=013895459, accessed September 9, 2016.

Malhotra, A., & Van Alstyne, M. (2014). The dark side of the sharing economy … and how to lighten it. *Communications of the ACM, 57*(11), 24–27.

McKenna, B. (2016). Digital platform more than taxi service: Is Uber an app economy paradigm? *Computer Weekly*, 4–6.

Nica, E., & Potcovaru, A.-M. (2015). The social sustainability of the sharing economy. *Economics, Management & Financial Markets, 10*(4), 69–75.

Our story. (n.d.). Uber. https://www.uber.com/our-story/, accessed May 20, 2016.

CASE STUDY #3
Apple: Can the Company Pull Off Another Disruptive Innovation?

No company in history has captured the world's imagination quite the way Apple has. Especially since 2001 when Apple released the first iPod, the company has enjoyed a long string of triumphs (Figure 3-1). Its share price soared and the company's market value topped $500 billion in 2016, making it one of the most valuable companies in the world.

But Apple's share price tumbled by more than 20% following the release of Apple Watch in 2015. What happened? Is the world's high-tech darling running out of steam, with no new blockbuster products on the horizon? The company is still enormously profitable, but margins are shrinking, and in 2016, the company reported its first drop in revenue in 13 years. Is the slide due to wildly unrealistic expectations, or is Apple really a "broken" company, as some analysts suggest? With Steve Jobs's death in 2011, Tim Cook became CEO, and some wonder whether Apple's magic is fading.

Apple's Innovations and the "Blue Ocean" Strategy

Apple's huge successes have hinged on the company's ability to come up with innovations and strategies that create new markets for products, the so-called "blue ocean" approach. The iPod and iTunes combination, for example, brought digital music to the masses as it gave consumers something new that was effortless to use. The combination did not just replace audio cassette players and the clunky MP3 players from other manufacturers. It was a disruptive innovation that upended the music business, which had relied heavily on album sales based on CDs. Music lovers quickly abandoned the albums for single songs and retired their CD players for a much smaller device that could hold thousands of songs.

The iPad is another innovation that tapped a blue ocean and created a new market. While tablets had been around, none had the appeal and usability of the iPad, with its intuitive interface, small size, and long battery life. Within just two years of its launch, Apple sold more than 100 million iPads. More than 25% of those were sold to people who had never purchased an Apple product before. People over age 65 who don't use a regular computer are among the iPad's most promising new customers.

Network Effects and Switching Costs

Besides emphasizing elegant design and usability, Apple creates competitive advantage through network effects and high switching costs. The iPhone, for example, benefited from

FIGURE 3-1

Sample Apple innovations and adjusted share prices, 2000–2016.

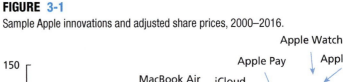
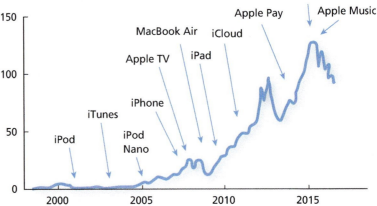

its early lead in market share, which attracted thousands of developers who built apps to make the iPhone even more valuable to users. While apps for Androids quickly caught up with the volume of iPhone apps, Apple gained an early head start.

Apple also integrates its products tightly, making it much easier to stick with the whole product line. The millions of people who store their music on iCloud, for example, have easy access to it from their Apple devices. Because of this, they might be reluctant to purchase non-Apple tablets or smartphones to avoid the heavy switching costs, or at least they would think twice.

Other high-tech industries tend to move toward openness and modular products, so consumers can match one brand with another without too much difficulty. For example, you can insert a USB drive from any manufacturer into any computer with a USB port. Whether Apple can preserve its integrated approach that tends to lock its customers into the company's product line is an open question.

Missteps with Apple Maps

Apple is well known for brilliant product design, but the company has made an occasional blunder. In 2012, for example, Apple launched its own mapping application to compete with Google Maps and other navigation aids. Apple had high hopes for Apple Maps, which included new features such as integration with its personal assistant, Siri.

Unfortunately, Apple Maps launched with many errors and out-of-date information, and users mocked the application with slideshows of humorous mistakes. "Apple brings back Woolworths" showed a store that had been closed for years. The application even misplaced Apple's own stores on the maps.

In Australia, police complained that the flawed maps were actually dangerous, and drivers should avoid them in certain geographic areas. Some people following the maps found themselves stranded in a deserted park with scorching temperatures and no food or water, many miles away from the town they were trying to reach. They were forced to walk long distances before they were able to reach a location where they had phone reception. Apple CEO Tim Cook apologized for all the glitches and promised to fix them.

Apple's Legal Battles for Patent Protection

Apple is notoriously secretive about its designs, and the company also defends its patents with lawsuits. The company once sued Microsoft, claiming that Windows illegally copied the Macintosh graphical user interface. That suit was unsuccessful, partly because Apple originally took much of the design from Xerox, which had done the early research.

The iPhone's major competitor is Samsung, the South Korean manufacturer that makes smartphones that use Google's Android operating system. Apple sued Samsung for patent infringement and a California court initially awarded Apple an astounding $1.05 billion in damages. Samsung is appealing the case all the way to the Supreme Court, and analysts worry that the court's decision could hinder innovation and consumer choice. The U.S. patent system is extremely old, and the outcome for cases like this one can be hard to predict. Intellectual property rights are important, but so are competition and consumer interests.

What Is Apple's Next "Blue Ocean"?

In 2015, Apple broke new ground with the Apple Watch and quickly dominated the smartwatch market. The watch offers features to support text messaging, medical sensors, news headlines, and music. But shipments fell the following year, suggesting that while many consumers like the product, it isn't a "must have."

Another area that seems ripe for Apple's style of disruptive innovation is the TV business. Consumers constantly grumble about paying high prices for hundreds of cable channels they don't watch, clunky set-top boxes, and a coffee table full of complicated remote controls. Some subscribers are canceling their cable or satellite subscriptions out of frustration and relying instead on services such as Netflix, Hulu, and free network TV for entertainment.

With its cash on hand, Apple also has many opportunities that aren't quite so disruptive but that might lead to growth in new areas. Possibilities include investment in original entertainment or experiments with self-driving cars. With the drop in Apple's share price, investors do not seem confident that Apple is capable of pulling off one more major disruptive innovation. But the company has done it before, and it may have many more surprises in store.

Discussion Questions

1. What are the key factors that make Apple successful, and how does each of these accomplish that?
2. When Apple sued Samsung to protect its intellectual property rights, it won. What might be the adverse effects on consumers of Apple's victory in the smartphone market?
3. During a student's college career, a wide variety of information systems are used in his or her classes and in his or her personal life. Is this non-integrated abundance of information systems another "blue ocean" market, and how might a company like Apple exploit such an opportunity?
4. Is Apple so successful that it cannot fail? What might Apple do to weaken its market leadership and lose its competitive advantage?

Sources

Alstyne, M. W. V., Parker, G. G., & Choudary, S. P. (2016). Pipelines, Platforms, and the New Rules of Strategy. *Harvard Business Review, 94*(4), 54–62.

Carr, A. (2013). What you don't know about Apple. *Fast Company, 174*, 35–38.

Eddy, N. (2016, January 25). Apple, Google Self-Driving Car Projects Impress Daimler CEO. *InformationWeek*, http://www.informationweek.com/it-life/apple-google-self-driving-car-projects-impress-daimler-ceo/d/d-id/1324037, accessed September 9, 2016.

Fox, J. (January 29, 2013). Apple versus the strategy professors. *Harvard Business Review*, HBR Blog Network, http://blogs.hbr.org/fox/2013/01/apple-versus-the-strategy-prof.html, accessed September 9, 2016.

Gross, G. (2016). Supreme Court to hear Samsung's appeal in Apple design patents case. *CIO.com*, http://www.cio.com/article/3046417/supreme-court-to-hear-samsungs-appeal-in-apple-design-patents-case.html, accessed September 9, 2016.

Hayward, A. (2016). Apple TV vs. Amazon's Fire TV: The gaming match-up. *Macworld—Digital Edition*, 16–23.

LaPorte, N. (2016). Revenge of the Nerds. *Fast Company, 205*, 68–96.

Thompson, N. (December 10, 2012). Apple Maps flaw could be deadly, warn Australian Police. *CNN Tech*, http://www.cnn.com/2012/12/10/tech/apple-maps-australia-flaw, accessed September 9, 2016.

Vizard, S. (2016). Apple must shake off perception it has lost its edge. *Marketing Week*, 8–10.

CASE STUDY #4
Managing the Federal Government's IT Project Portfolio

Tracking how much the U.S. federal government spends on IT investments and how well or poorly that money is spent are not simple tasks. Projected federal spending on IT projects for FY 2017 tops $80 billion, but that figure does not include everything, such as spending on classified IT projects.

How well is this money being spent? Much of it goes toward operating and maintaining older legacy systems still in use. A large chunk is spent on projects to implement new systems with advanced functionality. But according to reports by the Government Accounting Office, the picture on those projects is mixed, with many going way over budget, failing to meet deadlines, or failing entirely. For example:

- The Office of Personnel Management finally canceled its "Retirement Systems Modernization Program" after years of unsatisfactory progress and an outlay of more than $230 million. The system was supposed to relieve the retirement claims backlog, which took more than 150 days for processing.
- The Department of Health and Human Services' Healthcare.gov website suffered a disastrous rollout, and the whole project encountered cost increases, schedule slips, and delayed functionality.
- Human resource management at the Department of Homeland Security involves more than 400 fragmented systems, and the project to implement an integrated and updated approach, begun in 2003, has been stalled for many years.
- Rather than continue with a faltering project, the Department of Defense canceled the Air Force Expeditionary Combat Support System after spending more than $1 billion.

Although the terminated projects are no longer costing money, many projects still under way are struggling. There also appears to be considerable duplication for ongoing projects, with some agencies unaware that another agency has a similar IT project under way.

Overseeing the IT Portfolio

To improve accountability and reduce duplication, the Office of Management and Budget (OMB) requires agencies to do IT portfolio reviews, looking for redundant projects that should be terminated. The process is called "PortfolioStat," and it helps agencies develop better strategies for managing a portfolio that could include hundreds of ongoing projects. The reviews are designed to uncover wasteful duplication on a variety of information systems, such as email, financial systems, or collaboration tools. They also flag mismanaged projects with unclear objectives.

Efforts to Reduce Costs

PortfolioStat tracks each agency's progress toward several important goals intended to reduce wasteful government IT spending. One goal involves greater use of cloud computing. OMB encourages agencies to implement cloud-based services, although some agency officials resist the effort, citing security concerns. Cloud vendors are not always aware of federal security requirements, but as the services mature, cloud computing should reduce costs.

Another major goal is to consolidate federal data centers, which multiplied into the thousands as agencies operated independently. As of 2015, 3,179 data centers closed down, saving billions of dollars. The General Services Administration led the way, closing 88 of its 124 data centers. Progress takes time, however, partly because agencies must inventory all their applications before they can consolidate. They also need to evaluate opportunities to consolidate across agencies, and not just combine their own data centers.

Streamlining procurement can also dramatically reduce costs, and another goal is for the federal government to buy as one customer rather than separate departments. CIOs at the agencies are also taking on more responsibility for overseeing IT purchases.

The IT Dashboard

The government tracks its project portfolio using the publicly accessible IT dashboard (www.itdashboard.gov). Agencies submit detailed information about their IT investments and the projects that make them up; visitors to the website can then slice and dice the data. They can drill down to individual investments in each agency, viewing charts and graphs of costs, schedules, and overall ratings of each project's status by the agency's chief information officer. Green means the project is on track, yellow indicates that it needs attention, and red points to significant concerns. The charts in Figure 4-1 illustrate the output for the Department of Education.

Visitors can download various data files from the dashboard for further analysis using Excel or other analytical tool. For example, one download includes a column to identify

FIGURE 4-1

Sample IT dashboard output for the Department of Education.

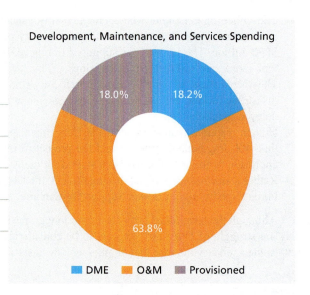

Investment Highlights

Total FY2016 Spending	**$689M**
Projects on Schedule	**75%**
Projects on Budget	**81%**
Major Investments	**40**
FY2016 Spending on Majors	**87%**

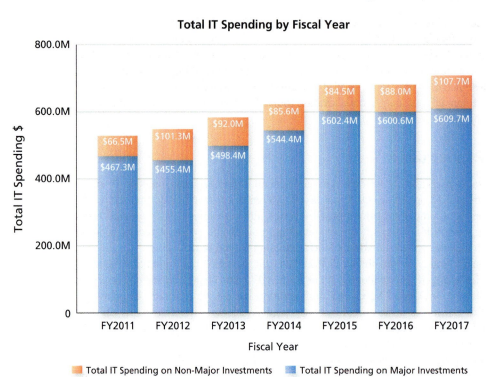

Source: IT Dashboard, USA.Gov.

FIGURE 4-2

Breakdown of software development methods used in federal agency IT projects.

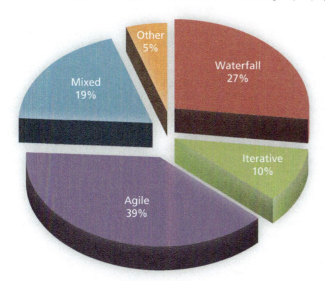

Source: File downloaded from itdashboard.gov, accessed May 23, 2016.

the type of software development method used for projects (if they involve development) (Figure 4-2). Federal CIOs encourage agile and iterative methods and also want to restrict waterfall methods to shorter time frames to avoid their high failure rates. Dashboards like this should make the government's project portfolio more transparent, but they also have drawbacks and critics. Some project managers complain about the bureaucratic overhead and the time-consuming job of collecting data from every team leader to find out the status of each project. Managers know that people report differently as well. Many want to avoid showing up as red, and they don't want to stay in the yellow for very long, so they can be reluctant to share bad news. Top-level management may not be aware that disaster looms until the deadline nears and there is no way to hide the problems.

The dashboard is only as useful as the data submitted by the agencies, and the quality of the data they submit is mixed. Much of it is out of date by the time it appears on the dashboard. Also, many agencies don't submit complete reports, or they submit questionable ratings. For example, the General Accounting Office (GAO) found that many agencies judged their projects to be less risky than they probably were. The sheer volume of projects is a challenge, especially for the larger agencies with thousands of ongoing projects.

Can the PortfolioStat sessions and an IT dashboard with better quality data lead to proper oversight of federal IT spending and rein in costs? An OMB initiative called TechStat was launched in 2010, with the goal of reviewing the viability of risky projects with cost overruns or missed deadlines. The meetings were intended to identify needed improvements, or to agree to just terminate the project if necessary. Optimism was initially high, but the number of TechStat sessions trailed off over time, suggesting they were not achieving the OMB's goals.

Whether PortfolioStat meets the same fate as TechStat remains to be seen. But expert portfolio management backed up by a dashboard with high quality and timely data is an essential ingredient for a well-functioning, 21st-century government.

Discussion Questions

1. What unique challenges does the federal government face in managing its IT project portfolio?
2. The federal government CIO focused primarily on asking agencies to identify high-risk projects. What other information might be valuable for the CIO to receive from agencies?
3. The current communication effort is focused on identifying and managing high-risk projects across federal agencies. What are other ways in which the CIO could use communications across federal agencies to improve performance?
4. What are the relevant human considerations in reporting high-risk projects?

Sources

Douglas, M. (August 3, 2010). Federal CIOs TechStat initiative seeks to diagnose troubled IT initiatives and deliver quick treatment. *Public CIO*, http://www.govtech.com/gt/articles/767303?id=767303, accessed September 9, 2016.

Government Accountability Office. (2016). *2016 annual report: Additional opportunities to reduce fragmentation, overlap, and duplication and achieve other financial benefits* (No. GAO-16-375SP). Washington, DC, http://www.gao.gov/products/GAO-16-375SP, accessed September 9, 2016.

Government Accountability Office. (2015). *High-risk series: An update* (No. GAO-15-290). Washington, DC, http://www.gao.gov/products/GAO-15-290, accessed September 9, 2016.

Malykhina, E. (March 28, 2013). Federal CIO announces PortfolioStat 2.0. *Information Week*, http://www.informationweek.com/government/information-management/federal-cio-announces-portfoliostat-20/240151930, accessed April 1, 2013.

Marks, J. (March 12, 2013). Measuring open government. *Emerging Tech*, http://www.nextgov.com/emerging-tech/emerging-tech-blog/2013/03/measuring-open-government/61828/, accessed September 9, 2016.

Office of Management and Budget. (2016). *Analytical perspectives budget of the U.S. government, fiscal year 2017*. Washington, DC, https://www.whitehouse.gov/sites/default/files/omb/budget/fy2017/assets/spec.pdf, accessed September 9, 2016.

Petty, A. (March 5, 2013). Federal government continues to lose billions to waste, fraud, and abuse annually. GovWin Network, http://govwin.com/apetty_blog/federal-government-continues-to-lose/843038, accessed April 1, 2013.

Powner, D. A. (2015). *Information technology additional actions and oversight urgently needed to reduce waste and improve performance in acquisitions and operations* (No. GAO-15-675T). Washington, DC, http://www.gao.gov/products/GAO-15-675T, accessed September 9, 2016.

Ziadeh, B. A. (February 19, 2016). Agency dashboards added to analytics.usa.gov. *GCN*, https://gcn.com/articles/2016/02/19/agency-analytics.aspx, accessed September 9, 2016.

Glossary

A

acceptable-use policy   An organizational policy that describes what employees are allowed to do with IT resources and what activities are disallowed; employees agree to the policy before gaining access to IT resources.

agile software development methods   Development strategies involving cohesive teams that include end users and in which many activities occur simultaneously rather than sequentially to accelerate delivery of usable software.

AJAX   A mix of technologies that builds on JavaScript and draws on live data to create interactive online displays.

anchoring   The tendency for people to rely too heavily on one piece of information to adjust their estimates, even if it is irrelevant.

application programming interface (API)   Set of routines and protocols that specify how software components should interface with one another in a standardized way.

application software   The type of software used to support a wide range of individual and business activities, such as transaction processing, payroll, word processing, and video editing.

artificial intelligence (AI)   The capability of some machines to mimic aspects of human intelligence, such as learning, reasoning, judging, and drawing conclusions from incomplete information.

ASCII code   A code that defines how keyboard characters are encoded into digital strings of ones and zeros.

assistive technologies   Devices and software that help people with disabilities, such as screen readers for the visually impaired.

autonumbering   Process that assigns incremental numbers to records as they are created to ensure that each record has a unique primary key.

availability bias   The tendency for people to judge the likelihood of events based on how readily they come to mind rather than their actual likelihood.

B

bandwidth   The maximum amount of information in bits per second that a particular channel can transmit.

batch processing   The process of sequentially executing operations on each record in a large batch.

benchmark   A reference point used as a baseline measurement.

best of breed   An approach used by organizations in which they procure the best systems for each application, regardless of the vendor, and then build interfaces among them.

big data   Collections of data that are so enormous in size, so varied in content, and so fast to accumulate that they are difficult to store and analyze using traditional approaches.

bitcoins   An online virtual currency that is not issued by a government and instead is valued based on market demand; transactions are difficult to trace.

bits per second (bps)   The measurement of transmission speed, defined as the number of bits transmitted each second; each bit is a single zero or one, and a string of 8 bits makes up a byte.

black swan   Used to describe an extremely rare event that is difficult or nearly impossible to predict, but which can have an immense impact in areas such as technology, finance, and science; black swans pose enormous challenges for strategic planners.

blog   Short for "web log" and used to facilitate collaboration and knowledge sharing. Posts are displayed in reverse chronological order so that the most recent appears on top.

Bluetooth   A technology that uses radio waves for connectivity, commonly used for wireless connections over very short distances.

Bluetooth low-energy (BLE) beacon   Low-cost, battery-powered device that broadcasts Bluetooth signals to nearby smartphones; used in proximity marketing at retail stores, conferences, sports stadiums, and other locations.

botnet   A combination of the terms *robot* and *network* referring to a collection of computers that have been compromised by malware and used to attack other computers.

bullwhip effect   Describes the distortions in a supply chain caused by changes in customer demand, resulting in large swings in inventory levels as the orders ripple upstream from the retailer to the distributor and manufacturer.

business continuity   The maintenance of the organization's operations in the event of disaster or disruption.

business intelligence   The information managers use to make decisions, drawn from the company's own information systems or external sources.

business process   A set of activities designed to achieve a task; organizations implement information systems to support, streamline, and sometimes eliminate business processes.

business process management (BPM)   Focuses on designing, optimizing, and streamlining business processes throughout the organization.

business process reengineering (BPR)   The design and analysis of workflows in an organization with the goal of eliminating processes that do not add value.

business to business (B2B)   E-commerce relationship in which businesses can buy and sell products or services online to one another.

business to consumer (B2C)   E-commerce relationship in which businesses offer products for online sale to consumers.

byte   Measurement unit for computer storage capacity; a byte holds eight zeros and ones and represents a single character.

C

CAPTCHA   A test created by software developers that the visitor must pass before continuing to register or enter the site; designed to thwart software bots.

cascading style sheets (CSS)   The part of a website template that controls the fonts, colors, and styles that appear when an editor identifies some text as a page heading, a paragraph title, or some other style.

central processing unit (CPU)   The brain of a computer, which handles information processing, calculations, and control tasks.

change control process   A process organizations use to manage and prioritize requests to make changes or add new features to an information system.

change management   A structured approach to the transition employees must make as they switch from their existing work processes to new ones, especially with the introduction of a new information system.

chief information officer (CIO)   The person who heads the department responsible for managing and maintaining information systems and ensuring they support the organization's strategic goals.

click-through rate (CTR)   A metric used to assess the impact of an online ad; computed as the number of visitors who click on the ad divided by the number of impressions.

clickstream data   Business intelligence data that includes every click by every visitor on a website, along with associated data such as time spent on the page and the visitor's IP address.

client-server network   A type of network in which the workload for running applications is shared between the server and the client devices, such as desktop computers, laptops, or smartphones.

closing processes   Processes that formally end the project in an orderly way; they include a signoff by the sponsor confirming that all deliverables have been received and accepted.

cloud computing ICT architecture in which users access software applications and information systems remotely over the Internet rather than locally on an individual PC or from servers in the organization's data center.

coaxial cables Wired medium, initially used for cable TV, consisting of a single inner conductor wire (typically copper) surrounded by insulation, which is then surrounded by a mesh-like conductor.

code review A peer review process in which programmers check over one another's work to ensure its quality.

cognitive bias A common human tendency to make systematic mistakes when processing information or making judgments; cognitive biases can distort strategic planning.

commercial off-the-shelf (COTS) Commercially available computer software that is ready to buy, install, and use.

communities of practice Groups of individuals who come together to learn from one another and share knowledge about their professions; they typically rely on online discussion forums, shared workspaces, wikis, blogs, and other social media.

competitive advantage Anything that gives a firm a lead over its rivals; it can be gained through the development and application of innovative information systems.

computer Any electronic device that can accept, manipulate, store, and output data and whose instructions can be programmed.

confirmation bias The human tendency to choose information to examine that supports the person's view, but ignore data that might refute that view.

consumer to business (C2B) E-commerce relationship in which individual consumers can sell products or services to businesses.

consumer to consumer (C2C) E-commerce relationship in which individual consumers can buy and sell to one another over the Internet.

content management system Software used to manage digital content in collaborative environments. The web content management system supports teams that develop and maintain websites.

cookie A small text file left on a website visitor's hard drive that is used to personalize the site for the visitor, or track web activities.

creative destruction What happens in an industry when disruptive innovations threaten the established players.

crisis management team The team in an organization that is responsible for identifying, assessing, and addressing threats from unforeseen circumstances that can lead to crisis situations.

critical path The longest path through the project, which identifies those tasks that can't be delayed without affecting the finish date. Monitoring tasks that fall along the critical path is especially important.

crowdsourcing Delegating tasks to large diffuse groups or communities who often volunteer their contributions.

customer relationship management (CRM) Encompasses the strategies, processes, and information systems an organization uses to build and maintain relationships with its current and prospective customers.

customer relationship management (CRM) system An information system used to build customer relationships, enhance loyalty, and manage interactions with customers.

D

dashboard A graphical user interface that organizes and summarizes information vital to the user's role and the decisions that user makes.

data Individual facts or pieces of information.

data definition Specifies the characteristics of a field, such as the type of data it will hold or the maximum number of characters it can contain.

data dictionary Documentation that contains the details of each field in every table, including user-friendly descriptions of the field's meaning.

data mining A type of intelligence gathering that uses statistical techniques to explore records in a data warehouse, hunting for hidden patterns and relationships that are undetectable in routine reports.

data model A model used for planning the organization's database that identifies what kind of information is needed, what entities will be created, and how they are related to one another.

data steward A combination of watchdog and bridge builder, a person who ensures that people adhere to the definitions for the master data in their organizational units.

data warehouse A central data repository containing information drawn from multiple sources that can be used for analysis, intelligence gathering, and strategic planning.

data-driven decision making Decision making that draws on the billions of pieces of data that can be aggregated to reveal important trends and patterns.

database An integrated collection of information that is logically related and stored in such a way as to minimize duplication and facilitate rapid retrieval.

database management system (DBMS) Software used to create and manage a database; it also provides tools for ensuring security, replication, retrieval, and other administrative and housekeeping tasks.

database schema A graphic that documents the data model and shows the tables, attributes, keys, and logical relationships for a database.

deliverables The products, documents, or services that will be delivered to the sponsor during the course of a project.

demand forecast accuracy (DFA) The difference between forecasted and actual demand.

digital rights management (DRM) Technologies that software developers, publishers, media companies, and other intellectual property owners use to control access to their digital content.

digital subscriber lines (DSL) Technology that supports high speed two-way digital communication over twisted pair phone lines.

direct implementation A type of implementation in which all the modules of a new information system are launched at the same time and the old system is turned off; also called the "big bang" approach.

disaster recovery The procedures and documentation the organization puts into place to prepare for a disaster and recover the technical infrastructure.

disruptive innovation A new product or service, often springing from technological advances, that has the potential to reshape an industry.

distributed denial of service (DDoS) An attack in which computers in a botnet are directed to flood a single website server with rapid-fire page requests, causing it to slow down or crash.

document management systems Systems that manage electronic documents, often converted from paper sources, making them searchable and easily transmitted.

Domain Name System (DNS) The hierarchical naming system that maps a more memorable URL to the actual IP address.

E

e-commerce The buying and selling of goods and services over the Internet or other networks, encompassing financial transactions between businesses, consumers, governments, or nonprofits.

e-discovery The processes by which electronic data that might be used as legal evidence are requested, secured, and searched.

e-government The application of ICT to government activities, especially by posting information online and offering interactive services to citizens.

e-learning A varied set of instructional approaches that all depend on ICT, especially the Internet, to connect trainees with learning materials and also with their instructors and other trainees.

e-marketplace A website that facilitates transactions by bringing together buyers and sellers from all over the world.

ecosystem An economic community that includes the related industries making complementary products and services, the competitors themselves, the suppliers, and also the consumers.

electronic data interchange (EDI) An electronic bridge between partner companies in a supply chain that is used to transmit real-time information about orders, inventories, invoices, and other data.

encryption Technique that scrambles data using mathematical formulas so that it cannot be read without applying the key to decrypt it.

enterprise architecture (EA) A roadmap created by an organization to describe its current situation and where it should head to achieve its mission, focusing on business strategy and the technology infrastructure required to achieve it.

enterprise content management (ECM) An overarching approach to organizing and managing all different kinds of content throughout their life cycles, from creation to updating, archiving or deleting, to include documents, images, videos, web pages, and other types.

enterprise resource planning (ERP)   Integrated application suite to support the whole enterprise that includes modules to manage financials, human resources, supply chain, customer relationships, and other business processes.

escalation of commitment   The tendency to continue investing in a project, despite mounting evidence that it is not succeeding; often comes about because people mistakenly let sunk costs affect decision making rather than weighing the value of further investment.

Ethernet   A communication protocol widely used for local area networks.

ethics   A system of moral principles that human beings use to judge right and wrong and to develop rules of conduct.

executing processes   All the coordinating efforts that ensure the tasks on the work breakdown structure are carried out properly.

expert system   Software that mimics the reasoning and decision making of a human expert, drawing from a base of knowledge about a particular subject area developed with the expert's assistance.

explicit knowledge   Knowledge that can be documented and codified, which is often stored in information systems, on websites, in spreadsheets, or in handbooks and manuals.

eXtensible Business Reporting Language (XBRL)   Part of the XML family of standardized languages specialized for accounting and business reports; tags identify data elements to make them transparent and also computer-readable.

extract, transform, and load (ETL)   A common strategy for drawing information from multiple sources by extracting data from its home database, transforming and cleansing it to adhere to common data definitions, and then loading it into the data warehouse.

extreme programming (XP)   A team-based agile method that features frequent releases of workable software, short time boxes, programmers who work in pairs, and a focus on testing.

F

feasibility study   Part of the information system planning process that examines whether the initiative is viable from technical, financial, and legal standpoints.

field   An attribute of an entity. A field can contain numeric data or text, or a combination of the two.

file transfer protocol (ftp://)   A URL component that indicates the resource is a file to be transferred.

financial management system   Enterprise information system that supports financial accounts and processes, including accounts payable, accounts receivable, procurement, cash management, budget planning, assets, general ledger, and related activities.

firewall   A defensive technical control that inspects incoming and outgoing traffic and either blocks or permits it according to rules the organization establishes. The firewall can be a hardware device or a software program.

focused niche strategy   A company strategy that involves differentiating a product or service for a particular market niche.

forecasting   A statistical decision support tool used to analyze historical trends and other business intelligence to estimate some variable of interest, such as customer demand.

foreign keys   Primary keys that appear as an attribute in a different table are a foreign key in that table. They can be used to link the records in two tables together.

functionally dependent   For each value of the table's primary key, there should be just one value for each of the attributes in the record, and the primary key should determine that value; the attribute should be functionally dependent on the value of the primary key.

G

Gantt chart   A graphic showing the tasks on the work breakdown structure along with each task's projected start and finish dates.

global positioning systems (GPS)   Electronic devices that receive signals from orbiting satellites that transmit time and location data; GPS devices help drivers navigate and keep managers in touch with their transportation fleets.

goal seeking   A decision support tool, often based on an Excel model, in which the user sets a target value for a particular variable, such as profit/loss, and tells the program which variable to change to try to reach the goal.

group decision support system (GDSS)   Collaborative technology that helps groups brainstorm and make decisions in face-to-face meetings, led by facilitators. Participants can contribute anonymously via their computers.

H

hashtag   Microblogging tool invented by web users in which posts on a similar topic all include a keyword prefixed by a #.

hertz (Hz)   The number of cycles per second of a wave.

hierarchical website architecture   Website structure in which the top-level home page contains links to second-level pages, which then link to further relevant pages.

hindsight bias   The human tendency to think an unusual event was (or should have been) predictable, once they know it actually happened.

human capital   The competencies and knowledge possessed by the organization's employees.

human capital management (HCM)   Encompasses all the activities and information systems related to effectively managing an organization's human capital. The HCM information system includes applications and modules with the employee as the central element.

human resources management (HRM) system   Typically the heart of the HCM system, the HRM system tracks each employee's demographic information, salary, tax data, benefits, titles, employment history, dependents, and dates of hire and termination.

hypertext markup language (HTML)   The original language used to create web pages; HTML specifies the web page's format using tags in angle brackets that browsers can interpret and put into reader-friendly output.

hypertext transfer protocol (http://)   A URL component that specifies the resource is a web page containing code the browser can interpret and display.

I

IMAP (Internet mail access protocol)   A protocol for handling incoming email.

in-memory computing   Refers to the use of primary storage as the main place information is stored, rather than in secondary storage devices such as hard drives, to vastly increase speed.

incident response plan   A plan that an organization uses to categorize a security threat, determine the cause, preserve any evidence, and also get the systems back online so the organization can resume business.

infomediary   Focuses on informing visitors and empowering them with aggregated information about products from different suppliers.

information   Data or facts that are assembled and analyzed to add meaning and usefulness.

information and communications technology (ICT)   The term encompasses the broad collection of information processing and communications technologies, emphasizing that telecommunication technology is a significant feature of information systems.

information privacy   The protection of data about individuals.

information security   A term that encompasses the protection of an organization's information assets against misuse, disclosure, unauthorized access, or destruction.

information system   A system that brings together four critical components to collect, process, manage, analyze, and distribute information; the four components are people, technology, processes, and data.

information technology (IT)   The hardware, software, and telecommunications that comprise the technology component of information systems; the term is often used more broadly to refer to information systems.

infrastructure as a service (IaaS)   Cloud hosting service provides computer resources such as virtual servers, storage, and processing power, allowing clients to configure the resources as they choose.

initiating processes   Processes that lay the groundwork for the project by clarifying its business value; setting its objectives; estimating the project's length, scope, and cost; identifying team members; and obtaining approval.

instant messaging (IM)   Also called "chat." IM consists of real-time text-based interactions over a network.

instructional designer   The person on an e-learning development team who brings the knowledge and skills about what strategies work best for e-learning.

intellectual capital (IC)   All the intangible assets and resources of an enterprise that are not captured by conventional accounting reports, but still contribute to its value and help it achieve competitive advantage.

intellectual property (IP)   Intangible assets such as music, written works, software, art, designs, movies, creative ideas, discoveries, inventions, and other expressions of the human mind that may be legally protected by means of copyrights or patents.

intelligent agents   Software programs or "bots" that are sent out to conduct a mission and collect data from web pages on behalf of a user.

intelligent character recognition (ICR)   Software that can interpret handprinted text written on paper forms.

interactive voice response (IVR)   A technology that facilitates access to the database from signals transmitted by telephone to retrieve information and enter data.

Internet Corporation for Assigned Names and Numbers (ICANN)   The nonprofit organization charged with overseeing the Internet's naming system, establishing policies, and resolving disputes.

Internet of Things (IoT)   The network of physical objects that contain sensors and technology that enable them to collect and exchange data.

Internet Protocol Version 6 (IPv6)   The next generation protocol for the Internet, which will support far more IP addresses compared to the current scheme.

intranet   An organization's private web space. It relies on TCP/IP and web browsers, but it is password-protected and accessible only to authorized individuals through the organization's portal.

iterative software development methods   Strategies that compress the time horizon for software development, partly to reduce the impact of changing business needs and the resulting rework. They focus on the time available until the next release, or iteration, and the development team determines how many of the requirements it can deliver in that timeframe.

J

JavaScript   A language used to add interactivity to web pages.

K

key performance indicators (KPIs)   The quantifiable metrics most important to the individual's role and the organization's success.

knowledge management (KM)   A set of strategies and practices organizations use to become more systematic about managing intellectual capital. It is also a field of study in which researchers investigate all the roles these intangible assets play, how they contribute to competitive advantage and productivity and how human behavior interacts with efforts to capture and share knowledge.

L

learning management system (LMS)   An information system used to deliver e-learning courses, track student progress, and manage educational records. Such systems also support features such as online registration, assessments, collaborative technologies, payment processing, and content authoring.

learning object   A self-contained digital resource embedded in an e-learning course that can be edited and reused for other purposes.

legacy systems   Older information systems that remain in use because they still function and are costly to replace.

local area network (LAN)   A network that connects devices such as computers, printers, and scanners in a single building or home.

low cost leadership strategy   A company strategy that involves offering a similar product at a lower price compared to competitors.

M

malware   Malicious software designed to attack computer systems.

management information systems (MIS)   The study of information systems—how people, technology, processes, and data work together. Also used to describe a special type of information system that supports tactical decision making at the managerial level.

market basket analysis   A statistical technique that reveals customer behavior patterns as they purchase multiple items.

mashup   An approach to aggregating content from multiple internal and external sources on customizable web pages that relies on Web 2.0 technologies.

massive open online course (MOOC)   An online course usually offered by a college or university through a third party for free or very low cost, with open enrollment and often very large volume.

master data management   An approach that addresses the underlying inconsistencies in the way employees use data by attempting to achieve consistent and uniform definitions for entities and their attributes across all business units.

media richness   A measure of how well a communication medium can reproduce all the nuances and subtleties of the messages it transmits.

metadata   Data about data that clarifies the nature of the information.

microblogging   A form of blogging in which the posts are quite short and especially suitable for mobile devices. As in a blog, the entries appear in reverse chronological order.

microformats   A set of formats that rely on the XML family of standards to represent metadata in HTML code and that support electronic exchange of business cards, calendar appointments, and other kinds of data.

microwave transmission   The technology involving signals in the gigahertz range that are transmitted to relays in the line of sight.

middleware   Software used as a bridge to integrate separate information systems and synchronize data across multiple systems.

mobile commerce (m-commerce)   The use of wireless, mobile devices to conduct e-commerce.

monitoring and controlling processes   Processes that track a project's progress from start to finish, pinpointing any deviations from the plan that must be addressed.

Moore's Law   A principle named for computer executive Gordon Moore, which states that advances in computer technology, such as processing speed or storage capabilities, doubles about every 2 years.

multidimensional website architecture   Website structure with multiple links to pages at all levels, allowing visitors multiple paths through the site.

multifactor authentication   A combination of two or more authentications a user must pass to access an information system, such as a fingerprint scan combined with a password.

N

n-tier   Type of network architecture in which several servers, specialized for particular tasks, may be accessed by a client computer to perform some activity, such as retrieving a bank balance.

natural laws and rights   An ethical system that judges the morality of an action based on how well it adheres to broadly accepted rules, regardless of the action's actual consequences.

near field communication (NFC)   A set of standards that supports communication between mobile devices when the two are very near one another.

network   A group of interconnected devices, such as computers, phones, printers, or displays, that can share resources and communicate using standard protocols.

network effects   The increased value of a product or service that results simply because there are more people using it.

neural network   An information system that attempts to mimic the way the human brain works; often used to spot suspicious activity in financial transactions.

normalization   A process that refines entities and their relationships to help minimize duplication of information in tables.

NoSQL DBMS   Flexible database management systems that do not require a fixed data schema with clear data definitions and that do not enforce strict constraints; data storage is typically spread across many servers.

O

object-oriented programming   A type of software programming that focuses on "objects" rather than lists of instructions and routines to manipulate data.

online analytical processing (OLAP)   Software that allows users to "slice and dice" or drill down into massive amounts of data stored in data warehouses to reveal significant patterns and trends.

open source software   A type of software whose licensing terms comply with criteria such as free distribution, so other people can access the source code to improve it, build upon it, or use it in new programs.

operating system (OS)   The category of system software that performs a variety of critical basic tasks, such as handling device input and output, maintaining file structures, and allocating memory.

operations management The area of management concerned with the design, operation, and improvement of the systems and processes the organization uses to deliver its goods and services.

optical character recognition (OCR) The capability of specialized software to interpret the actual letters and numbers on a page to create a digital document that can be edited rather than a flat picture.

optical fiber Cables that transmit bits by means of light pulses along a glass or plastic fiber instead of electrical signals over a conductor; ideally suited for long distances.

optical scanners Electronic devices that capture text or images and convert them to digital format.

optimization An extension of goal seeking in which the user can change many variables to reach some maximum or minimum target, as long as the changes stay within the constraints the user identifies.

P

packet switching A technology used by networks in which data is broken into segments, called packets, for transmission. The packets contain information about their destination and position in the whole message, and they are reassembled at the receiving end.

parallel implementation A type of implementation in which the new system is launched while the old one it is replacing continues to run so output can be compared.

payment gateway An e-commerce application that facilitates online shopping by mediating the interconnections to the merchant's bank, the bank or other entity that issued the card, and then back to the original website to approve or decline the purchase.

peer-to-peer network A type of network in which there is no central server and computers can share files, printers, and an Internet connection with one another.

phased implementation A type of implementation in which the modules of a new information system are launched in phases rather than all at once.

phishing An attempt to steal passwords or other sensitive information by persuading the victim, often in an email, to enter the information into a fraudulent website that masquerades as the authentic version.

planning processes The processes in project management that focus on planning how the project will be executed.

platform as a service (PaaS) Cloud hosting service provides computer resources and also operating systems, application development environments, and often a database management system.

portal A gateway that provides access to a variety of relevant information from many different sources on one screen; for an enterprise, the portal provides a secure gateway to resources needed by employees, customers, and suppliers.

power of buyers The advantage buyers have when they have leverage over suppliers and can demand deep discounts and special

services. This is one of Porter's five competitive forces.

power of suppliers The advantage sellers have when there is a lack of competition and they can charge more for their products and services. This is one of Porter's five competitive forces.

predecessors The tasks that must be completed in a project before a particular task can begin.

predictive analytics Data mining approaches and statistical techniques used to predict future behavior, especially to unlock the value of business intelligence for strategy.

presence awareness IM software feature that allows users to display their current status to their contacts, colleagues, or buddy list.

primary activities Activities directly related to the value chain process by which products and services are created, marketed, sold, and delivered.

primary key A field, or a group of fields, that makes each record unique in a table.

private branch exchange (PBX) Technology that manages all the office phone lines, voice mail, internal billing, call transfers, forwarding, conferencing, and other voice services.

process diagrams Graphical representations that trace how each process that a new information system will support operates from beginning to end.

product differentiation strategy A company strategy that involves adding special features to a product or unique add-ons for which customers are willing to pay more.

program management office (PMO) The part of an organization that oversees all the projects going on throughout the organization and provides project management training, software, and support.

programming language An artificial language used to write software that provides the instructions for the computer about how to accept information, process it, and provide output.

project A temporary activity launched for a specific purpose, to carry out a particular objective.

project charter A document that authorizes a project that includes a clear statement of objectives, estimated start and end dates, the names of the relevant people and their roles, a tentative budget, criteria for success, and other pertinent information.

project management A systematic approach to project planning, organizing, and managing resources, resulting in a project that successfully meets its objectives.

project management plan The roadmap and guide for executing a project that includes information such as an organizational chart, a detailed description of the work to be performed, information about the schedule, details about meetings and reviews, success metrics, and notations about any information systems or project monitoring tools that will be used.

project portfolio management A continuous process that oversees all the projects for an organization, selecting which projects to pursue and which ones to terminate.

proxy An intermediary server that receives and analyzes requests from clients and then directs them to their destinations; sometimes used to protect privacy.

public key encryption A security measure that uses a pair of keys, one to encrypt the data and the other to decrypt it. One key is public, widely shared with everyone, but the other is private, known only to the recipient.

R

radio frequency identification (RFID) A technology placed on tags with small chips equipped with a microprocessor, a tiny antenna to receive and transmit data, and sometimes a battery that stores information on the tagged object's history.

random access memory (RAM) A computer's primary temporary storage area accessed by the CPU to execute instructions.

ransomware A type of malware that encrypts the victim's files, and the attacker demands a ransom payment to provide the codes to unlock them.

rapid application development (RAD) A strategy in which developers quickly bring up prototypes to share with end users, get feedback, and make corrections before building the fully functional version.

record A means to represent an entity, which might be a person, a product, a purchase order, an event, a building, a vendor, a book, a video, or some other "thing" that has meaning to people. The record is made up of attributes of that thing.

referential integrity A rule enforced by the database management system that ensures that every foreign key entry actually exists as a primary key entry in its main table.

relational database The widely used database model that organizes information into tables of records that are related to one another by linking a field in one table to a field in another table with matching data.

request for information (RFI) A request sent to software vendors containing a high level description of the information system an organization needs, so that vendors can describe their products that may fit.

request for proposal (RFP) An invitation to software companies to submit a formal proposal, including a detailed description of their products, services, and costs. The RFP details the requirements developed in the analysis phase and also includes information about the organization's architecture, staffing, and other relevant details.

requirements analysis The process by which stakeholders identify the features a new information system will need and then prioritize them as mandatory, preferred, or nonessential.

requirements definition document (RDD) A document that specifies the features a new information system should have, prioritized by stakeholders. It also includes assumptions and constraints that affect the system, such as the need to migrate and possibly reformat data from an existing system.

resource description framework (RDF) Part of the XML family of standards, RDF is used to describe online resources and their properties for the semantic web.

risk matrix A matrix that lists an organization's vulnerabilities, with ratings that assess each one in terms of likelihood and impact on business operations, reputation, and other areas.

rivalry among existing competitors The intensity of competition within an industry. Intense rivalry can reduce profitability in the industry due to price cutting or other competitive pressures. This is one of Porter's five competitive forces.

S

scalability A system's ability to handle rapidly increasing demand.

scope creep A term that refers to the way in which features are added in an uncontrolled way to a project, often without considering the impact on the budget or timeline.

Scrum An agile process for software development that relies on tightly knit, cohesive teams that do "sprints" of 2 to 4 weeks each.

search engine optimization (SEO) An Internet marketing strategy used to increase the quantity and quality of traffic from search engines, often by improving the site's position in result lists.

semantic web A web with meaning, in which online resources and their relationships can be read and understood by computers as well as human beings.

semi-structured information Information category that falls between structured and unstructured information. It includes facts and data that show at least some structure, such as web pages and documents, which bear creation dates, titles, and authors.

sentiment analysis A capability of specialized software to scan text input surveys, blogs, or other user-generated content and classify the opinions as pro, con, or neutral toward the company or product.

sequential website architecture Website structure that guides visitors step by step through a transaction, survey, or learning module.

serious game A game designed for useful purposes beyond pure entertainment.

service-oriented architecture (SOA) A set of design principles in which systems are assembled from relatively independent software components, each of which handles a specific business service.

shadow system Smaller databases developed by individuals outside of the IT department that focus on their creator's specific information requirements.

Sharable Content Object Reference Model (SCORM) A set of standards that govern how e-learning objects communicate with the LMS on a technical level, so a user can import a SCORM-compliant object to any LMS that supports the standard.

shared workspace An area on a server in which team members can post documents, maintain membership lists, feature news and announcements, and collaborate on edits and updates.

shopping cart software Computer software that tracks purchases as customers navigate an e-commerce site and click "add to cart" as they go. The software tallies the purchase, calculates taxes based on the customer's location, computes shipping costs, and also posts a discount if the customer enters a valid promotional code.

single sign-on A gateway service that permits users to log in once with a single user ID and password to gain access to multiple software applications.

SMTP server Mail server using the simple mail transfer protocol; handles outgoing email.

social capital The number and quality of all the relationships an organization's employees maintain, not just with one another, but with clients, customers, suppliers, and prospective employees.

social engineering The art of manipulating people into breaking normal information security procedures or divulging confidential information.

social network analysis (SNA) A technique that maps and measures the strength of relationships between individuals and groups, represented as nodes in the network. The measures provide insights into network clusters and the roles different people play as leaders or connecting bridges to other networks.

social networking sites Online communities of people who create profiles for themselves, form ties with others with whom they share interests, and make new connections based on those ties.

software The computer component that contains the instructions that directs computer hardware to carry out tasks.

software as a service (SaaS) A type of commercially available software that is owned, hosted, and managed by a vendor and accessed by customers remotely, usually via the Internet.

source code All the statements that programmers write in a particular programming language to create a functioning software program.

strategic enabler The role information systems play as tools to grow or transform the business, or facilitate a whole new business model.

structural capital The knowledge stored as documentation, often electronically, about business processes, procedures, policies, contracts, transactions, patents, research, trade secrets, and other aspects of the organization's operations.

structured information Facts and data that are reasonably ordered, or that can be broken down into component parts and organized into hierarchies.

Structured Query Language (SQL) A standard query language, widely used to manipulate information in relational databases.

subject matter expert The person on an e-learning development team who knows what content should be included in the course and possesses the content expertise.

supply chain management (SCM) Strategies that optimize the flow of products and services from their source to the customer.

support activities Activities performed as part of the value chain model that are not primary; support activities include administration and management, human resources, procurement, and technology support.

sustaining technologies Technologies that offer improvements to streamline existing processes and give companies marginal advantages.

switching costs Costs that customers incur when they change suppliers.

system software The type of software that controls basic computer operations such as file management, disk storage, hardware interfaces, and integration with the application software.

systems development life cycle (SDLC) The process that describes the seven steps in the life of an information system: planning, analysis, design, development, testing, implementation, and maintenance.

systems integrator A consultant who ensures that the hardware and software components of an information system work together when they come from different vendors.

T

table A group of records for the same entity, such as employees. Each row is one record, and the fields of each record are arranged in the table's columns.

tacit knowledge Knowledge that encompasses the insights, judgment, creative processes, and wisdom that come from learning and long experience in the field, as well as from many trials and errors.

tag cloud A visual depiction of keywords related to the search, with font size and position indicating relevance.

talent management As part of the HCM system, the talent management module focuses on the employee life cycle, including recruitment, performance evaluations, career development, compensation planning, e-learning, and succession planning after retirement or departure.

TCP/IP Abbreviation for Transmission Control Protocol and Internet Protocol; used for Internet communications.

telepresence The impression created when remote participants in an interactive video meeting are almost life-sized and vividly clear; useful for sensitive negotiations.

text mining A technique used to analyze unstructured text that examines keywords, semantic structures, linguistic relationships, emotion-laden words, and other characteristics to extract meaningful business intelligence.

third-party cookies Small text files that a website leaves on a visitor's computer that are not deposited by the site being visited; used by ad networks to track customer behavior across all their client websites.

threat of new entrants The threat new entrants into an industry pose to existing businesses; the threat is high when start-up costs are very low and newcomers can enter easily. This is one of Porter's five competitive forces.

threat of substitutes The threat posed to a company when buyers can choose alternatives that provide the same item or service, often at attractive savings. This is one of Porter's five competitive forces.

top-level domain The last string of letters in a URL that indicates the type of organization or country code.

transistor A small electrical circuit made from a semiconductor material such as silicon.

twisted pair wires The most common form of wired media, these wires consist of thin, flexible copper wires used in ordinary phones.

U

unified communications (UC) Technology that integrates multiple communications channels and applications into a single interface, which is accessible from many different devices.

unified procurement An approach used by organizations in which they prefer systems from a single vendor, especially to avoid the need to build interfaces.

uniform resource locator (URL) The unique global address for a web page or other resource on the Internet.

unstructured information Information that has no inherent structure or order and the parts can't be easily linked together.

usability Refers to the ease with which a person can accomplish a goal using some tool, such as a website, a mobile phone, or a kiosk.

use case diagram Diagrams that show how different types of users will interact with the system.

user-generated content (UGC) The content contributed to a system by its users.

utilitarianism An ethical system that judges whether an act is right or wrong by considering the consequences of the action, weighing its positive effects against its harmful ones.

utility software The category of system software that includes programs to perform specific tasks that help manage, tune, and protect the computer hardware and software.

V

value chain model A model developed by Michael Porter that describes the activities a company performs to create value, as it brings in raw resources from suppliers, transforms them in some way, and then markets the product or service to buyers.

version control software A type of software that tracks versions of the source code during development, enforcing checkout procedures to prevent developers from writing over one another's files.

virtual reality Describes what people experience when some of their sensory input is not from the real world, but from a computer-generated one. Technologies such as stereoscopic goggles and specially wired gloves enhance the illusion of physical immersion.

virtual world A graphical, often 3D environment in which users can immerse themselves, interacting with virtual objects and one another using avatars.

virtualization Cost-cutting approach to servers in which multiple operating systems run concurrently on a single physical PC server.

visibility Describes how easily managers can track timely and accurate supply chain metrics.

voice over IP (VoIP) The technologies that make voice communications across networks using packet switching feasible, including those used over the Internet.

W

war room A large area in which team members on the same project work closely together, surrounded by whiteboards, large digital displays, and other tools to facilitate impromptu meetings and smooth collaboration.

waterfall software development method Method in which the systems development life cycle tasks occur sequentially, with one activity starting only after the previous one has been completed.

wavelength The distance between one peak of an electromagnetic wave to the next.

Web 2.0 The second generation of web development that facilitates far more interactivity, end-user contributions, collaboration, and information sharing compared to earlier models.

web accessibility Refers to how easily people with disabilities can access and use web resources.

web beacon (or web bug) A tiny, invisible image, typically a single pixel with a unique identifier, used on websites to track visitors.

web browser The software application that retrieves, interprets, and displays web resources.

web conferencing Technology that supports online meetings or "webinars" via the Internet. Participants join the meeting from their own computers or smartphones.

web feed Standardized and regularly updated output from a publisher, such as CNN or Weather.com, that can be embedded in a customized mashup.

what-if analysis A simulation model, often constructed using Excel, that calculates the relationships between many variables; users can change some variables to see how others are affected.

wifi Short for wireless fidelity; it refers to a computer network in which connections rely on radio waves at frequencies of 2.4 GHz or 5 GHz for transmission.

wiki Web software frequently used to build knowledge bases that allows users to add and edit interlinked web pages.

wireless router A device connected to a computer network that emits signals from its antenna and enables wireless connectivity to the network.

workforce management module As part of the HCM system, the workforce management module helps track time and attendance, sick leave, vacation leave, and project assignments.

World Wide Web Consortium (W3C) An international body that establishes and publishes standards for programming languages used to create software for the web.

Index

Note: Page number followed by f indicate figures and page numbers in **bold** indicate definitions.

OTHER MIS TITLES OF INTEREST

Introductory MIS

Experiencing MIS, 7/e
Kroenke & Boyle ©2017

Using MIS, 10/e
Kroenke & Boyle ©2018

Management Information Systems, 15/e
Laudon & Laudon ©2018

Essentials of MIS, 12/e
Laudon & Laudon ©2017

IT Strategy, 3/e
McKeen & Smith ©2015

Processes, Systems, and Information: An Introduction to MIS, 2/e
McKinney & Kroenke ©2015

Information Systems Today, 8/e
Valacich & Schneider ©2018

Introduction to Information Systems, 3/e
Wallace ©2018

Database

Hands-on Database, 2/e
Conger ©2014

Modern Database Management, 12/e
Hoffer, Ramesh & Topi ©2016

Database Concepts, 8/e
Kroenke, Auer, Vandenburg, Yoder ©2018

Database Processing, 14/e
Kroenke & Auer ©2016

Systems Analysis and Design

Modern Systems Analysis and Design, 8/e
Hoffer, George & Valacich ©2017

Systems Analysis and Design, 9/e
Kendall & Kendall ©2014

Essentials of Systems Analysis and Design, 6/e
Valacich, George & Hoffer ©2015

Decision Support Systems

Business Intelligence, Analytics, and Data Science, 4/e
Sharda, Delen & Turban ©2018

Business Intelligence and Analytics: Systems for Decision Support, 10/e
Sharda, Delen & Turban ©2014

Data Communications & Networking

Applied Networking Labs, 2/e
Boyle ©2014

Digital Business Networks
Dooley ©2014

Business Data Networks and Security, 10/e
Panko & Panko ©2015

Electronic Commerce

E-Commerce: Business, Technology, Society, 13/e
Laudon & Traver ©2018

Enterprise Resource Planning

Enterprise Systems for Management, 2/e
Motiwalla & Thompson ©2012

Project Management

Project Management: Process, Technology and Practice
Vaidyanathan ©2013